ROUTLEDGE HANDBOOK ON THE GREEN NEW DEAL

Edited by
Kyla Tienhaara and Joanna Robinson

Routledge
Taylor & Francis Group
LONDON AND NEW YORK

Cover image: by Ricardo Levins Morales. It was originally created for the Green New Deal Arts Kit, available at art.350.org/green-new-deal-arts and is reproduced here with the permission of Mr. Levins Morales and 350.org

First published 2023
by Routledge
4 Park Square, Milton Park, Abingdon, Oxon OX14 4RN

and by Routledge
605 Third Avenue, New York, NY 10158

Routledge is an imprint of the Taylor & Francis Group, an informa business

British Library Cataloguing-in-Publication Data
A catalogue record for this book is available from the British Library

Library of Congress Cataloging-in-Publication Data
A catalog record has been requested for this book

ISBN: 978-0-367-62804-8 (hbk)
ISBN: 978-0-367-62805-5 (pbk)
ISBN: 978-1-003-11088-0 (ebk)

DOI: 10.4324/9781003110880

Typeset in Bembo
by codeMantra

This book is dedicated to everyone who worked on the frontlines - whether in a hospital, warehouse or classroom - through the COVID-19 pandemic and sacrificed their physical and mental health to keep us safe. You deserve better.

We also dedicate this book to all those who work tirelessly for a more equitable, just and sustainable world.

CONTENTS

Notes on contributors *x*
Foreword *xvi*
Avi Lewis
Acknowledgements *xix*

Introduction 1
Kyla Tienhaara and Joanna Robinson

PART I
Political economy of the Green New Deal **21**

1 The Green New Deal, climate breakdown, and power 23
Ann Pettifor

2 Financing the Green New Deal: The Modern Money Theory approach 35
Yeva Nersisyan

3 Central banks and Green New Deals: What role can they play? 47
Ray Galvin

4 Avoiding the pitfalls of capitalism in the Green New Deal 73
John McCollum

5 A Green New Deal for agriculture: Whither capitalism? 88
Benjamin Selwyn

6 Worktime reduction and the Green New Deal 108
Juliet B. Schor and Kyla Tienhaara

7 Reshaping global trade and investment law for a Green New Deal 120
Todd N. Tucker and Timothy Meyer

PART II
Tackling injustice through the Green New Deal **139**

8 Jobs, justice, and the Green New Deal 141
Joanna Robinson

9 Lessons for a Green New Deal: Race, the New Deal legacy, and environmental justice in Detroit 157
Josiah Rector

10 The Seventh Fire and the Sitting Bull Plan: An Indigenous Green New Deal 173
Winona LaDuke

11 A Feminist Agenda for a Green New Deal: Challenges and opportunities 194
Frances Roberts-Gregory

12 Democratizing the Green New Deal 211
Julie L. MacArthur, Christina E. Hoicka and Runa R. Das

13 A Green New Deal beyond the "North": Both promise and peril 231
Vijay Kolinjivadi and Ashish Kothari

PART III
The Green New Deal in practice **257**

14 Chinese Green Job Guarantee: A roadmap for sustainable prosperity 259
Vincent (Yijiang) Huang

15 South Korea's Green New Deal 2.0: Old wine in new bottles? 279
Kyla Tienhaara, Sun-Jin Yun and Ryan Gunderson

16 Decarbonization without democracy: Tennis-ball politics and the EU Green Deal 299
David Adler and Pawel Wargan

17 The evolution of the UK's Green New Deal: "Green Industrial Revolution," "Building Back Better," and beyond 315
Daniel Bailey and Elena Hofferberth

18 A made-in-Canada Green New Deal 331
Seth Klein

19 Cities and the Green New Deal: Addressing the financialization of urban production 353
Christopher W. Gibson

Appendix: Examples of Green New Deals and legislative proposals 373

Index *489*

CONTRIBUTORS

David Adler is a political economist and General Coordinator of the Progressive International. He is co-founder of the Green New Deal for Europe campaign.

Daniel Bailey is a Senior Lecturer in International Political Economy at the Future Economies Centre at Manchester Metropolitan University. His research addresses the relationship between environmental unsustainability, the global economy, and the state's institutions, objectives, and strategies. He has published research in *New Political Economy*, *Environmental Politics*, *Competition and Change*, *Local Government Studies*, *British Politics*, and *Renewal* amongst other academic journals, has co-authored reports for the *New Economics Foundation* and *Foundation for European Progressive Studies*, and collaborated on an edited collection with Prof. Colin Hay. He has previously worked at the University of Manchester, the University of Sheffield, and the University of York.

Runa R. Das is an Associate Professor in the College of Interdisciplinary Studies at Royal Roads University. Her research is motivated by holistic understandings of sustainability and focusses on energy-related topics, including the human dimensions and determinants of energy use, energy poverty, the energy efficiency of buildings, and energy transitions.

Ray Galvin has a diverse, interdisciplinary background including engineering, philosophy, social psychology, policy studies, and economics. Over the past decade his research has focussed on energy consumption behaviour and policy, with empirical work on buildings, transport and electricity supply. More recently he is investigating the effects of increasing economic inequality on access to energy services in OECD countries. He uses both qualitative and quantitative research methods and has contributed to theoretical discussion on field research methods. Ray is an Affiliated Researcher in Energy Economics at RWTH-Aachen University, Germany. He also tutors postgraduate students in interdisciplinary sustainability issues at Cambridge University, UK, and serves as an expert research evaluator for the European Commission.

Christopher W. Gibson is Assistant Professor of Sociology at California State University, Fullerton. With a doctorate from the Department of Sociology at UC Irvine and an MA in

Global Studies from UC Santa Barbara, his research focusses on the intersection of economic markets and social policy, with special attention to environmental governance. He hopes that his work will highlight ways that we can best prepare our governance institutions to equitably address the challenges of climate change. His current research project examines water management in California to understand the role of financial markets in shaping policy decisions.

Ryan Gunderson is an Associate Professor in the Department of Sociology and Gerontology and Affiliate of the Institute for the Environment and Sustainability at Miami University. His research interests include environmental sociology, the sociology of technology, social theory, political economy, and animal studies.

Elena Hofferberth is a postgraduate researcher in economics at the University of Leeds. In her research, she scrutinizes the macroeconomic and political economy underpinnings of a social-ecological transformation, including proposals for Degrowth, Post-Growth, and the Green New Deal. She is a member of the Economics and Policy for Sustainability Research Group at the University of Leeds, the international Post-Growth Economics Network, and the Scientific Working Group on Sustainable Money.

Christina E. Hoicka is an Associate Professor and Canada Research Chair for Urban Planning for Climate Change in the Department of Geography and Department of Civil Engineering at the University of Victoria. She studies the diffusion of low-carbon innovations, renewable energy transitions, energy democracy, and energy justice.

Vincent (Yijiang) Huang is a heterodox economist with the primary fields of political economy of China and East Asia, money and banking, and ecological economics. He is a Teaching Assistant Professor of Economics at the University of Denver and a Research Scholar at the Global Institute for Sustainable Prosperity. Vincent received his Interdisciplinary PhD degree in Economics and Social Science Consortium at the University of Missouri – Kansas City in 2020.

Seth Klein is the Team Lead for the Climate Emergency Unit (a project of the David Suzuki Institute). Previously, Seth served for 22 years as the founding British Columbia Director of the Canadian Centre for Policy Alternatives, a public policy research institute committed to social, economic, and environmental justice. He is a writer, speaker, and policy consultant, and an adjunct professor with Simon Fraser University's Urban Studies programme. He writes a bi-monthly column for *Canada's National Observer*. Seth's book – *A Good War: Mobilizing Canada for the Climate Emergency* – was published in September 2020.

Vijay Kolinjivadi is a brother, friend, partner, son, neighbour, and uncle. He is also a post-doctoral researcher at the Institute of Development Policy, University of Antwerp. His research explores the uneven environments generated from "greening" interventions like payments for ecosystem services (PES) in North America and in Central and South Asia. His current research explores the spatial and temporal processes of dehumanization and ecological simplification that characterize the replication of plantation logics. In particular, he explores how plantation ecologies are both resisted and reinforced within the so-called Anthropocene through "green" thinking. He is also a writer with the Earth Negotiations Bulletin, following multilateral environmental processes and co-editor of Uneven Earth, a website focussing on environmental politics. In addition to academic publications, he has been published in *Al Jazeera*, *New Internationalist*, *Truthout*, *The Conversation*, and *Mongabay*.

Ashish Kothari is a founder-member of Kalpavriksh (https://kalpavriksh.org), a 40-year civil society organization in India focussing on environment and development issues. He taught at Indian Institute of Public Administration, is Professor of Practice at National Law School and University (Bengaluru), and guest faculty in several other universities in India and abroad. He coordinated India's National Biodiversity Strategy & Action Plan, served on Indian government committees to formulate the National Biodiversity Act and National Wildlife Action Plan, and served on boards or steering committees of two IUCN commissions, Greenpeace International & India, and the ICCA Consortium (www.iccaconsortium.org). A long-standing member or supporter of several people's movements, he helps coordinate Vikalp Sangam (www.vikalpsangam.org), Global Tapestry of Alternatives (www.globaltapestryofalternatives.org), & Radical Ecological Democracy (www.radicalecologicaldemocracy.org) processes. He is (co)author/(co)editor of several books, including *Birds in Our Lives* (2007), *Churning the Earth* (2012), *Alternative Futures* (2017), and *Pluriverse: A Post-Development Dictionary* (2019).

Winona LaDuke is an internationally renowned activist working on issues of sustainable development renewable energy and food systems. She lives and works on the White Earth reservation in northern Minnesota and is a two-time vice presidential candidate with Ralph Nader for the Green Party. As Program Director of the Honor the Earth, she works nationally and internationally on the issues of climate change, renewable energy, and environmental justice with Indigenous communities. And in her own community, she is the founder of the White Earth Land Recovery Project, one of the largest reservation-based non-profit organizations in the country and a leader in the issues of culturally based sustainable development strategies, renewable energy, and food systems. In this work, she also continues national and international work to protect Indigenous plants and heritage foods from patenting and genetic engineering. She is the author of six books, including, most recently, *To Be a Water Protector.*

Julie L. MacArthur is an Associate Professor and Canada Research Chair in Reimagining Capitalism in the School of Business at Royal Roads University. Her research focusses on the political economy of energy transitions, energy policy and community energy. Her most recent books include Empowering Electricity (2016 UBC Press) analyzing the political economy of electricity co-operatives in Canada and Politics and Environmental Politics and Policy in Aotearoa New Zealand (with Maria Bargh, Auckland University Press 2022). She sits on the President's Advisory Committee for Regenerative Sustainability at Royal Roads University.

John McCollum is a dual-appointed professor in Sociology and Political Science at Minot State University, North Dakota. He received his PhD at the University of California, Irvine, where his dissertation work focussed on the developmental possibilities and consequences of Indonesia's palm oil sector and the efforts of labour and environmental NGOs to alter these outcomes. Broadly, his work examines class, environment, and globalization. His current research examines the possibilities of booms in commodity prices and extractive industries to open opportunities for organized labour to make gains recruitment and bargaining demands. This research looks at the established unions in North Dakota's Bakken Oil Shale region to examine how the late 2000s oil boom altered their organizations. Lastly, he is interested in theory and the social imaginary, including youth movements and the Green New Deal.

Timothy Meyer is Professor of Law and co-Director of the Center for International and Comparative Law at Duke University Law School. He is an expert in public international law, with specialties in international trade and investment law and international energy governance. His current research examines how international economic agreements relate and respond to concerns about economic opportunity and inequality, as well as the role of the constitutional separation of powers in US international economic policymaking. His past research has examined the interaction of international and local rules on energy subsidies, the role of local governments in free trade agreements, and the creation of non-binding "soft law" obligations. Professor Meyer has testified before the US Senate Committees on Foreign Relations and the Judiciary and has served as both counsel and an expert in cases raising international law and trade issues in US courts, including litigation challenging the Trump Administration's "national security" tariffs under Section 232 of the Trade Expansion Act. Professor Meyer entered the legal academy after practising law for several years at the Office of the Legal Adviser, US Department of State. He earned his BA and MA in history from Stanford University, and his JD and PhD from the University of California, Berkeley.

Yeva Nersisyan is an Associate Professor of economics at Franklin and Marshall College in Lancaster, PA. She received her BA in economics from Yerevan State University in Armenia, and her MA and PhD in economics and mathematics from the University of Missouri-Kansas City. She is a macroeconomist working in the Modern Money Theory, Post Keynesian, and Institutionalist traditions. Her research interests include banking and financial instability, fiscal and monetary theory and policy. She has published a number of papers on the topics of shadow banking, liquidity creation, the Glass-Steagall Act, the Green New Deal, and Modern Money Theory. Currently, she is working on editing the *Elgar Companion to Modern Money Theory* with L. Randall Wray.

Ann Pettifor was one of few to predict the Great Financial Crisis in *The Coming First World Debt Crisis* (Palgrave 2006). In 2008 she jointly co-authored the original *The Green New Deal* (New Economics Foundation). In 2017 she published *The Production of Money* (Verso) on the nature of money, debt, and banking. In 2019 her book *The Case for The Green New Deal* (Verso) was published. She is director of Policy Research in Macroeconomics (PRIME) – a network of mainly Keynesian economists. In 2018 Germany's Heinrich Boll Foundation awarded Pettifor the Hannah Ahrendt Prize. She is a fellow of the New Economics Foundation, and a trustee of the PREP Foundation for pluralist economics. In 2000 the University of Newcastle awarded her an honorary doctorate for leading an international movement for cancellation of $150bn of debt owed by 35 poor countries, *Jubilee 2000.* In 2004–2005 Pettifor worked with Nigerian Finance Minister, Ngozi Okonjo-Iweala to clear debts of $30 billion owed to official creditors.

Josiah Rector is an Assistant Professor of History at the University of Houston. He is the author of *Toxic Debt: An Environmental Justice History of Detroit* (2022).

Frances Roberts-Gregory is an ecowomanist ethnographer, feminist political ecologist, and former Future Faculty Fellow in the School of Public Policy & Urban Affairs at Northeastern University. Frances completed her undergraduate studies at Spelman College in Environmental Science, Sociology, and Anthropology, and graduate research at the University of California, Berkeley, in Environmental Science, Policy, & Management. Her feminist activist research explores how Black and Indigenous women navigate contradictory relationships with energy and petrochemical industries, resist environmental racism, and devise solutions for environmental, energy, and climate justice. Frances is also a co-founding and steering committee member of the Feminist Agenda for a Green New Deal, former environmental educator for the Deep South Center for Environmental Justice, advisory board member for the Hive Fund for Climate & Gender Justice, and former resource developer for the New Orleans and C40 Women4Climate Mentorship Program. From 2018 to 2021, Frances taught courses on gender, environmental racism, digital activism, climate justice, and sustainable development at Tulane University, Bard Early College New Orleans, and the University for Peace in Costa Rica. Most importantly, Frances looks forward to nurturing healing justice as feminist climate justice as a Climate Justice Program Officer at the Foundation for Louisiana. Reach her via Facebook, Twitter, or Instagram @BlackngreenPhD or via her website blackngreenphd.org.

Joanna Robinson is Associate Professor in the Department of Sociology and Interim Director of the Glendon School of Public and International Affairs at Glendon College, York University, Toronto, Canada. Her research focusses on environmental politics, climate change, and social movements in a cross-national comparative perspective. Her first book, *Contested Water: Anti-Water Privatization in the United States and Canada*, examines cross-sectoral movements that emerge in response to water privatization. Her current research focusses on the role of labour and environmental movements in shaping the transition to a green economy in the United States and Canada.

Juliet B. Schor is an economist and sociologist at Boston College. Schor's research focusses on work, consumption, and climate change. Her most recent book is *After the Gig: How the Sharing Economy Got Hijacked and How to Win It Back* (2020), which won the Porchlight Management and Workplace Culture Book of the Year. Schor's previous books include the national best-seller *The Overworked American: The Unexpected Decline of Leisure* (1992), *The Overspent American: Why We Want What We Don't Need* (1998) and *True Wealth: How and Why Millions of Americans are Creating a Time-Rich, Ecologically Light, Small-Scale, High-Satisfaction Economy* (2011, previously published as *Plenitude*). Schor is a co-founder of the Center for a New American Dream (newdream.org), a national sustainability organization where she served on the board for more than 15 years. She chairs the board of the Better Future Project, a Massachusetts-based climate justice organization. She is a co-founder of the South End Press and the Center for Popular Economics.

Benjamin Selwyn teaches and researches about labour, food, global value chains, and development in the Department of International Relations, University of Sussex, UK. His publications include *The Struggle for Development* (2017).

Kyla Tienhaara is an Assistant Professor and Canada Research Chair in Economy and Environment in the School of Environmental Studies and the Department of Global Development Studies at Queen's University, Kingston. Her research explores the impacts of economic globalization on environmental governance. Her book *Green Keynesianism and the*

Global Financial Crisis (Routledge, 2018) explored the green stimulus measures adopted in five countries in 2008/09. More information on her green new deal-related research can be found at http://greennewdealinfo.com

Todd N. Tucker is a political scientist and Director of Industrial Policy & Trade at the Roosevelt Institute, where he helps lead research on global governance, democracy, and the administrative state. He is author of *Judge Knot: Politics and Development in International Investment Law* (2018), along with other academic research published by journals at Cambridge University Press, Oxford University Press, and others. His current book project examines whether and how veto points in governance institutions impact international competitiveness and a country's ability to respond to existential threats. A recognized expert on trade and political economy, Dr. Tucker has testified before legislatures and expert committees around the world. His writing has been featured in *Politico*, *Time Magazine*, *Democracy Journal*, the *Financial Times*, and *The Washington Post*. Prior to his doctoral work, he led research on international issues for Public Citizen and worked as an analyst at other think tanks.

Pawel Wargan is the Coordinator of the Secretariat of the Progressive International. He is co-founder of the Green New Deal for Europe campaign.

Sun-Jin Yun is a Professor in the Graduate School of Environmental Studies at Seoul National University, Seoul, Republic of Korea. Yun's research concentrates on the political economy of climate change, climate and energy policies, environmental and climate justice, anti-nuclear and energy transition movements, discourse analysis, common pool resource management, and environmental education.

FOREWORD

Avi Lewis

Is Mother Nature an accelerationist? One could be forgiven for thinking so.

Privileged populations in the global north are increasingly getting hammered by natural disasters, turbo-charged by climate change. In other words, what vulnerable communities everywhere have been experiencing for decades. Climate breakdown is indeed accelerating, and the existential threat is finally impossible to ignore in the halls of power.

This makes the debate about the Green New Deal (GND) – the big idea at the centre of this Handbook – a hugely consequential one, taking place at an inflection point in human history.

While this volume contains many useful definitions, the GND is at its core not a proposal, but a frame. A contested, evolving, and necessary space in which it is possible to consider solutions that embody the speed and scale necessary to meet the overlapping emergencies confronting all living things.

Because, of course, the climate emergency is not the only one we face on planet earth. There are other environmental crises, from mass extinction to biodiversity collapse to rapid deforestation. There are social crises, from housing bubbles to surging white supremacy, and public services shredded by decades of austerity, buckling under an immense burden of need. There are economic crises like spiralling inequality, concentration of wealth, and discounted women's labour. There are international crises of ever-increasing militarism, twenty-first-century colonialism, and the negative net transfer of wealth – the fact that the poorest countries on earth still pay the richest ones hundreds of billions of dollars a year for the privilege of staying poor.

And now there is the COVID-19 pandemic, which both exacerbates and is exacerbated by many of the emergences above.

The links of causation and amplification among all these intersecting disasters would take another book of this same impressive heft just to list. But in preface to a volume on the GND, it's worth noting at the outset that none of them can be solved in isolation. That's why this big idea has become so important to so many. The GND attempts to articulate a vision of transformative, holistic change in the face of cascading, connected emergencies. And it attempts to ground this vision in principles of justice, resting on a foundation of scientific necessity.

Transformation in the face of climate breakdown has long been the demand of Indigenous leaders, social movements and frontline communities. But those calls are now footnoted with empirical science – especially, and explicitly, since October 8, 2018.

That's the day the press release dropped for the Summary for Policymakers of the Intergovernmental Panel on Climate Change (IPCC)'s Special Report on Global Warming of 1.5°C (approved by governments.) Here's the first sentence, which as far as I'm concerned, says it all:

> Limiting global warming to 1.5°C would require rapid, far-reaching and unprecedented changes in all aspects of society, the IPCC said in a new assessment.

It is a baldly revolutionary sentiment. "Unprecedented changes in all aspects of society"! It's practically T-shirt-worthy (ok, for a very small subculture, but who wants a T-shirt that everyone is wearing?) The fact that it is found in a marketing document for the specific form of IPCC report that is subject to the compromises of political negotiation, is remarkable.

It's also an incredibly succinct expression of the scientific imperative for a Green New Deal.

I have found myself repeating these words, mantra-like. Meditating on them, making them the screensaver on my computer. I find that they magnify both the challenge and the opportunity of transformative climate action that addresses the very system which created the emergency. "Rapid, far-reaching and unprecedented changes...." It is both thrilling and terrifying. And it is also a relief: it acknowledges the scale of the problem, and provides a diagnosis that is commensurate.

These are words that just keep giving. "*Every* aspect of society." As a mid-career filmmaker and climate activist who has suddenly become an academic, I have only recently given any thought to the role of the university in the existential struggle for climate justice. It has been an unwelcome revelation for me, though I'm sure this has long been obvious to many readers: the academy itself requires "rapid, far-reaching and unprecedented changes" if it is to play an effective role in a society-wide mobilization around the climate emergency.

This book – the sheer expanse of it, both materially and intellectually – gives me hope that this change is beginning. It represents an explosion of work on the GND that is truly heartening to see. The span of voices from diverse disciplines, geographies, and ideologies is impressive. But what is also notable is the spirit of this collection. Even the most profound challenges to the very frame of the GND seem carefully designed to be constructive, respectful, generative.

As you read the many chapters of this book, you will encounter a far-flung community of scholars who may have important disagreements, but nonetheless treat this political moment as both consequential and precarious. The authors manifest a clear intention to move the GND forward in full awareness that the lives, health, and well-being of hundreds of millions of people are on the line, hanging in the balance of what kind of change we can win in the next short few years.

It has to be said that the political conditions are not yet ripe for the full implementation of a Green New Deal. There has been much excitement since 2018 that in the heart of global empire, insurgent young US politicians might not just crack the Overton window open, but knock it off its hinges. But that has not come to pass. It is true that GND-scale policies have finally been floated (and diluted) in the US Congress. But by and large, the fossil-fuelled forces of late-stage capitalism have once again proven that they are able to absorb and deflect movements that would shift the balance of forces in society toward climate justice.

And so we have entered a new era, which I have taken to calling The Co-optacene. It's a time when the titans of the global economy try to sound like Greta, while overseeing trillions of new investments in fossil fuel projects. A time when Canada's government trumpets its climate leadership even as it rams a bitumen pipeline through Indigenous territory, stuffed full of billions in fossil fuel subsidies.

This is the moment of double discourse that has arisen in tandem with – or perhaps in response to – the spectre of the Green New Deal. So as the floodwaters of climate anxiety rise around us, they are sand-bagged with vigorous greenwashing in the form of "Net-Zero by 2050" pledges from governments, corporations, and large financial institutions. These schemes are designed to assuage very real fears, but they do not stand up to any rigorous accounting. In fact, almost without exception, the impact of these plans will be to perpetuate the very status quo that is choking the planet. Taken together, they are a festival of false solutions, festooned with unproven technologies, borne on the wings of magical thinking.

And yet.

Nearly two decades ago, Naomi Klein unearthed an overlooked passage from Milton Friedman – one of the principal architects of the neoliberal order which has immeasurably accelerated the climate crisis. Those words have resonated far and wide, and they remain a powerful premise for work on the Green New Deal:

> Only a crisis – actual or perceived – produces real change. When that crisis occurs, the actions that are taken depend on the ideas that are lying around. That, I believe, is our basic function: to develop alternatives to existing policies, to keep them alive and available until the politically impossible becomes the politically inevitable.

The ideas lying around in these pages need to be ready to get up and leap into action. They need to be ready for prime time, whenever it arrives. And since we don't know when we'll reach that political tipping point, the work of debating, deepening, and defining the Green New Deal is a matter of true existential urgency. This book may be a little supersized. But so is its contribution to the most important work in the world.

ACKNOWLEDGEMENTS

The project to develop this Handbook was undertaken, in part, thanks to funding from the Canada Research Chairs Program. The editors would like to acknowledge that most of the contributors to the volume committed to the project before the outbreak of the COVID-19 pandemic and that many of them had to deal with a dramatic shift in work responsibilities as well as increased care responsibilities. We very much appreciate that they stuck with the project, and that they also demonstrated great patience with us when we were struggling to balance work and home obligations.

The editors would also like to acknowledge the excellent copy-editing of the entire manuscript by Emily Jeffers.

Both editors are also grateful to their families for their support throughout the process of compiling this Handbook.

INTRODUCTION

Kyla Tienhaara and Joanna Robinson

It is customary to begin volumes of this nature by spelling out in detail the dire situation that currently confronts humanity. To note the number of degrees of warming that are already unavoidable, and the devastating impacts that climate change will have. To count the species that have been lost, and the number of years we have left before there are no more coral reefs, or summer glaciers. To quantify the economic cost of more intense storms and rising sea levels. To acknowledge the human suffering that the ecological breakdown we are experiencing is already having around the world.

We could reiterate all of this. We could highlight that as we began writing this introduction, the West Coast of Canada was experiencing a previously unimaginable heatwave that would result in hundreds of sudden deaths and contribute to numerous devastating forest fires, one of which would obliterate the town of Lytton, British Columbia. But such a story, while shocking and raw for us in the moment, is likely to quickly become dated as we are all forced to absorb a seemingly relentless onslaught of news of "record-shattering" and "unprecedented" catastrophes. Indeed, less than a month later, we had moved on to being stunned by extraordinary flooding around the world, particularly in parts of Europe and in the Chinese city of Zhengzhou, which received a year's worth of rain over the course of only three days. As climate scientist Simon Donner notes, these types of events should not be described as the "new normal" because that would require that we had reached a point of stability, which, in turn, would require that we had stopped making the problem worse (Crawford 2021). Instead, we may well look back on this point in time as the "good old days" before things got *really* bad. That is, unless we choose to act.

And that is what we want this book to be about. Not about how bad things are or about where we are headed if we choose to keep our heads in the sand. We assume that if you have picked up this Handbook, you are already aware that the climate crisis and broader ecological crisis are real and urgently need to be tackled with the level of commitment and resources that governments have previously given to fighting wars (Klein 2020). If not, then there are numerous excellent sources available, including the most recent assessment report from the Intergovernmental Panel on Climate Change (IPCC 2021). What we would like to focus on instead is where we could be in a few decades if we embrace a different way of thinking about how we respond to ecological breakdown. This different way of thinking is captured in the Green New Deal (GND).

DOI: 10.4324/9781003110880-1

What is the Green New Deal?

The GND draws inspiration from the New Deal, which was a series of economic policies, government employment programs, and public works programs that were adopted by the US government during the tenure of President Franklin Delano Roosevelt (FDR) to tackle the Great Depression. As with the New Deal, providing employment is a central plank of the GND. However, a key difference between the two programs is that in addition to economic ills, the GND must also tackle a global ecological crisis of climate disruption, biodiversity loss, soil degradation, plastic pollution, and numerous other issues. Admittedly, some New Deal programs, like the Civilian Conservation Corps (CCC), had similar aims and would likely be deemed "green" if established today. Between 1933 and 1942, the CCC employed more than 3 million young men who, among other things, planted approximately 2 billion trees and developed 800 new state parks (Maher 2008). A contemporary proposal for a Civilian Climate Corps in the US was "[i]nspired by the ambition and impact" of the original CCC (Evergreen Action 2021).

There are some important limitations to the historical analogy, one of the most critical being that many New Deal policies were racist (see chapter by Rector, this volume) and "intimately tied to the entrenchment of settler colonialism in the United States" including "the continuation of the violence of Native American boarding schools" (Lehman and Johnson 2021). While it is certainly important to be cognizant of these limitations and work hard to ensure that such outcomes are not repeated, there is still value in tying the GND to a historical precedent. Crucially, it helps to address any concerns that the climate problem is just "too big" for us to tackle. Klein (2019) argues that:

> By looking decades backward and forward simultaneously, we are no longer alone as we confront our weighty historical moment. We are surrounded by both ancestors whispering that we can do what our moment demands just as they did, and by future generations shouting that they deserve nothing less.

The ability to draw on a successful economic and social mobilization from the recent past is particularly important at this moment when denial of climate science has largely been supplanted by strategies of climate delay (Lamb et al. 2020). Two of these strategies – to suggest that the change required to address the climate crisis is impossible or that we are doomed to failure because it is too late to stop catastrophic warming (Ibid.) – can be effectively countered with examples of how a society has beaten the odds before (see also Klein 2020, who examines the societal mobilization during World War II).

While it draws primarily on American history, the GND is not an exclusively American idea. For most of us, hearing the phrase "Green New Deal" immediately conjures an image of New York Congresswoman Alexandria Ocasio-Cortez (AOC) or an office of the US Congress filled with young protesters from the Sunrise Movement demanding "green jobs for all." While both have done much to popularize the term, proposals for a GND pre-date both the rise of youth-led climate activism and AOC's first political campaign in 2018. The GND first emerged in substantive form in the UK in 2008, with the publication of a proposal from the Green New Deal Group (GNDG) – a collective of academics, economists, journalists, and politicians (see chapter by Pettifor, this volume). Green New Deal platforms were subsequently adopted by Green parties in Europe and the US. Korea's 2009 stimulus package was dubbed a Green New Deal, although it was arguably a purely "green growth" platform (see chapter by Tienhaara, Yun and Gunderson, this volume). The United Nations Environment Programme (UNEP) also proposed a Global Green New Deal in 2009. In

2015, the Leap Manifesto – a "proto-Green New Deal" (Klein 2019) – was developed by a coalition of environmentalists, Indigenous, labor, and faith leaders, authors, and artists in Canada in the run-up to the 2015 federal election and Paris Conference of the Parties to the United Nations Conference on Climate Change.

Each of these GND proposals should be considered within the context of the domestic politics where it emerged, as well as the point in time in which it was developed (e.g., the UK GNDG, UNEP, and Korean versions were very much concerned with responding to the Global Financial Crisis). However, we would argue that most proposals share some assumptions and objectives. We will come to what those are in a moment, but first it is important to clarify the distinction that we make between "a GND proposal" and "the GND." The former is a specific list of policies for a given sector (e.g., a GND for Housing, a GND for Public Schools) or an entire economy (e.g., a GND for Europe). The broader narrative under which these proposals fit is "the GND."

A 2021 article in *The Atlantic* entitled "The Green New Deal Does Not, Strictly Speaking, Exist" (understandably) raised the hackles of many of those who have been working hard to develop specific GND proposals. In it, author Robinson Meyer observed that: "the Green New Deal is not a single policy to win, but a change in outlook and approach." Many authors have described the GND in similar terms, highlighting that the GND is an "agenda for governing" (Ajl 2021); "style of governance" (Aronoff 2021); "framework" (Adler and Wargan 2019); "political process" (Stilwell 2021: 162); or "civilizational *mission*" (Klein 2019). In addition to eschewing the notion that the GND is a single policy, or indeed a "wish list" or "grab-bag" of many policies (as it is often derisively described), most of these authors emphasize that the GND approach is categorically *different* from the (neoliberal) approaches that have dominated climate and environmental policy for more than 30 years. In other words, the GND is not a repackaging of old ideas under a new slogan. Adler and Wargan (2019) talk of "a radical reimagining of our societies," while Aronoff (2021) sees the GND as "the basis of a new social contract."

For our part, we think that the best definition of the GND was provided by Schor (2015: 532–533), who was not actually discussing the GND at the time but was instead describing what she felt we desperately needed to achieve progress on the key socio-ecological issues of our age: "an economic narrative that links human well-being to the well-being of the planetary eco-system." We think that this is apt for several reasons. First, we think that using the term "narrative" articulates better than "approach" or "framework" the fact that the GND tells a story of how the world could be better. Importantly, the story is optimistic in a different way than utopian visions of a post-carbon world that are based entirely on as-yet unjustified expectations about advances in technology. It is possible *today*. Second, it is important that the narrative is an economic one, not just because the economy is so central to society, but more crucially because it is our economic systems that fundamentally need to change if we are to avert ecological collapse. Finally, the definition connects the well-being of people to the well-being of the planet, in alignment with the focus of the GND on centering equity and justice in all decarbonization efforts.

Critiques of the GND

The GND gets attacked from the right, left, and center – for being too radical, not radical enough, or for getting "distracted" by issues that aren't "climate" (like health care or education; Aronoff 2021). We will not waste the readers' time on the claims that the GND is too radical (as noted above, there are lots of excellent sources out there for those not yet convinced that, as Aronoff, Battistoni, Cohen and Riofrancos [2019] put it, "the age of climate gradualism is over"). Those that argue that the GND is not radical enough make many excellent arguments, which are discussed more thoroughly below on a point-by-point basis. Because these critiques are often framed in terms of "the GND could be better if..." rather than "we should reject the GND outright," we consider them as part of an ongoing discussion in which the GND will evolve.

Before turning to these constructive critiques and discussions, we feel the need to address the centrist critique that the GND includes too many "non-climate" objectives. Klein (2019) describes often hearing this sentiment: "Lowering emissions is hard enough, we are told – why weigh it down by trying to fix so much else at the same time?" Authors at the ecomodernist Breakthrough Institute go so far as to suggest that Green New Dealers do not actually believe that climate change is an existential emergency because:

> the test of whether environmentalists take their own catastrophist warnings seriously is whether the solutions they propose diverge in any meaningful way from the sorts of things that environmentalists (and progressives) would want whether climate change were happening or not. The everything-ism of the Green New Deal, in this way, undermines the deadline-ism of the climate emergency.
>
> *(Nordhaus and Trembath 2019)*

The problem with this critique is twofold. First, it assumes that climate change is a technical problem, but it is in fact a political problem, "in the real sense of the word political, meaning a problem involving competing visions of the kind of world we want to live in" (Kallis 2019). Green New Dealers recognize that a broad coalition to support climate action cannot be built around interventions that will not make people's lives materially better and could even leave them much worse off. The "yellow-vest" backlash to a proposed raise in fuel taxes in France is an oft-cited example of how climate policy that ignores the interests of the working class will fail (Mehleb, Kallis and Zografos 2021).

Second, the use of the term "everything-ism" suggests that the GND includes issues that are unrelated, simply because they are desirable from a leftist political perspective. While it is certainly true that the solutions proposed within the GND are "the sorts of things that environmentalists (and progressives) would want whether climate change were happening or not," this does not change the fact that these "things" are also climate/environmental issues. As Hathaway (2020) states, the GND "recognizes the inequities of systemic power relations as root causes of climate change, and their redress as the only promising way forward."

What unites us

There has been a flurry of books, media articles, think tank reports, academic articles, and even a few poems written about the GND in the last few years. While we have read widely, we don't claim to have conducted an exhaustive review of the GND literature. Nevertheless, we feel confident in arguing that the vast majority of those that deploy the GND narrative agree on the following:

1. The market cannot lead a socio-economic transformation.
2. All economic policy must deliver positive outcomes for equity and justice in addition to decarbonization.
3. There is power in a message of "good hope."

The market cannot lead a socio-economic transformation

For as long as most of us can remember, environmental policy has been dominated by a single powerful idea: "that most (ideally all) of our environmental problems can be solved by the creation and enforcement of tradeable property rights in environmental 'goods' and 'bads'" (Eckersley 1993). In line with this idea, climate politics has been reduced to endless political battles over the establishment of carbon pricing schemes (carbon taxes or emissions trading). Biodiversity conservation circles have been similarly overtaken by an obsession with pricing "ecosystem services."

The rejection of a central focus on market mechanisms in the GND is critically important in distinguishing it from other "green" discourses. The GND diverges sharply from this "free market environmentalism" for four key reasons. First, while market mechanisms may be more economically *efficient* than other approaches, they have not proven to be effective in responding to most environmental issues in practice (Tvinnereim and Mehling 2018; Machin 2019; Green 2021). At best, market mechanisms deliver incremental improvements in terms of emissions reductions and other environmental benefits, which is simply inadequate in the current context. Second, market mechanisms are unlikely to deliver outcomes that also serve to improve equity and may even exacerbate inequality (e.g., regressive carbon taxes). Third, there is a more direct link to employment outcomes with a process of government planning than with a market approach (Stilwell 2021). Finally, and unsurprisingly given the equity and employment issues, pricing schemes tend to be unpopular with the public (Konisky and Carley 2021).

It should be noted that not all Green New Dealers reject market-based approaches outright, with many arguing, for example, that a carbon tax can play a role in a GND if is designed to consider equity and justice goals (e.g., a tax-and-dividend approach; Fischer and Jacobsen 2021; Konisky and Carley 2021). However, market mechanisms are always presented as part of a broader package and generally take a back seat to other forms of policy. Even those scholars on the left that are somewhat skeptical of the GND recognize that "rather than seeking environmental 'fine-tuning' through market mechanisms, it opens the possibility of a more transformative approach to employment, environment, equity and empowerment" (Stilwell 2021: 156).

Of course, it is logical to ask: if the market is not going to lead a socio-economic transformation, then who or what will? For most Green New Dealers, the response to this question is, first and foremost, the state. Acknowledging the limitations of the state, and the abysmal environmental record of most states, Green New Dealers nevertheless conclude, as Eckersley (2021: 261) does, that "states are better placed than any other actor or organisation to facilitate socio-ecological transformation given their powers to regulate, tax, spend, redistribute, and procure and to perform these tasks in ways that are more or less responsive and accountable to citizens." Furthermore, looking to past technological revolutions (e.g., the internet), almost all have involved a massive investment from the state (Mazzucato 2015). Given the pre-eminent role of the state, the GND is often characterized as "a leftist resurrection of federal industrial policy" (Meyer 2019). However, the range of policies that many GND proposals cover goes beyond steering "industry." For example, a just transition is also likely to require regional-focused rather than industry-focused policy in countries where fossil-fuel-dependent communities are highly concentrated in certain areas (e.g., Australia, Canada; Stilwell 2021). Furthermore, many discussions of "green industrial policy," do not delve into issues of race, gender, and economic equity (see, for example, Rodrik 2014; Altenburg and Assmann 2017).

There are notable tensions within the GND movement around the central role given to the state. Those that try to build on the GND with insights from degrowth, for example, worry about how compatible a "top-down" GND approach is with their preference for "bottom-up" grassroots initiatives (Mastini, Kallis and Hickel 2021). Concern is understandably greatest for those who have suffered the most under state oppression: racialized communities and Indigenous peoples. The authors of the Red Deal (discussed further below) are explicit about this: "States protect capital and its caretakers: the ruling class. They do not protect the people. Reformists who appeal to the state for change compromise our future by aligning with the interests of the ruling class" (Red Nation 2021).

It is also worth noting that there are an increasing number of GND proposals emerging at the sub-national level. A particularly inspiring example is the GND platform of Boston mayoral candidate Michelle Wu, which includes proposals to decarbonize and decommodify housing, make transit fare-free, and create jobs through an Urban Climate Corps (Wu Committee n.d.). Christopher W. Gibson discusses some of the challenges that local governments face in their efforts to adopt such radical reforms in the final chapter of this volume.

Equity and justice

At the core of the vision for the GND is the belief that policies should be designed to simultaneously address the ecological crisis and preserve "human values and dignity – for all humans, not just those who can pay" (Konisky and Carley 2021: 2). Green New Dealers argue that it is not possible to "fix" the emissions problem while leaving global inequities firmly entrenched (and even if we could, this would be an undesirable outcome).

The Resolution on the GND put before US Congress by AOC and Senator Ed Markey includes a call for "stopping current, preventing future, and repairing historic oppression of Indigenous Peoples, communities of color, migrant communities, deindustrialized communities, depopulated rural communities, the poor, low-income workers, women, the elderly, the unhoused, people with disabilities, and youth" (H. Res. 109, 2019). As Coleman (2019) notes, this wording "is starkly different from the color-blind, economically muffled message that mainstream environmental organizations have long favored."

Of course, the GND movement does not have a monopoly on equity and justice concerns. Environmental, ecological, and climate justice discourses have existed for decades and have been extensively studied (for an overview, see Agyeman, Bullard and Evans 2003; Pellow and Brulle 2005; Schlosberg 2007; Jafry 2019). There is also increasing recognition among mainstream NGOs of the critical role being played by Indigenous land defenders and water protectors in resisting further fossil fuel developments and other forms of extraction, and in preserving biodiversity. Environmental organizations have also been forced, by the power of the Black Lives Matter movement, to reckon with the racism of their founders (e.g., John Muir of the Sierra Club) and the ongoing exclusion of non-white voices from environmental policy discussions (NoiseCat 2019). Calls for "climate justice now" are, in 2021, very much in the mainstream. What distinguishes the GND from general calls for justice and equity is the way in which these principles are envisaged to be integrated into specific economic policy programs.

For example, the job guarantee (see further chapter by Huang, this volume), the centerpiece of the AOC–Markey proposal, is a "commitment to leaving no one behind amidst economic transformation and climate chaos" (Aronoff et al. 2019). It is also not enough for any jobs created under a GND to be "green" – they also need to be good (i.e., well paid, unionized; Tcherneva 2020). Furthermore, while the "green jobs" slogan generally conjures up images of men wearing hard hats and installing solar panels, the GND recognizes "the crisis of social reproduction" and aims "to expand work in the caring economy" (Eaton 2021: 7). Battistoni (2017) refers to jobs in teaching, nursing, and child/elderly care as "pink collar work" and notes that while this work is low carbon and critical to society, it is also often poorly paid and exploitative. She also points out that pink collar jobs are disproportionately occupied by women, immigrants and people of color. The focus on equality and justice in the GND demands that pink collar jobs be elevated along with other green collar jobs (see further Roberts-Gregory, this volume, and Robinson, this volume).

Although employment is central to the GND, it is not the only path through which inequality and injustice is to be addressed. As Gunn-Wright (2020) argues, the "green" parts of the GND are not distinct from the "equity" parts – all projects in a GND proposal should be designed to contribute to both. For example, in any energy-efficiency home retrofitting scheme, financial assistance for low- and middle-income households should be prioritized (Stilwell 2021). There are also important discussions about the role of Universal Basic Services in a GND (Vansintjan 2020) and the role that reparations (whether they be within a country – see Coleman 2019 – or globally, see further below) can play in furthering the goals of justice and equity. Obviously, there is still a lot of work to do and there are understandable concerns that what has been included in GND proposals to date is far from enough. Nevertheless, there are some exciting developments – like the Feminist GND discussed by Frances Roberts-Gregory in a chapter in this volume (see also Daniel and Dolan 2020) – that are pushing the conversation in the right direction.

There is power in a message of "good hope"

In her opening remarks at the launch of the Global Alliance for a Green New Deal in July 2021, UK MP Caroline Lucas noted that "none of us are prepared to limit our imaginations to simply tinkering around the edges and creating a world that is not quite as bad as the one we have now." Similarly, Naomi Klein (2019) argues that the GND can provide "a shared destination – somewhere distinctly better than where we are now. That kind of shared mission is something our late capitalist culture badly needs."

There is evidence in the academic literature to support these sentiments. Milkoreit (2017) argues that "imagination lies at the heart of social change" and that,

> Explicit visions of desirable (sustainable) and undesirable futures are necessary to motivate and guide any kind of change, but might be particularly important for triggering transformational change – a process of fundamentally altering the structure and character of a given system.
>
> *(see also Paterson 2020)*

Apocalyptic framings of a future of 3°C or more of warming abound (Bendell 2018; Wallace-Wells 2020). However, such visions are more likely to lead to "doomerism" or "bad despair" than to spur action (Foust and O'Shannon Murphy 2009; Robbins 2020). Similarly, techno-optimist utopian visions of a post-carbon world fall into the trap of "unvarnished daydreaming in the face of deeply structural problems" or "bad hope" (Robbins 2020: 5). We argue that the GND avoids excessive pessimism and excessive optimism by embracing what Robbins calls "good hope" and "good despair," in that it acknowledges "terrible realities, uneven injustices, and structural barriers, while moving towards revolutionary change" (2020: 5).

This mix of realism and optimism or "critical utopianism" is on full display in the short films produced by The Intercept and The Leap, *A Message from the Future* and *A Message from the Future II: The Years of Repair* (Howley 2020). The first film, narrated by AOC and animated by Molly Crabapple, opens decades in the future with the Congresswoman riding a bullet train from New York to Washington, D.C. She looks back to the "decade of the Green New Deal" (2020–2030) that brought about everything from a solar-powered smart grid to universal health and child care, and publicly funded election campaigns. While most of the future that is imagined in the film is positive, there is an acknowledgment that climate-related disasters still occurred along the way, such as Miami being permanently submerged. Howley (2020) argues that

> [l]ike all meaningful political art, the critical utopianism articulated through this provocative intervention is not simply a political-economic critique of the recent past, nor is it a dire warning for our precarious present. It is an animating force toward realizing a more sustainable future.

The second film is more somber, imagining another pandemic in 2023 as well as articulating more clearly how difficult the struggle will be to arrive at the destination presented in the first film. Nevertheless, it is still hopeful. As one of the film's creators, Avi Lewis (2021), explains, it provides "a map drawn in the colours of a liberatory imagination. And so we also imagine the treasure on that map: the territory under repair." Surely this kind of message is more likely to ignite a social movement than soulless calls for "net zero by 2050," which only seem to inspire those working in the PR departments of large corporations.

What should unite us, but hasn't always been made explicit

Naomi Klein (2019) notes that it was "really just one line in the Leap (Manifesto)" that caused a huge amount of uproar in Canada about the proto-GND proposal; the "no pipelines" line that ruled out the building of any further fossil fuel infrastructure. The AOC–Markey GND Resolution in the US avoided this particular confrontation by not explicitly targeting the fossil fuel industry. Greenpeace USA was quick to point out its concerns with this approach (Redman 2019), as was the Indigenous Environmental Network (IEN), which argued that "the most impactful and direct way to address the problem is to keep fossil fuels in the ground" (IEN 2019). Given that AOC participated in the Standing Rock resistance to the Dakota Access Pipeline, the omission of any call for supply-side climate policies in the Resolution would seem most likely to have been an attempt to "make the proposal more politically palatable for many of the Democrats' presidential contenders in 2020, as well as for labor groups that compose a powerful portion of the party's base" (Colman 2019) rather than a rejection of the keep-it-in-the-ground movement (see also Roberts 2019).

However, only a few years later it is clear that supply-side policy approaches are increasingly moving into the mainstream (Gaulin and Le Billion 2020; Piggot, Verkuijl, van Asselt and Lazarus 2020). President Biden cancelled the Keystone XL pipeline on his first day in office, and a growing number of countries have started to ban certain forms of fossil fuel extraction (e.g., fracking, offshore oil). Over 2000 academics, including more than 100 Nobel laureates, have called on governments to sign a Fossil Fuel Non-Proliferation Treaty. And in August 2021, Denmark and Costa Rica took a step in this direction by forming a Beyond Oil and Gas Alliance, calling on other countries to fix a date to phase out oil and gas production and to stop giving permits for new exploration. As such, it no longer seems as necessary as it might have in 2018 to sideline supply-side policy to make the GND "politically palatable." Furthermore, as fossil fuel extraction and infrastructure projects disproportionately impact Indigenous and racialized communities, it is inconsistent and unconscionable for Green New Dealers to remain silent on the need to keep fossil fuels in the ground.

Bernie Sanders' GND (2020) notably embraced a strong suite of supply-side policies, including banning offshore drilling, mountaintop removal coal mining, fracking, imports and exports of fossil fuels, as well as ending fossil fuel extraction on public lands and new permits for fossil fuel infrastructure. Furthermore, prominent writers on the GND do not shy away from advocating for such proposals. For example, Aronoff et al. (2019) argue that "Focusing exclusively on demand avoids attacking fossil fuel companies' core product, and more importantly fossil political power, head-on. That's a mistake a radical Green New Deal won't make."

What we are still figuring out

As is evident even in the above discussion about what unites Green New Dealers and what might be strategically omitted from some GND proposals, there are tensions within the movement. Schlosser (2021) has suggested that the differences between various GND proponents are irreconcilable because "even if they all hold rapid decarbonization as the end goal, they turn on very different understandings of what constitutes politics, social transformation, and what is or is not 'radical.'" However, the plurality of perspectives is, to some extent, a good thing – the GND needs to be a "big tent" because we can't possibly achieve a socio-economic transformation on the scale required if everyone stays in their own preferred policy camps. It should be instructive to the movement that there are very few disagreements among centrist and right-wing opponents of the GND, who all argue with one voice (even if with different motivations)[1] in favor of carbon pricing. What Green New Dealers need, then, are processes for working through disagreements and seeking common ground. We would note that there has already been an impressive amount of good will demonstrated by, for example, the Red Nation (2021) presenting its Red Deal not "as a counterprogram to the GND, but rather going beyond it" and prominent degrowthers proposing a Green New Deal *with degrowth* (Mastini et al. 2021) rather than launching further debates on the Green New Deal vs. degrowth.

In our view, the key issues that Green New Dealers will have to grapple with in coming years are: (i) how to pay for it; (ii) how much we can rely on technology; (iii) whether to explicitly or implicitly embrace degrowth; (iv) decolonization; and (v) working within or against capitalism.

How to pay for it

The rise of the GND in US policy discourse has been closely associated with the ascent of Modern Money Theory (MMT). In brief, MMT suggests that countries with sovereign control of their currencies can never run out of money (Kelton 2020). Following this logic, the appropriate question is not whether a government can "raise enough money" to pay for a GND, but what constraints on real productive resources (labor, technology, etc.) exist, and what spending limits are required to control inflation (Galvin and Healy 2020: 4). In Chapter 2 of this volume, Yeva Nersisyan explains this approach further and applies it to a costing of the US GND.

While MMT is increasingly popular, many GND proponents do not base their proposals on it, focusing instead on initiatives that can raise finance, such as progressive taxation (e.g., higher corporate taxes, wealth and luxury taxes) (Schroeder 2021). Naomi Klein (2019) has also proposed an international transaction tax to get a fairer share of the financial sector's massive earnings. While taxes of one sort or another are common in many GND proposals, there is not universal acceptance of this approach. In 2019, French economist Thomas Piketty and the former Greek Minister of Finance Yanis Varoufakis engaged in a back-and-forth over whether a European GND should be funded through taxes (Piketty's view) or a system of public green banks (Varoufakis' view; Brown 2019).

Green New Dealers also argue that resources can be redirected from other areas of government spending (Eaton 2021). While we suspect that there is universal agreement within the movement on the need to eliminate fossil fuel subsidies (which were estimated to be US$5.9 trillion in 2020: see Parry, Black and Vernon 2021), reducing or eliminating spending in other areas is more contested. The US Green Party's 2012 GND platform proposed cutting the military budget in half. The Red Nation (2021) goes much further in its proposal to divest from the military, police and prisons, freeing up $1 trillion in the US that could be reinvested in a Red Deal.

Importantly, much of the discussion about how to pay for the GND occurs within the Global North. The issues of funding GNDs in the Global South are even more complex. In addition to discussions about climate reparations (see below) there must be consideration of the constraints that the current system of global economic law places on countries in the Global South. As Muchhala (2020) articulates,

> [a] systemic reassessment of the norms and rules governing fiscal discipline, deficit financing and macroeconomic reporting is critical to salvage public financing for public systems if pandemic recovery, let alone a scaled up financing push for a Global Green New Deal, are to actualize.

Gallagher and Kozul-Wright (2019) propose numerous changes to the current multilateral economic system in their Geneva Principles for a Global Green New Deal.

Technology

There is no credible GND proposal in the world that does not see a critical role for renewable energy technologies, like solar and wind power, in the transformation of our economy from fossil-fuel-dependent to low-carbon. However, there is disagreement in GND discussions about the extent to which we can continue to grow the renewable energy sector indefinitely, given the impacts on communities and environments in the Global South where essential materials for renewable technologies are extracted (Riofrancos 2021; see also chapter by Kolinjivadi and Kothari, this volume), and the substantial land-use footprint of turbines and solar farms (Capellán-Pérez, de Castro and Arto 2017; Palmer-Wilson et al. 2019). The question of the extent to which we can rely on renewable energy technology must also be informed by recent research that suggests that the growth in renewable energy has not displaced fossil fuels but instead has expanded the overall amount of energy that is produced (York and Bell 2019).

Investments in efficiency measures can certainly help with reducing overall energy consumption; however, there are limits to what can be achieved and the potential for rebound effects. The technology issue is thus closely connected to the growth issue (see further below) and the discussion of the need to move toward "private sufficiency" and "public luxury" (Monbiot 2021). For example, should a GND heavily subsidize the automotive industry to spur the rapid uptake of electric vehicles, or focus primarily on expanding and improving public and active transportation options? Bernie Sanders' GND (2020) tried to do both, including US$2.09 trillion in grants to low- and moderate-income families and small businesses to trade in their fossil fuel-dependent vehicles for new electric vehicles, as well as investments in electric trucks for shipping, electric buses, and other upgrades to public transportation. Green New Dealers will have to find an appropriate balance between private and public transportation solutions, and it will be important to get the messaging around the importance of "fewer cars" not just "electric cars" right.

When it comes to other forms of technology, it is less clear what Green New Dealers agree to be appropriate. Should a GND include investments in nuclear power? Authors from the influential US think tank Data for Progress say "yes" (Carlock and Mangan 2018), whereas more than 500 non-profit organizations in the US say "no" (Green New Deal Letter 2019). What is the role of Carbon Capture and Storage (CCS) – is it an essential technology or a tool of the fossil fuel industry to delay meaningful action on climate change? What about biomass, large-scale hydro, and negative emissions technologies? Perhaps the best way to answer these questions is to examine them through the lens of the key principles of the GND. Professor M.V. Ramana and Schyler Edmunston (2020) argue, for example, that when considering nuclear, it is clear that the technology fails to live up to the objectives of the GND: it can't be scaled up quickly, it doesn't create a lot of jobs, and at both the point of uranium extraction and waste disposal, it disproportionally harms Indigenous communities.

Embracing degrowth (implicitly or explicitly)?

Since the publication in 1972 of *The Limits to Growth*, there has been a division between those in the environmental community who view economic growth as harmful to the environment, and those who argue that economic growth can be harnessed to achieve environmental objectives (i.e., "green growth"). In recent years, the degrowth movement, which argues for a move away from an overriding preoccupation with GDP growth in the Global North, has flourished, particularly in Europe. The degrowth movement shares many of the same objectives as the GND movement. However, as Eaton (2021: 7) points out,

> GND proposals would initiate large public investments, that, at least in the short term, would build out a tremendous amount of infrastructure…Whether [this] could be reconciled with no growth or degrowth economies is a question these movements have largely side-stepped.

One positive aspect of imagining a GND that centers investments in care work and "pink collar" jobs in education in health (discussed in the chapter by Robinson in this volume) is that it lessens the dependency on the renewable energy sector alone for job growth and relies largely on existing institutions and infrastructure.

Several prominent scholars have argued for a green growth approach in the GND and suggested that the growth produced by the GND justifies the spending required for it (Pollin 2018, 2019; Stiglitz 2020). Others have acknowledged that while some growth may occur at the outset of a GND as a result of the influx of government funding into green sectors, it is neither necessary nor desirable in the long-term (Aronoff et al. 2019; Pettifor 2019). In addition to deciding where to land in this debate (which is discussed in further detail in the chapter by Schor and Tienhaara, this volume), Green New Dealers will have to decide whether to be explicit about their views on economic growth, or instead to equivocate for strategic/political reasons. Unfortunately, degrowth is often misconstrued as a form of eco-austerity and critiqued by those concerned about the well-being of the working class in the Global North. Therefore, an explicit linking of the degrowth and GND movements could potentially hurt the prospects for a large-scale political mobilization. At least in North America, where the degrowth movement has yet to reach the mainstream, focusing on positive messages about jobs, public luxury, and "time wealth" (achieved through work-time reduction), rather than encouraging less consumption, is likely to be a more effective strategy for Green New Dealers. The one exception to this is when the target for reduced consumption is the wealthy: taxing the rich is a policy that has widespread public support in Canada and the US.

Decolonization

Perhaps the most important critique of the GND is that it has, thus far, only paid "lip service to decolonization" (Red Nation 2021). This critique has two distinct but related strands. First, there are concerns about how the GND incorporates the views and interests of Indigenous communities. The Indigenous Environmental Network (IEN 2019) in the US did not support the AOC–Markey GND Resolution because it would "leave incentives by industries and government to continue causing harms to Indigenous communities." Eaton (2021: 7) argues that even though there is interest in decolonization among Green New Dealers, "Indigenous sovereignty, rights, and the return of land" are "still marginal to the GND" (Eaton 2021: 7). We would argue that while this is certainly an area where more work needs to be done, there is now growing attention to indigenizing the GND and recognition within the movement of the importance of Indigenous knowledge about conservation, biodiversity, and reimagining the relationship between humans and nature. Winona LaDuke provides insights into what an Indigenous-led GND could look like in her chapter in this volume.

Second, there is a sense that the GND "has largely been trapped in national imaginations" (in the Global North), while "climate change is global and therefore its solutions, too, must be global" (Paul and Gebrial 2021). Scholars have highlighted the risk that GNDs could usher in "a new era of 'green colonialism'" (Paul and Gebrial 2021; see also Táíwò 2019; Sturman and Heenan 2021 and chapter by Kolinjivadi and Kothari, this volume).

Many Green New Dealers appear to have recognized the shortcomings of nationalist GND discourse, and there are numerous proposals for a global GND (Varoufakis and Adler 2019; Fawcett 2019). Climate debt payments or "climate reparations" to the Global South have emerged as a key proposal in writings about the need to decolonize the GND (Kaboub 2020; Muchhala 2020; Táíwò and Cibralic 2020; Ajl 2021; Red Nation 2021) and was also flagged by UK MP Caroline Lucas (2021) at the launch of a global alliance of lawmakers working on the GND. Clearly, while there has been progress here, there is still much to be done to expand on these proposals and to identify realistic pathways to implementing them.

Working within or against capitalism

Sturman and Heenan (2021: 152) point out that the GND has "come under fire from the left as a vehicle for the continuation of capitalism in crisis." Ajl (2021), who takes a clear anti-capitalist stance, sees a rather more diverse field of GNDs that variously act as "plans for preserving, strengthening, remolding, attacking, or abolishing capitalism." Certainly, the Red Deal is explicitly anti-capitalist, proposing a "full-scale assault on capitalism, using Indigenous knowledge and tried-and-true methods of mass mobilization as its ammunition" (Red Nation 2021).

However, most Green New Dealers are more ambiguous about their position on capitalism. There are certainly many who identify as eco-socialists, but there are also green Keynesians and those who reject all the "isms." We believe that the absence of explicit calls to abolish capitalism in the majority of GND proposals has more to do with pragmatism than a belief that "green capitalism" is sustainable in the long run. In particular, the urgency of responding to the climate crisis in a very short timeframe means that choices have to be made about which battles to prioritize. Eco-Marxist John Bellamy Foster describes the predicament well:

> We cannot deal with the climate crisis, much less the overall planetary ecological emergency, in an effective way while conforming to the logic of a globalized capitalist economy. But we currently live in such an economy, and we have a very short time in which to respond to climate change. So, it becomes a question of immediately choosing to steer society toward putting people and nature before profits, as opposed to what capitalism does, i.e., putting profits before people and nature. We have to go against the logic of the system even while living within it.
>
> *(Quoted in Triantafyllou 2019)*

Noam Chomsky has similarly argued that "a simple consideration of time scales reveals that the existential issues must be considered within the framework of state-capitalist systems" (Chomsky and Pollin 2020: 56). Stilwell (2021: 166) adds to this that, "[w]ishing for a different starting point is not helpful" and that, "the adoption of a GND would be just the start of a journey of socio-economic change, not an end point." The important question then becomes not whether the GND challenges capitalism head-on, but whether it opens "the possibility of moving subsequently to more radical transformations as the process develops" (Stilwell 2021: 166).

On this last point, it is important to note that Green New Dealers increasingly emphasize the need for an expansion of public ownership, particularly in the energy sector (see further the chapter by MacArthur, Hoicka and Das, this volume), but also in a wide range of other areas. For example, Vansintjan (2020) calls for GNDs to create "libraries for everything," from tools to seeds. Further, a major GND policy piece in the US focuses on expanding as well as decarbonizing public housing (Cohen et al. 2019, 2021). Expansion of public ownership and cooperative forms of ownership offers a potential pathway to a post-capitalist system even if they are not framed as anti-capitalist initiatives.

Several chapters in this volume address capitalism and the GND in greater depth, particularly those by John McCollum and Benjamin Selwyn.

Outline of the book

There are two key aims of this volume. The first is to explore significant conversations that we believe will contribute to the development of the GND narrative. The second aim is to decenter the US in GND discourse, because the ecological crisis is, after all, global. The contributors to come from a variety of disciplinary backgrounds and some take a purely scholarly approach, while others adopt a more activist lens. While we, the editors, would consider ourselves advocates[2] of the GND, many authors in the volume express a significant amount of skepticism about either the narrative itself or about specific GND policies and proposals.

We find all of the critiques presented by the authors to be constructive and helpful in driving the further refinement of the GND narrative.

We begin in Part I by exploring the political economy of the GND.

In Chapter 1, Ann Pettifor – one of the original members of the British Green New Deal Group – argues that the green movement missed an important target at birth by failing to engage with, challenge, and disarm the entrenched power of Wall Street and the sector's support for the fossil fuel industry. The GND has helped to change this, but Pettifor expresses concern that in the US, President Biden is still conceding too much power to the private authority of Wall Street institutions.

In Chapter 2, Yeva Nersisyan turns to the question of the affordability of the GND. She argues that the MMT approach allows us to reorient the conversation away from what is unimportant (finance) to what is essential (real resources). She suggests that taking this approach leads to completely different conclusions about both the affordability of the GND and the macroeconomic challenges that need to be tackled to make it possible.

In Chapter 3, Ray Galvin argues that central banks have an important role to play in monitoring possible inflationary and other structural economic effects of the substantial amount of government spending that GNDs entail. Central banks can sell or buy government (and other) bonds to stimulate or dampen inflation and can be required to trade bonds to the favor of green or at least climate-neutral enterprises. However, Galvin cautions that there may be resistance to such an approach from financiers who argue for complete independence of central banks from political/democratic control.

In Chapter 4, John McCollum provides a critique of the GND from an ecological Marxist perspective. He highlights three key concerns: that the GND will expand the "treadmill of production;" that the GND will widen the "metabolic rift" between the Global North and Global South; and that an expanded state bureaucracy could boost a new round of capitalist power, threatening to turn the GND into a crutch for capital, to the detriment of both equality and environment. McCollum stresses that his critique is meant to be constructive and to help the movement avoid poorly conceived GNDs that "could threaten the entire enterprise."

In Chapter 5, Benjamin Selwyn continues with the theme of capitalism, but focuses on the need for a GND for agriculture to combat environmental degradation, social inequality and labor exploitation. Selwyn identifies a number of areas for discussion and political action, such as the reorientation of state subsidies, workers' rights, agrarian reform, the decommodification of food, agroecology, possibilities for urban agriculture, the application of new technologies, and rewilding.

In Chapter 6, Juliet B. Schor and Kyla Tienhaara discuss the relationship between degrowth and the GND. They argue that the type of policies advocated by degrowth proponents – job guarantees, worktime reductions, wealth caps or taxes, etc. – also address inequality and are a natural fit for GNDs. They focus on how a shorter working week could be incorporated into GNDs.

In Chapter 7, Todd Tucker and Timothy Meyer turn to the role of the global legal infrastructure in facilitating or hindering GNDs and sketch out an approach to modernize the current rules. They outline changes to the World Trade Organization rules and new uses of domestic trade remedy laws. In their view, there is currently an opportunity to remake and green an international trade and investment architecture that is already in crisis.

In Part II, we turn to issues of justice (economic, gender, racial) and democracy.

In Chapter 8, Joanna Robinson discusses the possibilities of a combined Green New Deal/COVID-19 recovery plan that prioritizes economic and climate justice by focusing on creating decent, well-paying jobs in low- or zero-carbon sectors of the economy. In a context where the COVID-19 pandemic has laid bare the reality of social and economic injustice in our communities globally, Robinson calls for a plan that is truly transformative and justice oriented and supports the well-being of people.

In Chapter 9, Josiah Rector provides some historical lessons for Green New Dealers about how the original New Deal perpetuated environmental inequality in Detroit, Michigan, between the 1930s and the 1960s. Rector argues that the linkage between the New Deal and racial discrimination was historically contingent rather than inevitable, and that racially just Green New Deal is possible.

Winona LaDuke puts forward, in Chapter 10, a bold proposal for an Indigenous-led, women-led GND: the Sitting Bull Plan. In addition to calling for respect for Indigenous knowledge (e.g., in the management of forest fires), she provides practical solutions such as a new material economy built around hemp.

In Chapter 11, Frances Roberts-Gregory describes the Feminist Agenda for a Green New Deal, an evolving policy platform and ecofeminist manifesto that provides innovative and cross-cutting perspectives on how policymakers, activist organizations, and civil society should plan for greener, regenerative, and care-fueled futures for all. She argues that any GND that fails to center solutions devised by feminists and BIPOC communities will continue to exacerbate global inequality, as well as the rights of nature and human rights abuses.

Julie L. MacArthur, Christina E. Hoicka, and Runa R. Das take up the concept of energy democracy and the lessons it holds for our understanding of GNDs in Chapter 12. They argue that GND proposals lacking significant democratization components are unlikely to be deeply transformative and thus more likely to reproduce (or even intensify) existing socio-economic cleavages.

In the final chapter in this section, Vijay Kolinjivadi and Ashish Kothari argue that the ecological ramifications of colonialism and continued global dependence on cheap labor and resources have gone unnoticed in calls for GNDs. They conclude that centering ecological reparations, decolonization, and deliberative democracy is key to a truly just transition.

Many of the chapters in the first two parts of the book refer to the US context. The AOC–Markey Resolution and Bernie Sanders' GND have without a doubt been inspirational to many and have generated a rich literature on what the GND is and what it could be. Specific proposals for a GND for Housing and a GND for Public Schools have also demonstrated that umbrella proposals covering the entire economy are not the only path to achieving the GND. However, there has been much less attention given to how the GND has been articulated and implemented in other political contexts (see, however, Cohen and Riofrancos 2020 on the GND in Latin America). For this reason, Part III aims to shine a light on the GND in practice outside of the US.

In Chapter 14, Vincent (Yijiang) Huang proposes a centrally funded and locally administered Chinese Green Job Guarantee to eliminate China's 24.27 million in urban unemployment while also improving infrastructure, addressing environmental degradation, and preserving traditional culture. Huang argues that the program would pay for itself through increased GDP growth.

In Chapter 15, Kyla Tienhaara, Sun-Jin Yun, and Ryan Gunderson examine both of South Korea's GNDs. The first (in 2009) focused overwhelmingly on a controversial project to dam Korea's four major rivers and had a minimal impact on greening Korea's economy. The second (2020) is socially and environmentally superior to its predecessor, but still involves support for projects with questionable environmental outcomes and places too much faith in the possibility of green growth.

In Chapter 16, David Adler and Pawel Wargan critically examine another existing platform – the EU Green Deal. They argue that far from being a pathbreaking vision for an ecological future, the EU Green Deal is a historic effort to greenwash Europe's political and economic status quo. Importantly, they highlight that the lack of involvement of the labor movement in the push for a GND enabled EU policymakers to craft an agenda that was green on the outside, but hollow on the inside.

In Chapter 17, Daniel Bailey and Elena Hofferberth trace the political and economic development of the UK's version of the GND, from its conception shortly before the global financial crash of 2008 to the calls to Build Back Better during the COVID-19 pandemic and outline the ways in which its development has been shaped by the numerous dysfunctions and pathologies of contemporary British capitalism.

In Chapter 18, Seth Klein examines the call for a Made-in-Canada GND. He explores some of the unique Canadian challenges: while the overall economy is not heavily dependent on the extraction of fossil fuels, certain regions are, and the highly decentralized nature of the Canadian federation presents special barriers to effective action. But Klein explains how a robust just transition plan "that leaves no one behind" could help to overcome such challenges.

In the final chapter, Christopher W. Gibson considers another site for GNDs to emerge: the city. Numerous municipal GNDs have popped up in the US in recent years. However, Gibson argues that the financialization of urban production and governance can hinder environmental reform efforts by local governments. Ultimately, he argues that in pursuing a GND, we must be cognizant of the need for financial reform and adaptation because financial structures can prefigure the outcomes of well-intended social and environmental planning.

We recognize that there are numerous other issues and case studies that are deserving of inclusion in this volume. Indeed, we sought out chapters on GNDs in Africa, Latin America and Australia. Unfortunately, as privileged as many are in the academic sector, the pandemic still took a heavy toll, and several authors had to withdraw from this project to focus on more pressing issues. While we were sorry to lose the insights of those scholars in these pages, we see this Handbook as only the beginning of a conversation that we hope to continue with an ever-widening assemblage of scholars, activists, and policymakers in the years to come.

Acknowledgements

The authors would like to thank Pavel Graymason for his comments on an earlier draft of this chapter.

Notes

1 In June 2021, *Unearthed*, the investigative journalism branch of Greenpeace, released a recording of an ExxonMobil lobbyist explaining that the company had backed a carbon tax in an effort to stall more serious measures to combat the climate crisis (see further Carter 2021).

2 See Green (2020: 152) on why "As climate scholars, it is our professional responsibility to engage in climate politics and use our expertise to serve as advocates, to identify the political causes of climate inaction as well as solutions to overcome them."

References

Adler, D. and Wargan, P. 2019. Stop Polluting Our Green New Deal. *Jacobin*. 11 June. Available at: https://jacobinmag.com/2019/06/green-new-deal-europe-capitalism

Agyeman, J., Bullard, R.D. and Evans, B. 2003. *Just Sustainabilities: Development in an Unequal World*. Cambridge, MA: Earthscan/MIT Press.

Ajl, M. 2021. *A People's Green New Deal.* London: Pluto Press.

Altenburg, T. and Assmann, C. (Eds.) 2017. *Green Industrial Policy. Concept, Policies, Country Experiences.* Geneva, Bonn: UN Environment; German Development Institute/Deutsches Institut für Entwicklungspolitk (DIE).

Aronoff, K. 2021. *Overheated: How Capitalism Broke the Planet and How We Fight Back.* New York: Bold Type Books.

Aronoff, K., Battistoni, A., Cohen, D.A. and Riofrancos, T. 2019. *A Planet to Win: Why We Need a Green New Deal.* New York: Verso.

Battistoni, A. 2017. Living, Not Just Surviving. *Jacobin.* 15 August. Available at: https://www.jacobinmag.com/2017/08/living-not-just-surviving/

Bendell, J. 2018. Deep Adaptation: A Map for Navigating Climate Tragedy. *IFLAS Occasional Paper 2.* Available at: https://jembendell.com/2019/05/15/deep-adaptation-versions/

Brown, E. 2019. The Secret to Funding a Green New Deal. *Truthdig.* 19 March. Available at: https://www.truthdig.com/articles/the-secret-to-funding-a-green-new-deal/

Capellán-Pérez, I., de Castro, C. and Arto, I. 2017. Assessing Vulnerabilities and Limits in the Transition to Renewable Energies: Land Requirements under 100% Solar Energy Scenarios. *Renewable and Sustainable Energy Reviews.* 77: 760–782. Available at: https://doi.org/10.1016/j.rser.2017.03.137.

Carlock, G. and Mangan, E. 2018. A Green New Deal: A Progressive Vision for Environmental Sustainability and Economic Stability. Data for Progress. Available at: https://www.filesforprogress.org/pdfs/Green_New_Deal.pdf

Carter, L. 2021. Inside Exxon's Playbook: How America's Biggest Oil Company Continues to Oppose Action on Climate Change. *Unearthed.* 30 June. Available at: https://unearthed.greenpeace.org/2021/06/30/exxon-climate-change-undercover/

Chen, V.T. 2015. *Cut Loose: Jobless and Hopeless in an Unfair Economy.* Berkeley: University of California Press.

Chomsky, N. and Pollin, R. 2020. *Climate Crisis and the Global Green New Deal.* New York: Verso.

Cohen, D.A. and Riofrancos, T. 2020. Latin America's Green New Deal. *NACLA Report on the Americas.* 52(2): 117–121. Available at: https://doi.org/10.1080/10714839.2020.1768726

Cohen, D.A. et al. 2019. A Green New Deal for American Public Housing Communities. Data for Progress. Available at: https://www.filesforprogress.org/reports/green-new-deal-public-housing-national.pdf

Cohen, D.A. et al. 2021. A Green New Deal for Public Housing to Deliver Racial, Economic, and Climate Justice. *climate + community project.* Available at: https://www.climateandcommunity.org/a-gnd-for-public-housing

Coleman, A. 2019. How Black Lives Matter to the Green New Deal. *The Nation.* 14 March. Available at: https://www.thenation.com/article/archive/reparations-green-new-deal-aoc/

Colman, Z. 2019. Green New Deal Won't Call for End to Fossil Fuels. *Politico.* 4 February. Available at: https://www.politico.com/story/2019/02/04/green-new-deal-fossil-fuels-1142544

Crawford, T. 2021. B.C.'s Heat Wave: Intense Weather Event Is Linked to Climate Crisis, Say Scientists. *Vancouver Sun.* 26 June. Available at: https://vancouversun.com/news/bc-heat-wave-intense-weather-event-is-linked-to-climate-crisis-say-scientists/wcm/eba6b54f-cb59-46c8-a43a-7d535ea358d6/amp/

Daniel, T. and Dolan, M. 2020. Intersectionality and Collective Action: Visioning a Feminist Green New Deal in the US. *Gender & Development.* 28(3): 515–533. Available at: DOI: 10.1080/13552074.2020.1843829

Eaton, E. 2021. Approaches to Energy Transitions: Carbon Pricing, Managed Decline, and/or Green New Deal? *Geography Compass.* 15(2): 1–11. Available at: https://doi.org/10.1111/gec3.12554

Eckersley, R. 1993. Free Market Environmentalism: Friend or Foe? *Environmental Politics.* 2(1): 1–19. Available at: DOI: 10.1080/09644019308414061

Eckersley, R. 2021. Greening states and Societies: From Transitions to Great Transformations. *Environmental Politics.* 30(1–2): 245–265. Available at: https://doi.org/10.1080/09644016.2020.1810890

Evergreen Action. 2021. Evergreen Explains: What is a Civilian Climate Corps and Why Democrats Are Making it a Top Priority in Reconciliation. *Evergreen Action Blog.* 19 July. Available at: https://www.evergreenaction.com/blog/evergreen-explains-what-is-a-civilian-climate-corps?

Fawcett, J. 2019. The Global Green New Deal. People's Policy Project. Available at: https://www.peoplespolicyproject.org/wp-content/uploads/2019/06/GlobalGreenNewDeal.pdf

Fischer, C. and Jacobsen, G. 2021. The Green New Deal and the Future of Carbon Pricing. *Journal of Policy Analysis and Management*. 40(3): 988–995.

Foust, C. and O'Shannon Murphy, W. 2009. Revealing and Reframing Apocalyptic Tragedy in Global Warming Discourse. *Environmental Communication*. 3(2): 151–167. Available at: DOI: 10.1080/17524030902916624

Gallagher, K. and Kozul-Wright, R. 2019. *A New Multilateralism for Shared Prosperity: Geneva Principles for a Global Green New Deal*. Geneva: UNCTAD. Available at: https://unctad.org/webflyer/new-multilateralism-shared-prosperity-geneva-principles-global-green-new-deal

Galvin, R. and Healy, N. 2020. The Green New Deal in the United States: What It Is and How to Pay for it. *Energy Research & Social Science*. 67: 101529. Available at: https://doi.org/10.1016/j.erss.2020.101529

Gaulin, N. and Le Billon, P. 2020. Climate Change and Fossil Fuel Production Cuts: Assessing Global Supply-Side Constraints and Policy Implications. *Climate Policy*. 20(1). Available at: https://doi.org/10.1080/14693062.2020.1725409

Green, J. 2020. Less Talk, More Walk: Why Climate Change Demands Activism in the Academy. *Daedalus*. 149(4): 151–162.

Green, J. 2021. Does Carbon Pricing Reduce Emissions? A Review of Ex-Post Analyses. *Environmental Research Letters*. 16: 043004.

Green New Deal Letter. 2019. Letter to US Congress from Environmental NGOs Re: Legislation to Address the Urgent Threat of Climate Change. 10 January. Full list of Signatories. Available at: https://www.earthworks.org/cms/assets/uploads/2019/01/Green-New-Deal-ltr-to-Congress-20190110.pdf

Hathaway, J. 2020. Climate Change, the Intersectional Imperative, and the Opportunity of the Green New Deal. *Environmental Communication*. 14(1): 13–22. Available at: https://doi.org/10.1080/17524032.2019.1629977

Hickel, J. 2021. *Less Is More: How Degrowth Will Save the World*. London: William Heinemann.

Howley, K. 2020. Animating the Green New Deal: 'A Message from the Future with Alexandria Ocasio-Cortez' (2019). *Animation Studies 2.0 Blog*. Available at: http://blog.animationstudies.org/?p=3689

Indigenous Environmental Network (IEN). 2019. Talking Points on the AOC-Markey Green New Deal (GND) Resolution. 8 February. Available at: https://www.ienearth.org/talking-points-on-the-aoc-markey-green-new-deal-gnd-resolution/

IPCC. 2021. AR6 Climate Change 2021: The Physical Science Basis. *6th Assessment Report: Working Group I*. Intergovernmental Panel on Climate Change. Available at: https://www.ipcc.ch/report/ar6/wg1

Jafry, T. (Ed.). 2019. *Routledge Handbook of Climate Justice*. London: Routledge.

Kaboub, F. 2020. Green and Just. *New Internationalist*. 26 October. Available at: https://newint.org/features/2020/08/11/green-and-just

Kallis, G. 2019. A Green New Deal Must Not Be Tied to Economic Growth. *Truthout*. 10 March. Available at: https://truthout.org/articles/a-green-new-deal-must-not-be-tied-to-economic-growth/

Kelton, S. 2020. *The Deficit Myth: Modern Monetary Theory and the Birth of the People's Economy*. New York: Public Affairs.

Klein, N. 2019. *On Fire: The Burning Case for a Green New Deal*. Toronto: Alfred A. Knopf.

Klein, S. 2020. *A Good War: Mobilizing Canada for the Climate Emergency*. Toronto: ECW Press.

Konisky, D. and Carley, S. 2021. What We Can Learn from the Green New Deal about the Importance of Equity in National Climate Policy. *Journal of Policy Analysis and Management*. 40(3): 996–1002.

Lamb, W. F. et al. 2020. Discourses of Climate Delay. *Global Sustainability*. 3: E17. Available at: https://doi.org/10.1017/sus.2020.13

Lehman, J. and Johnson, E. 2021. Blue Imaginaries for a Green New Deal. In H.K. Paul and D. Gebrial (Eds.) *Perspectives on a Global Green New Deal*. London: Rosa Luxemburg Stiftung and The Leap. Available at: https://global-gnd.com/water/#blue-imaginaries-for-a-green-new-deal

Lewis, A. 2021. Epilogue. In Paul, H.K. and Gebrial, D. (Eds.): *Perspectives on a Global Green New Deal*. London: Rosa Luxemburg Stiftung and The Leap. Available at: https://global-gnd.com/category/epilogue/

Lucas, C. 2021. Opening Remarks – Launch of the Global Alliance for a Green New Deal. [video] Available at: https://www.youtube.com/watch?v=r5fTMg4aWaQ

Machin, A. 2019. Changing the Story: The Discourse of Ecological Modernization in the European Union. *Environmental Politics*. 28(2): 208–227.

Maher, N. 2008. *Nature's New Deal: The Civilian Conservation Corps and the Roots of the American Environmental Movement*. Oxford: Oxford University Press.

Mastini, R., Kallis, G. and Hickel, J. 2021. A Green New Deal without Growth? *Ecological Economics*. 179: 106832.

Mazzucato, M. 2015. *The Entrepreneurial State: Debunking Public vs. Private Sector Myths*. London: Anthem Press.

Mehleb, R.I., Kallis, G. and Zografos, C. 2021. A Discourse Analysis of Yellow-Vest Resistance Against Carbon Taxes. *Environmental Innovation and Societal Transitions*. 40: 382–394. Available at: https://doi.org/10.1016/j.eist.2021.08.005

Meyer, R. 2019. A Centuries-Old Idea Could Revolutionize Climate Policy. *The Atlantic*. 19 February. Available at: https://www.theatlantic.com/science/archive/2019/02/green-new-deal-economic-principles/582943/

Meyer, R. 2021. The Green New Deal Does Not, Strictly Speaking, Exist. *The Atlantic*. 13 July. Available at: https://www.theatlantic.com/science/archive/2021/07/the-green-new-deal-doesnt-exist/619424/

Milkoreit, M. 2017. Imaginary Politics: Climate Change and Making the Future. *Elementa: Science of the Anthropocene*. 5: 62. Available at: https://doi.org/10.1525/elementa.249

Monbiot, G. 2021. Private Sufficiency, Public Luxury: Land is the Key to the Transformation of Society. *40th Annual Schumacher Lecture*. Available at: https://www.thealternative.org.uk/dailyalternative/2021/3/28/monbiot-schumacher-public-luxury

Muchhala, B. 2020. Towards a Decolonial and Feminist Global Green New Deal. *Rosa Luxemburg Stiftung*. 24 August. Available at: https://www.rosalux.de/en/news/id/43146/towards-a-decolonial-and-feminist-global-green-new-deal

NoiseCat, J.B. 2019. The Environmental Movement Needs to Reckon with Its Racist History. *Vice*. 13 September. Available at: https://www.vice.com/en/article/bjwvn8/the-environmental-movement-needs-to-reckon-with-its-racist-history

Nordhaus, T. and Trembath, A. 2019. Is Climate Change like Diabetes or an Asteroid? *The Breakthrough Institute Blog*. 4 March. Available at: https://thebreakthrough.org/articles/is-climate-change-like-diabetes

Palmer-Wilson, K. et al. 2019. Impact of Land Requirements on Electricity System Decarbonisation Pathways. *Energy Policy*. 129: 193–205. Available at: https://doi.org/10.1016/j.enpol.2019.01.071.

Parry, I., Black, S. and Vernon, N. 2021. Still Not Getting Energy Prices Right: A Global and Country Update of Fossil Fuel Subsidies. International Monetary Fund. IMF Working Paper No. 2021/236.

Paterson, M. 2020. 'The End of the Fossil Fuel Age'? Discourse Politics and Climate Change Political Economy. *New Political Economy*. Available at: https://doi.org/10.1080/13563467.2020.1810218

Paul, H.K. and Gebrial, D. 2021. Climate Justice in a Global Green New Deal. In Paul, H.K. and Gebrial, D. (Eds.) *Perspectives on a Global Green New Deal*. London: Rosa Luxemburg Stiftung and The Leap. Available at: https://global-gnd.com/introduction/

Pellow, D.N. and Brulle, R.G. (Eds.) 2005. *Power, Justice, and the Environment: A Critical Appraisal of the Environmental Justice Movement*. Cambridge, MA: The MIT Press.

Pettifor, A. 2019. *The Case for the Green New Deal*. New York: Verso.

Piggot, G., Verkuijl, C., van Asselt, H. and Lazarus, M. 2020. Curbing Fossil Fuel Supply to Achieve Climate Goals. *Climate Policy*. 20(8): 881–887.

Pollin, R. 2018. De-Growth versus a Green New Deal. *New Left Review*. 112: 5–25.

Pollin, R. 2019. Advancing a Viable Global Climate Stabilization Project: Degrowth versus the Green New Deal. *Review of Radical Political Economics*. 51(2): 311–319.

Ramana, M.V. and Edmundson, S. 2020. "No" in "The Big Debate: Should Nuclear Energy be Part of a Green New Deal?" *The Toronto Star*. 30 June. Available at: https://www.thestar.com/opinion/contributors/thebigdebate/2020/06/30/the-big-debate-should-nuclear-energy-be-part-of-a-green-new-deal.html

Recognizing the Duty of the Federal Government to Create a Green New Deal. H. Res. 109, 116th Congress. 2019. Available from: https://www.congress.gov/bill/116th-congress/house-resolution/109/text.

Redman, J. 2019. Breaking: Green New Deal Still Needs to Face Fossil Fuel Industry. *Greenpeace USA*. 7 February. Available at: https://www.greenpeace.org/usa/news/breaking-green-new-deal-still-needs-to-face-fossil-fuel-industry/

Red Nation. 2021. *The Red Deal: Indigenous Action to Save the Earth*. Brooklyn, NY: Common Notions.

Riofrancos, T. 2021. The Rush to 'go electric' Comes with a Hidden Cost: Destructive Lithium Mining. *The Guardian*. 14 June. Available at: https://www.theguardian.com/commentisfree/2021/jun/14/electric-cost-lithium-mining-decarbonasation-salt-flats-chile

Robbins, P. 2020. Is Less More … Or Is More Less? Scaling the Political Ecologies of the Future. *Political Geography*. 76: 102018. Available at: https://doi.org/10.1016/j.polgeo.2019.04.010

Roberts, D. 2019. There's Now an Official Green New Deal. Here's What's in It. *Vox*. 7 February. Available at: https://www.vox.com/energy-and-environment/2019/2/7/18211709/green-new-deal-resolution-alexandria-ocasio-cortez-markey

Rodrik, D. 2014. Green Industrial Policy. *Oxford Review of Economic Policy*. 30(3): 469–491.

Sanders, B. 2020. The Green New Deal. *BernieSanders.com*. Available at: https://berniesanders.com/issues/green-new-deal/

Schlosberg, D. 2007. *Defining Environmental Justice: Theories, Movements, and Nature*. Oxford: Oxford University Press.

Schlosser, K. 2021. Contrasting Visions of the Green New Deal. *Environmental Politics*. 30(3): 477–481. Available at: DOI: 10.1080/09644016.2020.1847514

Schor, J. 2015. Climate, Inequality and the Need to Reframe Climate Policy. *Review of Radical Political Economics*. 47(4): 525–536.

Schroeder, S. 2021. A Kaleckian Wealth Tax to Support a Green New Deal. *The Economic and Labour Relations Review*. 32(2): 190–208.

Stiglitz, J. 2020. The Economic Case for a Green New Deal. In Prakash, V. and Girgenti, G. (Eds.) *Winning the Green New Deal: Why We Must, How We Can*. New York: Simon & Schuster.

Stilwell, F. 2021. From Green Jobs to Green New Deal: What Are the Questions? *The Economic and Labour Relations Review*. 32(2): 155–169.

Sturman, A. and Heenan, N. 2021. Introduction: Configuring the Green New Deal. *The Economic and Labour Relations Review*. 32(2): 149–154.

Táíwò, O. 2019. How a Green New Deal Could Exploit Developing Countries. *The Conversation*. 25 February. Available at: https://theconversation.com/how-a-green-new-deal-could-exploit-developing-countries-111726

Táíwò, O. and Cibralic, B. 2020. The Case for Climate Reparations. *Foreign Policy*. 10 October. Available at: https://foreignpolicy.com/2020/10/10/case-for-climate-reparations-crisis-migration-refugees-inequality/

Tcherneva, P. 2020. *The Case for a Job Guarantee*. London: Wiley.

Triantafyllou, V. 2019. A Green New Deal Is the First Step Toward an Eco-Revolution. *Truthout*. 9 February. Available at: https://truthout.org/articles/a-green-new-deal-is-the-first-step-toward-an-eco-revolution/

Tvinnereim, E. and Mehling, M. 2018. Carbon Pricing and Deep Decarbonisation. *Energy Policy*. 121: 185–189.

UNEP. 2009. Global Green New Deal. Policy Brief. Geneva: United Nations. Available at: http://www.unep.org/greeneconomy/sites/unep.org.greeneconomy/files/publications/a_global_green_new_deal_policy_brief.pdf

Vansintjan, A. 2020. Public Abundance is the Secret to the Green New Deal. *Green European Journal*. 27 May. Available at: https://www.greeneuropeanjournal.eu/public-abundance-is-the-secret-to-the-green-new-deal/

Varoufakis, Y. and Adler, D. 2019. It's Time for Nations to Unite around an International Green New Deal. *The Guardian*. 23 April. Available at: https://www.theguardian.com/commentisfree/2019/apr/23/international-green-new-deal-climate-change-global-response

Wallace-Wells, D. 2020. *The Uninhabitable Earth: Life after Warming*. New York: Tim Duggan Books.

Wu Committee. n.d. Our Policy Platform Is More than a Vision. Michelle for Mayor. Available at: https://www.michelleforboston.com/issues [Retrieved 24 October 2021].

York, R. and Bell, S. 2019. Energy Transitions or Additions? Why a Transition From Fossil Fuels Requires More than the Growth of Renewable Energy. *Energy Research & Social Science*. 51: 40–43.

PART I

Political economy of the Green New Deal

1

THE GREEN NEW DEAL, CLIMATE BREAKDOWN, AND POWER

Ann Pettifor

Introduction

> Climate Change is not just an environmental issue, it is an economic issue. All the smartest economists agree on this: The cost of fighting climate change now is nothing compared to the cost of suffering through it later.
>
> *(Yellen 2021)*

In 2008, and to little fanfare, the London-based New Economics Foundation (NEF) published a report called *The Green New Deal.* It had been argued over, drafted, and finally edited for months by a small informal group loosely associated with NEF called the Green New Deal group, which I'll refer to here as "the British group." The group included a macroeconomist, a political economist, an accountant, a journalist, a solar energy pioneer, and several distinguished environmentalists. The title of the report deliberately drew on, and was inspired by, US President Franklin D. Roosevelt's New Deal. Like Roosevelt, in his efforts to tackle simultaneously the crisis of unemployment and the Dust Bowl of the 1930s, the British group sought to forge a plan for both economic and ecological transformation. They had come together on the understanding that finance, the economy, and the ecosystem are all tightly bound together. Any attempt to address and transform the ecosystem required transformation of the economic system – financialized capitalism.

While this was a radical departure from traditional green manifestos, the group were not the first to use the term. In January 2007, Thomas L. Friedman had called for a Green New Deal (GND) in a *New York Times* column titled, "A Warning from the Garden." But Friedman's call was limited to technological change – for an "energy New Deal." "We need more of everything," he wrote, "solar, wind, hydro, ethanol, biodiesel, clean coal and nuclear power– and conservation."

Unaware of Friedman's call, the British group persevered through the financial crisis of 2007–2008 to develop their plan for addressing and averting financial breakdown, climate change and biodiversity collapse. It was not easy. The economists in the group (including, for transparency, myself) were overwhelmingly concerned with monetary policy and the impact of the finance sector on both the economy and the ecosystem. The environmentalists were singularly focussed on the fragility of the planet. Over regular,

DOI: 10.4324/9781003110880-3

informal evening meals in a central London apartment, there were ferocious disagreements when members of the group argued at cross purposes. Eventually, however, and thanks to our wise and convivial convenor, Colin Hines, the group arrived at a radical consensus, and the *Green New Deal* report was published in July 2008– just before the collapse of Lehman Brothers.

Ten years later, and after consultations between the British group and representatives of the United States' Justice Democrats (who had visited the United Kingdom), campaigning in America began around the GND, with Alexandria Ocasio-Cortez and the Sunrise Movement at the forefront. This was an effort to galvanize Democrat candidates and their supporters; first in the 2018 congressional primaries, and later in the 2019 Bernie Sanders campaign for the presidency. The outcome of that grassroots advocacy, and of wider international campaigning pressure led by Greta Thunberg, was the welcome, albeit very late launch of a radical climate plan by President Joe Biden in January 2021.

The eerie silence of a clamorous climate movement

Climate and environmental advocacy have a long and honourable history. Campaigners stood on the shoulders of far-seeing scientists like Svante August Arrhenius (1859–1927), a Swedish physicist who as far back as 1896 warned of the effects of carbon dioxide in his paper, "On the Influence of Carbonic Acid in the Air upon the Temperature of the Ground" *(Barral 2019)*. The scientist James Hansen alerted the US Congress in 1988 to an earth that was warmer than at any time in the history of instrumental measurements. Hansen went on to warn that "global warming has reached a level such that we can ascribe with a high degree of confidence a cause and effect relationship between the greenhouse effect and observed warming" (Shabecoff 1988).

These scientific breakthroughs helped launch the global environmental movement. It has now been in existence in an organized form for at least 60 years. Over that time, hundreds of thousands of climate campaigners – collectively dubbed "the largest movement in the world" by Paul Hawken in his book *Blessed Unrest* (2007) – drew the attention of the media, politicians, and officials to threats posed by climate breakdown and biodiversity collapse. Throughout this period, there were wins at the local level (on environmental standards, for example) and big wins at the international level – including the Montreal Protocol (1987), the Kyoto Protocol (1997), and the Paris Agreement (2015).

As Hawken noted at the time, "there are over one – and maybe even two – million organizations [worldwide] working toward ecological sustainability and social justice." And yet, he went on to argue, the movement is "atomized" and "largely ignored." There was no organized effort leading society toward a legislative framework that would tackle the powerful, urgently drive down greenhouse gas emissions across the board and begin to sequester carbon dioxide.

The green movement and the economy

In 1997, Friends of the Earth and the US National Wildlife Federation launched Quantum Leap – a new initiative on the economics of climate change aimed at training campaigners to become financially literate and influence the private finance sector. Five years later, in 2002, over 100 civil society organizations gathered in the Italian village of Collevecchio and issued a *Declaration on Financial Institutions and Sustainability*. In 2004, a new organization – BankTrack – was established to campaign on projects co-financed by private banks, such as the OCP pipeline in Ecuador, the Chad–Cameroon oil pipeline, the Camisea gas project in Peru, and the financing of oil palm plantations in Indonesia and Malaysia.

And yet, while there were victories, for many years there was no real and meaningful impact on governmental decision-making. In the words of Kumi Naidoo in 2011, then the executive director of Greenpeace: "We are winning very significant battles, but we are losing the planet" (Duke 2011).

The BBC pointed out that Greenpeace "was born from the fight against nuclear weapons and enjoyed quick success. Just one year after its first protest against nuclear testing – at Amchitka Island, Alaska in 1971 – the US government turned on its heels and left" (Duke 2011).

The fight to save the planet has been less successful. "When we add up all the victories, it does not equal the level of change that we need now," said Naidoo. "We have to recognize that a lot of damage has been done" (Duke 2011).

For years, the green movement's focus had relied on concerns expressed by scientists (often cautiously expressed and dogged by jargon) and on individual and community action: "change your lightbulbs, eat local," or "recycle, repair, reuse, reduce, localize." With the exception of the Dutch Friends of the Earth initiative of 1997, there were few demands of the state, or of states, for structural or legislative (regulatory) changes to ensure sustainability – demands that could help to build a united movement at both national and international levels.

Historically, other successful global movements had adopted demands for structural change. Campaigns like the international anti-slavery movement fought to change the structure of society, the economy and of laws that legitimized slavery. The suffragette movement demanded societal changes and the abolition of discriminatory laws on the right to vote. The American civil rights movement demanded legal recognition and federal protection for the citizenship rights of Black people, as enumerated in the Constitution and in federal law. The global anti-apartheid movement demanded structural changes to South African society and apartheid laws.

These demands for structural change addressed power directly and were unifying and motivating in their demand for action. They united behind active slogans like: "Votes for Women," "All Power to the People," "Black Power," "End Apartheid," "No Taxation without Representation."

Compared to these great movements, the climate change movement was massive and yet remained fractured, atomized, and largely ignored. This, despite public opinion surveys such as one conducted by Yale University and Gallup in September 2007, which found that "nearly half of Americans now believe that global warming is either already having dangerous impacts on people around the world or will in the next 10 years." The authors noted then that this was "a 20-percentage-point increase since 2004," representing "a sea change in public opinion… and a growing sense of urgency" (YaleNews 2007).

It is my contention that it was not until the late 1990s and early 2000s that some, very few, in the green movement began to address the financial and economic causes of ecological imbalances. And it was not until the launch of the British *Green New Deal* that the global environmental movement found a unifying slogan or banner. Before that, the links, the connection between rates of financial and economic activity and the extraction of ecosystem assets was not often made by most environmentalists. The focus tended to be on *the outcome* of economic activity. Just as recently, environmentalists have become vociferous in opposition to economic "growth." Growth, however, is an *outcome* of excessive and extractive financial and economic activity, not a cause.

James Speth helped explain the reasons for the movement's blinkered approach to outcomes in an October 2008 column:

> Environmentalists see solutions coming largely from within the environmental sector. They may worry about the flaws in and corruption of our politics, for example, but that is not their professional concern. That's what Common Cause or other groups do. Similarly, environmentalists know that the prices for many things need to be higher, and they are aware that environmentally honest prices would create a huge burden on the half of American families that just get by. But universal health care and other government action needed to address America's gaping economic injustices are not seen as part of the environmental agenda.
>
> *(Speth 2008)*

So, by 2008, the year the NEF's *Green New Deal* was published, the largest movement in the world had won some important victories but had not yet become an effective force for transformation.

The global movement and the 2009 Copenhagen conference

The weakness of the global green movement had consequences. As someone active in the leadership of Operation Noah – a climate change campaign based in Britain's churches and faith organizations – I witnessed firsthand the lack of unity among Britain's richly varied environmental campaigns in advance of the 2009 Copenhagen Summit. The movement, such as it was, boasted of its divisions not as a weakness, but as "diversity." A thousand flowers were allowed to bloom. Campaigners marched onward to Copenhagen with a suite of different and often competing demands of those powerful statesmen and corporations that were driving climate breakdown. That confusion met with the Obama administration's own political timidity and China's resistance, so the Conference predictably fell into disarray and almost collapsed.

The failure of Copenhagen delayed for many years the struggle to tackle and prevent climate breakdown and biodiversity collapse. It led one US Senator, Sheldon Whitehouse of Rhode Island, to deliver 279 weekly "Time to Wake Up" speeches on the US Senate floor for the 12 years after the Copenhagen conference (C-Span 2021). He only wound up his deliveries in the week of 27 January 2021 – after President Biden issued his Climate Plan.

The failure to challenge entrenched power

The weakness of what can broadly be described as "the green movement" was not confined to the environmental sector. The political left as a whole was weakened and fractured in the decades after the collapse of the Bretton Woods international financial system in 1971 and the Soviet Union in 1989. Those events were followed by decades of financial deregulation and trade "liberalization" – defined as globalization – which, in turn, led to an immense expansion in extractive economic activity. Worse, globalization increased the power of the globalized private finance sector over democratic nation-states, the international economy and ultimately, the ecosystem. Throughout this period, as the documentary filmmaker Adam Curtis has noted, progressives remained ambivalent about globalization and failed to challenge the power that governments had conceded to the finance sector – Wall Street and the City of London – over the most important levers of the economy. These included the creation of credit; the determination of rates of interest for loans across the spectrum of lending – short- and long-term, safe and risky and in real terms; the exchange rate; cross-border capital mobility and trade. These economic levers ultimately impact not just the economy, but also the ecosystem, and were now controlled by unaccountable capital markets – deliberately detached from oversight by the regulatory democracy of states.

The deregulation of credit creation by (a) traditional commercial banks and (b) the shadow banking sector, combined with global capital mobility, led to a vast expansion in the availability of "easy money." Excessive credit creation led, predictably, to the build-up of a mountain of debt that by 2021 (at more than 360% of global GDP) loomed over the global economy (Campos 2020). Credit fuels consumption and production, which, in turn, fuel emissions. But credit issued at high rates of interest demands high rates of return for repayment.

As an example: in February 2021, at the height of the global coronavirus pandemic, the South African government battled to pay for vaccines and drugs. To help finance the budget, the government cut public sector pay and public services for a population in which 43% were unemployed. Yet the South African government simultaneously issued bonds on globalized markets at a yield (effectively the interest) of more than 8% to attract foreign, speculative capital. Servicing and repaying these bonds will inevitably lead to the extraction of South Africa's scarce ecological and human "assets" and will require the mining of minerals, the logging of forests, the fishing of seas, the burning of fossil fuels and the exploitation of labour.

Instead of recognizing the role that financialized globalization played in the era of deregulation and capital mobility (extracting and exploiting scarce ecological assets), progressive civil society turned inward, and built new organizational forms which sought to build a world, as Curtis argued,

> ...where the counter-culture could flourish, free of governments...Through the connection of computers and networks you could have a system where all individuals could connect with each other through feedback, no one would be in charge, and somehow out of that world would come this stability – including ecosystems, nature as a model – with no one in charge.
>
> Take the Occupy Movement which engaged in "horizontal organizing." They borrowed those ideas from cyberspace utopianism....and created *a picture of a world without power.*
>
> *(Chapo Trap House 2019)*

One notable exception was the international Rainforest Action Network (the Network), which in 2019 began monitoring and analysing funding from the world's major banks for the fossil fuel sector. While progressive movements spent decades building a utopian world without power, Wall Street was wielding its power to make vast capital gains by fuelling greenhouse gas emissions. In 2020, the Network reported that:

> [thirty-five] banks from Canada, China, Europe, Japan, and the US have together funneled USD $2.7 trillion into fossil fuels in the four years since the Paris Agreement was adopted (2016–2019). The biggest fossil bank over that time was JPMorgan Chase, followed by its U.S. peers: Wells Fargo, Citi, and Bank of America. Over those four years, RBC was the biggest fossil bank in Canada, MUFG in Japan, Barclays in Europe, and Bank of China in China. BNP Paribas was the biggest European fossil bank in 2019,

> despite its policy on unconventional oil and gas financing, and along with Santander and CIBC saw the biggest percentage increase in its fossil financing from 2018–2019. The biggest absolute increase in fossil financing last year came from Bank of America.
>
> *(Rainforest Action Network 2020)*

Civil society movements have missed an important target by failing since the birth of the green movement to engage with, challenge, and disarm the entrenched power of Wall Street and the sector's support for the fossil fuel industry. Instead, the movement focussed on the emissions of the world's individuals, households, and firms, and by doing so, missed another strategically important target: namely, the activities of around 10% of the global population, responsible for almost 50% of global carbon emissions; or the 20% of citizens responsible for 70% of emissions, as Professor Kevin Anderson of Manchester University reminds us (2018).

Anderson went on to argue that if governments were to impose a limit on the per capita carbon footprint of the top 10% of global emitters – including billionaires like Bill Gates traversing the earth in their own private jets – cutting their emissions down to the equivalent of an average European citizen could reduce global emissions by fully one-third in a matter of a year or two.

The green movement rises

In the United States, the distinguished American environmentalist Bill McKibben began to lead an international campaign that sought to cut off the source of fossil fuel financing.

In 2007, McKibben co-founded the 350.org campaign (based on 350 parts per million or ppm of carbon dioxide, identified as the safe upper limit to avoid a climate tipping point). The goal of that campaign seemed paradoxical – almost as if 350 ppm was the aim. But in 2012, McKibben and thousands of young campaigners moved away from a focus on outcomes (i.e., reductions in carbon emissions) and aimed instead at the sources of financing for the fossil fuel industries – the pension funds and endowments of universities, local governments, and churches (Suzuki 2020). The campaign began by targeting a small college in rural Maine with an endowment of US$8 million and went on to persuade the managers of US$14 trillion in endowments and portfolios to divest from fossil fuels.

These effective campaigners then turned the movement's attention to Wall Street and its billions in financing for the fossil fuel sector. On 17 September 2019, McKibben filed a stunning piece in *The New Yorker* titled: "Money is the Oxygen on Which the Fires of Global Warming Burns." In January 2020, a coalition of climate, youth, and Indigenous organizations launched a major new mobilization: *"Stop the Money Pipeline" (Nelson 2020).*

Finally, the US green movement was connecting the dots and preparing to engage with the real, entrenched power of a sector that, as McKibben articulated so clearly, fuels the fire of global warming.

The American Green New Deal movement

While it is the case that a combination of extreme weather events and the worldwide climate movement applied immense pressure on Democrats in the run up to the US presidential election of 2020, it was the home-grown Green New Deal mobilization led by the Sunrise Movement and left-leaning Democrats that had the greatest influence on the incoming Biden administration.

First, the call for an American GND became a unifying banner behind which a number of organizations could gather. There were different interpretations of what constituted an American GND; nevertheless, the slogan's resemblance to the radical New Deal of the 1930s was quickly understood by a wide swathe of American society. Most importantly, green organizations with different priorities could easily marshal their demands behind the banner or under the umbrella of the GND.

Unity was the consequence – and unity made the movement far more cohesive and powerful.

Second, the US GND embraced, as part of the environmental agenda, universal health care and other government action needed to address what Speth had called "America's gaping economic injustices."

The American Green New Deal Congressional Resolution (2019)

The American Green New Deal, as formalized by a resolution submitted to the US Congress by Rep. Alexandria Ocasio-Cortez, Democrat-N.Y., and Sen. Ed Markey, Democrat-Mass., on 5 February 2019, is a federal government-led mobilization working alongside, and integrating, the private sector within GND programs.

In drafting the GND, Justice Democrats, Senator Markey, and Congresswoman Ocasio-Cortez drew heavily on the work of Professor Mariana Mazzucato, whose research has shown that contrary to myth, public organizations have played a critical role as "investor of first resort" in the history of technological change and advancement. From the iPhone to Google Search, the world's most popular products were funded, Mazzucato (2015) concludes, not by private companies but by the taxpayer.

The American GND, through Resolution 109, "Recognizing the duty of the Federal Government to create a Green New Deal," seeks to achieve five major goals in the course of a ten-year mobilization:

- to reach net-zero greenhouse gas emissions through a fair and just transition for all communities and workers;
- to create millions of good, high-wage jobs, and ensure prosperity and economic security for all people of the United States;
- to invest in the infrastructure and industry of the United States to sustainably meet the challenges of the twenty-first century;
- to secure clean air and water, climate and community resilience, healthy food, access to nature, and a sustainable environment for all;
- to promote justice and equity by stopping current, preventing future, and repairing the historic oppression of frontline and vulnerable communities.

The American GND in social and political terms was more ambitious than the UK GND. In the words of the veteran climate campaigner Bill McKibben, the US GND seeks to "remake not just a broken planet, but a broken society." Members of "frontline and vulnerable communities" were placed front and centre as beneficiaries of the GND. The drafters of the resolution were acutely conscious of the 1930s New Deal's "intimate partnership with those in the South who preached white supremacy," and of the deliberate and racist exclusion of many Black people from the economic gains of that era.

However, the US GND addresses in only vague terms how the five major goals outlined above are to be financed. The key assumption is that the state will provide and leverage

> adequate capital… including through community grants, public banks and other public financing… for communities, Federal, State and local government agencies and businesses working on the Green New Deal mobilization.
>
> *(H. Res. 109 2019)*

Demond Drummer and Rhiana Gunn-Wright led the policy work on the resolution. When asked how the GND would be paid for, they said: "to be clear: it's a question of how we will pay for it – not if we can afford to pay for it. America can afford what we decide to do" (Pettifor 2019, p. 12).

The United Kingdom's Green New Deal (2008)

The United Kingdom's Green New Deal differed from the American version in a number of respects. The US GND was and is focussed on the domestic economy (The Green New Deal Group 2008). The UK GND, by contrast, demanded systemic change to the global economic order and regarded such change as an essential precondition for addressing climate breakdown.

In the opening paragraphs of our report, we argued that:

> The triple crunch of financial meltdown, climate change and "peak oil" has its origins firmly rooted in the current model of globalization. Financial deregulation has facilitated the creation of almost limitless credit. With this credit boom have come irresponsible and often fraudulent patterns of lending, creating inflated bubbles in assets such as property, and powering environmentally unsustainable consumption.

The UK GND is in this sense Keynesian, as Keynes' most urgent priority after the debacle of the 1919 Versailles Treaty was the reconstruction of the international system, the gold standard – the globalization of its day. He sought to help rebuild an international system governed not by *private* authority, but by *public* authority (Rauchway 2015). Keynes also understood that transformation of the domestic economy required transformation of the international system. Acknowledged widely as the greatest economist, Keynes was also primarily a monetary theorist who devised an economics in which money and credit were fully integrated (Tily 2016). Recall that his most famous work is titled *The General Theory of Employment, Interest and Money* – not the General Theory of "tax and spend," as it is often wrongly derided. Keynes' economics was based on money understood properly as a social technology rather than as a form of barter: "real exchange." For Keynes, economic failure was a result of the failures of the monetary or financial system.

Keynes argued – and persuaded Roosevelt – that in order to manage the domestic economy and address the huge economic failure of the 1920s and 1930s, it was important to manage monetary policy and the international financial system. As Geoff Tily explains, his remedies included the need for an international clearing union (to replace control over the world's reserve currency by a hegemon) and capital control; a permanently low bank rate and extensive changes to government debt management policy. His conclusion was "that the interests of finance and wealth are wholly opposed to the interests of society as a whole."

Roosevelt took Keynes' theory to heart. In his inaugural address on 4 March 1933, the new president pledged to expel the "money changers" from the temple of American democracy: "faced by failure of credit they had proposed only the lending of more money. They knew only the rules of self-seekers and had no vision, and when there is no vision the people perish" (Pettifor 2019, p. 48). He explained that his administration would adopt "lines of attack" and "safeguards" against a return of the old order; that there would be strict supervision of all banking, credits, and investments; an end to speculation with other people's money, and provision for an adequate but sound currency. That very night (a Saturday) he began the process of taking the United States off the gold standard, and by Monday morning, Roosevelt was well into the dismantling and transformation of the "barbaric relic" that was the globalized financial system.

Roosevelt's New Deal is often hailed as "Keynesian" with its emphasis on fiscal (tax) policy, government investment, and spending. But, in this author's estimation, that is wrong and a deliberate misnomer, for two reasons. First, what was genuinely Keynesian and radical about Roosevelt's New Deal were his monetary policies. By ending the gold standard and revaluing the currency, his administration was freed from shackles imposed by Wall Street over the exchange rate and fiscal policy. By dismantling the gold standard, Roosevelt and his advisers challenged the arrogance of Wall Street tycoons. His administration subordinated "global market forces" to the priorities of a democratically elected president. By suspending both the system and the neoclassical ideology of the gold standard, Roosevelt courageously freed up his administration to resolve the banking crisis, to address the needs of millions of unemployed and poor Americans and to tackle soil erosion across the Great Plains of America – the Dust Bowl.

We in the British GND group were clear that to restore the global ecosystem to stability, it was necessary to transform financialized capitalism: re-regulate capital flows and credit creation, and restore policy autonomy to governments. In other words, we sought changes to the international system to ensure that powers to manage money creation could be restored to regulatory democracies with public authority over the international financial system. The purpose of such changes would be to ensure credit creation is managed and aimed at productive, sustainable activity, not speculation. Furthermore, we considered it vital that finance should be made available for the transformation of the economy at low real rates of interest, because high real rates of interest had driven the need for excessive rates of return on investment – hence the compulsion to strip forests, empty the seas, and exploit labour –to generate returns needed to repay debts.

Like the US GND authors, we advocated for the creation and training of what we termed a "carbon army" of workers to provide the human resources for a vast environmental reconstruction program.

Finally, the British GND adopted a more internationalist perspective than the American versions of the program, calling on OECD governments to help finance massive investment in low-income countries aimed at climate change adaptation and clean energy.

Globalization and the reinstatement of Wall Street power

Today the United States and the world are once again effectively governed by an international financial system that closely resembles the liberal framework of the gold standard. As Rana Foroohar of the *Financial Times* has argued, the US economy (and therefore the world economy) "is dangerously dependent on the whims of Wall Street" with "mounds of global debt, falling credit quality, and decades of low interest rates driving asset prices to unsustainable levels." She states that this dependency has grown "little by little, since the 1970s onwards… [and] is the result of policy changes driven by both Democrats and Republicans" (2020).

Public authority was replaced by private authority over the international monetary and financial system, with the US dollar as the dominant, reserve currency. Almost immediately the system became prone to crises.

Conclusion

By February 2021, the green movement in the United States had made spectacular gains with the election of a Democrat administration that enjoyed a majority in both Congress and the Senate and which immediately published a radical Climate Plan (White House 2021a).

In announcing the plan, President Biden's Envoy on Climate, John Kerry, and National Climate Advisor Gina McCarthy addressed the media in the White House Briefing Room (White House 2021b). They repeatedly reminded the audience that the Climate Plan was based on the creation of "good paying union jobs" in low-carbon industry sectors – a mantra that echoed an earlier speech by the President. John Kerry simultaneously appealed to Wall Street's powerful billionaires for help in creating "good paying union jobs."

He began the press conference by welcoming a recent letter to investors by the CEO of BlackRock, in which the billionaire acknowledged "that climate risk is investment risk. But we also believe the climate transition presents a historic investment opportunity" (White House 2021b).

Kerry praised the letter as indicating "the new awareness among asset managers about the need to be putting resources into this endeavour." Later in the Briefing, Kerry made a direct appeal to Wall Street:

> What the financiers, the big banks, the asset managers, private investors, venture capital, are all discovering is that there is a lot of money to be made in the jobs to be created in these sectors…

Gina McCarthy, National Climate Advisor, drove home the point, saying: "The question won't be, will the private sector buy into it? The private sector is going to drive it…"

In a *Financial Times* article titled "Wall Street's new mantra: green is good," Gillian Tett noted that BlackRock had "exploded in size and power this century by amassing exchange traded funds and 'passive' strategies that automatically track mainstream indices, such as the S&P 500… [which] include fossil fuels, so BlackRock is heavily exposed to that by default" (Tett 2021).

BlackRock's Fink, described by some as one of "the greatest greenwashers of them all," was clearly delighted to be placed effectively in the driving seat of Biden's Climate Plan. As he excitedly told Tett in the *Financial Times*:

> This [climate story] reminds me of the formative years when I was a mortgage-backed securities trader…In five straight years we elevated it to becoming a dominant component of global capital markets. It might take ten years, not five years, for sustainability. But the underlying potential is huge.
>
> *(Tett 2021)*

As Gillian Tett commented, Fink's activities as a mortgage-backed securities trader "went to crazy extremes this century, triggering the 2008 crisis."

Undeterred and unlike President Roosevelt's administration, the mighty US government is, in 2021, conceding its great power to implement a Green New Deal, to transform the economy, to fix humanity's and nature's life support systems, to create jobs and to strengthen trade unions – to the private authority of Wall Street institutions like BlackRock.

If Biden's Climate Plan were to fail because his administration relied too heavily on Wall Street to drive the Plan forward, then the political consequences would be dire. Ultimately, much of the blame would fall on the green movement for failing to effectively challenge power. Not just the power of Wall Street to make capital gains from financing fossil fuels, but also the power exercised by 10% of global elites, responsible for 50% of greenhouse gas emissions (Anderson 2018).

References

Anderson, K. 2018. Response to the IPCC's 1.5C Special Report. Policy@Manchester: University of Manchester [online]. 8 October. Available from: http://blog.policy.manchester.ac.uk/posts/2018/10/response-to-the-ipcc-1-5c-special-report/

BankTrack. History Page [online]. Available from: https://www.banktrack.org/page/history

Barral, M. 2019. Svante Arrhenius, the Man Who Foresaw Climate Change. *OpenMind BBVA*. 19 February. Available from: https://www.bbvaopenmind.com/en/science/leading-figures/svante-arrhenius-the-man-who-foresaw-climate-change/.

Campos, R. 2020. Global Debt to Hit Record $277 Trillion by Year End. *Reuters* [online]. 18 November Available from: https://www.reuters.com/article/us-global-debt-idUSKBN27Y239.

Chapo Trap House. 2019. No Future Feat. Adam Curtis | Chapo Trap House | Episode 65 FULL. *YouTube*. 2 February. Available from: https://www.youtube.com/watch?v=AZypbVJ16Jk

C-Span. 2021. Senator Whitehouse Ends 12-Year Run of Climate Change Speeches. 27 January. Available from: https://www.c-span.org/video/?c4941865/senator-whitehouse-ends-12-year-run-climate-change-speeches

Duke, S. 2011. Has the Green Movement Failed? *BBC World Service* [online]. 30 September. Available from: https://www.bbc.co.uk/news/science-environment-15109093.

Foroohar, R. 2020. US Economy Is Dangerously Dependent on Wall Street Whims. *Financial Times* [online]. 9 March. Available from: https://www.ft.com/content/ef3539ec-5f96-11ea-b0ab-339c2307bcd4.

Friedman, T. 2007. A Warning from the Garden. *New York Times* [online]. 19 January. Available from: https://www.nytimes.com/2007/01/19/opinion/19friedman.html.

Green New Deal Group. 2008. *A Green New Deal: Joined Up Policies to Solve the Triple Crunch of the Credit Crisis, Climate Change and High Oil Prices*. London: New Economics Foundation. July. Available from: https://neweconomics.org/uploads/files/8f737ea195fe56db2f_xbm6ihwb1.pdf

Hawken, P. 2007. *Blessed Unrest: How the Largest Movement in the World Came into Being and Why No One Saw It Coming*. New York: Viking.

Mazzucato, M. 2015. *The Entrepreneurial State: Debunking Public vs. Private Sector Myths*. London: Anthem Press.

Nelson, K. 2020. The Climate Movement Is Going After Wall Street. *Greenpeace.org*. 5 January. Available from: https://www.greenpeace.org/usa/news/the-climate-movement-is-going-after-wall-street/.

Pettifor, A. 2019. *The Case for the Green New Deal*. London: Verso.

Rainforest Action Network. 2020. Banking on Climate Change: Fossil Fuel Finance Report 2020. Available from: https://www.ran.org/wp-content/uploads/2020/03/Banking_on_Climate_Change__2020_vF.pdf

Rauchway, E. 2015. *The Money Makers: How Roosevelt and Keynes ended the Depression, Defeated Fascism and Secured a Prosperous Peace*. New York: Basic Books.

Recognizing the Duty of the Federal Government to Create a Green New Deal. H. Res. 109, 116th Congress. 2019. Available from: https://www.congress.gov/116/bills/hres109/BILLS-116hres109ih.pdf

Shabecoff, P. 1988. Global Warming has Begun Expert Tells Senate. *New York Times* [online]. 24 June. Available from: https://www.nytimes.com/1988/06/24/us/global-warming-has-begun-expert-tells-senate.html

Speth, J. 2008. Environmental Failure: A Case for a New Green Politics. *Yale Environment* 360 [online]. 20 October. Available from: https://e360.yale.edu/features/environmental_failure_a_case_for_a_new_green_politics

Suzuki. K. 2020. Bill McKibben on the Divestment Movement. *The Allegheny Front* [online]. 9 July. Available from: https://www.alleghenyfront.org/bill-mckibben-on-the-divestment-movement/.

Tett, G. 2021. Wall Street's New Mantra: Green Is Good. *Financial Times* [online]. 29 January. Available from: https://www.ft.com/content/e5b57ece-0c31-4f42-9229-c8981bc9fd34.

Tily, G. 2016. As If Keynes Had Never Lived. *Policy Research in Macroeconomics (PRIME)*. 7 October. Available from: https://www.primeeconomics.org/articles/geoff-tily-presents-at-cambridge-keynes-conference/

White House. 2021a. *Executive Order on Tackling the Climate Crisis at Home and Abroad.* 27 January. Available from: https://www.whitehouse.gov/briefing-room/presidential-actions/2021/01/27/executive-order-on-tackling-the-climate-crisis-at-home-and-abroad/#content

White House. 2021b. Press Briefing by Press Secretary Jen Psaki, John Kerry and Gina McCarthy. *YouTube*. 27 January. Available from: https://www.youtube.com/watch?v=XtKXI94aBNs&feature=youtu.be

YaleNews. 2007. Americans Consider Global Warming an Urgent Threat, Poll Finds. Yale University [online]. 1 October. Available from: https://news.yale.edu/2007/10/01/americans-consider-global-warming-urgent-threat-poll-finds.

Yellen, Janet [SecYellen]. 2021. [Twitter] 5 February. Available from: https://twitter.com/SecYellen/status/1357820760748867584.

2

FINANCING THE GREEN NEW DEAL

The Modern Money Theory approach

Yeva Nersisyan

Introduction

The Green New Deal resolution introduced by US Congress Representative Alexandria Ocasio-Cortez and Senator Ed Markey jumpstarted a global conversation about the need for comprehensive reforms to address climate change, rising inequality, joblessness and inadequate access to food, shelter, healthcare and affordable education. Advocates of the Green New Deal (GND) believe these problems to be interconnected, thus emphasizing the need to address them with reforms that tackle a broad range of problems.[1]

One of the first questions that comes up when discussing the GND is how we are going to pay for it. Indeed, as soon as the Ocasio-Cortez/Markey resolution was introduced, economists and think tanks started crunching numbers to determine its price tag. While the range of estimates varied widely, one thing that was common was the methodology: they all estimated the costs of various programs in financial terms, adding them up to come up with the total cost of the GND. They then tried to determine the appropriate combination of tax hikes, spending cuts and bond financing to pay for the program.

In this chapter, I argue that approaching the cost of the GND as a financial problem is misguided. A relatively new economic theory, the Modern Money Theory (MMT), which has gained wider acceptance since the global financial crisis of 2007–2008 and especially in the aftermath of the COVID-19 crisis, informs my analysis. As MMT demonstrates, a government which issues its sovereign currency is not constrained in terms of finance (Wray 1998, 2015). Whether or not it can afford a particular spending program depends on the availability of real resources. Instead of quibbling over where we are going to find the money to pay for the GND, we need to determine whether we have the real resources (labor, materials, etc.) to implement it. If the resources are not available, finance cannot provide a solution to the problem. If resources are available, then worrying about where to find the money is not useful.

In sum, to answer the question of whether the GND is affordable requires estimating the amount of resources it will require, as well as the amount it will potentially release. This will allow us to come up with the net resource needs of the program (and the boost to aggregate spending it will entail). If this increase in aggregate spending takes us beyond our productive capacity, then the GND could be inflationary (see also Galvin's discussion of inflation

DOI: 10.4324/9781003110880-4

in Chapter 3 of this volume). In this case, we will need to implement counter-inflationary measures, such as tax increases, but also (potentially) rationing, price controls, etc. While estimating the real resource costs of major programs over a long period of time is necessarily ripe with uncertainty, the methodology I employ is still more useful as a guide to the affordability of the GND than the financial "pay for" approach espoused by most.

The rest of the chapter is structured as follows: Section 2 introduces the mainstream approach to government finances, contrasting it with the MMT approach. In Section 3, I explain the MMT approach to costing the GND. Section 4 addresses what taxation policy might be appropriate for a GND, while Section 5 concludes.

Two approaches to costing the Green New Deal

The conventional approach

Perhaps the most often cited GND cost estimate is the conservative American Action Forum's (AAF) study which came out shortly after the introduction of the GND resolution (see Holtz-Eakin et al. 2019). It estimates the cost of the GND in financial terms, adding up the projected costs of the various programs (greening the economy, Medicare for All (M4A), Job Guarantee (JG), etc.). While the authors of the report admit that due to "spillovers" between the different programs, "an ideal analysis would be to consider them simultaneously," they still merely add up the costs to come up with a scandalous price tag of US$93 trillion over ten years. They further assume tax hikes are needed to "pay for" this program, which would be confiscatory at best and would bankrupt our grandchildren at worst. It is worth noting that the highest "costs" accrue due to the "economic agenda," including the job guarantee and the expansion of Medicare, rather than the program of fighting climate change by greening the economy itself. As I will explain in Section 3, both of these programs will likely mobilize real resources to be used in greening the economy. In other words, they will be a source of real resources, rather than a cost.

The AAF approach is just one case of the so-called "pay for" approach to government spending. This mainstream approach is espoused by most liberal and progressive economists (see, e.g. Pollin et al. 2018; Pollin 2019). Even one of the most progressive politicians in the United States, Bernie Sanders, has a complete cost accounting for his GND and Medicare for All programs, explaining what tax increases and spending cuts would be implemented to "pay for" the increased spending.[2]

The conventional approach to costing government programs is based on mainstream economic theory regarding government spending and taxation, accepted by most economists and policymakers. Mainstream economists posit a government budget constraint, similar to the household budget constraint. The government has three sources for financing its spending: tax revenue, selling bonds or printing money. Tax revenue is, of course, constrained because there are limits to how much the government can tax. Selling bonds has limits too, because at some point the government might get shut out of the bond market with investors refusing to lend to it (or demanding very high interest rates). Printing money is one of the biggest taboos in economics. It gives rise to images of hyperinflation where people are using money as wallpaper or lugging wheelbarrows full of cash to buy groceries.

The conventional approach treats government finances as equivalent to those of private sector entities, such as households and firms. Just like a household, the government needs to try to "live within its means," at least over the longer term. While a household might be able to run deficits for a short period of time, these are not sustainable because they lead to accumulation of debt creating the potential for a default. It implies that governments have to do a financial cost accounting for their programs; to spend a trillion dollars, they need to raise taxes or cut spending elsewhere to finance that spending. And if they cannot raise all of the needed revenue, they will be adding the remainder of that spending to the government's existing pile of debt by issuing bonds. Too much debt could then lead a country to the brink of default.

Most economists would admit that the US government has more leeway than a typical household because it can borrow more and for extended periods of time (after all, a household has an "end," while the government does not). They would also allow for increased borrowing when interest rates are low. More recently, Paul Krugman (2020) and Olivier Blanchard (2019) have said that as long as interest rates are low, the government can/should borrow and invest. Thus, while borrowing to spend might be warranted under certain conditions, such as low interest rates, it is not desirable as a regular policy approach.

The Modern Money Theory approach

Although the above discussion of government finances is taken at face value without much questioning by most economists, policymakers or the general public, surprisingly most of it is false. In the past two decades a heterodox macroeconomic body of theory called Modern Money Theory has sprung to prominence by questioning all of the tenets held true by the mainstream (for foundational works in MMT, see Mosler 1996; Wray 1998; Bell 2000; see also Wray 2015; and Nersisyan and Wray 2016). Modern Money Theory, largely based in Post-Keynesian economic thinking, argues that mainstream ideas about government finances do not apply to governments with their sovereign currency. Sovereign currency is defined as currency issued by a sovereign government which is not backed by a metal (like gold) or any other currency.[3] The government does not promise to convert its own currency into anything else at a fixed exchange rate (while you can convert dollars to euros, you cannot demand conversion from the government at a fixed rate. Similarly, you can buy gold at the market price, but you cannot demand a certain amount of gold from the government for a given amount of dollars).[4] While the United States has been on and off some kind of precious metal standard for most of its history, it finally abandoned the fixed convertibility in 1971 when President Nixon suspended the conversion to gold basically setting off the demise of the post-WWII global money system, known as the Bretton Woods system (Elwell 2011). Since then, the US dollar has been a truly sovereign currency.

How does a sovereign currency change the financial constraints the government faces? Simply put, a government that issues its own sovereign currency cannot run out of that currency (Wray 1998, 2015). It therefore does not face any inherent financial constraints on its spending.[5] The analogy between households and the government is false because households are users of the currency while the government is the (monopoly) issuer. While the users of the currency must get hold of it before they can spend it, the issuer of the currency must spend the currency before it can collect it back. In terms of government taxation and spending, it means the government must spend first and tax later because taxes can only be paid in the government's own currency. So unless currency has entered the economy through government spending (or lending, as in lending done by the central bank), the private sector won't have the currency with which to pay its taxes. This means that taxes cannot be a source of financing for the sovereign government.[6] In sum, the government never has or does not have currency. The currency gets issued when the government spends – it is spent into existence (Bell 2000; Wray 2015).[7]

Some of the misunderstanding about government finances is due to the broad misunderstanding about the nature of money. Most mainstream textbooks tell a story (embraced without much historical understanding by most economists) that money was originally a commodity that was chosen to serve as a universal medium of exchange to alleviate the difficulties associated with bartering. Leaving aside the historical inaccuracy of this origins story (see Graeber 2012), whatever the history of money, today money is simply an IOU, an obligation of the issuer. This IOU does not exist until it has been issued. In case of government IOUs, they are issued through spending or lending (Tymoigne 2014; Wray 2015). Similarly, when the issuer collects its IOU back (let's say in tax payments in case of the government), it does not need to "save" them because the IOUs are worthless in the issuer's hands (e.g. your own IOU would be worthless in your own pocket/wallet). If money was a commodity, like gold or silver, things would be somewhat different. The government would need to get hold of the commodity before it could create the currency and spend.[8] This is what the current misunderstanding about government finances stems from – thinking that the government needs to tax first (collect the commodity) before it can spend (use the commodity to buy other commodities).

Another factor that obscures how governments actually spend and tax is the presence of the banking system which intermediates payments from and to the government (Bell 2000; Fullwiler 2010; Wray 2015; Nersisyan and Wray 2016). When the government makes payments, it doesn't send piles of cash to the recipients of its spending. The recipient simply gets a credit to their bank account. Similarly, when we pay our taxes, we do so through our checking accounts. Most of us don't usually deal in government currency directly. However, what MMT has elucidated is what happens between the Treasury, the central bank and the private banking system as payments are made and received (Tymoigne 2014). Simply put, all payments to and from the government take the form of debits and credits of central bank money, reserves. Just like we have accounts at commercial banks, banks have accounts at the central bank. It is through these accounts that banks make payments to the Treasury, whether for tax payments on our behalf or for purchases of bonds. What on the surface seems like a payment made to the Treasury through your checking account has another layer to it; your bank is making a payment to the Treasury through its account at the Federal Reserve (in the case of the United States). The balances in these accounts are the liabilities of the Fed, i.e. obligations of the US government. Thus all government spending in the first instance involves crediting the reserve accounts of banks, i.e. issuing government IOUs (Wray 1998; Tymoigne and Wray 2013; Wray 2015).

Real resource constraints

The MMT claim that the government is not financially constrained should not be taken as an assertion that the government faces no constraints. The most important one is the constraint imposed by real resources available to the country (either domestically or through its ability to import). While MMT de-emphasizes financial constraints as irrelevant to sovereign governments, it elevates the importance of real resource constraints and policies governments can engage in to increase their real resource space (Nersisyan and Wray 2019, 2020b).

If there are idle resources available for sale in a country's currency, of which the government is the monopoly issuer, it can afford to buy them (Wray 2015). If the economy is at full employment, however, attempting to buy more will simply bid up prices rather than stimulating more production (the government can always outbid the private sector). When there are idle resources the private sector does not want to buy/employ, the government can use its currency issuing power to buy/hire them without bidding up prices. An example of this would be the Great Recession and the consequent anemic recovery, or the Great Depression when unemployment and underemployment were high and widespread. If the government were to hire these workers, it would not be bidding them away from the private sector (and thus would not put pressure on wages, and consequently, prices). Even eight years after the Great Recession officially ended, there were still, according to some estimates, more than 15 million people either unemployed or underemployed (Wray and Dantas 2017).

Mainstream economists often claim that "there is no such thing as a free lunch," i.e. every resource bought by the government takes it away from the private sector. This of course stems from the belief/assumption that the economy is at full employment or that government spending today will be offset by more taxation in the future (a dubious theory without any empirical support). However, when there are unemployed resources, the government is basically getting a "free lunch" (or a very cheap one if we account for other resources that it might need).

On the other extreme, when resources are limited in supply, government competition for them will crowd out the private sector by bidding up prices. As a case in point, when the COVID-19 pandemic got to the United States, there was a shortage of Personal Protective Equipment (PPE), toilet paper and other necessities. In such a situation, a government trying to buy more of what is already in short supply would be able to get more only at the expense of the private sector (and with the consequence of higher prices; Nersisyan and Wray 2020b). As it was reported in the media, US states were bidding up prices of PPE in their struggle to get hold of it. More money, which the US government could easily throw at this problem, would not have solved it, at least not in the short run (it could have stimulated companies to try to produce more, especially if this change in demand was perceived to be longer-lasting or permanent). Another historical case when we hit supply constraints in a more global scale was during WWII when the United States had to resort to rationing and price controls as well as fiscal measures, such as tax increases, to control inflation as a large part of our output was moved to the military (Nersisyan and Wray, n.d.).

What we conclude is that when resources are idle, a government can use them without displacing the private sector. When they are in short supply, more money will not necessarily solve the problem; the solution lies in increasing productive capacity to be able to produce more. Therefore, if there is any sense in which "paying for" government spending makes sense, it is in terms of real resources; a country always pays for things in terms of the real output it can produce or can net import from others. Only at full employment does a country face trade-offs for real resource use. Thus excessive spending manifests itself not in terms of government insolvency, but in terms of inflation due to the pressure on resources.

The MMT approach to costing the GND

The implications of Modern Money Theory for the Green New Deal are clear and stark. Financing the GND is not a money problem (financing is a misnomer in some sense). Financially, we can afford the GND; the US federal government has the means to do so. It doesn't require any changes to the government's spending procedures. We don't need to "print money" or have the Fed finance this spending any more than it finances any other government spending.[9] Instead, Congress needs to appropriate the budget, while the Treasury will fulfill this budgeted spending, a process which also involves the Fed as the government's bank. Whether we need to raise taxes or not is not a question that can be answered *a priori* without an analysis of the resource needs of the GND. Just because government spending needs to go up does not mean taxes must increase as well.

The affordability of the GND, therefore, should be viewed as a resource availability and allocation problem.[10] Evaluating it requires determining which programs would be a source of real resources and which ones would be a cost (Nersisyan and Wray 2019, 2020a). Ideally, we would calculate the number and type of workers and other resources needed for the various components of the GND (e.g. greening the economy) and the resources that would be freed up (e.g. due to the elimination of the fossil fuel industry). We would also evaluate whether resources made available would be suitable for use in other parts of the program, e.g. whether resources freed in the private healthcare sector would be suitable to be used in greening the economy.

A less perfect, but still acceptable approach (and one I adopt here following Nersisyan and Wray 2019) is to estimate whether the various programs will lead to more or less spending (regardless of whether the public or private sectors will be doing that spending) and netting them out. What we are trying to determine is whether GND reforms as a whole will push the amount of spending beyond our productive capacity, since this could be inflationary (and is really the limit to spending, as explained in Section 2).

It is also worth explaining how spending is related to resource use. This point stems from the simple macroeconomic principle that someone's spending is someone else's income. If we are spending less on pharmaceuticals and medical procedures, for instance, it means someone is earning less (the drug company and consequently those who get their income from this company; similarly, if we eliminate private health insurance, anyone who currently earns their income through this sector will lose it). Those earning less will be spending less as well, which translates into using fewer resources and leaving some that would be previously consumed idle. This can range from restaurant meals to yachts – the composition of that spending may be important. However what is important is the overall macroeconomic impact. Lower spending creates room in the economy for other kinds of spending, such as that on greening the economy. At the level of employment, less spending means less employment. This will be especially clear with respect to administrative workers currently employed by medical insurance companies and doctors' offices. Many of these workers would likely become redundant in a Medicare for All system (at the same time, we might need more medical assistants, nurses, doctors and other healthcare workers to meet the increased demand for healthcare). The same is true of workers in the fossil fuel industry, who will likely lose their jobs as we gradually phase out the industry.

Transitioning to green energy

In this subsection, I explain whether the three major programs included in the GND – "greening the economy," Medicare for All and the job guarantee – would be a source of resources or would represent a use of resources.[11] Would transitioning to a fully renewable energy system, which involves eliminating the use of fossil fuels, require real resources or will it free them up? The answer is that it can be both. Transitioning to green energy will involve stopping investment in oil and gas exploration in the near term and eliminating the exploitation of existing capacities in the longer term. This will free up labor and other resources currently employed in the fossil fuel industry (indeed, the unemployment this will create is often seen as one of the negative effects of getting rid of fossil fuels). Eventually we will also spend less on environmental cleanup. At the same time, spending on green energy will increase tremendously. We will need to devote more workers and other resources to building wind turbines and solar panels, on increasing energy efficiency, creating infrastructure for public transport, a high-speed rail system, etc. In other words, as a society we will be spending more than before to green the economy.

Evaluating how much it will cost to green the economy from a real resource perspective requires netting out the resources needed and resources freed up. Since phasing out fossil fuels will be gradual, we can ignore the resource savings from this. However, we can count the resource savings from stopping investment in fossil fuels today because committing to green energy implies not investing in new sources of fossil fuel energy. On net, greening the economy will represent a demand on resources (labor and otherwise) and will add to spending at the macroeconomic level (in other words, it will be stimulative and potentially inflationary, all else equal). Nersisyan and Wray (2020a) estimate a net increase in aggregate spending equal to about 5% of US GDP per year over a ten-year period. This is the estimate I use going forward.

Universal single-payer healthcare (Medicare for All)

The universal single-payer system, or Medicare for All (M4A), is deemed the most expensive GND program. Most commentators emphasize the fact that the government will be spending more on healthcare than it currently does, which is true. Hence they claim we will need to raise taxes on employers and employees to "pay for" this spending. What they ignore, however, is that as a society we will be spending less on healthcare. In other words, M4A will lead to a decrease in spending at the macroeconomic level (decreased use of resources) rather than an increase.

The United States is an outlier among OECD countries in terms of its spending on healthcare – around 17%–18% of US GDP in 2018 compared to an OECD average of 10%, an outcome likely driven by unusually high prices and administrative costs. Anderson et al. (2003) demonstrate that prices account for much of the higher healthcare spending in the United States, a result confirmed more recently by Anderson, Hussey and Petrosyan (2019). They conclude that the United States was not then, and is still not, devoting more real resources (hospital beds, physicians and nurses) to providing healthcare compared to the OECD median. Nor do Americans receive more care – in fact, by some measures they actually receive less (fewer visits to physicians, for example). Similarly, the United States spends about 8% of total national health expenditures on governance and administration, compared to a range of 1%–3% in comparable countries (Papanicolas, Woskie and Jha 2018; see also Mueller, Hagenaars and Morgan 2017, who calculate an OECD average of about 3%). Further, over 24% of US hospital spending is on administration, compared to 12.9% in Canada (Woolhandler, Campbell and Himmelstein 2003). To the extent that Medicare for All will bring US spending on healthcare in line with other developed countries, it will reduce spending in the economy on aggregate (i.e. it will be deflationary).

There is a range of estimates for how much M4A would "cost," and consequently how much it could save or add to the country's spending on healthcare (estimates for savings range from about 1.6% to 5% of GDP; see Nersisyan and Wray 2019). The savings stem from eliminating the private insurance industry, lower spending on pharmaceuticals and other medical services due to cost controls in a single-payer system, as well as savings on administrative expenses. In the longer term, universal access to healthcare will likely improve people's health, thus further lowering our spending on healthcare. Nersisyan and Wray (2019) estimate that in the short term M4A could save about 3.7% of GDP while providing healthcare to more people than before.

Guaranteed jobs

The broader Green New Deal package also includes some kind of a guaranteed jobs program. The job guarantee has always been an important part of MMT as a way to achieve true full employment and price stability (Wray 1998; Tcherneva 2018, 2020; Wray et al. 2018). MMT economists have long argued that managing aggregate demand to try to achieve full employment would probably cause too much inflation long before reaching that goal. Instead, they have proposed a job guarantee program, which offers a basic wage and benefits and provides a job to anyone willing to work. This operates like a commodity price support program, ensuring wages do not fall below the program wage without competing with the private sector to push wages higher. Private employers can always recruit from the pool if they need workers, paying at least the program wage.

The job guarantee, while a cost in financial terms, represents both a cost (consumption by workers) and a source of real resources for other GND projects. In particular, JG workers (most of whom, importantly, are currently not employed by the private sector) can be engaged in many of the GND projects, such as small construction and retrofitting projects, environmental cleanup, etc. Nersisyan and Wray (2019) estimate that the JG would be using an amount of resources equal to about 2% of GDP, while supplying an amount of resources for greening projects equal to 1% of GDP. Hence, the net cost in terms of resource use comes out to 1% of GDP.

Tallying the above estimates leads us to conclude that the net cost of the GND would be 2.3% of GDP (5% of GDP for greening plus 1% for the job guarantee minus 3.7% for Medicare for All). Nersisyan and Wray (2019) also include an estimate for cutting spending on "forever wars" equal to 1% of GDP, something that many advocates of the GND support. With that, the net cost of the GND comes out to 1.3% of (2017) GDP per year for ten years. While an annual addition of spending equal to 1.3% of GDP is not insignificant, it is not unmanageable either.

The above discussion demonstrates that analyzing government spending from a real resource perspective leads to completely different conclusions compared to when we approach it like that of a household. Medicare for All is a stark example of that. Most economists and policymakers believe we need to raise taxes to pay for it. But our analysis shows that M4A is actually a deflationary macroeconomic policy, since the economy as a whole will be spending less on healthcare services than before (despite the fact that the government will be shouldering more of that cost). Hence, if anything, this program would require the government to further stimulate the economy to offset the decrease in spending, let's say through a tax cut, rather than increasing taxes. In other words, we reach the complete opposite conclusion compared to the "pay for" approach discussed in Section 2.

Lastly, what we miss by approaching financing the GND as a problem of "finding money" is that a comprehensive GND is desirable in comparison to a piecemeal approach (Nersisyan and Wray 2021). If one looks at the GND from the perspective of financing, the conclusion is that the whole package costs too much and is unaffordable because it requires excessive tax hikes. However, our analysis shows that the various parts of GND complement each other as some release resources, while others require more. For instance, trying to "green" the economy by itself could be inflationary. At the same time, implementing M4A on its own could be deflationary. But by combining the two we get the benefit of one offsetting the other to some extent.[12] Similarly, a job guarantee combined with greening the economy works especially well because unemployed workers can be put to work in greening projects. It also acts as a safety net and a transition program for those workers who are left unemployed, whether from fossil fuel, medical insurance or administrative sectors.

Inflation and tax policy for a Green New Deal

What kind of tax policy is appropriate for a Green New Deal? The mainstream approach is to determine the amount of increase in government spending and then try to find revenue through taxes. To answer that question from the MMT perspective, we need to first move away from the idea that tax revenue finances government spending. As already explained in Section 2, sovereign governments finance their spending by issuing their IOUs. Taxes simply return government IOUs back to the government, making them worthless in the government's own "hands"; they are not a source of finance for the government. Just because government spending goes up (as it will if we implement the GND) doesn't mean taxes need to go up as well.

Instead, MMT economists approach taxes functionally, i.e. they need to be used based on their functions (i.e. their effect on the economy). These include, for instance, disincentivizing certain behaviors (e.g. smoking or drinking soda), addressing income and wealth inequality, and withdrawing income from the economy (see Ruml 1946 for a discussion of the various functions of taxes). By removing purchasing power from the private sector, taxes create the real resource space for the government to spend in a noninflationary manner.

The GND is likely to increase aggregate spending, although it is not a foregone conclusion that this increase in the demand for resources will be beyond our capacities. A lot depends on the starting point of the economy. Prior to the COVID-19 recession, many economists and policymakers believed the economy did not have much room to absorb increased spending without triggering inflationary pressures (whether or not that was true is up for debate). As of this writing, it is not clear how long the COVID-19 recession will last and most importantly, the amount of idle resources there will be. The state of the labor market is currently close to what it was at the peak of the Great Recession. If this becomes a more permanent situation as businesses close and permanently fire their workers, we might have a starting point that's more like the Great Recession in terms of idle capacity rather than the peak of a cycle. This means there could be much more room in the economy to absorb additional spending than there was just a year ago.

In any case, with well-targeted spending, we might be able to implement the GND without sparking inflation. Not all sectors of the economy and parts of the labor force are affected equally when the economy grows. Some reach full capacity, while others lag behind. By carefully directing GND spending to underutilized resources, where possible, we might be able to avoid significant inflation.

If the GND does push us beyond full employment, and inflation becomes a threat, we can also use the tax system, among other measures, to address it. However, if taxation were used as a tool to regulate demand, the kind of taxes imposed would be important (while if we approach them as a source of revenue, the kind of taxes we impose doesn't matter as much). The key is to structure taxes so as to reduce the demand for resources to create room in the economy for GND spending. For instance, a financial transactions tax, often advocated by progressive politicians and economists, will likely not lower the demand for resources by much if at all, although it might be useful in curbing financial speculation – a worthy goal. Similarly, taxing the rich will contribute positively to reducing income inequality (an important goal of GND advocates), but it will likely not lower the demand for resources by much. The rich need to be significantly less rich for their consumption to be affected (and for real resources to be released). The GND can/should still include a tax on high incomes and wealth as a way to lower income inequality. However, viewing this as a source of financing for the GND will be counterproductive. Lastly, taxes on workers' income will be more effective in withdrawing purchasing power and spending, although they are not necessarily desirable (see Nersisyan and Wray, 2021 for a tax proposal for controlling inflation).

Conclusion

Paul Krugman (2019) remarked that heterodoxy (meaning MMT) does not help when it comes to deciding whether spending programs are affordable. He used the example of Medicare for All to argue that the government would be spending more were we to adopt such a system, causing inflation. What I have demonstrated in this chapter is that MMT does help as it reorients the conversation away from what's unimportant (finance) to what is essential (real resources). While most economists who are working to estimate the costs of the GND are looking at finances and trying to devise ways to find the money to pay for this spending package, MMT demonstrates that we are looking in the wrong place and for the wrong thing. What we need to find is not money, but the real resources and the technology to transition to a fully green economy as soon as possible, while also fulfilling other important objectives, such as providing healthcare and jobs to all. Once we reorient the conversation away from finances toward real resources, we reach completely different conclusions regarding both the affordability of the GND and the macroeconomic challenges that need to be tackled to make it possible (e.g. inflation as opposed to, say, government insolvency).

What I would like to emphasize is the methodology used in this chapter, rather than any particular cost estimates for the GND. The mainstream approach assumes the economy is at full employment and hence there are always trade-offs, which is clearly not true in the real world. The important issue is whether the GND will take us beyond full employment, and if it does, what the appropriate method for dealing with the potential inflation is.

Those who argue that tackling climate change and economic problems such as inadequate access to healthcare, shelter and food is too difficult, too expensive or too inflationary should be reminded of the formidable challenge of WWII and how the United States successfully dealt with it. In climate change, we have a challenge which is the moral equivalent of WWII and is equally urgent, although it does not require the same degree of resource mobilization. With WWII we achieved the kind of mobilization of economic resources which had hitherto seemed impossible (and in a very short period of time).[13] The US government met this challenge, using the financial system for the appropriate purpose of mobilizing the available real resources, as well as increasing our productive capacity. They did so rather successfully and without triggering much inflation (Nersisyan and Wray 2021). What WWII shows is that an extensive mobilization of resources is possible, in terms of financing, real resources and public planning. MMT explains why we should stop worrying about financing and instead focus on real resource availability.

Notes

1 Since there are a variety of proposals referred to as the Green New Deal, it is important to clarify which one of these I am going to discuss in this chapter. In European countries, for instance, many of which already have some type of universal healthcare, childcare and free or affordable higher education, the GND refers more strictly to transitioning the economy to renewable energy. In the United States, Senator Bernie Sanders' GND program is also largely a program of greening the economy (Senator Sanders also has separate proposals for a Medicare for All, Free College, etc.). In this chapter, I will use a broad definition of the Green New Deal which includes fully transitioning to renewable energy in ten years, a Medicare for All (M4A) program and a job guarantee program. As I will demonstrate, such a comprehensive approach is the right way to go.

2 See https://berniesanders.com/issues/how-does-bernie-pay-his-major-plans/

3 Further, if the government issues any other obligations, such as bonds, they have to be denominated in its own currency as well. This is unfortunately not the case for many developing countries.

4 Note that by this definition, the euro is not a sovereign currency for its member countries. Hence, the fact that Greece was forced to default on its debt is not surprising.

5 There can be self-imposed constraints, such as debt limits/a debt ceiling, limitations on direct purchases of bonds by the central bank, etc.
6 As MMT explains, taxes play an important role in our money system – they drive the demand for government's currency, its IOUs. The government creates the need for its own IOUs by imposing a debt (a tax) on the population and demanding that it be paid back only in its IOUs.
7 It follows from this discussion that a government with sovereign currency cannot be forced to default on its debt (see Wray 2015 for an in-depth discussion of this point).
8 Note that the precious metal would not become currency until stamped by the government.
9 Some economists mistakenly believe MMT is all about "print and spend" (see Buiter 2020, for example).
10 To the extent that the state will also be involved, it's a matter of public planning, something that the original New Deal did as well (e.g. the Tennessee Valley Authority), but an approach that the US government has increasingly replaced with private sector incentives.
11 The discussion largely follows that of Nersisyan and Wray (2019 and 2020a).
12 Clearly, resources released by the shift from private insurers to single payer may not be well suited to alternative uses (such as other GND projects). Released resources will need to be retrained, and this can take time.
13 Indeed, the original New Deal, which reshaped the US economy for generations didn't even get close to WWII in terms of the increase in government spending and resource mobilization.

References

Anderson, G. F., Hussey, P. S., and Petrosyan, V. 2019. "It's Still the Prices, Stupid: Why the US Spends So Much on Health Care, and a Tribute to Uwe Reinhardt." *Health Affairs* 38(1): 87–95.

Anderson, G. F., Reinhardt, U. E., Hussey, P. S., and Petrosyan, V. 2003. "It's the Prices, Stupid: Why the United States Is So Different from Other Countries." *Health Affairs* 22(3): 89–105.

Bell, S. 2000. "Do Taxes and Bonds Finance Government Spending?" *Journal of Economic Issues* 34(3): 603–620.

Blanchard, O. 2019. "Reexamining the Economic Costs of Debt. Testimony." *US House Committee On the Budget Hearing*. 15 November.

Buiter, W. 2020. "The Helicopters Are Coming." *Project Syndicate*. 26 March. Available at: https://www.project-syndicate.org/commentary/helicopter-money-coronavirus-responseby-willem-h-buiter-1-2020-03?barrier=accesspaylog

Dantas, F., and Wray, L. R. 2017. "Full Employment: Are We There Yet?" *Public Policy Brief No. 142*. Annandale-on-Hudson, NY: Levy Economics Institute of Bard College. February.

Elwell, C. K. 2011. "Brief History of the Gold Standard in the United States." *Congressional Research Service Report for Congress*. 23 June.

Fullwiler, S. T. 2010. Modern Money Theory-a Primer on the Operational Realities of the Money System. Available at SSRN 1723198.

Graeber, D. 2012. *Debt: The First 5000 Years*. Brooklyn, N.Y.: Melville House.

Holtz-Eakin, D., Bosch, D., Gitis, B., Goldbeck, D., and Rossetti, P. 2019. *The Green New Deal: Scope, Scale, and Implications*. Washington, DC: American Action Forum. 25 February.

Krugman, P. 2019. "How Much Does Heterodoxy Help Progressives?" *New York Times*. 12 February.

Krugman, P. 2020. "The Case for Permanent Stimulus (Wonkish)." *New York Times*. 7 March.

Mosler, W. 1996. *Soft Currency Economics*. Christiansted, St. Croix: Valance Co.

Mueller, M., Hagenaars, L., and Morgan, D. 2017. "Administrative Spending in OECD Health Care Systems: Where Is the Fat and Can It Be Trimmed?" In *Tackling Wasteful Spending on Health*. Paris: OECD Publishing. https://www.oecd-ilibrary.org/social-issues-migration-health/tackling-wasteful-spending-on-health_9789264266414-en

Nersisyan, Y. and Wray, L. R. 2016. "Modern Money Theory and the Facts of Experience." *Cambridge Journal of Economics* 40(5): 1297–1316.

Nersisyan, Y. and Wray, L. R. 2019. "How to Pay for the Green New Deal." *Levy Economics Institute Working Papers No. 931*.

Nersisyan, Y. and Wray, L. R. 2020a. "Can We Afford the Green New Deal?" *Levy Economics Institute Public Policy Brief No. 148*.

Nersisyan, Y. and Wray, L. R. 2020b. "The Most Important Economic Lesson from the COVID-19 Crisis: It's Time to Ditch "pay-for" Politics." *Dollars & Sense*. May/June.

Nersisyan, Y. and Wray, L. R. 2021. "Can We Afford the Green New Deal?" *Journal of Post Keynesian Economics* 44(1): 68–88.

Papanicolas, I., Woskie, L. R., and Jha, A. K. 2018. "Health Care Spending in the United States and Other High-Income Countries." *JAMA* 319(10): 1024–1039.

Pollin, R. 2019. "How Do We Pay for a Zero-Emissions Economy?" *The American Prospect*. 5 December. Available at: https://prospect.org/greennewdeal/how-to-pay-for-a-zero-emissions-economy/

Pollin, R. et al. 2018. *Economic Analysis of Medicare for All*. Amherst, MA: Political Economy Research Institute. 30 November.

Ruml, B. 1946. "Taxes for Revenue Are Obsolete." *American Affairs* 8(1): 35–39.

Tcherneva, P. 2018. "The Job Guarantee: Design, Jobs, and Implementation." *Working Paper No. 902*. Annandale-on-Hudson, NY: Levy Economics Institute of Bard College. April.

Tcherneva, P. 2020. *The Case for a Job Guarantee*. Cambridge: Polity Press.

Tymoigne, E. 2014. "Modern Money Theory and the Interrelation between the Treasury and the Central Bank: The Case of the United States." *Journal of Economic Issues* 48(3): 641–662.

Tymoigne, E. and Wray, L. R. 2013. "Modern Money Theory 101: A Reply to Critics." *Working Paper No. 778*. The Levy Economics Institute of Bard College. November.

Woolhandler, S., Campbell, T., and Himmelstein, D. U. 2003. "Costs of Health Care Administration in the United States and Canada." *New England Journal of Medicine* 349: 768–775.

Wray, L. R. 1998. *Understanding Modern Money: The Key to Full Employment and Price Stability*. Northampton, MA: Edward Elgar.

Wray, L. R. 2015. *Modern Money Theory: A Primer on Macroeconomics for Sovereign Money Systems*. New York: Palgrave Macmillan.

Wray, L. R. et al. 2018. "Public Service Employment: A Path to Full Employment." *Research Project Report*. Annandale-on-Hudson, NY: Levy Economics Institute of Bard College. April.

3

CENTRAL BANKS AND GREEN NEW DEALS

What role can they play?

Ray Galvin

Introduction

Much has been written recently about the concept and structure of green new deals (see review in Galvin and Healy 2020). There were numerous proposals in the late twentieth and early twenty-first centuries that advocated government stimulus funding for climate change mitigation, and a survey of these found they were often modelled on US President Franklin D. Roosevelt's New Deal of the 1930s (Luke 2009). These advocate decarbonizing the economy and protecting the environment while also reducing income inequality. The US Green New Deal advocated by US Congresswoman Alexandra Ocasio-Cortez and Senator Ed Markey (H.Res. 109 2019) was constructed along these lines. Its content was fleshed out in Senator Bernie Sanders' presidential campaign policies with minor modifications (Sanders 2019) and later incorporated more or less intact in President Joe Biden's pre-election policy briefs (Biden 2020). Policy statements and cabinet appointments since Biden's election and inauguration indicate that he fully intended to implement a policy very much like this (Deutsche Welle 2021; Sanders 2021), though he is not openly calling it a green new deal.

All three of these versions of a climate change mitigation project have the character of a Roosevelt-style New Deal and are designed to be government-led and mostly government-funded. Biden's version, like that of Sanders, envisages very large deficit funding inputs in the region of 1–2 trillion US dollars over multiple years. The entire US federal budget in 2019 was $4.45 trillion, so an extra deficit of around one-quarter to one-third of that is very large. It is entirely proper that there should be vigorous discussion on how this would affect the economy.

Most studies on the financing of green new deals look at these from the perspective of a government, via its ministry of finance, spending money on projects that will decarbonize the economy, reduce inequalities and improve social justice.

In this chapter I want to explore the issue from the perspective of a different arm of government, namely, the central bank. Most governments have two distinct arms with respect to finance: the ministry of finance (called the Treasury in the United States and Britain); and the central bank (called the Federal Reserve or "Fed" in the United States and the Bank of England in Britain). The ministry of finance is headed by a cabinet minister appointed by the highest democratically elected member of government: the President in the United States and the Prime Minister in Britain, Australia, New Zealand and similar countries.

DOI: 10.4324/9781003110880-5

Whenever a government spends money, it does so via its ministry of finance,[1] and it can only spend what Congress (in the United States) or Parliament (in Britain and similar countries) approves. The same applies when money flows in the reverse direction: the government can only demand taxes that are approved by Congress or Parliament. Governments' spending and demanding of money is therefore fully under democratic, political control.[2]

The other financial arm of government, the central bank, is several steps removed from democratic, political control and is more akin to a specialized, technical, quasi-independent body run by civil servants. Central banks have a crucial role in countries' economies because they have broad powers to create and dissolve money and use this to meet inflation targets and stabilize financial markets, as well as serving as the government's bank and a kind of super-bank where commercial banks hold their reserve accounts. Central banks are a relatively modern phenomenon. Britain was the first country to have a central bank, established in 1694 to act as the English government's banker, nationalized in 1946 by the government of Prime Minister Clement Atlee and given independence in its basic roles in 1998. The roles, purpose and powers of central banks have evolved somewhat over the past 200–300 years, and most central banks today are based on the British model. The Federal Reserve is the United States's third central bank, following the First Bank of the United States in 1791–1811 and the Second Bank of the United States in 1817–1836.

In order to better understand how a green new deal can work or fail, we need to understand how a country's ministry of finance and central bank interact and how their roles are demarcated. Some central banks are already acting independently to steer financial markets away from climate-damaging investment, and some are going further by favouring green firms in their bond-buying and financing activities. In this respect, central banks themselves are assessing climate-related risks and making decisions as to where best to target money. But the main role central banks would play in a green new deal would be to act in support of government decisions on large-scale spending for climate change mitigation and social equity initiatives, which would include both providing finance and acting to discipline financial markets to avoid inflation. In this situation the traditional role of central banks in controlling inflation and ensuring financial stability takes on a special focus. In a nutshell, we need to ask what central banks must do to ensure that inflation stays within acceptable limits amid the large amounts of money that governments will inject into the economy via a green new deal.

To understand this requires an understanding of what money is and how it regularly comes into existence and is dissolved out of existence. I will therefore begin the discussion by briefly explaining this in the context of modern central banking. I also comment on the shifting relationship between central banks and the political, elected arm of government. I will then outline recent moves by central banks to adjust their role in relation to the financial challenges that climate change and its mitigation are bringing. Later, I report on further moves, especially by the United Kingdom's central bank, to be more proactive in shifting the economy toward decarbonization. I then outline a further proposal, from the European Greens, that could link central banks' money-creation activities much more closely to the climate change mitigation aims of European governments. Finally I take a detailed look at what the roles of a central bank would be if a government adopted a fully fledged green new deal.

Central banks and democratic control

One of the main roles of central banks today is to create and dissolve money for the ministry of finance, or "Treasury." In this role they act in a purely technical capacity as the servant of the elected government. At the precise moment the government spends money in accordance with what Congress or Parliament have approved, the central bank credits the amounts to the reserve accounts of the recipients' banks (see Box 3.2 in this chapter). The central bank always pays the money, irrespective of how high the spending is, or how good the government's balance sheet is at the time. A government that is sovereign over its currency (such as the United States, the United Kingdom, Canada, Australia, Britain, Japan and New Zealand) can never run out of money because the central bank simply creates it as the government spends it into existence – though this does not mean a government should spend however much it wants to, as I will explain later. Money in most countries today is "fiat" money, an expression we hear frequently in discussions of central banks. "Fiat" is a Latin word meaning "a command or act of will that creates something without, or as if without, further effort."[3] More broadly, the word fiat is used in English to mean "by decree or dictate." The expression "fiat money" is used because the central bank creates money out of nothing, by dictate. It usually does this by computer keystrokes, and there are no physical or metaphysical limits on the amount it can spend. There are, however, some very important practical limits, as I will discuss toward the end of the chapter.

In this respect, then, a central bank is fully under the control of the elected government and is therefore subject to the politics of the day. It has to follow democratically enforced mandates but has considerable leeway as to how to meet these. Most central banks are required to adjust key aspects of the money supply to ensure "price stability," which in most high-income countries currently means keeping consumer price inflation at or just under 2% in the long run. In the United States, the Fed is also required to aim for "maximum employment" and "financial stability" (Federal Reserve 2020a). In New Zealand, in addition to similar goals, the central bank has to aim for "monetary policy's best contribution to the prosperity and well-being of New Zealanders, and to a sustainable and productive economy" (Reserve Bank of New Zealand 2020). Note that the term "monetary policy" refers to the rules and norms that guide central banks' money creation, distribution and dissolution, whereas "fiscal policy" refers to the elected government's spending and sequestering of money.

This chapter applies first and foremost to countries that are sovereign over their own currencies and have relatively well-functioning economies that produce about as much value, in goods and services, as they consume. It does not apply directly to countries like Bahrain, Djibouti and Jordan, which peg their countries to the US dollar, nor to some former French colonies in Africa which peg theirs to the euro. Nor does it apply to countries that would be heavily dependent on foreign aid or investment to buy equipment for infrastructure needed to decarbonize key features of their energy industry such as their electricity grid. Further, it applies only with modifications to the 19 Eurozone countries. Although the Eurozone as a whole is sovereign over its currency, the individual Eurozone countries are not. For example, under normal circumstances they cannot make their own rules about how far to go into debt, even if going deeper into debt would lift their economies and mitigate inequality in the long run (Piketty 2014; 2019). I will mention some implications for Eurozone countries along the way, but the chapter would be too long if I went into these in detail.

Central banks are more or less left to themselves to decide how to achieve the monetary policy aims that are given to them by government. Much has been written about the unprecedented initiatives central banks took in 2008 and subsequently, beginning with the Fed and the Bank of England, to stabilize financial systems as the global financial crisis unfolded. Vogl (2017) maps the details of hastily convened committee meetings, back-room deals, input from heads of corporations and agreements made and unravelled between the Fed and British banks, which led to the unprecedented emergence of "quantitative easing" (QE). The Fed and the Bank of England came to the view that huge injections of money needed to go to major private financial corporations such as Bear Sterns and publicly traded companies such as the Federal National Mortgage Association to prevent their collapse and thereby prevent a cascade of collapses in financial institutions which would catastrophically derail global financial systems. They achieved this by buying bonds and other non-cash instruments held by these institutions on a massive scale (for an explanation of what "bonds" are, see Box 3.1).

Box 3.1 What are "bonds" and "yields"?

A **bond** is a form of IOU. In its crudest form it is a signed piece of paper promising to pay the holder a specified sum of money at a particular point in time, called its "**maturity**" date, plus regular interest payments at a specified rate. To give a much simplified example, a firm named Solar Investors needs $10 million for a wind farm project. It offers an auction of 1,000 five-year bonds each of face value $10,000 with an interest rate of 4% per year. Potential investors bid for a specific number of these bonds and compete against each other by naming their discount rate, i.e. the percentage above the face value of the bonds that they would be willing to pay. Solar Investors accepts offers with the highest discount rate covering 1,000 bonds, so that it will have to pay back as little as possible.

Suppose a successful investor, Fiona, bought two of these bonds for $10,100 each. She can then sell her bonds on to others. This is called selling on the "secondary market." Her bonds are earning 4% of 2 × $10,000 interest, i.e. $800 per year. A potential purchaser, Henry, offers $10,200 per bond to secure this annual income of $800 from the two bonds. The "**yield**" of a bond is the annual income you get for the bond as a percentage of the price you paid. Fiona's yield per bond was $400 divided by the price she paid for them ($10,100), i.e. 3.96%. Henry's yield is lower: $400/$10,200 = 3.92%. Hence, for a specific bond, the higher the bond's price, the lower its yield.

Private companies issue bonds to get money, often for investments in expansion or new projects. Governments and their central banks issue bonds to withdraw money from circulation. In quantitative easing (QE), central banks buy bonds to inject money into the market. A very large portion of the bonds that central banks buy are central or local government bonds, but central banks usually avoid government bond auctions and only buy government bonds on the secondary market. However, the Canadian central bank buys government bonds at auction after private bidders have set the discount rate.

In the United States, government bonds are called Treasury bonds, or "**treasuries.**" Most bonds have long maturity periods, up to 30 years. Those with short maturity periods are usually called "**bills.**" Of course, today bonds exist and are bought and sold electronically rather than on the elegant paper formats of past days.

There is a basic difference between bonds purchased by central banks and bonds purchased by the private sector. When the central bank purchases a bond it does so by creating new money to pay for the bond. When a private firm or citizen buys a bond, existing money is simply shifted from one bank account to another.

The buying and selling of government bonds on the "secondary market" (also see Box 3.1) has long been a regular activity of central banks in managing the quantity of money in the banking system, as one of the tools of price stabilization (Epstein 2006; Barrowclough 2020). The money they use to buy bonds is fiat money, created out of nothing. As central banks faced the global financial crisis of 2008, they increased this practice massively and also bought up a large quantity of less secure bonds issued by private firms. This "QE" approach was seen as a success, and QE was continued in the United States, Britain and other countries and is now a regular activity. QE enjoyed a resurgence in many countries when the coronavirus pandemic struck. Using QE, the Bank of England created and injected £695 billion into the financial markets between November 2009 and November 2020, increasing its total injection of money by around £80 billion per year (Bank of England 2021b). This is about equal to the amount the UK government spends each year on the military plus transport combined, or about 80% of the education budget (HM Treasury 2018). Currently the Eurozone's central bank, the European Central Bank (ECB), is injecting €1,850 billion of new money into the economy via financial markets over a period of about 18–20 months in 2020–2021, in its Pandemic Emergency Purchase Programme. The total amount of "high-powered" or "narrow" money (see below for definitions) in circulation in euros in December 2019 was €9,500 billion, so this round of QE will increase the Eurozone's narrow money supply by 19.5% (European Central Bank 2020).

Whatever one thinks of the technical efficacy of this approach, a key point is that it happens outside of direct democratic and political control. This is not inherently intended as a criticism, but it is important to note, in relation to the large shifts in spending and finance that decarbonization will entail. Prior to central banks gaining greater operational independence toward the end of last century, it was not unusual for politicians to use their central banks' money-creation powers to crank up the economy prior to an election, which led to inflation after the election, which had to be reigned in after the election with austerity-type actions such as high interest rates and severely reduced government spending (Blancheton 2016; Barrowclough 2020, 152). Nevertheless, when a quasi-independent body is able to make very large impacts on the economy, the question of accountability has to be visited and revisited.

For example, I have argued elsewhere, rightly or wrongly, that it might have been more pragmatically effective in 2008–2009 for the Fed to feed money directly to households to prevent them defaulting on their mortgages, possibly by buying a stake in their homes or mortgages, as this would have taken pressure off both the households and the banks and consequently the wider financial system, rather than just the latter two (Galvin 2020a). It might have made even more sense in 2020 for central banks to support households and businesses directly, as these were the immediate casualties of the COVID-19 lockdowns. Instead, central banks saw their role as supporting the commercial banks and corporations whose ability to serve the economy was endangered by the shortages of cash among their customers, i.e. households and productive businesses. It was left to the Treasury to support households and productive businesses, and this was done rather patchily in many countries. Barrowclough (2020) and the United Nations Conference on Trade and Development (UNCTAD) (2019, 151) argue that elected governments are largely to blame for this type of imbalance, through making central banks independent to the extent that their own options for supporting their objectives are severely limited.

Whatever one's views on the technical issues of how central banks should have acted, or what social and political influences have led to central banks' independence and somewhat narrow options for intervention in an economy, it is important to understand that they are now regularly creating and dissolving huge sums of money in comparison to government spending. If we are to consider the role that they can have in climate change mitigation and green new deals, we need to address the issue of accountability. Of course, being democratically elected does not guarantee adequate skill or motivation to spend money wisely, but there are clear lines of accountability in a democratically elected government, from the top right down to the voters. With central banks, accountability is much more blurred.

Further, as Barrowclough (2020) points out, the day-to-day actions of central banks are never politically or morally neutral, since they involve decisions such as which private enterprises to support financially with bond trading, how high or low to let interest rates go (thereby benefiting ether savers or borrowers), and how much collateral commercial banks must have in their reserve accounts (thereby influencing how much they can lend to customers).

This raises the important question of how central banks evolved to have such enormous power in modern economies. Tognato (2012) explores the links between central banks' legitimacy, public support and independence, and how these have developed over the past 100 years. In particular, he examines the social and cultural underpinnings of central bank power. He argues that central banks' legitimacy stems primarily from the cultural support we give them, rather than from a deliberative democratic process. For example, he shows how the (West) German central bank, the Bundesbank, won popular admiration in the decades immediately after the Second World War for its disciplined control of the money supply that contributed to the German currency, the Deutschmark, persistently increasing in value alongside the US dollar and British pound. Consumer prices in West Germany and the reunited Germany increased by an average of 3.21% per year from 1960 to 1999, when the euro replaced the Deutschmark, while in the United States, Britain and New Zealand, prices increased by 4.40%, 6.76% and 7.20% per year respectively (author calculations based on data from World Bank 2020). Germany's inflation was therefore less than half that of Britain's. Figure 3.1 shows the annual increase in the consumer price index in each of those years. This graphically indicates how the Bundesbank's monetary discipline helped to prevent the huge spikes in inflation seen in other countries due to the oil price shocks of the 1970s and the shift to floating[4] currencies in the 1980s.

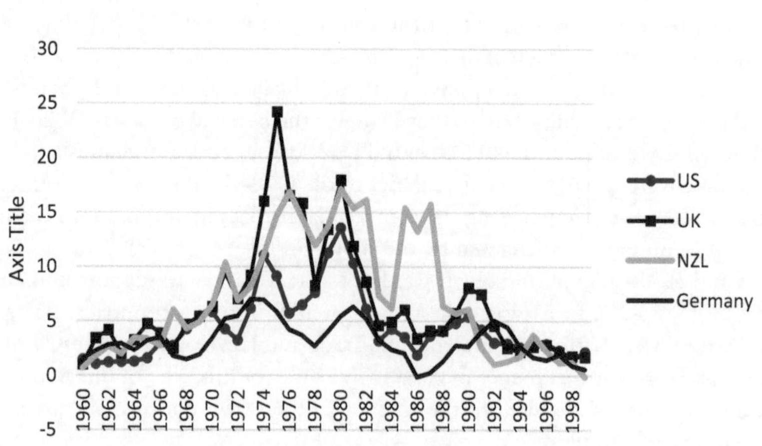

Figure 3.1 Annual consumer price increase (%) 1960–1999, the United States, the United Kingdom, New Zealand and Germany

Data source: World Bank.

Tognato (2012) then shows how German popular support for the Bundesbank's model heavily influenced both the unwritten and written rules and codes of the Eurozone's central bank, the European Central Bank (ECB). This, he argues, is largely why the ECB pursued such harsh austerity measures in the aftermath of the global financial crisis. He applies the same method to understanding the responses of US and other countries' central banks to the global financial crisis. The implication is that one of the reasons central banks chose to save the economy by propping up the financial markets rather than households and businesses in the real economy who were suffering financial ruin – largely due to the profligacy of those very same financial markets – was not primarily because they were constrained to do so by their governments. Rather, this was their culture. In addition, there was and is a constant interplay of financial personnel between central bank boards and the corporate financial world. Membership of central bank committees is constantly recycled among actors from corporate finance. There is a deep, culturally entrenched understanding among some of these actors that central banks are a kind of addendum to the financial world and are beholden to it, rather than to parliaments or Congress.

Vogl (2017) looks at this at an even deeper level. He tracks the interactions and mutual understandings between financial institutions, including commercial and central banks, over the past 300 years. He shows how the dynamics of modern finance rest on complex and constantly evolving relationships between private financial institutions and the state. He takes the issue further than Tognato, arguing that there is a kind of tacit understanding of how finance should be done, not just between private financial institutions and central banks, but also in the heart of many ministries of finance among their civil servants. Legislation governing central banks allows these banks to set their own norms, practices and implicit rules, and these tend to be influenced by actors in the financial world.

On the other hand, Blancheton (2016) tracks the history of the degree of independence central banks have enjoyed over the past century, suggesting that government influence over their actions is always either real or not that far away, and tends to ebb and flow according to shifts in the types and degree of economic challenges and crises. He suggests that central banks effectively lost control of price stability after the global financial crisis of 2008 (inflation got stuck at too low a rate even though the broad money supply reached unprecedented levels) and that this has to some extent weakened governments' trust in the ability of central banks to act independently.

A further perspective is given by Barrowclough (2020) and UNCTAD (2019, 151), who point out that in the 1930s–1980s central banks were more directly subject to their governments' economic and social policy aims and played a much more direct role in providing economic firepower and restraint, as needed, for the success of these policies. These authors, among others, argue that it was the dominance of neoliberalism that severed this relationship and left central banks with a much narrower focus on the financial markets.

These issues need to be taken into account in mapping out a role for central banks in relation to a green new deal. Governments may have to decide what aspects of independence are appropriate for central banks in the age of climate disruption, where government actions and spending for decarbonization will be ramped up substantially. There might also be strong resistance among some central bankers if they feel governments are trespassing on their territory. At the same time, there are dangers in making central banks simply the money-pumping tools of financially irresponsible governments.

In the midst of these unresolved issues, an interesting development is that many central banks have already begun to respond to a coming regime of ramped-up climate change mitigation activity and are responding on several levels. I will now survey these before exploring what their role might be in a fully fledged green new deal.

Central banks as defenders of the financial system

Most studies of central banks in relation to climate change look at what may be called "central banks as defenders of the financial system." As I mentioned above, most central banks have a mandate to support price stability so that inflation remains within a narrow margin, usually around 1.5%–2.0%, and to support the stabilization of financial markets.

It is well understood among academic observers that climate change will impact on the financial sphere. As Dafermos et al. (2018, 232) argue, "The fundamental changes that are expected to take place in the climate system in the next decades are likely to have severe implications for the stability of the financial system." Battiston and Monasterolo (2019) develop models to quantify these risks and the financial damage they could cause in a 2-degree global heating scenario. Meanwhile, Cormack et al. (2020) offer a method to quantify financial risks due to a transition to climate-friendly technologies such as decarbonization of the European electricity grid.

Many central banks therefore now see climate change as a threat to the health of the financial system. In the words of the supervisors of central banks in Britain, France and the Netherlands in 2019,

> That is why 34 central banks and supervisors – representing five continents, half of global greenhouse gas emissions and the supervision of two-thirds of the global systemically important banks and insurers – joined forces in 2017 to create a coalition of the willing: the Network for Greening the Financial System (NGFS).
>
> *(Carney et al. 2019)*

While "greening the financial system" might sound extraordinarily ambitious and radical, the goals of the NGFS are primarily reactive rather than proactive, geared to keep the financial system running smoothly in the face of climate shocks and stresses, rather than to initiate or foster climate change mitigation actions. The main goal is to "integrate the monitoring of climate-related financial risks into day-to-day supervisory work, financial stability monitoring and board risk management" (Carney et al. 2019; see also the NGFS website).[5] More specifically, Carney and other central bank heads urged central banks to ensure that the corporations and banks they buy bonds from or support are adequately addressing climate risks in their business activities so that they do not get hit by financially damaging climate impacts. Carney and colleagues point out, for example, that insured losses have risen five-fold in the past 30 years and that climate change events are damaging infrastructure, productivity, private property and human health, as well as destroying other forms of wealth. They also note that reducing carbon emissions to reach net zero by 2050 will require massive reallocations of capital and that "If some companies and industries fail to adjust to this new world, they will fail to exist."

Hence two main types of interrelated disruption are envisaged: (1) disruption to investments and capital caused directly by climate change, such as hurricanes, floods, wildfires, heatwaves and sea-level rise; and (2) disruption originating within the financial system itself due to massive shifts in investment priorities for climate change adaptation and mitigation (cf. UNCTAD 2019, 151). In a more detailed report, Francois Villeroy de Galhau, Governor of Banque de France, categorizes these as "physical risks" of climate change and "transactional risks" of climate change mitigation (Villeroy de Galhau 2019).

The new governor of the Bank of England, Andrew Bailey, has repeatedly reiterated the Bank's commitment to this agenda. In a speech in November 2020 he affirmed: "Our goal is to build a UK financial system resilient to the risks from climate change and supportive of the transition to a net-zero economy." Referring to how decisively the Bank of England responded to financial disruption due to the COVID-19 pandemic, he went on to say,

> We need that same ambition in our approach to climate change. But what is different with climate change is that we know now it is coming, so we can identify where risks will arise and start managing them in advance.

This will require that:

> ...firms must assess how climate risks could impact their business and review whether additional capital needs to be held against this. Investments that look safe on a backward look may be existentially risky given climate risks. And investments that might have looked speculative in the past could look much safer in the context of a transition to net zero.
>
> *(Bailey 2020)*

In relation to climate change and its physically and transactionally induced shocks, these central bankers see their role as responding to the financial disruption due to climate change and its mitigation through a range of instruments to keep financial systems stable and functional. Barrowclough (2020) discusses an even fuller range of possible tools central banks could use for this. I call these "reactive" responses as they are geared to support, defend and protect financial markets and systems from shocks and failures due to climate change, rather than to address the problem of climate change directly. They can contribute to climate change mitigation by encouraging firms to shift investment out of carbon-intensive activities early, so as to be seen by the central bank as unlikely to get caught out with stranded assets in the future. But there are also indications of central bank interest in proactive responses, which I discuss in the following section.

Toward a proactive approach: buying green bonds

Several studies point out that central banks have an interest in being proactive, taking the initiative to help mitigate climate change, if only to dampen physical risks and get more control over transactional risks. As early as 2016, a paper from the Bank of England drew attention to the climate-damaging tendency of the financial sector if left without controls:

> ...the decision of financial institutions to fund activities that are intensive in CO_2 emissions can contribute to increasing the climate-related physical risks, albeit indirectly; and conversely, their financing of technologies that help reduce CO_2 emissions can contribute to a reduction of climate-related physical risks.
>
> *(Batten et al. 2016)*

In response to these risks, Dafermos et al. (2018), UNCTAD (2019, 151) and Barrowclough (2020) propose "green quantitative easing" (green QE), in which central banks bid on the open market to buy bonds issued by green enterprises. There are various ways central banks could pursue green QE: introduce a bias in favour of environmentally sound companies for their bond-buying (Anderson 2015); run parallel QE programs of both regular and green bond purchases (Campiglio et al. 2018); or fund agencies that have specific remits to work for climate change mitigation (Ryan-Collins 2013). Durrani et al. (2020) point out that approaches such as these would usually require central banks to seek regulatory changes to include environmental bias in their asset purchase programs. Alternatively, governments could initiate such changes in their central bank legislative frameworks.

Having a bias in favour of green bonds brings several advantages. It increases the supply of loan money for private sector projects designed to mitigate climate change such as wind farms, battery peak load shavers, photovoltaics, etc., and in doing so reduces the interest rates that such enterprises must pay to finance these investments. In more technical language, it reduces the "yield" (see Box 3.1) on green bonds while increasing their price. In Dafermos et al.'s words, "The reduction in the green bond yield leads to a lower cost of borrowing for firms and a lower reliance on bank lending. This increases overall investment, including green investment" (2018, 232).

A further payoff is that green bonds become more financially desirable in comparison to other bonds. As Dafermos explains, "the yield of green bonds declines relative to the yield of conventional bonds and the share of desired green investment in total investment goes up." As firms then invest more in green capital (renewables, energy efficiency, etc.), this "leads to lower CO_2 emissions and slower global warming than what would otherwise be the case."

In parallel with this idea, Mark Carney, until recently the governor of the Bank of England, strongly advocated the need for the private sector to develop a mature green bond market with international connectivity (Carney 2016). This would provide a coherent market niche for at least a portion of central bank bond buying.

Since green bonds are now relatively well established in markets (though still a small sector), Reboredo and Ugolini (2020) examined data from October 2014 to June 2019 to estimate how their performance correlates with that of other financial instruments and indicators. They found their performance is not closely linked to that of the stock market, wider energy markets or high-yield corporate bond markets, but tends to follow government bond markets and the value of the US dollar. This makes green bonds a good hedge for investors, as they are less likely to fall in value when mainstream investments fall. It also gives weight to the idea that green projects are moving at least a small part of the economy in a new direction. These factors provide both a pragmatic and an ethical argument for central banks to boost the proportion of green bonds on their balance sheets.

A preference for green bonds would also begin to free central banks from their tendency to support climate-damaging financial ventures and corporations. Campaglio et al. find evidence that current and past QE programs have "inadvertently favoured large carbon-intensive companies, reflecting their relatively strong credit ratings and the fact that many low-carbon firms are too small to issue corporate bonds." This can have a snowball effect, reducing the cost of borrowing further for climate-damaging firms as central bank investments in them give the market the impression that they are more stable and safer than smaller, green firms (2018, 465).

The Bank of England's new governor, Andrew Bailey, admitted that the Bank's bond-buying during the COVID-19 crisis inadvertently supported carbon-intensive investment, claiming this was inevitable in a severe economic crisis. Concern about this was raised by the UK House of Commons' Environmental Audit Committee in January 2021. The committee stated that buying bonds from companies with a high climate impact contravenes government policies on climate change. Committee Chairman Philip Dunne wrote to the

Governor of the Bank of England: "The Bank must begin a process of aligning its corporate bond purchasing programme with Paris Agreement goals as a matter of urgency" (Milliken 2021). The Bank of England holds corporate bonds in proportion to the amounts issued in bond markets, and this tends to favour climate-damaging firms as these are the wealthiest and issue the most bonds. In January 2021, 19% of the bonds the Bank of England held were issued by electricity companies, 9% by gas and other energy companies, and 11% by industrial and transport firms, making a total of 39% in support of carbon intensive businesses (Milliken 2021; see also Bank of England 2021a).

A shift toward more green bonds and less from carbon-intensive firms could come via the stress tests to which central banks regularly subject commercial banks and other financial institutions. Central banks usually have powers to require these institutions to increase their reserves or take other measures in response to their stress test performance. The Bank of England is to conduct "green stress tests," called the "2021 Biennial Exploratory Scenario" (BES), in June 2021 (Bank of England 2020a). The Bank of England's statement on stress testing and climate change states:

> The objective of the Climate BES is to test the resilience of the largest banks, insurers and the financial system to different possible climate pathways and provide a comprehensive assessment of the UK financial system's exposure to climate-related risks. The Climate BES will ask firms to consider three scenarios, which will be based on the scenarios published by the Network for Greening the Financial System (NGFS).

Proactive central bank interventions such as these can put pressure on markets to increase their holdings of green bonds and reduce holdings of bonds from carbon-intensive industries which are more likely to suffer transactional shocks caused by government-led initiatives toward carbon neutrality.

A related strategy is for central banks to support and set guidelines for "green banking." When central banks buy a firm's bonds, this not only puts money in the firm's bank account, it also boosts the balance sheets of the commercial banks with which these firms do their banking. Park and Kim (2020) explore how central banks could thereby regulate, advise or put pressure on commercial banks to adopt green investment policies for their own lending activities. The effect would be to bring even more bias toward green and climate-friendly investment in the real economy.

Approaches such as these would begin to carve out a role for central banks in support of their governments' climate change mitigation programs. Nevertheless, as Breitenfellner et al. (2019) argue, approaches such as these would not be sufficient to reduce CO_2 emissions deeply enough to meet climate goals, and there would still need to be government-directed investments and management to go the rest of the distance.

Further, all such approaches give the initiative to the central bank, which is one or two steps removed from democratic control, as discussed above. Some recent studies argue that since money and climate change are so closely related there needs to be a more synergistic realignment of central bank activity with the political, democratically led climate aims of elected government. It is essential, argue Langley and Morris (2020), that central bank interventions "are animated by normative, politically prior and oppositional questions about what central banks could and should do," and this "will most likely necessitate the democratic transformation and fundamental repurposing of central banking itself" (p. 1447. See also Mann 2010). Before looking more closely at what this alignment might look like in a green new deal, there is one further in-between initiative to consider.

A step further toward government control

A proposal by the European Parliament's Greens/European Free Alliance (EFA) group (Anderson 2015) envisions a shift away from central bank control over the choice of firms and corporations that get favourable treatment on the basis of their green credentials. Here, the European Central Bank (ECB) would channel QE funding via the European Investment Bank, which would make the decisions as to which green bonds to purchase (i.e. which green enterprises to fund). The European Investment Bank is a publicly owned international financial institution whose shareholders are the EU member states. It was established in 1958 under the Treaty of Rome as a "policy-driven bank" which would use financing operations to further EU policy goals such as European integration and social cohesion. The EU member states set the bank's broad policy goals and oversee its decision-making bodies: the board of governors and board of directors. It is the world's largest international publicly owned lending institution. Two of its six priority objectives are support for small and medium-sized enterprises, and environmental sustainability. This combination fits well with the idea of accelerated funding for the aims of a green new deal, but via private enterprise rather than government stimulus funding. As of 2019 the European Investment Bank requires at least 25% of its loans to go to projects that mitigate climate change (UNCTAD 2019), so there is already a precedent for directing investment to this aim.

The amounts provided by the ECB would be in accordance with its statutory monetary stabilization responsibilities, but the ECB would have no say as to which bonds are purchased. Since not all EU countries use the euro, the non-Eurozone members of the EU would participate in the scheme via their own central banks, which would create additional QE money for the European Investment Bank to use in green bond purchases.

The Eurozone is a special case in that its member countries' central banks do not have unlimited money-creation power, which is reserved for the European Central Bank. However, we can also imagine the model working in a currency-sovereign country such as the United Kingdom, New Zealand or the United States, where a Green Investment Bank would be established to purchase green bonds using QE money from their central banks, with the purchases in line with the government's green new deal aims. The day-to-day decisions of a country's Green Investment Bank would be directly accountable to the government.

Nevertheless, a scheme such as this still suffers at least three major drawbacks. First, the amount of funding for green enterprises would vary according to the central banks' price stabilization mandates, rather than the investment needs of climate change mitigation enterprises: a flood of money during economic downturns and a mere trickle when markets are performing well.

Second and closely related to this, the type of investment needed for climate change mitigation is often very long-term and oriented toward infrastructure development (UNCTAD 2019; Barrowclough 2020), whereas central banks' monetary interventions tend to be short-term, as they have to respond nimbly to economic shocks and vicissitudes. However, public investment banks could still run long-term green investment operations financed from their current base, alongside the more fluctuating investment activities from QE money.

A third limitation is that such a scheme feeds money to private initiatives only. Certainly the private sector has a huge role to play in climate change mitigation, but this is will not be sufficient even if the government provides guidance and direction for the private sector through regulations. Christophers (2017) argues that approaches such as these rest on the neoliberal assumption that the markets will bring the desired result if left to themselves, but some of the major investments needed are unlikely to turn a profit quickly enough for private sector investment. Some are very large-scale and would best proceed with government investment and leadership, often in concert with private sector involvement – such as decarbonizing an entire national electricity grid.

However, the concept of an investment bank that sits between central banks and the private sector for the purposes of QE is worth considering. This would relieve central bankers of normative and inevitably political decisions as to which firms to favour for bond purchases, leaving them to focus on their more specialist technical skills of assessing when financial interventions are needed and by how much. Meanwhile a different set of technical skills is needed to assess which firms' proposed projects best further the goals of climate change mitigation, while normative issues are ultimately the domain of elected governments.

This also raises the issue of the role of public banks in general in a green new deal, i.e. banks owned by central or local government or by intergovernmental agencies. While this issue is beyond the scope of this chapter, it is worth pointing out that there are already many such banks, and that more and more of these are becoming oriented toward green investment (for a fuller discussion, see McDonald et al. 2020).

A more directly accountable role would be for central banks to act in support of government-led climate change mitigation initiatives, such as green (new) deals and other forms of green stimulus programs. This would work in much the same way that they currently fund regular government expenditure and act to dampen shocks in the economy where government spending (or lack of it) has unintended consequences. I turn now to consider this approach.

Toward a combined monetary-fiscal approach

Green New Deals and government deficits

As mentioned earlier in this chapter, a common feature of green new deal proposals is "deficit" funding. The classic deficit model is that the parliament (or Congress in the United States) votes to authorize government spending, the government then spends the money (which is created by the central bank), and in terms of bookkeeping, the government's financial position is debited by the amount spent. If government receipts (mostly from taxes, fees and fines) in a particular year are less than its expenditure, the government is said to be in deficit.

However, this can be deceptive because, as Yeva Nersisyan points out in Chapter 2 of this book, a government that is sovereign over its currency relates to money very differently from households. A household can only spend money that it gets from somewhere outside itself. If a household spends more than it possesses, it is in debt to particular people or businesses and needs to get money from somewhere outside itself to repay the debts. Governments, however, create money out of nothing by spending it into existence. When a government "spends" money it simply uses computer keystrokes to credit the amount to the bank account of the recipient, while the central bank simultaneously credits the recipient's bank's reserve account (see Box 3.2) at the central bank by the same amount (for a more detailed account, see Wray 2015). The amount the government has spent is written as a debit in its ledger at the central bank. If the sum of all government spending in a particular year is greater than the government's income (from taxes, fines and fees), the government is said to be in deficit. This is very different from a household being in deficit, because a government that is sovereign over its currency and has a deficit in that currency only, cannot go bankrupt. There can be other unhappy consequences of too high a government deficit, as I explain below, but bankruptcy is not one of them.

Box 3.2 Reserve accounts

The diagram gives a simplified view of how commercial banks' reserve accounts are related to customers' accounts and the money-creating function of the central bank.

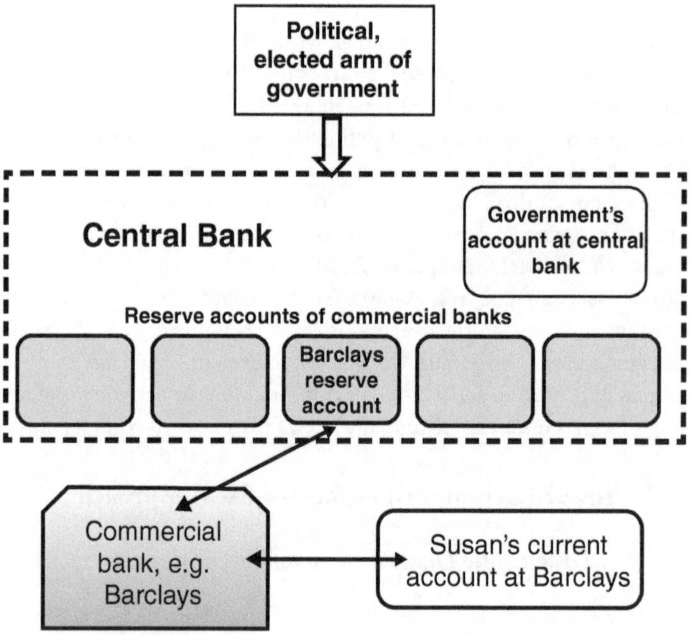

Suppose the government pays Susan's monthly wages, say $4,000 net. Susan's current account is held at Barclays Bank. The central bank, acting on the government's behalf, increases the balance in Barclays' reserve account at the central bank by $4,000. In doing so it injects 4,000 new dollars into the economy. It does this simply by computer keystrokes, a kind of government IOU. But note that this is high-powered money, as reliable as the institution of government itself. At about the same moment, Barclays increases the balance in Susan's current account by $4,000. This is a bank IOU, as reliable as the bank (plus any government guarantee there might be).

The next day Susan pays her rent with $1,000 by making an online transfer to Maria, who banks with Lloyds. At that point, Barclays reduces the balance in Susan's account by $1,000, Lloyds increases the balance in Maria's account by $1,000, and (most important!) Barclays prepares to shift $1,000 from its reserve account to Lloyds' reserve account by the end of the working day. Because there have been hundreds of thousands of similar transactions criss-crossing the banking system throughout the day, the banks calculate which bank owes which other bank how much, on balance, at the end of the day, and they reconcile their accounts by shifting money between their reserve accounts.

If a bank finds itself short of what it needs to pay others, it can either borrow from other banks' reserve accounts at the interbank rate or, if this rate is too high that day, it might find it cheaper to borrow from the central bank at the overnight interest rate.

Note that the government does not need to use a commercial bank for its day-to-day transactions. Its account is held at the central bank. Also, the government's spending power is not limited by however much it has in this account, but only by the dictates of Parliament or Congress. Think of the government's account as a kind of buffer rather than a store of what the government is financially worth.

This does not apply, of course, to a government that borrows money in a different currency from its own. Doing so runs the risk that the exchange rate will shift and substantially increase the amount of debt from the point of view of the government's own currency. But regular deficit budgeting in a government's own currency is a normal part of governance.

In fact, governments have to be in deficit if the economy is to grow due to population growth or growth in GDP, because the money supply has to increase continually to prevent these leading to deflation (Tymoigne 2019). I explain this in relation to one currency sovereign country, New Zealand, in Box 3.3.

Box 3.3 Why a healthy economy needs a government fiscal deficit: an example from down under

Population growth

If the population of a country is increasing, there will need to be more money in circulation so that everybody has enough. If the same amount of money were shared among more people, they would each have less, on average. For example, New Zealand's population increased from 3.333 million in 1988 to 4.782 million in 2019, an increase of 43.47%. If the total amount of high-powered money in circulation had stayed constant in that period, average wages and savings per person would have reduced by about one-third. This would have produced a deflationary spiral, where economic activity falls dangerously low because people put off purchases in the hope that prices will keep falling. The government avoided this by spending more money into existence each year than the year before: classic deficit spending. But the increase in population led to more people working and spending and paying taxes, so the deficit did not accumulate. It fluctuated between 32% and 52% of GDP, sometimes falling from year to year, sometimes rising.

Increase in GDP per capita

GDP per capita has also steadily increased in New Zealand (and most other countries) in recent decades: by 56.5% in New Zealand in 1988–2019. Therefore, the country not only has needed more money each year to satisfy the needs of an increasing population, it has also needed to enable each of them to produce and buy the increased volume and quality of goods and services on offer. Again, government deficit spending provided the steadily increasing supply of money to enable this to happen. And again, this did not lead to ever-increasing levels of government debt because the increasing amount of wages and purchases led to more tax being paid.

Inflation

Most high-income countries today aim for an inflation rate of just under 2%. An inflation rate of 2% means that a basket of goods and services purchased this year will be 2% more expensive than an equivalent basket last year. There is a very subtle but important reason why some inflation is inevitable in a healthy economy. Because of persistent improvements in technology and industrial processes, many workers produce a great deal more economic value today than equivalent workers did 50 years ago or even a decade ago. If the goods they produce were the same price today as 50 years ago, today's production workers would earn a phenomenally high wage. However, many other workers provide services rather than goods. For example, a schoolteacher today teaches a class of about 30 children and has about the same output as a schoolteacher of 50 or even 100 years ago. It is much the same for a police officer, priest, social worker, politician or tax administrator. Some of these may be more productive today due to better support systems and technology, but their increase in productivity has been nowhere near that of a car assembly worker or grain farmer. But because society needs these professions, it has to pay them far more per unit output today than their counterparts earned 50 years ago so that their spending power keeps pace with that of workers in industry. This balancing out of wages against productivity is inevitably inflationary. New Zealand's inflation in 1988–2019 averaged 3.31% per year, leading to a 98.1% increase in prices over that period. Again, increases in government spending provided the money to enable this to happen, leading to deficit spending – but again, the increased tax take it brought prevented the deficit accumulating unduly.

Adding these figures for New Zealand suggests that the supply of high-powered money needed to increase to about 300% of what it was in 1988 to satisfy the demand due to these three factors. There should be at least three times as much high-powered money in commercial banks' reserve accounts plus notes and coins in circulation and in bank vaults in 2019 as there was in 1988. In fact, there was 2.94 times as much, from $NZ87.8 billion in 1988 to $NZ258.3 in 2019, an increase of $NZ170.5 billion. Where did this enormous amount of money come from? The New Zealand government spent it into existence through deficit spending.

Nevertheless, most governments do not go on creating money willy-nilly, as this would have two major detrimental effects. The first is higher-than-desired inflation caused by government spending in the productive economy.

Inflationary pressures in the productive economy

If government expenditure simply gives more spending power to consumers without also increasing the amount of goods and services they can purchase, this can increase competition for scarce goods and services, leading to price increases.

However, this effect is greatly mitigated if the projects the government funds have high Keynesian multiplier effects, meaning they cause a greater value of goods and services to be produced than the amount the government has spent. For example, if a government funds the building of a hydrogen pipeline, the workers spend most of their wages locally, stimulating local business which may then employ more workers, who spend money locally, and so on. Meanwhile, the pipeline may enable private firms to invest in photovoltaic arrays and electrolysis plants that produce hydrogen for the pipeline, stimulating production of technical equipment, and so on. If government spending does not lead to the production of more goods and services, it could drive spending beyond the capacity of the economy to absorb it, and so be inflationary (Landau 2021; Pattanaik 2021). However, a recent survey of leading finance experts and central bankers from around the world found that green and climate change mitigating projects generally are considered to have high Keynesian multipliers, mostly in the range of 2–3 (Hepburn et al. 2020; and see a summary of this in Galvin 2020a).

Critical studies of green new deals also tend to find that government-led climate change mitigation funding is unlikely to lead to inflation as long as it utilizes unused capacity in the economy, boosts the total amount of goods and services on offer, and does not compete heavily with other sectors for specialist labour and expertise (see review in Nersisyan and Wray 2019, and discussion in Chapter 2 by Nersisyan).

A factor that mitigates inflation is that each time money gets spent or paid as wages in the real, productive economy, a portion of it is paid back to the government in taxes. At this point it is withdrawn from the economy, effectively dissolved into nothing (though it may appear as a credit on the government's books). Money invested in projects that have high Keynesian multiplier effects tends to get spent and re-spent, or lead to other money getting spent and re-spent and therefore taxed and re-taxed, so normal everyday taxes tend to drain the extra money out of the economy, putting downward pressure on inflation.

Another possible cause of inflation in a green new deal would be wage increases due to competition for skilled workers. There are also questions as to whether there are enough unemployed or under-employed people, skilled or unskilled, to fill the extra jobs a green new deal would generate. If there are not, this pushes up the cost of labour, leading to inflation (Palley 2019). However, the transition to a green economy will see jobs disappearing as well as being created, and it remains to be seen how this will balance out. Nersisyan makes some important comments on this in Chapter 2.

Possible inflationary consequences will therefore need to be closely monitored. This is a traditional role for the central bank, and as Landau (2021) argues, central bank personnel's skills and experience will play an important role in monitoring and forecasting short and longer-term impacts of green new deal stimulus on the productive economy, plus bond trading to reduce inflationary pressure if need be. Ironically, over the past ten years central banks have struggled to keep inflation high enough to satisfy the 2% target, but we cannot guarantee this will persist.

The effects of increasing "high-powered" money

The second possible problem is more subtle and hardly discussed in literature. When governments create money by spending it into existence, this is often called "high-powered" money or "narrow" money, i.e. money that is as reliable as the sovereignty of the government and can be exchanged for anything that is for sale (Lothian 1976; see also Federal Reserve 2020). Physical cash is one form of high-powered money, and so are the electronic balances in commercial banks' reserve accounts (see Box 3.2) at the central bank; the sum of these equates to what central banks in many countries call M1. The money I have in my bank account is of a lesser kind; it is only a commercial bank's IOU. If the bank fails, my "money" disappears – except for the first few tens of thousands which often have a government-backed guarantee. Normally, tax can only be paid with high-powered money (Wray 2015) via a three-stage process in which (1) my order to pay is received by my bank, which then (2) deposits the amount from its own reserve account at the central bank into the government's bank account at the central bank and (3) reduces the value of its IOU to me by that amount, i.e. reduces my bank balance by that amount. The payment of taxes thereby withdraws high-powered money from circulation, effectively dissolving it into nothing.[6]

The absolute qualitative difference between high-powered and lower-powered forms of money is seen in the fact that only the central bank can increase the total amount in commercial banks' reserve accounts by bringing new money into existence. Commercial banks can exchange money between each other's reserve accounts; they can deposit money in their reserve accounts that they receive cash in the form of deposits from customers or as earnings from elsewhere in the economy; but nobody but the government via its central bank, or the central bank acting on its own initiative (e.g. in bond buying), can add to the total stock of money in commercial banks' reserve accounts by creating new money.

Therefore, when governments create money by spending it into existence, such as in a green new deal, this not only increases the total balances of individuals' and businesses' bank accounts, i.e. their banks' IOUs to them, *it simultaneously increases the total amount of commercial bank reserves held at the central bank.* Workers paid by the government for green projects such as decarbonizing the electricity grid see their bank balances increase on payday, but these are just commercial bank IOUs. The real, high-powered, newly created money lands in the reserve accounts of the workers' banks at the central bank. Further, when the workers pay their energy bills by bank transfer or buy food or furniture using a debit card, the recipients' bank accounts are increased only in that their banks increase the level of their IOUs to them. Meanwhile the equivalent high-powered money simply shifts from one bank's reserve account to another at the central bank. The exception is if the workers withdraw money in cash (notes and coins), which effectively reduces both the bank's IOU to them and its reserves at the central bank – but usually not by much because most people do not carry much cash.

Generally, then, whatever a government spends ends up in commercial banks' reserve accounts at the central bank. Conversely, whatever the government demands in taxes, fees and fines comes back from commercial banks' reserve accounts at the central bank, to the government – where it is effectively dissolved, as it is withdrawn from circulation.

A key issue is that commercial bank depositors are making thousands of bank transfers during the day – a huge network of payments criss-crossing the economy, and each of these requires the equivalent payment in high-powered money from one bank to another. At the end of each working day the commercial banks have to reconcile their reserve accounts with each other, and this is not difficult if, on balance, they all owe each other about the same amounts. But banks are wise to have sufficient high-powered money in their reserve accounts just in case they have an unlucky day. If they do not, they have to borrow from one another at the interbank interest rate – the rate commercial banks charge each other for outstanding amounts on interbank account reconciliation. If a bank cannot borrow from others, it borrows from the central bank at the overnight interest rate, which is usually set higher than the interbank rate.

Why is this important? Banks also use their reserve accounts as collateral for making loans. If they have large reserves and the interbank rate is low, they generally feel confident about offering large loans to customers. The more liberal they are with lending, the more (lower-powered, commercial bank-created) money circulates in the economy and the more upward pressure there is on inflation. Therefore, if commercial banks have very large reserves, this makes it harder for the central bank to dampen inflation by putting upward pressure on interest rates by raising its overnight interest rate. A government can step in and help drain commercial banks' reserves by raising taxes, but this can be unpopular and have other undesired effects.

Large commercial bank reserves and a low interbank rate can therefore lead to high levels of bank lending and therefore high inflation. When commercial banks lend to households and businesses, they too are creating money by keystrokes, though it is a "lower" form of money than government-created money because it is effectively just a commercial bank's IOU. Commercial banks' total lending is usually many times higher than their balances in their reserve accounts at the central bank, which are simply treated as collateral to leverage a much higher amount of lending. Some central banks put limits on the lending to reserve ratio (often around 10 : 1), but the real constraint on commercial bank lending is their perception of how well-stocked their reserve account is and how easy it will be to reconcile their reserve accounts at the central bank at the end of each day, which depends heavily on the interbank interest rate, which tends to be lower if reserves are higher. *A green new deal would put upward pressure on the size of commercial banks' reserve accounts at the central bank, thereby increasing the possibility of inflation via too-liberal bank lending.*

Again, however, a mitigating factor is that customers who borrow commercial bank money have to pay tax on it as soon as they spend it, and the people they pay the money to have to pay tax on it when they spend it, and so on. The taxes are paid as described above, i.e. with high-powered money from commercial banks' reserve accounts. The government effectively gets a free lunch: it did not put up the money for the loan but it gets high-powered money whenever the bank loan money is spent and re-spent.

In fact, governments use all sorts of tricks to drain high-powered money out of the economy via taxation. In Germany, for example, certain households who consume electricity generated by their own photovoltaic panels have to pay tax of about 7 eurocents on every kilowatt-hour they use (Galvin 2020b). No money changes hands between citizens whatsoever, but the government withdraws 7 eurocents of high-powered money from the economy for each kilowatt-hour generated and used in the home.

Further, inflation does not automatically follow when central banks have large reserves of high-powered money. In the years after the 2008 global financial crisis and again during the coronavirus pandemic, central banks struggled to get commercial banks to lend money, despite filling up their reserve accounts with trillions of dollars from bond purchases (on which see below). At times such as these, larger reserve account balances due to government stimulus spending could actually save central banks a lot of work and worry as it could free up bank lending and add further stimulus to the economy. At the time of writing, the Bank of England was so concerned about getting banks to lend more liberally that it was asking commercial banks to prepare for the possible advent of a negative overnight interest rate by mid-2021 (Bank of England 2020b; Inman and Makerotof 2021).

But we cannot guarantee these conditions will persist in subsequent years, and a green new deal will persist for at least a decade. Bloated reserve account balances could conceivably lead to excess lending and therefore unacceptably high inflation.

In a green new deal, then, central banks would need to monitor the amount of money in commercial banks' reserve accounts, just as they do in other times. They might need to drain these accounts by selling government bonds to the commercial banks, just as they have always done when there is too much money in their accounts. But in times of persistently low inflation and sluggish investment in the real economy, such as over the past decade, this might not be necessary on a large scale, especially since a government's green new deal investment will increase the volume of goods and services and move the economy toward full employment, thereby increasing the tax take.

Government spending on the real economy also has the advantage of bypassing non-productive financial markets. Instead of banks and other financial institutions getting money directly from the central bank via bond sales – money which they can then leverage for speculative investments in assets such as shares, casino-type financial instruments and property markets – the high-powered money that lands in commercial bank reserve accounts is already committed to the banks' depositors via their accounts. This might not stop the banks leveraging it for some amount of loans and even speculative investment, but it puts pressure on the banks to take less risk with their ventures because they will have to pay the money out if their depositors demand it, such as for tax payments or for transfers to customers of other banks.

Real economic growth and asset price inflation

Feeding the money for a green new deal into the real economy rather than the financial system has a further advantage with respect to inflation. Official inflation rates track consumer price increases, which have tended around 2% in high-income economies over the past decade, but this is not the only type of inflation that should be considered. There is also asset price inflation, which refers to increases in the buying and selling price of assets such as real estate, shares, exotic financial instruments, gold and artworks. High asset price inflation can be devastating for potential homeowners. Annual average house price inflation in 2015–2020 was 4.0% per year in the United Kingdom, 6.7% in the United States, 7.0% in New Zealand, 7.2% in Germany, 7.3% in Canada and 9.3% in Luxembourg (author's calculations from OECD 2020), and the average annual increase in share prices in the Euro countries was 6.2% per year. But real economic growth averaged only around 2%–3%. Asset price inflation thereby made the average worker between 2% and 7% poorer each year, cumulatively, in terms of her or his ability to accumulate assets such as a house and shares.

Asset price inflation also favours individuals and corporations who already have a lot of high-value assets, as they can use these to leverage the purchasing of more, which contributes to even more asset price inflation. But asset price inflation is not taken into account by central banks in their definition of "price stability."

A study of US consumer price inflation and government deficit figures by Tymoigne (2019) indicates there is little if any empirical evidence of a correlation between government deficits and consumer price inflation, at least in the United States. However, there is overwhelming evidence that central bank action in boosting financial markets leads to asset price inflation. For almost every high-income country, there is a revealing pattern when we track the total amount of money injected into the financial markets by the central bank, against key indicators such as house prices, nominal real economic growth (inflation × population growth × GDP/capita growth) and nominal real economic growth per person (inflation × GDP/capita growth). We find that house prices increase in line with money growth, while real economic growth per person lags far behind. Figure 3.2 illustrates this for the United Kingdom for the years 1986–2019 (data from World Bank 2020). The variable "broad money" includes both high-powered money and most credible types of low-powered money. It gives an indication of how much credit and cash is available for buying financial assets as well as investing in productive industry and buying food and necessities. "Total reserves" is the high-powered money in commercial banks' reserve accounts at the central bank. It indicates the level of money creation and dissolution that central banks see as necessary to keep the broad money supply high enough for what they regard as a well-functioning economy. Looking at Figure 3.2, it is clear that both broad money and total reserves increased at much higher rates than growth in GDP per capita or even the combined effects of population, GDP growth and inflation. The ratio of broad money to personal spending power was 4.5 times as

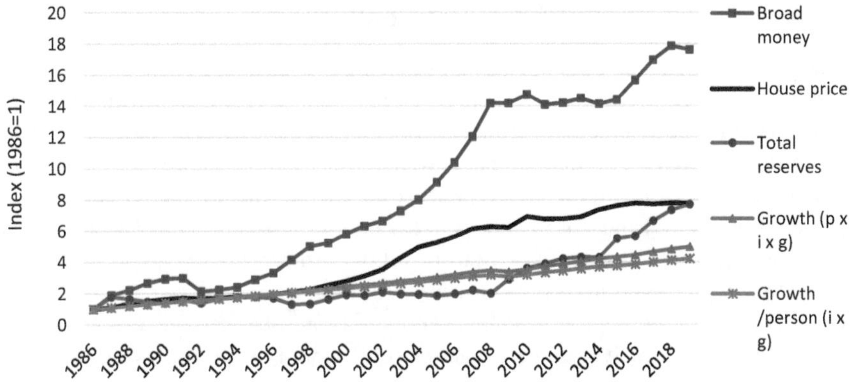

Figure 3.2 UK house prices, broad money, total reserves, growth (inflation × population × GDP/capita growth) and growth per person (inflation × GDP/capita growth), 1986–2019, indexed to 1 for 1986

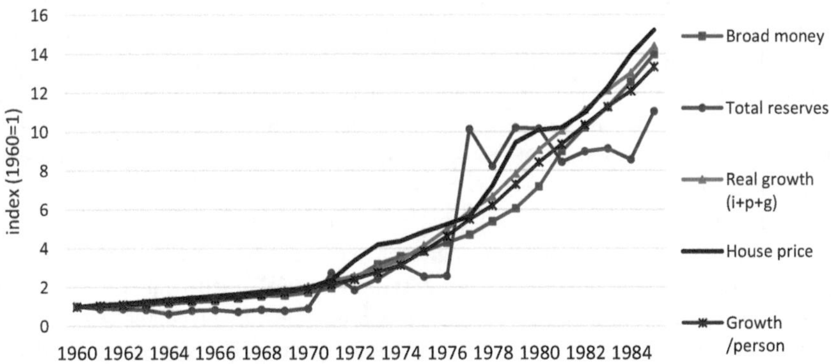

Figure 3.3 UK growth in broad money, total reserves and "real" economy (inflation×pop×GDP/capita), 1960–1985. Author's calculations from World Bank database

high in 2019 as it was in 1986. The Bank of England's attempts to stimulate the economy by channelling money into the financial markets failed to produce real economic growth and instead fuelled substantial asset price inflation (cf. Blancheton 2016).

A similar graph for 1960–1985 (Figure 3.3) shows that in that earlier period, broad money, house prices and personal spending power tracked each other almost one-to-one. In this graph we see a spike in total reserves in the late 1970s, which was initiated in response to the oil price hikes. We also see that this and other central bank action kept broad money on track to almost seamlessly serve the needs of the real economy, as broad money increased in the same proportions as real growth, growth per person and house prices. But since the mid-1980s this focus on the real economy has given way to a tendency for central banks to focus on serving the financial markets – a position outlined in revealing detail by commentators such as Vogl (2017), Tognato (2012), Wray (2015) and Barrowclough (2020).

A major advantage of a green new deal would be to work against this trend, since government funding goes directly into the real, productive economy. This would support the aims for equity and social justice that are one of the central pillars of green new deals. Central banks can be left to focus more directly on their technical tasks of adjusting the narrow money supply to serve the needs of price stability.

Conclusions

This chapter has considered the possible role of central banks in the context of a green new deal. Central banks are already realizing that commercial banks and the financial system are likely to be severely buffeted by the shocks of climate change. This is because of the physical damage caused by extreme climate events as well as transactional shocks due to shifts in investment away from CO_2-intensive enterprises toward green investment. Green investment will come increasingly from within the private sector and be hugely accelerated by shifts in government spending as green new deals or similar projects get underway. Some central banks are already preparing stress tests for banks in this scenario.

As well as this reactive approach, some prominent central bankers are advocating a more proactive approach in which quantitative easing (QE) would be weighted toward green enterprises and the banks that support them.

Both these approaches fit within the broad mandate of central bankers to act independently, based on their professional expertise, to support price stability and act to prevent severe disruptions in the financial system and therefore in the economy. However, it is asking too much of central bankers to make normative, political decisions that are properly the domain of elected governments that are accountable to voters and supported by democratically maintained institutions. The European Greens/EFA have proposed a more politically responsive and democratically accountable approach where central banks' creation of money via QE would be channelled via the European Investment Bank, which is under the control of government ministries and would ensure that QE money is all invested in green, climate-friendly enterprises. A limitation is that the volume of QE money fluctuates according to financial market parameters, so the supply would be unsteady. However, the European Investment Bank and public banks in other countries could take a greater role in directing bond purchases by central banks, alongside their other ongoing investments in green and green-deal-related projects.

The step that is most needed, however, is a green new deal financed and led by the political, elected arm of government, which would decide what projects to initiate and support and would spend the money for these into existence by deficit spending. Central banks' main roles would then be to monitor price stability in the real economy and sell or buy government (and other) bonds to stimulate or dampen inflation; and to monitor the levels of high-powered money accumulating in commercial banks' reserve accounts to keep these at a level that stimulates appropriate levels of bank lending. Again, the central bank would buy or sell bonds to keep these reserves at a suitable level. This could be combined with the European Greens/EFA suggestion that bond sales and purchases would be channelled via a government-controlled investment bank.

In such an approach the central bank would lose much of its autonomy. It would be required to trade bonds to the favour of green or at least climate-neutral enterprises – though some leading central bankers are already advocating this – or trade via a government-controlled investment bank. It would also have much less scope for quantitative easing because the government would be injecting money directly into the productive economy via green new deal projects, and this would provide much of the stimulus that central banks currently feel obliged to provide via quantitative easing.

Further, the central bank's board membership might need to be re-ordered so that there is more direct communication with the political arm of government and with the scientific expertise on climate change and its mitigation.

Although such an approach might seem straightforward and reasonable, there could be stiff resistance from circles of financiers who are deeply embedded in aspects of central bank culture that favour radical independence from political and therefore democratic control of the creation and distribution of newly created money. Although central banks are literally an institution of government, some are culturally habituated to make their own decisions and have often supported powerful financial players rather than households and businesses in the everyday real economy. Democratically elected governments might find there is a discursive and possibly even obstructionist backlash against green new deals and will need to take fuller responsibility for the overall direction of monetary policy in order to have the space to pursue a green new deal persistently. However, recent moves by central banks to support climate change mitigation investment, such as those promoted by the Network for Greening the Financial System, indicate that there may already be a groundswell of support among central bankers for a major transition to an age of green new deals.

Notes

1 Except in some limited areas where other ministries have spending rights, such as emergency social welfare payments.
2 Of course, sometimes governments find ways to circumvent Congress' or Parliament's scrutiny. There is always a risk of corruption and nepotism with government spending. But generally, the ministry of finance's money activities are designed for democratic control of government finances, and a functional Congress or Parliament has the means, at least in principle, to direct these.
3 Definition from the Merriam-Webster Dictionary
4 A currency is said to be floating when there are no regulatory levers to adjust its value in relation to other countries' currencies: its value is determined by the level of demand for it. From 1946 until 1971 the US dollar was tied to a gold standard: $35 per ounce of gold, while other high-income countries pegged their currencies to the value of the dollar. US President Nixon changed the standard to $38 in August 1971 and made US dollars no longer automatically convertible to gold. His government increased this again in 1973 to $48 per ounce but then completely decoupled the dollar from gold or any other objective standard. Over the next decade and a half most high-income countries decoupled their currencies from the US dollar; they floated their currencies and have left them floating ever since.
5 https://www.ngfs.net/en/news/communique-de-presse
6 Governments can, of course, confiscate assets, such as stately homes or even works of art, in lieu of tax payments when taxpayers are broke or bankrupt, but the default position is that paying taxes causes high-powered money to be withdrawn from circulation.

References

Anderson, V. 2015. *Green money: Reclaiming quantitative easing. Money creation for the common good.* Green/EFA Group in the European Parliament. Available from: https://mollymep.org.uk/wp-content/uploads/Green-Money_ReclaimingQE_V.Anderson_June-2015.pdf.

Bailey, A. 2020. "The time to push ahead on tackling climate change." Speech by Andrew Bailey, given at the Corporation of London Green Horizon Summit, Mansion House. 9 November. Available from: https://www.bankofengland.co.uk/speech/2020/andrew-bailey-speech-corporation-of-london-green-horizon-summit

Bank of England. 2020a. "Climate change." Available from: https://www.bankofengland.co.uk/climate-change

Bank of England. 2020b. "Information request: Operational readiness for a zero or negative bank rate." Letter from Sam Woods, Deputy Governor, Prudential Regulation CEO, Bank of England Prudential Regulation Authority. Available from: https://www.bankofengland.co.uk/-/media/boe/files/prudential-regulation/letter/2020/info-request-operational-readiness-policy-rates.pdf?la=en&hash=E973B09B00A6EC1D2B5AB9B845BF20EB5EF7BBB6

Bank of England. 2021a. *Asset purchase facility quarterly report – 2020 Q4*. Available from: https://www.bankofengland.co.uk/asset-purchase-facility/2020/2020-q4

Bank of England. 2021b. "How much quantitative easing have we done in the UK?" Available from: https://www.bankofengland.co.uk/monetary-policy/quantitative-easing

Barrowclough, D. 2020. "Coronavirus and the evolving roles of Central Banks: Avoiding a "Climate Minsky Moment". In D. McDonald, T. Marois, D. Barrowclough, eds. *Public banks and Covid-19: Combatting the pandemic with public finance.* Kingston: Municipal Services Project; Geneva: UNCTAD; Brussels: Eurodad. pp. 85–112. Available from: https://publicbankscovid19.org/index.php/publications

Batten, S., Sowerbutts, R. and Tanaka, M. 2016. "Let's talk about the weather: The impact of climate change on central banks." Bank of England Staff Working Paper No. 603. Available from: https://www.bankofengland.co.uk/working-paper/2016/lets-talk-about-the-weather-the-impact-of-climate-change-on-central-banks

Battiston, S. and Monasterolo, I. 2019. "A carbon risk assessment of central banks' portfolios under 2°C aligned climate scenarios." Vienna University of Economics and Business, Working Paper. Available from: https://pdfs.semanticscholar.org/20ca/e100c005ce8f6524b67e46e6cba86efe17d7.pdf

Biden, J. 2020. "The Biden Plan for a clean energy revolution and environmental justice." Available from: https://joebiden.com/climate-plan/

Blancheton, B. 2016. "Central bank independence in a historical perspective: Myth, lessons and a new model." *Economic Modelling* 52: 101–107. Available from: http://dx.doi.org/10.1016/j.econmod.2015.02.027

Breitenfellner, A., Pointner, W. and Schuberth, H. 2019. "The potential contribution of Central Banks to green finance." *Vierteljahrshefte zur Wirtschaftsforschung* 88(2): 55–71. http://dx.doi.org/10.3790/vjh.88.2.55

Campiglio, E., Dafermos, Y., Monnin, P. et al. 2018. "Climate change challenges for central banks and financial regulators." *Nature Climate Change* 8: 462–468.

Carney, M. 2016. "Resolving the climate paradox." Speech given by Mark Carney, Governor of the Bank of England, Chair of the Financial Stability Board. Arthur Burns Memorial Lecture, Berlin. 22 September. Available from: www.bankofengland.co.uk/publications/Pages/speeches/default.aspx

Carney, M., Villeroy de Galhau, F. and Elderson, F. 2019. "The financial sector must be at the heart of tackling climate change." *The Guardian.* 17 April. Available from: https://www.theguardian.com/commentisfree/2019/apr/17/the-financial-sector-must-be-at-the-heart-of-tackling-climate-change

Christophers, B. 2017. "Climate change and financial instability: Risk disclosure and the problematics of neoliberal governance." *Annals of the American Association of Geographers* 107(5): 1108–1127. Available from: DOI: 10.1080/24694452.2017.1293502

Cormack, C. et al. 2020. "Estimating financial risks from the energy transition: Potential impacts from decarbonisation in the European power sector." Paper submitted to Elsevier. Available from: https://www.researchgate.net/profile/Chris_Cormack/publication/341821387_Estimating_Financial_Risks_from_the_Energy_Transition_Potential_Impacts_from_Decarbonisation_in_the_European_Power_Sector/links/5ed60c0f299bf1c67d3290ba/Estimating-Financial-Risks-from-the-Energy-Transition-Potential-Impacts-from-Decarbonisation-in-the-European-Power-Sector.pdf

Deutsche Welle. 2021. "Biden's climate plans: A 'historic tipping point'?" [online]. Available from: https://www.dw.com/en/bidens-climate-plans-a-historic-tipping-point/a-55542191

Durrani, A., Rosmin, M. and Volz, U. 2020. "The role of central banks in scaling up sustainable finance – what do monetary authorities in the Asia-Pacific region think?" *Journal of Sustainable Finance & Investment.* Available from: https://doi.org/10.1080/20430795.2020.1715095

Epstein, G. 2006. "Central banks as agents of economic development." Research Paper No. 2006/54. United Nations University – World Institute for Development Economics Research (UNU-WIDER).

European Central Bank. 2020. "Pandemic emergency purchase programme (PEPP)." Available from: https://www.ecb.europa.eu/mopo/implement/pepp/html/index.en.html

Federal Reserve. 2020a. "What economic goals does the Federal Reserve seek to achieve through its monetary policy?" Available from: https://www.federalreserve.gov/faqs/what-economic-goals-does-federal-reserve-seek-to-achieve-through-monetary-policy.htm

Federal Reserve. 2020b. "US Federal Reserve Code of Federal Regulations 12 CFR § 204.5. Maintenance of required reserves." Available from: https://www.law.cornell.edu/cfr/text/12/204.5

Galvin, R. 2020a. "Yes, there is enough money to decarbonize the economies of high-income countries justly and sustainably." *Energy Research & Social Science* 70. Available from: https://doi.org/10.1016/j.erss.2020.101739

Galvin, R. 2020b. "I'll follow the sun: Geo-sociotechnical constraints on prosumer households in Germany." *Energy Research & Social Science* 65. Available from: https://doi.org/10.1016/j.erss.2020.101455

Galvin, R. and Healy, N. 2020. "The Green New Deal in the United States: What it is and how to pay for it." *Energy Research & Social Science* 67. Available from: https://doi.org/10.1016/j.erss.2020.101529

Hepburn, C. et al. 2020. "Will COVID-19 fiscal recovery packages accelerate or retard progress on climate change?" Smith School Working Paper 20-02. Available from: https://www.lagone.it/wp-content/uploads/2020/05/STUDIO-STIGLITZ-ART4.pdf

HM Treasury. 2018. Budget 2018. Available from: https://assets.publishing.service.gov.uk/government/uploads/system/uploads/attachment_data/file/752202/Budget_2018_red_web.pdf

Inman, P. and Makoretof, K. 2021. "Bank of England: Rapid GDP rebound likely as vaccines take effect." *The Guardian*. 4 February. Available from: https://www.theguardian.com/business/2021/feb/04/uk-banks-given-six-months-to-prepare-for-negative-interest-rates

Landau, J.-P. 2021. "Inflation and the Biden stimulus." Vox EU CEPR. 8 February. Available from: https://voxeu.org/article/inflation-and-biden-stimulus

Langley, P. and Morris, J. 2020. "Central banks: Climate governors of last resort?" *Environment and Planning A: Economy and Space* 52(8): 1471–1479. Available from: https://doi.org/10.1177/0308518X20951809

Lothian, J. 1976. "The demand for high-powered money." *American Economic Review* 66(1): 56–68.

Luke, T. 2009. "A green new deal: Why green, how new, and what is the deal?" *Critical Policy Studies* 3(1): 14–28.

Mann, G. 2010. "Hobbes' redoubt? Toward a geography of monetary policy." *Progress in Human Geography* 34(5): 601–625.

McDonald, D., Marois, T. and Barrowclough, D. eds. 2020. *Public banks and Covid-19: Combatting the pandemic with public finance*. Kingston: Municipal Services Project; Geneva: UNCTAD; Brussels: Eurodad. Available from: https://www.municipalservicesproject.org/publication/public-banks-and-covid-19-combatting-pandemic-public-finance

Milliken, D. 2021. "Bank of England told to stop buying 'high carbon' bonds." *Reuters*. 25 January. Available from: https://www.reuters.com/article/ukDomestic/idUSKBN29U00T?il=0

Nersisyan, N. and Wray, L.R. 2019. "How to pay for the Green New Deal, Levy Economics Institute." Working Papers Series 931. Available from: https://www.econstor.eu/handle/10419/209174

Network for Greening the Financial System (NGFS). [website] Available from: https://www.ngfs.net/en

OECD. 2020. House Prices 2015–2020. Available from: https://data.oecd.org/price/housing-prices.htm#indicator-chart

Palley, T. 2019. "Macroeconomics vs Modern Money Theory: Some unpleasant Keynesian arithmetic." Post-Keynesian Economics Society, Working Paper 1910.

Park, H. and Kim, J. 2020. "Transition towards green banking: Role of financial regulators and financial institutions." *Asian Journal of Sustainability and Social Responsibility* 5(5): 1–25. Available from: https://doi.org/10.1186/s41180-020-00034-3

Pattanaik, S. 2021. "Breakingviews – If Joe Biden doesn't stoke inflation, no one can." *Reuters*. 9 February. Available from: https://www.reuters.com/article/instant-article/idUSKBN2A92CP

Piketty, T. 2014. *Capital in the twenty-first century*. Translated from the French by Arthur Goldhammer. Cambridge, MA: Belknap-Harvard University Press.

Piketty, T. 2019. *Capital et Ideologie*. Paris: Éditions du Seuil.

Reboredo, J., Ugolini, A. 2020. "Price connectedness between green bond and financial markets." *Economic Modelling* 88: 25–38. Available from: https://doi.org/10.1016/j.econmod.2019.09.004

Recognizing the duty of the Federal Government to create a Green New Deal. H. Res. 109, 116th Congress. 2019. Available from: https://www.congress.gov/bill/116th-congress/house-resolution/109/text

Reserve Bank of New Zealand. 2020b. "Memorandum of understanding between the Minister of Finance and the Reserve Bank of New Zealand regarding the use of alternative monetary policy tools." Available from: https://www.rbnz.govt.nz/about-us/memoranda-of-understanding/memorandum-of-understanding-between-the-mof-and-rbnz

Ryan-Collins, J. et al. 2013. *Strategic quantitative easing: Stimulating investment to rebalance the economy.* London: New Economics Foundation. Available from: https://neweconomics.org/uploads/files/e79789e1e31f261e95_ypm6b49z7.pdf

Sanders, B. 2019. "Sanders and Ocasio-Cortez announce the green new deal for public housing act." Press Release. 14 November. Available from: https://www.sanders.senate.gov/newsroom/press-releases/sanders-and-Ocasio-Cortezannounce-the-green-new-deal-for-public-housing-act.

Sanders, B. 2021. "Joe Biden must put an end to business as usual. Here's where to start." *The Guardian.* 20 January. Available from: https://www.theguardian.com/commentisfree/2021/jan/20/joe-biden-action-bernie-sanders

Tognato, C. 2012. *Central Bank Independence: Cultural codes and symbolic performance.* New York: Palgrave Macmillan.

Tymoigne, E. 2019. "Debunking the public debt and deficit rhetoric." *Challenge* 62(5): 281–298. Available from: DOI: 10.1080/05775132.2019.1639412.

UNCTAD (United Nations Conference on Trade and Development). 2019. Trade and Development Report 2019. Financing a Global Green New Deal. Available from: https://unctad.org/webflyer/trade-and-development-report-2019

Villeroy de Galhau, F. 2019. "Greening the financial system: The new frontier." *Banque de France, Financial Stability Review.* June. Available from: https://publications.banque-france.fr/en/financial-stability-review/june-2019

Vogl, J. 2017. *The ascendancy of finance.* Translated from the German by Simon Garnett. Cambridge UK and Malden MA: Polity Press.

World Bank. 2020. "Inflation, consumer prices." Available from: https://data.worldbank.org/indicator/FP.CPI.TOTL.ZG

Wray, L.R. 2015. *Modern money theory: A primer on macroeconomics for sovereign monetary systems.* New York: Palgrave Macmillan.

4

AVOIDING THE PITFALLS OF CAPITALISM IN THE GREEN NEW DEAL

John McCollum

Introduction

The Green New Deal (hereafter GND) is one of the most exciting social programs emerging from progressive politics in the contemporary era. The US version of the plan is consciously modeled on President Franklin D. Roosevelt's New Deal of the 1930s, which saw vast expansion of US federal governmental power to restart the economy after the Great Depression. The New Deal excited many socialists, communists, and the labor left through its programs, which sought full employment, farm price guarantees, and the possibility of fully democratizing the US economy. Of course, many of these programs halted in the shift of class power in favor of the business elite of both Democratic and Republican parties in the 1950s. Nevertheless, the New Deal illustrated the viability of sweeping social programs to combat poverty, put power and dignity into the hands of workers after years of unemployment, and rebuilt the confidence of the polity in the efficacy of the government when faced with a major crisis of legitimacy. The GND makes many of the same broad, sweeping promises. The recession triggered by the COVID-19 outbreak, racial injustice, and deep cuts to social spending under a neoliberal political, economic, and social framework illustrate the urgency of such a program.

There are now a variety of GND proposals across the globe. Proposals in the United Kingdom (see Bailey and Hofferberth, this volume) and Canada (see Klein, this volume) make similar provisos. The GND's welfare measures would be a major shift from the neoliberal policies of the past 50 years, which have been so commonplace in both core and periphery states of the world system. Many different activist organizations have added their own demands to the GND, and its supporters include many anti-racist groups seeking to ensure that its measures include people of all racial and ethnic backgrounds (Kahn 2019). The US version of the GND includes provisions for racial equity (Ocasio-Cortez 2019). The GND promises to rectify the deliberate exclusion of people of color from the original New Deal (see Rector, this volume). Indigenous activists have drafted their own plan in the United States, known as the "Red New Deal" (Estes 2019).

While there are variations in GND proposals within and across different national contexts, all share the idea that a massive government spending plan is required to transition to renewable energy. There are some issues inherent in a social-democratic framework of vastly

DOI: 10.4324/9781003110880-6

increased state spending – economic expansion and the material basis of this expansion – that should give pause to progressive forces of all stripes. The welfare states of Scandinavia, often cited as "ideal typical" welfare state models for the United States by its progressive left, are also examples of states that make efforts to back renewable energy development and other environmental reforms. Norway's dependency on gas and oil extraction in the North Sea to fund its welfare provisions, as well as the questionable ability of the other Scandinavian states to achieve sustainability, should raise a degree of caution about using these states as models to emulate. Further "green reform" along the lines of ecological modernization (Mol 2001) within these states may never create a fully sustainable level of carbon emissions, to use one environmental outcome, and it should serve as a warning to GND proponents about the end goal of this sweeping social program.

Many of these issues relate to the nature of capitalist production. Although the GND offers a potential remedy to many of the ecological and social problems of our contemporary society, its implementation may worsen some of the ecological problems it is intended to resolve. Similarly, it does not offer a solution to the political and economic problems of the social relations of capitalist societies, namely the class power of a bourgeoisie that controls the flow of investment capital. In order to reverse centuries of ecological degradation under capitalism and improve the lives of low-income racialized individuals and communities, a GND will have to confront two major issues: entrenched political power and the problem of capital accumulation as the present driver of economic production. The concepts of the "treadmill of production" and the "metabolic rift" frame the debate around capital accumulation, and I frame the issue of entrenched political power around the problem of "state capitalism" and management, rather than the political resistance to the GND as a third area of critique.

Many of the present versions of the GND in different national contexts threaten to undermine the very reasons behind the GND, especially appropriation of material inputs and the reliance on capitalist control and management of its programs. Avoiding these issues is of paramount importance in ensuring the GND meets both its environmental and social goals. Fortunately, the Marxist tradition in which I base my critiques has a rich and growing theoretical tradition of examining these issues. John Bellamy Foster and his collaborators have found a number of areas in which Marx in his writing as early as the 1830s examined the relationship of capitalism to ecology (Foster 2000). Similarly, James O'Connor also explored this relationship in his work on the "second contradiction of capitalism." Allan Schnaiberg's work on the "treadmill of production" in the 1980s left an indelible mark on the sociology of the environment. His innovations were later adopted by the growing school of ecological Marxism, who adapted Schnaiberg's models and questions into a Marxist framework (Clausen and York 2008; Foster 2005; Jorgenson and Clark 2009; Jorgenson and Rice 2005). Their critiques of capitalism and its relationship to ecology are deeply relevant to many of the questions surrounding the GND. Here, I seek to lay out their critiques in relation to the GND and offer some solutions to many of the issues they raise. In particular, I explore three Marxist critiques of the GND: (1) that the GND will increase environmental problems through expanded production and consumption; (2) that the GND will widen the "metabolic rift" in nutrient cycling, extraction and waste disposal between the Global North and South; and (3) that the GND is a form of "state capitalism" that does not move beyond the issues raised in critiques one and two, presenting a unique problem from the view of entrenched political interests and class relations. Unless pushed toward the resolution of these class and political contradictions, this may wreck the GND over the long term.

My intention in this piece is not to disparage the GND. The advancement of broad welfare measures after decades of neoliberalism would lift millions of people from desperate poverty and social exclusion. In the United States, where welfare measures historically have lagged behind those of European states, survey work has shown the popularity of the GND in the US electorate (McElwee 2019). Its social-democratic promise for the United States would be an unprecedented political, economic, and social program of stability and security. However, it has some signs that it may worsen our ecological crisis, undermining the reasons for its creation. I root my critique here in a political-economic critique of capitalism. I understand fully that many supporters of the GND are not Marxists, but a critique of the GND in Marxist perspective offered in good faith can only support the GND in its planning and implementation. I hope they will accept this critique in the same spirit of critique and debate in which it is written and that some solutions offered at the end of this chapter might help us all avoid these pitfalls.

The treadmill of production

The basis of the first critique lies with the production and consumption patterns of the treadmill of production (Schnaiberg 1980). A major problem of the GND will be the appropriation of a new material to build renewable energy infrastructure, convert homes and other buildings to be more energy efficient, and build new public transportation systems. While these will certainly increase the efficiency of energy usage and help eliminate fossil fuel extraction and burning, they will result in a high short-term increase in energy consumption. At present, the percentage of US energy production from renewables is around 20% (US EIA 2020). To move toward 100%, and to ensure a reliable supply of energy when conditions do not favor wind or solar energy production, a tremendous amount of new wind farms, solar farms, geothermal sites, biomass plants, and a national electrical grid to deliver power from these sources to regions without suitable production conditions will need to be constructed, requiring a high initial investment of energy. Regardless of the particular "mode of production" – be it socialist, capitalist, or otherwise – it is difficult to see how this would not increase environmental impacts. However, a massive undertaking like this under a prevailing capitalist political, economic, and social system threatens the entire enterprise. Capitalism's imperative of growth in production and consumption means that even renewable energy will need to increase output to fuel production and consumption year after year; otherwise employment, state finances, and household budgets will enter a state of stagnation and collapse. This necessitates some serious thinking on the part of GND proponents to overcome the contradiction of the need for growth with the need for a sustainable level of production and consumption. A central problem is capitalism's endless pursuit of profit. It operates by investing capital into productive enterprise and selling the goods and services produced at a profit after costs are accounted for. A portion of the profits are then reinvested into expanded production of goods and services. A cycle of accumulation then results in which capital invested in production and consumption returns more capital, only to be reinvested once again. These resulting cycles depend on continuously increasing levels of consumption and production. Workers find themselves unequally tied into the system as wage earners dependent on employment from capitalists.

As economic growth expands the amount of goods produced and consumed, the treadmill must run at an increasingly faster pace and scale. If capital should not expand fast enough, and not enough commodities are produced and consumed, the treadmill will cease to function, resulting in a recession or depression. Workers "buy into" the treadmill for several reasons. Arguably the most compelling reason is their dependency on the treadmill for employment and wages. If capitalists cannot expand their capital at a sufficiently fast pace or amount, then layoffs and pay cuts are likely. Workers are compelled to work, despite the threat the treadmill poses to their livelihoods, health, and their opportunities to enjoy the aesthetic values of both a "wild" nature and their own neighborhoods and living spaces. Another issue is that workers' wages do not keep up with the continually increasing pace of production and consumption. Workers' wages are kept steady so as not to threaten profits or to maximize them. Faced with few good options, workers actively participate in the expansion of the treadmill. Frequently, they face on-the-job issues such as exposure to toxic chemicals, but whole cities and neighborhoods where workers live can face massive environmental issues. Local people are forced to support these industries since they are a major source of employment and wages. Similarly, moving out of a recession or depression may lead to political calls for overcoming environmental regulations to cheapen the cost of natural resources and their disposal, creating a temporary boost in profits, sold to workers as an opportunity for employment following the introduction of ecologically and socially disruptive technologies (Gould, Pellow and Schnaiberg 2004).

Both perspectives on the treadmill nature of capitalist societies note the inability of environmental and labor movements to halt or end the pernicious effects of capitalist production and consumption on their own. The labor movement's emphasis on raising wages and improving working conditions will not alter the fundamental assumptions of the treadmill. If workers continue to buy into the treadmill, its continued production of environmental problems will continue. The "first contradiction of capitalism" is the tendency toward stagnation in accumulation and profits as the ability to produce goods eventually outstrips the ability of workers to buy what they produce. When this happens on a large scale, a recession or depression results. James O'Connor (1988) has noted a second environmental contradiction: capitalism tends to wear down the ability of nature to produce resources and absorb and dispose of waste, leading to a breakdown in the viability of the system. Ideally, workers would be capable of using the productive capacity of the treadmill to meet human needs, rather than simply producing more and greater profits. Both theories suggest that the failure to "break up" the treadmill will lead to ecological collapse and impoverishment for the working class.

To summarize, one of the central problems of capitalism and the environment is the tendency toward the constant increase in the consumption of natural resources and disposal of waste. Quantitative analyses of the treadmill show that on a global scale, the treadmill is creating the pattern that Schnaiberg and his later collaborators theorized. Despite the claims of the ecological modernization school, growing ecological consciousness and green reforms have not made a substantial impact on the connection between economic growth and resource consumption (Mastini, Kallis and Hickel 2021; York, Rosa and Dietz 2003, 2008). Evidence of "decoupling" resource use and economic growth in countries with high levels of environmental reform often ignores that environmental damage is frequently outsourced to other countries (Vaden et al. 2020).

The GND is premised on many of the same political-economic assumptions as our prevailing methods of economic expansion and increasing prosperity for working people *à la* treadmill of production. This leads to a short set of options for both increasing working-class prosperity and curbing climate change. The first option is a furthering of ecological modernization. The conversion of the US energy grid to entirely renewable sources, as well as the probable increase in energy production and consumption in the years under the GND and post-GND, will result in an expansion of the treadmill, in terms of overall material inputs, energy production, and consumption. The GND could prime a new cycle of treadmill expansion, worsening the environmental problems the GND meant to solve.

One of the most pressing problems is the narrow time horizon needed to cut CO_2 production before global production hits a point of irreversible damage (IPCC 2018). Although an entirely green energy grid may cut CO_2 emissions, it may not do so on a sufficient time scale to avert these problems, and the initial burning of fossil fuel to construct and install renewables will worsen the situation. Another issue for the future is the lack of any planning around a ceiling for energy production. The Jevon's Paradox suggests that the efficiency gains from the construction of renewable sources will lead to an overall increase in the total production and consumption of energy from renewable sources (Clark and Foster 2001). In the absence of a ceiling on power production, total electricity production will likely increase beyond present levels today, even without burning any fossil fuels. This presents a problem in halting greenfield developments and space usages.

Expanding this issue into the social realm, the increase to aggregate demand from the high wages of the GND could push increased household consumption of consumer goods, increasing resource consumption and disposal. Although the GND challenges some of the assumptions of free market capitalism, especially regarding employment and wages, there are some aspects of it that closely resemble the political-economic relations of the treadmill of production. The issue of the interconnection between growth in working-class living standards and constant manufacture of green infrastructure, greater energy efficiency, and the need to continually expand the measures of the GND should give us pause. Could the GND become a new "green" treadmill, requiring continuous injections of funds, material and maintenance to keep the labor force employed? Here, we enter the realm of speculation, but past experiences with growing energy efficiency suggest that increasing efficiencies merely lead to greater resource usage. A vigorous state sector enjoys certain advantages over the free market in providing a decent living standard to workers, but it runs up against many of the same issues as a capitalist system. Constant modernization of the forces of production, dislocations, and periodical unemployment or other forms of adjustment to the prevailing labor conditions may still be a feature of the post-GND economy and society. In other words, the GND may not be breaking the treadmill of production, but rather attempts to mollify an intractable problem in a less harmful, but ultimately ineffective way.

Elsewhere in this volume, degrowth economics is discussed as a potential solution to the problem of the treadmill (see Schor and Tienhaara, this volume). A transition to an economics of sufficiency over growth holds great promise in this respect, but I offer for consideration that it holds growth, rather than social relations, as the prime characteristic of capitalism. The treadmill of production holds the social relations between labor and "producers" (we might reinterpret Gould, Pellow and Schnaibergs' terminology to read "capitalists") as the driver behind the treadmill. Breaking the treadmill will undoubtedly involve boosting the political power of labor over capital. I have great optimism for degrowth economics, but it will likely have to follow the conclusion of labor's victory over capital, rather than trying to supplant one economic model for another, as I find it unlikely that capital is going to allow such a transition without serious resistance.

The metabolic rift

The basis of the second critique concerns the "metabolic rift" (Clark and Foster 2009; Foster, Clark and York 2011). A GND may result in a widening of the metabolic rift in both spatial and temporal terms as extraction, processing, production, installation, consumption, and disposal of materials take place on a major scale. A few examples will show how this process might work. I focus here on the production of "green" technologies.

Solar panels, wind turbines and hybrid vehicle engines are examples of technologies that will require substantial material inputs. These technologies also require rare earth metals, which comprise 17 chemical elements and their compounds (Atwood 2012). Lithium, one of the most commonly used rare earth metals, comes largely from South American sources. China is also a major location of rare earth metal deposits, producing as much as 90% of the world's supply (USGS 2002). As the GND accelerates the production of renewables, these mineral resources will be extracted. Unfortunately for these Global South states, extraction and processing of rare earth metals is a highly toxic process (Rim 2016). Investigative reporting on China's rare earth metal processing in Outer Mongolia demonstrates how extraction and refinement of these elements have severely impacted water supplies and human health in the region, specifically the city of Baotou (Kaiman 2014).

The environmental damage borne by countries meeting US demands for rare earth metals will not be matched by the benefits the United States sees from these technologies. A rigorous debate on "ecologically unequal exchange" (see *inter alia* Givens, Huang Jorgenson 2019) has accompanied these questions. As the United States grows from these technologies and reduces its emissions, source countries will experience a worsening environmental situation. If the GND's main goals are to reduce carbon emissions, then accelerating rare earth metal extraction will do the opposite. The need for continuing development and growth in the Global South, potentially at the expense of the environment, will prove difficult to balance against the need for environmentally sound extraction of these minerals. Similarly, moving production of green tech to the Global South threatens to accelerate a growing global divide between those who make the green goods and those who use them to improve their emissions' profile.

The exigencies of accomplishing the transition to an all-renewable energy profile in the United States and conversion to more energy-efficient buildings and vehicles mean that the rare earth metal sources outside the United States will need to be exploited. The GND's current outlines lack any guarantees of preventing or mitigating environmental damage outside the United States. If the GND seeks to avert a climate catastrophe by cutting CO_2 emissions, it must do so at a global level, not just within the United States (see Kolinjivadi and Kothari, this volume). Otherwise, the metabolic rift – opened both between regions and the ability of the earth to absorb and mitigate this damage – will widen.

State capitalism and the problem of entrenched political power

Our next important area for critiquing the GND in Marxist perspective is the state. The question of whether the working class can advance its interests through the state remains a heated debate in Marxist political thought. Marxist political theorist Ralph Miliband held that the state could be turned toward working-class interests through parliamentary means. The state reflected capital's interests because of the capitalist class's occupation of decision-making power and influence over the parliamentary process. Miliband believed that the working class could capture some degree of political power in national politics and affect change in that manner. A case in point was the rise to power of the Labour Party after World War II in Miliband's native United Kingdom. The social-democratic nature of the GND highlights the hopes of its supporters to advance the GND through national parliaments and congresses, rather than, say, through revolutionary means. Given that the state will remain intact, we should look further into what this means for the class nature of the GND and the problems this may create, socially and environmentally.

Capitalism has some political contradictions that the GND may exacerbate, particularly in terms of environmental sustainability. Capital wants free markets to produce and sell, and it requires a state to do this. However, that same state also constrains capital in ways that prevent the endless accumulation of capital. This gives an outward appearance of tension between the state and capital. However, the state's longer-term provision of stability to the entire system is in the benefit of capital. Despite some of the limitations on the worst environmental abuses, the state also facilitates access to new markets for natural resources, labor pools, and market rules that favor capitalist interests at the expense of the environment and human well-being. State efforts to mitigate pollution have not superseded the pace of resource consumption or built a sustainable economy. Although the GND has and will continue to provoke serious political opposition, the political issues around the GND go deeper to the nature of the state in capitalist society. For the GND to be successful in the long run, it will need to overcome many of these issues, even in a state in which the GND is an overarching political, economic, and social policy set.

One intractable problem is the question of material provision of the GND and the benefits that this could provide in boosting capitalism, despite the GND's radical demands in the present conjuncture of political and economic forces. The GND is in an embryonic stage, but for it to make a rapid dent in environmental issues like CO_2 emissions, the projects will need to begin rather quickly. To do so, it will require a high number of private suppliers to appropriate and provide materials, land, maintenance, and services for the infrastructural projects. In normal federal building practices, private contractors bid to perform services on infrastructure. As the GND develops, the appropriation of materials, land, and machinery to perform the labor will boost a new "green fraction of capital" to the forefront of the program. The influx of public funds to private ends will secure profits for this social class. For some time, the inherent opposition between workers and capital will be mediated by state support to both capital and labor, likely creating a corporatist state.

The environmental problems of capitalism are threatening the long-term economic viability of capitalism, necessitating new state forms to manage these problems. In times of great threat to the system, the state may take on new roles to reestablish legitimacy and initiate a new cycle of accumulation, exemplified by many states' reactions to the Great Depression. In the US context, the New Deal encountered a great deal of opposition from capitalists, but the loss of political legitimacy gave President Roosevelt an unusually wide berth in implementing policy (Piven and Cloward 1971: 84–88). The extension of new welfare benefits, including unemployment protections, reduced the political threat of mass insurgency and civil unrest. In this same sense, the GND may bolster state legitimacy while also alleviating some of the worst environmental problems. Unlike the original New Deal, the GND's dual focus on environmental issues and social equality means that new contradictions must also be considered.

In economic terms, the state may bolster both aggregate demand and political legitimacy through a centralized wealth redistribution mechanism. The Scandinavian welfare states are an example of this dynamic. After many decades of struggle, the powerful labor movements in the Scandinavian countries settled into a long period of peace in industrial relations. The healthcare, education, and welfare systems of these countries act to maintain a high level of social equality and a decent living standard for most citizens in these countries. However, these states are still capitalist in their economic framework. These states invest capital, both foreign and domestic, and wage labor remains the dominant form of labor relations. The same export of capital from a Scandinavian state drives the same forms of environmental damage as capital exported by the United States, though the per capita damage is lower. While many Americans admire their political and economic system (exemplified by Bernie Sanders' 2016 and 2020 presidential nomination campaigns' vision of "socialism"), it is important to remember that this same system is facing serious political pressure to undergo neoliberal reforms of the social welfare system and labor market, most notably in Sweden (Harvey 2005: 112–115). A need to remain "globally competitive" for investment drives much of the political argument in favor of reducing the welfare state and the bargaining power of unions in the region.

A GND might not go far enough as a state form capable of preventing catastrophic climate change in the necessary timeframe. The Scandinavian countries exemplify many of the goals of a GND in the US context already. They typically have a high level of regulation of pollution, state investment in green technology, and public transit systems. However, they are not totally sustainable. Sweden, a noted environmental reformer, has made considerable strides in environmental efficiency, but net sustainability is lagging (Lidscog and Elander 2012; Vail 2008). Norway remains a "petrostate" whose generous welfare measures depend on its oil production. The cold climates of these states necessitate burning a considerable amount of fuel to keep citizens warm in its long winters. Under their present social-democratic frameworks, in which capitalism operates alongside welfare supports but essentially has the same systemic requirement for capital accumulation, a completely sustainable economy remains out of reach.

As the GND gains traction, the United States has the potential to transform into a social democracy akin to the Scandinavian states. Although these states remain leaders in green reform, they still have some distance to go toward environmental sustainability, Norway particularly (Norgaard 2011). To push forward into a "true" sustainability, deeper transformation toward a socialist economy is necessary. A boosted middle class under the GND is unlikely to want to go in this political, economic and social direction, if past experiences are an indication. This poses a thorny political and social problem. Just as the radical demands and riots of the 1960s and 1970s eventually cooled as welfare measures expanded in the United States, the GND could put a "cap" on the demands of the working class for even broader welfare measures once more people become integrated into GND projects.

My third critique of the GND, the problem of entrenched political power, is meant to highlight the problems of the state, capital and environment, particularly in welfare states. The problems of the state as presently understood could undermine the GND's environmental goals as the state provides its generous welfare measures. The ecological modernization of the Scandinavian states shows the limits of their social model in confronting climate change. The social relations of such states are similar in many respects to those of other capitalist states. State managers ease the conflict between workers and management in private industry. Meanwhile, these states export a high percentage of capital and import material from the Global South. The Green New Deal may replicate these structures while being unable to deal with their environmental and social problems. The GND needs to move beyond the environmental limits of social democracy if it is to build a truly sustainable society.

There are other, more grounded problems of provision and finance related to the state to consider; a major question hanging over the GND in a Marxist perspective is the question of its financing and management. The social relations under capitalism compel the working class to sell its labor for wages in a free market with some limitations. The bourgeoisie uses that labor to accumulate capital, paying some of their earnings on the market as wages, but keeping a large part as profits. A middle stratum of management directs the work process and receives a boost over the wages of most workers. The GND in its present form replicates many of these same relations, including sourcing capital from private industry and its social relations. For this reason, I posit the critique that the GND may encourage a form of "state capitalism" that reproduces many of the problems of capitalism and the GND, albeit with a vigorous state sector. This critique centers around two social phenomena: the capitalist social relations prevailing in a "productivist" state program and the possibility that the state will become the main provider of capital, labor control, and return on investment in a new form of "state capitalism."

The capitalist relations of our present society necessitate management to stir workers to labor in order to produce profit. Through their labor, initial investment garners a suitably high return to make it worth an investor's risk. A middle stratum of skilled managers directs and supervises those members of the working class with less skill. The United States, like many higher-income countries, has a large middle-class relative to peripheral states in the world system. Directing a socially transformative project like the GND will require a large body of managers and technicians to implement policy goals. Their increased size will play a stabilizing role in the US polity and economy, providing a high degree of upward mobility to a wide swathe of society. President Lyndon B. Johnson's "Great Society" programs of the 1960s largely succeeded in creating a class of Black professionals to administer these programs – possibly a greater economic and social impact than the poverty-alleviating programs themselves.

Middle-class professionals will be needed in large numbers to direct Green New Deal programs. These managers will use their bureaucratic authority to compel workers to maximize their productivity while minimizing their costs, including wages. Add to this the high likelihood that much of this work will be unpleasant (e.g., cleaning toxic waste sites), and it is possible, if not probable, that management-labor disputes will arise. Like the New Deal, these social relations could threaten the viability of the GND as a sweeping social project. Erik Olin Wright identified the "contradictory positions" that the middle class occupies in capitalist society as both manager and worker. A GND-boosted middle class would face many of these same contradictory priorities to stir other workers to productivity while also displaying some measure of solidarity with the working class (Wright 2015).

An interesting historical example of social relations in a program comparable to the GND is the original New Deal. Scholars of the New Deal celebrate its transformative vision and the boost it gave to many areas of the United States marked by constant grinding poverty, especially the US South. However, some aspects of the New Deal resembled the social relations of the non-state sector in troubling ways. Despite the promises of employment guaranteed by the New Deal, wages in its programs tended to be quite low for the laborers employed in projects like building hydroelectric dams. The wage structure of the Works Progress Administration, the main program boosting employment under the New Deal, deliberately offered lower wages than the private sector so as not to create a competing economic sector that would drive wages upward (Piven and Cloward 1971: 94–98). Also, many of the democratic initiatives in model towns, like Norris, Tennessee (a project in which Eleanor Roosevelt became personally invested), failed to attract many local working-class people to town meetings and other markers of elevated class status within the "utopian" communities surrounding New Deal projects (Isenberg 2016: 221–222). We might surmise that the work requirements of these programs caused many participants to view them as "work" rather than as transformative social projects and to approach them with the same alienated distance as any other type of industrial or service work.

A new capitalist class will likely be able to dominate the political processes surrounding the GND, directing funds and resources in favor of this class. The previous New Deal offers some interesting examples. The Southern Democrats in President Roosevelt's electoral and legislative coalition welcomed additional federal spending the Southern states, including large infrastructural projects. However, these groups succeeded in denying Black domestic and agricultural laborers social protections like Social Security, as well as limiting their ability to organize unions under pro-labor legislation. A GND could see much of the same process.

Although this critique risks opening some of the oldest wounds among Western European and North American Marxists, as well as their Asian, African and Latin American counterparts, we must be cognizant that the primary Marxist states, i.e., the Soviet Union and present-day China, were or are extremely "productivist" in their approach to raising living standards (Castoriadis 1985). This includes constant increases in production and resource consumption, including the creation and maintenance of "resource periphery" countries supplying raw materials. The environmental consequences have been devastating. Capital may not have circulated freely in these states, but the mere absence of free market capitalism did not eliminate environmental issues. Cuba's successes in reforestation, organic agriculture and disaster preparedness came as a result of the US embargo on essential fossil fuels, not an original "green" state policy (Latouche 2009). Just as a GND alone will not "fix" environmental problems, neither will blind faith in an anti-capitalist/post-capitalist GND (Fotopoulos 2009; Kallis 2010). Regardless of the type of economic and social system, growth is perceived as the solution to many social ills. Degrowth scholars have pointed to this contradiction and have proposed some useful solutions to the problem of increasing human well-being without degradation of the natural environment. The Marxist left would benefit from serious considerations of these scholars (see *inter alia* Demaria et al. 2013).

Alone, however, degrowth may not challenge the political control of a capitalist class. Capitalism, in many definitions, is a system based on wage labor as the dominant form of labor control and social relations. Imagining capitalism without growth is difficult, but it may not be wholly inconceivable that the present relationship of class forces could continue under the political control of a capitalist elite, albeit one that may focus more on rent collection than expanding their capital. Pre-capitalist economic and social systems certainly saw control by small elites, even without the constant expansion of the economy. A degrowth economy without democratic control of the means of production would not solve many of the political and economic issues surrounding our current economy. In summation, anti-capitalism without degrowth won't solve economic, social, and environmental issues alone, and, likewise, degrowth without considering class relations won't solve them, either. I am not alone in this consideration; degrowth scholars have written about where degrowth crosses from capitalism to socialism or somewhere in between (Gorz 1994; Jackson 2009; Latouche 2009). The challenge is to create a system in which management of such a system allows for autonomy, political legitimacy and democratic input while achieving environmental sustainability.

The New Deal offered many Marxists and other segments of the left a transformative vision of a vigorous state sector capable of redirecting investment toward social needs with a high degree of electoral input. However, the managerial nature of state bureaucrats in contemporary welfare states and the state socialism of the Soviet Union highlight another set of contradictions under a managerial state – be it socialist, capitalist, or any other system with a large state bureaucracy. At the beginning of this final critique, I noted the possibility that new class relations could be established as state managers push workers to higher levels of productivity. In order to make the GND a financial success, workers might be pushed to work long hours for relatively little pay. Like the New Deal before it, this program will require extensive state appropriations of land, materials and labor. Political power will certainly be wielded by employers to make the GND as cheap as possible, much as the New Deal was unable to offer wages or working conditions that would hamper private employment. Projects for community gardening, tree planting, and the Americorps program (a US national community service program that does not pay a living wage whose main attraction is student debt relief) illustrate that a GND might only attract a segment of middle-class youth, who feel attracted to the sense of belonging and social transformation of the program, and will most certainly pass from GND jobs into middle-class professions. Achieving working-class inclusion into a GND with long hours, relatively low pay, little room for promotion and hard-driving management could politically doom the program. The union jobs promised by many GND supporters could run into considerable opposition from workers themselves and put state managers in the contradictory position of promising high wages with good benefits and simultaneously keeping GND project as cheap as possible.

This critique is not meant to disparage the GND as a class project that progressives or the left (or anyone wanting to live on a livable planet) should avoid. However, the political task of moving beyond capitalism, rather than attempting to build a green welfare state, is wholly necessary to the achievement of the GND as a program. The COVID-19 recovery plans of many countries show that crisis can push the state to adopt stabilizing reform, even against the backdrop of decades of austerity. Increasing the breadth of this new wave of state spending into environmental reform and welfare state (re)construction can build a valuable constituency for the GND. Already, the Biden administration in the United States is floating green spending as a cornerstone of COVID recovery. The political question is whether we can go beyond these limits. Failure to prepare for new class antagonisms that might emerge from public works programs or to foresee political backlash as the program might transform into a public investment program that boosts capitalist production could make the GND dead on arrival.

Moving past the "pitfalls of capitalism"

Throughout this volume, other scholars will be positing many ways to overcome the hurdles I present here. I will, however, comment briefly on a few potential solutions to avoiding the "pitfalls of capitalism" in the GND. Degrowth economics offers a path forward in the macroeconomic transformation of society's production and consumption (see Schor and Tienhaara, this volume). From an ecological Marxist perspective, the one issue I raise with degrowth is its premise that growth, not the social relations of capitalism, is the basis for the environmental problems of capitalism. These relations are the dominance of a capitalist class over the productive process. I have doubts that capitalism can continue without growth, but a focus on ending growth rather than building an inclusive labor movement that can disrupt the production process to negotiate and/or supersede capital, puts the cart before the horse. This is the realm of pure speculation, but it is not inconceivable that capitalism could continue without growth, as long as a capitalist class can dominate the productive process. Feudal social relations could be said not to involve growth, as rents extracted from peasants were not reinvested in expanding production, but this did not impede the dominance of the feudal aristocracy. Rather than not expanding a store of capital, a degrowth economy could simply extract rent to be spent by an owning class. I understand that degrowth economists would never call for such a thing, but a degrowth perspective without a call to shift social relations, especially through a rigorous labor movement, would be unlikely to open the political space for degrowth economics, anyway.

In conjunction with that, a direct form of reducing both the class inequalities and excessive consumption of capitalist economies is greater redistribution of wealth from the wealthiest to the poorest. At the national level, many of the most destructive forms of consumption are thanks to the wealthiest in society. An excess of large homes, multiple boats, cars, imported luxury foods and other forms of "conspicuous consumption," as well as global travel by the ultra-wealthy, mean that the consumption of the wealthiest vastly exceeds that of the poorest. A redistribution of wealth would curb a great deal of unsustainable consumption and pollution by these individuals.

A redistribution of wealth would also interrupt the ease with which the wealthy influence the political system. The vast network of media outlets funded by the Koch brothers, Rupert Murdoch, and other figures hell-bent on countering the GND would become more difficult to sustain through private and corporate donations. Local "not-in-my-backyard" or "NIMBY" campaigns to protect the real estate values of the wealthy will also become less "affordable." The fungibility of money into political influence will become more difficult for those in a class position to hamper the GND's growth and spread.

At the global level, reining in consumption by wealthy countries and spreading global wealth through foreign aid as grants, not loans, could also bring about a greater distribution of the benefits of a global GND and the excessive consumption enjoyed by the relatively large middle classes of Europe, North America, Australia, Japan, and New Zealand. This would help to close the ecological debt owed by the core states of the world system to the peripheral states. Ideally, such spreading of the global wealth could push for GNDs throughout the Global South. Removing harmful patent protections on green technologies would further their spread. Also, these funds could pay for environmental cleanup from rare earth minerals extraction and the other material inputs required in the GND, closing the metabolic rift between Global North and South.

Affecting this shift in wealth means shifting social relations. If the present political moment teaches us anything, capitalists refuse to "go quietly" toward sharing their wealth. A powerful protest movement of the working class that can disrupt politics and economics "as usual" is required to grab hold of the wealth made and extracted from working people. Unlike the past, this shift in relations is likely to involve more than the "traditional" labor movement. As capitalists have reorganized and dismantled the welfare state in much of the developed world, the traditional labor movement has lost ground in numbers, a conducive legal environment, and the industrial workplaces that form its traditional organizing ground. New forms of organization, including movements of immigrants, movements for racial and ethnic equality, and Indigenous movements, will have to fill this gap to effect change. These groups have historically been excluded from the labor movement, but the manner in which racialized communities have served as regions from which to extract value and saddle with waste means their inclusion in the GND is absolutely necessary and can broaden the "popular front" pushing for the GND.

Another possibility to avoid these pitfalls is the reduction of the work week. Rather than boost wages, a worthy goal in any event, workers could be rewarded with more leisure time. To put things in terms Marx might have used, this would be a reduction in the production of absolute surplus value after workers get their share from the production of relative surplus value in an efficiently run workplace. Compensating workers in this way would have a discernable impact on emissions without creating rebound effects. Less time spent commuting would mean a reduction in emissions. Workplaces would see a reduction in power consumption for running machinery, electronics, and heating and cooling. Similarly, a reduction of the work week would lead to a reduction in unemployment as employers would hire more workers to make up for the reduction in hours each employee could work. Some international comparative work suggests that reducing the work week has a noted effect on emissions in many national contexts (Fitzgerald, Jorgenson and Clark 2015; Fitzgerald, Schor and

Jorgenson 2018). The increase in wages and public goods, such as housing, boosted by the GND would further reduce the need for many to work as many hours as they do at present, furthering the possibilities of increased leisure time under the GND. The GND has the potential to improve access for millions of people to public parks, public transit, and the arts, if it follows in the same vein as the social programs of the original New Deal. These activities would likely have low environmental impacts as these are collectively enjoyed forms of leisure and relaxation. Expropriating empty vacation homes, condos and luxury sporting goods like fishing boats and turning them into reservable public property could give everyone a chance to enjoy "the good life." Furthermore, such public goods need not generate profit for private corporations and individuals, breaking up the treadmill of production while affording working-class people time to enjoy themselves. Reclaiming the weekend, making the traditional workweek only four or even three days long, and having more time for families and friends would be difficult for any opponent of the GND to undo. This would also create powerful constituencies of GND supporters and avoid the "hard sell" of decreasing consumption in consumer society.

Conclusion

In this chapter, I employed the concepts of the treadmill of production, metabolic rift, and class-based issues of welfare states to critically examine the Green New Deal as currently proposed within the United States. I hope that these critiques will drive a further debate on the GND for others working on similar proposals around the world. The GND is exciting, beyond a doubt. However, a poorly conceived GND could threaten the entire enterprise and expend an incredible amount of political capital that may be irrecoverable. Though these critiques may, at times, seem pessimistic about the whole initiative, I hope that other scholars will take them into consideration and negate the issues they raise. Financing the GND and generating new forms of worker management are tasks that I hope economists, natural scientists, managers, social scientists and political organizers will see as challenges to meet, rather than critiques that doom the Green New Deal.

References

Atwood, D. 2012. *The Rare Earth Elements: Fundamentals and Applications*. Hoboken, NJ: Wiley-Blackwell.

Castoriadis, C. 1985. Reflections on "Rationality" and "Development." Thesis. 10/11, 18–35.

Clark, B. and Foster, J.B. 2001. "William Stanley Jevons and the coal question: An Introduction to Jevons's 'Of the Economy of Fuel.'" *Organization & Environment* 14(1): 93–98.

Clark, B. and Foster, J.B. 2009. "Ecological Imperialism and the Metabolic Rift: Unequal Exchange and the Guano/Nitrates Trade." *International Journal of Comparative Sociology* 50(3–4): 311–334.

Clausen, R. and York, R. 2008. "Global Biodiversity Decline of Marine and Freshwater Fish: A Cross-National Analysis of Economic, Demographic, and Ecological Influences." *Social Science Research* 37(4): 1310–1320.

Demaria, F. et al. 2013. "What Is Degrowth? From an Activist Slogan to a Social Movement." *Environmental Values* 22(2): 191–215.

Energy Information Administration. 2020. "What Is US Electricity generation by Source?" Available from: https://www.eia.gov/tools/faqs/faq.php?id=427&t=3. Retrieved 24 June 2020.

Estes, N. 2019. "A Red Deal." *Jacobin*. Available from: https://www.jacobinmag.com/2019/08/red-deal-green-new-deal-ecosocialism-decolonization-indigenous-resistance-environment. Retrieved 8 March 2021.

Fitzgerald, J.B., Jorgenson, A.K. and Clark, B. 2015. "Energy Consumption and Working Hours: A Longitudinal Study of Developed and Developing Nations, 1990–2008." *Environmental Sociology* 1(3): 213–223.

Fitzgerald, J.B. et al. 2018. "Working Hours and Carbon Dioxide Emissions in the United States, 2007–2013." *Social Forces* 96(4): 1851–1874.
Foster, J.B. 2000. *Marx's Ecology: Materialism and Nature*. New York: Monthly Review Press.
Foster, J.B. 2005. "The Treadmill of Accumulation Schnaiberg's Environment and Marxian Political Economy." *Organization & Environment* 18(1): 7–18.
Foster, J.B., Clark B. and York, R. 2011. *The Ecological Rift: Capitalism's War on the Earth*. New York: Monthly Review Press.
Fotopoulos, T. 2009. *The Multi-Dimensional Crisis and the Inclusive Democracy*. English translation provided in *International Journal of Inclusive Democracy*. Available from: https://www.inclusivedemocracy.org/fotopoulos/english/brbooks/multi_crisis_id/multi_crisis_id.htm. Original Greek version published in Athens: Gordios (2005).
Givens, J., Huang, X. and Jorgenson, A.K. 2019. "Ecologically Unequal Exchange: A Theory of Global Environmental Injustice." *Sociological Compass* 13(5): 1–15.
Gorz, A., 1994. *Capitalism, Socialism, Ecology*. London: Verso.
Gould, K.A., Pellow, D.N. and Schnaiberg, A. 2004. "Interrogating the Treadmill: Everything You Wanted to Know, but Were Afraid to Ask." *Organization and Environment* 17(3): 296–316.
Harvey, D. (2005). *A Brief History of Neoliberalism*. Oxford: Oxford University Press.
Intergovernmental Panel on Climate Change. 2018. "Summary for Policymakers of IPCC Special Report on Global Warming of 1.5°C Approved by Governments." Available from: https://www.ipcc.ch/2018/10/08/summary-for-policymakers-of-ipcc-special-report-on-global-warming-of-1-5c-approved-by-governments/. Accessed 24 June 2020.
Isenberg, N. 2016. *White Trash: The 400-Year Untold History of Class in America*. New York: Penguin.
Jackson, T., 2009. *Prosperity without Growth: Economics for a Finite Planet*. London: Earthscan.
Jorgenson, A.K. and Clark, B. 2009. "The Economy, Military, and Ecologically Unequal Exchange Relationships in Comparative Perspective: A Panel Study of the Ecological Footprints of Nations, 1975–2000." *Social Problems* 56(4): 621–646.
Jorgenson, A.K., and Rice, J. 2005. "Structural Dynamics of International Trade and Material Consumption: A Cross-National Study of the Ecological Footprints of Less-Developed Countries." *Journal of World-Systems Research* 11(1): 57–77.
Kahn, B. 2019. "More Than 600 Environmental Groups Just Backed Ocasio-Cortez's Green New Deal." *Earther*. Retrieved 24 June 2020.
Kaiman, J. 2014. "Rare Earth Mining in China: The Bleak Social and Environmental Costs." *The Guardian*. Available from: https://www.theguardian.com/sustainable-business/rare-earth-mining-china-social-environmental-costs. Accessed 24 June 24, 2020.
Kallis, G. 2010. "In Defence of Degrowth." *Ecological Economics* 70: 873–880.
Latouche, S. 2009. *Farewell to Growth*. Cambridge: Polity Press.
Lidskog, R. and Elander, I. 2012. "Ecological Modernization in Practice? The Case of Sustainable Development in Sweden." *Journal of Environmental Policy & Planning* 14(4): 411–427.
Mastini, R., Kallis, G. and Hickel, J. 2021. "A Green New Deal without Growth?" *Ecological Economics* 179. Available from: https://doi.org/10.1016/j.ecolecon.2020.106832. Accessed 4 March 2021.
McElwee, S. 2019. "People Actually Like the Green New Deal." *New York Times*. Available from: https://www.nytimes.com/2019/03/27/opinion/sunday/green-new-deal-mcconnell.html. Accessed 16 July 2020.
Mol, A.P.J. 2001. *Globalization and Environmental Reform: The Ecological Modernization of the Global Economy*. Cambridge, MA: MIT Press.
Norgaard, K.M. 2011. *Living in Denial: Climate Change, Emotions, and Everyday Life*. Cambridge, MA: MIT Press.
O'Connor, J. 1988. "Capitalism, Nature, Socialism: A Theoretical Introduction." *Capitalism, Nature, Society* 1(1): 11–38.
Piven, F.F. and Cloward, R. 1971. *Regulating the Poor: The Functions of Public Welfare*. New York: Random House.
Recognizing the Duty of the Federal Government to Create a Green New Deal. H. Res. 109, 116th Congress. 2019. Retrieved June 23, 2020. Available from: https://www.congress.gov/bill/116th-congress/house-resolution/109/text.
Rim, K-T. 2016. "Effects of Rare Earth Elements on the Environment and Human Health: A Literature Review." *Toxicology and Environmental Health Sciences* 8, 189–200.
Schnaiberg, A. 1980. *The Environment: From Surplus to Scarcity*. Oxford: Oxford University Press.

United States Geologic Survey (USGS). 2002. "Rare Earth Element Mines, Deposits, and Occurrences." Available from: https://mrdata.usgs.gov/ree/. Accessed 24 June 2020.

Vadén, T.V. et al. 2020. "Decoupling for Ecological Sustainability: A Categorisation and Review of Research Literature." *Environmental Science & Policy* 112: 236–244.

Vail, B. 2008. "Ecological Modernization at Work? Environmental Policy Reform in Sweden at the Turn of the Century." *Scandinavian Studies* 80(1): 85–108.

Vestas. 2012. *2 MW.* Product Brochure 04/2012-EN, Vestas Wind Systems A/S.

Wishart, R., Jamil Jonna, R. and Besek, J. 2020. "Metabolic Rift: A Selected Bibliography." Available from: https://monthlyreview.org/commentary/metabolic-rift. Accessed 13 July 2020.

Wright, E.O. 2015. *Understanding Class.* London: Verso.

York, R., Rosa, E. and Dietz, T. 2003. "Footprints on the Earth: The Environmental Consequences of Modernity." *American Sociological Review* 68(2): 279–300.

York, R., Rosa, E. and Dietz, T. 2008. "The Ecological Footprint Intensity of National Economies." *Journal of Industrial Ecology* 8(4): 139–154.

5

A GREEN NEW DEAL FOR AGRICULTURE

Whither capitalism?*

Benjamin Selwyn

Introduction

Even before the coronavirus (COVID-19) pandemic, the InterAcademy Partnership characterized the world's food system as broken. Over 800 million people were hungry, 600 million suffered from obesity and another 2 billion people were overweight, while one-third of food produced globally (over 1 billion tonnes) are wasted every year (Carrington 2018). The outbreak of COVID-19 has exacerbated many of the system's worst aspects. It has also highlighted the conditions under which zoonotic diseases (those that spread between animals and humans) emerge. If there ever was a time to reconsider the possibilities of establishing a new food system, this is it. Unsurprisingly, then, within the current conjuncture there is a stampede across the political spectrum toward visions of a green transformation, with the idea of a Green New Deal (GND) at the forefront.

The rationale for such a transformation is clear. On the one hand, the world economy is set to triple in size by 2050 – entailing three times more production, consumption and trade based upon current trends (Hawksworth and Chan 2015). On the other hand, the 2018 Special Report from the Intergovernmental Panel on Climate Change (IPCC) warns that "limiting global warming to 1.5°C would require rapid, far-reaching and unprecedented changes in all aspects of society" (IPCC 2018). Failure to do so threatens an "existential risk to humanity" (Spratt and Dunlop 2019).

The global food system is a major contributor to climate breakdown, contributing directly to the sixth mass extinction of wildlife (Intergovernmental Science-Policy Platform on Biodiversity and Ecosystem Services 2019). It generates between 20% and 35% of anthropogenic greenhouse gasses, uses 70% of global fresh water and 40% of global land (Clapp, Newell and Brent 2018, 80). The livestock sector (especially industrial-scale beef production) has a particularly severe impact on climate breakdown: 33% of global croplands are devoted to feed crops, and 26% of the world's ice-free land is used for livestock grazing, and the subsector generates around 15% of total greenhouse gas (GHG) emissions (FAO 2012; Garnett et al. 2017, 27).

* This chapter was adapted with permission from Benjamin Selwyn (2021) A green new deal for agriculture: for, within, or against capitalism?, *The Journal of Peasant Studies*, 48:4, 778–806, DOI: 10.1080/03066150.2020.1854740.

DOI: 10.4324/9781003110880-7

This chapter shows how the capitalist food system, in particular its agro-industrial segment, depends upon two core relations: accumulation-driven commodification and the exploitation of labor and nature, which, in turn, cause many of the maladies mentioned above. The policies and investments that support capitalist agro-industry are, arguably, a leading contributor to ecocide – massive damage caused to the planet's flora and fauna (Higgins 2012).

The relative novelty of GND-type transformations means that their form, content and trajectory have not yet been firmly determined. Are they part of a project to save capitalism from itself through generating an epoch of green capitalism? Or do they have a more transformative potential? If the latter, then they must confront and transform the core relations (of accumulation-driven commodification and exploitation) of the contemporary agro-industrial food system. If the former, then it is quite likely that these relations will remain in place, to contribute further to social polarization and ecocide.

A growing number of green transformations are *pro*-capitalist. These aim to boost capital accumulation, including through new rounds of commodification/marketization of nature (see further chapter by McCollum, this volume). Examples of these include the European Union's Green Deal (see further chapter by Adler and Wargan, this volume) and Joseph Biden's Climate Deal (see further chapter by Pettifor, this volume). Other programs aim to operate *within* capitalism while delivering important social reforms for laboring classes. An example is the UK Labour Party's Labour for a Green New Deal (see further chapter by Bailey and Hofferberth, this volume).

The ultimate challenge for a socialist GND is to restore the metabolic interaction between humans and nature through a new, non-exploitative society where the "conscious and rational treatment of the land as permanent communal property" is "the inalienable condition for the existence and reproduction of the chain of human generations" (Marx 1981, 754). This chapter introduces a range of criteria and policies that, it suggests, constitute a socialist GND, to be implemented as one lever *against* capitalism.

Following this introduction, the rest of this chapter is organized as follows: first it outlines a brief conception of a socialist transition to establish a benchmark against which to assess non-socialist GNDs. It then identifies the inherent environmental, financial and social unsustainability of capitalist agriculture, in particular agro-industry. This is followed by a discussion of win-win green ideologies – based upon the core assumption that business and the environment can benefit mutually from the right policy packages. Finally, the chapter outlines a number of key areas in agrarian political economy for academic research and political conversation.

Notes on a socialist transition

Considering the possibilities of a progressive GND in the USA, Raj Patel and Jim Goodman (2020, 449) argue for a "GND bloc" involving "labour, movements fighting for gender and racial justice and decolonization… and the span of groups pushing for social control over finance." This chapter concurs, but suggests that more should be said about the direction of travel of such a social movement-powered GND. Is the endgame a better, greener capitalism or a transcendence of capitalism, and what are the implications of the answers to these questions for political strategy? Such questions should be addressed as the campaigns for the form and content of GNDs continue, as part of maintaining the coherence and power of the bloc. At the time of writing, in the USA and across the EU, the Black Lives Matter, Extinction Rebellion, school-students/Sunrise movements (but still not yet the trade union movement en masse), represent progressive forces that could potentially contribute to establishing such a bloc.

Answering these questions within the scope of a single chapter requires some space-saving assumptions. The assumptions made here are, first, that a GND bloc emerges and wins political office through democratic elections in one country (generating some leverage over state power), before contributing to the internationalization of other GND blocs and (potentially) states. Second, once in office, the political representation (probably a party of sorts) of the bloc begins to implement a GND within a capitalist economic system. Third, the objectives of the GND are simultaneously to fortify the bloc, initiate decisive actions to avoid climate breakdown and contribute to a transition to socialism. It must always be kept in mind that the new system develops "from within an antithesis to the existing development of production and the inherited, traditional relations of property" (Marx 1993, 278).

How then, do we conceive of (a) a movement toward socialism within a capitalist system and (b) a GND for agriculture as a lever in that process? There are two key aspects here: decommodification and a decisive shift in the balance of class power. Gøsta Esping Andersen (1990, 37) refers to decommodification as "…the degree to which individuals, or families, can uphold a socially acceptable standard of living independently of market participation. When work approaches free choice rather than necessity, decommodification may amount to de-proletarianization." Esping Andersen notes, however, that policies and processes of decommodification have existed, and can support, varied political economic regimes – from Bismarck's social programs to the 1945 Labour government's welfare state.

What, then, makes a process of decommodification co-constitutive of socialist deproletarianization? It is the equalizing of class power. Just as working classes cease to exist as servants of capital, so too do capitalist classes cease to exist as masters of labor. Michael Lebowitz (2010) uses the concepts of "inroads" and "encroachments" into capital's power over labor to describe the *process* of establishing socialism. Such inroads would entail laboring classes taking over capital's decision-making functions, such as resource allocation and investment, in part through political economic programs such as a socialist GND. Assessing whether a GND is designed to strengthen capitalism, exist within it (albeit with important concessions to labor) or transcend it, therefore, requires a sense of whether it is contributing to decommodification, class equalization and ultimately to deproletarianization.

COVID-19 and the unsustainability of capitalist agro-industry

Proponents of capitalist agriculture, and agro-industry in particular, identify its ability to produce high yields cheaply to feed the world's expanding population (Collier 2008; World Bank 2015). At the aggregate level, such arguments appear reasonable. After all, humanity continues to accelerate away from a Malthusian trap. Productivity increases in agriculture pushed up per capita food availability from about 2,716 calories per person per day at the turn of the millennium to 2,904 calories in 2015–2017 (Global Agriculture 2020).

However, such productivist narratives occlude ways in which agro-industry destroys the natural environment and contributes directly to pandemics such as COVID-19, and ignore how capitalism fails to feed approximately 800 million people adequately and how the food system contributes to a situation where over 2 billion people are either obese or overweight. Rather than a system orientated to meet human need through environmentally sustainable practices, the global agro-industrial system is one where "people, animals, plants and the environment [are] controlled in order to maintain order, authority and predictability" (Lang and Heasman 2004, 279).

Figure 5.1 The unsustainability of capitalist agro-industry

Contrary to liberal fantasies (of the existence, or at least the possibility, of self-sustaining and regulating markets), capitalist agro-industry is fundamentally unsustainable; that is, it cannot sustain itself on its own basis (Figure 5.1).

This is so in four ways. First, it ruins the natural environment upon which it depends. As Bernard and Lux (2017, 1280) put it: "Heavy use of pesticides, fertilisers, irrigation, intensive ploughing and large-scale monocropping systems" are leading to the "degradation of soil and water systems, erosion and salinisation, loss of soil fertility and lead to displacement and loss of biodiversity." A consequence of these processes is that globally, an estimated "10 million hectares of agricultural land are lost" every year (Branford 2011, 5). Parts of the UK may have only 100 harvests left due to topsoil degradation (Case 2014).

Such ecocidal dynamics are powered by the market system. Capitalist agriculture requires the prior and continually reproduced commodification of nature (especially land), labor and food (Marx 1990; Polanyi 2001). Capitalist nature is simultaneously commodified and externalized – where its use and destruction are either not incorporated as a cost into production or is done so very cheaply (Moore 2015). It is not just disaffected environmentalists and Marxists who understand this! In one of its reports, the consultancy firm KPMG noted that the full environmental costs of the US food sector amounted to 224% of its earnings (KPMG 2012, 100). As Patel and Goodman (2020, 448) note, "[e]ither the industry is profitable by dint of its externalities, or it stops making food and money."

The agro-industrial livestock sector is responsible for much of GHG emissions *within* the total agro-food sector (Weis 2013) and around 15% of total GHG emissions (Garnett et al

2017). This is through (1) the conversion of forests and other natural ecosystems to pasture and the associated loss of organic matter in soils; (2) the enteric generation of methane by ruminant animals; (3) the decline in landscapes' carbon-sequestration capacity as they are simplified according to monoculture imperatives; (4) the use of fossil fuels for farm machinery, the manufacture, transport and application of chemical fertilizers and pesticides, and the operation of processing facilities (from hatcheries to slaughterhouses); (5) and the longer and denser "food miles" required to bring meat to markets, entailing associated refrigeration and storage costs (Weis 2013, 134–135). As Mike Davis notes:

> The world icon of industrialised poultry and livestock production…Tyson Foods… which kills 2.2 billion chickens annually, has become globally synonymous with scaled-up, vertically coordinated production; exploitation of contract growers; visceral anti-unionism; rampant industrial injury; downstream environmental dumping; and political corruption.
>
> *(Davis 2006, 83)*

A second font of unsustainability is that commodification and intense labor exploitation is central to the reproduction of global agriculture:

> [O]f the 1.3 billion people employed in agriculture… there are some 450 million waged workers, over half of whom are women. Seventy per cent of child labour globally takes place in agriculture… and agriculture produces over 170,000 work-related deaths annually. Agricultural workers are twice as likely to die at work than in any other sector. Between three to four million pesticide poisonings occur each year, some 40,000 of them fatal…chronically high rates of malnutrition occur among agricultural workers.
>
> *(Rossman 2012, 61)*

These dynamics are present throughout the global agro-industrial system, including it its core in the USA. For example, as the US national farm worker ministry puts it: "Annually, the average income of crop workers is between $10,000 to $12,499 for individuals and $15,000 to $17,499 for a family… [T]he federal poverty line is $10,830 for an individual or $22,050 for a family of four (in 2009)" (National Farm Worker Ministry 2010). It is doubtful whether contemporary capitalist agro-industry could exist without vast pools of impoverished workers.

The third way in which agro-industry is unsustainable is its dependence upon the global fossil fuel subsidy regime, which cheapens inputs (from chemical fertilizers to farming equipment), transportation, storage, packaging and ultimately the retail of its produce. Global energy subsidies,

> as measured by the difference between what consumers should be paying for fossil fuel energy to cover supply costs, environmental costs, and general consumption taxes, and what they actually pay – are… estimated [to be] $5.3 trillion for 2015, or 6.5% of global GDP.
>
> *(Coady et al. 2017, 21)*

Finally, the agro-industrial sector relies heavily upon direct public subsidies. Approximately US$530 billion of an annual US$700 billion of global public support is paid to farmers engaged in high-input, chemically intensive, monocrop-based farming (Food and Land Use Coalition 2019, 54).

Before the advent of capitalist agriculture, farming was predominantly small-scale, determined overwhelmingly by local ecology and based upon internally dependent nutrient cycles. Nutrients and energy sources (e.g., manure) were recycled within and through a relatively self-reproducing system (Mazoyer and Roudart 2007). Capitalist agriculture has increasingly broken apart the previously unified process of production – as land, labor and inputs were commodified – and producers became increasingly market-dependent, a process dialectically related to the rise of agricultural science (Lievens 2010, 9). Agriculture has been transformed from an internally dependent to an externally dependent system reliant "upon the continued purchase and application of various external inputs in order to produce commodities for sale" (Weis 2007, 58; Berlan 1991). Marx's concept of the metabolic rift (unearthed by Foster 1999), captures the inherent unsustainability of capitalist agriculture:

> All progress in capitalist agriculture is a progress in the art, not only of robbing the worker, but of robbing the soil; all progress in increasing the fertility of the soil for a given time is a progress toward ruining the more long-lasting sources of that fertility.... Capitalist production... only develops the techniques and the degree of combination of the social process of production by simultaneously undermining the original sources of all wealth – the soil and the worker.
>
> *(Marx 1990, 638)*

Agro-industry contributes to environmental breakdown, is economically unsustainable, is based upon the exploitation of workers and degradation of nature, and contributes directly to pandemics such as COVID-19. As Rob Wallace notes:

> Agribusiness as a mode of social reproduction must be ended for good if only as a matter of public health. Highly capitalised production of food depends on practices that endanger the entirety of humanity, in this case helping unleash a new deadly pandemic. We should demand food systems be socialised in such a way that pathogens this dangerous are kept from emerging in the first place. That will require reintegrating food production into the needs of rural communities first. That will require agroecological practices that protect the environment and farmers as they grow our food. Big picture, we must heal the metabolic rifts separating our ecologies from our economies. In short, we have a planet to win.
>
> *(Wallace 2020)*

While globalized capitalist agriculture – and in particular its agro-industrial variant – is inherently unsustainable, this chapter does not view former Soviet/Eastern Bloc agriculture as representing an alternative. Rather, following Cliff (1996), it understands these regions as variants of "state capitalist" catch-up development, where agricultural (and industrial) production were subordinated to military-industrial competitive accumulation. Cliff described how Stalin's agricultural collectivization:

> ...resulted in the freeing of agricultural products for the needs of industrial development, the 'freeing' of the peasantry from its means of production, the transformation of a section of them into reserves of labour power for industry, and the transformation of the rest into part-workers, part-peasants, part-serfs in the kolkhozes.
>
> *(Cliff 1996, 66; For China and Cuba, see Harris 1978 and Binns and Gonzales 1980, respectively.)*

While the world's agro-industrial system is viewed with increasing suspicion across much of the globe, many green solutions to climate breakdown not only eschew any critique of the capitalist system within which it exists and contributes to reproducing, but also are couched in avowedly pro-capitalist terms.

The lure of win-win solutions for business and environment

Arguments for green capitalism and green growth have become mainstream over the last decade and a half, at least since the Stern review (Stern 2007), and inform much of the thinking/strategy of contemporary "green recovery" plans (e.g., see Partington 2020). Such arguments are often framed in win-win/positive-sum terms (good for the environment, good for capital) and tend to offer technical solutions to climate breakdown. However, as Thomas Wanner notes, the mainstreaming of green thinking represents an attempt to re-establish the power of hegemonic social forces by adopting what was previously the language of subaltern groups: "Economic growth (now known as green growth) is constructed as the solution to all social, environmental and economic problems" (Wanner 2015, 35).

Pro-capitalist advocates of green growth present it as potentially saving capitalism from itself and saving the climate from "old/industrial capitalism" through generating new profit opportunities. Portraying the climate crisis as "our third world war" (in terms of resource mobilization), Joseph Stiglitz argues that:

> The war on the climate emergency...would actually be good for the economy – just as the Second World War set the stage for America's golden economic era... The Green New Deal would stimulate demand, ensuring that all available resources were used; and the transition to the green economy would likely usher in a new boom...More jobs by far will be created in renewable energy than will be lost in coal.
>
> *(Stiglitz 2019)*

Stiglitz does not mention how in the original New Deal the US government introduced wage and price controls and seized factories, land and services (such as the appropriation of the department store chain Montgomery Ward in 1944 to settle a labor dispute; Bozuwa 2019, 44). Nor does he note how these moves underpinned the state's war-time mobilization of the economy.

The World Bank and other international institutions propose that climate-smart agriculture (CSA) represents not just win-win, but a triple-win scenario:

> Climate-Smart Agriculture sustainably increases productivity, resilience (adaptation), reduces/removes greenhouse gases (GHGs) (mitigation), while enhancing the achievement of national food security and development goals.
>
> *(FAO 2010)*

Positive evidence provided by CSA proponents is the reduction of chemical application and reduced plowing (and hence lower levels of soil loss) through no-till agriculture. Technically, there are merits to such methods (Montgomery 2017). However, as Marcus Taylor (2018) shows, the CSA agenda is being rolled out in the service of expanding agro-industry (such as animal feed-oriented soy production), which contributes directly to climate breakdown. By bracketing out questions of power, hierarchy and exploitation (of humans and nature), CSA serves, like arguments for green growth more generally, to legitimize continued capitalist expansion.

The Intergovernmental Panel on Climate Change's 2019 report *Climate Change and Land* complements the above approaches to combatting climate breakdown. While it includes potentially useful technical solutions to climate breakdown, which could be incorporated into a transformative socialist strategy, it eschews anti-capitalist sentiments. It defines sustainable land management as:

> ...the stewardship and use of land resources, including soils, water, animals and plants, to meet changing human needs, while simultaneously ensuring the long-term productive potential of these resources and the maintenance of their environmental functions.
>
> *(IPCC 2019, 24, f.n. 33)*

Examples of potentially useful sustainable land management include:

> ...agroecology (including agroforestry), conservation agriculture and forestry practices, crop and forest species diversity, appropriate crop and forest rotations, organic farming, integrated pest management, the conservation of pollinators, rainwater harvesting, range and pasture management, and precision agriculture systems.
>
> *(Ibid.)*

The report does not mention land reform. It does advocate enhancing local and community collective action, the promotion of Indigenous rights and women's empowerment, albeit entailing "improved access to markets for inputs, outputs and financial services..." (ibid. 32).

Win-win/pro-capitalist conceptions of green transformations obscure how capitalism is hierarchical, exploitative and based upon endless commodification of nature and labor. They therefore preclude, rhetorically and in practice, the kinds of measures required to make inroads into capitalist power. Such inroads would entail the nationalization and effective closing down of the US$4.65 trillion fossil fuel industry (the 1,500 oil and gas firms listed on stock exchanges; Casella 2018). As Richard Seymour (2019) notes, making the GND work will require "a shattering blow to current circulations of value and profit." The states, firms and international organizations that support these (and other environmentally destructive) industries could, in the future, be tried for ecocide (Higgins 2012). If found culpable, their assets could be expropriated and used to address the ecocidal impacts of their prior investments.

There is another problem with win-win perspectives. They promise to deepen even further the existing relations that underpin climate breakdown. While the Stern review (2007) was concerned about how the costs of global warming may dampen economic growth, this is not so across the board. Capitalism's inherent unevenness means that far from representing a barrier to capitalist expansion *in toto*, environmental disasters and risk can be made profitable. Carbon markets, pollution permits, climate derivatives and catastrophe bonds all generate new profit opportunities for financial investors (Klein 2007; Keucheyan 2016). Moreover, without the transformation of social relations (entailing different forms of production, consumption and divisions of labor and wealth), technological solutions to climate change such as a large-scale shift to renewable energy promise new rounds of "renewable extractivism" (Zehner 2012; see also chapter by Kolinjivadi and Kothari, this volume).

Win-win perspectives also occlude historical causes of ecological ruination and ideologically shield actors that promoted such actions. The World Bank promoted the green revolution and structural adjustment programs, heralding the former as boosting crop yields and the latter of boosting allocative efficiency through exposure to heightened competition, respectively. Yet both programs contributed to environmental degradation through increased monocropping and capitalization of agriculture (Patel 2013). Win-win perspectives, from CSA to the IPCC's proposed solutions to environmental breakdown, are predicated upon yet deeper commodification (through market integration) of land and labor.

The rationale for conceiving a socialist GND for agriculture is that capitalist commodification and exploitation are fundamental drivers of climate breakdown. For example, the average carbon footprint of the top 1% of the world's population is around 175 times that of the poorest 10% (Gore 2015). Dario Kenner (2019) identifies how a "polluter elite" of 88 billionaires (in 2015) invested in and profited from fossil fuel industries. Moreover, the poorest segments of the world's population are the most vulnerable to, and least able to cope with, the effects of climate breakdown "with women facing greater risks than men, rural communities often more exposed than urban ones and groups marginalized because of race, ethnicity or other factors likely to be disproportionately affected" (Gore 2015, 5).

That said, what kinds of transformations will be required, and will be possible, within the agricultural sector, as part of a larger-scale socialist GND? The following section outlines some key areas for academic research and political discussion.

Agendas for academic research and political conversations

A GND/green recovery could represent the system-wide reorganization required to begin to address the double threat of climate breakdown and the onset of a pandemic epoch. The key question, however, is what kind of reorganization will such an approach facilitate? One that entrenches capitalist social relations and profit-driven economic growth? Or one that encroaches upon, with the aim of transcending, these social relations and replaces them with new relations between humans and nature? These end goals will determine every aspect of a green, system-wide reorganization. On the agricultural front they will confront, transform and build upon several key areas. The following section introduces eight of these as a way of generating further academic research and political conversations around potential green transformations.

Subsidies

In liberal mythology markets do, or at least can (in theory), exist freely of state interference. But as Karl Polanyi (2001, 146–147) noted:

> The road to the free market was opened and kept open by an enormous increase in continuous, centrally organised and controlled interventionism.... [T]he introduction of free markets, far from doing away with the need for control, regulation and intervention, enormously increased their range.

What will be the role of centrally provided funds in any green transformation? At present the global agro-food sector is supported by multiple subsidies, whether indirect (to the fossil fuel industry, as noted above) or direct (through PL480 in the USA and the Common Agricultural Policy (CAP) in the EU). In the EU, for example, in 2013 the "twin pillars" of the CAP budget (direct subsidies to farmers and payments to support rural development) was 57.5 billion euros (BBC 2013).

The above-noted subsidies are "market making" – designed to increase investment and output for profit realized through product markets. An alternative would be to conceive of subsidies as "market reducing." Here, agricultural subsidies could be used to support food production for laboring classes or reducing workers' market dependence by lessening markets' role in resource allocation (see below). Complementary objectives would include facilitating more equal land ownership and ecologically sustainable use through agrarian reform, encouraging nutritious food production by supporting agricultural sector incomes.

Workers' rights

Under the contemporary corporate food regime, labor across myriad agricultural subsectors is characterized by informality and disproportionately high rates of poverty compared to other economic sectors (McMichael 2013; Akram-Lodhi 2015; Scoones 2015). Globally, alongside construction and mining, agriculture is one of the three most dangerous occupational sectors. Historically, many national agricultural sectors have often been excluded from progressive extension of workers' rights (such as minimum wages, collective bargaining or access to social services) (Hurst, Termine and Karl 2007).

Pro-capitalist green approaches (such as the EU's Green Deal) view the extension of workers' rights as complementing the establishment of legally binding property rights and better-functioning labor markets. While most progressives would welcome the establishment of basic rights where they did not previously exist, the extension of workers' rights can also be conceived in anti-market ways. First, progressives could argue for the establishment of more extensive rights than just the minimum. Some International Labour Organization (ILO) conventions provide the basis for establishing "social democratic" relations in agriculture.

ILO Convention 141 on agricultural worker's organizations obliges governments to support the "establishment and growth of strong and independent rural workers' organisations" (ILO 1975). Convention 184 and Recommendation 192 on Safety and Health in Agriculture commit governments to extending to agricultural workers the same rights and protections as enjoyed by workers in other sectors (e.g., ILO 2001).

Convention 99 on a minimum wage (for individual workers) could serve as the basis for formulating and implementing a living wage (for workers' families) across the sector. It should

> ensure that all members of the family have permanent access to quantitatively and qualitatively adequate and sufficient food, that is in conformity with the cultural traditions of the family concerned, without having to sacrifice other basic human rights, such as the right to education or to housing.
>
> *(De Schutter 2009, 7)*

The rollout of basic social democratic rights could begin undermining one of the corporate food system's principal foundations – of cheap and expendable labor – and constitute a significant encroachment onto the terrain of capital in the food system. Another way of putting this is that the costs of food production would have to be internalized and/or socialized by the agricultural system to a significantly greater extent than at present. However, such social democratic rights would be insufficient to properly encroach upon or take over capital's power in agriculture without addressing questions of land ownership.

Agrarian reform

The global concentration of land is a product of capitalist market imperatives and state support for land-based capital and imperialism (Akram-Lodhi 2015). Throughout the twentieth century, state-led agrarian reform was a key demand of the international left. From the 1990s onwards, market-led agrarian reform gained prominence among liberal circles (including the World Bank) as a means of better allocating resources and lessening market distortions in land (Lahiff et al. 2007). More recently it has become a demand of some "authoritarian populist" regimes (as in South Africa and Zimbabwe; Scoones et al. 2018), while others such as Bolsonaro are avowedly anti agrarian reform.

How would a left/socialist movement differentiate its agenda for agrarian reform from statist, liberal and authoritarian populist variants? The above-noted liberal approaches to land reform regarded it as a process potentially leading to the better operation of rural markets. Statist and some variants of authoritarian populism perceive it as a tool for shoring up stronger state control over national resources. The essence of a socialist agrarian reform would be to engender (a) the democratization of public wealth by encroaching upon the power of capital and (b) the decommodification of social life (especially food) in ways that sustain and enhance laboring class power. Such a program would be supported by the combination of redirected subsidies and enhanced workers' rights noted above. As Borras (2020), inspired by Bernstein (2010, chapter 8) and Shviji (2017) argues, part of such an agenda would be for the left to reclaim from the right the concept of community, which requires a nuanced and non-essentialist conception of class. For example, Bernstein's (ibid.) notion of classes of labor illuminates how workers depend directly *and indirectly* (i.e., through a whole host of survival strategies) upon the sale of their labor power for their daily reproduction.

Other areas that a socialist program of agrarian reform would have to address would be the preservation and protection of Indigenous lands, the transformation of large landed property into worker and community-managed and publicly owned enterprises, the establishment of community-run farms in rural and peri-urban areas, and the transformation of unused urban spaces into community-run urban gardens and agricultural units.

Decommodifying food

Even on the political right there is a dawning recognition that states must play a role in ensuring that their populations have access to sufficient and healthy food.[1] At present, however, the commodification of food (i.e., people's dependence upon incomes to buy it) discriminates against laboring classes by reducing their ability to purchase sufficient volumes of nutritious food (Guthman 2011). A program to decommodify food, perhaps through state-supported community restaurants (Selwyn 2020), could respond to such negative pressures, while maintaining a popular support base for a socialist administration.

A coping strategy for austerity-afflicted laboring classes is "substituting less costly items, cutting out more expensive items and replacing them with filling foods, sacrificing safety, taste and familiarity for volume and price" (Scott-Villiers et al. 2016, 7). Such dynamics are associated with the rise of "empty calories" and the forced under-consumption of laboring classes across the globe (Dixon 2009, 326; see Mintz 1986 for a longer historical analysis). Domestic food preparation is one of the realms through which unequal gender relations are reproduced (see Jabs and Devine 2006).

The current COVID-19 pandemic has seen ostensibly liberal governments engaging in decidedly non-liberal actions such as ensuring workers receive pay even while not working.

Witness the UK government's "eat out to help out" subsidy scheme during August 2020 (Rayner 2020). Under these circumstances a program of state subsidies to establish community restaurants serving free and cheap food does not seem so far-fetched. How would a socialist GND differentiate itself from avowedly anti-socialist policies that, on the surface, appear to represent attempts at decommodifying social life? Part of the answer is that socialist decommodification would aim to reduce, continually, workers' market dependence, leading to a situation where the latter no longer function as central resource allocators in society.

Agroecology

Virtually all green visions wax lyrical about (or at least pay lip-service to) the benefits of a more "natural" approach to agriculture, where chemical inputs are replaced by more "organic" techniques. Agroecological principles include the reliance upon biodiversity to regulate and reproduce ecosystems; multifunctional (diverse) agricultural systems such as polycultures to safeguard the human–nature metabolic interaction and provide diverse food sources; and use of traditional knowledge (including farmer innovations and technologies; Rosset and Altieri 2017). Aspects of agroecology include agroforestry; facilitating, building and conserving soil fertility; using biological controls for diseases, insects and weeds; intercropping, seed saving and selection; smaller-scale multiple harvesting cycles; and the integration of small-scale pasturing and grazing (Weis 2010, 334; see also chapter by LaDuke, this volume).

As Rosset and Altieri (2017) note, however, agroecology is now a buzzword within international institutions, where practices such as CSA are promoted as embodying agroecological principles. They also note that agroecology is more than a set of techniques, and that it entails shifts in scale (smaller-sized farms), scope (more varied cropping systems) and provenance of inputs (respect for, and greater reliance upon local/historical knowledge), all of which generate greater equity in land ownership and power throughout the food system.

Can agroecology feed the world? The Ten Years for Agroecology (TYFA 2018) research exercise has modeled how a future EU could increase food production and reduce food imports through the adoption of agroecological methods, to the extent that it would be able to feed Europe's projected population of approximately 530 million people. It recognizes that yields would fall as a consequence of the phase-out of chemical inputs but shows how this would be more than compensated by reallocation of land away from feed crops and livestock toward food crops (Food, Farming and Countryside Commission 2019). Similarly, for the USA, the Rodale Institute's Farming Systems Trial found that agroecological methods can reduce direct use of fossil fuel inputs in agricultural production, enable organic agriculture to play a role in carbon sequestration, and maintain high crop yields (Lasalle and Hepperly 2008, 5).

However, these scenarios depend upon a different system of land use where the industrial grain and livestock complex (Weis 2007) shrinks and yields hectarage to agroecological production. This means that green recovery plans, such as the European Green Deal, which do not aim to confront the mega-power of the industrial food system, cannot easily claim to support an extensive rollout of agroecological production.

Beyond the power of industrial agriculture, there lies the issue of the divisions of labor that agroecological farming would engender. There is a tendency on the left to suggest that an eco-socialist agricultural system would increase labor intensity and the numbers working in agriculture.[2] For example, Naomi Klein (2011) argues that sustainable agriculture "is much more labor intensive than industrial agriculture, which means that farming can once again be a substantial source of employment." And Tony Weis (2010, 334) holds that "Agricultural systems must be vastly more labour intensive and biodiverse....There is no substitute for skillful and dense human labour, decentralized agricultural knowledge and careful, passionate stewardship."

So, would a socialist GND for agriculture (or any agroecological GND for that matter) entail an increase in labor intensity in farming? In a socio-economic system where workers' wages are necessary for the purchase of subsistence goods, it may be that greater labor intensity in farming represents a path to full employment. This may be especially so under COVID-19 conditions and looming mass unemployment. However, a program for a socialist transformation – based upon decommodification of social life, equalization of class relations and social production for workers' needs – could propose wide-ranging substitution of labor by technology designed to reduce the working day to the minimum (across all economic sectors), thereby increasing time for democratic participation and leisure (Selwyn 2018; Bastani 2019; Huber 2019).

Technology

Under capitalism, new technologies, even when they have the potential to reduce or eliminate human drudgery, are often applied in ways that increase labor exploitation (Braverman 1998). So where would technology fit into a vision of socialist transformation? Certainly, the technological determinism of some strands of Marxism (in particular Stalinism) represent more the stagism of modernization theory than any conception of human emancipation through changed social relations. More pressingly, technology-based solutions, if not married to a strategy of reduced economic growth, risk exacerbating climate breakdown (Paterson 2007). The Jevons paradox illuminates how efficiency gains and reduced costs of use (e.g., of coal in his day, but potentially of green technology in ours) increase the rate of use of a given technology.

But there are technologies that could be deployed under changed (and contributing to further changing) social relations that could meet the socialist criteria of providing healthy food for laboring classes, reducing the work-effort required for their production and simultaneously healing the metabolic rift.

A potentially world-changing solution is being developed by a small company, Solar Foods, funded by the European Space Agency's business incubation program (Monbiot 2018; Solar Foods 2018). The company produces a wheat flour-like compound called Solein, with a 50%–60% protein, 5%–10% fat and 20%–25% carbohydrate content. It is made using electricity from solar panels to electrolyze water (splitting water cells) in a bioreactor (similar to a fermentation tank for beer) to create hydrogen. The hydrogen is then combined with carbon dioxide and other nutrients (phosphorus, sodium and potassium) and soil-derived microbes. Producing Solein, it is claimed, requires 20,000 times less land than for the same amount of soy-based food. It can substitute for protein in processed foods, could replace animal fodder, and could produce palm oil substitutes. Solein has the potential to vastly reduce humanity's reliance upon land-based grain-crop farming, thereby freeing up land for other activities (see below).

Automation of food production through hydroponics (growing plants without soil) in vertical farms is another potential transformative boon. Vertical farms could be established in unused or newly constructed high-rise urban buildings or built in rural areas (Despommier 2009). Such techniques have reportedly enabled the production of greens (lettuce and herbs) using up to 90% less water while yielding 30 times more crops per acre of land than some forms of land-based farming (Smith 2018). In other cases, soilless hydroponics have led to four- to five-fold yield increases of tomatoes and cucumbers compared to soil cultures (Resh 2012, 8). Technological advances combined with strategically directed finance could enable such investments to be combined with solar-generating energy (either directly through photovoltaic panels built onto the vertical farms) and/or through a solar powered national grid.

Computerization and robotization can potentially raise the productivity of land-based farming while reducing the labor burden. Agro-robots are capable of identifying and using lasers to destroy 800 different types of weeds, hugely reducing the need for chemical fertilizers. Soon they could map the land, plant seeds, weed and harvest crops (Harris 2018).

Whether or not such technologies are put to good use for laboring classes and planet or for a new phase of "green" corporate agriculture is a political question. While some advocates of agroecology do not engage with the human development potential of high-tech (Altieri and Nichols 2020), this seems to be an obvious area for research and politics for advocates of a socialist transition.

Rewilding

Agrarian reform, replacing the industrial grain and livestock complex with increasingly plant-based agriculture, and new technologies have the potential to liberate vast tracks of land for reforestation/rewilding to sequester atmospheric carbon. Most GNDs/Green recovery programs advocate a degree of nature preservation, and the debate is not whether, but how much, and how to preserve natural environments?

Even in the relatively population-dense UK, there is land available for such projects. For example, 1.3 million hectares in England, Scotland and Wales are covered by grouse moor estates, and 1.8 million hectares in Scotland are comprised of deer stalking estates (Rewilding Britain 2019, 11). With a shift away from livestock and feed crop production, still more land would become available. In the UK, "supporting native woodland re-establishment, the restoration and protection of peatbogs and heaths, and species-rich grasslands over a total of 6 million hectares...could sequester 47 million tonnes of CO_2 per year," which is more than a tenth of current UK greenhouse gas emissions (Rewilding Britain 2019, 4). The cost of such an endeavor would be approximately £1.9 billion (compared to the current £3 billion of the UK's Common Agricultural Policy subsidies) (Ibid.).

E.O. Wilson's (2017) "Half-Earth" proposal – where 50% of the planet's surface area is dedicated to nature – is an influential iteration of this theme which highlights strengths and weaknesses of rewilding under existing capitalist social relations. Wilson's arguments do not address how humanity would exist in half-earth urban environments. Nor do they identify capitalism's dynamics of endless accumulation and economic growth as the prime cause of climate breakdown. Further, they risk generating mass social displacement of people to make way for "nature" (Napoletano 2018). Surprisingly perhaps, Wilson's ideas have been taken up by some on the left, who propose that compulsory veganism (leading to the elimination of the industrial grain and livestock complex) would free up the necessary land (Vettesse 2018). Such solutions highlight the authoritarian risks associated with rewilding programs.

From a socialist perspective, rewilding could occur through agrarian reform and incorporating private land into public democratic spheres, in conjunction with, for example, agroecological food systems such as agroforestry. The metabolic rift entails the privatization of the land and its subjection to the demands of competitive capitalist accumulation. Rewilding could contribute to overcome this rift, through common ownership of the land and its use for public leisure and environmental education.

Urban greening and agriculture

Healing the metabolic rift requires, in part, overcoming the damage done to laboring classes and to the environment by the urban-rural divide. Urban greening – the establishment of "public landscaping and urban forestry projects that create mutually beneficial relationships between city dwellers and their environments" – represents a potential first step (Capital Roots 2020).

Urban agriculture also has some potential to contribute to a socialist GND for agriculture. However, there are potential dangers here too. Prince Charles is an advocate of increased food self-provision, though hardly a socialist! Cuba's experience – where urban agriculture restored national calorie intake to the levels prior to Russia's collapse – is admirable. However, assuming that its successes can be replicated in any socialist transition is unduly risky. Rather, given the technological potential for new forms of farming noted above, urban agriculture could perform an altogether different role in a socialist transition (Altieri et al. 1999; Ewing 2008).

In a context of reducing working hours brought about by redistributive degrowth, the establishment of urban agricultural centers could generate novel social opportunities. Urban agricultural extension services can offer training and assistance to those who want to participate in urban gardening. Such services can be coordinated with public health bodies and community restaurants to produce seasonal and healthy foods. Education services (for all ages) can be partially reoriented to include training in healthy food production.

More generally, changes to urban land use would make urban living more pleasant, and could, for example, generate dynamic new opportunities for environmental education for children and adults alike. Unused buildings can be transformed into greenhouses; flat roofs can be used as new growing spaces; unnecessary roads can be transformed into fields, allotments and parks; and home and public gardening will be encouraged and facilitated through provision of inputs, technologies and permaculture education (see Trainer 1996, 139).

Conclusions

The collective barbarism of environmental collapse, climate breakdown and pandemic is now afflicting ever-greater numbers of the world's population, and will increase if capitalism is not limited in its expansionary drive and ultimately transcended. The longer the current trajectory continues, the more radical any response will have to be if it is to have any chance of succeeding.

This chapter shows how capitalist agro-industry is a major contributor to climate breakdown. Contrary to free market mythology, global agro-industry is reliant upon a four-fold subsidy regime comprised of: the externalization of environmental use and degradation, cheap fossil fuel inputs, massive direct subsidies and a higher degree of labor exploitation than in other economic sectors. The case for a socialist GND for agriculture is that while these subsidies can be reversed, and new relations (between humans, and between humans and nature) can be established through innovative state policies, doing so will require a shattering blow to the political economic infrastructure upon which capitalist agro-industry depends.

The agricultural component of a GND will be key to any socialist transformation because food represents one of the most fundamental human requirements and, under capitalism, one of the most basic wage goods. To transform this wage good from a commodity produced for profit to a decommodified social right is to transform social life more generally.

The core argument advanced in this chapter is that transcending the metabolic rift – the damaging set of relations between humans and nature derived from capitalism's core dynamics of competition and exploitation – requires a socialist GND. The latter simultaneously aims to forestall climate breakdown through a profound transformation of social relations. Such a transformation must be one based upon redistributive, rather than growth-based human development, the decommodification of social life and the equalization of class relations.

Notes

1 Witness the UK Conservative government's belated attempts to tackle rising levels of obesity (Boseley 2020).
2 The remainder of this paragraph draws on Huber (2019b).

References

Akram-Lodhi, A.H. 2015. Accelerating towards food sovereignty. *Third World Quarterly*. 36(3), 563–583.
Altieri, M.A. et al. 1999. The greening of the "barrios": Urban agriculture for food security in Cuba. *Agriculture and Human Values*. 16(2), 131–140.
Altieri, M.A. and Nicholls, C.I. 2020. Agroecology and the reconstruction of a post-COVID-19 agriculture. *The Journal of Peasant Studies*. 47(5), 881–898.
Bastani, A. 2019. *Fully automated luxury communism*. London: Verso Books.
BBC. 2013. Q&A: Reform of EU farm policy. 13 July. Available from: https://www.bbc.co.uk/news/world-europe-11216061
Berlan, J.P. 1991. "The Historical Roots of the Present Agricultural Crisis." In *Towards a New Political Economy of Agriculture*, edited by W. Friedland, L. Busch, F. Buttel, and A. Rudy, 115–136. Boulder, CO: Westview.
Bernard, B. and Lux, A. 2017. How to feed the world sustainably: An overview of the discourse on agroecology and sustainable intensification. *Regional Environmental Change*. 17(5), 1279–1290.
Bernstein, H. 2010. *Class dynamics of Agrarian change*. Boulder, CO: Kumarian Press.
Binns, P. and Gonzalez, M. 1980. Cuba, Castro and socialism. *International Socialism Journal*. 2(8), 1–36.
Borras Jr., S.M. 2020. Agrarian social movements: The absurdly difficult but not impossible agenda of defeating right-wing populism and exploring a socialist future. *Journal of Agrarian Change*. 20(1), 3–36.
Boseley, S. 2020. New UK obesity plan fails to address underlying problems. *The Guardian*. 27 July. Available from: https://www.theguardian.com/society/2020/jul/27/new-uk-obesity-plan-fails-to-address-underlying-problems
Bozuwa, J. 2019. The politics and potential of the Green New Deal. *IPPR Progressive Review*. 26(1), 39–50.
Branford, S. 2011. The great global land grab. In: M. Gerwin, ed. *Food and democracy*. Krakow: Polish Green Network. pp. 79–82. Available from: https://aa.ecn.cz/img_upload/b397cb5367c764a2f19867d8032c9d0c/Food_and_Democracy.pdf
Braverman, H. 1998. *Labor and Monopoly Capital: The Degradation of Work in the Twentieth Century*. New York: NYU Press.
Capital Roots. 2020. Urban greening: Planting green communities. Available from: https://www.capitalroots.org/programs/urban-greening/urban-greening1/
Carrington, D. 2018. Global food system is broken, say world's science academies. *The Guardian*. 28 November. Available from: https://www.theguardian.com/environment/2018/nov/28/global-food-system-is-broken-say-worlds-science-academies
Case, P. 2014. Only 100 harvests left in UK farm soils, scientists warn. *Farmers Weekly*. 21 October. Available from: https://www.fwi.co.uk/news/only-100-harvests-left-in-uk-farm-soils-scientists-warn
Cassella, C. 2018. When the fossil fuel industry pops, it will be way bigger than the 2008 financial crisis. *Science Alert*. 5 June. Available from: https://www.sciencealert.com/fossil-fuel-industry-pops-way-bigger-than-2008-financial-crisis-renewable-energy
Clapp, J., Newell, P. and Brent, Z.W. 2018. The global political economy of climate change, agriculture and food systems. *The Journal of Peasant Studies*. 45(1), 80–88.

Cliff, T. 1996. *State capitalism in Russia*. London: Bookmarks.

Coady, D., Parry, I., Sears, L. and Shang, B. 2017. How large are global fossil fuel subsidies? *World development*. 91, 11–27.

Collier, P. 2008. The politics of hunger: How illusion and greed fan the food crisis. *Foreign Affairs* 87(6), 67–79.

Davis, M. 2006. *The monster at our door: The global threat of avian flu*. Toledo: Owl Books.

De Schutter, O. 2009. Report of the Special Rapporteur on the right to food: Agribusiness and the right to food. United Nations. Available from: http://www.srfood.org/images/stories/pdf/officialreports/20100305_a-hrc-13-33_agribusiness_en.pdf

Despommier, D. 2009. The rise of vertical farms. *Scientific American*. 301(5), 80–87.

Dixon, J. 2009. From the imperial to the empty calorie: How nutrition relations underpin food regime transitions. *Agriculture and Human Values*. 26(4), 321.

Eat Lancet Commission. 2019. *Healthy diets from sustainable food systems*. Available from: https://eatforum.org/content/uploads/2019/07/EATLancet_Commission_Summary_Report.pdf

Esping-Andersen, G. 1990. *The three worlds of welfare capitalism*. Princeton: Princeton University Press.

Ewing, E. 2008. Cuba's organic revolution. *The Guardian*. 4 April. Available from: https://www.theguardian.com/environment/2008/apr/04/organics.food

FAO. 2010. *"Climate-Smart" Agriculture*. Food and Agriculture Organization of the United Nations. Available from: https://www.fao.org/3/i1881e/i1881e.pdf

FAO. 2012. *Livestock and landscapes*. Food and Agriculture Organization of the United Nations. Available from: http://www.fao.org/3/ar591e/ar591e.pdf

FAO, IFAD, UNICEF, WFP and WHO. 2019. *The state of food security and nutrition in the World 2019. Safeguarding against economic slowdowns and downturns*. Rome: FAO.

Food and Land Use Coalition. 2019. *Growing better: Ten critical transitions to transform food and land use*. Available from: https://www.foodandlandusecoalition.org/wp-content/uploads/2019/09/FOLU-GrowingBetter-GlobalReport.pdf

Food, Farming and Countryside Commission. 2009. *Our future in the land*. Available from: file://smb-home.uscs.susx.ac.uk/bs94/Downloads/Report-rsa-ffcc-our-future-in-the-land%20(4).pdf

Foster, J.B. 1999. Marx's theory of metabolic rift: Classical foundations for environmental sociology. *American Journal of Sociology*. 105(2), 366–405.

Garnett, T. et al. 2017. *Grazed and confused? Ruminating on cattle, grazing systems, methane, nitrous oxide, the soil carbon sequestration question-and what it all means for greenhouse gas emissions*. Oxford: FCRN.

Global Agriculture. 2020. *Hunger in times of plenty*. Available from: https://www.globalagriculture.org/report-topics/hunger-in-times-of-plenty.html

Gore, T. 2015. *Extreme carbon inequality: Why the Paris climate deal must put the poorest, lowest emitting and most vulnerable people first*. London: Oxfam.

Green New Deal Group. 2020. *Green New Deal Group*. Available from: https://greennewdealgroup.org/

Guthman, J. 2011. *Weighing in: Obesity, food justice, and the limits of capitalism*. Berkeley: University of California Press.

Harris, N. 1978. *The mandate of heaven: Marx and Mao in Modern China*. London: Quartet.

Harris, J. 2018. "We'll have space bots with lasers, killing plants": The rise of the robot farmer. *The Guardian*. 20 October. Available from: https://www.theguardian.com/environment/2018/oct/20/space-robots-lasers-rise-robot-farmer

Hawksworth, J. and Chan, D. 2015. *The World in 2050: Will the shift in global economic power continue?* PriceWaterhouseCoopers. Available from: https://www.pwc.com/gx/en/issues/the-economy/assets/world-in-2050-february-2015.pdf

Higgins, P. 2012. *Eradicating ecocide*. London: Shepheard Walwyn (Publishers), Ltd.

Huber, M. 2019a. Ecological politics for the working class. *Catalyst*. 3(1), 1–29.

Huber, M. 2019b. Ecosocialism: Dystopian and scientific. *Socialist Forum*. Available from: https://socialistforum.dsausa.org/issues/winter-2019/ecosocialism-dystopian-and-scientific/

Hurst, P., Termine, P. and Karl, M. 2007. *Agricultural workers and their contribution to sustainable agriculture and rural development*. ILO, FAO, IUF. Available from: http://agris.fao.org/agris-search/search.do?recordID=GB2013203664

Intergovernmental Science-Policy Platform on Biodiversity and Ecosystem Services. 2019. *Global assessment report on biodiversity and ecosystem services*. Available from: https://www.ipbes.net/global-assessment-report-biodiversity-ecosystem-services

International Labour Organization. 1975. *Rural Workers' Organisations Convention, 1975 (No. 141)*. Available from: https://www.ilo.org/dyn/normlex/en/f?p=NORMLEXPUB:12100:0::NO::P12100_ILO_CODE:C141

International Labour Organization. 2001. *C184: Safety and Health in Agriculture Convention, 2001*. Available from: https://www.ilo.org/dyn/normlex/de/f?p=NORMLEXPUB:12100:0::NO::P12100_INSTRUMENT_ID:312329

IPCC. 2018. *Global Warming of 1.5 °C: Summary for Policymakers*. Available from: https://www.ipcc.ch/site/assets/uploads/sites/2/2019/05/SR15_SPM_version_report_LR.pdf

Jabs, J. and Devine, C.M. 2006. Time scarcity and food choices: An overview. *Appetite*. 47(2), 196–204.

Kenner, D. 2019. *Carbon inequality: The role of the richest in climate change*. London: Routledge.

Keucheyan, R. 2016. *Nature is a battlefield: Towards a political ecology*. Cambridge: Wiley.

Klein, N. 2007. *The Shock doctrine: The rise of disaster capitalism*. London: Macmillan.

Klein, N. 2011. Capitalism vs climate. *The Nation*. Available from: https://www.thenation.com/article/capitalism-vs-climate/

KPMG. 2012. *Expect the unexpected: Building business value in a changing world*. Amstelveen: KPMG International Cooperative. Available from: https://assets.kpmg/content/dam/kpmg/pdf/2012/08/building-business-value-part-1.pdf.

Lahiff, E., Borras Jr., S.M. and Kay, C. 2007. Market-led Agrarian reform: Policies, performance and prospects. *Third World Quarterly*. 28(8), 1417–1436.

Lang, T. and Heasman, M. 2004. *Food wars*. London: Earthscan.

LaSalle, T. J., and Hepperly, P. 2008. *Regenerative organic farming: A solution to global warming*. Rodale Institute.

Lebowitz, M. 2010. *The socialist alternative: Real human development*. New York: NYU Press.

Lievens, M. 2010. Towards an eco-marxism. *Radical Philosophy Review*. 13(1), 1–17.

Marx, K. 1981. *Capital, Vol. 3*. New York: Vintage.

Marx, K. 1990. *Capital: A critique of political economy, Vol.1*. London: Penguin.

Marx, K. 1993. *Grundrisse*. London: Penguin.

Mazoyer, M. and Roudart, L. 2007. *A history of world agriculture: From the neolithic age to the current crisis*. Routledge.

McMichael, P. 2013. *Food regimes and agrarian questions: Agrarian change and peasant studies*. Nova Scotia, Canada: Fernwood Publishing.

Mintz, S.W. 1986. *Sweetness and power: The place of sugar in modern history*. London: Penguin.

Monbiot, G. 2018. Electric food – the new sci-fi diet that could save our planet. *The Guardian*. 31 October. Available from: https://www.theguardian.com/commentisfree/2018/oct/31/electric-food-sci-fi-diet-planet-food-animals-environment

Montgomery, D.R. 2017. *Growing a revolution: Bringing our soil back to life*. New York: W.W. Norton & Company.

Moore, J.W. 2015. *Capitalism in the web of life: Ecology and the accumulation of capital*. London: Verso Books.

Napoletano, B. 2018. Half-earth: A biodiversity 'solution' that solves nothing. *Climate and Capitalism*. Available from: https://climateandcapitalism.com/2018/10/02/half-earth-a-biodiversity-solution-that-solves-nothing/

National Farm Worker Ministry. 2010. Low wages. Available from: http://nfwm.org/resources/low-wages/

Partington, R. 2020. UK should prioritise green projects to kickstart economy, says IMF. *The Guardian*. Available from: https://www.theguardian.com/business/2020/jul/02/uk-should-prioritise-green-projects-to-kickstart-economy-says-imf

Patel, R. 2013. The long green revolution. *The Journal of Peasant Studies*. 40(1), 1–63.

Patel, R. and Goodman, J. 2020. The long new deal. *The Journal of Peasant Studies*. 47(3), 431–463.

Paterson, M. 2007. *Automobile politics: Ecology and cultural political economy*. Cambridge: Cambridge University Press.

Polanyi, K. 2001. *The great transformation: The political and economic origins of our time*. Boston, MA: Beacon Press.

PricewaterhouseCoopers (PWC). 2015. *The World in 2050: Will the shift in global economic power continue?* Available from: https://www.pwc.com/gx/en/issues/the-economy/assets/world-in-2050-february-2015.pdf

Rapidtransition.org. 2019. The post-Cold War Cuban food experiment. Available from: https://www.rapidtransition.org/stories/the-post-cold-war-cuban-food-experiment/

Rayner, G. 2020. Sunak mini-budget shifts coronavirus agenda to economy as crisis spending hits £188bn. *Daily Telegraph*. Available from: https://www.telegraph.co.uk/politics/2020/07/08/rishi-sunak-shifts-covid-agenda-economy-mini-budget-crisis-spending/

Resh, H.M. 2012. *Hydroponic food production: A definitive guidebook for the advanced home gardener and the commercial hydroponic grower*. Santa Barbara: CRC Press.

Rewilding Britain. 2019. *Rewilding and climate breakdown: How restoring nature can help decarbonise the UK*. Available from: https://s3.eu-west-2.amazonaws.com/assets.rewildingbritain.org.uk/documents/Rewilding-and-Climate-Breakdown-a-report-by-Rewilding-Britain.pdf

Rosset, P.M. and Altieri, M.A. 2017. *Agroecology: Science and politics*. Warwickshire: Practical Action Publishing.

Rossman, P. 2012. Food workers' rights as a path to a low carbon agriculture. In: N. Räthzel and D. Uzzell, eds. *Trade unions in the green economy*. Milton Park, NY: Routledge. pp. 74–79.

Sanders, B. 2019. *The Green New Deal*. Bernie Sanders. Available from: https://berniesanders.com/en/issues/green-new-deal/

Scoones, I. 2015. *Sustainable livelihoods and rural development*. Rugby, UK: Practical Action Publishing.

Scoones, I., Edelman, M., Borras Jr., S.M., Hall, R., Wolford, W. and White, B. 2018. Emancipatory rural politics: Confronting authoritarian populism. *The Journal of Peasant Studies*. 45(1), 1–20.

Scott-Villiers, P., Chisholm, N., Wanjiku Kelbert, A., and Hossain, N. 2016. *Precarious lives: Food, work and care after the global food crisis*. Brighton: IDS.

Selwyn, B. 2018. A manifesto for socialist development in the 21st century. *Economic and Political Weekly*. 53(36), 47–55.

Selwyn, B. 2020. *Community restaurants: Decommodifying food as socialist strategy*. Socialist Register 2021. New York: Merlin Press.

Selwyn, B. 2021. Community restaurants: Decommodifying food as socialist strategy. *Socialist Register 2021*. 57. New York: Merlin Press.

Settele, J., Díaz, S., Brondizio, E., and Daszak, P. 2020. COVID-19 Stimulus Measures must save lives, protect livelihoods, and safeguard nature to reduce the risk of future pandemics. *The intergovernmental science-policy platform on biodiversity and ecosystem services*. Available from: https://ipbes.net/covid19stimulus

Seymour, R. 2019. What's the deal with the Green New Deal? *MR Online*. Available from: https://mronline.org/2019/04/27/whats-the-deal-with-the-green-new-deal/

Shivji, I. 2017. The concept of 'working people'. *Agrarian South: Journal of Political Economy*. 6(1), 1–13.

Smith, N. 2018. America's first autonomous robot farm replaces humans with 'incredibly intelligent' machines. *The Guardian*. 8 October. Available from: https://www.theguardian.com/us-news/2018/oct/08/robot-farm-iron-ox-california

Solar Foods. 2018. *Solein: Food out of thin air*. Available from: https://solarfoods.fi/

Spratt, D. and Dunlop, I. 2019. Existential climate-related security risk: A scenario approach. *Breakthrough – National Centre for climate restoration*. Available from: https://docs.wixstatic.com/ugd/148cb0_a1406e0143ac4c469196d3003bc1e687.pdf

Stern, N. 2007. *The economics of climate change: The Stern review*. Cambridge: Cambridge University Press.

Stiglitz, J. 2019. The climate crisis is our third world war. It needs a bold response. *The Guardian*. 4 June. Available from: https://www.theguardian.com/commentisfree/2019/jun/04/climate-change-world-war-iii-green-new-deal

Taylor, M. 2018. Climate-smart agriculture: What is it good for? *The Journal of Peasant Studies*. 45(1), 89–107.

Taylor, M. 2019. Labour members launch green new deal inspired by US activists. *The Guardian*. 22 March. Available from: https://www.theguardian.com/politics/2019/mar/22/labour-members-launch-green-new-deal-inspired-by-us-activists

United Nations. 1948. *United Nations Declaration of Human Rights*. Available from: http://www.claiminghumanrights.org/udhr_article_25.html#at27

Vettese, T. 2018. Vettese: To freeze the thames. *New Left Review*. 111, 63–86.

Wallace, R. 2020. Coronavirus: Agribusiness would risk millions of deaths [interview]. *Marx21*. Available from: www.marx21.de/coronavirus-agribusiness-would-risk-millions-of-deaths

Wanner, T. 2015. The new 'passive revolution' of the green economy and growth discourse: Maintaining the 'sustainable development' of neoliberal capitalism. *New Political Economy*. 20(1), 21–41.

Weis, T. 2007. *The global food economy: The battle for the future of farming.* London: Zed Books.
Weis, T. 2010. The accelerating biophysical contradictions of industrial capitalist agriculture. *Journal of Agrarian Change.* 10(3), 315–341.
Weis, T. 2013. *The ecological hoofprint: The global burden of industrial livestock.* London: Zed Books.
World Bank. 2015. *Ending poverty and hunger by 2030: An agenda for the global food system.* Washington, DC: World Bank.
Zehner, O. 2012. *Green illusions: The dirty secrets of clean energy and the future of environmentalism.* Lincoln, Nebraska: University of Nebraska Press.

6

WORKTIME REDUCTION AND THE GREEN NEW DEAL[1]

Juliet B. Schor and Kyla Tienhaara

Introduction

> Shorter working hours would not only be good for the economy, but they are going to be crucial for boosting mental health and tackling climate change. A four-day week would signal a critical shift in the design of our economies towards the wellbeing of people and nature, as we prioritise the urgent need to bring down carbon emissions to safe levels.
>
> *(Ryle et al. 2020)*

The COVID-19 pandemic has provided an opportunity to rethink work, not only in terms of where work is done, but also how much of it is done. Seizing this opportunity could improve the lives of many and increase the chances of avoiding catastrophic climate change. Academics and the media alike have underscored the benefits of remote work (or "teleworking") over the course of the pandemic. Teleworking reduces commuting, which frees up time and potentially results in significant reductions in greenhouse gas emissions (GHGs) (Morrisette, Deng and Messacar 2021). Public pronouncements from companies and worker surveys suggest that remote work is both successful and popular (Barrero, Bloom and Davis 2021; PWC 2021; Strack et al. 2021).

The shift to teleworking in 2020–2021 was global in scale (albeit limited to certain sectors) and largely involuntary. By contrast, experiments to reduce working time have been localized and intentional. However, they too have been broadly popular (Liu 2020; Pinsker 2021). Beginning in 2015, 2,500 city and national government employees in Iceland transitioned to 35- or 36-hour workweeks with successful results on productivity, stress, and well-being (Haraldsson and Kellam 2021). Large and small firms have also experimented with worktime reductions. Microsoft conducted a highly successful trial in Japan in 2019 (Paul 2019), and Unilever began a yearlong pilot of a four-day week in New Zealand in December 2020 (Kelly 2020). These experiments are now receiving greater attention as governments and businesses assess how to reduce unemployment post-pandemic. New Zealand's Prime Minister Jacinda Ardern and Scotland's First Minister Nicola Sturgeon both support the four-day week. A three-year trial of a four-day workweek (with government incentives

 DOI: 10.4324/9781003110880-8

for firms that participate) will soon launch in Spain, and a six-month pilot project (with government funding for research on the economic, social and environmental impacts) will begin in Ireland in January 2022 (Fox 2021). In Japan, economic policy guidelines released by the government in 2021 include a recommendation that companies permit their staff to opt to work only four days a week (Westfall 2021).

As with teleworking, reductions in working hours can have environmental benefits, including cutting GHGs. If properly designed, worktime reduction can also reduce income inequality. Thus, worktime reduction policies appear to be a natural fit with the objectives of green new deal proposals. While a number of scholars and non-profits that research and advocate for worktime reduction have called for inclusion of such policies in green new deals, there has not been substantial uptake of this idea from green new deal advocates themselves (an exception is the Green New Deal for Europe campaign, discussed below). In this chapter, we argue for more serious consideration of worktime reduction in green new deals alongside policies such as the job guarantee (see further chapter by Robinson, this volume).

We situate our argument within the broader debate about economic growth and green new deals. We advocate an agnostic stance, or what Jeroen van den Bergh has termed a-growth (van den Bergh 2011). A-growth abandons the presumption of growth and regards it as a means rather than an end. This is not a particularly radical position as even mainstream economic theory is agnostic about growth. In the standard model, the optimal rate of growth depends on workers' preferences for goods and leisure. If workers prefer to take their productivity growth in the form of shorter hours, the labor market equilibrates with fewer hours supplied. Indeed, mainstream economists lack an analytic rationale for taking an unquestioning attitude to growth. Even Marxist economists, who certainly adopt a firm-level growth imperative, have less argument for growth in the aggregate. We know that some capitalist countries have operated with low or near-zero growth for extended periods of time. Population trends are also relevant to aggregate growth rates. Almost half the global population (48%) lives in countries with sub-replacement fertility, including all of the European Union (EU), the United States, China, Russia, Brazil, and Japan (UNDESA 2017).

Agnosticism with respect to growth requires that we start with the goals of economic and climate policy, and then determine what level of GDP growth is compatible with them. Some climate scientists suggest a "brutal" answer to that question (Anderson 2012). In the Global North, required emissions reductions are far beyond what has been achieved to date, particularly once carbon embedded in imports and exports is included. Given that global emissions need to fall by more than 7% a year through 2030 (UNEP 2019), and that rich countries' required levels are significantly above that rate, double-digit emissions reductions are in order for those who can afford them. As we explain further in the next section, under this requirement, feasible GDP growth is likely at zero or below. In other words, what rich countries need to do is "power down," or "degrow," i.e., engineer a reduction of the material size of the global economy alongside a radical redistribution of resources. It's important to note that this is a conclusion that's relevant to the wealthy nations of the Global North. While Global South countries must also achieve massive emissions reductions, the degrowth paradigm is typically directed at the rich.

Several prominent green new deal advocates have written about the need to transcend a preoccupation with economic growth. Klein (2019) argues for a green new deal that doesn't just improve the efficiency of the economy but also reduces "the amount of material stuff that the wealthiest 20 percent of people on the planet consume." Aronoff et al. (2019) take the view that while a green new deal may lead to growth in the short term to jumpstart the necessary transformation of the economy, this should not be a long-term objective. Pettifor's

(2019) vision for a green new deal also resoundingly rejects growth (although she eschews the term "degrowth," arguing that it reinforces the growth framing) and instead sets out a plan for a steady-state economy. Furthermore, one of the ten pillars of the Green New Deal for Europe campaign is "ending the dogma of endless growth" (GNDE n.d.). Degrowth is not an alternative to conventional energy policies such as the shift to clean renewables and improvements in energy efficiency, which are the core of virtually all climate policies, including nearly all green new deals. Rather, it builds on changes in energy use with additional elements such as a job guarantee, worktime reduction and wealth/luxury taxes. Furthermore, contrary to the position espoused by some opponents of degrowth, these policies are popular and may be crucial to achieving political support for a green new deal.

Although Mastini, Kallis and Hickel (2021, 7) acknowledge that some of the more "radical" green new deal proposals reject growth and that there are areas of convergence between green new deal and degrowth visions, they also see "tensions…that some may find irreconcilable." One of these tensions is the "more statist spirit" of a green new deal with an "emphasis on top-down action" which "does not sit necessarily easily with degrowth's emphasis on bottom-up actions and prefigurative, grassroots politics" (ibid.). We argue in this chapter that worktime reduction policies can bridge the statist/top-down approach of a green new deal with the bottom-up grassroots approach of degrowth. We suggest that government support for (or mandating of) a four-day working week opens up possibilities for expanding the low-impact living approaches championed by the degrowth movement.

The debate about growth and the Green New Deal

Many proposals for green new deals have emerged around the world since February 2019, when Congresswoman Alexandria Ocasio-Cortez (AOC) and Senator Ed Markey first put forward their Green New Deal resolution in the US Congress (H. Res. 109, 2019). These proposals share some common features. They are all rooted in a shift to non-carbon energy sources and investments to increase energy efficiency, and often also include some recognition of the need for a "just transition" for fossil-fuel-dependent workers and communities. There's also general agreement that poor countries cannot be asked to bear the burden of emissions reductions any more than is absolutely necessary. However, while these aspects of green new deals are standard and widely accepted as necessary, there is a debate over whether they are sufficient. Put differently, proponents of green new deals differ on whether the magnitude of required emissions reductions can be achieved while leaving the basic structures of the economy unchanged. In particular, some who see value in a green new deal framework question whether achieving the demanding emissions reductions that are required is compatible with high levels of economic growth in the Global North.

We would argue that while the AOC–Markey resolution was short on policy specifics, it is significant that it does not start from the premise of GDP growth. Instead, it starts with goals for decarbonization (set by science) and human needs. However, Mastini et al. (2021, 5) contend that it is nevertheless "implicit in the text" that the Green New Deal will promote growth. Furthermore, as Hickel (2021a) points out, the Green New Deal has been "picked up and repackaged by some media pundits" into a more standard green growth message that "transitioning to clean energy will liberate capitalism from any concerns about ecology." Indeed, green new deals in other parts of the world, such as the European Green Deal (see chapter by Adler and Wargan, this volume) and the Korean New Deal (see chapter by Tienhaara, Yun and Gunderson, this volume) are explicit in viewing investments in renewable energy and other "green" sectors as a mechanism to increase GDP growth.

Some prominent academic proponents of a (global) green new deal also see economic growth as critical in terms of both achieving decarbonization targets and galvanizing political support for the project. Nobel Prize-winning economist Joseph Stiglitz (2020, 105), for example, notes:

> The Green New Deal is not only affordable and not only would we save money by acting on it now but it would actually be *good* for the economy. The war on climate change, if correctly waged, would benefit the country in the same way that World War II set the stage for America's golden economic era, with the fastest rate of growth in its history amid shared prosperity.

Pollin (2018) also centers growth – specifically "egalitarian green growth" – in his vision for a green new deal.

Those who advocate for green growth assume that absolute decoupling of emissions from GDP is possible in a timeframe that would allow us to avoid dangerous climate change. However, a large body of research indicates little support for this assumption. A major study of decoupling by Jorgenson and Clark (2012), analyzed three national-level territorial carbon emissions measures: total emissions, per capita emissions and emissions per unit of GDP from 1960 to 2005 (see also Jorgenson 2014; Longhofer and Jorgenson 2017). They find a strong relationship between per capita emissions and GDP per capita in Global North nations that is stable through time. In the Global South, the emissions/GDP per capita linkage has increased over time although it is smaller than in developed countries. For total emissions, in the Global North there is some evidence of relative decoupling. Thombs (2018) replicates the findings of Jorgenson and Clark (2012) across all three measures of territorial emissions and extends the time period. This body of work provides some evidence of relative decoupling, but not the absolute decoupling required to achieve emission targets.

Accounting for embodied emissions in trade and cyclical variations gives a less positive picture. Knight and Schor (2014) find no decoupling using consumption (i.e., trade adjusted) rather than territorial carbon emissions. Cohen et al (2018) find that emissions are pro-cyclical, that consumption emissions are more coupled than production and that almost no countries (with Germany as a notable exception) have been able to decouple GHGs from GDP over time. The United States is estimated to have a long-term GHG elasticity of 0.6.

There are some researchers who contend that decoupling is occurring. A blog post by climate scientist Zeke Hausfather (2021) argues that 32 countries absolutely decoupled between 2005 and 2019, including for consumption emissions. While the emissions reductions for some nations are so small as to be negligible (e.g., Norway, Poland, Mexico), others have achieved notable reductions in CO_2 emissions according to Hausfather's data (e.g., Ireland, Romania, Spain). However, this analysis is subject to several caveats. First, it includes only carbon emissions, and not emissions from other fossil fuels, land use changes, international shipping and aviation. For example, the shift from coal to natural gas reduced carbon use but raised methane emissions, which Hausfather excludes. Depending on the amount of methane leakage in the natural gas supply chain, the shift from coal to gas can actually produce greater near-term warming, according to some estimates (Howarth 2014, although there continues to be debate on these effects; see Tanaka et al. 2019). Furthermore, it may be more useful to look at the EU as a whole, than as individual countries, given that it is such a highly integrated area. Twenty-one of the thirty-two countries that Hausfather claims have absolutely decoupled are part of the EU. A third point is that this analysis relies on bi-variate correlations, unlike most of the literature, which estimates models that control for other factors; it's possible that a third variable is driving the results, rather than a true delinking of GDP with GHGs. That said, it's possible that we have entered a new period in which GDP and emissions are no longer so tightly coupled in Global North countries. However, the evidence for that position remains scant. A recent review of the evidence on decoupling in 835 peer-reviewed articles concluded that "large rapid absolute reductions of resource use and GHG emissions cannot be achieved through observed decoupling rates, hence decoupling needs to be complemented by sufficiency-oriented strategies and strict enforcement of absolute reduction targets" (Haberl et al. 2020, 1).

Whatever the latest evidence on decoupling, the issue is not just whether we can achieve it, but whether we can do so in a timeframe that would allow us to remain with the carbon budget for 1.5°C. On those grounds the evidence is decidedly more pessimistic. First, most of the scenarios assume widespread use of negative emissions technologies; without them, the rate of decoupling required to meet decarbonization targets is greater than what models would suggest is feasible (Hickel and Kallis 2020). Virtually all scenarios modeled by the Intergovernmental Panel on Climate Change (IPCC) and the International Energy Agency (IEA) rely on large-scale negative emissions later in the century – the equivalent of pulling a rabbit out of a hat, given the state of negative emissions technology. To address this, Keyßer and Lenzen (2021, 11) model several "degrowth pathways" and find that they "exhibit the lowest relative risks for feasibility and sustainability when compared with established IPCC SR1.5 pathways" and should be "widely and thoroughly considered and debated." Schröder and Storm (2020) provide a compelling account of feasible GDP growth rates; they calculate that to achieve even an 85% emissions reduction target by 2050, per capita global GDP growth must be negative.

To put the matter rather simply, for Global North countries, the annual emissions reductions which are necessary, and which incorporate a modicum of global equity, are in the double-digit range. These are far beyond the 1%–2% rates of relative decoupling of near-term historical experience. We are in unchartered waters in terms of the speed and depth of the decarbonization and emissions reductions that are needed to prevent catastrophe. Schröder and Storm (2020) correctly conclude that we are at a fork in the road, in which we either face a future of Hothouse Earth following consensus growth pathways, or we need to drastically alter the operation of our economies. This is of course a conclusion reached by many advocates of green new deals.

That said, we must still reckon with the question of whether Global North countries can tolerate low or negative growth. We believe that they can, but such a regime will require progressive reductions in working hours to absorb excess labor, especially if decarbonization spurs productivity growth, as it may well do. Energy transition and low or negative growth will also both require a major and likely growing state role in the investment process and mechanisms to create more equally distributed wealth. These issues have been addressed via economic modeling in (Victor 2009) and informally by Schor (2010) and Jackson (2005) as well as in numerous papers by Victor and Jackson, who are developing a new macroeconomics for a post-growth world (Jackson and Victor 2016). For the purposes of this chapter, we will focus on the issue of worktime reduction and the important role that it can play in green new deals.

Worktime reduction: social and environmental benefits

Worktime reduction is an example of a double- or multiple-dividend policy. While attention to working hours waned as wages stagnated and inequality rose in the early twenty-first century, in an earlier era, economists, trade unionists, and others recognized the benefits of shorter hours (Schor 1992). Shorter hours of work have historically been enacted as a remedy for unemployment, for example, during the Great Depression, and in Western Europe after the 1980 recession. As noted in the introduction, interest in a shorter working week has substantially increased with the COVID-19 pandemic and associated economic downturn (Coote, Harper and Stirling 2021). Worktime reduction has also historically been a major factor in maintaining high employment when labor-saving technical change occurs. As artificial intelligence eliminates the need for many jobs, it may prove to be a vital policy response. Shorter working hours can also contribute to reduced stress, better physical and mental health, and higher quality of life (Schor 2010).

A growing body of research demonstrates that shorter hours of work can be an important part of the effort to reduce GHGs. There is a large and significant relationship between annual hours of work and emissions in wealthy countries (Knight, Rosa and Schor 2013; Fitzgerald, Jorgenson and Clark 2015). Fitzgerald et al. (2015) estimate that for every 1% decline in hours, energy consumption in wealthy nations is reduced by 0.4%. This relationship is even larger across US states, as Fitzgerald, Schor and Jorgenson (2018) find that a 1% decline in weekly hours results in emissions reductions ranging from 0.55% to 0.67%, depending on the model used. Mallinson and Cheng (2022) replicated their research using a more recent set of data (2014–2017) and found an even stronger relationship of close to 1% lower emissions for every 1% decline in weekly hours.

There are two pathways through which hours and emissions are likely related. The first and larger one is what we have termed the scale effect (Schor, Knight and Rosa 2013): countries that take more productivity growth in the form of shorter hours expand output less than they might. Casual observation reveals that the few countries that have managed to achieve significant emissions reductions, such as Germany, have done so with low rates of GDP growth. The second pathway is the composition effect, which measures how time availability affects the composition of household activities and consumption, following the classic insights of Gary Becker (1965) and Steffan Linder (1970). The intuition is that time-stressed households engage in more carbon-intensive activities (e.g., carbon-intensive commuting, pre-made meals – see Mompelat 2021 for further examples). In the cross-national studies, the composition effect is much smaller, and in some models nonsignificant; however, in the US cross-state models it is similar in magnitude to the scale effect (Fitzgerald, Schor and Jorgenson 2018).

This body of work suggests that policies to reduce working hours can be an important tool for lowering emissions, while also boosting employment and improving workers' health and well-being (Schor 2013). If worktime reduction is tied to productivity growth, it can be achieved without reducing workers' income, but as an alternative to higher wages. This avoids the well-known problem of loss aversion as well as the preference endogeneity that develops when incomes rise – a phenomenon Schor has described as the "work-and-spend cycle" (Schor 1992). In the United States, working hours have risen substantially for the most highly educated workers (Jacobs and Gerson 2005), who are also disproportionate carbon emitters. Focused policies that target members of this group, who have historically been most interested in trading time for money, could reduce both income inequality and emissions. Recent work by Fitzgerald (2021) finds significant interactions between domestic inequality and working hours, such that at higher levels of inequality, working hours have a larger relationship to emissions. The potential to address inequality through worktime reduction policies is significant for our discussion in this chapter, given that this is a core objective of most green new deals. As Fremstad, Paul and Underwood (2019) argue, there is a strong case for worktime reduction – even if it would play a relatively minor role in reducing emissions – because of its social benefits, including the possibility of reaching full employment.

In 2020 and 2021, as the COVID-19 lockdown affected people around the world, worktime re-emerged as a popular alternative to pre-pandemic working patterns. In addition to demands for remote work and higher pay, widespread dissatisfaction with long hours of work helped spur a movement for a four-day week. As noted above, governments began to voice interest in testing four-day weeks, with Spain and Scotland officially involved in pilot programs. Because these trials involve no reduction in pay, and expectations of increased work intensity (to fit five days of work into four days) they are unlikely to have large impacts on carbon emissions. However, if the four-day week movement creates ongoing momentum for worktime reduction, it will soon involve trading productivity growth for shorter hours and will likely yield the emissions reductions expected from the scholarly literature.

Incorporating worktime reduction policies into Green New Deals

There are several possible models for worktime reduction that could be adopted in green new deals. While the employment consequences of shorter hours are complex and vary with the type of reductions, it can be concluded that large reductions in working hours are more conducive to employment expansion. A key question is whether the reduction should be in the form of fewer hours worked per day, fewer days worked per week, or longer periods of vacation and other forms of annual leave. As noted above, current advocacy is focused on the four-day week, which has certain advantages from an environmental perspective (King and van den Bergh 2017). Unlike shorter workdays, a shorter workweek allows for reduction in commuting. A common "day off" also allows for office closure, and thus a reduction in energy use for lighting/heating etc., which longer periods of vacation or annual leave – if they are not taken at the same time by all staff – do not.

Another question is how a "top-down" green new deal would bring about a shorter working week or other forms of worktime reductions. Options available include policies that support individualized, voluntary changes in working patterns (e.g., through policies that give employees rights to reduce their hours – see further Pullinger 2014); worktime reduction in the public sector (as in Iceland); government incentives for private firms to reduce working hours; or a legislated mandate for worktime reduction.

Individualized changes in working hours would not provide the benefits of an additional day of office closure but could still reduce commuting and consumption-driven emissions. Shortening the working week in the public sector only would be easier to achieve than an economy-wide policy, but would have a smaller impact on emissions, at least initially. However, to remain attractive to employees, the private sector might follow suit. Hickel (2021b) suggests as much in his proposal for a job guarantee program set at 30 hours per week instead of the standard 40. Coote et al. (2021) also suggest that new jobs as part of a green new deal should "be created on the basis of a shorter working week with guarantees of a living wage."

The Green New Deal for Europe's "Blueprint for Europe's Just Transition" employs the third option and aims to incentivize the private sector by providing a "transitional subsidy for firms that move to a four-day workweek without cutting staff or pay" (GNDE 2019, 51). The subsidy starts at 100% of the firm's costs associated with the shorter workweek and then is slowly phased out (50% in the second year, 25% in the third year). The Spanish government appears likely to adopt a similar model to cover the costs for firms that are involved in the three-year trial of a four-day working week (Kassam 2021).

While it may seem optimistic to think that countries would legislate worktime, there is a long history of worktime legislation. In the United States, President Franklin Delano Roosevelt signed the Fair Labor Standards Act of 1938, which set the 40-hour workweek as a standard and required time-and-a-half pay for overtime work. In July 2021, US Congressman Mark Takano introduced legislation that would lower the maximum hours threshold for overtime compensation under this law from 40 hours to 32 hours (Takano 2021). The American Federation of Labor and Congress of Industrial Organizations, the largest federation of unions in the United States, supports the bill. However, it is not clear at this point whether the legislation, if passed, would lead to any substantial reduction in working hours or simply greater amounts of work being classified as "overtime."

A key design question is whether the worktime reductions should occur with or without a change in wages. As noted above, existing trials for shorter working hours/weeks involve no reduction in pay, and most contemporary four-day working week advocates adopt this model. As Kallis et al. (2013, 1561) note, cutting weekly wages through reduced working hours is "a policy of regressive redistribution from labor to capital" and is "not the policy advocated by Keynes or by degrowth precursors in the 1970s such as Andre Gorz." However, from the perspective of a green new deal, a potential drawback of this approach is that it may not result in lower emissions. One option would be to enact a shift to a four-day week without loss of pay now and to incorporate policies that lead to an economy-wide path in which future productivity growth is used to reduce hours rather than expand production. Firms could be required, or given incentives, to offer that option to employees. Another policy, which exists in the Netherlands, is the right to reduce hours within a job without loss of promotion opportunities. Of course, programs that facilitate trading income for time are more likely to be taken up by high-income earners, thus reducing both consumption and income inequality. For lower earners, complementary policies such as higher minimum wages, universal basic income, and universal basic services can ensure that workers are financially better off if they also opt to work fewer hours (Mompelet 2021, 12).

There are other complimentary policies that should be included in green new deals to ensure maximum social and environmental benefits from worktime reduction. Policies that promote "convivial consumption," including investments in "convivial infrastructures" such as public squares, parks, and theaters, are critical for ensuring that everyone is equally able to participate in low-carbon forms of leisure (Kallis et al. 2013). Luxury taxes on high-carbon activities – flights, for example – can also help to reduce behavioral changes, such as more weekend travel, that lead to higher emissions.

There is a clear connection between top-down policies that can be adopted by governments through "statist" green new deals – both in terms of reducing working hours and the complementary policies to support low-income earners and convivial consumption – and the kind of bottom-up community initiatives that can break the work-and-spend cycle and create what Schor (2010) has called an economy of "plenitude." These policies will enable workers to reclaim their time, as many currently do not have either the option or the luxury of choosing to reduce their working hours. This new free time can then be invested in ecologically restorative activities such as growing food and repairing goods and homes. More time also enables citizens to be more politically active, which should be a boon to both democracy and the environment.

Conclusions

Kevin Anderson and Alice Bows have admonished their fellow climatologists for allowing economists to lead them into the "misguided belief that commitments to avoid warming of 2°C can still be realized with incremental adjustments to economic incentives," by which they mean continued economic growth. "Put bluntly, climate change commitments are incompatible with short- to medium-term economic growth (in other words, for 10 to 20 years)." A growing number of scholars, and even the European Environment Agency (EEA 2021), have come to the same conclusion. The simple point about growth is that it makes the very high mountain that we need to climb even steeper. Why rule out an important source of emissions reductions before we've even started? Furthermore, given that the type of policies advocated by degrowth proponents – job guarantees, worktime reductions, wealth caps or taxes, etc. – also address inequality, they are a natural fit for a green new deal.

Some green-growthers claim that abandoning growth as a policy goal is politically infeasible. We believe that this perspective is rooted in an earlier political reality which has already been superceded. The association of growth with higher inequality and the urgent need for targeted interventions to address health, education, housing and other basic needs have made the postwar growth-centricity increasingly obsolete. The public seems to understand that growth does not necessarily yield well-being for the majority any longer. In our view, a people-centric rather than growth-centric approach is precisely the politics that can mobilize populations and maintain ongoing support for decarbonization. The popularity of the AOC–Markey Green New Deal, which did not center GDP-growth, demonstrates this. By contrast, green growth approaches are typically far more tied to the status quo, less oriented to equity, and avoid the major structural changes that are necessary to simultaneously achieve decarbonization and human well-being.

The popularity of the four-day workweek is certainly clear; a recent global survey found 74% of workers support it (Liu 2021). However, this does not mean that achieving it will be easy. In this respect, it is important to highlight the key role of the labor movement in bringing about worktime reductions both in the past and more recently. For example, unions in Iceland (which represent 90% of workers) were instrumental in negotiating the trials for shorter working hours and in having those trials turned into a permanent policy. However, in many parts of the world, decades of neoliberal policy have severely undermined the capacity of unions to effectively bargain for their members (Coote et al. 2021). Green new deal supporters must therefore work with unions to drive a renewal of the labor movement, including through the reform or repeal of laws that have limited the power of labor to organize (Stuart, Gunderson and Peterson 2020; Coote et al. 2021; Huber 2021).

In closing, we would stress that worktime reduction is not a panacea. Indeed, the contribution that it makes to emissions reductions may be small in some contexts and will be largely determined by how it is complemented by other policies. Nevertheless, it is a policy that can provide climate benefits while simultaneously enhancing people's lives by reducing stress and improving mental health. It can reduce income inequality. And it has the potential to bring about a more radical shift in the way that people view their relationships with work, material consumption, and the planet. For all of these reasons, it should be considered a critical component of green new deals.

Note

1 This chapter was adapted with permission from Juliet B. Schor and Andrew K. Jorgenson, 2019, "Is it too late for growth?," *Review of Radical Political Economics*, 51(2): 320–329.

References

Anderson, K. and Bows, A. 2012. A new paradigm for climate change. *Nature Climate Change*. September. Available at: http://www.nature.com/nclimate/journal/v2/n9/full/nclimate1646.html?WT.ec_id=NCLIMATE-201209

Aronoff, K. et al. 2019. *A Planet to Win: Why We Need a Green New Deal*. New York: Verso.

Barrero, J., Bloom, N. and Davis, S. 2021. Why working from home will stick. *National Bureau for Economic Research Working Paper 28731*. Available at: DOI 10.3386/w28731

Becker, G. 1965. A theory of the allocation of time. *Economic Journal*. 75: 493–517.

Cohen, G. et al. 2018. The long-run decoupling of emissions and output: Evidence from the largest emitters. *Energy Policy*. 118: 58–68.

Coote, A., Harper, A. and Stirling, A. 2021. *The Case for a Four-Day Week*. Cambridge: Polity.

European Environment Agency. 2021. Growth without economic growth (briefing paper). Available at: https://www.eea.europa.eu/publications/growth-without-economic-growth

Fitzgerald, J. 2021. Working time, inequality and carbon emissions in the United States, 2005–2015. Department of Sociology, Oklahoma State University. Working Paper.

Fitzgerald, J., Jorgenson, A.K. and Clark, B. 2015. Energy consumption and working hours: A longitudinal study of developed and developing nations, 1990–2008. *Environmental Sociology*. 1: 213–223.

Fitzgerald, J., Schor, J.B. and Jorgenson, A.K. 2018. Working hours and carbon dioxide emissions in the United States, 2007–2013. *Social Forces*. 96: 1851–1874.

Fox, M. 2021. Will the post-Covid world include a 4-day workweek? As Kickstarter tests it out, some predict it will catch on. *CNBC*. 6 July. Available at: https://www.cnbc.com/2021/07/06/post-covid-4-day-workweek.html

Fremstad, A., Paul, M. and Underwood, A. 2019. Work hours and CO2 emissions: Evidence from U.S. households. *Review of Political Economy*. 31(1): 42–59. Available at: DOI: 10.1080/09538259.2019.1592950

Green New Deal for Europe (GNDE). n.d. 10 Pillars of the green new deal for Europe. Available at: https://gnde.diem25.org/10-pillars/

Green New Deal for Europe (GNDE). 2019. Blueprint for Europe's just transition (Edition II). Available at: https://report.gndforeurope.com/cms/wp-content/uploads/2020/01/Blueprint-for-Europes-Just-Transition-2nd-Ed.pdf

Haberl, H. et al. 2020. A systematic review of the evidence on decoupling of GDP, resource use and GHG emissions, part II: Synthesizing the insights. *Environmental Research Letters* 15: 065003

Haraldsson, G.D. and Kellam, J. 2021. *Going Public: Iceland's Journey to a Shorter Working Week*. London: Autonomy. Available at: https://autonomy.work/wp-content/uploads/2021/06/ICELAND_4DW.pdf

Hausfather, Z. 2021. Absolute decoupling of economic growth and emissions in 32 countries. *The Breakthrough Institute Blog*. 6 April. Available at: https://thebreakthrough.org/issues/energy/absolute-decoupling-of-economic-growth-and-emissions-in-32-countries

Hickel, J. 2021a. *Less Is More: How Degrowth will Save the World*. London: William Heinemann.

Hickel, J. 2021b. Stimulus is an environmental disaster waiting to happen. *Foreign Policy*. 23 February. Available at: https://foreignpolicy.com/2021/02/23/stimulus-is-an-environmental-disaster-waiting-to-happen/

Hickel, J. and Kallis, G. 2020. Is green growth possible? *New Political Economy*. 25(4): 469–486. Available at: DOI: 10.1080/13563467.2019.1598964

Howarth, R. 2014. A bridge to nowhere: Methane emissions and the greenhouse gas footprint of natural gas. *Energy Science & Engineering*. 2: 47–60. Available at: https://doi.org/10.1002/ese3.35

Huber, M. 2021. Why the Green New Deal has failed — so far. *Jacobin*. 10 May. Available at: https://jacobinmag.com/2021/05/green-new-deal-climate-change.

Jackson, T. 2009. *Prosperity Without Growth: Economics for a Finite Planet*. London: Routledge.

Jackson, T. and Victor, P. 2016. Does slow growth lead to rising inequality? Some theoretical reflections and numerical simulations. *Ecological Economics*. 121(C): 206–219.

Jacobs, J. and Gerson, K. 2005. *The Time Divide: Work, Gender, and Family Inequality*. Cambridge, MA: Harvard University Press.

Jorgenson, A.K. 2014. Economic development and the carbon intensity of human well-being. *Nature Climate Change*. 4: 186–189.

Jorgenson, A.K. and Clark, B. 2012. Are the economy and the environment decoupling? A comparative international study, 1960–2005. *American Journal of Sociology*. 118: 1–44.

Kallis, G. et al. 2013. "Friday off": Reducing working hours in Europe. *Sustainability*. 5: 1545–1567. Available at: https://doi.org/10.3390/su5041545

Kassam, A. 2021. Spain to launch trial of four-day working week. *The Guardian*. 4 March. Available at: https://www.theguardian.com/world/2021/mar/15/spain-to-launch-trial-of-four-day-working-week

Kelly, J. 2020. Now that working from home has proven successful, unilever is trying out a four-day workweek. *Forbes*. 1 December. Available at: https://www.forbes.com/sites/jackkelly/2020/12/01/now-that-working-from-home-has-proven-successful-unilever-is-trying-out-a-four-day-workweek/?sh=128788091ab0

Keyßer, L.T. and Lenzen, M. 2021. 1.5°C degrowth scenarios suggest the need for new mitigation pathways. *Nature Communications*. 12(1): 1–16.

King, L. and van den Bergh, J. 2017. Worktime reduction as a solution to climate change: Five scenarios compared for the UK. *Ecological Economics*. 132: 124–134.

Klein, N. 2019. *On Fire: The Burning Case for a Green New Deal*. Toronto: Alfred A. Knopf.

Knight, K. Rosa, E. and Schor, J.B. 2013. Could working less reduce pressures on the environment?: A cross-national panel analysis of OECD countries, 1970–2007. *Global Environmental Change*. 23: 691–700.

Knight, K. and Schor, J.B. 2014. Economic growth and climate change: A cross-national analysis of territorial and consumption-based carbon emissions in high-income countries. *Sustainability*. 6(6): 3722–3731.

Linder, S.B. 1970. *The Harried Leisure Class*. New York: Columbia University Press.

Liu, J. 2020. 74% of office workers support a 4-day workweek—here's how the pandemic could make it more common. *CNBC*. 23 November. Available at: https://www.cnbc.com/2020/11/23/74 percent-of-office-workers-support-a-4-day-workweek-in-new-survey.html

Longhofer, W. and Jorgenson, A.K. 2017. Decoupling reconsidered: Does world society integration influence the relationship between the environment and economic development? *Social Science Research*. 65: 17–29.

Mallinson, G. and Cheng, K. 2022. The relationship between state-level carbon emissions and average working hours in the United States: A replication study. *Environmental Sociology* 8(1): 88–93.

Mastini, R., Kallis, G. and Hickel, J. 2021. A Green New Deal without growth? *Ecological Economics*. 179: 106832.

Mompelat, L. 2021. Stop the clock: The environmental benefits of a shorter working week. 4 Day Week (UK)/Platform London. Available at: https://6a142ff6-85bd-4a7b-bb3b-476b07b8f08d.usrfiles.com/ugd/6a142f_5061c06b240e4776bf31dfac2543746b.pdf

Morissette, R., Deng, Z. and Messacar, D. 2021. Working from home: Potential implications for public transit and greenhouse gas emissions. Statistics Canada. Available at: https://doi.org/10.25318/36280001202100400005-eng

Pettifor, A. 2019. *The Case for the Green New Deal*. New York: Verso.

Pinsker, J. 2021. Kill the 5-day workweek. *The Atlantic*. 17 June. Available at: https://www.theatlantic.com/family/archive/2021/06/four-day-workweek/619222/

Pollin, R. 2018. De-growth versus a Green New Deal. *New Left Review*. 112: 5–25.

Pullinger, M. 2014. Working time reduction policy in a sustainable economy: Criteria and options for its design. *Ecological Economics*. 103: 11–19

PWC. 2021. It's time to reimagine where and how work will get done: PwC's US Remote Work Survey. Available at: https://www.pwc.com/us/remotework

Recognizing the duty of the Federal Government to create a Green New Deal. H. Res. 109, 116th Congress. 2019. Available at: https://www.congress.gov/bill/116th-congress/house-resolution/109/text.

Ryle, J. et al. 2020. Open Letter to World Leaders, 15 November 2020. 4 Day Week Campaign (UK). Available at: https://www.4dayweek.co.uk/latest-news

Schor, J.B. 1992. *The Overworked American: The Unexpected Decline of Leisure*. New York: Basic Books.

Schor, J.B. 2010. *Plenitude: The New Economics of True Wealth*. New York: Penguin Press.

Schor, J.B. 2013. Why solving climate change requires working less, in Coote, A. and Franklin, J.J. (eds.) *Time on Our Side: Why We All Need a Shorter Working Week*. London: New Economics Foundation.

Schor, J.B., Knight, K. and Rosa, E. 2013. Reducing growth to achieve environmental sustainability: The role of work hours, in Pollin, R. and Wicks-Lim, J. (eds.) *Capitalism on Trial: Explorations in the Tradition of Thomas Weisskopf*. Cheltenham: Edward Elgar.

Schröder, E. and Storm, S. 2020. Economic growth and carbon emissions: The road to "Hothouse Earth" is paved with good intentions. *International Journal of Political Economy.* 49(2): 153–173. Available at: DOI: 10.1080/08911916.2020.1778866

Stiglitz, J. 2020. The economic case for a Green New Deal, in Prakash, V. and Girgenti, G. (eds.) *Winning the Green New Deal: Why We Must, How We Can.* New York: Simon & Schuster.

Strack, R. et al. 2021. *Decoding Global Ways of Working.* Boston Consulting Group. Available at: https://www.bcg.com/en-us/publications/2021/advantages-of-remote-work-flexibility

Stuart, D., Gunderson, R. and Peterson, B. 2020. *Climate Change Solutions beyond the Capital-Climate Contradiction.* Ann Arbor: University of Michigan Press.

Takano, M. 2021. Rep. Takano introduces legislation to reduce the standard workweek to 32 hours. 27 July. Available at: https://takano.house.gov/newsroom/press-releases/rep-takano-introduces-legislation-to-reduce-the-standard-workweek-to-32-hours

Tanaka, K., Cavalett, O., Collins, W.J. et al. 2019. Asserting the climate benefits of the coal-to-gas shift across temporal and spatial scales. *Nature Climate Change.* 9: 389–396. Available at: https://doi.org/10.1038/s41558-019-0457-1

Thombs, R. 2018. The transnational tilt of the treadmill and the role of trade openness on carbon emissions: A comparative international study, 1965–2010. *Sociological Forum.* 33(2): 422–442.

UN Department of Economic and Social Affairs (UNDESA). 2017. *World Fertility Report 2015.* Available at: https://www.un.org/development/desa/pd/sites/www.un.org.development.desa.pd/files/files/documents/2020/Feb/un_2015_worldfertilityreport_highlights.pdf

United Nations Environment Programme (UNEP). 2019. Cut global emissions by 7.6 percent every year for next decade to meet 1.5°C Paris target. 26 November. Available at: https://www.unep.org/news-and-stories/press-release/cut-global-emissions-76-percent-every-year-next-decade-meet-15degc

Van den Bergh, J. 2011. Environment versus growth — A criticism of "degrowth" and a plea for "a-growth." *Ecological Economics.* 70: 881–890

Victor, P. 2008. *Managing Without Growth: Slower by Design, Not Disaster.* Cheltenham, UK: Edward Elgar.

Westfall, S. 2021. Japan proposes four-day workweek as idea gains purchase amid pandemic. *Washington Post.* 24 June. Available at: https://www.washingtonpost.com/world/2021/06/24/japan-four-day-work-week/

7

RESHAPING GLOBAL TRADE AND INVESTMENT LAW FOR A GREEN NEW DEAL

Todd N. Tucker and Timothy Meyer

Introduction

Little more than a year after the Green New Deal (GND) was introduced in the US Congress, it captured the imagination of a wide range of parties. Chief among them is US President Joe Biden, who has called it "a crucial framework for meeting the climate challenges we face."[1] While Biden has not wholly embraced the GND brand, he has proposed a suite of standards, investments and justice initiatives that are qualitatively similar. Both his plan and the European Commission's Green Deal (which envisions a distinct set of policy tools) aim to reduce net carbon emissions in the United States and Europe by 2050.

Rapid decarbonization would fundamentally change how national and global economies function. The process would likely generate trade and investment disputes even if countries were using identical policy instruments applied at the same speed and intensity. But given that countries are on track to use different instruments at varying speeds and intensities, trade and investment conflicts are almost certain. There are several strategies policymakers could pursue to make such conflicts less likely. One approach would change the rules themselves to make the global governance regime more compatible with the climate objectives. Another approach is to water down the decarbonization agenda to make compliance with trade and investment agreements more likely.

First we describe the approaches to decarbonization on both sides of the Atlantic. Then we examine how trade and investment law might limit the options for decarbonization and lay out options for enhancing the compatibility of these initiatives with existing trade and investment law. The section that follows flips this analysis, and looks at how the trade and investment rules could be rewritten to facilitate an aggressive decarbonization. Finally, we conclude that in order to respond to the moral and existential threat of climate change, we must fundamentally overhaul global trade and investment law.

The distinct approaches to decarbonization in the United States and Europe

Climate change is one of the most serious threats to national and international security and prosperity that the world has ever seen. If the Earth does not reach carbon neutrality by the year 2050, we will see higher sea levels, more storms and droughts, and widespread

DOI: 10.4324/9781003110880-9

displacement of human and animal populations. Even the climate-change-skeptical Trump administration predicted a seven-degree-Fahrenheit increase in global temperatures by 2100, a level that scientists say will kill off many coral reefs, put parts of Miami and Manhattan underwater, and unleash extreme heat waves (Eilperin, Dennis and Mooney 2018).

Nonetheless, the political will to reverse warming and weather changes has been lacking – even though economists have found there are imminently plausible technical and political means for doing so (Paul, Mason and Fremstad 2019). Part of the difficulty has been the US political system's high number of veto points. Individual senators from tiny states have enormous capacity to block legislation from moving forward, while US courts exercise judicial review in a manner that seems increasingly biased against major policy reform. Meanwhile, countervailing institutions like labor unions that could overcome or pressure against these veto points have been decimated (Tucker 2019). As for Europe, the European Commission also faces a wide range of veto points that, in some cases, require unanimity of all the member state governments to take the boldest types of climate action (Marcu, Mehling and Cosbey 2020).

Past US climate efforts have attempted to deal with these veto points by circumventing them. This strategy has a certain logic. After all, in 1997, the US Senate preemptively rejected the Kyoto Protocol, and in 2009 never took up the American Clean Energy and Security Act (also known as the Waxman-Markey climate bill), which had been passed by the House. As a result, the Obama administration relied on regulatory tools and non-treaty instruments when it came to climate policy – strategies that have been partly wound down by the Trump administration and courts (Aschwanden 2015).

A newer generation of political leadership is attempting to address this stalemate not through avoiding politics but by changing them. In February 2019, Representative Alexandria Ocasio-Cortez (D-N.Y.) unveiled the Green New Deal – a ten-year proposed mobilization to completely decarbonize the US economy by 2030. She and the broader progressive community aim to do so by politically embedding climate solutions in a popular anti-inequality agenda, creating high-paying union jobs and addressing racial and gender inequities in the process (H.Res. 109). This proposal is backed by sound research: regional, class and racial disparities are associated with higher rates of emissions (Holmberg 2017). The "yellow vest" protests faced by French President Emmanuel Macron in 2018 reinforce why many environmentalists see climate and inequality as inextricably linked. French policymakers sought to use the revenue from carbon taxes (which fall most heavily on poor and working-class people) to fund government budget deficit reduction (Mufson and McAuley 2018). In contrast, many social scientists think that (at a minimum) revenue needs to be recycled to citizens through a carbon dividend. In the United States, the debate among reformers is whether a payoff is enough, or whether a more inclusive and participatory New Deal-level mobilization is needed (Hook 2019). In this latter view, much as disruptive trade liberalization in the mid twentieth-century was embedded in domestic social contracts that elevated labor unions, welfare states and restrictions on finance (Ruggie 1982), the GND's advocates seek a twenty-first-century "embedded decarbonization."

The localism of the GND begs the question: what would its international dimension look like? The GND is not yet elaborated in detailed legislation, but rather takes the form of a resolution outlining five goals, 14 projects, and 15 requirements to evaluate said projects. Immediately upon its launch, it was criticized for its supposed lack of detail on the international ramifications. For instance, economist Noah Smith of Bloomberg tweeted that,

> because the US only produces 14% of global carbon emissions (and falling every day), the Green New Deal won't actually reduce climate change… [it] doesn't focus on the

international aspect at all. In other words, the current GND just doesn't look like it'll do much to actually save the planet.

(*Smith 2019*)

In fact, the GND framework has both explicit and implicit international dimensions. Most of these components are explicitly international in focus or are framed in an open-ended fashion that would allow for an international dimension. Indeed, only three of the goals, six of the projects (43%), and three of the requirements (20%) are explicitly national in focus. The remaining 57% of the projects and 80% of the requirements are either explicitly or potentially international in scope. These are summarized in Table 7.1.

Note that there is not a neat bifurcation between national and international dimensions, even on those aspects that appear to be one or the other. For instance, many of the "explicitly national" aims could entail the use of foreign inputs and technologies, as there is no strict "Made in America" provision. Moreover, not all of the explicitly international items take a collaborative form. Requirement K is ambiguous as to whether these reformed trade rules need be in the form of new international agreements: the language is capacious enough that it could be achieved via domestic legislation. Requirement N appears to contemplate expansive extraterritorial application and enforcement of the Sherman Act and other anti-trust statutes, discouraging not only domestic but also international monopolies. Only Project N appears to be partly collaborative, encouraging trade not only to advance US leadership, but also to promote internal domestic mobilizations within other countries. Finally, the vast majority of the projects and requirements are neither explicitly national nor explicitly international. For instance, Requirement G promotes labor unionization, and Requirement M promotes the prior informed consent of Indigenous Peoples. From its wording, there would be no reason this would have to be limited to situations in the United States. Indeed, Goal A is arguably a global goal of net-zero emissions with a just transition. If so, GND policy would not be limited to unionizing solar power installers in Cleveland or protecting the Standing Rock tribe in the Dakotas. Indeed, it would equally trigger the use of diplomatic tools to promote union rights in Mexico and Indigenous rights in Canada.

Biden's Build Back Better (BBB) climate plan borrows heavily from the GND, and makes greater mention of the international dimensions of climate policy. The core of the plan is a $2 trillion investment over four years that would aim to reach net-zero emissions in the electricity and transportation sectors by 2035, and in the economy as a whole by 2050. To generate political support for such an ambitious agenda, the plan commits the US government to purchasing virtually exclusively domestic manufacturing, services and agricultural outputs through so-called "Buy American" conditions. It also commits to a wide range of local content requirements for green subsidy schemes. Academic research indicates that such linking to local economies is an effective way to overcome resistance to the economic costs of decarbonization (Meyer 2015; Stokes 2016; Hess et al. 2018). Finally, 40% of the benefits of this investment will go to disadvantaged communities, and the plan commits every US government agency to making environmental justice a part of its core mission – including explicitly the promotion of Indigenous rights at home and abroad.[3]

While many Europeans have swooned over the GND, the European Commission has opted for a distinct approach. Some changes are cosmetic, dropping the "new" in favor simply of a Green Deal. The major difference has to do with the fact that European countries have two decades of experience operating under an emissions trading scheme. The GND and Biden plans eschew that mechanism, as well as carbon taxes (the two tools favored most by mainstream economists) in favor of a set of standards, investments and justice initiatives

Table 7.1 Green New Deal – International and National Dimensions

Section	*Explicitly National (denoted e.g., "in the US")*	*Explicitly International (denoted e.g., "overseas")*	*Potentially International (no explicit qualifier)*
(1) Goals	(B) Job creation and prosperity (C) Sustainable infrastructure and industrial policy (D) Healthy future		(A) "achieve net-zero greenhouse gas emissions through a fair and just transition for *all* communities and workers" (emphasis added) (E) Protecting "frontline and vulnerable communities" (FVCs)
(2) Projects	(B) US infrastructure (C) US power demand met through 100% clean energy sources (E) Decarbonizing US buildings (F) Decarbonizing US manufacturing (G) Decarbonizing US farming (H) Decarbonizing US transportation	(N) Promote "international exchange of technology, expertise, products, funding, and services, with the aim of making the United States the international leader on climate action, and to help other countries achieve a Green New Deal."	(A) Resilient community-defined projects (D) Smart grids (I) Mitigation (J) Conservation and reforestation (K) Restore damaged ecosystems (L) Clean hazardous sites (M) Identify and clean up new emission sources
(3) Requirements	(C) Training and higher education with focus on FVCs so all Americans "can be full and equal participants" (H) "guaranteeing a job with a family-sustaining wage, adequate family and medical leave, paid vacations, and retirement security to all people of the United States" (O) US social safety net and rights (health, housing, security, water, air, food, access to nature)	(K) "enacting and enforcing trade rules, procurement standards, and border adjustments with strong labor and environmental protections – (i) to stop the transfer of jobs and pollution overseas; and (ii) to grow domestic manufacturing in the United States" (N) "ensuring a commercial environment where every businessperson is free from unfair competition and domination by domestic or international monopolies"	(A) Public resources to communities, agencies, businesses – with public stakes and return (B) Environmental and social accounting through old and new laws (D) Public investment in new tech (E) Just transition (F) Democratic participation in planning, implementation, administration (G) Creation of [only] high quality union jobs [and local hiring][2] (I) Collective bargaining rights (J) Labor standards (L) Protecting public patrimony/oceans and not abusing eminent domain (M) Indigenous rights

that amount to an intersectionally conscious industrial policy. Because Europe has a significantly different starting point, the Green Deal utilizes a different set of tools intended to graft the climate strategy onto the trading scheme. Following the sectoral rollout of the carbon trading scheme, the EU's plan imagines sectoral efforts to decarbonize the economy, focusing on, for instance, the transport and energy sectors as well as the carbon footprint of buildings. The plan also includes a Just Transition Mechanism that aims to direct 100 billion euros to geographic regions adversely impacted by the move to a green economy. Such a plan reflects a recognition that environmental policies, like trade policies, have different impacts in different regions. Holding adversely affected regions harmless is key to ensuring the long-term political viability of green policies, just as it is a key element of sustaining support for the global trade regime.

How to reconcile decarbonization with existing trade and investment rules

Since the creation of the World Trade Organization (WTO) in 1995, reams of academic writing have been produced attempting to show how trade rules would not pose a hurdle to environmental and other public interest policymaking. In 2019, the WTO ruled that the Buy Local components of seven American states' renewable energy plans violate trading rules. The case followed similar decisions against Buy Local requirements (also referred to as "local content requirements") in renewable energy laws in Canada and India, the latter in a case brought by the United States (Dumont et al. 2019). Moreover, WTO panels and the Appellate Body have generally declined to simply uphold defendants' invocation of the so-called environmental and other public interest exceptions to the trading rules if the measure can be construed as overtly favoring domestic products over imports (Moran 2017). Instead, WTO dispute resolution reports tend to find at least some fault with the defendants' measures, forcing defendants to revisit their policies.

Matters are hardly more favorable in the investment policy regime. Since the 1990s, thousands of bilateral investment treaties have been signed – many of which lack even the type of (inadequate) environmental exception clauses found in trade agreements. From the infamous early *Methanex* case against Mexican toxic waste dump regulations to the more recent *Bilcon* case against Canadian environmental impact assessment procedures, investors have brought highly controversial claims against sovereign governments' most politically sensitive domestic laws – increasingly with the use of speculative third party financing of legal fees. As a result, many policymakers are considering major changes to the investment treaty system, ranging from more institutionalization and appellate review of arbitration decisions (the EU's favored approach) to paring back of investors' access to any arbitral options (the United States' favored approach; Tucker 2018a; Dafe and Williams 2021).

The upshot of the ongoing existence of trade and investment agreements is that governments that adopt aggressive decarbonization policies are likely to face adverse rulings from trade and investment tribunals (Tienhaara and Cotula 2020). Governments will either have to be willing to suffer the consequences, including potential trade retaliation or monetary damages in investment cases, or water down their decarbonization efforts to comply with international legal rules. Those who argue that international rules do not present this tension generally insist that nondiscriminatory measures will survive review. But this claim is tautological. A nondiscriminatory measure does not, of course, violate rules against discrimination, but the question in these cases is usually what counts as "discriminatory." Moreover, in investment law, expansive interpretations of fair and equitable treatment or expropriation doctrines create the possibility of adverse judgments even in the absence of discrimination.

An intolerance for discriminatory measures also can prevent green measures from being adopted. Green policies, by their nature, create public goods that are diffuse. Those public goods are, in turn, undersupplied unless they are linked to more narrowly defined benefits. Linking green policies to local economic development is thus a critical political tool to making green policy feasible. Yet under trade law, the links between green policies and local economic development are likely to be found discriminatory. That has been the fate of Buy Local requirements in green subsidies. The EU's efforts to decarbonize its transport sector via renewable energy face a similar challenge (Fischer and Meyer 2020). The EU created incentives for the use of renewable fuels in the transport sector in the hope that the program would both reduce emissions in that sector and provide support for the EU's domestic biodiesel industry. When a significant portion of the EU's share of its own market was absorbed by low-cost, subsidized biodiesel from Indonesia and Argentina, the EU responded first with duties on imports of biodiesel. After the WTO found those duties unlawful under trade rules, the EU responded with an environmental regulation, the 2018 Renewable Energy Directive, that will phase out incentives for palm-based biodiesel (from Indonesia and Malaysia, principally) on the grounds that palm-based biodiesel creates an unacceptable risk of environmentally harmful indirect land use changes. Now Indonesia has lodged a challenge to the 2018 Renewable Energy Directive and its implementing regulations, alleging that they unlawfully discriminate against Indonesian biodiesel. Forbidding discrimination for environmental measures is not just a technical issue, then, but a major substantive constraint on nations' ability to actually enact green policies.

One policy area in particular could receive an early test and also provides an illustrative example of the problems that trade and investment law can create. Today, approximately 40 governments worldwide – including Japan, the European Union, Canada, and state governments within the United States – have regulations and/or carbon pricing schemes of one form or another that can raise the cost of production to domestic producers. However, the globalization of manufacturing has made it harder for these schemes to be effective. The problem is this: if a country pushes its industries to make costly adjustments to reduce carbon emissions and other countries do not follow suit, its manufacturers may head offshore. After all, if Vietnam or Indonesia allows firms to pollute freely, it quickly becomes an attractive business proposition to relocate there and sell cheap products back to US or European consumers. This so-called "carbon leakage" problem is not only an economic competitiveness problem but also an environmental one, as net carbon emissions have not been reduced – simply relocated. A recent study concluded that a moderate domestic carbon tax could induce up to a 19% increase in overseas emissions (Barron et al. 2018).

How to make domestic measures more effective in a world of globalized markets? One possibility is a border adjustment measure on carbon-intensive imports. Such a measure could take the form of a so-called border carbon adjustment (BCA), carbon adjustment fee (CAF), or simply, a carbon tariff. By raising the price of carbon-intensive imports that are not subject to stringent climate policies in the country where they are produced, a carbon tariff would reduce the incentive to shift production offshore and contribute to net emissions reductions (Böhringer et al. 2018; Mehling et al. 2019). The adjustment could be calculated in several ways. First, if a government is assessing a carbon tax or an equivalent measure on domestic industry, the same rate could be applied to imports. The downside to this approach is that foreign production could be significantly more polluting than domestic industry, so an identical rate could still incentivize carbon leakage. Moreover, recent meta-analyses have found that domestic carbon prices and taxes contribute far less to decarbonization than do other regulations, while causing significant political feasibility problems (Cullenwald and Victor 2020; Green forthcoming).

Second, where a tax on domestic producers is not being assessed, an implicit price could be calculated that estimates the regulatory burden for domestic firms to comply with each policy instrument, and then estimates a tariff equivalent to that price to be imposed on foreign producers. Where green subsidies lower the cost of production for foreign producers, countervailing duties equivalent to the value of the subsidy can be imposed. But this approach is exceedingly complicated computationally, and puts a focus on inventorying policy *instruments* in foreign countries, rather than *achieved emissions reductions*.[4]

A final approach that addresses the drawbacks of the previous two methods would calculate the so-called "embedded carbon" in foreign production, subtract the embedded carbon levels in US production, and apply a rate equal to the social cost of carbon to the differential.[5]

After years of debate, both in national capitals and at the WTO, momentum finally seems to be gathering for carbon border measures. The European Union recently introduced a proposal for a BCA as part of its EU Green Deal. President Biden has likewise proposed a CAF or quota on imports that do not meet US environmental standards (Holtzman 2020). Jennifer Hillman, a widely respected former WTO Appellate Body member, wrote an influential policy paper arguing that a nondiscriminatory carbon border tax would be consistent with WTO rules – a view that is increasingly widespread (Hillman 2013).

But the devil is in the details. As noted above, WTO panels and the Appellate Body have tended to nitpick, finding health and environmental measures in violation of trade rules on the grounds that relatively insignificant exceptions to blanket rules create impermissible discrimination.[6] A recent report by the Roundtable on Climate Change and Sustainable Transition identified five major design choices that could affect whether a European BCA would survive WTO scrutiny (Marcu, Mehling and Cosbey 2020). Most, though not all, of these design choices implicate a trade-off between the measure's ability to achieve its decarbonization goals and the measure's consistency with trade rules. We recount the design choices here to demonstrate how these trade-offs are likely to work in practice:

1 *Coverage of trade flows*. A BCA could apply just to imports, or alternatively also apply to exports. In the latter scenario, European exporters would get a rebate to compensate them for their higher cost of production relative to countries that don't decarbonize. A two-sided adjustment would be the most beneficial for Europe's economic competitiveness. However, from a trade law perspective, the optimal policy would be imports-only coverage, as an export adjustment could be considered a prohibited subsidy. In other words, a trade-compliant border adjustment would sacrifice European companies' global competitiveness.
2 *Geographic scope*. Europe could apply a BCA to products from all countries. Alternatively, it could exempt products from certain countries on the basis of their lower level of economic development (as is common in many trade policy regimes) or offer credits to producers based on foreign carbon pricing policies to which they are subject. From a climate perspective, the optimal policy would be to reward producers that are decarbonizing. However, from a trade law perspective, those rewards create the possibility of the border adjustment being challenged as unlawfully discriminatory. Explicitly discriminating on the basis of other nations' carbon policies raises the likelihood of adverse trade action most directly, but even origin-neutral policies that focus on the carbon associated with individual products and production methods run the risk of being found de facto discriminatory, in violation of trade rules.

3 *Sectoral scope*. Because measures that focus on foreign government policies are more problematic under trade law, a BCA is likely to focus on products and production methods. But assessing the carbon intensity of imported products is a difficult regulatory task. For that reason, some BCA proposals would apply only to the most energy-intensive and trade-exposed (EITE) industries. A common example is steel, the production of which utilizes a lot of carbon, and for which small increases in price could seriously damage Europe's competitiveness with low-cost Chinese producers. By applying a BCA only to steel imports, regulators have a manageable task and also make non-steel exporters to Europe happy. For that reason, the course of action is also most likely to survive trade law scrutiny. Contrarily, to maximize decarbonization benefits, Europe should apply a BCA to as many sectors as possible. Focusing only on steel, for instance, will place European producers that use steel as an input at a competitive disadvantage with their foreign competitors, weakening the political will within Europe for a BCA and/or leading to carbon leakage as producers move overseas to acquire steel without the costs imposed by the BCA.

4 *Emissions scope*. In producing goods, firms produce both direct and indirect emissions. The narrowest category of emissions for producing, say, an automobile, would include only those emitted by the auto factory. In contrast, a more expansive look would incorporate emissions made by the suppliers to the auto factory as well. As with the other design criteria, the best solution for the environment (inclusion of indirect emissions) is the most problematic from a trade law perspective, as it increases the chance of discrimination that cannot be justified under trade rules.

5 *Determination of embedded emissions*. There are numerous ways for customs authorities to assess how much carbon is embedded in a given shipment. The most labor-intensive is to calculate and apply different BCA rates to every single item that enters their custom areas based on a careful carbon audit of each. This would be extremely burdensome, and few border authorities would be likely to undertake it. An alternative approach is to make simplifying assumptions and come up with benchmark rates based on criteria like the source country for the imports, the lowest common denominator practices globally, or the best decarbonization practices globally. These would imply, respectively, treating all goods from the United States based on the average carbon intensity of the whole US economy (even if some industries and producers have a higher-than-average green record), treating all US goods as bad as the worst-polluting country (China or Saudi Arabia), or treating all US goods as good as microstates that emit very little carbon. Here, the best solution for both trade law and decarbonization purposes is the most labor-intensive and probably non-feasible: shipment-by-shipment rates. One solution to this problem is to employ simplifying assumptions but to allow importers to challenge the default in their individual case. If the simplifying assumptions are reasonable, such an approach will avoid the need for case-by-case inquiries in many instances, reducing the administrative burden on regulatory authorities. At the same time, the possibility of challenging the default rule as applied to you both improves accuracy from a climate point of view and makes the measure more likely to survive trade law review (by reducing the risk that a panel will find the measure arbitrarily or unjustifiable discriminatory).

In sum, there are certainly ways to design climate policy so that it maximizes the chance of surviving trade law scrutiny. But those ways may decrease the feasibility, decarbonization benefits, or both.

How to rewrite the trade rules to accommodate decarbonization

The foregoing analysis gives little hope that aggressive decarbonization policies will get a seal of approval under the existing international trade and investment rules. There are several principled reasons for concern about this looming conflict of laws. First, it may poison the well on international collaboration needed to reduce planetary emissions. If countries are litigating against one another, there may be less capacity and will to negotiate binding climate rules. Second, the conflict of laws gives domestic opponents of the GND/BBB a rhetorical resource to mobilize. Imagine major polluters like Exxon, who oppose attempts to regulate their behavior, all of a sudden finding a new passion for ensuring that the US lives by its international law obligations. Third, sustained non-compliance with international legal obligations could weaken the already fragile authority of international economic institutions like the WTO, or international law more generally – authority that can be useful for advancing global progress on a wide range of issues. Put differently, even if there is not a conflict of law problem in a strict legal sense, there could be political value in suspending extant international obligations as a way of focusing the public's attention on the mobilization. For instance, even unmeritorious challenges to GND/BBB policies could lead to an erosion of public support. In the effort to mobilize an entire economy to meet the existential threat of climate change, a challenge akin to wartime mobilization, these distractions may prove unacceptable. In short, it would be far preferable to cultivate both the impression and reality of harmony between the economic and carbon regime complex (Keohane and Victor 2011).

For the remainder of this section, we will examine progressively more ambitious options for remaking trade law. There are broadly similar reforms that could be made of investment law, though investment law is primarily embodied in bilateral treaties, so offers less bang for the diplomatic buck. As we explain, the simplest course for investment law would be either suspending those treaties until decarbonization is achieved or exempting green policies from investment dispute settlement. First, we will examine how modernized trade rules could allow more recourse to measures that link economic development to green policies, such as the BBB Buy American requirements that Joe Biden has proposed for the United States. Second, we will consider how domestic trade law could be marshaled to affirmatively battle the climate crisis. Finally, we will consider a more fulsome remaking of the trade system to facilitate all the elements of the GND.

Making trade safe for green economic development policies

As discussed above, green economic development policies are more politically feasible when they link local economic development objectives, which create concentrated benefits, to green policies that create more diffuse benefits. Examples of such policies include Buy American requirements in government procurement measures aimed at greening sectors such as infrastructure and transportation; local content requirements in subsidy programs, which require the private recipient of a government subsidy to buy local; and environmental measures that create a disparate impact on imports from countries with poor environmental practices.

The pledge to robustly enforce Buy American requirements in government procurement, as Joe Biden has promised, will likely require changes to US commitments under the WTO Agreement on Government Procurement (GPA). Under the GPA, the United States must not discriminate against goods and services from other GPA partners. In effect, the United States must treat goods from other GPA members as if they were domestically produced when it comes to applying the preference margins mandated in Buy American rules. Given that most major economies have joined (European Union and Japan) or are in the process of doing so (China and Russia), this will effectively "grandfather" into Buy American much of the global economy, significantly limiting the United States' ability to keep domestic tax dollars in the US economy.

One reform option would be to remove the nondiscrimination rules from the GPA. However, since that is the single most important element of the pact, the truncated remainder would have little commercial value for anyone. (As it happens, the US Government Accountability Office has concluded that the GPA has little economic benefit as it stands, and less for the United States than for its trading partners [GAO 2019].) Thus, a more straightforward approach would be to withdraw the United States from the GPA altogether, or work with allies to terminate the treaty. The Trump administration reportedly drafted an executive order for a US exit (Baschuk 2020), so it would be simple for the Biden administration to set that policy in motion.

Local content requirements tied to subsidy programs to incentivize the private consumption of domestic green products and services are trickier. The WTO's General Agreement on Tariffs and Trade (GATT), General Agreement on Trade in Services (GATS), Agreement on Technical Barriers to Trade (TBT), Agreement on Sanitary and Phytosanitary Measures (SPM), Agreement on Subsidies and Countervailing Measures (SCM), and Agreement on Trade-Related Investment Measures (TRIMS) contain nondiscrimination rules that, as interpreted, make it difficult for subsidy schemes to give preference to local goods and services, again as Joe Biden has proposed to do on a large scale. These nondiscrimination rules in general prohibit (1) a covered measure (such as a tax or regulation) (2) from treating "like" imported goods or services (3) less favorably than either domestic products or imports from a third country. Local content requirements like Buy American rules violate these nondiscrimination rules on their face.

Facially neutral environmental regulations that protect domestic production from competition with environmentally unsustainable imports can run afoul of these same nondiscrimination rules if the regulations are found to be de facto discriminatory. The EU's 2018 Renewable Energy Directive, discussed above, is a prime example of a facially neutral environmental regulation that is facing claims that it violates the WTO's nondiscrimination rules.

Even if a law is deemed discriminatory, either on its face or as a de facto matter, the discrimination can be excused if the measure is justified under various exceptions (such as GATT Article XX) as necessary or related to a permissible regulatory objective. Unfortunately, the Appellate Body has also interpreted these exceptions narrowly, for example, by asking whether a government has chosen the least trade restrictive measure.

Given the fragility of the global economy post-COVID and the need to rebuild alliances while also mobilizing domestic support for climate change, the United States might find value in engaging with allies to modify how WTO nondiscrimination rules and exceptions apply to these two categories of green economic development policies.

One option would be for WTO members to clarify that a complainant challenging a facially neutral government policy as discriminatory must demonstrate *both* that (1) the purpose of the policy is to treat imports less favorably (rather than say, build political support for decarbonization, supply chain reshoring and other governing priorities), and (2) the complaining party suffered adverse effects (i.e., they lost business they already had). Even if the measure is deemed discriminatory, either on its face or under this test, dispute panels should be required to excuse the measure under applicable exceptions (such as GATT art. XX(b) or XX(g)) if it makes a "material contribution" to addressing climate change. Such a rule makes clear that addressing climate change is imperative, justifying a wider margin of appreciation for WTO members than any other permissible regulatory objective. These changes could be accomplished either through explicit amendments to WTO agreements or through a binding understanding negotiated in connection with resolving the current impasse over WTO dispute resolution.

Narrowing the test for nondiscrimination has precedent within WTO/GATT legal practice. In the early and mid-1990s, the United States urged panels to use the so-called "aim and effect" test (Hudec 1998). To determine whether a facially neutral measure is discriminatory, that test required dispute panels to look at the purpose and application of a measure in assessing whether two products or services are "like" and thus capable of comparison. If two products are not "like" in light of the aim and effect of the distinctions drawn by a domestic regulatory regime, then no unlawful discrimination can occur. In 2011, a WTO panel in the *US-Clove Cigarettes* dispute adopted a similar test for likeness, again at the urging of the United States. Unfortunately, the Appellate Body rejected the test in both of these contexts, first in the *Japan-Alcoholic Beverages* in 1996 and then again in its 2012 *US-Clove Cigarettes* decision.[7]

Instead, the WTO Appellate Body has interpreted nondiscrimination rules to allow WTO panels to find discrimination without a showing of *either* discriminatory purpose or effect. The Appellate Body has said that a measure is discriminatory if it denies imported products the "effective equality of opportunities for imports to compete" with like domestic products. And instead of considering the regulatory purpose and effect of product distinctions drawn in facially neutral measures, WTO jurisprudence directs dispute panels to determine "likeness" with respect to a series of abstract traits such as the physical characteristics of the product, its various end-uses and consumer tastes. This test, and the "obsession" with likeness, has been rightly criticized by commentators and practitioners alike (Pauwelyn 2008).

Since nondiscrimination rules mark the boundary between permissible and impermissible uses of domestic regulatory power, assessing the legality of product distinctions without considering the regulatory purpose and effect of those distinctions makes little sense. A test that focused on both purpose and effects would thus better capture the intent behind the WTO's nondiscrimination rules (Hudec 1998). This course of action would also move WTO nondiscrimination law closer to US constitutional nondiscrimination rules. For instance, under the equal protection clause of the 14th Amendment, US courts will only find a facially neutral law discriminatory if a plaintiff can show *both* discriminatory purpose and discriminatory effect. Under dormant commerce clause jurisprudence, a facially neutral law can be found discriminatory upon a showing of either discriminatory intent or purpose. And even if a law is found discriminatory, it can survive if the government can demonstrate that the discrimination serves a sufficiently important government interest (Chemerinsky 2013: 473–474).

An alternative approach would be for WTO members, as well as parties to investment treaties, to agree to a peace period under which the WTO Dispute Settlement Understanding and investment dispute settlement procedures would not apply to policies related to decarbonization, including policies aimed at boosting local content, until economies get to net-zero emissions. This approach could be diplomatically easier to achieve. Rather than modify nondiscrimination rules generally, it would suspend their operation for measures related to decarbonization. Such an approach would follow the Obama administration's approach to preventing challenges to tobacco control measures in the Trans-Pacific Partnership. Such an approach could build support for decarbonization measures while deferring disagreements with allies over the future of WTO and investment rules more generally.

Using domestic trade law to decarbonize

What if the Biden administration finds a WTO membership totally unwilling to reform? It has a range of options under US domestic law. Using domestic law to impose decarbonizing trade measures first could provide leverage to negotiate subsequent reform to international rules. This constructive role for unilateral action in the trade space is well understood. Unilateral US enforcement of GATT rules during the 1980s under Section 301 of the Trade Act of 1974 gave other nations an incentive to replace the ineffective GATT dispute settlement system with the more robust WTO system. Unilateral action in the trade space complements a wide range of unilateral actions the administration could take to spur climate ambition abroad (Shaia and Colgan 2020).

These options could include incorporating environmental standards into domestic anti-dumping law. This was proposed by Dani Rodrik, as well as senators Tammy Baldwin (D-Wis.) and Jeff Merkley (D-Ore.). The latter's legislative proposal amends the US anti-dumping laws so that the so-called "normal cost" of production is "increased by an amount equal to the estimated cost of producing the merchandise under conditions under which all employees receive adequate wages and sustainable production methods are maintained." Environmental and labor groups would then be able to bring a case claiming that high-carbon imports are being dumped on the US market. If successful, the government would be obligated to increase duties to the level where the cost of pollution is internalized by the foreign producers.

Another approach would be to impose a carbon border adjustment measure. Such a measure could be difficult to get via legislation. An increasingly polarized Congress might struggle to pass a statute that would authorize a carbon border adjustment – particularly in the absence of Democratic super-majorities. But even without new legislation, presidential administrations still have a lot of delegated authority in the form of general statutes like the Clean Air Act on which they can fall back. Indeed, this domestic regulatory authority is how President Obama intended to implement the commitments his administration made in the 2015 Paris Agreement. Major policies implemented by the executive branch alone, though, must still go through often slow administrative processes, like those required by the Administrative Procedure Act, which are designed to inject deliberation and public input into executive branch policymaking. On the other side of those administrative processes, inevitable court challenges can tie up an administration's policies for months or years.

For a carbon border adjustment, though, a US president has a far easier path forward. A Cold War-era law known as Section 232 of the Trade Expansion Act of 1962 gives the president the authority to "adjust the imports" of any product that "threatens to impair the national security" of the United States. While the phrase "national security" makes most people think of defense and foreign affairs, Congress made clear that it wanted the president to take a much broader view. In assessing threats, Congress directed the president to "recognize the close relation of the economic welfare of the Nation to our national security" and to consider

> the impact of foreign competition on the economic welfare of individual domestic industries; and any substantial unemployment, decrease in revenues of government, loss of skills or investment, or other serious effects resulting from the displacement of any domestic products by excessive imports,

as well as any other factors the president deems relevant. The president can then act on his or her assessment without further authorization by Congress.

Put simply, Section 232 links national security to economic security and, in doing so, gives the president carte blanche to regulate imports that he or she decides affect some aspect of the nation's economic well-being. Section 232 also gives the president his or her choice of policy instrument; the president can impose tariffs, fees or quotas. Congress even gave advance consent to international agreements that adjust imports. Taking Congress up on its broad invitation, President Trump used Section 232 to impose tariffs on steel and aluminum imports, and he threatened to impose tariffs on auto imports as well. Past presidents have used these powers to "adjust the imports" of oil and for other purposes. Section 232 thus provides a US president with all the authority he or she needs to impose a carbon border adjustment measure.

Carbon border adjustment measures would be a much more defensible use of the broad 232 authorities than Trump's erratic approach. The US Department of Defense has already concluded that climate change poses a threat to national security, even as conventionally understood. Significant research suggests that decarbonizing the economy need not slow economic growth and is even likely to support greater economic productivity. Moreover, Section 232's ex ante grant of authority to conclude international agreements allows the president to work with US allies on carbon tariffs, rather than antagonizing them through unilateral action. Indeed, having on hand a Department of Commerce report that recommends security-motivated restrictions on carbon-intensive imports (even if the president does not ultimately impose the restrictions) can motivate allies and competitors alike to come to the table.

A global Green New Deal?

The most ambitious version of a trade/investment/climate reconciliation would be to internationalize the GND proposal advanced by Ocasio-Cortez. What might this look like?

First, nations could implement a two-track treatment of the flow of goods under a Global GND. For nations that agree to implement domestic GNDs and decarbonize their economies, tariffs on all goods would go to zero for ten years. For those that do not join the Global GND, existing tariffs would remain in place or could even rise, for instance to the equivalent of tariffs like those the United States maintains on products from countries (currently Cuba and North Korea) to which it has not extended normal trading relations status. This would represent a significant expansion on the ambitions of the Environmental Goods Agreement. Rather than reduce tariffs only on green products (many of which are already subject to low tariffs), a Global GND would link a reduction in all tariffs to the implementation of a domestic decarbonization scheme. As suggest above, for the ten-year duration of the Global GND, the dispute resolution provisions of extant international trade treaties could be temporarily suspended with regard to treaty obligations that may be inconsistent with the Global GND.[8] The Global GND could also be made enforceable through the WTO's existing structure. During the ten-year mobilization, Global GND countries would, every six months, perform and make public a full audit of their progress toward domestic implementation of the "embedded decarbonization" agenda. The WTO's Trade Policy Review Mechanism, suitably modified, could provide an existing institutional structure to promote transparency and peer review of members' domestic efforts. If member states breach their Global GND commitments, they would be subject to legal challenge at the WTO's Dispute Settlement Body. If necessary, Global GND members could set up a dedicated arbitration system to enforce the arrangement, similar to the Multi-Party Interim Appeal Arbitration Arrangement set up under article 25 of the

Dispute Settlement Understanding to serve as a makeshift appeals mechanism during the Appellate Body's incapacitation. At the end of the ten-year period, countries would hold a negotiation to decide whether to keep the Global GND in place (as perhaps more time will be needed), return to WTO obligations, or develop an entirely new treaty framework. Indeed, the WTO rules and tools have proved to be more enforceable than the international climate regimes (and governments have familiarity with how to use them); we do not have to create a new enforcement mechanism out of whole cloth.

Second, all investment treaty obligations could be similarly suspended for a ten-year timeframe. In their place, ad hoc arbitration would be available to any investor or civil society group that alleges a government is not upholding its obligations under the Global GND. As with a similar proposal made elsewhere on labor rights (Tucker 2018b), the immediate function here is naming and shaming, though sustained violation by a country could be a precursor to trade sanctions under the alternative WTO scheme mentioned above. Alternatively, investment treaty obligations (or simply the dispute resolution provisions with respect to those obligations) could be suspended only to the extent that they are inconsistent with the Global GND.[9] This strategy is perilous, however. Investment legal standards are so flexible that creative lawyers could probably find a way to parse policy regimes such that some GND-related policy could be challenged (Ortino 2020). Moreover, retaining *any* investment rules risks creating the wrong focal point for policy and politics at a time when investor expectations *need* to shift rapidly to take into account the impact of aggressive government action on climate.

Table 7.2 Possible Global Counterparts of a Domestic Green New Deal

US Green New Deal	*Global Green New Deal*
(A) Public investment	(A) Green Climate Fund/Financial Transaction Tax
(B) Environmental and social accounting	(B) Bringing more environmentally friendly regulatory review rules into next-generation trade and investment agreements
(C) Training and higher education with focus on FVCs	(C) Best practices exchange
(D) Public investment in new tech	(D) Technology transfer to poor countries
(E) Just transition	(E) Enforceable economic development chapter
(F) Democratic participation in planning, etc.	(F) Private right of action in climate disputes
(G) Creation of union jobs	(G) Worker Power Agreement
(H) Job guarantee	(H) Full Employment Mandate at IFIs
(I) Collective bargaining rights	(I) Worker Power Agreement
(J) Labor standards	(J) Worker Power Agreement / ILO
(K) Pro-labor, pro-environment trading rules	(K) Ten-year two-tier trade pact
(L) Protecting public patrimony	(L) Global oceans treaty
(M) Indigenous rights	(M) United Nations Declaration on the Rights of Indigenous Peoples +
(N) Anti-monopoly policy	(N) Effective Competition standard in trade pact
(O) Social safety net and rights	(O) Four Freedoms / Second Bill of Rights

Finally, a suite of policies complementary to the GND requirements could be put in place in international economic law and foreign policy practice as outlined in Table 7.2, including:

- A financial transaction tax, which could increase the coffers of the Green Climate Fund (Goering 2017);
- The United States could transfer all publicly funded green technology for free to poor countries (but can still require US production for local US projects to meet the US full employment objectives);
- Economic development obligations could be enforced through the new trade rules, which would compel each nation to engage in robust community-wide adjustment assistance for frontline and vulnerable persons and regions (Meyer and Sitaraman 2018);
- A worker power agreement and strengthened International Labor Organization could ensure that countries increase union density (Tucker 2018b);
- The UN could accelerate work on a global oceans treaty (Nyman et al 2018);
- An effective competition standard – instead of the consumer welfare standard – could be enforced via the new trade rules (Lynn 2020); and
- The United States could revive Franklin Roosevelt's call for a Second Bill of Rights and Four Freedoms (Paul, Darity and Hamilton 2018; Flynn and Holmberg 2019).

Conclusion

An adequate climate response must be both national and international. The United States has the lion's share of responsibility for past carbon emissions, so it must be a part of the solution. Meanwhile, the United States is responsible for only 15% of current emissions, and failure to get other countries on board means that emissions will simply "leak" overseas – along with US jobs.

As this chapter indicated, there are numerous potential conflicts between ambitious domestic climate policy and current international trading rules. Yet this need not be a barrier to action. The ten-year mobilization of the Green New Deal (and similar efforts under Build Back Better) offers an opportunity to remake and green an international trade and investment architecture that is already in crisis. The ideas discussed in this chapter contribute to a growing literature on how to best internationalize the GND and address potential conflicts between climate and trade policy (Beachy 2016; Kaufman 2018; Castano Tierno 2019). Although many specific routes are open, it is vital that the campaign for a new economy be accompanied by new and more just economic rules – both at home and abroad.

Notes

1 https://joebiden.com/climate-plan/

2 The official resolution does not call for only union jobs to be created, but does call for hiring of local workers (perhaps an indirect way of making it national in scope). Accompanying fact sheets feature the reverse of each clause.

3 See https://joebiden.com/clean-energy/; https://joebiden.com/supplychains/; https://joebiden.com/made-in-america/; https://joebiden.com/environmental-justice-plan/

4 Indeed, "green" subsidies can be problematic in terms of their impact on carbon emissions. Some such incentives, such as greening the electrical grid, both lower the cost to producers (through enhancing economic efficiency) *and* lower emissions. Other so-called green subsidies – such as free emissions allowances for national champion firms – actually increase emissions. Indeed, that was the criticism in a recent US Department of Commerce decision, which found that certain EU emissions allowances amounted to a countervailable subsidy under US domestic trade law. See (Maeder 2020).

5 This is essentially the method proposed by Mehling and Ritz (2020), though they further assume that a domestic carbon tax will be levied.
6 *United States-Measures Affecting the Production and Sale of Clove Cigarettes*, WT/DS406/AB/R (adopted April 24, 2012); *European Communities-Measures Prohibiting the Importation and Marketing of Seals Products,* WT/DS400/AB/R (adopted June 18, 2014).
7 *US-Clove Cigarettes* involved a claim under article 2.1 of the Technical Barriers to Trade (TBT) Agreement. Under that provision specifically (but not other WTO nondiscrimination rules), the AB said that no discrimination occurs if "like" imported products are treated less favorably due exclusively to a legitimate regulatory distinction. The TBT Agreement does not have exceptions like GATT article XX, necessitating policy space within the primary nondiscrimination obligation itself. Because this approach requires that any discrimination stem "exclusively" from a legitimate regulatory distinction, it is still narrower than the standard we suggest.
8 Policymakers could also consider making the Paris Climate Agreement enforceable at the WTO, along with other multilateral environmental agreements, and create a non-sustainable economy designation (similar to non-market economy designation). This would turn the WTO into a sort of "climate club," as explored by Nobel-winning economist William Nordhaus.
9 Similar proposals have been made with respect to COVID response measures (e.g., Bloomer et al. 2020).

References

Aschwanden, C. 2015. "A Lesson from Kyoto's Failure: Don't Let Congress Touch A Climate Deal." *FiveThirtyEight.* 4 December. Available from: https://fivethirtyeight.com/features/a-lesson-from-kyotos-failure-dont-let-congress-touch-a-climate-deal/.

Barron, A.R. et al. 2018. "Policy Insights from the EMF 32 Study on US Carbon Tax Scenarios." *Climate Change Economics* 9(1): 1840003.

Baschuk, B. 2020. "Trump Considers Withdrawing From WTO's $1.7 Trillion Purchasing Pact." *Bloomberg.com.* 4 February. Available from: https://www.bloomberg.com/news/articles/2020-02-04/trump-mulls-withdrawal-from-wto-s-1-7-trillion-purchasing-pact.

Beachy, B. 2016. "A New, Climate-Friendly Approach to Trade." Discussion Paper. Washington, DC: Sierra Club. Available from: http://www.sierraclub.org/sites/www.sierraclub.org/files/uploads-wysiwig/climate-friendly-trade-model.pdf" http://www.sierraclub.org/sites/www.sierraclub.org/files/uploads-wysiwig/climate-friendly-trade-model.pdf.

Bloomer, P. 2020. *Call for ISDS Moratorium During COVID-19 Crisis and Response.* New York: Columbia Center on Sustainable Development. Available from: http://ccsi.columbia.edu/2020/05/05/isds-moratorium-during-covid-19/

Böhringer C., Carbone, J., and Rutherford, T. 2018. "Embodied Carbon Tariffs." *The Scandinavian Journal of Economics* 120(1): 183–210.

Castano Tierno, P. 2019. "A Green New Deal for Europe." *Jacobin.* 11 May. Available from: https://jacobinmag.com/2019/05/europe-ecosocialism-green-new-deal-labour-melenchon-podemos.

Chemerinsky, E. 2013. *Constitutional Law: Principles and Policies*, 4th ed. New York, NY: Aspen Publishers.

Cullenward, D. and Victor, D.G. 2020. *Making Climate Policy Work.* Cambridge: Polity Press.

Dafe, F. and Williams, Z. 2021. "Banking on Courts: Financialization and the Rise of Third-Party Funding in Investment Arbitration." *Review of International Political Economy* 28(5): 1362–1384. Available from: https://doi.org/10.1080/09692290.2020.1764378.

Dumont, A.J., Ridings, P.J. and Rodriguez Mendoza, M. 2019. United States - Certain Measures Relating to the Renewable Energy Sector (Report of the Panel), No. WT/DS510/R. World Trade Organization. 27 June 27.

Eilperin, J., Dennis, B. and Mooney, C. 2018. "Trump Administration Sees a 7-Degree Rise in Global Temperatures by 2100." *Washington Post.* 28 September. Available from: https://www.washingtonpost.com/national/health-science/trump-administration-sees-a-7-degree-rise-in-global-temperatures-by-2100/2018/09/27/b9c6fada-bb45-11e8-bdc0-90f81cc58c5d_story.html.

Fischer, C., and Meyer, T. 2020. "Baptists and Bootleggers in the Biodiesel Trade: EU–Biodiesel (Indonesia)." *World Trade Review* 19(2): 297–315.

Flynn, A. and Holmberg, S.R. 2019. "America Needs Economic Rights. Now Is the Time to Push for Them." *The Nation*. 11 January. Available from: https://www.thenation.com/article/franklin-roosevelt-economic-bill-rights/.

GAO. 2019. "International Trade: Foreign Sourcing in Government Procurement." GAO-19–414. Washington, DC: Government Accountability Office. Available from: https://www.gao.gov/products/GAO-19-414.

Goering, L. 2017. "Innovative Finance Needed to Find $300 Billion a Year for Climate." *Reuters*. 15 May. Available from: https://www.reuters.com/article/us-climatechange-finance-idUSKCN18B21Z.

Green, J.F. Forthcoming. "Does Carbon Pricing Reduce Emissions? A Review of Ex-Post Analyses." *Environmental Research Letters*.

Hess, D.J. et al. 2018. "Local Matters: Political Opportunities, Spatial Scale, and Support for Green Jobs Policies." *Environmental Innovation and Societal Transitions* 26(March): 158–170. Available from: https://doi.org/10.1016/j.eist.2017.03.003.

Hillmann, J. 2013. "Changing Climate for Carbon Taxes: Who's Afraid of the WTO?" German Marshall Fund of the United States, Climate & Energy Paper Series 2013.

Holmberg, S.R. 2017. *Boiling Points: The Inextricable Links Between Inequality and Climate Change*. New York: Roosevelt Institute. Available from: https://rooseveltinstitute.org/boiling-points/.

Holtzman, J. 2020 "Biden Could Seek Carbon Taxes with Same Strategy Trump Used for Steel, Aluminum." *S&P Global Market Intelligence*. 11 December. Available from: https://www.spglobal.com/marketintelligence/en/news-insights/latest-news-headlines/biden-could-seek-carbon-taxes-with-same-strategy-trump-used-for-steel-aluminum-61685494.

Hook, L. 2019. "Surge in US Economists' Support for Carbon Tax to Tackle Emissions." *Financial Times*. 17 February. Available from: https://www.ft.com/content/fa0815fe-3299-11e9-bd3a-8b2a211d90d5.

Hudec, R. 1998. "GATT/WTO Constraints on National Regulation: Requiem for an Aim and Effects Test". *International Lawyer* 32, 619–649.

Kaufman, A.C. 2018. "New NAFTA Deal Omits Climate Change, and Hands Oil and Gas yet Another Win." Grist (blog). 1 October. Available from: https://grist.org/article/new-nafta-deal-omits-climate-change-and-hands-oil-and-gas-yet-another-win/.

Keohane, R.O. and Victor, D.G. 2011. "The Regime Complex for Climate Change." *Perspectives on Politics* 9(1): 7–23. Available from: https://doi.org/10.1017/S1537592710004068.

Lynn, B.C. 2020. *Liberty from All Masters: The New American Autocracy vs. the Will of the People*. New York: St. Martin's Publishing Group.

Maeder, J. 2020. "Forged Steel Fluid End Blocks from Italy." Investigation. Washington, DC: US Department of Commerce, International Trade Administration. 7 December. Available from: https://enforcement.trade.gov/frn/summary/italy/2020-27336-1.pdf.

Marcu, A., Mehling, M.A. and Cosbey, A. 2020. *Border Carbon Adjustments in the EU: Issues and Options*. Geneva: The European Roundtable on Climate Change and Sustainable Transition. Available from: https://ercst.org/border-carbon-adjustments-in-the-eu-issues-and-options/.

Mehling, M.A., Van Asselt, H., Das, K., Droege, S., and Verkuijl, C. 2019. "Designing Border Carbon Adjustments for Enhanced Climate Action." *American Journal of International Law* 113(3): 433–481.

Mehling, M.A. and Ritz, R.A. 2020. "Going beyond Default Intensities in an EU Carbon Border Adjustment Mechanism." Cambridge Working Papers in Economics. Cambridge: University of Cambridge Faculty of Economics. September.

Meyer, T. 2015. "How Local Discrimination Can Promote Global Public Goods". *Boston University Law Review* 95, 1937–2025.

Meyer, T. and Sitaraman, G. 2018. *A Blueprint for a New American Trade Policy*. New York: Great Democracy Initiative.

Moran, N. 2017. "The First Twenty Cases Under GATT Article XX: Tuna or Shrimp Dear?" In *International Economic Law: Contemporary Issues*. Adinolfi, G. et al. (eds.). New York: Springer International Publishing, pp. 3–21. Available from: https://doi.org/10.1007/978-3-319-44645-5_1.

Mufson, S. and McAuley, J. 2018. "France's Protesters Are Part of a Global Backlash against Climate-Change Taxes." *Washington Post*. 4 December. Available from: https://www.washingtonpost.com/world/europe/frances-protesters-are-part-of-a-global-backlash-against-climate-change-taxes/2018/12/04/08365882-f723-11e8-863c-9e2f864d47e7_story.html.

Nyman, E. et al. 2018. "71 Countries Are Negotiating a New Biodiversity Treaty. Here's What You Need to Know." *Washington Post*. 19 September. Available from: https://www.washingtonpost.com/news/monkey-cage/wp/2018/09/19/the-world-has-begun-negotiating-a-marine-biodiversity-treaty-heres-what-you-need-to-know/.

Ortino, F. 2020. *Taming the Chaos in Investment Treaty Protection*. New York: Columbia Center on Sustainable Development. Available from: http://ccsi.columbia.edu/files/2018/10/No-294-Ortino-FINAL.pdf.

Paul, M., Darity, W.Jr. and Hamilton, D. 2018. "An Economic Bill of Rights for the 21st Century." *The American Prospect*. 5 March. https://prospect.org/article/economic-bill-rights-21st-century.

Paul, M., Mason, J.W. and Fremstad, A. 2019. *Decarbonizing the US Economy: Pathways Toward a Green New Deal*. New York: Roosevelt Institute. Available from: http://rooseveltinstitute.org/decarbonizing-the-us-economy/.

Pauwelyn, J. 2008. "The Unbearable Lightness of Likeness." In *GATS and the Regulation of International Trade in Services*. Panizzon, M., Pohl, N. and Sauvé, P. (eds.). Cambridge: Cambridge University Press, pp 358–369.

Recognizing the Duty of the Federal Government to Create a Green New Deal. H. Res. 109, 116th Congress. 2019. Available from: https://www.congress.gov/bill/116th-congress/house-resolution/109/text.

Ruggie, J.G. 1982. "International Regimes, Transactions, and Change: Embedded Liberalism in the Postwar Economic Order." *International Organization* 36(2): 379–415. Available from: https://doi.org/10.2307/2706527.

Shaia, F. and Colgan, J.D. 2020. *Presidential Climate Action on Day One: A Foreign-Policy Guide for the Next U.S. President*. Providence, RI: Watson Institute for International and Public Affairs, Brown University. October. Available from: https://watson.brown.edu/files/watson/imce/news/explore/2020/Final%20CSL%20Report.pdf.

Smith, N. [Noahpinion]. 2019. [*The problem is that because the U.S. only produces 14% of global carbon emissions (and falling every day), the Green New Deal won't actually reduce climate change. Thus, we'll be paying for both the Green New Deal AND the hurricanes, floods, droughts, wildfires, etc.*]. [Twitter]. 9 February. Available from: https://twitter.com/Noahpinion/status/1094110992638693377

Stokes, L.C. 2016. "Electoral Backlash against Climate Policy: A Natural Experiment on Retrospective Voting and Local Resistance to Public Policy." *American Journal of Political Science* 60(4): 958–974. Available from: https://doi.org/10.1111/ajps.12220.

Tienhaara, K. and Cotula, L. 2020. "Raising the Cost of Climate Action? Investor-State Dispute Settlement and Compensation for Stranded Fossil Fuel Assets." Land, Investment and Rights Series. London: International Institute for Environment and Development. October. Available from: https://pubs.iied.org/17660IIED/.

Tucker, T.N. 2018a. *Judge Knot: Politics and Development in International Investment Law*. London: Anthem Press.

Tucker, T. 2018b. *Seven Strategies to Rebuild Worker Power for the 21st Century Global Economy: A Comparative and Historical Framework for Policy Action*. New York: Roosevelt Institute. Available from: http://rooseveltinstitute.org/seven-strategies-rebuild-worker-power/.

Tucker, T. 2019. *Fixing the Senate: Equitable and Full Representation for the 21st Century*. New York: Roosevelt Institute. Available from: https://rooseveltinstitute.org/wp-content/uploads/2020/07/RI_Fixing-The-Senate_report-201903.pdf

PART II

Tackling injustice through the Green New Deal

8

JOBS, JUSTICE, AND THE GREEN NEW DEAL

Joanna Robinson

August 2021: the present

Climate change is wreaking havoc around the world. Deadly fires, floods, heat waves and hurricanes have become the new norm. The West Coast of North America is burning. Over the last two months in British Columbia, Canada, alone, 1,511 wildfires burned close to 800,000 hectares of land in what is likely the worst fire season in recorded history (Emergency Management BC 2021). Fires destroyed the entire town of Lytton, B.C. at the same time as heat records were shattered across the province, resulting in over 500 lives lost from the deadly heat dome. Parts of Southern Europe and North Africa are aflame. Deadly floods killed over 200 people in Western Europe last month (Dewan 2021). The US Gulf Coast has just been walloped by the second-worst hurricane in recorded history, destroying homes and wiping out power for millions of people (Kozlov 2021).

July 2021 earned the distinction of being the world's hottest month ever recorded, according to the National Oceanic and Atmospheric Association's (NOAA) National Centers for Environmental Information (NOAA 2021). In August the Intergovernmental Panel on Climate Change (IPCC) released its latest Report, sounding the loudest alarm yet about the dangers of climate change – pointing to its severe and often irreversible effects in all regions of the globe – and calling for "immediate, rapid and large-scale reductions" to avoid planetary catastrophe (IPCC 2021a). Without concrete and dramatic measures to reduce greenhouse gas emissions (GHGs) and lower global temperatures, the kinds of impacts the world witnessed recently – from fires and floods to extreme temperatures – will only increase in frequency and severity.

The report is just the latest iteration of similar calls for action over the last decade by the IPCC and other international environmental bodies and climate activists – calls that have too often been ignored by governments that have largely failed to take the kind of bold action necessary to reverse the path of climate change devastation. As Greta Thunberg, Swedish climate activist, recently proclaimed at the Youth4Climate conference: "Words that sound great, but so far have led to no action. Our hopes and dreams drown in their empty words and promises" (Carrington 2021).

To make matters worse, the alarming news about climate change has occurred simultaneously with the devastation wrought by the COVID-19 pandemic globally, including

DOI: 10.4324/9781003110880-11

billions of people sickened, millions of deaths and unprecedented job losses, particularly for women who left the workforce in unforeseen numbers (Ellingrud and Hilton Segel 2021). The pandemic also revealed weaknesses in the social safety net and the stark inequalities within and between countries; its impacts made worse by a world polarized politically – one telling example being the attempted coup by rioters who stormed the US Capitol and tried to subvert democracy at the end of President Trump's term in January 2021 (Barry, McIntire and Rosenberg 2021).

The pandemic exposed the underlying inequalities that had long been ignored by policy makers and revealed that the burden of these crises fell disproportionately on racialized and low-income people (Evelyn 2020). Racialized and low-income individuals and families are disproportionately impacted by the devastation of climate change as well as measures to combat it such as carbon taxes and regulations (Gardiner 2020). This bleak period should not have come as a surprise. Scientists, activists and policy makers have sounded the alarm for decades about climate devastation (Bell 2021), growing inequality and poverty (Picketty 2014), the dangers of a global pandemic (Beck 1992) and political polarization (Abramowitz and McCoy 2019) – issues that are inextricably linked. Measures to combat poverty, inequality, the erosion of public trust and health risks must be part of any credible and effective climate change plan.

Let's be clear. The roots of the climate crisis and the crisis created by the COVID-19 pandemic are intricately connected. Many communities around the world have been living on the frontlines of both the climate crisis and the inequality crisis for decades. In Canada, a shockingly high number of First Nations reserves have no access to clean drinking water or adequate housing, despite decades of promises by provincial and federal governments (McGregor 2012). First Nations schools in Canada are also chronically underfunded. In 2020, Canada spent almost $5,000 more per pupil for off-reserve schools than they did for on-reserve schools, reflecting a 30% funding gap between First Nations and non-First Nations schools (Drummond and Kachuck Rosenbluth 2013).

For low-income workers – largely women and racialized individuals – wages have stagnated, poverty is on the rise, and access to secure, adequate housing is declining (Galabuzzi and Block 2018). An increasing number of workers are employed in jobs that do not provide a living wage or provide benefits such as sick leave and pensions, the impact of which was revealed when COVID-19 hit (Enriques and Goldstein 2020).

Given the dire circumstances, it is hard not to despair and feel powerless to enact the massive reforms needed to mitigate these near-term catastrophes. Yet hope is not lost. From the climate activists around the world who are fighting to make climate justice a central focus of governments to the Indigenous land defenders across the globe, many people work tirelessly to protect their lands and livelihoods from ecological collapse and economic devastation. More broadly, a new sense of urgency and cautious optimism is emerging. Even the 2021 IPCC report contains clear pathways to a sustainable climate future, if we act quickly and boldly (IPCC 2021b). What would that world look like? And how do we get there?

Fast-forward to August 2050: a green and just new world

Can we imagine a better world? One that addresses the climate and inequality crises together? If we truly prioritize the health and well-being of people and the planet, it is possible to get to what Naomi Klein characterizes as, "a future world radically better than our own" (Klein 2020a). A radically better world prioritizes health and well-being, child care, gender equity, ending racial discrimination, affordable housing, human rights, environmental justice, Indigenous reconciliation and a just transition to a zero-carbon economy through investments in clean energy and the expansion of secure, living-wage jobs in a caring economy. This is a vision that can replicate in countries around the world.

How do we get there? Close your eyes and imagine the future of a country like Canada.

The first step came when the Canadian government passed the first well-being budget in the history of the country in 2021, as part of a COVID-19 recovery plan and to set the stage for a secure climate future. The goal was to create the conditions for a just and equitable society. Modeled on the 2021 New Zealand well-being budget (Government of New Zealand 2021), it moved beyond the idea of reducing deficits and growing GDP as measures of economic strength, and treated money as a tool for enhancing the health and well-being of people and the environment. No longer were budgets based on the politics of the electoral cycle, but rather on the notion of caring for people and the planet (The Leap Manifesto n.d.).

The second major reform was the passing of a Green New Deal for Canada in 2022 with the goal of eliminating poverty and creating millions of jobs in renewable energy, care work, health and education (The Leap 2021). The Green New Deal transformed the economy and society, allowing for workers to be retrained to work in zero-carbon sectors, prioritizing jobs and training for Indigenous, racialized and low-income communities. Millions of well-paying jobs were created, the tax base was expanded, and the crises of underfunded housing, health and education were addressed head-on, all while building a robust and sustainable economy (Ibid.).

Massive investments in solar, wind, and water – paid for through a significantly increased carbon tax and by redirecting fossil fuel subsidies to supporting the clean energy sector – created a realistic pathway to transition to a 100% renewable energy economy by 2050 (Government of Canada 2021). Imagine: solar panels on every house, building, and factory across the country. Electric cars in driveways. Cities redesigned to be carbon neutral with expanded green public transit systems. High-speed trains connecting major Canadian and US cities. Renewed and retrofitted homes providing energy-efficient affordable housing. The creation of thousands of kilometers of bike paths, and legislation enacted requiring all vehicles on all our roads to be electric by 2035 (Transport Canada 2021). Investing in this massive transition led Canada to become more innovative and competitive as a world leader in green energy production and manufacturing as well as sustainable living (Cruickshank 2020) and enabled it to ascend to the top of the United Nations Human Development Index.[1]

At the same time, one of the most important steps that Canada took was to finally commit to full reconciliation with Indigenous Peoples. In 2015, the Truth and Reconciliation Commission (TRC) – which documented the history and lasting impact of the Canadian Indian residential school system – released 94 Calls to Action to address the multiple consequences of residential schools, including in the areas of child welfare, education, justice, health, culture and language (TRC 2015). In 2022, governments across Canada began to implement the TRC Calls to Action. At first progress was slow, but by 2030 all 94 Calls to Action were acted upon, transforming the nation-to-nation relationship with Indigenous Peoples and the Crown. This was a pivotal moment for Canada to address its colonial past and the depth of harm caused to Indigenous Peoples and begin to right past wrongs. True reconciliation allowed Indigenous communities to become key partners in conservation and protecting biodiversity, enhancing environmental stewardship through Indigenous governance and knowledge systems (Garnett et al. 2018).

How did Canada do it? It wasn't easy. And it could not have happened without the social movements that fought for social and environmental justice, including the youth climate justice movement, the Indigenous land-back movement and Black Lives Matter. These movements seized the political opportunities that emerged from the COVID-19 pandemic to build a stronger, more equitable and just society. And they showed us that another world was possible.

A Green New Deal for all: providing good jobs and protecting the environment

How do we move from the current precarious state of the planet in 2021 to a just and sustainable world by 2050? How does this vision become reality? What are the key elements of the radically better future? Many scholars and activists have referred to the change we need as being rooted in the concepts of "care and repair," stressing the need both to care for people through living wages and good clean jobs, and care for the planet through repairing and respecting fragile ecosystems (Klein 2020b). This means investing not only in the renewable energy sectors, but also in health, social services and education. It means, importantly, affordable high-quality child care, investments to enable lifelong learning for all, and investments in research. It means making sure parents have supports to house, nourish and feed their children with healthy food and ensuring that individuals can afford their prescription medications.

In terms of repairing the planet, the 2021 IPCC report also offers hope for a positive pathway forward, maintaining that as long as we act now, with rapid and bold solutions, we can meet the challenge of climate change and begin to reverse the devastation it has wrought as well as prevent future catastrophes (IPCC 2021c). This cautiously hopeful pathway coincides with both increasing public support for climate change mitigation and adaptation and the COVID-19 pandemic recovery initiatives emerging around the world – initiatives that rely heavily on visions laid out in the global versions of a Green New Deal (Tienhaara 2019). In many countries, COVID-19 recovery has focused on public investments in infrastructure and services that focus on green energy and low-carbon sectors. Many plans also emphasize a gender-inclusive recovery to ensure the re-entry of women into the workforce (OECD 2021; Solomon et al. 2020).

What scholars and activists make clear is that an effective Green New Deal (GND) must be bold, transformative and implemented at an unprecedented scale. While iterations of the GND have existed for years and have been gaining traction in the public policy arena, mainstream politics and elected governments have generally been slow to link job growth to climate change, particularly when it concerns economic justice. Many of the GND proposals around the world offer little more than the status quo or mere tweaks to the economic system (see Adler and Wargen and Klein, this volume) rather than a plan: "to charge forward with a Green New Deal that offers a program of economic transformation, grounded […] in the world's best climate science, with a vision on the scale of an existential threat to human civilization" (Aronoff et al. 2020). As Greta Thunberg recently reminded us, governments and policy makers must go beyond words and promises, to concrete action (Carrington 2021).

What are the possibilities of a combined GND/COVID-19 recovery plan that prioritizes economic and climate justice by focusing on creating decent, well-paying jobs in low- or zero- carbon sectors of the economy? In a context where the COVID-19 pandemic has laid bare the reality of social and economic injustice in our communities globally, how can we ensure a plan that is truly transformative and justice-oriented? Despite the devastation wrought by the COVID-19 pandemic, one silver lining is the growing awareness of the need for robust public policy to prevent economic collapse and support the well-being of people. COVID-19 recovery proposals include a call for investments in green infrastructure, while also recognizing the need to create strong protections for workers, such as better wages and benefits, stronger labor policies and investments in affordable housing. From US President Joe Biden's Build Back Better agenda (White House n.d.) to Canada's green recovery plan,[2] governments around the world are increasingly linking recovery policies to climate change mitigation, targeting investments to areas of the economy that will both create jobs and contribute to reducing greenhouse gas emissions.

The jobs-versus-the-environment dilemma is a false dichotomy used to resist decarbonization, particularly from the oil and gas industry and other high carbon-intensive sectors, which have the backing of powerful unions that fight to preserve jobs in these sectors (Robinson 2020). Traditional carbon-intensive sectors such as oil and gas, forestry and auto-manufacturing have generally provided well-paid, secure jobs that allowed millions of workers – mostly male breadwinners – to rise into the middle class in North America (Chen 2015; Robinson 2020). Research on transition to green jobs reveals that these workers and the unions that represent them are concerned about shifting to jobs that are low paid and precarious (Robinson 2020). This is reinforced by the increase in poverty-wage, precarious work – often in care work or the service sector.

Research on the post-industrial organization of work points to increasing income inequality in Canada and internationally, resulting in part from the shift from a manufacturing to a service-sector economy. A consequence of this shift is an increasingly segmented labor market for recent immigrants, visible minorities and women (Chun 2009; Zuberi 2013). Scholars argue that growing inequality and poverty is directly related to the rapid expansion of poverty-wage jobs and temporary and precarious employment in the service sector (Fuller and Vosko 2008; Zuberi 2006). At the same time, much of this research focuses on workers in the rapidly expanding service sector. Scholars often accept as inevitable the decline of the manufacturing sector and the disappearance of well-paid, secure work. Yet the possibility of a just GND adds a new dimension to debates about the loss of manufacturing and the rise in precarity. Policy makers often focus on the renewable energy sector while neglecting other critically important sectors of the economy, such as health services, child care and education, as important to a low-carbon economy (Klein 2020b; Aronoff et al. 2020). Investing in these sectors is potentially transformative and could simultaneously address the climate crisis and inequality as long as there is a guarantee that these jobs are well paid and secure.

While some opponents of the GND argue that job losses in oil and gas and other carbon-intensive sectors such as the transportation, manufacturing and automotive industries will lead to economic devastation, research shows that transition to a net-zero economy through a GND will create more jobs than an extractive economy (U.S. Department of Energy 2017). The experience of countries that have invested in transition and retraining for workers in green jobs reveals the positive impact of climate change for employment, often ignored by governments and policy makers (Lipsig-Mummé 2013; McBride and Shields 2011). Investing in green jobs can create millions of good new jobs beyond the energy sector, in education, health and social services, while also tackling poverty and inequality and providing a pathway out of the jobs-versus-the-environment trap. A justice-oriented GND offers a clear path forward that includes retraining for energy sector workers, jobs for underrepresented populations, investments in other sectors beyond renewable energy, such as care work, health care, education and housing (Aronoff et al. 2020). The COVID-19 economic recovery may be just the catalyst we need to get us there through a justice-oriented GND that tackles both inequality and climate change.[3]

This chapter and other chapters in this volume point to the potential of the COVID-19 pandemic recovery to unite the concerns of climate activists with social and economic justice activists by advocating for jobs, justice and a Green New Deal to be the central platform of recovery policies. In the section below, I lay out a five-point plan for achieving a just transition to a zero-carbon economy made possible by a version of a GND that focuses on good jobs in renewable energy and beyond, including care work, health, education and housing – areas of the economy impacted severely by the COVID-19 pandemic. Investing in these sectors can potentially result in a massive reduction in GHG emissions while also addressing inequality, poverty and racial discrimination.

A five-point plan for a just transition

We are facing twin crises: climate change and inequality. We need to merge the climate crisis with the inequality crisis by reorienting the focus toward an economy based on renewables and care work (Aronoff 2021; Klein 2020a). As Naomi Klein points out, the COVID-19 pandemic revealed the deep deficit in care (Klein 2020b): care for the elderly; care for the immunocompromised; care for essential workers; care for women who disproportionately lost their jobs and/or needed to care for children at home due to school closures; care provided largely by racialized, low-income, front-line communities that bore the brunt of COVID-19, from risks of contracting the virus to the mitigation measures implemented. And now we see a care deficit for our children who are heading back to school to face the highly contagious delta variant, potentially creating a nightmare scenario of sick children. At the same time, the climate crisis – laid bare by recent catastrophic events like forest fires, floods and hurricanes – has revealed, as Naomi Klein shows, the deep deficit in care for the planet, reminding us that it is time to invest in caring for people and the planet (Klein 2020b).

How do we solve the care deficit? Below, I offer a five-point plan for a radically better world.

Invest in training and jobs in renewable energy and transportation to ensure just transition

A key part of any transformative GND requires transitioning energy production and transportation away from fossil fuels to renewables. In Canada, for example, while there have been important efforts to switch to clean energy by phasing out coal production, most of the gains from this transition in terms of emissions reductions have been offset by increased emissions in two sectors: transportation, and oil and gas (Plumtre 2018). Two of the biggest challenges to shifting away from fossil fuels, particularly in North America, include political opposition to a GND in areas that depend on the oil and gas sector for employment and economic growth, and anxiety over job losses in the oil and gas sector and the impact on communities (Robinson 2020).

Governments and policy makers need to address these concerns with targeted programs and investments in regions that are most likely to be impacted by limiting fossil fuel production. The good news is that the renewable energy and emissions-free public transportation sectors can create millions of jobs around the globe to offset losses in the oil and gas industry (Doherty 2019). At the same time, research on potential sites for renewable energy production demonstrates that regions where current fossil fuel hubs are located have the "greatest potential for both wind and solar electricity generation," thus potentially limiting political opposition as long as there is a strategic and coordinated effort to retrain workers in renewable energy sectors (Tomer, Kane and George 2021).

Key pillars in the transition to renewable energy jobs include:

- Investing in skills training and re-training to support transitioning workers from carbon-intensive sectors (oil and gas, auto manufacturing, etc.) to jobs in renewable energy, such as solar and wind, and connecting them to employers in renewable energy;
- Ensuring that workers are further supported through labor and employment policy by enacting living wage legislation, expanding access to employment insurance, increasing eligibility for pension plans and upholding the right to collective bargaining;
- Working in partnership with educational institutions, labor unions and local communities to ensure that the needs of workers, their families and communities are met during the transition;
- Supporting economic development and diversification through subsidies to renewable energy projects and investments in research and development, particularly in areas where the oil and gas sector is a large sector of the economy (Ibid.);
- Using a combination of regulation and incentives to ensure investments in renewable energy;[4]
- Applying an equity lens to job creation: target jobs and training to racialized and low-income communities, which have often been excluded from accessing decent employment opportunities (Aldana Cohen et al. 2021);
- Investing in the expansion of public transportation, cycling and pedestrian infrastructure in urban areas and in high-speed rail to connect regions. Expanding emissions-free public transit reduces greenhouse gas emissions, creates good – often unionized – jobs, and enhances social justice by expanding access to low-income communities (Beckles 2020; Doherty 2019).

At the same time, it is crucial that policy makers and activists work together with unions and workers to build support for just transition. Research on workers in carbon-intensive sectors of the economy shows high levels of support for climate change initiatives among workers, but also concerns about job losses and transition to lower-wage jobs with less security and fewer benefits (Allan and Robinson 2022). Research on unions and transition to a green economy also reveals that support for green jobs is contingent upon those jobs being unionized to provide financial security (Robinson 2020).

Support a caring economy through investments in education and health to ensure social justice is a pillar of the GND

A key area for a GND investment is care work (Aronoff 2021). While the link between a GND and job creation in renewable energy and transportation sectors is evident, there is growing awareness of and attention to sectors of the economy that have always been "green" in that they produce few emissions and where transition re-training is not necessary, including health care, education and social services. Investments in these sectors to expand employment and increase security through better wages, work conditions, and benefits have the potential to address climate change and ensure social justice through supporting good jobs for women and racialized workers and newcomers, who often fill jobs in these sectors (Ibid.). From nurses to cleaners, personal support workers and teachers, workers in the care economy have shown us that they are the ones who supported and steered us through the pandemic.

Historically ignored and not a central part of a green jobs strategy, scholars and activists are increasingly calling attention to the importance of care work in building a long-term, sustainable economy (Ibid.). Recently, activists, scholars and academics have begun to center the GND on the concept of care. From Naomi Klein's call to "repair our broken infrastructures of care" (Klein 2020a) to AOC's vision of a GND that includes paid family leave and childcare (Klein 2019), care work is at the center of a green recovery. Caring for people and the planet, these experts argue, is the necessary pathway forward for a GND that is just and sustainable (see also Roberts-Gregory, in this volume).

The rise in precarious work and the consequences of the COVID-19 pandemic on low-income workers, their families and their communities demonstrate that a true recovery plan needs to incorporate caring for people as a central component to well-being. As the last 18 months have made abundantly clear, care work is critically important to the well-being and resilience of our communities. The toll COVID-19 wrought on front-line workers – often racialized, low-income workers – as well as the excessive deaths in long-term care homes and the exodus of women from the job market demonstrate that a truly transformative recovery plan should prioritize care work and policies that support women's re-entry into the labor market. We have the unique opportunity to address the challenges revealed by the pandemic while also tackling the climate crisis by investing in a care economy, including in the health, education and social service sectors and by ensuring that these jobs are good jobs – with decent pay, benefits and security.

Key pillars to prioritizing care work in a GND include:

- Implementing reforms in the long-term care sector, such as improving work conditions, increasing wages, and improving standards of care (conditions and pay), which would also reduce risks in future pandemics (Armstrong et al. 2020);
- Ensuring that long-term care residential services are part of universal, publicly funded, accessible health services;[5]
- Expanding home care and access to personal support workers for an aging population;[6]
- Expanding paid parental leave programs and ensure the right to return to work;
- Implementing publicly funded, universal and accessible high-quality child care;
- Investing in early childhood education programs and making them accessible to all families;[7]
- Increasing funding for public education, particularly for schools in low-income neighborhoods;
- Investing in Indigenous education by increasing funding for on-reserve First Nations schools and expanding access to post-secondary education for Indigenous populations;[8]
- Expanding access to mental health services and supports, especially for vulnerable populations.

A secure and sustainable future depends on providing the tools for ensuring resilience for people and the environment. Investing in care work, including health care, education, childcare and social services, is the most effective way to expand low-emissions jobs and reduce vulnerability through increased access to services and better wages and benefits. Care work also tackles the problem of women's unemployment and precarity in the workforce by increasing their participation, thus expanding the tax base and boosting economic growth. Investing in universal child care and early childhood education, for example, allows women into the workforce in greater numbers while also increasing tax revenue, thus reducing the cost of the program (Fortin 2017).

Build affordable, sustainable housing to ensure an inclusive GND

A critically important area for the GND should be the expansion of sustainable, affordable housing. In many cities around the world, the housing crisis has reached a tipping point. Many Canadians, including new graduates from post-secondary institutions, immigrants, and refugees, are struggling to find affordable housing, a situation exacerbated by the COVID-19 crisis as people face job losses, decline in income and even eviction. The focus on new private sector housing has targeted better-off families while the shortage of rentals available, the lack of affordable housing, and the declining public investment in housing exacerbate these challenges (see United Way 2011). Racialized communities are particularly impacted by discrimination, (un)affordability and displacement (Springer 2021).

When housing affordability declines in urban centers, more people get pushed out of the city into substandard housing in the outer suburbs, requiring them to rely more on private cars as access to public transit decreases (Weiner and Kammen 2019). The lack of affordable rental housing also contributes to homelessness, a major issue in cities globally. An inclusive GND helps alleviate this challenge, while also reducing emissions in the housing sector, by building sustainable housing and focusing on initiatives such as infill, densification and retrofits.

While governments around the world have implemented or promised policies for sustainable housing, most tend to focus on subsidies for home retrofits such as green homes programs (see the Canada Greener Homes Grant, for example; Natural Resources Canada n.d.). While these are commendable, they fail to provide affordable housing for those in need, they do not prioritize rental housing retrofits, and they ignore the importance of job retraining or decent wages and benefits. An inclusive GND focused on housing would expand affordable housing, prioritize rental retrofits, reduce emissions, and expand training and jobs for communities in need. For example, the United States Green New Deal for Public Housing Act introduced by Bernie Sanders and Alexandria Ocasio-Cortez would potentially create nearly 250,000 jobs in the housing sector and increase affordable housing (Sanders 2021). Investing in affordable housing not only addresses climate change, but also reduces poverty and racism, and increases community resilience and well-being (Aldana Cohen et al. 2021).

Key pillars for an inclusive GND housing strategy include:

- Creating green community infrastructure by investing in energy-efficient renovations of existing public housing stock;[9]
- Prioritizing worker training, especially for unionized and disadvantaged workers for jobs in green building and retrofits (Aldana Cohen et al. 2021; Robinson 2020);
- Investing in and building sustainable housing through rapid access to government funding (see Canada's Rapid Housing Initiative, CMHC 2021);
- Focusing on new urban planning and inclusionary zoning to ensure infill and densification, and making urban neighborhoods more walkable (Dembicki 2020a);
- Expanding supportive housing through programs to address homelessness and housing affordability challenges, particularly for racialized or Indigenous populations.[10]

A Green New Deal for housing would recognize that climate and housing are inextricably linked. Targeted action on housing, including expanding and/or retrofitting green rental housing and re-training workers for green construction and retrofits would reduce pollution, lower GHG emissions and provide much-needed secure and sustainable housing and jobs to disadvantaged communities.

Make decolonization and Indigenous justice a key pillar of the GND

In Canada, the United States and beyond, a critically important pillar of climate justice is the recognition of the rights of Indigenous Peoples through policies that ensure decolonization and reconciliation. Colonization has displaced Indigenous Peoples, disconnecting them from their traditional lands and cultures and excluding them from economic development (Yellowhead Institute 2021). At the same time, colonization has polluted lands and waterways through the development of large-scale resource extraction projects that threaten the health and security of Indigenous Peoples and their traditional way of life (Lavoie 2018; Raygorodesky 2018).

Indigenous-led GND and climate justice movements in Canada, the United States and around the globe remind us of our obligation to listen to Indigenous Peoples and fight for the climate solutions they propose (Yellowhead Institute 2021). As Winona LaDuke suggests in this volume, we need a bold proposal for an Indigenous-led GND – what she calls "the Sitting Bull Plan" – that would respect Indigenous knowledge of the land and biodiversity while also including Indigenous Peoples as partners in a new sustainable materials economy (for example, one built around the production of hemp) (see LaDuke, in this volume). Other Indigenous activists call for restoring Indigenous economies through expanding the jurisdiction of Indigenous Peoples over their traditional territories (Yellowhead Institute 2021). Recent research demonstrates that Indigenous-managed lands globally are more resilient and far better at protecting biodiversity than non-Indigenous-managed lands (Tauli Corpez 2020).

Key pillars for an Indigenous-led GND include:

- Ensuring environmental and economic justice by developing energy projects sustainably and equitably, which would involve investing in Indigenous-led and -owned renewable energy projects (such as wind and solar power) and training for jobs in these sectors (Yellowhead Institute 2021);
- Engaging in meaningful consultation with Indigenous communities for resource projects on traditional territories;
- Supporting transformative solutions transferring power over land and resources to Indigenous communities (Dembicki 2020b; Yellowhead Institute 2019);
- Transforming from extractive, pollutive infrastructure (such as oil pipelines and mining) to life-sustaining infrastructure (such as water pipelines and biodiversity projects) that are central to sustainable economies (LaDuke and Cowen 2020);
- Working with Indigenous communities on conservation and biodiversity to ensure the protection of water and forests through recognition of land title rights and jurisdictional control (Raygorodesky 2018);
- Fully implementing the United Nations Declaration on the Rights of Indigenous Peoples (United Nations General Assembly 2007).

Centuries of colonial extractive economies have resulted in a crisis for Indigenous Peoples globally. From the forcible removal from traditional lands to broken promises on housing, education and access to economic justice, Indigenous Peoples have borne the brunt of an economic system based on extraction and commodification (Bernauer 2019; Crook, Short and South 2018). The time is now to repair the harm done, through restitution, reconciliation and justice-based climate solutions.

Work in partnership with social movements to ensure a justice-oriented Green New Deal

Political responses to the climate crisis – including developments of a justice-oriented GND – must include the voices of social movements and the millions of climate activists from around the world. All social movements are political by nature. Social movement activists and organizations develop common political agendas, mobilize constituencies to make demands on the state, and push elected leaders to fulfill their responsibilities and obligations to their citizens. Engaging with political parties creates leverage for a movement's demands by providing access to decision-making channels (Tarrow 2012). Ultimately, social movements are a necessary part of the political process and democracy, where citizen-led pressure from below makes action occur from the top down. It is the interactions between movements and the state that create possibilities for political change to occur (Ibid.).

For social and political change to occur, political channels need to be open and inviting to allow social movements to have a say in decision-making processes by governments. This is essential for inclusive and democratic change. In a world faced by increasingly complex and challenging social and environmental problems, we cannot afford to leave decision-making to elected parties alone. Social movements are essential vehicles for fostering social transformation through sustained pressure and engagement with mainstream political parties.

We need what Avi Lewis calls "a movement-electoral coalition" (Savage 2021), whose pillars include:

- Ensuring that citizen-led movements are at the table when negotiating climate agreements at multiple governance levels;
- Incorporating participatory democracy tools and transparency into government decision-making bodies, especially those focused on climate policy;
- Working with local communities when planning transition projects – such as from oil and gas to renewables or in climate mitigation strategies such as building retrofits, infill and densification – to ensure buy-in and support from local citizens, including promoting co-resource management and co-ownership (see Doukas et al. 2020; Schiffer 2017);
- Supporting, listening to and enacting policy recommendations from Indigenous-led movements such as Land Back to ensure both environmental and economic justice;[11]
- Working with labor movements to ensure the concerns of workers (racialized and low-income workers, in particular) about just transition and climate mitigation are heard (Robinson 2020).

To ensure a radically better world and a justice-oriented GND, policy makers and governments must listen to and support climate activists and work in partnership with social movements – from the youth-led Sunrise Movement to Indigenous Land Back movements and labor movements – to ensure that the voices of those at the margins are heard and concerns about climate justice are incorporated into climate policies.

Conclusion

The 2050 vision described above must not remain a dream but become a reality. Time is running out to create a just and sustainable world and prevent the catastrophic events that will continue to devastate the planet and people as a result of climate change and growing inequality. As Avi Lewis reminds us: "This is our shot. We need to get it right" (Savage 2021).

The chapters in this volume demonstrate that we have the evidence we need. We have the science. We have the technology and traditional knowledge to get us out of the climate crisis, reduce emissions and save the planet. We have the means to pay for a just transition. There are millions of climate justice activists and land defenders around the world who are on the frontlines of action to protect the planet and the people. We also have the social policy tools to deal with the inequality crisis – with countless examples of successful policy initiatives in countries internationally, from investments in renewable energy and a care-based economy. What we lack so far is the political will.

Climate change is increasingly a political problem. We need a bold political vision to address this crisis; a robust, bold and effective Green New Deal that will ensure a just transition to a carbon-neutral economy that lifts people up, protects the environment, and links climate action with social justice. The key is to advance the policy agenda and turn the tide of politics from one of denial, apathy and inaction to rapid intervention and effective action. The good news is that we now have growing public support for an inclusive GND as well as a paradigm shift with regard to rapid governmental policy responses due to the COVID-19 pandemic, which creates the opportunity for a new path forward for people and the planet. Public opinion is shifting, and governments are increasingly acknowledging the severity of the climate change crisis and the urgency to act quickly and with bold policies. From Biden's Build Back Better Agenda in the United States (White House n.d.) to New Zealand's Well-being Budget (Government of New Zealand 2021), policy makers are increasingly focusing on policies that work to enhance well-being and inclusion and reduce GHG emissions (see also Seth Klein's chapter in this volume for a discussion on the need for a massive mobilization of resources on the scale of World War II in order to solve the climate crisis).

The stakes are higher than ever. We need to act now, with robust and bold policies to reduce emissions and address the growing challenge of rising poverty, inequality, precarious work, and the care deficit. The five-point plan to an inclusive GND offered in this chapter – investing in renewable energy and retraining workers, expanding the care economy and sustainable housing, supporting the rights of Indigenous Peoples and their jurisdiction over traditional lands, and working in partnership with social movements around the world – offers a concrete pathway to a just and sustainable world that is radically better, more sustainable and more equitable.

Notes

1 See: http://hdr.undp.org/en/content/human-development-index-hdi

2 The Canadian government's 2021 budget includes investing $17.6 billion in a green recovery (Department of Finance Canada 2021).

3 For example, in a recent study of COVID-19 fiscal recovery policies around the globe, Hepburn et al. (2020:17) found that "recovery packages that seek synergies between climate and economic goals have better prospects for increasing national wealth, enhancing productive human, social, physical, intangible, and natural capital."

4 Examples include California's Million Solar Roofs campaign, Canada's carbon tax regimes and subsidies for home retrofitting.

5 Armstrong and her colleagues (2020: 3) demonstrate that privately run LTC homes in Canada "have lower staffing levels, more verified complaints, and more transfers to hospitals, as well as higher rates for both ulcers and morbidity."

6 For example, in Canada, the "Age Well at Home Initiative" part of the federal budget in 2021 focuses on supporting seniors in their home so they can stay healthy and secure (in an aging population this is particularly key). See AGE-WELL 2021.

7 Expanding access to high-quality child care and early childhood education has been demonstrated to reduce poverty and decrease inequality by providing the foundation for children to thrive while

also expanding jobs in this sector that disproportionately help women and allow for women to return to the workforce (see Boeckmann et al. 2015)

8 This is a key recommendation in the Truth and Reconciliation Commission of Canada report (Government of Canada n.d.)

9 Retrofitting rental homes is beneficial beyond reducing emissions and has the added benefit of lowering utility costs for renters and reducing exposures to toxins such as lead and asbestos (Aldana Cohen et al. 2021).

10 For example, Finland has spent 250 million euros for their Housing First program, which creates new homes and provides social service support for those transitioning from homelessness or unsecure housing. Research on Finland's Housing First program demonstrates savings in emergency health care, services and prison costs of more than 15,000 euros per person housed. See DW 2020. https://www.dw.com/en/finland-solving-homelessness/av-49047542

11 The Land Back movement in Canada centers Indigenous models of governance and law and advocates for the return of land to Indigenous Peoples (Yellowhead Institute 2019).

References

Abramowitz, A. and McCoy, J. 2019. United States: Racial Resentment, Negative Partisanship and Polarization in Trump's America. *Annals of American Academy of Political and Social Sciences.* 681(1): 137–156.

AGE-WELL. 2021. Federal Budget Provides Supports for Older Canadians at Home and in Long-Term Care. *Age-Well.* Available at: https://agewell-nce.ca/archives/11726

Aldana Cohen, D. et al. 2021. A Green New Deal for Public Housing to Deliver Racial, Economic, and Climate Justice. *climate + community project.* 19 April. Available at: https://www.climateand-community.org/a-gnd-for-public-housing

Allan, K. and Robinson, J.L. 2022 [forthcoming]. Working Towards a Green Job? The Role of Auto-manufacturing Sector Workers in the Transition to a Low-carbon Economy. *Journal of Industrial Relations.* 64(4): 1–23.

Armstrong, P. et al. 2020. Re-imagining Long-term Residential Care in the COVID-19 Crisis. Canadian Centre for Policy Alternatives. Available at: https://www.policyalternatives.ca/sites/default/files/uploads/publications/National%20Office/2020/04/Reimagining%20residential%20care%20COVID%20crisis.pdf

Aronoff, K. et al. 2020. We Can Waste Another Crisis, or We Can Transform the Economy. *Jacobin Magazine.* 14 March. Available at: https://jacobinmag.com/2020/03/green-new-deal-coronavirus-stimulus

Aronoff, K. 2021. Care Work Is Climate Work. *The New Republic.* 9 April. Available at: https://newrepublic.com/article/161998/care-work-climate-work

Barry, D., McIntire, M. and Rosenberg, M. 2021. 'Our president wants us here': The Mob that Stormed the Capitol. *New York Times.* 10 January. Available at: https://www.nytimes.com/2021/01/09/us/capitol-rioters.html

Beck, U. 1992. *Risk Society: Towards a New Modernity.* London: Sage.

Beckles, J. 2020. We Need a Green New Deal for Public Transit. *Jacobin Magazine.* 19 August. Available at: https://www.jacobinmag.com/2020/08/green-new-deal-public-transit-east-bay

Bell, A. 2021. Sixty Years of Climate Change Warnings: The Signs that Were Missed (and Ignored). *The Guardian.* 5 July. Available at: https://www.theguardian.com/science/2021/jul/05/sixty-years-of-climate-change-warnings-the-signs-that-were-missed-and-ignored

Bernauer, W. 2019. The Limits to Extraction: Mining and Colonialism in Nunavut. *Canadian Journal of Development Studies.* 40(3): 404–422.

Boeckmann, I., Misra, J. and Budig, M.J. 2015. Cultural and Institutional Factors Shaping Mothers' Employment and Working Hours in Postindustrial Countries. *Social Forces.* 93(4): 1301–1333.

Carrington, D. 2021. 'Blah, blah, blah': Greta Thunberg Lambasts Leaders Over Climate Crisis. *The Guardian.* 28 September. Available at: https://www.theguardian.com/environment/2021/sep/28/blah-greta-thunberg-leaders-climate-crisis-co2-emissions

Chen, Victor Tan. 2015. *Cut Loose: Jobless and Hopeless in an Unfair Economy.* Berkeley: University of California Press.

Chun, J.J. 2009. *Organizing at the Margins: The Symbolic Politics of Labor in South Korea and the United States.* Ithaca: Cornell University Press.

CMHC. 2021. Rapid Housing Initiative (RHI). Canada Mortgage and Housing. 23 June. Available at: https://www.cmhc-schl.gc.ca/en/professionals/project-funding-and-mortgage-financing/funding-programs/all-funding-programs/rapid-housing

Crook, M., Short, D. and South, N. 2018. Ecocide, Genocide, Capitalism and Colonialism: Consequences for Indigenous Peoples and Glocal Ecosystems Environments. *Theoretical Criminology*. 22(3): 298–317.

Cruickshank, A. 2020. A Green COVID-19 Recovery: How Canada Can Chart a Sustainable Path Forward for the Economy. *The Narwhal*. 7 July. Available at: https://thenarwhal.ca/green-covid-19-recovery-canada-economy/

Dembicki, G. 2020a. How Rethinking Affordable Homes Connects with the Climate Fight. *The Tyee*. 30 November. Available at: https://thetyee.ca/News/2020/11/30/Rethinking-Affordable-Homes-Climate-Fight/

Dembicki, G. 2020b. Indigenous Housing Solutions, Built on Empowerment. *The Tyee*. 18 December. Available at: https://thetyee.ca/News/2020/12/18/Indigenous-Housing-Solutions-Empowerment/

Department of Finance Canada. 2021. Budget 2021: A Recovery Plan for Jobs, Growth and Resilience. Government of Canada. *News Release*. 19 April. Available at: https://www.canada.ca/en/department-finance/news/2021/04/budget-2021-a-recovery-plan-for-jobs-growth-and-resilience.html

Dewan, A. 2021. Germany's Deadly Floods Were up to 9 Times More Likely Because of Climate Change, Study Estimates. *CNN*. 24 August. Available at: https://www.cnn.com/2021/08/23/europe/germany-floods-belgium-climate-change-intl/index.html

Doherty, E. 2019. Green New Deal Must Include a Transportation Transformation. *National Observer*. 18 May. Available at: https://www.nationalobserver.com/2019/05/18/opinion/green-new-deal-must-include-transportation-transformation

Doukas, H. et al. 2020. The Green Versus Green Trap and a Way Forward. *Energies*. 13(20): 5473.

Drummond, D. and Kachuck Rosenbluth, E. 2013. The Debate on First Nations Education Funding: Mind the Gap. Queen's University Policy Studies. Working Paper #49.

DW. 2020. Finland: Solving Homelessness. *DW.com*. 26 March. Available at: https://www.dw.com/en/finland-solving-homelessness/av-49047542

Ellingrud, K. and Hilton Segel, L. 2021. COVID-19 Has Driven Millions of Women Out of the Workforce. Here's How to Help them Come Back. *Fortune*. 13 February. Available at: https://fortune.com/2021/02/13/covid-19-women-workforce-unemployment-gender-gap-recovery/

Emergency Management BC. 2021. B.C. Wildfires: Quick Statistics. Forests, Lands, Natural Resource Operations and Rural Development. BC Gov News. Government of British Columbia. 16 August. Available at: https://news.gov.bc.ca/releases/2021FLNRO0069-001613

Enriques, D. and Goldstein, A. 2020. COVID-19's Socioeconomic Impact on Low-Income Benefit Recipients: Early Evidence from Tracking Surveys. *Socius*. 6.

Evelyn, K. 2020. 'It's a racial justice issue': Black Americans Are Dying in Greater Numbers from Covid-19. *The Guardian*. 8 April. Available at: https://www.theguardian.com/world/2020/apr/08/its-a-racial-justice-issue-black-americans-are-dying-in-greater-numbers-from-covid-19

Fortin, P. 2017. What Have Been the Effects of Quebec's Universal Childcare System on Women's Economic Security? Brief Submitted to the Standing Committee on the Status of Women (FEWO) of the House of Commons, Ottawa, March 2017. Available at: https://www.ourcommons.ca/content/Committee/421/FEWO/Brief/BR8806290/br-external/FortinPierre-e.pdf

Fuller, S. and Vosko, L. 2008. Temporary Employment and Social Inequality in Canada: Exploring Intersections of Gender, Race, and Migration. *Social Indicators Research*. 88(1): 31–50.

Galabuzzi, G.E. and Block, S. 2018. *Persistent Inequality: Ontario's Colour-coded Labour* Market. Ottawa: Canadian Centre for Policy Alternatives. 11 December. Available at: https://www.policyalternatives.ca/sites/default/files/uploads/publications/Ontario%20Office/2018/12/Persistent%20inequality.pdf

Gardener, B. 2020. Unequal Impact: The Deep Links Between Racism and Climate Change. Yale School of Environment. *Yale Environment 360*. 9 June. Available at: https://e360.yale.edu/features/unequal-impact-the-deep-links-between-inequality-and-climate-change

Garnett, S.T. et al. 2018. A Spatial Overview of the Global Importance of Indigenous Lands for Conservation. *Nature Sustainability*. 1: 369–374. Available at: https://doi.org/10.1038/s41893-018-0100-6

Government of Canada. 2021. Net-Zero Emissions by 2050. Canada.ca. Page Dated 2021-08-13. Available at: https://www.canada.ca/en/services/environment/weather/climatechange/climate-plan/net-zero-emissions-2050.html

Government of Canada. n.d. Truth and Reconciliation Commission of Canada. Canada.ca Page dated 2021–06–11. Available at: https://www.rcaanc-cirnac.gc.ca/eng/1450124405592/1529106060525

Government of New Zealand. 2021. Wellbeing Budget 2021: Securing Our Recovery. Budget 2021. The Treasury. Government of New Zealand. 20 May. Available at: https://www.treasury.govt.nz/publications/wellbeing-budget/wellbeing-budget-2021-securing-our-recovery

Hepburn, C. et al. 2020. Will Covid-19 Fiscal Recovery Packages Accelerate or Retard Progress on Climate Change? *Oxford Review of Economic Policy*. 36(S1): S359–S381.

IPCC. 2021a. Climate Change Widespread, Rapid, and Intensifying – IPCC. Intergovernmental Panel on Climate Change. 9 August. Available at: https://www.ipcc.ch/2021/08/09/ar6-wg1-20210809-pr/

IPCC. 2021b. *AR6 Climate Change 2021: The Physical Science Basis*. Intergovernmental Panel on Climate Change. 9 August. Available at: https://www.ipcc.ch/report/ar6/wg1/

IPCC. 2021c. Summary for Policymakers. In Masson-Delmotte, V. et al. (eds.): *Climate Change 2021: The Physical Science Basis. Contribution of Working Group I to the Sixth Assessment Report of the Intergovernmental Panel on Climate Change*. Cambridge University Press. Available at: https://www.ipcc.ch/report/ar6/wg1/downloads/report/IPCC_AR6_WGI_SPM.pdf

Klein, N. 2019. A Message from the Future with Alexandria Ocasio-Cortez. *The Intercept*. 17 April. Available at: https://theintercept.com/2019/04/17/green-new-deal-short-film-alexandria-ocasio-cortez/

Klein, N. 2020a. A Message from the Future II: The Years of Repair. *The Intercept*. 1 October. Available at: https://theintercept.com/2020/10/01/naomi-klein-message-from-future-covid/

Klein, N. 2020b. Care and Repair: Left Politics in the Age of Climate Change. *Dissent Magazine*. Winter 2020. Available at: https://www.dissentmagazine.org/article/care-and-repair-left-politics-in-the-age-of-climate-change

Kozlov, M. 2021. Hurricane Ida Forces Louisiana Researchers to Rethink their Future. *Nature*. 9 September. Available at: https://www.nature.com/articles/d41586-021-02456-z

LaDuke, W. and Cowen, D. 2020. Beyond Wiindigo Infrastructure. *The South Atlantic Quarterly*. 119(2): 244.

Lavoie, J. 2018. Nowhere Else to Turn: First Nations Inundated by Oil Sands Projects Face Impossible Choices. *The Narwhal*. 30 June. Available at: https://thenarwhal.ca/nowhere-else-turn-first-nations-inundated-oilsands-face-impossible-choices/

Lipsig- Mummé, C. (ed). 2013. *Climate@Work*. Winnipeg, MB: Fernwood Publishing.

McBride, S. and Shields, J. 2011. Industrial Strategies for Green Jobs: Opportunities and Obstacles in the Ontario Case. Work in a Warming World Working Paper #2011–03. 17 pages.

McGregor, D. 2012. Traditional Knowledge: Considerations for Protecting Water in Ontario. *The International Indigenous Policy Journal*. 3(3). Available at: http://ir.lib.uwo.ca/iipj/vol3/iss3/11

Natural Resources Canada. n.d. Canada Greener Homes Grant. Government of Canada. Page dated 2021–08–13. Available at: https://www.nrcan.gc.ca/energy-efficiency/homes/canada-greener-homes-grant/23441

NOAA. 2021. It's Official: July was Earth's Hottest Month on Record. National Oceanic and Atmospheric Association. 13 August. Available at: https://www.noaa.gov/news/its-official-july-2021-was-earths-hottest-month-on-record

OECD. 2021. OECD Policy Responses to Coronavirus (COVID-19): Towards Gender-Inclusive Recovery. Organisation for Economic Co-operation and Development. 19 May. Available at: https://www.oecd.org/coronavirus/policy-responses/towards-gender-inclusive-recovery-ab597807/

Picketty, T. 2014. *Capital in the 21st Century*. Cambridge: Harvard University Press.

Plumtre, B. 2018. Three Takeaways from Canada's Latest Greenhouse Gas Emissions Data. Pembina Institute. 12 July. Available at: https://www.pembina.org/blog/three-takeaways-canadas-latest-greenhouse-gas-emissions-data

Raygorodesky, G. 2018. Indigenous Peoples Defend Earth's Biodiversity – But they're in Danger. *National Geographic*. 16 November. Available at: https://www.nationalgeographic.com/environment/article/can-indigenous-land-stewardship-protect-biodiversity-

Robinson, J. 2020. Building a Green Economy: Advancing Climate Justice through Labour-Environmental Alliances. *Mobilization*. 25(2): 245–264.

Sanders, B. 2021. NEWS: Sanders and Ocasio-Cortez Rollout Green New Deal for Public Housing Act. News Release. sanders.senate.gov. 19 April. Available at: https://www.sanders.senate.gov/press-releases/news-sanders-and-ocasio-cortez-rollout-green-new-deal-for-public-housing-act/

Savage, L. 2021. Avi Lewis: Ecosocialism Is on the March in Canada. *Jacobin*. 24 August. Available at: https://jacobinmag.com/2021/08/avi-lewis-interview-ndp-british-columbia-climate-movement-green-new-deal/

Schiffer, A. 2017. *Shared Ownership in Scotland: Opening up Citizen Participation in Renewable Energy*. Technical Report. Friends of the Earth Scotland, Edinburgh.

Solomon, A., Hawkins, K. and Morgan, R. 2020. Hawaii and Canada: Providing Lessons for Feminist Pandemic Recovery Plans to COVID-19. The Gender and COVID-19 Working Group. Available at: https://genderandcovid-19.org/resources/hawaii-and-canada-lessons-for-feminist-economic-recovery-from-covid-19/

Springer, A. 2021. Living in Colour: Racialized Housing Discrimination in Canada. *Homeless Hub*. Toronto. 2 March. Available at: https://www.homelesshub.ca/blog/living-colour-racialized-housing-discrimination-canada

Tarrow, S. 2012. *Power in Movement: Social Movements and Contentious Politics*. New York: Cambridge University Press.

Tauli Corpez, J. 2020. Voices of the Landscape: Land Transitions towards Securing Legal and Customary Land Tenure of Indigenous Peoples and Decolonizing Conservation. *Global Landscapes Forum Biodiversity Digital Conference*. White Paper.28–29 October 2020. Available at: https://events.globallandscapesforum.org/wp-content/uploads/sites/2/2020/10/GLF-Biodiversity-2020-white-paper-Voices.pdf

The Leap. 2021. Let's Talk about a Green New Deal. The Leap. Available at: https://theleap.org/portfolio-items/green-new-deal/

The Leap Manifesto. n.d. Available at: https://leapmanifesto.org/en/the-leap-manifesto/

Tienhaara, K. 2019. The Green New Deal Is Going Global. *The Conversation*. 6 May. Available at: https://theconversation.com/the-green-new-deal-is-going-global-115961

Tomer, A., Kane, J.W. and George, C. 2021. How Renewable Energy Jobs can Uplift Fossil Fuel Communities and Remake Climate Politics. Brookings Institution. 23 February. Available at: https://www.brookings.edu/research/how-renewable-energy-jobs-can-uplift-fossil-fuel-communities-and-remake-climate-politics/

Transport Canada. 2021. Building a Green Economy: Government of Canada to Require 100% of Car and Passenger Truck Sales Be Zero-Emission by 2035 in Canada. Government of Canada. Canada.ca. 29 June. Available at: https://www.canada.ca/en/transport-canada/news/2021/06/building-a-green-economy-government-of-canada-to-require-100-of-car-and-passenger-truck-sales-be-zero-emission-by-2035-in-canada.html

TRC. 2015. Truth and Reconciliation Commission of Canada: Calls to Action. Truth and Reconciliation Commission of Canada. Available at: https://ehprnh2mwo3.exactdn.com/wp-content/uploads/2021/01/Calls_to_Action_English2.pdf

United Nations General Assembly. 2007. United Nations Declaration on the Rights of Indigenous Peoples. Resolution adopted by the General Assembly. 2 October 2007. A/RES/61/295. Available at: https://www.un.org/development/desa/indigenouspeoples/wp-content/uploads/sites/19/2018/11/UNDRIP_E_web.pdf

United Way. 2011. Vertical Poverty: Poverty By Postal Code 2. United Way. January. Available at; https://www.unitedwaygt.org/document.doc?id=89

U.S. Department of Energy. 2017. U.S. Energy and Employment Report. Available at: https://www.energy.gov/sites/prod/files/2017/01/f34/2017%20US%20Energy%20and%20Jobs%20Report_0.pdf

White House. n.d. The Build Back Better Agenda. WH.gov. Available at: https://www.whitehouse.gov/build-back-better/

Wiener, S. and Kammen, D. 2019. Why Housing Policy is Climate Policy. *New York Times*. 25 March. Available at: https://www.nytimes.com/2019/03/25/opinion/california-home-prices-climate.html

Yellowhead Institute. 2019. *Land Back: A Yellowhead Institute Red Paper*. October. Available at: https://redpaper.yellowheadinstitute.org/wp-content/uploads/2019/10/red-paper-report-final.pdf

Yellowhead Institute. 2021. *Cash Back: A Yellowhead Institute Red Paper*. May. Available at: https://cashback.yellowheadinstitute.org/wp-content/uploads/2021/05/Cash-Back-A-Yellowhead-Institute-Red-Paper.pdf

Zuberi, D. 2006. *Differences that Matter: Social Policy and the Working Poor in the United States*. Ithaca, NY: Cornell University Press.

Zuberi, D. 2013. *Cleaning Up: How Hospital Outsourcing Is Hurting Workers and Endangering Patients*. Ithaca, NY: Cornell University Press.

9

LESSONS FOR A GREEN NEW DEAL

Race, the New Deal legacy, and environmental justice in Detroit

Josiah Rector

Introduction

Recent debates about the Green New Deal (GND) in the United States have taken a detour into familiar territory for US urban and labor historians. GND advocates point to the original New Deal as a successful precedent for large-scale public investments in infrastructure, jobs, housing, social welfare, and wilderness conservation that they argue are necessary to simultaneously combat climate change, inequality, and poverty. The text of House Resolution 109, sponsored by Representative Alexandria Ocasio-Cortez (D-NY), and the writings of GND proponents, also acknowledge a longstanding critique of the original New Deal as structurally racist (H. Res. 109; Aronoff et al. 2019; Prakash et al. 2020). Those who emphasize the shortcomings of the New Deal for African Americans, in particular, often reference the historical literature on redlining and the exclusion of farm and domestic workers from Social Security (Katznelson 2013; Coates 2014; Rothstein 2017). More recently, some scholars working in the historical materialist tradition have critiqued liberal accounts of racism and the New Deal for downplaying the role of private capital in shaping these discriminatory policies (Jenkins 2017; Reed 2020).

While acknowledging the New Deal's problematic aspects, GND advocates argue that it contains progressive elements which could be adapted for a racially and environmentally just twenty-first-century version. The infrastructure, housing, and labor policies outlined in House Resolution 109 would have profound consequences for cities, which are both leading carbon polluters and on the frontlines of climate impacts. Few participants in this debate, however, have considered the relationship between the original New Deal and urban environmental inequalities. Studies by urban environmental historians and sociologists provide relevant evidence for such an analysis (Hurley 1996; Washington 2005; Sicotte 2016). Some historians have examined the racial politics of the New Deal-era National Park Service and Civilian Conservation Corps (Young 2009; McCammack 2017), and the impact of New Deal conservation and infrastructure policies on Native Americans (Weisiger 2011; Needham 2014; Estes 2019). However, few scholars have explicitly analyzed the implications of New Deal housing and labor policies for urban environmental inequality.

DOI: 10.4324/9781003110880-12

In the context of the GND, grappling with this history will be necessary to avoid the mistakes of the past and achieve environmental justice in the twenty-first century. Using Detroit, Michigan as a case study, this chapter analyzes the relationship between environmental inequality and the original New Deal in order to better evaluate the prospects for the GND. I argue that, while New Deal policies benefited both Black and white workers, improving public health and creating jobs and housing opportunities, they also contributed to racialized environmental inequality. Racially discriminatory "redlining" by the Federal Housing Administration (FHA) and the real estate industry excluded African Americans from housing opportunities beyond the inner city, resulting in higher rates of lead poisoning, tuberculosis, and industrial pollution exposure between the 1930s and the 1960s. And while New Deal labor laws gave Detroit auto workers the right to strike and bargain collectively, they provided few protections from occupational discrimination, which disproportionately relegated Black workers to jobs that caused silicosis and other occupational diseases.

I also make an equally important corollary argument. Although Black Detroiters benefited less from New Deal policies than whites, they also suffered more from their dismantling between 1980 and 2020, in terms of both economic security and environmental health. Following decades of deindustrialization and white flight to the suburbs, neoliberal policies of deregulation, privatization, tax cuts, austerity and "welfare reform" gutted the New Deal welfare and regulatory state and hollowed out the public sector. These policies contributed directly to the mass water shutoffs and lead poisoning that ravaged twenty-first-century Detroit and Flint, with devastating consequences for African Americans (and, especially in Flint, some working-class and poor whites and non-Black people of color). For this reason, if we are to achieve environmental justice in the twenty-first century, we must recognize both the flaws and the virtues of the original New Deal. Ultimately, I agree with GND advocates that the most progressive aspects of the New Deal provide a valuable precedent for policies that could make environmental, racial, and economic justice possible for Detroit and other frontline communities, but only if we learn from the past.

The Great Depression and the New Deal in Detroit

Located in southeast Michigan on the US–Canadian border, Detroit became the global epicenter of auto manufacturing and Fordist assembly line production between 1910 and 1930. By 1929, the Ford Motor Company's River Rouge complex, located southwest of the Detroit city limits, was the world's largest factory, with over 98,000 workers producing over 1 million cars per year (Freeman 2018). As Detroit became a magnet for southern migrants during the Great Migration, its African American population rapidly increased from 5,741 in 1910 to 120,066 in 1930. Housing discrimination, including the ubiquitous use of racial deed restrictions (backed by the Detroit Real Estate Board), trapped most Black migrants in the city's Paradise Valley and Black Bottom neighborhoods on the Near East Side (Boyle 2004). As overcrowding increased, the Black death rate from tuberculosis in Detroit increased from 4.7 times the white rate in 1926 to 6.9 times the white rate in 1930 (Van Duser 1947).

During the 1920s, African American men replaced Eastern and Southern European immigrant men as the primary labor force in Detroit foundries and paint shops, where white managers restricted most to dangerous, lower-wage jobs. The Ford Motor Company employed roughly half of all African American workers in the auto industry before World War II, the bulk of them at River Rouge. Ford's Employment Office assigned 46% of all African American workers hired between 1918 and 1947 to foundries, compared with only 5% of white workers (Foote et al. 2003). Racist labor practices widened Black-white disparities in death from infectious diseases like tuberculosis, as well as in occupational diseases like silicosis (Rector 2022).

The stock market crash of 1929 and the ensuing decade of depression hit Detroit harder than any other large industrial city in the United States. Car and truck sales in the United States plummeted 75% between 1929 and 1932, and 45% of Detroit auto workers were unemployed by 1933. Detroit's assessed tax revenues declined by 45.2% between 1930 and 1935, pushing the city to the edge of bankruptcy (Wengert 1939). By 1932, the Detroit Department of Welfare (DDW) relief rolls had swelled to more than 50 times their 1928 level, reaching a total of 229,000. Forced to pay its own workers in scrip, the administration of Mayor Frank Murphy struggled to feed the hungry, shelter the homeless and give work to the unemployed. Those who retained their jobs were disproportionately native-born white men in the salaried middle classes and the skilled trades. Whereas only 3.8% of Detroit's native-born whites were on relief in July 1932, 10.2% of foreign-born immigrants and 17% of African Americans were on relief (Fine 1975). The Great Depression also produced a water affordability crisis in Detroit. Because of unpaid water bills, water revenues at the Detroit Department of Water Supply (DDWS) fell from $6.2 million in 1930–1931 to $5.4 million in 1932–1933, and by March 1934 over 100,000 water counts were "delinquent," or past due and in danger of shutoffs. Landlords, who relied on payments from DDW to cover rent for poor tenants, often refused to pay water bills until tenants paid full rent, resulting in skyrocketing delinquencies (Smith 1933).

In February 1933, the administration of Mayor Frank Murphy defaulted on Detroit's debts to Wall Street banks, and Michigan became the first US state to close its banks. Detroit was at the leading edge of a national crisis that brought down 11,000 banks, leading President Roosevelt to declare a national bank "holiday" only two days after his inauguration in March 1933. The Emergency Banking Act, passed by Congress that month, stabilized the US banking system with emergency loans from the Reconstruction Finance Corporation and the Federal Reserve, a system of federal deposit insurance (the Federal Deposit Insurance Corporation), and financial regulations that established a firewall between commercial banks, investment banks, securities firms and insurance companies to reduce systemic risk (Kennedy 1991).

It was only in June 1933, once these emergency measures were in place, that Detroit reached an agreement with Wall Street banks to refinance its entire municipal debt. The agreement converted all Detroit's bond debt due within the next ten years to long-term debt, or "callable sinking fund bonds," not due for 30 years. By reducing short-term debt service obligations, the agreement enabled DDWS to meet operating expenses and extend consumer credit to prevent water shutoffs. No less significantly, the Public Works Administration (PWA) and the WPA funneled federal aid into the DDWS budget, allowing the city to put unemployed Detroiters to work building new water and sewer infrastructure (Wengert 1939).

During the 1930s, the Works Progress Administration (WPA) alone created nearly 100,000 public works jobs in the city, building water and sewer lines, parks and schools, and improving roads, hospitals, fire houses and police stations. WPA workers doubled the flow capacity of Detroit's water mains by replacing 8-inch water pipes with 16-inch ones, and improved thousands of miles of sewer tunnels in Detroit and the surrounding suburbs. The WPA and the PWA contributed $15 million for the construction of a $27.3 million sewage treatment plant, which allowed Detroit to treat its municipal sewage for the first time in a century. African Americans disproportionately obtained WPA jobs in Detroit, although primarily as unskilled laborers under white foremen. In 1939, African Americans made up less than 10% of Detroit's population, but 35% of the WPA workers in the city (Wolcott 2001; Clemens 2008).

New Deal infrastructure projects improved the quality of Detroit's drinking water and reduced sewage pollution in the Detroit River, finally eliminating waterborne diseases like typhoid that had dogged public health officials since the nineteenth century. Numerous other features of the New Deal helped bring down tuberculosis death rates in Detroit during the 1930s and 1940s: federal funding for the Detroit Health Department, via the US Public Health Service that improved medical care and accelerated the development of antibiotics; WPA programs in city hospitals; and expanded access to healthcare through union contracts for blue-collar workers and Aid to Families with Dependent Children (AFDC) for indigent families. The combination of New Deal policies and full employment created by wartime defense production helped bring down racial disparities in tuberculosis death rates. The ratio of Black-to-white tuberculosis deaths in Detroit fell from 6.9:1 in 1930 to 3.7:1 in 1945 (Van Duser 1947).

The New Deal's most harmful legacy for African Americans was in the area of housing policy. Rather than challenging the racist deed restrictions and appraisal practices of the real estate and banking industries, the Home Owners Loan Corporation (HOLC) and the Federal Housing Administration (FHA) made them federal policy. In 1947, the year before the US Supreme Court ruled that restrictive covenants were not legally enforceable in *Shelly v. Kraemer*, restrictive covenants barred the sale or rental of over 90% of the housing units in metropolitan Detroit to African Americans (Sugrue 1996). The HOLC and FHA downgraded the credit rating of any neighborhood without racial deed restrictions, and classified over 90% of Detroit neighborhoods with African American residents as "hazardous" for mortgage lenders (Nelson et al. 2019). Federal loan appraisers embraced racial segregation, moreover, at a time when New Deal policies were making home mortgages more affordable than ever before. Between 1945 and 1972, the FHA subsidized mortgages for 11 million families and home improvements for another 22 million families (Jackson 1987). While subsidizing the build-out of suburbs across the United States, the FHA continued to redline African American communities and openly incentivized the maintenance of whites-only developments until the Fair Housing Act of 1968 (Taylor 2018).

The HOLC, which operated from 1933 until 1954, did not refuse all mortgage loans to African Americans in Detroit. In 1940, the HOLC reported 880 mortgage refinancing loans on Black-owned single-family homes in Detroit, an estimated of 44.7% of Black homeowner mortgages in the city. Indeed, the proportion of Black homeowner mortgages held by the HOLC in Detroit was higher than in most cities, including Chicago, New York, Philadelphia, Cleveland and Los Angeles. African American Ford Workers in the Detroit suburbs, especially in River Rouge and Ecorse but also a few in Inkster, also received HOLC loans, although none were in segregated white neighborhoods (Michney and Winling 2019).

The FHA also provided home loans to African Americans, even as it practiced redlining and encouraged racial restrictive covenants. Like the HOLC, the FHA narrowly circumscribed where African Americans could purchase homes. In the 1940s, FHA officials even required a developer to build a wall between Black and white neighborhoods in Detroit's 8 Mile–Wyoming neighborhood before insuring loans for nearby white homeowners (Sugrue 1996). Despite the FHA's support for a literal apartheid wall, African Americans in Detroit had obtained a higher percentage of FHA loans than in most cities by 1950. As historians Todd M. Michney and LaDale Winling have shown, "Detroit was the only major Black homeownership center where [African Americans] garnered even a roughly equitable share" of FHA loans in the early postwar era (Michney and Winling 2019). In part, this reflected the growth of Detroit's Black middle class and the city's robust manufacturing economy. Nevertheless, because of the combination of FHA policies and racial discrimination by realtors, builders and white homeowners, 16 Detroit suburbs had zero Black homeowners as late as 1968 (Darden et al. 1987).

In the area of labor policy, the New Deal had mixed results for African Americans. Detroit auto workers won a series of hard-fought labor battles between 1935 and 1941, employing innovative tactics like the sit-down strike and taking advantage of New Deal labor legislation, including the Wagner Act of 1935 and the Fair Labor Standards Act of 1938. However, it was only pressure from African American labor organizers, from A. Philip Randolph's March on Washington Movement to wildcat strikes by Black foundry workers at Ford and Packard, that opened defense production jobs to African Americans during World War II. Black labor activists forced President Roosevelt to sign Executive Order 8802, which established the temporary Fair Employment Practices Committee (FEPC) (Meier and Rudwick 2007; Lewis-Colman 2008). New Deal labor legislation recognized the right to strike for the first time in US history, and created a system of federally arbitrated collective bargaining that established a legal framework for negotiating union contracts. However, apart from the temporary FEPC (1941–1946), it lacked any substantive protections against job discrimination or unsafe working conditions. As a result, both problems remained endemic in Detroit auto factories, and African Americans suffered the most from both (Sugrue 1996).

While they had ultimate control over hiring, production, and promotion decisions, employers were not solely to blame for job discrimination. Many African American auto workers believed that Walter Reuther, who served as President of the United Auto Workers (UAW) from 1946 to 1970, was either complacent or complicit in job discrimination in auto plants and union halls. While Reuther supported federal civil rights legislation, he was reluctant to challenge Jim Crow practices by southern UAW locals or to antagonize white skilled tradesmen who excluded African Americans from apprenticeship programs in his own northern backyard (Boyle 1995). The persistence of discrimination within the union would lead to the founding of the Trade Union Leadership Council (TULC) by Black UAW activists in 1957, which lobbied to open the skilled trades to Black Workers and for Black leadership positions in the union (Lewis-Colman 2008).

Within the realm of collective bargaining, UAW leaders secured enviable wage gains and health care, unemployment and pension benefits for unionized auto workers, exemplified by the 1946 and 1950 UAW–GM contracts. Between 1947 and 1960, average wages in the automobile industry nearly doubled to $6,000 per year, although recessions and layoffs made work unstable and insecure for many Detroit auto workers. Younger auto workers benefited less from union fringe benefits than older workers with seniority, and white skilled tradesmen enjoyed higher wages and more job security than women or African Americans, who remained largely shut out of those occupations. Nevertheless, living standards improved for most unionized Detroit auto workers across lines of race and gender (Clark 2018). In 1950, one in four white workers in the Detroit metropolitan area worked in a skilled occupation. By contrast, only one in eight Black workers was in a skilled occupation. A decade later, this picture remained virtually unchanged. In 1960, while Black workers made up 45% of the production workers at Dodge Main in Hamtramck, none of the 1,500 skilled workers were Black. On the other side of the metropolitan area, Black workers made up 65% of production workers at the Rouge, but a mere 3.5% of the skilled workers (US Commission on Civil Rights 1960; Boyle 1995).

An epidemiological study of automobile foundry workers from 1970 reveals the price African Americans paid for concentration in hazardous jobs. That year, the Detroit-based

Michigan Health and Social Security Research Institute (MHSSRI) conducted a study of 14,000 Ford workers in three foundries (Dearborn Iron Foundry, Dearborn Specialty Foundry and Cleveland Castings) and three non-foundry plants (Wayne Assembly, Sterling Axle and Ypsilanti Parts). They found that Black workers in the Dearborn Iron Foundry had a death rate 79.37% higher than average workers; white workers in the foundry had a death rate 34.78% above average. Black foundry workers had the highest cancer death rates: 25.1% of them died of cancer, compared with 21% of Black non-foundry workers, 17.59% of white foundry workers, and 19.7% of white non-foundry workers. Thus, the concentration of African American workers in hot, dust-filled foundries disproportionately sentenced them to an early death (Rector 2022).

Housing and postwar environmental inequality

While job discrimination increased African Americans' exposure to pollution at work, housing discrimination increased their exposure to pollution at home. An air pollution study by the US–Canadian International Joint Commission (IJC), conducted between 1949 and 1960, revealed how environmental inequalities had widened since 1939. Working with the IJC, William Fredrick of the Detroit Bureau of Industrial Hygiene led a comparative study of morbidity in "high pollution" and "low pollution" census tracts in Detroit. Fredricks and his assistants made two separate comparisons: one between all-white areas with "high" and "low" levels of pollution, and another between areas "having non-white population" with high and low levels. They found that while most whites in metropolitan Detroit lived in low-pollution areas, all but one of the census tracts "having non-white population" (census tract 305, at the intersection of Livernois and 8 Mile Road on the west side) were high-pollution areas (International Joint Commission 1960).

In 1967, Detroit had the highest rate of Black home ownership of any large city in the United States. The rate of home ownership in Detroit had more than tripled among African Americans since 1940, rising from 15% to 48%. This remained well below the white rate of 69%, however. And while Black Detroiters' median income increased by 6% between 1949 and 1965, it fell as a percentage of white median income from 79% to 62%. The Black unemployment rate was 11% in 1967, over triple the white rate (Fine 1989). The combination of racial discrimination in housing, jobs and policing, and the disproportionate impact of deindustrialization and destructive urban renewal and highway projects on African Americans, help explain why the deadliest urban rebellion of the 1960s occurred in Detroit in 1967 (Sugrue 1996).

While African Americans comprised 40% of Detroit's population, they made up over 82% of the residents of substandard housing in 1967, including an estimated 29,600 households (Fine 1989). Epidemiological studies revealed an epidemic of lead poisoning in Detroit's substandard housing units. According to a 1973 Detroit Health Department report, blood tests revealed that 10% of Detroit children had "abnormal levels of lead in their blood," and an estimated 80,000 Detroit children between the ages of one and five faced "a high risk of being lead poisoned" (Detroit Health Department 1973). Most African Americans in Detroit lived in the "lead belt" of 375,000 units of pre-World War II housing south of McNichols Road, built when lead-based paint was both unregulated and ubiquitous on exterior and interior surfaces. Redlining had starved lead belt neighborhoods of capital for home improvements, contributing to structural dilapidation, flaking paint and corroded pipes. Well into the twenty-first century, rates of child lead poisoning in Detroit were between four and ten times as high as in the city's suburbs in Wayne, Macomb and Oakland Counties (Katz 1977; Detroit News 2017).

Postwar deindustrialization also eroded inner city job opportunities, contributing to high rates of Black unemployment. In this respect, Detroit exemplified a national pattern (Wilson 1996). Between 1950 and 1983, Detroit and its industrial suburbs lost 335,000 manufacturing jobs, while four nearby counties gained over 123,000. In 1990, only 62,000 manufacturing jobs remained in Detroit, and by 2007 there were only 23,000 left. Factories in suburban Wayne County still employed an estimated 60,000 workers, but they were increasingly automated, and regional manufacturing employment had plummeted 37.3% since 2000 (McDonald 2015). In 2018, General Motors announced plans to close the Detroit-Hamtramck Assembly plant, which straddled the border of Detroit and the suburb of Hamtramck. This left only one auto assembly plant in the city of Detroit: the Fiat-Chrysler Jefferson North Assembly Plant, which employed 5,000 workers. Detroit had become the "motor city" in name only (DeVito 2019).

Race, neoliberalism, and environmental health disasters

Racial segregation persisted in twenty-first-century Detroit, ensuring that African Americans bore the brunt of unemployment and poverty in the aftermath of deindustrialization. As white flight continued, the proportion of Detroit's population classified as "white" fell from 55.5% to 34.4% in the 1970s. Poverty rates in Detroit increased from three times the suburban level in 1970 to four times in 1980 (Darden et al. 1987; Jacobs 1999; Anieri 2007). By 1999, 34.8% of Detroit children and youth were living below the federal poverty line; over three times the national average. By 2009, this percentage had risen to 46%, and by 2012 it was a staggering 59.4% (Data Driven Detroit 2012; Michigan League for Public Policy 2017).

In 2016, the gap in average life expectancies between Detroit and its surrounding suburbs – the majority of which remained between 80% and 95% white – was over ten years, and in some cases was as high as 16 years. In 2019, the population of Detroit was 78.6% African American, and 36.4% of residents lived below the federal poverty line. In 2014–2018, per capita incomes were only $17,338. A University of Michigan study of Detroit's labor market released in October 2019 found that

> up to 140,000 working-age Detroit residents are not in the labor force, with many facing multiple barriers to work such as lack of a high school diploma, having no car, and having been out of work in the past year.
>
> *(Detroit News 2016; Holzer and Rivera 2019)*

The toxic legacies of housing and job discrimination, white flight, and inner-city plant closures in majority African American cities like Detroit and Flint had already produced concentrated poverty and urban fiscal crises by 1980. Over the next 40 years, neoliberal policies dismantled key components of the "New Deal order" in Detroit: unionized manufacturing jobs, federal aid to cities, banking regulations, progressive taxation, and welfare and public health programs. These policies contributed directly to mass home foreclosures, mass water shutoffs, and lead poisoning disasters that devastated working-class and poor African American families between the late 1990s and the 2010s. Predatory subprime lending by deregulated Wall Street banks led to the global financial crash of 2007–2008 and caused over 200,000 home foreclosures in Detroit, precipitating a municipal fiscal crisis and state takeover, and radical austerity policies that further gutted the public sector and endangered urban public health (Rector 2022). In all of these respects, the unmaking of the "New Deal order" has disproportionately harmed African Americans in Detroit.

In 1999, President Bill Clinton signed the Financial Services Modernization Act, followed by the Commodity Futures Modernization Act in 2000. Whereas the first bill repealed the Glass-Steagall Act, stripping away the New Deal-era firewall between commercial banks, investment banks, securities firms and insurance companies, the second deregulated the swaps market. As a direct result of deregulation, the market for credit default swaps metastasized from $180 billion in 1998 to $6 trillion in 2004 and $57 trillion by the summer of 2008. Investment banks' aggressive marketing of high-risk swap deals to municipalities, from Detroit to Chicago to San Francisco, facilitated the growth of this market (US Senate 2011; Tabb 2012).

Financial deregulation enabled new forms of predatory lending to municipalities in fiscal distress, a trend that Detroit exemplified. Between 2001 and 2005, the Detroit Water and Sewerage Department (DWSD) made a series of interest rate swap deals with creditors, which constituted bets that interest rates would rise. If they fell, the city would be forced to pay "swap termination payments." In 2005, the city entered a particularly risky $1.44 billion deal with UBS AG and Merrill Lynch Capital Services (later acquired by Bank of America). As the *Detroit Free Press* reported in 2013, the deal "involved two layers of speculative financial instruments," including variable rate debt to fund city worker pensions, and an interest rate swap to fund DWSD. The deal constituted a bet that interest rates would rise rather than fall, and after interest rates plummeted as a result of the 2008 financial crisis, Detroit lost the bet, increasing its pension debt to over $770 million. The banks also charged DWSD over $547 million in "swap termination fees" (City of Detroit 2012; Guyette 2014). By 2012, debt service to the banks was consuming 40% of revenues at DWSD (Preston 2012).

Financial deregulation also enabled the mass marketing of adjustable-rate "subprime" mortgage loans to working-class African American communities, which banks had historically redlined. Here as well, Detroit stood at the forefront of a national trend. In 2005, 68% of the mortgages in Detroit were subprime, compared with 27% in Michigan as a whole, and 21% in the United States. Between 2005 and 2007, Detroit had the highest rate of subprime mortgage foreclosures in the United States (US Senate 2011). Between 2005 and 2015, over a third of the properties in Detroit (139,699 out of 384,672) entered into foreclosure. Mass home foreclosures contributed to Detroit's 25% population decline between 2000 and 2010, from 951,270 to 713,777 (MacDonald and Kurth 2015). The 2008 financial crash, and the foreclosure crisis it accelerated, caused median home prices in Detroit to collapse by over 68% in 2007–2010, causing a sharp contraction in an early severely eroded municipal tax base (Atahuene and Berry 2019).

During the same period, "welfare reform" eviscerated utility bill assistance for families living under the federal poverty line. Following President Clinton's signing of the Personal Responsibility and Work Opportunity Reconciliation Act in 1996, the number of welfare recipients in metropolitan Detroit fell from 107,869 in 1992 to 24,752 in 2000 (Allard 2001). The bill abolished Aid to Families with Dependent Children (AFDC), which had guaranteed cash assistance to impoverished single mothers and their children since the New Deal, replacing it with a more limited, punitive and short-term program called Temporary Assistance for Needy Families (TANF). The bill also devolved control over welfare spending to the states. In October 2002, as part of welfare reform, Michigan's conservative Republican Governor John Engler eliminated the Vendor Pay Program, whereby the Family Independence Agency assisted TANF recipients with utility bills to prevent shutoffs. As a result, nearly 30,000 people in Wayne County became immediately vulnerable to shutoffs. As the Michigan Welfare Rights Organization (MWRO) February 2003 newsletter noted, "[t]his is when our telephones at MWRO began to ring off the hook," as thousands of impoverished households faced gas, electricity and water shutoffs (MWRO 2003).

The number of Detroit households living without running water, which had already been rising as a result of "welfare reform," exploded in the aftermath of the 2008 financial crash. Between 2012 and 2019, the City of Detroit shut off water for 141,000 households, including more than a quarter-million people, or over a third of the residents of the city (Kurth and Wilkinson 2020). While some residents had water service restored within 24 hours, others lived without running water for weeks, months, and in some cases years at a time. In response to the worst water affordability crisis since the New Deal, DWSD opted for a much harsher policy toward ratepayers behind on their bills than their predecessors in the 1930s. Those deprived of water in Detroit were nearly all African Americans living below the federal poverty line, and they were disproportionately disabled, single mothers and their children, or elderly people living on fixed incomes. By making it impossible for families to properly bathe, clean, or even flush their toilets, water shutoffs created unsanitary conditions and contributed to the spread of viral infections and exacerbated existing chronic diseases like hypertension, diabetes, cancer and asthma. Perhaps worst of all, water shutoffs were an assault on dignity. They created embarrassing situations and increased fears that the authorities would condemn houses and separate children from parents, adding to the already acute psychosocial stress of living in poverty (Orduño 2018; Gaber et al. 2020).

In addition to the cruel and inhumane policy of depriving human beings of running water, industrial pollution and dilapidated public infrastructure added to the burden of chronic and infectious disease in Detroit. According to a 2017 study by Community Action to Promote Healthy Environments (CAPHE), a research partnership sponsored by the University of Michigan School of Public Health, air pollution caused an average of 690 excess deaths, 1,800 hospitalizations, and 3,400 asthma-related doctor's visits in Detroit every year. Indeed, they estimated that "ambient air pollution represents 7% of deaths in the city," more than all the lives lost to homicide (Community Action to Promote Health Environments 2017). Industrial polluters, and their emissions of fine particulate matter, ozone, sulfur dioxide, diesel exhaust and other air contaminants, annually killed more Detroiters than perpetrators of gun violence (Community Action to Promote Healthy Environments 2017).

Moreover, early twenty-first-century Detroit was experiencing a lead poisoning epidemic even worse than the more widely publicized case of Flint, Michigan. The elimination of Detroit's lead abatement program in 2012, partly due to Republican Governor Rick Snyder's cuts in state revenue sharing, reversed the city's slow progress in bringing down child lead poisoning rates. So, too, did a recklessly executed municipal "blight removal" program under Mayor Mike Duggan, which blanketed Detroit neighborhoods with lead dust from demolition debris. As a result of these ill-advised state and municipal policies, rates of childhood lead poisoning in Detroit increased from 6.9% to 8.8% between 2015 and 2016, a rate over twice as high as in Flint in the aftermath of that city's toxic water disaster (Bouffard and MacDonald 2017; Detroit Health Department 2017).

All of these conditions exacerbated the risks of morbidity and mortality in a respiratory pandemic, which arrived with COVID-19 in 2020. By the end of January 2021, 1,717 Detroiters had died from COVID-19 (State of Michigan 2021). In March–July 2020, African Americans in Michigan were dying of COVID-19 at over six times the rate of whites (Zelner et al. 2020). The "COVID Depression" of 2020 also had racially disproportionate impacts. A survey conducted by the University of Michigan Detroit Metro Area Communities Survey in March–April 2020 found that 43% of employed Detroiters had lost their jobs due to the pandemic, pushing Detroit's unemployment rate to 48%, a situation worse than the Great Depression. African Americans were not only more likely to be unemployed than whites, but were also likelier to be high-risk "essential workers" in medicine, retail and healthcare, on the front lines of exposure to the virus. An estimated 90% of the Detroit zip codes in Detroit with the highest number of COVID-19 deaths were low-income, with populations 90% or more African American (Detroit Metro Area Communities Study 2020; Henrie-Nick and Hudak 2020).

Detroit and the Green New Deal

For decades before the COVID-19 pandemic, Detroit activists had challenged these race and class inequalities, and demanded fundamental structural change. In the face of a manifestly broken political and economic model, environmental justice activists in Detroit established alternative food, water and energy systems, from urban farms to free water stations to windmills and solar installations (Boggs 1998; Boggs and Kurashige 2011; Rector 2022). However, many activists also recognized the need for larger policy solutions. The sheer scale of Detroit's economic and environmental challenges, as well as those of other frontline communities, clearly illustrates the pressing need for progressive public policies that can supplement and give breathing space to local experiments.

In many respects, the GND – as introduced in House Resolution 109 and elaborated on by advocates like Rhianna Gunn-Wright, Varshini Prakash, and the contributors to this volume – represents the potential for such structural change. A federal guarantee of a living-wage, unionized job with "adequate family and medical leave, paid vacations, and retirement security," combined with a guaranteed income for those unable to work, would go a long way toward ending poverty in Detroit and the United States more broadly (H. Res. 109). These policies would disproportionately benefit working-class and poor people of color in frontline communities across the United States. In cities like Detroit, they could end the mass suffering created by structural unemployment, while completing long-overdue infrastructural repairs and improvements to remediate toxic contamination, weatherize homes, decarbonize the electrical grid, and make water and sewer systems resilient in the face of increasingly extreme weather (Tcherneva 2020).

Promises of green jobs in Detroit are nothing new. During the presidential campaign in 2008, Barack Obama spoke of creating "5 million green jobs." According to the Council of Economic Advisors, the $90 billion in "Clean Energy" spending in the Obama administration's 2009 American Recovery and Reinvestment Act created only 720,000 jobs. In Michigan, which had the nation's highest unemployment rate, the Detroit Free Press reported in November 2009 that the stimulus had created only 22,500 jobs, of which over 13,000 went to education and over 3,000 to summer youth programs (Spangler 2009; Aldy 2013).

Of those, the City of Detroit reported 342 "projected" jobs, based on a $10 million grant for 14 public works projects in the city. However, none of those jobs had been created by the end of 2009. Detroit ultimately received $170 million in federal stimulus, but the city could only spend $16.8 million by February 2010 because the grants required up-front payments prior to reimbursement. The city, which faced a $330 million deficit, could only afford a small fraction of the up-front payments. By 2011, federal stimulus funds had added over $10 million to Detroit's public works budget, primarily for road repair projects (Helms 2011). However, fixing potholes and sheet asphalt did nothing to decarbonize the transportation sector, let alone the electrical grid, or to remediate brownfield sites, lead paint and other environmental health hazards in the city. No less importantly, a few hundred public works jobs had no appreciable impact on mass unemployment in Detroit. In 2010–2011, only 45% of Detroit residents in the 18–64 age range were classified as "employed" (19% were officially "unemployed" and 36% were classified as "not in labor force") (Holzer and Rivera 2019).

In the face of a crisis comparable to the Great Depression, federal policies remained a feeble echo of the New Deal.

Yet, both the needs and possibilities for green job creation in Detroit remained very large. In 2000, the EPA estimated that the city had 45,000 contaminated brownfield sites; other estimates reached as high as 90,000 (Sierra Club 2013). Donele Wilkins, who sat on the board of the Detroit Brownfield Redevelopment Authority, estimated in 2015 that there were 60,000 parcels of contaminated land in the city (Wilkins 2015). Moreover, the city's water, sewer, and energy infrastructure were aging and demanded upgrading. By 2018, the average water or sewer line in Detroit was 95 years old, and the city had an estimated 125,000 lead service lines that posed a toxic contamination risk for residents. The city's Combined Stormwater Overflow system periodically backed up during rainstorms, causing raw sewage to frequently back up into basements in parts of the city. A 2018 survey of approximately 1600 residents by the Detroit Office of Sustainability found that a majority experienced flooding in their homes (13% reported flooding "very often," 23% "somewhat often," and 32% "occasionally") (Kassem et al. 2019).

The city's electrical infrastructure was similarly dilapidated. In 2016, an estimated 40% of Detroit's 88,000 streetlights did not work, and the city's private electrical utility, DTE Energy, shut off electricity and gas service for thousands of Detroiters every week for unpaid bills. A 2017 survey of residents of Highland Park, a majority-African American suburb surrounded by the city of Detroit, found that "close to half of those polled had trouble paying their electricity bills," and a quarter had experienced utility shutoffs. Activists in Soulardarity, a Highland Park-based non-profit, advocated replacing DTE Energy with a public or cooperative utility that would support community-controlled renewable energy and implement progressive utility rate structures (Koeppel et al. 2019).

Remaking Detroit's infrastructure for the twenty-first century to meet ambitious climate mitigation and adaptation goals could create unionized, living-wage jobs on a scale that matches Detroit's equally severe problems of poverty and structural unemployment. Green jobs training programs in Detroit have also produced promising results. In 2007, the non-profit Detroiters Working for Environmental Justice (DWEJ) launched a Green Jobs Training Program. With funding from the National Institute of Environmental Health Service, the program accepted over 300 applications in its first year. The program included technical training for energy auditing, green landscaping, lead and asbestos abatement, hazardous waste operations and emergency response (HAZWOPER) positions, and Occupational Safety and Health Administration (OSHA) workplace certification, among others (Campbell 2009).

In 2010, DWEJ co-founder Donele Wilkins started a new non-profit called the Green Door Initiative (GDI). In a 2015 interview, she described the GDI's "green jobs" training program. The GDI provided training for "environmental lead removal, asbestos removal, deconstruction and all that kind of stuff." They also involved weatherization, energy auditing and the operation of wastewater treatment plants. Wilkins said that people receiving job training at her organization were "on average making, like, 18 bucks an hour." She estimated that roughly a third were formerly incarcerated, "and we target African American men, primarily between the ages of 22 and 35. And we've been pretty successful, and have about a 92 percent job placement rate." Cleaning up Detroit's brownfield sites could provide safe, living-wage jobs for Detroiters, including those facing employment discrimination due to past convictions and gaps in their work history (Wilkins 2015).

In a study of urban green jobs programs, political scientist Sekou Franklin argues that successful initiatives require "building relationships between the skilled trades (labor unions and trade associations) and groups representing people with severe barriers to employment, such as low-skilled workers, formerly incarcerated persons, homeless and transitional housing residents and poor youth." Similar programs include Sustainable South Bronx's BEST Program, the Oakland Job Corps, and Newark, New Jersey's Green-Collar Apprenticeship Program (Franklin 2017). In Detroit, DWEJ has collaborated with the Regional Energy Efficiency Partnership Training Program (REEPTP), whose partners include the Laborers' International Union of North America, the International Brotherhood of Electrical Workers, and other building trades unions (DiRamio and Coxen 2012).

If we examine the original New Deal through the lens of environmental justice, particularly from the perspective of frontline communities, we can discern both worthy lessons to emulate and clear mistakes to avoid for a twenty-first-century GND. On the positive side, New Deal public works programs compare favorably with the small-scale grants provided by the 2009 American Recovery and Reinvestment Act. In places like Detroit, the unemployment and infrastructure problems of the Great Recession equaled those of the Great Depression, but the federal government response was comparatively paltry. The latest downturn produced by the COVID-19 pandemic, and projections of increased extreme weather produced by climate change models, only underscore the need for public investments on the scale of (if not greater than) the original New Deal (Prakash and Girgenti 2020).

On the negative side, the history of housing and job discrimination against African Americans in Detroit demonstrates that public investment, labor rights and an expanded social wage do not automatically produce racial justice. New Deal policies subsidized banking, real estate and manufacturing industries that denied equal housing and job opportunities to African Americans, and institutionalized those practices as a matter of federal policy (above all through mortgage redlining). In light of this history, racial justice and anti-discrimination must be at the center of Green New Deal policies, and public investments must prioritize frontline communities that have historically borne the brunt of disinvestment and concentrated poverty. As Rhianna Gunn-Wright, the Climate Policy Director at the Roosevelt Institute, has observed, "an economic mobilization that ignores justice and equity is a danger to both marginalized people and decarbonization." A GND "won't succeed if it is not just and equitable" (Gunn-Wright 2020).

Theresa Landrum, a veteran African American environmental justice activist in Detroit, recently offered a lucid and powerful description of what the GND could mean for her community. Landrum grew up in and around zip code 48217 in Southwest Detroit, in the shadow of a Marathon Oil refinery (Landrum 2019). In 2010, University of Michigan researchers classified 48217 the most polluted zip code in the state of Michigan (Lam 2010). In a 2020 interview, Landrum described her desired vision of the GND in Detroit, which embedded environmental justice in a broader conception of racial and economic justice. She said:

> It would be a future for my children and grandchildren to have air that is not brown, that is not gray, that is not black with pollution. It would be where my children can run barefoot on the grass, and their feet not be burned up from chemicals that may be hidden in there from surrounding industries. It would be healthcare for every American that did not have the ability to buy their own private insurance. It would be a plate of food three times a day on the table for the people that don't have food. It would be a strong educational system where my kid can have the same advantages of white children. It would be an equitable deal where we can have economic development where we can create our own jobs and have Black and Brown people establishing their own businesses.

> The poor would have equity as well as the rich. A Green New Deal would be the end of usage of the fossil fuels that contaminates my air. That's what a Green New Deal would be if I could construct it.
>
> *(Generation Green New Deal Podcast 2020)*

Ultimately, whether the Green New Deal succeeds in addressing the problems facing frontline communities will depend on the involvement of people like Theresa Landrum. In addition to learning from the mistakes and achievements of the past, Green New Deal advocates must allow frontline communities to take the lead in constructing an environmentally just, post-carbon future.

Bibliography

Aldy, J. 2013. "A Preliminary Assessment of the American Recovery and Reinvestment Act's Clean Energy Package." *Review of Environmental Economics and Policy* 7(1), 136–155.

Allard, S.W.P. 2001. "Race, and Work: The Dynamics of Welfare Reform in Metropolitan Detroit." *Brookings Institution Survey Series* (September), 1–11.

Anieri, P.J.D. 2007. "Regional Reform in Historic Perspective: Metropolitan Planning Institutions in Detroit, 1950–1990." Ph.D. diss., University of Michigan.

Aronoff, K. et al. 2019. *A Planet to Win: Why We Need a Green New Deal*. New York: Verso.

Atahuene, B. and Berry, C. 2019. "Taxed Out: Illegal Property Tax Assessments and the Epidemic of Tax Foreclosures in Detroit." *UC Irvine Law Review* 9(4), 847–886.

Boggs, G.L. and Kurashige, S. 1998. *Living for Change: An Autobiography*. Minneapolis: University of Minnesota Press.

Boggs, G.L. and Kurashige, S. 2011. *The Next American Revolution: Sustainable Activism for the Twenty-First Century*. Berkeley: University of California Press.

Bouffard, K. and MacDonald, C. 2017. "Detroit Kids' Lead Poisoning Rates Higher Than Flint." *Detroit News*. 15 November.

Boyle, K. 1995. *The UAW and the Heyday of American Liberalism*. Ithaca: Cornell University Press.

Boyle, K. 2004. *Arc of Justice: A Saga of Race, Civil Rights, and Murder in the Jazz Age*. New York: Henry Holt & Company.

Campbell, E. 2009. "DWEJ Gives Detroiters a Chance." *Michigan Citizen*. 11 February.

City of Detroit. 2012. "Comprehensive Annual Financial Report for the Fiscal Year Ended June 30, 2012." Available from: https://www.scribd.com/document/195004314/EP731053-EP567459-EP968879.

Clark, D.J. 2018. *Disruption in Detroit: Auto Workers and the Elusive Postwar Boom*. Urbana: University of Illinois Press.

Clemens, E. 2008. *The Works Progress Administration in Detroit*. Chicago: Arcadia Press.

Climate Justice Alliance. 2020. "Protect, Repair, Invest, and Transform: A People's Orientation to a Regenerative Economy." June. Available from: https://climatejusticealliance.org/wpcontent/uploads/2020/06/ProtectRepairInvestTransformdoc22x.pdf.

Coates, T. 2014."The Case for Reparations." *The Atlantic*. June. Available from: https://www.theatlantic.com/magazine/archive/2014/06/the-case-for-reparations/361631/.

Community Action to Promote Healthy Environments. 2017. *Public Health Action Plan: Improving Air Quality & Health in Detroit 2017*. Available from: http://caphedetroit.sph.umich.edu/wpcontent/uploads/2017/05/CAPHE-PHAP-Full-Report-and-Executive-Summary-5-10-17.pdf.

Darden, J.T. et al. 1987. *Detroit: Race and Uneven Development*. Philadelphia: Temple University Press.

Data Driven Detroit and the Skillman Foundation. 2012. "The State of the Detroit Child 2012." Available from: https://www.skillman.org/wpcontent/uploads/2017/12/2012_Detroit_Child_report-min.pdf.

Detroit Health Department. 1973. "Childhood Lead Poisoning in Detroit: An Overview." Library of Michigan, Lansing, MI.

Detroit Health Department. 2017. "Task Force Recommendations for Improving Demolition Safety and Health Standards." Available from: https://detroitmi.gov/sites/detroitmi.localhost/files/2018-05/Task%20Force%20Recommendations.pdf

Detroit Metro Area Communities Study. 2020. "2020--COVID-19 Rapid Response." Spring. Available from: https://detroitsurvey.umich.edu/wp-content/uploads/2020/04/Wave-7-Toplines-Final.pdf

DeVito, L. 2019. "Backlash Against General Motors Is Helping Plants the Seeds for a Green Revolution." *Metrotimes*. 30 January.

DiRamio, M. and Coxen, T. 2012. "Working Toward a Sustainable Detroit: Investing in Sustainable Industry and 'Green Collar' Careers for Residents in Detroit." Detroit Regional Workforce Fund, United Way for Southern Eastern Michigan. May. Available from: https://edauniversitycenter.uic.edu/wp-content/uploads/sites/16/2018/09/Working-Towards-a-Green-Detroit.pdf.

Eichenhorn, S. 1977. "A Return to the 'Fires of Hell': Workers Revisit Abandoned Ford Foundry." *Detroit News*. 19 October.

Estes, N. 2019. "A Red Deal." *Jacobin*. 6 August.

Fine, S. 1975. *Frank Murphy: The Detroit Years*. Ann Arbor: University of Michigan Press.

Fine, S. 1989. *Violence in the Model City: The Cavanagh Administration, Race Relations, and the Detroit Riot of 1967*. Ann Arbor: University of Michigan Press.

Foote, C.L., Whatley, W.C. and Wright, G. 2004. "Arbitraging a Discriminatory Labor Market: Black Workers at the Ford Motor Company, 1918–1947." *Journal of Labor Economics* 21(July), 593–532.

Franklin, S. 2017. "Race, Class and Green Jobs in Low-Income Communities in the US: Challenges for Community Development," in Shaw, M. and Mayo, M. eds., *Class, Inequality and Community Development*. Bristol: Policy Press. pp. 77–92.

Freeman, J. 2018. *Behemoth: A History of the Factory and the Making of the Modern World*. New York: W.W. Norton.

Gaber, N. et al. 2020. "Water Insecurity and Psychosocial Distress: Case Study of the Detroit Water Shutoffs." *Journal of Public Health* (September), 43(4), 1–7.

Generation Green New Deal Podcast. 2020. "Episode 5: Detroit, Engine of the Green New Deal." October. Available from: https://www.generationgreennewdeal.com/podcast-s1e5.

Gunn-Wright, R. 2020. "Policies and Principles of a Green New Deal," in Prakash, V. and Girgenti, G. eds., *Winning the Green New Deal: Why We Must, How We Can*. New York: Simon & Schuster. pp. 67–93.

Guyette, C. 2014. "Bad Interest Rate Swaps Contribute to Detroit Water Crisis and Financial Crisis." *Metro Times*. 6 August.

Helms, M. 2011. "Detroit to Fix $53M Worth of Major Roads, Side Streets." *Detroit Free Press*. 17 February.

Henrie-Nick, M. and Hudak, J. 2020. "Social Distancing in Black and White Neighborhoods in Detroit: A Data-Driven Look at Vulnerable Communities." *Brookings Institution*. 19 May. Available from: https://www.brookings.edu/blog/fixgov/2020/05/19/social-distancing-in-black-and-white-neighborhoods-in-detroit-a-data-driven-look-at-vulnerablecommunities/.

Holzer, H.Z. and Rivera, J. 2019. "The Detroit Labor Market: Recent Trends, Current Realities." University of Michigan. October. Available from: https://poverty.umich.edu/files/2019/10/Detroit-Labor-Market-1213.pdf.

H.Res.109. 2019. Recognizing the Duty of the Federal Government to Create a Green New Deal. 116th Congress, 7 February. Available from: https://www.congress.gov/bill/116th-congress/house-resolution/109/text.

Hurley, A. 1996. *Environmental Inequalities: Class, Race, and Industrial Pollution in Gary, Indiana, 1945–1980*. Chapel Hill: University of North Carolina Press.

International Joint Commission. 1960. *Report of the International Joint Commission on the Pollution of the Atmosphere in the Detroit River Area*. Washington, DC and Ottawa: International Joint Commission.

Jackson, K.T. 1987. *Crabgrass Frontier: The Suburbanization of the United States*. New York: Oxford University Press.

Jacobs, A.J. 1999. "Intergovernmental Relations and Uneven Development in the Detroit and Nagoya Auto Regions." Ph.D. diss., Michigan State University.

Jenkins, D. 2017. "Who Segregated America?" *Public Books*. 21 December. Available from: https://www.publicbooks.org/who-segregated-america/.

Katz, D. 1977. "Blood Lead Level Tests Urged for City Children." *Detroit Free Press*. 1 August.

Katznelson, Ira. 2013. *Fear Itself: The New Deal and the Origins of Our Time*. New York: W.W. Norton.

Kennedy, S.E. 1991. *The Banking Crisis of 1933*. Lexington: University Press of Kentucky.

Koeppel, J., Bozuwa, J. and Veazey, L. 2019. "The Green New Deal Must Put Utilities Under Public Control." *In These Times*. 1 February.

Kurth, J. and Wilkinson, M. 2020. "I Hate to Complain, But I haven't had Water in a Year." *Bridge Magazine*. 17 February.

Lam, T. 2010. "48217: Life in Michigan's Most Polluted Zip Code." *Detroit Free Press*. 20 June.

Landrum, T. 2019. Oral History Interview by Josiah Rector, Detroit, Michigan. 24 May.

Lewis-Colman, D. 2008. *Race Against Liberalism: Black Workers and the UAW in Detroit*. Urbana: University of Illinois Press.

MacDonald, C. and Kurth, J. 2015. "Volume of Abandoned Homes 'Absolutely Terrifying': Since 2005, More Than 1-in-3 Detroit Properties Have Been Foreclosed Because of Mortgage Defaults or Unpaid Taxes." *Detroit News*. 14 May.

Mayor's Interracial Committee. 1926. *The Negro in Detroit*. Detroit, MI: Detroit Bureau of Governmental Research.

McCammack, B. 2017. *Nature and the Great Migration in Chicago*. Cambridge, MA: Harvard University Press.

Meier, A. and Rudwick, E.W. 2007. *Black Detroit and the Rise of the UAW*, 2nd Ed. Chapel Hill: University of North Carolina Press

Michigan League for Public Policy. 2017. "Poverty-Children Ages 0–17–SAIPE: Detroit, Michigan." Available from: http://datacenter.kidscount.org/data/tables/1692-poverty--children-ages-0-17--saipe?loc=24&loct=3#detailed /3/58/false/869,36,868,867,133/any/3591,13134.

Michigan Welfare Rights Organization. 2003. "Recent History of Utility Shut-offs for Detroit's Poor, Disabled, and Seniors." Available from: https://www.mwro.org/past_actions.htm

Michney, T. and Winling, L. 2019. "New Perspectives on New Deal Housing Policy: Explicating and Mapping HOLC Loans to African Americans." *Journal of Urban History* (January), 1–31.

Needham, A. 2014. *Power Lines: Phoenix and the Making of the Modern Southwest*. Princeton: Princeton University Press.

Nelson, R.K. et al. 2019. "Mapping Inequality: Redlining in New Deal America," in Nelson, R.K. and Ayers, E.L. et al., eds., *American Panorama*, University of Richmond Digital Scholarship Lab. Available from: https://dsl.richmond.edu/panorama/redlining/#loc=10/42.348/-83.45&city=detroit-mi

Orduño, S. 2018. Oral History Interview by Josiah Rector, Detroit, Michigan. 20 July.

Prakash, V. and Girgenti, G. eds. 2020. *Winning the Green New Deal: Why We Must, How We Can*. New York: Simon & Schuster.

Preston, D. 2012. "Detroit Shows Wall Street Never Loses on Bad Swaps." *Bloomberg*. 12 September.

Rector, J. 2022. *Toxic Debt: An Environmental Justice History of Detroit*. Chapel Hill: University of North Carolina Press.

Reed, T. 2020. *Toward Freedom: The Case Against Race Reductionism*. New York: Verso.

Shaw, T.C. 2009. *Now is the Time! Detroit Black Politics and Grassroots Activism*. Durham: Duke University Press.

Sicotte, D. 2016. *From Workshop to Waste Magnet: Environmental Inequality in the Philadelphia Region*. New Brunswick: Rutgers University Press.

Sierra Club. 2013. "The State of Detroit's Environment: An Initial Assessment Using the Framework of Environmental Justice." April. Available from: http://www.crainsdetroit.com/sites/default/files/assets/2946531/State_of_Detroit_s_Envioonment.pdf.

Smith, H.F. 1933. "At War with the Depression in the Detroit Water Department." *Journal of the American Water Works Association* 25(12), 1681–1689.

Spangler, T. 2009. "Federal Stimulus Impact: Billions for State, But Where Are Jobs?" *Detroit Free Press*. 15 November.

State of Michigan. 2021. "Cases and Deaths by County (Public Use Datasets)." 29 January. Available from: https://www.michigan.gov/documents/coronavirus/Cases_and_Deaths_by_County_2021-01-07_712368_7.xlsx.

Sugrue, T.J. 1996. *The Origins of the Urban Crisis: Race and Inequality in Postwar Detroit*. Princeton: Princeton University Press.

Tabb, W.K. 2012. *The Restructuring of Capitalism in Our Time*. New York: Columbia University Press.

Taylor, D. 2014. *Toxic Communities: Environmental Racism, Industrial Pollution, and Residential Mobility*. New York: New York University Press.

Tcherneva, P.R. 2020. *The Case for a Job Guarantee*. Medford, MA: Polity Press.

US Census Bureau. 2019. "Quickfacts: Detroit City, Michigan Population Estimates, July 1, 2019 (V2019)." Available from: https://www.census.gov/quickfacts/fact/table/detroitcitymichigan/HSD410218.

US Commission on Civil Rights. 1961. *Hearings Before the United States Commission on Civil Rights: Hearings Held in Detroit, Michigan, December 14, 1960 and December 15, 1960.* Washington, DC: US Government Printing Office.

US Senate, Majority and Minority Staff Report, Permanent Subcommittee on Investigations. 2011. "Wall Street and the Financial Crisis: Anatomy of a Financial Collapse." 13 April. Available from: http://www.hsgac.senate.gov/imo/media/doc/Financial_Crisis/FinancialCrisisReport.pdf?attempt =2.

Van Duser, A. 1947. "Tuberculosis in the Negro: A Comparison of the Negro of Detroit with the White." M.A. Thesis, University of Michigan.

Washington, S.H. 2005. *Packing Them In: An Archaeology of Environmental Racism in Chicago, 1865–1954.* Lanham, MA: Lexington Books.

Weisiger, M. 2011. *Dreaming of Sheep in Navajo Country.* Seattle: University of Washington Press.

Wengert, E.S. 1939. *Financial Problems of the City of Detroit in the Depression.* Detroit: Detroit Bureau of Governmental Research.

Wilkins, D. 2015. Oral History Interview by Josiah Rector, Detroit, Michigan. 14 July.

Wilson, W.J. 1996. *When Work Disappears: The New World of the Urban Poor.* New York: Knopf.

Wolcott, V. 2001. *Remaking Respectability: African American Women in Interwar Detroit.* Chapel Hill: University of North Carolina Press.

Young, T. 2009. "'A Contradiction in Democratic Government': W.J. Trent, Jr., and the Struggle to Desegregate National Park Campgrounds." *Environmental History* 14 (October), 651–682.

Zelner, J. et al. 2020. "Racial Disparities in Coronavirus Disease 2019 (COVID-19) Mortality Are Driven by Unequal Infection Risks." *Clinical Infectious Diseases* 72(5), 1–8.

10

THE SEVENTH FIRE AND THE SITTING BULL PLAN

An Indigenous Green New Deal

Winona LaDuke

> *The world is undergoing an initiation. The ancient knowledge of our ancestors and elders is needed now more than ever as we navigate through times of illness, painful division and social disruption. It's time to call on the world's spiritual midwives – those who can bridge us to the new paradigm.*
> *(Angaangaq)*

Now is the time. One prophecy and one instruction can guide a life. *It can guide a social movement and a transformation.* In the time of the Seventh Fire, the Anishinaabeg were told that we would have a choice between two paths: one well worn, but scorched; a second not well worn, but green. We are instructed to make a choice. For those of us who choose the Green Path, there is another fire that is called the Eighth Fire.

There, the Anishinaabeg are told that we will find a more peaceful time and return to our teaching of *Mino Bimaatisiiwin* (the Good Life). That is the goal... *Light the fire*, I say.

Timing could not be better. The world is changing. That is to say, despite all intentions, technology and proclamations, our world is being transformed. The Technological world created by men has been transformed by the Natural world – in this case, by a virus. *It's never a good idea to pick a fight with Mother Nature. You won't win.* The fact is that this world is changing, and it's time to be the change.

> Coronavirus has made the mighty kneel and brought the world to a halt like nothing else could... Historically, pandemics have forced humans to break with the past and imagine their world anew. This one is no different. It is a portal, a gateway between one world and the next. We can choose to walk through it, dragging the carcasses of our prejudice and hatred, our avarice, our data banks and dead ideas, our dead rivers and smoky skies behind us. Or we can walk through lightly, with little luggage, ready to imagine another world. And ready to fight for it.
> *(Roy 2020)*

Roy's statement is about walking through that portal to the next world – the one we will make. There are many names for this time of change; all I am sure of is that we need some directions on how to get there. For some, it is called the Green New Deal, referencing Franklin Delano Roosevelt's rebuilding of America during the Great Depression. In Canada,

DOI: 10.4324/9781003110880-13

the transition has also been encapsulated in the LEAP Manifesto (2015). Harkening to the times of the Marshall Plan, which saw the United States direct funds toward the rebuilding of Europe after World War II, the transformation will require social movements, political will and a huge amount of structural change. In honor of one of the greatest political leaders of North America, I often refer to this as the Sitting Bull Plan. Its time is now.

The groundwork and much of the thinking has been laid out and, indeed, has been transforming this world for years, though largely unnoticed by journalists and politicians who often seem to seek big-ticket items and miss the forest for the trees. Essential elements of Just Transition carry across territories. In January of 2020, Indigenous Peoples gathered in Fairbanks, Alaska, to talk about a Just Transition.

During these discussions, the organization Native Movement proposed that the term *Kohtr'elneyh*, which means "We Remember" in Benhto "Kenaga," the lower Tanana Dene Athabaskan language, be embedded in the Just Transition framework, and that traditional knowledge would be a guiding light in this work. Enei Begay of Native Movement reminds us that the Just Transition framework:

> upholds relationships that stem from time immemorial and must recognize it was not people who governed the land, but rather the land and the spiritual beings of the land prescribed relationships among humans and their relationships to the land....We acknowledge the depth of Indigenous knowledge rooted in the long inhabitation of a particular place offers answers as we search for a more satisfying and sustainable way to live.
> *(cited in LaDuke 2020)*

That transition is happening, and it needs a plan. In addition to the pandemic, social, economic and ecological movements are currently transforming the world we know. Icons are falling, from the statues of Columbus to those of confederate soldiers and conquistadors. The icons of capitalism are also falling. Fossil fuel companies have lost their glitter as for the first time in 50 years – there are none on the top ten of the S&P index. In fact, Exxon, once the world's largest corporation, has been kicked out of the Dow Jones index (Egan 2020).

Globalization is increasingly in question. Globalization has a lot of hidden risk and costs, and most of these are "offshored" and unfathomable. That's why we get child labor in Pakistan, the destruction of rainforests, and a garbage dump in the middle of the ocean that is twice the size of Texas (Rice 2018). These are "economic externalities" for corporations, but they are real life. At a more basic level, we are simply moving way too much stuff around, and we don't know the costs of that. For example, a shrimp raised in Scotland gets sent to China to be deveined and then is shipped to a Walmart near you. That's not the healthiest idea in the world for a whole bunch of reasons, the least of which being that shrimp should not travel that far.

The COVID-19 pandemic has shown us another dark side of globalization. Historically, epidemics have been spread through two common forms of human movement: trade and war. In the Middle Ages, it took a decade or so for the Bubonic Plague (the Black Death) to spread from China through the Silk Roads and Mongolian conquests to Europe. In 1918, the Spanish flu spread from Spain to France and Britain by June and to the United States and Canada by the fall of that same year. That pandemic followed battle lines and military movements during World War I. COVID-19 took only a few days to spread from Wuhan to other Chinese cities in late 2019, and then it moved along trade routes. By March 2020 it had hit 72 countries. Dun & Bradstreet (2020) estimates that at least 51,000 companies around the world have "Tier 1" suppliers in the impacted region of China, and 5 million companies have one or more "Tier 2" suppliers in the impacted region. As Kim Moody (2020) notes: "The emphasis for the last two or three decades on lean production, just-in-time delivery, and, more recently, 'time-based competition,' along with updated transportation and distribution infrastructure, has accelerated the speed of transmission."

Somehow, it is not surprising that the single-largest hotspot for COVID-19 in April 2020 was the Smithfield Meats plant in Sioux Falls, South Dakota (Lussenhop 2020). That plant was a centerpiece for butchering millions of pigs raised at industrial faming facilities, known as Confined Animal Feeding Operations, or CAFOS. All of these systems are collapsing.

This is the end of "Wiindigo Economics," or the Economics of a Cannibal, as we know it. In turn, social movements are surging. There's a tide of change. *It's time to surf.*

What is certain is the need for structural change. For decades, the World Bank and the International Monetary Fund have required developing countries to comply with structural adjustment plans. Now is the time for the first world to adjust – and there are plenty of opportunities. The reality is that we will need to make major adjustments in food, infrastructure, energy and materials economy systems to weather the storms ahead. Beyond that, we will need to adjust and transform how we relate to each other, to the Natural world and to our terrestrial relatives, whether they have fins, roots, wings or hooves. The time, as the Santee philosopher John Trudell would tell us, is a time for "Peace with Earth." Let's begin. *Skoden.*

The Sitting Bull Plan – just transition

Let us put our minds together to see what life we will make for our children.

(Tatanka Yotanka)

Sitting Bull, or Tatanka Yotanka, was a Hunkpapa Lakota political and spiritual leader during the most complex times for the Oceti Sacowin. His people saw the destruction of the buffalo (the center of their way of life), the coming of the military and Indian Wars (targeting his nation), and the coming of George Hearst and subsequently the Homestake Mine, one of the largest and most profitable gold mines in the world, in the heart of the Pahá Sápa (sacred land of the Lakota, also known as the Black Hills mountain range). His vision led to the defeat of George Armstrong Custer at the Battle of the Little Bighorn in June 1876, and his military and strategic leadership decisions have been widely regarded as some of the most brilliant in war and civil society. His vision was great, and he lived in epic times. These are such times as well.

Indigenous Peoples have fought for centuries to protect the sacred. We honor that and continue that protection – from the Arctic National Wildlife Refuge (the Gwich'in people have regarded the Coastal Plain of the Arctic Refuge as *Iizhik Gwats'an Gwandaii Goodlit* or "The Sacred Place Where Life Begins") to the Yanomami lands of the Amazon. From the Arctic to the Amazon, literally, we must honor the sacred and protect it. Why? Because life is there.

Where the wild things are

On a worldwide scale, Indigenous Peoples represent about 4% of the world's population, but care for about 75% of the world's biodiversity. Protect those places; they have life. Indigenous Peoples use thousands of medicines and plants in a world where industrialization has limited plants to those provided mostly by corporations and governments. The boreal forests of the

North and the forests of the South, like the Amazon, are places where peoples and our relatives remain, including "uncontacted tribes" or First Nations in the Far North of Canada.

In America, there are 52 million acres of Indian land (4% of the continental United States), and our treaty territories are much larger. We live where there are wolves, bears, buffalo, sturgeon, geese, eagles and salmon. Our lands also retain agro-biodiversity of thousands of seeds grown for millennia as well as the grasses and forests to support life. Our territories contain sacred places and sacred landscapes; all of which are the places where we are able to reaffirm and recharge our relationship with Mother Earth. Stand with these people. Because there is life where we live.

Respect our knowledge. We know more than what Western society gives us credit for, by a long shot. Take the heartbreaking story of Australian wildfires, a story of devaluing Indigenous knowledge of landscape while a continent burned. Over the past decade, scientific journals have discussed Indigenous fire management. Indeed, fire is a powerful tool, when harnessed. North American Indigenous Peoples often burned the prairies to make grass and keep back trees. New grass is good for buffalo, and many plants actually require fire to germinate. The Australian story is the same. Unlike hazard reduction burning, cultural burns are cooler and slower moving, usually no taller than knee height, leaving tree canopies untouched and allowing animals to take refuge from the flames. Small fires are lit with matches, instead of drip torches, and burn in a circular pattern. Northern Australia fires burned 57% fewer acres than in previous years, where Aboriginal people managed land for fire. Dean Yibarbuk, chairman of Warddeken Land Management, has 150 Aboriginal rangers working. "We are very lucky in the north to be able to keep our traditional practices," Yibarbuk said (quoted in Fuller and Abbott 2020). "There's a pride in going back to the country, managing it and making a difference." Sadly, our knowledge is generally not valued, and instead is pushed aside by scientists and experts (Nunn 2020). George Nicholas (2018) writes:

> On the one hand, these types of knowledge are valued when they support or supplement archaeological, or other scientific evidence. But when the situation is reversed – when Traditional Knowledge is seen to challenge scientific "truths" – then its utility is questioned or dismissed as myth. Science is promoted as objective, quantifiable, and the foundation for "real" knowledge creation or evaluation while Traditional Knowledge may be seen as anecdotal, imprecise and unfamiliar in form.

In short, we must protect and value life and those who understand how to live for thousands of years in a place without destroying it. Those are some good lessons.

Seeds are life

> They tried to bury us, but they forgot we were seeds.
>
> *(Zapatista proverb)*

Grow the future. Remember the victory gardens of World War II and create gardens for the future. Indeed, during the pandemic of 2020, seed sales grew dramatically, and homebound families returned to the gardens (Picchi 2020). Seeds are about promise, hope and commitment. Seeds are about life. Indigenous and heritage seeds are intelligent seeds; genetically modified seeds are not. Here is why, simply stated: plants have an ability to adapt and have more systems of adaptation than a corporate seed company will ever have. Mother Nature and her rooted children are intelligent beings. Anyone who has grown a multitude of crops and varieties can see adaptation and genius in plants; different weather conditions bring forth different plants; abundance varies.

In the meantime, major corporations like Monsanto and Syngenta talk about climate-change-adapting varieties they are introducing, using billions of dollars to create "climate-smart" varieties. The seed scholar Patrick Mooney tells an Indigenous Slow Food Gathering in Meghalaya, India, that the average cost for climate-smart seeds per species is US$136 million (Mooney 2015). In the meantime, Indigenous nations worldwide are adapting our pre-petroleum varieties to the times ahead. Combined, Indigenous and peasant farmers are producing today 70% of the world's food (Mooney 1996). One might want to stick with the ancient, time-tested wisdom of food.

The return of Indigenous seeds is referred to as "rematriation." As Mohawk scholars Elizabeth Hoover and Rowen White (2018) say:

> The word rematriation reflects the restoration of the feminine seeds back into the communities of origin. The Indigenous concept of rematriation can also encompass the reclaiming of ancestral remains, spirituality, culture, knowledge, and resources. It simply means back to Mother Earth, a return to our origins, to life and cocreation, honoring the life-giving force of the Divine Feminine.

Many of these seeds are highly nutritious. Heritage varieties are often higher in magnesium and amino acids (Agriculture and Agri-Food Canada 2018). As the plants are pre- and post-petroleum, they are not addicted to industrial agriculture. What you plant matters. Don't plant iceberg lettuce, plant kale. That will take you into winter.

Then there is the just transition from industrial agriculture. What has come to be called "conventional agriculture" is really an aberration of thousands of years of agriculture. It is essentially the agriculture of the Green Revolution: plants created in laboratories and slathered with water and fossil fuels. Organic and restorative agriculture sequesters carbon, rebuilds topsoil and cleans water. It is estimated that organic agriculture on a worldwide scale could sequester up to a quarter of the carbon in the atmosphere today (Nargi 2017). Simply stated, carbon belongs in the soil, not in the air. Rattan Lal, a soil scientist based at Ohio State University, estimates that since the beginning of the Industrial Revolution, more than a quarter of all carbon added to the atmosphere has come from plowing, which speeds up the decomposition of the soil's organic matter and exposes soil to wind and rain, thereby increasing erosion (Gewin 2020).

Today, 15%–20% of total annual greenhouse gas emissions are attributed to agriculture, much of that from plowing (Gewin 2020). Carbon can be put back into the soil by no-till farming practices, perennialized agriculture, the application of compost and manure, and the holistic grazing of livestock, such as chickens or buffalo. This is how life is restored. The Marin Carbon Project finds that a single layer of compost less than an inch thick applied to the surface of pasture stimulates microbial and plant activity, resulting in the sequestration of 5 tons of carbon per acre on a continual basis. Feed the topsoil, that's where the life comes from, and feed the Earth.

Buffalo Nation, Buffalo Commons, Buffalo Treaty

Restore the largest ecosystem in North America, the prairies. The Great Plains region spans across 40% of the United States but holds just a small fraction of its population. By comparison, the Prairie Ecozone of Canada spans across 5% of Canada's landmass. It is estimated that over half of the remaining native grassland in Canada is in the Mixed Grass Prairie, which is found in southern Saskatchewan, Alberta and Manitoba (Callaghan 2017). Time to restore peace with those lands.

Grazing animals create extraordinary environments in a reciprocal relationship with plants and water. These are marked upon the Serengeti plains and tallgrass prairies of the United States. "Where original grasslands are still intact, they are abundant lands with carbon-rich soils. They benefit from the activity of migratory herds that cluster tightly for protection; munch grasses to the crown; disturb the soil with their hooves, intermixing their urine and feces; and then move on…" (Noss 1994).

Managed grazing imitates the natural cycle, addressing two key variables: how long livestock graze in a specific area and how long the land rests before animals return. Managed grazing techniques can improve soil health, carbon sequestration, water retention, and forage productivity. Frank and Debra Popper, demographers from Rutgers University, proposed "the Buffalo Commons," or the restoration of that biome to a buffalo-based ecosystem, full of the grazing animals and pre- and post-petroleum economics (Popper and Popper 1999). That is what we need for the future, a Buffalo Commons.

In 2017, 11 First Nations from the cross-border region of the Northern Plains signed the Northern Tribes Buffalo Treaty. The Buffalo treaty encompasses 6.3 million acres of land held by the Blackfeet Nation (in the United States and Canada), the Blood Tribe, the Siksika Nation, the Piikani Nation, the Assiniboine and Gros Ventre Tribes of Fort Belknap Reservation, the Assiniboine and Sioux Tribes of Fort Peck Reservation, the Confederated Salish and Kootenai Tribes, and the Tsuu T'ina Nation. These First Nations are largely in the Montana and Alberta region. They have come together to restore the buffalo – or *iiniwaa,* in the Blackfeet language – to its natural territory. That's the beginning of the affirmation of relationship again (Drimal 2019)

Within the United States, 41 separate tribes now belong to the Intertribal Bison Cooperative, whose sole mission is buffalo restoration. On reservations from Taos Pueblo to Standing Rock in North Dakota, Native communities are actively welcoming home their relations. In 2019, the Buffalo Treaty was signed again, this time with officials from tribes based in Alberta, South Dakota and Wyoming signing on to the agreement, bringing the total number of signatories to more than 30. The hope is that over time, wildlife – specifically, buffalo corridors – can be created between the entities, to restore the Buffalo Nation. The Buffalo Treaty marks one of the first Indigenous treaties of this millennium and reminds us that treaties and agreements should be made to benefit all. Restore the buffalo and we will restore the prairies. That's how the land and plants absorb the carbon in the air and how the water of the land is returned.

Infrastructure justice

Build infrastructure that matters for people, public health and Mother Earth, not multinational corporations. Infrastructure matters. It is not the exciting stuff of Trump Towers and flashy museums; it's the stuff that connects the country, heats it, powers it, waters it and tries to take care of the sewage and waste. Infrastructure constitutes the body of the Wiindigo – the beast of Anishinaabe legend. Roads and rails, pipelines and dams, prisons and borders have all worked to carve up Turtle Island into preserves of settler jurisdiction, while entrenching and hardening the very means of settler economy and sociality into tangible material structures. Yet infrastructure is not inherently violent – it is also essential for transformation; a pipe can carry fresh water as well as toxic sludge. Infrastructure matters and needs investment. The American Society of Civil Engineers has graded America a "D" in infrastructure, whether water or electrical (Longley 2019). That is a killer problem. Take, for example, the California Camp Fire of 2019. That fire – caused by faulty electric lines at the power company, Pacific Gas and Electric (PG&E) – killed 85 people (Eavis and Penn 2019). In comparison, the Blue Lake Rancheria, an Indigenous tribe in northern California, saved lives during the PG&E power outage, as their one-megawatt solar microgrid continued to operate (Neumann 2020). Climate change brings disaster, but also opportunity.

Consider the water infrastructure of a city like Flint, Michigan (Edwards 2016). Residents should have access to clean drinking water – as should Native people, who, from the north of Canada to the Navajo Reservation, lack adequate water infrastructure. The injustice of infrastructure is not only about lack – for instance, when clean water infrastructures do not reach northern Indigenous communities on James Bay or urban Black communities on the Great Lakes, or when public transit infrastructures do not reach racialized neighborhoods, which are increasingly pushed to the fringes of gentrifying cities (LaDuke and Cowen 2020).

Simply stated, instead of building mega pipelines for tar sands oil projects, build pipelines for cities and people: water pipelines, sewer pipelines and gas pipelines to replace leaking lines in urban areas. Save water, save energy and save lives. Pipeline expert Trudy Bell reported the following in 2015:

> In 2013 and 2014, a team of researchers from Duke University, Stanford University, and other organizations drove every street in Boston and Washington, D.C., measuring methane in the ambient air and issuing from manholes. In Boston there were more than 3,000 gas leaks, and in the District of Columbia nearly 5,900, including a dozen telecommunications manholes where natural gas exceeded 50,000 parts per million – that is, 5% gas in air, the minimum explosive limit. Independently, in 2012, New York City's two distributors of natural gas reported finding over 9,900 leaks in their systems combined. All those leaks mean that collectively, the nation's consumers annually pay at least $20 billion for gas they are not receiving, revealed a 2013 report. The report also documented 796 "significant incidents" in the nation's gas distribution system between 2002 and 2012, including several hundred explosions, 116 fatalities, 465 injuries, and nearly $811 million in property damage.
>
> *(See Bell 2015 for cited research)*

Saving resources is always the best plan.

Think about this: a study completed by the Lawrence Livermore National Laboratory and the US Department of Energy showed that some 59% of energy was "rejected" by the system between point of production and point of consumption, with the two largest sectors of waste found in the transportation sector and in electricity production (US Department of Energy 2015). Efficiency creates jobs and reduces inequalities and conflict.

Solutionary Rail

Solutionary Rail is a grassroots proposal to reconfigure the aging fossil fuel train system in the United States into an electric train system (Solutionary Rail n.d.). In Italy 64% of trains are electric; in France, 52%; and in Germany, 48%. In the United States, only 1% of trains are electric (Solutionary Rail n.d.). Electrifying the train system would reduce emissions from the trains themselves, and the train routes can be used as transmission corridors for renewable energy. Indigenous communities have already taken on renewable energy projects.

For example, the Blackfeet Reservation in Montana – which is connected by railroads and transmission lines – has some of the highest and most constant wind speeds in the world (wind power classes ranging from three to seven) and has been taking on wind projects since 1994 (Blackfeet Nation n.d.). The Mandan, Hidatsa and Arikara, have over 17,000 times more wind power than they are able to use on the Fort Berthold reservation where they live in North Dakota (LaDuke 2018). Solutionary Rail could move electricity coming off the Northern Plains to other parts of the country. Therein lies the possibility of rebuilding a distributive energy plan and creating better distribution infrastructure for people and the Earth. And we recognize that many of the right of ways for the railways pass through Native lands. Justice is found in good agreements.

Transform the materials economy

Annie Leonard's telling film, *The Story of Stuff* (see https://www.storyofstuff.org/), really summarizes the problem: we have too much stuff, and we don't need it. Nearly 70% of the US economy is based on private consumption (CEIC 2021). That's a lot of stuff. About half of it will end up in a landfill within six months; and as it goes, we do not have anywhere left to dump it (Katz 2019).

China is not taking our garbage anymore, nor is most of Asia or Africa. We have a gob of plastic in the ocean the size of Texas, and soon there will be more plastic than fish in the ocean. That's the kind of stuff the US Navy force should clean up in a demilitarized economy. They certainly have the equipment and money.

Before any of this "stuff" exists, the first part of the equation is the extraction and production processes required to make stuff – that is, mining and fossil fuel-based plastics. Mining is an especially inefficient process. Pretty soon, the mining projects may become so inefficient that we might as well be looking for "Unobtanium," the stuff of legend in the film *Avatar.*

There is a huge minerals complex that surrounds the Great Lakes. Here is an example of the end of the era of mining and Wiindigo Economics. The website of Minnesota's PolyMet Mining says it estimates NorthMet Project ore reserve at 290 million tons of proven and probable reserves grading 0.288% copper and a further 795 million tons grading 0.234% copper. Copper mining is the most inefficient product to produce from a big dig, as the recovery ratio for copper is 0.16%, much smaller than the average for other metals (4.5%). In other words, you need to remove 1,000,000,000 tons of material to recover 1.6 tons of copper. The only substance with a lower recovery rate is gold. Metal mining consumes more energy than both coal and mineral mining, and between the three is the least efficient. That's really the bottom of the barrel. And it's time to move on.

The solution is pretty simple. Stop single-use containers, move on from plastics, and start washing some bottles. The Bayern Brewery in Missoula, Montana, is an example of a company pursuing the transition. That company uses 1–100% recycled bottles, washes the bottles and reuses them to distribute a number of beverages throughout the region, refilling those same bottles (Bayern Brewing 2020). Reusing glass, rather than crushing it and making it anew, is a huge energy and materials resource savings.

Energy justice

Having provided a huge amount of energy to the US and Canadian economies over the past hundred years has exacted a devastating toll on Indigenous Peoples. Almost every mega dam has flooded our best lands, our heartlands, changing how we relate to water. Uranium extraction, coal mining and the tar sands all lay waste to vast Indigenous territories. Energy justice means that we are at the center of the next energy economy, but under different terms.

Consider the statistics reported by Rob Capriccioso in 2009: "Tribal lands have an estimated 535 billion kilowatt-hours per year (kWh/year) of wind power generation potential" and "an estimated 17,000 billion kWh/year of solar electricity generation potential, about 4.5 times total US annual generation" (Capriccioso 2009).

Blue Lake Rancheria is a federally recognized tribe in northern California. In 2016, the tribe built a microgrid, which has proven to be a model for the future. The microgrid includes 500 kilowatts of solar photovoltaics with a 1 megawatt-hour (MWh) battery storage system (Blue Lake Rancheria n.d.). The microgrid is connected to the Pacific Gas and Electric distribution grid and operates autonomously. A 2019 report from the California Energy Commission stated the following:

> Energy savings to the Blue Lake Rancheria was about $160,000 in 2017 and beginning in 2018 will increase to nearly $200,000 annually...The greenhouse gas emission reductions for 2017 are estimated to be 159 tons carbon dioxide equivalent (CO2e) and are expected to reach 175 tons CO2e/year in 2018 and beyond.
>
> *(Carter et al. 2019)*

Standing Rock, the site of the ongoing battle over the Dakota Access Pipeline, is also emblematic of the transition being led by Native nations. In 2019, the Cannon Ball Community Solar Farm came online, adding 300 kilowatts into the grid. This is the largest solar project in North Dakota, a state which is the second-largest oil producer in the country (Funes 2019).

Another example is Navajo Solar. After decades of a forced structural adjustment of the Dine[1] (or Navajo) economy from a land-based, pastoral economy to an energy powerhouse of coal strip mining, coal generation, and uranium mining and gas operations, the Navajo nation is transitioning. Coal-fired generators are closing on the reservation, and there's plenty of transmission infrastructure, not to mention a skilled energy work force. The challenge is powering it. The Kayenta solar project was the first utility-scale project on Navajo territory (the Navajo nation itself boasts one of the highest levels of renewable energy production, largely due to the remote and rural housing of the Nation). At 26 megawatts, the Kayenta project generates enough energy to power 13,000 homes (Associated Press 2017). More will come as coal strip mines and power plants close. The opportunity is clear.

In a 2019 article published by *Earther* (on Gizmodo), David Suzuki Foundation fellow Melina Laboucan-Massimo stated that, "It's pretty amazing that we see indigenous communities adopting renewable energy from coast to coast...For me, as an indigenous person, it's also a lot more in alignment with our indigenous worldview and philosophy about reciprocity and connection to the Earth and ensuring we protect the Earth, we protect the water, the land" (quoted in Funes 2019).

Get local: small is beautiful and resilient

Get local on energy. Each megawatt of community solar generates US$1.87 million in total economic impact during construction, operation, and maintenance. Community solar projects allow families of all income levels, communities, tribal governments, and municipalities to combine efforts to go solar. Nationally, 75% of all Americans face physical or financial barriers to adopting solar technologies. Community solar initiatives allow people who may not have suitable locations, rooftops, or with financial or regulatory barriers, to access solar. That increases local energy security.

There are lessons to be learned from the Puerto Rico Electric Power Authority's 97.5% fossil fuels plan in the face of tremendous solar potential. Today, there's a concerted effort between NGOs and corporations to relocalize and build a solar grid in that country. Hawaii, another neo-colony, has extremely high energy costs: 2016 data showed that the average price per kWh for electricity in Hawaii was 27.5 cents, while the US average was 12.5 cents per kWh (US Energy Information Administration 2018). Rather than spinning its wheels with exports in exchange for fuels, the state of Hawaii could benefit from localized renewable energy production, satisfying local electricity needs and reducing costs for the islands' residents and businesses.

The New Green Revolution: cannabis

It's said that 100 years ago or so, we had a choice between a carbohydrate economy and a hydrocarbon economy. We made the wrong choice. We are going to make the right choice now and create the New Green Revolution.

Cannabis has the ability to transform our materials economy and our textiles economy; return carbon to the soil; be a central material in sustainable housing and heating; provide health and well-being; and be a path to restorative justice. This narrative and potential apply to the plants known as industrial hemp and marijuana. In a world of technological fixes, it turns out that the future should have more plants in it, not less. And those plants have power, from biodiversity to carbon sequestration.

Cannabis sativa is a plant that can change our world. And she will, once we work on our relationship with her. She's complex and has many expressions: hemp and marijuana are the two most common varieties. Marijuana refers to the plant used as a psychotropic drug (either medicinal or recreational), and is genetically distinct from the hemp plant, which is used for a variety of products and in textile manufacturing. Hemp plants are defined as any cannabis plant that has 0.3% or less THC (Johnson 2019). THC, short for tetrahydrocannabinol, is the primary psychoactive compound in cannabis. The more THC you consume, the more changes you will notice in your cognition and how you feel. In essence, THC gets you "high." Even a plant with 0.4% THC would be regulated as marijuana, despite the fact that 0.4% isn't going to have a noticeable psychoactive effect. Both varieties have great value.

The cannabis economy is exploding in North America. Legalization opens a door for economic justice and well-being for all. Cannabis has known medical benefits, but more research is warranted. In 2017, the United States imported US$1.9 million worth of hemp textiles and 312 tons of hemp yarn valued at US$2.7 million, according to data from the US Department of Commerce's Office of Textiles and Apparel (Lotus 2019). Retail sales of hemp textiles in 2016 were about US$96.3 million, according to a report from the Hemp Industries Association (Ibid.). By 2019, the United States had become the third-largest producer of hemp in the world, with China and Canada being the second and first-ranked producers, respectively (HempToday 2019).

In terms of the other plant, there is speculation that the US cannabis industry for recreational and medical marijuana could reach US$37 billion by 2024 (McVey 2020).

Most "modern" textiles are produced by petrochemicals, and the cotton industry uses a massive amount of pesticides, defoliators and other toxic chemicals. Ninety-eight million tons of oil were used in the textile industry in 2015 (Morlet et al. 2017). By 2050, that number is expected to be 300 million (Panne 2019). Textile production is one of the most polluting industries, producing 1.2 billion tons of CO_2 equivalent (CO2e). Half the world's clothing is cotton, about 20 million tons produced annually. It can take more than 5283 gallons of water to make a single T-shirt and pair of jeans, and 73% of global cotton harvest comes from irrigated land (Newell 2016).Groundwater is getting contaminated. Agriculture is the largest source of pollution in most countries. Cotton occupies 2.4% of the world's crop land and yet it accounts for 24% and 11% of the global sales of insecticide and pesticides respectively (Amberoot n.d.).

Hemp is about three times the tensile strength of cotton, mold and UV resistant, uses very little water, pesticides or fertilizers, builds soil… and until the 1920s was about 80% of the clothing made in the United States. Minnesota itself had 11 hemp mills (Winona's Hemp n.d.). Hemp produces twice as much fiber per acre as cotton.

The National Council of Textile Organizations reported that in 2015, the US textile industry saw $2 billion in capital investments (NCTO 2017). In addition to new greenfield investment, existing textile companies that weathered the downturn are retooling their businesses and automating the work process. The United States is currently the world's third-largest exporter of textiles (Land 2017). Now we just need to rebuild the industry so that the materials are organic and grown here; hemp may be the answer.

In addition to textiles, hemp can also be used as a building material. Concrete is the most widely used manmade material in the world. It is also the source of about 8% of the world's carbon dioxide (CO_2) emissions (Lehne and Preston 2018). As BBC journalist Lucy Rodgers put it in 2018: "If the cement industry were a country, it would be the third largest emitter in the world – behind China and the United States. It contributes more CO_2 than aviation fuel (2.5%) and is not far behind the global agriculture business (12%)" (Rodgers 2018).

One potential alternative to concrete is hempcrete. Like many other hemp industries, hemp has been used for centuries as a building material and is now being adapted with a variety of techniques into new construction. Unlike concrete, which involves mining and smokestacks to produce, hemp is a plant, and its growth draws in huge amounts of carbon dioxide. In its application, hempcrete is a porous material and has the ability to retain carbon dioxide and moisture in large quantities (Berg 2020).

Hemp could also replace fossil-fuel-based plastics. Hemp plastics biodegrade and could be used for many products.

Justice in the New Green Revolution

People of color made up 86% of marijuana possession arrests in New York in 2017 – 48% Black and 38% Hispanic (Cheney 2018). These figures stand in stark contrast to estimates suggesting that only 1% of legal marijuana dispensaries in 2018 were owned by African Americans (Douglas and Ordoñez 2018). According to a 2013 American Civil Liberties Union (ACLU) report, "On average, a Black person is 3.64 times more likely to be arrested for marijuana possession than a white person, even though Black and white people use marijuana at similar rates…" (ACLU 2013). A *Vice* report filed by Rachel Browne looked at statistics from 2015 to 2017 and found that, "Indigenous people in Regina were nearly nine times more likely to get arrested for cannabis possession than white people during that time period" (Browne 2018).

That's a snapshot of how economic justice can work in marijuana. This industry, perhaps more than any other, holds the potential to develop an equitable economy. As previously mentioned, indicators from business reviews show that total US sales could rise as high as US$37 billion by 2024 (McVey 2020), yet the statistics above show the discrepancies in terms of who is treated as a legal participant in the marijuana economy and who is positioned to benefit from the profits. In a 2020 Forbes article about equity in the cannabis industry, Jason Ortiz, President of the MCBA Minority Cannabis Business Association was quoted as follows:

> If we do not center the opportunities for those impacted by the racist war on drugs, our communities will continue to purchase from and support unlicensed sales, and marijuana will continue to be seen as a clear example that the United States is racist in its policy and racist in its economics.
>
> [The] cannabis industry is providing us a chance to turn the corner and begin the process of healing [but not] without a full accounting of the damage done, and public policy that directs resources to heal that damage. Until we get there, there will continue to be a divide between communities of color and the wealthy white-dominated corporations of "the industry
>
> *(quoted in Burns 2020)*

Tribal nations hold large land areas, about 4% of the United States, and can produce on that land a variety of food crops, buffalo and energy. As well, some of those tribes can produce cannabis. People of color are demanding access to the industry as the hemp renaissance begins. Over the past five years, Indigenous cannabis growers and industry have blossomed, from the Nuwu Paiute dispensary off the strip in Las Vegas, Nevada; to the Indigenous hemp collaboratives evolving in the northern plains (Hernandez 2019).

Restorative justice

An eye for an eye and a tooth for a tooth doesn't work out. The United States and Canada have punitive versus restorative justice systems, and there's really no justice for people of color. We treat people like throwaways. And there are too many of them. Wendy Sawyer and Peter Wagner of the Prison Policy Initiative reported the following statistics in 2020: "The American criminal justice system holds almost 2.3 million people in 1,833 state prisons, 110 federal prisons, 1,772 juvenile correctional facilities, 3,134 local jails, 218 immigration detention facilities, and 80 Indian Country jails as well as in military prisons, civil commitment centers, state psychiatric hospitals, and prisons in the U.S. territories" (Sawyer and Wagner 2020). The United States has more people in prison per capita than any other country. Making a business out of incarceration is not a sustainable strategy, while restorative justice and reintegrating offenders rebuilds communities. The communities most impacted are those of color. On a worldwide scale, movements toward restorative justice are taking shape, often founded on teachings of Indigenous nations.

Restorative economics

The business of cleaning up should be financed by the corporations who made the mess, that's for sure, and they are going to fight it. Take Enbridge's pipeline proposals as an example. They have aging lines and 800 spills under their belt. Rather than clean up legacy contamination (chemicals that remain in an environment long after they are introduced to an area through industry) they want to put in a new pipe in a new corridor and make a new mess. The cost of cleanup and removal of their old Line 3 (built in the 1960s before the Clean Air and Water Acts) is about US$2 billion, and of course that is not what the company wants to do. Removing all of Enbridge's pipelines in the United States would cost approximately US$23 billion (American Risk Management Resources Network 2019). Let me point out that the billions of dollars are not for new hardware, it is all labor. That's some jobs. Restorative economies are full of employment at their foundation. That's to say, that cleaning up the messes from the pipelines to the ocean garbage dump is a substantial amount of work. The goal, however is restoring balance, soil, water and life systems, that's restorative economics.

Price tags for this: Lester Brown (2009) estimates that US$110 billion per year will start that up. How's it financed? Make corporations pay their share, divest/invest. And, we could always turn the peacetime military loose on this.

Transition economics

One day I was sitting by the water in Sitka, Alaska, watching eagles dive for salmon and looking out at the immensity of the ocean. As I watched, an enormous cruise ship entered from the left of my vision. Disturbing my beautiful moment, I watched that cruise ship come into the harbor, and then, to my amazement, I watched this cruise ship turn on a dime, do a complete 180 and leave my line of sight. That's basically what we have to do, turn the cruise ship on a dime.

These past years, increasing numbers of scholars have come together to address sustainability issues. Paul Hawken et al. (authors of *Drawdown*, Penguin Books), Lester Brown (Earth Policy Institute) and the Finnish scientific community (Järvensivu et al. 2018), like Indigenous communities, are all discussing the transition we will make to the Green Path, the Eighth Fire or to sustainability. Economists like Lester Brown of the Earth Policy Institute have done remarkable analysis of the macro structures and costs associated with repairing and restoration. Brown, in *Plan B 4.0* explains a number of strategies from organic agriculture and reforestation to efficiency and demilitarization. Brown suggests the following:

> Let your political representatives know that a world spending more than $1 trillion a year for military purposes is simply out of sync with reality, not responding to the most serious threats to our future. Ask them if $187 billion a year, the Plan B budget, is an unreasonable expenditure to save civilization. Ask them if diverting one eighth of the global military budget to saving civilization is too costly. Remind them of how the United States mobilized during World War II.
>
> *(p. 267)*

Indigenous just transition: killing the Wiindigo

I once sat with a Nuchalnuth Chief discussing clear-cut logging in his territory; territory claimed by the Canadian government. He said to me, "sitting down and talking to the Canadian government is a lot like sitting down and talking to a Cannibal. You can make as much small talk as you want, but in the end, you know exactly what he wants." That's true, and the time of the Wiindigos is over. The economics of Wiindigos is that of cannibals. It doesn't work out in the end. In response to the UN's 2019 Global Sustainable Development Report authored by the Finnish scientists mentioned above, the website Living Resilience wrote:

> The team of researchers from various academic institutions throughout Finland who wrote the report gave a sobering assessment of the planet's future if the current economic

order continues unabated. Namely, that all rich Western countries have based their societies on an abundance of cheap energy, which the scientists say is no longer a reality.

> Economies have used up the capacity of planetary ecosystems to handle the waste generated by energy and material use.... [D]ominant economic theories as well as policy-related economic modeling rely on the presupposition of continued energetic and material growth. The theories and models anticipate only incremental changes in the existing economic order. Hence, they are inadequate for explaining the current turmoil.
>
> *(Living Resilience 2018)*

The report outlines some of the essential structural elements of the transformation that are necessary. What they propose is what the World Bank and predatory first world countries have done to third world countries for the past century: structural adjustment. Now's the time. They argue that the scale of transformation necessary requires a worldwide coordinated plan, referring to it as the Marshall Plan. As discussed, we've already changed that name to the Sitting Bull Plan. The backgrounder to the report notes that:

> In view of the challenges encountered today in implementing meaningful international agreements, the most likely option for initiating transitions to sustainability would be for a group of progressive states to take the lead. This would require economic thinking that enables large public investment programs on the one hand and strong regulation and environmental caps on the other. In the modern global economy, states are the only actors that have the legitimacy and capacity to fund and organize large-scale transitions.
>
> *(Järvensivu et al. 2018, 6)*

I would note that in addition to "progressive states," First Nations can take on a leadership role. We have the legitimacy and are already doing much of the necessary work. Internationally, by 2013, over a thousand communities had begun discussing what is known as the Transition Town movement, tackling issues of "degrowth" (see Schor and Tienhaara, this volume), self-sufficiency, and energy descent plans using efficiency and the concept of "negawatts."[2] As climate change increases the instability of local, national and international economies, more towns and regions are transitioning for security. The movement is here, and it's growing.

Time to put our minds together to see what kind of future we can make for our children. And maybe we just mobilize the military for this transition. That would be about making peace. That's this plan. The Sitting Bull Plan, or the Eighth Fire.

Land back and restorative justice

> The only compensation for land is land.
>
> *(Oren Lyons, Haudenosaunee Peacekeeper)*

Settler colonialism stands on shaky ground. From the issuance of soldier scrips to military recruits during the Revolutionary War, allocating Native lands to military veterans, to the appropriations of national parks, there is plenty of opportunity for a land back movement for Indigenous nations. Some of that is underway. More needs to happen. And, after that is settled, this same land back movement needs to happen with poor people and people of color.

Nationally, the fact is that the National Parks and Wildlife Refuges hold more land than Native people. As Keller and Turek point out in *American Indians & National Parks,* "tribes today contain 50 million acres; the Park Service controls approximately 80 million" (Keller and Turek 1998). That's ironic and tragic. In the long arc of history, we find that enlightenment is possible. I am reminded that the brutality of history only finds redress in reparations and justice.

The Black Hills, or the Paha Sapa, are one of the flagships of appropriation, from the theft of the Black Hills from the Lakota nation to the carving of four American presidents into the heart of the Paha Sapa, things have always been wrong there. On 3 July 2020, as US President Donald Trump rallied at the base of Mt. Rushmore, the Lakota once again came to the Black Hills to demand justice. "Mount Rushmore is on stolen Lakota land and its very existence is a symbol of white supremacy" says Nick Tilsen, NDN Collective President and CEO. "In opposing the ongoing desecration of our sacred land and asking for return of Lakota lands where Mount Rushmore is situated, we're not saying anything that our parents, grandparents and great grandparents haven't already said" (NDN Collective 2020).

Ruth Hopkins described the historical context of these lands in *Indian Country Today* in 2014:

> The 1868 Treaty of Fort Laramie ended Red Cloud's War when it set aside the Black Hills of western South Dakota and other lands and hunting rights in South Dakota, Wyoming, and Montana for the Oceti Sakowin (The Great Sioux Nation). Once gold was discovered however, prospectors began crossing into Black Hills territory, in violation of the treaty. The Oceti Sakowin rightfully defended their legally protected lands. The U.S. government responded by passing a law that took the Black Hills land away from the Oceti Sakowin in 1877.
>
> In *United States v. Sioux Nation of Indians* (1980), the U.S. Supreme Court ruled that the Black Hills had been illegally taken, and that the Oceti Sakowin were owed the sum of US$105 million for the Black Hills plus an additional $44 million for the lands outside of the Black Hills.
>
> *(Hopkins 2014)*

The Lakota did not take the settlement, and 40 years later, that money still remains in the bank. The Lakota want the land. As Loretta Afraid of Bear from the Oglala Lakota puts it, "We come from the Hills. They are a part of us" (Ibid.).

On 21 October 2019, Tuluwat, known as Indian Island, was returned to the Wiyot Tribe of northern California. The Wiyots are Algonquin speakers, a linguistic miracle, thousands of miles from the rest of our linguistic family. "This is the first known transfer of land from a city to a tribe of this kind," Eureka Councilwoman Natalie Arroyo said. "We are all responsible to do what we can to actively participate in healing. I will be so bold to say under current conditions Eureka owns the land, but it was never truly ours" (Greenson 2019). "The vote to return the Tuluwat island to the Wiyot Tribe was unanimous and the motion passed," Eureka Mayor Susan Seaman said (Slavey 2019).

To the west, the Pikuni or Blackfeet Nation is pushing for more access to Glacier Park. The Lame Bull Treaty of1855 recognized the Blackfeet lands as well as the lands to the north and south in Glacier occupied by Kootenai and Salish people, respectively. The Blackfeet were starved into transferring more land to the federal government for US$1.5 million in 1895 (Ashby 1985). When the land was declared a national park in 1910, Blackfeet hunting and fishing rights were revoked, but gathering rights remained. Since then, Blackfeet people have been arrested and challenged in court.

In the fall of 2019, the Blackfeet announced their own national park project. Led by Ed DesRosier, a 30-year veteran of park tourism, owner of Sun Tours, and Loren BirdRattler, project manager for the Blackfeet Nation's Agricultural Resource Management Plan, a Blackfeet Park is in the making. Approximately 55% of Montana's biodiversity is present on Blackfeet Nation's 1.5 million acres, and as tourism revenues do not benefit the Blackfeet nation, the Blackfeet are looking to create their own park, to begin reversing this process (Weber 2019).

"Land acknowledgements" are a start, Indigenous People's Day declarations begin a process, but the only compensation for land is land.

The Dish with One Spoon Treaty and the rights of Mother Earth

In 1701, the Anishinaabe and the Iroquois made an agreement, known as the Dish With One Spoon Treaty. It was recorded in a wampum belt. That agreement held that the Anishinaabe and the Haudenosaunee lived and hunted in the same territory and ate from the same dish. Sharing a spoon means that we are relatives and should have peace. That is a teaching for all. Indigenous knowledges and agreements have a permanence that precedes and antecedes industrial societies and the laws of modern nation-states. The precepts and canons of Indigenous law need to be applied. On a worldwide scale, they are now coming to the surface as the Rights of Nature.

For Native people, the Holy Land is here. Whether Bear Butte, Manitoulin Island, Mni Sose, or Gitchi Gummi, people who have lived on this land for 10,000 years know this as the Holy Land, not elsewhere. This recognition is growing into a body of law, not just in North America, but worldwide. Indigenous People will say that it's time to return to the Creator's law. These laws are considered the Rights of Nature, or the Rights of Mother Earth, a body of new jurisprudence which is growing internationally.

In 2017, *The Guardian* reported that Mount Taranaki in New Zealand was granted the same legal rights as a person, in turn, becoming the third major geographical feature in New Zealand to be granted a "legal personality" (Ainge Roy 2017). In 1978, the mountain was returned to the people of Taranaki by federal jurisdiction (Mount Egmont Vesting Act 1978). This legal designation followed a set of similar acknowledgements made by India, which granted the Himalayan glaciers, rivers, streams, lakes, air, meadows and forests the same legal rights as persons, joining India's sacred Ganges and Yamuna River as having standing under the law (O'Donnell and Talbot-Jones 2017). These legal recognitions are intended to protect those living beings. This new set of international rulings represents the most significant creation of new legal rights for Nature since 2010, when Bolivia passed the Law of Mother Earth as a part of their constitution (Ibid.), with a similar law being passed by the Ponca Nation of Oklahoma (2017) and the Ho Chunk nation of Wisconsin (de la Terre 2015).

The reality is that American, Canadian and other legal institutions are not capable of regulating the intergenerational violence of technology. What is done in war and in industry exceeds the experience of any generation before us in scope and damage, and our regulatory institutions have no framework for understanding the impact of these decisions.

Sadly, rather than being cautious, the legal institutions to which Native people are asked to subjugate themselves are inadequate to address regulatory prudence or, indeed, justice. Historically, North American legal systems have protected the rights of private property holders, not Nature herself. Private corporations continue to pillage the commons, transferring toxic poisons from their world into the world of rivers, mountains and sacred places.

The leadership on the transition to a more enlightened set of legal canons is being provided by Indigenous Peoples. That's because our legal systems pre-date and will post-date those of the church and the nation-states.

Oceans away, the question of the life of a river has taken on a new legal meaning. In 2012, the Whanganui River became a legal entity (APNZ 2012), and in 2017, it was given the same status as a person under New Zealand law (Warne 2019). In an agreement between the Maori and the Crown, the river has been given legal status under the name Te Awa Tupua, and two guardians – one from the Crown and one from the Maori – have assumed the responsibility to protect the river. This responsibility is a reaffirmation of Indigenous practice and has the ability to transform the laws of nation-states. One can easily argue that many "stakeholders" in an American or Canadian regulatory process are only interested in their rights, and rarely interested in their "responsibilities." In contrast, recently signed treaties between Indigenous nations, like the Buffalo Treaty and the Treaty of the Salish Sea, pledge to make humans responsible in relationship to these great spiritual beings, the Buffalo Nation and the Salish Sea.

Here on Turtle Island, another river is recognized. In May of 2019, the Yurok Tribal Council voted unanimously in favor of a resolution establishing the Rights of the Klamath River (Schertow 2019), which spans through Modoc, Hoopa, Karuk territory (in regions of Oregon and California) to the Pacific Ocean. John Ahni Schertow reported the following:

> According to the Yurok Tribe, the resolution "establishes the Rights of the Klamath River to exist, flourish, and naturally evolve; to have a clean and healthy environment free from pollutants; to have a stable climate free from human-caused climate change impacts; and to be free from contamination by genetically engineered organisms."
>
> *(Ibid.)*

Now is the time to make legal institutions that reflect the world we live in, not the anthropocentric world we fantasize is a reality. It really is not prudent to regulate watersheds until there is no water in a river. Now is the time to make laws which reaffirm the spirit of place, of beings, and reaffirm the relationship between humans and the Holy Land. *Omaa Akiing.*

It is clearly time to think intergenerationally and to think about justice and peace. This is between ourselves, our relatives, and our Mother Earth. This is our gift to our descendants. Our prophecies and instructions give some clear guidance on the restoration of the covenant between the humans and the natural world. Now is the time. Light the Fire.

Notes

1 *Dine* means "the people" in the Navajo language.
2 A negawatt is a term coined by Amory Lovins – it represents a watt of energy that has not been used as a result of energy conservation or the use of energy-efficient products.

References

ACLU. 2013. The War on Marijuana in Black and White. American Civil Liberties Union. June. Available at: https://www.aclu.org/report/report-war-marijuana-black-and-white

Agriculture and Agri-Food Canada. 2018. The Three Sisters: Optimizing the Value and Food Potential of an Ancestral Indigenous Crop System. Scientific Achievements in Agriculture. *Government of Canada*. 14 November. Available at: https://agriculture.canada.ca/en/news-agriculture-and-agri-food-canada/scientific-achievements-agriculture/three-sisters-optimizing-value-and-food-potential-ancestral-indigenous-crop-system

Ainge Roy, E. 2017. New Zealand Gives Mount Taranaki Same Legal Rights as a Person. *The Guardian*. 22 December. Available at: https://www.theguardian.com/world/2017/dec/22/new-zealand-gives-mount-taranaki-same-legal-rights-as-a-person

Amberoot. n.d. How Good Is Wearing Cotton for You and for the Environment? *Amberoot.com*. Available at: https://amberoot.com/blogs/blog/how-good-is-wearing-cotton-for-you-and-for-the-environment

American Risk Management Resources Network. 2019. An Analysis of The Enbridge Financial Assurances Offered to the State of Michigan on Matters Related To The Operation of The Enbridge Line 5 Pipeline At the Straits of Mackinac, Prepared For The State of Michigan The Michigan Department of Attorney General The Michigan Department of Environment, Great Lakes and Energy The Michigan Department of Natural Resources. Available at: https://www.michigan.gov/documents/ag/Master_Michigan_Enbridge_10_29_final__670367_7.pdf

APNZ. 2012. Agreement Entitles Whanganui River to Legal Identity. *NZ Herald*. 30 August. Available at: https://www.nzherald.co.nz/nz/news/article.cfm?c_id=1&objectid=10830586

Ashby, C. 1985. *Blackfeet Agreement o 1895 and Glacier National Park: A Case History*. PhD thesis. University of Montana. Available at: https://scholarworks.umt.edu/cgi/viewcontent.cgi?referer=&httpsredir=1&article=2703&context=etd

Associated Press. 2017. Navajo Nations First Solar Project Now Producing Enough Electricity for about 13,000 Homes. *AZcentral*. 29 August. Available at: https://www.azcentral.com/story/money/business/energy/2017/08/29/navajo-nations-first-solar-project-now-producing-electricity-13-000-homes/613443001/

Bayern Brewing. 2020. *Bayern Brewery Sustainability*. Bayern Brewing Inc. Available at: https://www.bayernbrewery.com/sustainability

Bell, T. 2015. Pipelines Safety and Security: Is It No More Than A Pipe Dream? *The Bent of Tau Beta Pi*. Winter. Available at: https://www.tbp.org/pubs/Features/W15Bell.pdf

Berg, N. 2020. Out of Hemp's Many Promising Uses, One of the Best Could be in Construction. *GreenBiz*. 22 October. Available at: https://www.greenbiz.com/article/out-hemps-many-promising-uses-one-best-could-be-construction

Blackfeet Nation. n.d. Commercial Wind Development. Blackfeet Reservation, Montana. Available at: https://www.bia.gov/sites/bia.gov/files/assets/as-ia/ieed/ieed/pdf/idc010175.pdf

Blue Lake Rancheria. n.d. A Low Carbon. *Community Scale Microgrid [Info Sheet]*. Available at: https://bluelakerancheria-nsn.gov/wp-content/uploads/2017/08/BLR-Microgrid-2-Page-Summary-Flyer.pdf

Brown, L. 2009. *Plan B 4.0: Mobilizing to Save Civilization*. Earth Policy Institute. New York: W.W. Norton & Company. Available at: http://www.earth-policy.org/images/uploads/book_files/pb4book.pdf

Browne, R. 2018. Black and Indigenous People are Overrepresented in Canada's Weed Arrests. *Vice*. 18 April. Available at: https://www.vice.com/en/article/d35eyq/black-and-indigenous-people-are-overrepresented-in-canadas-weed-arrests

Burns, J. 2020. Make No Mistake: Cannabis Equity Can't Wait. *Forbes*. 8 January. Available at: https://www.forbes.com/sites/janetwburns/2020/01/08/in-2020-cannabis-equity-cant-wait/

Callaghan, C. 2017. What Is a Prairie? Canadian Wildlife Federation Blog. 22 June. Available at: https://blog.cwf-fcf.org/index.php/en/what-is-a-prairie/

Capriccioso, R. 2009. Groups Press for Tribe-Friendly Renewable Energy Policies. *Indian Country Today*. 2 January. Available at: https://indiancountrytoday.com/archive/groups-press-for-tribe-friendly-renewable-energy-policies

Carter, D. et al. 2019. Demonstrating a Secure Reliable Low-Carbon Community Microgrid at Blue Lake Rancheria. *California Energy Commission*. 31 January. Available at: https://www.energy.ca.gov/publications/2019/demonstrating-secure-reliable-low-carbon-community-microgrid-blue-lake-rancheria

CEIC. 2021. United States Private Consumption: % of GDP. *Quarterly Report*. June. Available at: https://www.ceicdata.com/en/indicator/united-states/private-consumption--of-nominal-gdp#:~:text=United%20States%20Private%20Consumption%20accounted,an%20average%20share%20of%2063.2%20%25 [Accessed September 20, 2021]

Cheney, B. 2018. Racial Disparities Persist in New York City Marijuana Arrests. *Politico*. 13 February. Available at: https://www.politico.com/states/new-york/city-hall/story/2018/02/13/racial-disparities-continue-in-new-york-city-marijuana-arrests-248896

Cultural Survival. n.d. Sacred Homelands Returned to Wiyot Tribe. *Cultural Survival*. Available at: https://www.culturalsurvival.org/news/sacred-homelands-returned-wiyot-tribe [Accessed September 16, 2020]

de la Terre, J. 2015. Ho-Chunk Nation Adds 'Rights of Nature' to Their Constitution. *Global Alliance for the Rights of Nature*. 20 September. Available at: https://therightsofnature.org/ho-chunk-nation-rights-of-nature-constitution/?cli_action=1572378434.619

Douglas, W. and Ordoñez, F. 2018 Majority Minority: The Challenges for People of Color in the Legal Pot Business. Impact 2020. *McClatchy Washington Bureau*. 20 April. Available at: https://www.mcclatchydc.com/podcasts/majority-minority/article209437519.html

Drimal, S. 2019. Buffalo Treaty Demonstrates Collaboration for Bison Conservation. *Greater Yellowstone Coalition*. 6 November. Available at: https://greateryellowstone.org/blog/2019/buffalotreaty

Dun & Bradstreet. 2020. *Business Impact of the Coronavirus: Business and Supply Chain Analysis Due to the Coronavirus Outbreak*. Available at: https://www.dnb.com/content/dam/english/economic-and-industry-insight/DNB_Business_Impact_of_the_Coronavirus_US.pdf

Eavis, P. and Penn, I. 2019. California Says PG&E Power Lines Caused Camp Fire That Killed 85. *The New York Times*. 15 May. Available at: https://www.nytimes.com/2019/05/15/business/pge-fire.html

Edwards, M. 2016. Understanding Flint's Water Infrastructure Crisis: Water Infrastructure Inequality in America. *Flint Water Study Updates*. 9 December. Available at: http://flintwaterstudy.org/2016/12/understanding-flints-water-infrastructure-crisis-water-infrastructure-inequality-in-america/.

Egan, M. 2020. Exxon Was the World's Largest Company in 2013. Now It's Being Kicked out of the Dow. *CNN*. 25 August. Available at: https://www.cnn.com/2020/08/25/investing/exxon-stock-dow-oil/index.html?fbclid=IwAR0gs-p_qRht-WOYphzrcCdBUwnLyOyLKERGZhvkmUZBjXBkDeI6dbAiOyY.

Fuller, T. and Abbott, M. 2020. Reducing Fire, and Cutting Carbon Emissions, the Aboriginal Way. *New York Times*. 18 January. Available at: https://www.nytimes.com/2020/01/16/world/australia/aboriginal-fire-management.html

Funes, Y. 2019. North Dakota's First Solar Farm Opens on Standing Rock Tribal Land. *Gizmodo*. 26 July. Available at: https://gizmodo.com/north-dakotas-first-solar-farm-opens-on-standing-rock-t-1836732750

Gewin, V. 2020. The World Food Prize Winner Says Soil Should Have Rights. *Civil Eats*. 15 July. Available at: https://civileats.com/2020/07/15/the-world-food-prize-winner-says-soil-should-have-rights/

Greenson, T. 2019. Duluwat Island is Returned to the Wiyot Tribe in Historic Ceremony. *North Coast Journal*. 21 October. Available at: https://www.northcoastjournal.com/NewsBlog/archives/2019/10/21/duluwat-island-is-returned-to-the-wiyot-tribe-in-historic-ceremony

HempToday. 2019. U.S. Jumps to No. 3 Among Top Hemp Growing Nations. *HempToday*. 18 February. Available at: https://hemptoday.net/us-third-biggest-hemp-grower/

Hernandez, D. 2019. 'The Tribe Has Taken over': the Native Americans Running Las Vegas's Only Cannabis Lounge. *The Guardian*. 11 November. Available at: https://www.theguardian.com/us-news/2019/nov/10/nevada-cannabis-lounge-paiute-las-vegas.

Hoover, E. and White, R. 2018. Seed Rematriation. *Sierra Seeds*. 19 March. Available at: https://sierraseeds.org/seed-rematriation/

Hopkins, R. 2014. Reclaiming the Sacred Black Hills. *Indian Country Today*. 28 June. Available at: https://indiancountrytoday.com/archive/reclaiming-the-sacred-black-hills

Järvensivu, P. et al. 2018. Global Sustainable Development Report 2019. Background Document on Economic Transformation to Chapter: Transformation: The Economy. Group of Independent Scientists. *BIOS Research Unit*. 14 August. Available at: https://bios.fi/bios-governance_of_economic_transition.pdf

Johnson, R. 2019. *Defining Hemp: A Fact Sheet*. Congressional Research Service. 22 March. Available at: https://fas.org/sgp/crs/misc/R44742.pdf.

Katz, C. 2019. The World's Recycling Is in Chaos. Here's What Has to Happen. *Wired*. 13 March. Available at: https://www.wired.com/story/the-worlds-recycling-is-in-chaos-heres-what-has-to-happen/

Keller, R.H. and Turek, M.F. 1998. *American Indians and National Parks*. Tucson, AZ: University of Arizona Press.

LaDuke, W. 2018. Three Affiliated Tribes at a Crossroads: Which Energy Path? *Indian Country Today*. 12 September. Available at: https://indiancountrytoday.com/archive/three-affiliated-tribes-at-a-crossroads-which-energy-path

LaDuke, W. 2020. Native Activists Are Forging a Just Transition to Renewable Energy. *Truthout.org*. 1 March. Available at: https://truthout.org/articles/native-activists-are-forging-a-just-transition-to-renewable-energy/

LaDuke, W. and Cowen, D. 2020. Beyond Wiindigo Infrastructure. *South Atlantic Quarterly*. 119(2): 243–268. Available at: https://doi.org/10.1215/00382876-8177747

Land, B.H. 2017. Textile Industry Making a Comeback in the U.S. Southeast. Area Development. *Halcyon Business Publications, Inc*. 18 April. Available at: https://www.areadevelopment.com/advanced-manufacturing/Q2-2017/textile-industry-making-comeback-in-US-southeast.shtml

Leap Manifesto, The. 2015. Available at: https://leapmanifesto.org/en/the-leap-manifesto/#manifesto-content

Lehne, J. and Preston, F. 2018. Making Concrete Change: Innovation in Low-Carbon Cement and Concrete. *Chatham House Report*. 13 June. Available at: https://reader.chathamhouse.org/making-concrete-change-innovation-low-carbon-cement-and-concrete

Living Resilience. 2018. Capitalism Must Die For Environment to Live. *Living Resilience*. 28 August. Available at: https://livingresilience.net/capitalism-must-die-for-environment-to-live/

Longley, K. 2019. ASCE Gives Thanks in 2019. *Report Card For America's Infrastructure*. 21 November. Available at: https://www.infrastructurereportcard.org/asce-gives-thanks-in-2019/

Lotus, J. 2019. Hemp Textiles Made in U.S. Will Take Time, Experts Say. *UPI*. 5 August. Available at: https://www.upi.com/Top_News/US/2019/08/05/Hemp-textiles-made-in-US-will-take-time-experts-say/9861564531347/

Lussenhop, J. 2020. Coronavirus at Smithfield Pork Plant: The Untold Story of America's Biggest Outbreak. *BBC*. 17 April. Available at: https://www.bbc.com/news/world-us-canada-52311877

Marin Carbon Project. Available at: https://www.marincarbonproject.org/home

McVey, E. 2020. Exclusive: US Retail Marijuana Sales on Pace to rise 40% in 2020, Near $37 Billion by 2024. *MJBizDaily*. 30 June. Available at: https://mjbizdaily.com/exclusive-us-retail-marijuana-sales-on-pace-to-rise-40-in-2020-near-37-billion-by-2023/

Moody, K. 2020. How "Just-in-Time" Capitalism Spread COVID-19. *Spectre Journal*. 8 April. Available at: https://spectrejournal.com/how-just-in-time-capitalism-spread-covid-19/

Mooney, P.R. 1996. The Parts Of Life: Agricultural Biodiversity, Indigenous Knowledge, and the Role of the Third System. *Journal of the Dag Hammarskjöld Foundation*. Available at: http://www.daghammarskjold.se/wp-content/uploads/1996/08/DD1996_1-2.pdf

Mooney, P.R. 2015. Presentation in the Panel on 'Building a Network of Local Climate, Smart Crops and Citizen Scientists', *Indigenous Terra Madre Conference*, Meghalaya, India. 4 November 2015.

Morlet, A. et al. 2017. *A New Textiles Economy: Redesigning Fashion's Future*. Ellen MacArthur Foundation. Available at: https://www.ellenmacarthurfoundation.org/assets/downloads/publications/A-New-Textiles-Economy_Full-Report_Updated_1-12-17.pdf

Mount Egmont Vesting Act. 1978. New Zealand. Available at: https://www.legislation.govt.nz/act/public/1978/0038/latest/whole.html#DLM21219

Nargi, L. 2017. New Study Shows Organic Farming Traps Carbon in Soil to Combat Climate Change. *Civil Eats*. 18 September. Available at: https://civileats.com/2017/09/11/new-study-shows-organic-farming-traps-carbon-in-soil-to-combat-climate-change/

NCTO. 2017. 2017 State of the U.S. Textile Industry. National Council of Textile Organizations. *Press Release*. 24 March. Available at: http://www.ncto.org/2017-state-of-the-u-s-textile-industry/

NDN Collective. 2020. NDN Collective Calls for Closure of Mount Rushmore and for the Black Hills to be Returned to the Lakota. *NDN Collective [Press Release]*. 3 July. Available at: https://ndncollective.org/ndn-collective-calls-for-closure-of-mount-rushmore-and-for-the-black-hills-to-be-returned-to-the-lakota/

Neumann, E. 2020. California Reservation's Solar Microgrid Provides Power During Utility Shutoffs. *NPR*. 11 January. Available at: https://www.npr.org/2020/01/11/795248921/california-reservations-solar-microgrid-provides-power-during-utility-shutoffs

Newell, A. 2016. Quenching Cotton's Thirst: Reducing the Use of Water in the Cotton Lifecycle. *Triple Pundit*. 23 February. Available at: https://www.triplepundit.com/story/2016/quenching-cottons-thirst-reducing-use-water-cotton-lifecycle/57196

Nicholas, G. 2018. When Scientists 'Discover' What Indigenous People Have Known For Centuries. *Smithsonian Magazine*. 21 February. Available at: https://www.smithsonianmag.com/science-nature/why-science-takes-so-long-catch-up-traditional-knowledge-180968216/

Noss, R.F. 1994. Building a Wilderness Recovery Network. *The George Wright Forum*. 11(4): 17–40. Available at: http://www.jstor.org/stable/43598878 [Accessed September 1, 2020].

Nunn, G. 2020. Australia Fires: Aboriginal Planners Say the Bush 'Needs to Burn'. *BBC News*. 12 January. Available at: https://www.bbc.com/news/world-australia-51043828.

O'Donnell, E. and Talbot-Jones, J. 2017. Will Giving the Himalayas the Same Rights as People Protect their Future? *Pursuit*. The University of Melbourne. 20 April. Available at: https://pursuit.unimelb.edu.au/articles/will-giving-the-himalayas-the-same-rights-as-people-protect-their-future.

Panne, V.V. 2019. Fashion Is Quietly a Major Fossil Fuel Industry-Could a Sustainable Revolution Be around the Corner? *Salon*. 6 September. Available at: https://www.salon.com/2019/09/06/fashion-is-quietly-a-major-fossil-fuel-industry-could-a-sustainable-revolution-be-around-the-corner/

Picchi, A. 2020. Seed Companies Can't Keep up as More Americans Turn to Growing their Own Food. *CBS News*. 14 April. Available at: https://www.cbsnews.com/news/coronavirus-seeds-americans-grow-food/

Popper, D.E. and Popper, F.J. 1999. The Buffalo Commons: Metaphor as Method. *Geographical Review*. 89(4): 491–510. Available at: https://www.jstor.org/stable/216099

Rice, D. 2018. World's Largest Collection of Ocean Garbage Is Twice the Size of Texas. *USA Today*. 28 December. Available at: https://www.usatoday.com/story/tech/science/2018/03/22/great-pacific-garbage-patch-grows/446405002/

Rodgers, L. 2018. Climate Change: The Massive CO2 Emitter You May Not Know About. *BBC News*. 17 December. Available at: https://www.bbc.com/news/science-environment-46455844

Roy, A. 2020. The Pandemic Is a Portal. *Financial Times*. 3 April. Available at: https://www.ft.com/content/10d8f5e8-74eb-11ea-95fe-fcd274e920ca

Sawyer, W. and Wagner, P. 2020. Mass Incarceration: The Whole Pie 2020. *Prison Policy Initiative*. 24 March. Available at: https://www.prisonpolicy.org/reports/pie2020.html

Schertow, J.A. 2019. The Yurok Nation Just Established the Rights of the Klamath River. *Intercontinental Cry*. 20 May. Available at: https://intercontinentalcry.org/the-yurok-nation-just-established-the-rights-of-the-klamath-river/

Slavey, C. 2019. Tuluwat Returned to the Wiyot. *The Lumberjack*. 23 October. Vol 115. No. 8. Available at: https://issuu.com/hsulumberjack/docs/issue8

Solutionary Rail. n.d. Available at: https://www.solutionaryrail.org/ [Accessed September 10, 2020]

The Story of Stuff. 2007. Directed by A. Leonard. [Film] Available at: https://www.storyofstuff.org/movies/story-of-stuff/

US Department of Energy. 2015. Quadrennial Technology Review: An Assessment of Energy Technologies and Research Opportunities. September. Available at: https://www.energy.gov/sites/prod/files/2015/09/f26/Quadrennial-Technology-Review-2015_0.pdf

US Energy Information Administration. 2018. Electricity Prices Are Highest in Hawaii But Expenditures Are Highest in South Carolina. 13 February. Available at: https://www.eia.gov/todayinenergy/detail.php?id=34932

Warne, K. 2019. This River in New Zealand Is a Legal Person. How Will It Use Its Voice? *National Geographic*. 24 April. Available at: https://www.nationalgeographic.com/culture/2019/04/maori-river-in-new-zealand-is-a-legal-person/

Weber, S. 2019. The Blackfeet Nation Is Opening its Own National Park. *High Country News*. 23 April. Available at: https://www.hcn.org/articles/tribal-affairs-the-blackfeet-nation-is-trying-to-open-its-own-national-park

Winona's Hemp. n.d. Our Hemp. Winona's Hemp & Heritage Farm. Winonashemp.com. Available at: https://www.winonashemp.com/our-hemp

11

A FEMINIST AGENDA FOR A GREEN NEW DEAL

Challenges and opportunities

Frances Roberts-Gregory

Introduction

> To truly address the root causes, as well as the scope and scale of the climate crisis, the Green New Deal must be cross-cutting in its approach, steadfast in feminist principles, and strive to combat historical oppressions.
>
> *(Feminist Agenda for a Green New Deal Principles and Values)*

In the wake of economic, environmental, and political instability brought about by a rise in neoliberal policy and the consolidation of wealth amongst the global polluter elite, calls for greener economies have grown in strength and fervor (Galvin and Healy 2020; Stephens 2020). So much so, one of the newest iterations of the US Green New Deal (GND) was proposed by US congresswoman Alexandria Ocasio-Cortez and Senator Ed Markey in 2019 as a nonbinding resolution to champion green investment, community development and climate resilience (Daniel and Dolan 2020). Their green policy platform aimed to reverse decades of lackluster and nonexistent green investment through a focus on renewable energy and resource efficiency (Clemmons 2020; Galvin and Healy 2020). Nevertheless, the 2019 US GND was immediately attacked by conservatives and liberals alike – a reflection of the political stasis, unwillingness to radically decarbonize, and polarization within the US Congress under the white supremacist and misogynistic Trump administration (Hathaway 2019; Rao and Teixeira 2020).

Despite these ongoing criticisms, the US GND uniquely employs an intersectional approach to green infrastructure, public works projects and technology investment (Galvin and Healy 2020; Hathaway 2019). Thanks to Black feminist policy architect Rhiana Gunn-Wright, a crew of policy wonks housed at the nonprofit New Consensus, and support from youth associated with the US Sunrise Movement, the US GND also offers a broad vision for transformative social change while balancing a growth mindset and Keynesian economic policies (Clemmons 2020; Galvin and Healy 2020; Hathaway 2019; Stephens 2020). Feminist climate justice activists similarly applaud it for encouraging "input and collective determination from all stakeholders and emphasizing that the eventual policy content must be collaboratively generated for each sector" (Daniel and Dolan 2020, 516). Even so, the US GND as a proposed stimulus package of legislation arguably falls short of more radical

 DOI: 10.4324/9781003110880-14

analysis when compared to explicitly decolonial visions and ecofeminist recovery solutions devised by frontline, fenceline and adversely impacted grassroots groups.

In fact, those who experience misogyny, communities of color, queer communities, formerly colonized people(s), differently abled persons, the global feminized poor, and Indigenous People(s) have yet to fully realize (our) human rights or aspirations for self-determination and sovereignty in the current geopolitical order; nor have we experienced equitable and meaningful inclusion in environmental governance and climate policy (Cohen and MacGregor 2020; Stephens 2020). Under these constraints, it is no surprise that the US GND also lacks a thorough and sufficient focus on gender, women's rights, the rights of nature, and what feminist scholars and activists term economies of care and institutions of social reproduction (Cohen and MacGregor 2020). Without radical feminist intervention, the US GND likewise models economic stimulus and green recovery after FDR's problematic New Deal policies – policies that arguably hold a mixed record in relation to elevating the economic prosperity, well-being, and human rights of the oppressed and marginalized communities.

For example, many scholars highlight how New Deal policies intentionally excluded women and people of color; social security and national labor relations coverage excluded domestic workers and farmworkers, disproportionately harming Black and Mexican American women and families (Fdr4freedoms 2014; Johnson 2020; Walker 2019). Section 213 of the Economy Act similarly penalized working women, effectively forcing married women to resign from their government positions if their spouses were also employed by the federal government (Fdr4freedoms 2014). To appease racist southern politicians and corrupt segregationists, New Deal programs were also managed at the local level, and local managers reinstituted discriminatory hiring practices. Nevertheless, it is equally important to acknowledge the reality of messy "herstories" and the leadership of feminist, anti-racist policymakers and stateswomen during the New Deal era. First Lady Eleanor Roosevelt, Women's Division Chair of the Democratic National Convention and political organizer Molly Dewson, and civil rights leader and womanist educator Dr. Mary McLeod Bethune are just a few of the feminist, anti-racist leaders who unapologetically strove to include BIPOC[1] communities, women, and children in relief efforts (Fdr4freedoms 2014).

The early feminist and intersectional analysis of New Deal policy architect Frances Perkins,[2] a brilliant labor advocate, social worker, and the first female US Secretary of Labor and presidential cabinet member, are also noteworthy (Pusey 2017; Rao and Teixeira 2020). Perkins is responsible for many transformative social welfare programs including social security, unemployment insurance, minimum wage, maximum workday laws, child labor restrictions, support for immigrant communities, and improvements to public works (Fdr4freedoms 2014). Perkins also shaped practical policies to improve social infrastructure including schools and hospitals and strengthened labor and workplace safety regulations. Although Perkins' advocacy for BIPOC and African American (male) inclusion in New Deal programs such as the Civilian Conservation Corps (CCC) was modest and tokenistic by today's standards, she was undeniably a radical visionary who (unsuccessfully) lobbied for universal healthcare. She was even considered a political ally by the National Urban League and the unofficial Federal Council on Negro Affairs (Guzda 1980; Walker 2019).[3] Once we recover and relearn "sheroes" like Perkins and her contemporaries, it is apparent that feminist and anti-racist thought leadership catalyzed large-scale social transformation from the original New Deal to the present-day GND.

In the spirit of "passing the torch" to the next feminist generation, my activist colleagues and I collectively champion the Feminist Agenda for a Green New Deal (FEM GND). In

2019, transnational feminist climate activists collectively developed ten principles that center ecological concerns and gendered perspectives for a US Green New Deal. Aptly termed the FEM GND, this evolving policy platform and ecofeminist manifesto provides innovative and cross-cutting perspectives on how policymakers, activist organizations, and civil society should plan for greener, regenerative and care-fueled futures for all. Our coalition likewise raises political awareness of the intersections and amplifications of interlocking systems of oppression and explicitly centers feminist analysis based on decades of grassroots organizing around climate, reproductive, gender, and environmental justice. While we recognize that we all share the burden of rising greenhouse gases, we know we are not equally responsible for climate disaster or equally impacted by environmental violence. As feminists, we moreover say no to false solutions such as industrial agriculture and mining, greening the military, carbon offset programs, geoengineering, and carbon trading. We similarly reject energy policies that disenfranchise women and critically interrogate nuclear, natural gas extraction, mega dams, biofuels, bioenergy, and other technofixes (FEM GND 2021).

We also embrace feminist economics that revalue housework, child rearing, disability care, and elder work, in addition to other invisible and unpaid forms of labor (MacGregor 2017; Stephens 2020; Wichterich 2015). We further resist the political status quo characterized by fossil fuel subsidies, lax enforcement of environmental laws and regulations, industrial tax exemptions, and the normalization of environmental externalities. We demand participatory democracies, better representation of marginalized voices in climate policymaking, and respect for free speech so that feminists and climate justice activists are not persecuted or censured. Most importantly, we recognize that our societies depend upon care work, and such work should be quantified as low-carbon work. These are all crucial points to consider as we modernize electricity, increase weatherization programs and develop community-controlled renewable portfolio standards. Through the FEM GND and feminist, anti-racist, anti-oppressive leadership, there is hope to combat the crisis of climate inaction and create the caring world we know is possible (Baker 2021; Bauhardt 2014; Cohen and MacGregor 2020; J.A. Nelson and Morgan 2020; Stephens 2020).

The following chapter thus outlines and examines FEM GND principles for tensions and congruencies, and analyzes opportunities and challenges for coalition building and communicating across epistemic divides. As a co-founding and steering committee member of the FEM GND, I argue that economic, environmental and social policies that fail to center climate and COVID recovery solutions devised by feminists and BIPOC communities will continue to exacerbate global inequality and the abuse of both human rights and the rights of nature. Policy approaches that lack considerations of gender and reproductive justice will likewise consolidate white supremacist, fascist, neocolonial and patriarchal power across geopolitical borders. To manifest the liberatory vision(s) of the FEM GND, I believe that feminist policy advocates and educators must utilize communication strategies that appeal to more diverse and less insular audiences (including politically conservative audiences and technocratic policymakers). Feminist GND policy advocates must communicate and demonstrate the value of economies of care and feminist economics through targeted communication strategies that appeal to increasingly siloed audiences and heterogenous publics (Hathaway 2019; J.A. Nelson and Morgan 2020).

I furthermore advocate for a rethinking of multilateral processes and argue that our feminist collective must be intentionally and unapologetically guided by collective care and feminist fellowship. Although we are routinely faced with uncertainty, crisis, and concomitant grief, care practices aligned with healing justice[4] are crucial for the sustainability of our political activism (HiveFund 2020). This chapter finally historicizes and assesses the FEM

GND for what it uniquely offers to green economies and efforts to inject feminist analysis into environmental policies and politics. By aligning our movement's needs with ecologies of support and intersectional policy analysis, the FEM GND will undoubtedly contribute to meaningful social change, political conscientization, and radical institutional transformation.

FEM GND antecedents

As a roadmap for policy interventions for coming decades, the US GND has the potential to shape massive social transformation through economic and public health safety nets. Yet, it is not the first (nor last) GND policy platform. Previous GND policy platforms developed by Britain and other European Green Parties (2008 and 2019), the German Green Party (2008), South Korea (2009), labor activists and environmentalists associated with UNEP (2008) and the Rio+20 Earth Summit (2012), the US Green Party under Jill Stein and Howie Hawkins (2010 and 2012), and even the Obama administration (2009), similarly theorize the remaking of physical infrastructure with environment and equity in mind (Littig 2017; Wichterich 2015). Unfortunately, many GND policies were not widely adopted after the 2008 financial crisis due to their over-emphasis on energy efficiency, short-term clean energy projects, and market disincentives (Barbier and UNEP 2020; Bloomfield and Steward 2020).

Former GND policy platforms were likewise influenced by the UN Sustainable Development Goals (SDGs) and European ecological modernization that developed throughout the 1980s, 1990s, and 2000s. They were also shaped by ongoing critiques of the inefficacy of the UN climate talks that focus on GDP as an indicator of progress, lack a structural analysis of colonialism, and sanction extractivism (Bloomfield and Steward 2020; MacGregor 2017; Mellor 2017; Salleh 2020). Over time, many GND policy architects extended their analysis to critique renewable energy initiatives, transnational care networks, and efforts toward degrowth that cement socioeconomic inequality at the expense of the Global South (Cohen and MacGregor 2020; Dengler and Seebacher 2019; see also chapters in this volume by McCollum and by Kolinjivadi and Kothari). Transnational care networks (i.e., the outsourcing of paid and unpaid care work) structure the "transnational movement of labor" through, for example, migrant worker programs and live-in caregiver and nanny programs in Canada and the United States (Cohen and MacGregor 2020, 5). Such energy initiatives, transnational care chains, and efforts toward degrowth cement global inequality when they (1) fail to redistribute gendered care responsibilities, resources and wealth; (2) fail to shift production and consumption models; (3) reproduce neocolonial and patriarchal power relations; and (4) cause job losses for low-wage workers based in Global South export industries (Dengler and Seebacher 2019). Nevertheless, many GND policies lack an explicitly feminist analysis and often fail to cite critical scholarship produced by feminist academics, policymakers and grassroots activists that problematize these issues.

Finally, it is noteworthy that international support for multilateral climate agreements and domestic grassroots engagement with (and opposition to) environmental and climate politics heightened in the post 1960s–1970s era. Concomitant with President Lyndon B. Johnson's acknowledgement of the threat posed by greenhouse gas emissions, the rise of the women's movement, and the passing of civil rights legislation (including the Voting Rights Act of 1965), white US conservatives resisted social movement gains through anti-feminist, anti-environmental, and racist electoral activism. In fact, white evangelicals began to vote in earnest along Republican party lines and reinvigorate voter suppression and gerrymandering in majority-BIPOC voting districts (i.e., today's environmental, energy and climate justice communities; Cohen 2020; Glickman 2020; Hansley and Butler 2015; Lavelle 2015). Cohen (2020) likewise highlights missed opportunities for an explicitly feminist bloc to collectively engage electoral politics and combat the rise of reactionary right-wing conservatism from the 1970s to the 2000s. Nevertheless, contemporary coalitions of environmentalists, feminists and Black civil rights leaders have responded to conservative backlash through fervent anti-racist, anti-sexist, and pro-environmental electoral activism, including political education and mobilization work to manifest FEM GND values and principles.

Origins and principles of FEM GND

In early 2019, a collective of environmental justice advocates, climate activists and women's rights organizations assembled together to center visions, dreams, and solutions for an intersectional and feminist GND (Daniel and Dolan 2020). We tasked ourselves with theorizing the adoption and implementation of global care economies and multilateral climate action. Our analysis was built upon decades of feminist organizing around universal health care, workers' rights, reproductive, and gender justice, and increased minimum wage. After collectively generating ten values and principles to augment federal GND policies, we formally launched our collective in the fall of 2019 during the UN Climate Summit and Climate Week in New York (WEDO 2019). Calling ourselves the FEM GND, our transnational feminist collective articulated an alternative vision for addressing the climate crisis, care crisis and US climate inaction. Our principles, drafted through virtual consultations with dozens of feminists, exemplify the power of non-hierarchical feminist brainstorming and organizing.

The FEM GND ultimately rests upon the collective action and hard-won global solidarities of women's rights and climate activists within civil society, academia, community organizations, and NGOs (WEDO 2019). The founding members of the FEM GND thus include organizations, coalitions, and individuals who understand the connection between healthy communities and a healthy planet (see Tables 11.1 and 11.2). As proponents of the FEM GND,

Table 11.1 Kickstart Organizations, Coalitions, and Academics/Freelance Radicals (KOCAs)

Organizations	*Coalitions*	*Academics/Freelance Radicals*
Ginew Collective	Climate Justice Alliance (CJA)	Frances Roberts-Gregory
Gulf Coast Center for Law & Policy	Grassroots Global Justice Alliance (GGJA)	Tamara Toles O'Laughlin
International Center for Research on Women	Rede Social de Justiça e Direitos Humanos (Network for Social Justice and Human Rights), Brazil	
National Association for the Advancement of Colored People (NAACP)		
MADRE		
Planned Parenthood Federation of America		
Sierra Club		
Women's Environment and Development Organization (WEDO)		
Women's Earth and Climate Action Network (WECAN)		
WE ACT for Environmental Justice		

Table 11.2 Endorsing Organizations & Coalitions (EOCs). The Membership Is Still Growing as the Coalition Builds Support and Additional Allied Orgs Endorse Our Principles

Organizations and Coalitions	
ActionAid USA	International Women's Health Coalition (IWHC)
Alliance for Affordable Energy	JASS (Just Associates)
Asociación Regional Mujeres Ingenieras	L'Associació Drets Sexuals i Reproductius
CAP! Center for Advocacy Practices	Mujeres en Energía Renovable México
Chirapaq, Center of Indigenous Cultures of Peru	NC Interfaith Power and Light
ClimateMama	Oxfam
Climate Watch Thailand	Rachel Carson Council
EmpoderaClima / Care About Climate	Simona Getova, Central European University
Environmental Justice Advocates of Minnesota	Sunrise Movement
European Network for Community-Led Initiatives on Climate Change and Sustainability (ECOLISE)	Support for Women in Agriculture and Environment (SWAGEN)
Forests and Farmers Coalition, Thailand	Sustaining Way
Formidable Initiatives for Women and Girls, Liberia (FIWG-L)	The Imani Group
Freedom Squre / Плоштад Слобода	Utah Moms for Clean Air
Global Justice Center	Women's Environmental Network (WEN)
Initiative de la Société Civile pour les ODD en Côte d'Ivoire (ISCODDCI)	Women Organizing for Change in Agriculture and Natural Resource Management (WOCAN)
Institute for Policy Studies, Climate Policy Program	Women's Learning Partnership (WLP)
International Centre for Climate Change and Development (ICCCAD)	350.org
Women's Earth Alliance	

we argue that US GND interventions that lack feminist analysis will exacerbate gender inequality if care is not taken to ensure that new labor regimes are less time-consuming, exploitative, and energy intensive (Cohen and MacGregor 2020; Mellor 2017; Stephens 2020).

Since our initial formation, constituent members have published a variety of reports and think pieces to further expound upon our beliefs including "Towards a Feminist Foreign Policy in the United States," "Gender and Climate Change: A Read of Existing Research," and "Planning for a Feminist Economic Recovery" (Dolan 2020; Sellers 2020; L. Thompson et al. 2020). Our constituent members have likewise participated in civil society and governmental advocacy to "build back better" from the global COVID-19 pandemic and embrace anti-resilient recovery; in other words, we unequivocally reject the status quo of injustice that has historically reified gendered and racialized inequality and disinvestment (Baker 2021; Daniel and Dolan 2020).

Brief description of principles

We locate the roots of the environmental and climate crisis, Indigenous genocide, and widespread human rights abuses within white supremacist heteronormative imperial militaristic capitalist patriarchy. We also recognize that Indigenous People(s) protect over 25% of the world's land surface and 80% of the world's biodiversity (FEMGND 2021; Levi-Uyeda 2019;

MacGregor 2017; Sellers 2020). Furthermore, the enslavement, colonization, and labor exploitation of BIPOC communities historically institutionalized deeply entrenched gendered and racialized social inequality and environmental degradation via processes of alienation, commodification, and accumulation by dispossession. Put simply, normative processes of capitalist economic development and technological advancement without inherent rights-based approaches continue to devastate and displace Indigenous Peoples, disenfranchise peoples of color, and oppress women and other marginalized peoples. It is thus important to center the leadership and climate solutions of those most impacted by rising seas, unnatural disasters, and extractive economies. We believe that feminist principles of engagement will ensure a just, regenerative and equitable future for all (Daniel and Dolan 2020; FEM GND 2019).

The (ten) principles of the Feminist Green New Deal include:[5]

1. Requiring intersectional gender analysis
2. Recognizing the fallacy of domestic climate policy
3. Confronting institutional patriarchy and racism
4. Centering Indigenous People's rights and leadership
5. Confronting exploitative and unsustainable production patterns
6. Advancing reproductive justice
7. Ensuring community-led and democratic solutions
8. Rejecting false solutions for the climate crisis that ignore root causes
9. Creating regenerative and feminist economies that center feminist alternatives
10. Respecting youth leadership

Since the FEM GND unequivocally supports Indigenous self-determination, sovereignty, and land rights, we also recognize the rights of nature and support free, prior, and informed consent. We moreover advocate for a reinvestment in peace, reparations, and equity, while ending the criminalization of water protectors and environmental activists targeted by the state-corporate-military industrial complex. We demand financial support for decarbonization, mitigation, adaptation measures and transfer of technical expertise. We ultimately believe in accountability measures that acknowledge the role of the US state in national and global political instability; we champion defunding of the US military industrial complex, income redistribution within US borders, and an end to interventions in other countries (FEM GND 2019; Sellers 2020; WEDO 2019).

FEM GND contemporaries

Fortunately, a diverse chorus of feminist, anti-racist, and anti-imperial activists similarly articulate visionary frameworks for climate justice, worker rights and Indigenous sovereignty (WEDO 2020).[6] Our principles and values align with many of these global feminist and intersectional frameworks including the Thrive Agenda, the Gulf South for a Green New Deal, the Feminist Fossil Free Future, A Just and Feminist Future, and the UK Feminist Green New Deal. Like our colleagues, we center Indigenous Peoples' rights and leadership, confront exploitative and unsustainable production patterns, and promote democratically controlled community-led solutions. We also support energy democracy and energy sovereignty, investment in the global commons, sustainable agriculture and fisheries, environmental justice, and a gender-just transition to unionized, safe jobs. Most importantly, we enthusiastically support feminist economic recovery plans created by our colleagues in Hawai'i, Canada, and Austria that link green investment to an equitable and just COVID recovery. The Red Deal and the Decolonial and Feminist Global GND similarly imagine intersectional and sovereign futures (Burns and Reyes 2020; HSCSW 2020; Levi-Uyeda 2019; Muchhala 2020).

Feminist academics also play an important role in raising consciousness of feminist climate justice. Feminist scholarship within the loosely defined gender and environment canon spans more than five decades and draws on expertise from fields such as gender and development, sustainability, feminist science studies, feminist political ecology, queer ecologies, postcolonial and women of color feminisms, feminists economics, ecofeminism(s), and critical environmental studies (Cohen and MacGregor 2020; Harcourt and Nelson 2015; MacGregor 2010, 2017; J.A. Nelson and Morgan 2020). Feminist activist scholarship linking gender inequality, climate inaction, and women's environmental activism is likewise inspired by radical movements for human rights and the rights of nature. These movements and transnational examples of resistance include abolitionist, suffrage, civil rights, anti-toxics, women's health, reproductive justice, environmental justice, anti-nuclear, peace, Indigenous sovereignty, industrial hygiene and labor, vegan activist, and the Black women's club movements (Gaard 2018; MacGregor 2017). The FEM GND coalition moreover leverages feminist academic expertise to advance feminist political priorities.

Lastly, a global rise in young feminist and Indigenous organizing around climate is exemplified by the US Sunrise Movement, grantees of the FRIDA Young Feminist Fund, the women, gender, and youth constituencies at the UN climate negotiations, transnational pipeline resistance, the Youth Climate Strike and Fridays for the Future, and all of the networks and coalitions that comprise the FEM GND coalition (Clemmons 2020; FRIDA and YFA-AWID 2016; Stephens 2020). Youth activists and climate feminists historically and currently advocate for greater representation of women, youth, LGTBQI+ communities, communities of color, and Indigenous People(s) in climate negotiations, as well as support climate finance, the polluter pays principle, and the insertion of gender, human rights, and Indigenous Peoples in trade agreements. Young and seasoned climate feminists also critique the neoliberal imperative behind many public-private partnerships, the economization and financialization of nature, and the feminization of care work that disproportionately burdens women and communities of color (Wichterich 2015).

Tensions and congruencies

The FEM GND principles, however visionary, are not immune from contradiction and intrinsic tension. In our demands for a gender just transition to 100% renewable energy, we must fervently acknowledge the inherent human rights abuses and greenwashing involved in a renewable sector dominated by white male elites (Stephens 2020). We must similarly acknowledge that our principles, by aligning with the US GND, potentially legitimize the logic of "green" neoliberal growth and paternalistic mentalities embedded within sustainable development rhetoric. Furthermore, our principles, without care and intention, could be misconstrued to minimize feminist critiques of sustainable development, reify essentialized understandings of femininity, and erase diverse eco-masculinities. We must ensure that our principles, when centering women's experiences, do not uphold the false notion that gender justice is solely synonymous with justice for women and other femme-bodied individuals (Foster 2017; Sandler and Goetz 2020; Stephens 2020).

Moreover, it is important that our principles refrain from advancing the heteronormative expectation of women as good economic saviors. According to Foster (2017, 220), "it is the construction of women as victims of environmental degradation, superior environmental managers, and reproductive mothers that creates and sustains the conditions for [environmental governmentality]." Consequently, the tension between celebrating women and BIPOC communities as the natural caretakers of "Mother Earth" and women and BIPOC communities as unlimited resources for gendered and racialized labor exploitation within masculinist economies has yet to be resolved through our feminist theorizing. Our principles could thus be strengthened by acknowledging diverse gendered ecological relationships and ensuring the language we use to describe our work and values promotes the commons, interspecies kinship and Indigenous sovereignty (i.e., ecologies and relations) as opposed to commodification and privatization (i.e., resources).

Most importantly, our principles could be strengthened by rethinking multilateralism to make space for bilateral, transnational, regional, and even strategic unilateral processes. Despite the gains made at the 1995 World Conference on Women at Beijing, "the multilateral decision-making enabled by the United Nations (UN), as the world's only forum for negotiating agreements between almost all countries, has been both fertile and frustrating for advancing women's rights" (Sandler and Goetz 2020, 239). As pragmatic and visionary feminists, we must acknowledge the reality of hybrid, fragmented and polycentric multilateralism institutionalized after the Paris Agreement. While we can and should debate the ideal *lateralisms* that will bring about international cooperation around climate change and gender equality, we must not ignore the growing disillusionment with globalization and distrust of state-centric multilateral institutions such as the UN. By rethinking multilateralism, we center the expertise and power of nonstate and substate actors including civil society, transnational corporations, feminist activists, and city mayors involved in the ICLEI, Global Covenant of Mayors for Climate & Energy, and C40 networks[7] (Bäckstrand et al. 2017; Liu and Lo 2021). We also promote reforms that enable greater responsibility, effectiveness, and inclusivity.

Our principles finally reify a problematic binary between the United States/Global North and the Global South during discussions of climate debt. For example, when we proclaim that the "US has been the world's largest historic carbon polluter, while those in the Global South have suffered its worst impacts," we erase US-based environmental justice communities struggling for reparations in sacrifice zones located within the borders of the Global North (Foster 2017; Sandler and Goetz 2020). Moreover, although our principles advocate for the leadership of "frontline, impacted communities," they do not necessarily provide concrete guidance on how to best mobilize and respect subaltern perspectives and voices that are routinely delegitimized in environmental decision-making and natural resource management. Nor do our principles discuss the need for robust and targeted funding for mentorship programs to increasing frontline, femme, and nonbinary representation in male-dominated policy, climate science, and environmental decision-making spaces (Stephens 2020). Despite these tensions, we are excited to promote the FEM GND principles as a feminist framework and abolitionist offering that uniquely links heteropatriarchal norms and global political inequality to the environmental and climate crisis.

Additional challenges

Every coalition has its challenges, and the FEM GND must address tensions that arise when building solidarities among transnational feminists. For example, it is difficult at times to coordinate busy schedules across multiple time zones, facilitate deep engagement from our constituent members, and ensure equitable representation of diverse voices from multiple geographies. It is always challenging to make space for rest, recovery, and community care during periodic seasons of burnout and simultaneously respond to urgent political developments in a timely and collective fashion. It is equally difficult to balance grant writing and fundraising with on-the-ground movement building. We need more financial support to amplify our official messaging in multiple languages and reach coalition members and grassroots communities with differing literacies and gendered identities (i.e., nonbinary, transgender, genderqueer, and "two-spirit" persons).

With the rise in techno-optimism and conservative calls for austerity, it is likewise challenging to convince public officials and the general public that centering care and women's labor is hard, as opposed to soft work. Outside of explicitly feminist circles and allies that sympathize with feminist analysis, it can be difficult to build consensus around the need for real solutions (i.e., feminist economies of care) versus false solutions for climate change (i.e., carbon pricing, nuclear, and geoengineering) (Cohen and MacGregor 2020). We similarly desire more funding for our under-resourced feminist constituent organizations to make the education, policy, and organizing work sustainable (FRIDA and YFA-AWID 2016). Although we object to unequal hierarchies that develop when our constituent organizations are cast as subgrantees, we recognize that financial assistance is required to sustain our work over the short and long terms. Since our work is radical and unapologetic, there is likewise a need for greater capacity building, planning for leadership transitions, and security measures in the light of backlash and other threats (FRIDA and YFA-AWID 2016).

We also recognize the inherent tensions of employing "insider-outsider strategies," i.e., working both with and against states to ensure regulation and enforcement of environmental policies in an era marked by heightened surveillance, spying, infiltration, assassination and neocolonial territorial expansion (Daniel and Dolan 2020; Dengler and Seebacher 2019; Hasler, Walters and White 2020). Recognizing the risks of liberal cooptation, we must navigate participation in official – at times hostile – UN spaces (where there has arguably been a lack of progress in attaining sustainable development goals) with mobilization in more grassroots and radical spaces such as the World Social Forum and civil society spaces adjacent to and outside of the official UNFCCC COP[8] decision-making body (Barbier and UNEP 2020). Since many mainstream climate action groups continue to miss the conversation on the value of the care economy, we need stronger data connections between greening initiatives, care work investment, and equitable policy outcomes. We must explicitly quantify and qualify what it means to combat the devaluation of those who experience misogyny, racism and othering within mainstream economics (Cohen and MacGregor 2020; Littig 2017; Mellor 2017; Sellers 2020).

Finally, it is increasingly important that we move beyond a deficit model of communication that assumes our detractors can be persuaded by rational feminist arguments. According to emerging scholarship within environmental and climate communications, scientific data and well-reasoned arguments about social inequality do not necessarily spur behavioral change and increase support for climate action or feminist politics (Hathaway 2019). Instead, it is pertinent that we engage in multi-directional dialog, meet people where they are (i.e., not where we think they should be), and patiently promote unlearning while nurturing seeds of decolonial thinking. By working with communication scholars and practitioners, we can disrupt narratives that demonize male workers in the oil fields and victimize female caregivers (Roberts-Gregory 2020). Communication strategists can likewise assist in debunking the notion that the US GND will primarily serve elites and technocrats (Cohen and MacGregor 2020; Hathaway 2019). While we adjust and develop targeted, heterogenous approaches to communication, we simultaneously should focus on feminist consciousness-raising among our allies and plan for feminist energy and policy systems informed by the historical legacy of feminist New Deal thought leaders (Bell, Daggett and Labuski 2020). We must also ensure that our work is accessible to feminist newcomers and long-term activists, while making space for internal ideological differences.

Opportunities

The FEM GND is a timely and necessary intervention that holds the potential to legislate a just transition to fossil-fuel-free-*ish* futures and create new opportunities for US-led climate action shaped by human rights, the rights of nature, and other ethical principles. The FEM GND also promises to bring more justice and accountability to international climate negotiations and redress gendered and racialized disparities in healthcare, housing, transportation, economic opportunity, agriculture, conservation, biodiversity, and education. By shifting from a pro-privatization and limitless growth mindset, the FEM GND can increase awareness of more cooperative, collective, resilient, and regenerative models within public discourse, while disrupting masculinist and androcentric power systems.

There are likewise opportunities to promote our Building Feminist Policies for Climate Justice Policy Screening and Resource Guide. Launched in March of 2021, this policy tool and resource guide provides new accountability measures to ensure policymakers and other GND decision-makers create actionable policies and intersectional climate legislation that center the voices, solutions and leadership of frontline, youth, feminist, and BIPOC communities. Geared toward policymakers working at local, regional, national, and international levels, our policy tool and resource guide will potentially transform municipal, state, and federal climate policymaking and bring greater attention to global gender mainstreaming and feminist foreign policy (Daniel and Dolan 2020; FEM GND 2021). We will moreover continue to promote feminist foreign policy and hybrid models of multilateral engagement through our participation in the Commission on the Status of Women and co-leadership of the Feminist Action on Climate Justice Action Coalition at the historic 2021 Generation Equality Forum.[9] Since we recognize that patriarchy knows no gender, we will finally use our feminist policy platform to call out individuals from all genders who fail to uplift feminist values and perpetuate harm through neoliberal logics and warmongering.

We are also excited to address voter suppression and encourage those who experience misogyny and environmentally minded allies to vote for feminist climate solutions; women, youth and BIPOC communities tend to favor positive climate action compared to their older white male counterparts (FEM GND 2019; Sellers 2020). Although we similarly recognize that feminist futures are contradictory and contentious, we believe radical and transformative change is required to confront rising wealth inequality and neoliberal logic embedded within GND policies and repackaged sustainable development rhetoric (Barbier and UNEP 2020; Harcourt and Nelson 2015). We will consequently continue to address environmental sexism, heterosexism, and speciesism, and promote feminist approaches to climate action through research, advocacy, and popular education (Gaard 2018; Harcourt and Nelson 2015; Wichterich 2015). Most importantly, we will continue to demand a new feminist social contract that values reinvestment in social infrastructure and social reproduction (Cohen and MacGregor 2020). In imagining decolonial and feminist futures, we unequivocally embrace multiple worlds, diverse tongues, and a plurality of knowledges and everyday approaches to feminist futures (Salleh 2020).

We furthermore plan to build stronger relationships with feminist climate funders such as the Hive Fund for Climate and Gender Justice, the Global Greengrants Fund, and the

FRIDA Young Feminist Fund to institutionalize healing justice, collective care, and holistic security within our movement spaces. We will nurture opportunities for feminist fellowship and self-care through our feminist science fiction reading group, our upcoming collective care and healing justice virtual gathering, and our community care working group. We will likewise increase feminist activist research on the transition from extractive to care economies by focusing on divestment from fossil fuels and industrial subsidies and reinvestment in living wages, affordable housing, and care industries (i.e., child, disability and elder care; hospitality and gig economies; healthcare; early childhood learning; and education) (Cohen and MacGregor 2020; FRIDA and YFA-AWID 2016; Sellers 2020). Future research will also explore divestment from carceral systems and policing in relation to care economies and will support initiatives such as the Canadian Care Economy Collective and the Action Nexus for Generation Equality Global Feminist Economic Justice Agenda. There are similarly exciting opportunities to experiment with consensus models and participatory rule, digital feminism(s), artivism, and other creative and unconventional change-making strategies (FRIDA and YFA-AWID 2016).

Our collective will finally continue to analyze major federal climate and care plans within the Biden-Harris administration and develop future multilingual resources for feminist climate legislation (Daniel and Dolan 2020). Portions of the Biden administration's 2021 American Rescue, Jobs, and Families plans (i.e., the Build Back Better Agenda) were recently repackaged into a proposed $1.2-trillion bipartisan infrastructure framework and $3.5-trillion budget resolution bill. These approved and/or upcoming proposals provide COVID relief, expand Medicare coverage, support worker protections, and encourage investment in climate-resilient infrastructure, clean energy and approximately $400 billion in home care infrastructure (Wilkie 2021). Nevertheless, these plans insufficiently promote equitable employment in these industries and only indirectly recognize care jobs as green jobs. They also fall short of radical feminist care infrastructure proposals developed by care work advocates such as the National Domestic Workers Alliance (NDWA)[10] (Palladino and Gunn-Wright 2021). Most importantly, we look forward to promoting opportunities for wealthy, colonizing nations to learn from their formerly colonized counterparts on how to live less carbon-intensive lives without romanticizing and homogenizing ecological solutions from the Global South (Dengler and Seebacher 2019). We cherish opportunities to link peace, decarbonization, human rights, and the rights of nature through feminist stimulus and economic recovery (Dolan 2020).

Moving forward

The FEM GND will continue to champion principles of feminist engagement that radically reimagine fossil-fuel-free-*ish* futures via feminist foreign policy, feminist COVID recovery, and feminist economies of care (Cohen and MacGregor 2020; Dolan 2020; HSCSW 2020). We will continue to collaborate with the Feminist COVID Response Collective to promote their Feminist Response to COVID-19 Principles, Feminist Monitoring & Advocacy Toolkit, and feminist collective storytelling project. We look forward to deepening relationships with care work advocates working at the intersection of COVID-19 recovery and climate justice through our recently published Care & Climate Policy Brief (Palladino and Gunn-Wright 2021). We also plan to increase member participation and leadership within our various policy, coordination, community care, care economy, and communications working groups. We ultimately look forward to growing our coalition and developing better strategies to influence Congress and global policymakers through targeted and heterogenous communication, determining catalysts for investments in care at the local, state and federal levels, and collaborating intersectionally and intergenerationally across the political spectrum.

We will also continue to center climate solutions from the Global South and embrace feminist ecological concepts such as South America's buen vivir and Southern Africa's ubuntu (Dengler and Seebacher 2019; Lyric Thompson 2020). We are eager to promote global justice within US climate discourse and global feminist solidarity through the THRIVE Agenda and other progressive and radical recovery platforms. Our constituent members such as WEDO, moreover, currently offer virtual climate negotiation trainings for first-time women delegates from least-developed countries (LDCs) and advocate for more robust gender mainstreaming and the Gender Action Plan (GAP) within UNFCCC negotiations. Another coalition member, WECAN, promotes Indigenous women's food sovereignty programs in the Gulf South, facilitates Indigenous rights workshops for financial institutions to move beyond the Paris Climate Agreement, and advocates for the Escazú Agreement in Latin America and the Caribbean to support criminalized and persecuted environmental defenders. All our members support water protectors through the #defundline3 and similar campaigns. In 2021, we will also launch a feminist futures animation to visually articulate our feminist and decolonial imaginings for a care-fueled and regenerative future for all.

We additionally look forward to raising global awareness of feminist climate sheroes such as Eunice Foote[11] on social media platforms and building stronger alliances with individuals who experience misogyny and othering in climate science associated with the Intergovernmental Panel on Climate Change (IPCC) (Schwartz 2020). We recognize the importance of centering the voices and stories of women, feminist activists, and scientists who inspire our contemporary activism yet are often relegated to historical obscurity, such as Eunice Foote and Frances Perkins. We likewise anticipate the need to facilitate critical dialog on how to rethink multilateralism; despite utopian yearnings, there is no guarantee that multilateralism will produce the feminist and climate-just futures we desire if powerful conservative and antifeminist nation-states are able to undermine, neglect, or defund programs that promote gender equality and women's rights. By engaging feminist allies through initiatives such as the C40 Women4Climate initiative,[12] FEM GND members and women's rights allies will nurture innovative partnerships, forestall conservative backlash against feminist priorities, and obtain more reliable finance for the democratization of outdated decision-making processes and feminist monitoring of UN performance and parity measures (Sandler and Goetz 2020).

Regardless of multilateralism's future, our feminist climate collective will continue to employ bottom-up and "insider-outsider" strategies at UNFCCC COP events, build solidarity with transnational feminists and allies, and advocate for gendered climate finance within UN spaces that serve to facilitate urgent, if asymmetrical, climate negotiations (Daniel and Dolan 2020). Productive tensions and congruencies with the aforementioned radical and feminist policy platforms will also ensure feminist accountability and make space for diverse feminist understandings of our principles, multiple cosmologies, and heterogenous approaches to feminist worldmaking (Daniel and Dolan 2020). Our collaborative relationships will ultimately ensure that our principles can withstand social and economic uncertainty, as well as enable us to remix and adapt our principles to changing political conditions with nimbleness, deftness, and flexibility.

Time will tell how we as a coalition navigate challenges and opportunities for building transnational solidarity and ensure our collective is not dominated by Global North perspectives and political priorities (Dengler and Seebacher 2019). Time will tell if our policy suggestions and insights will contribute to a centering of those who experience misogyny and racism in emerging green economies, a restructuring of the global gendered pay gap, and a revaluation of essential workers as caregivers (Cohen and MacGregor 2020; Daniel and Dolan 2020). Time will also tell if our principles will inspire feminists to join the climate justice movement (and vice versa) and bridge silos between policy, movement, philanthropic, civil society, nonprofit, and academic spaces. Irrespective of these challenges, the FEM GND offers a unique opportunity to increase global awareness of the linkages between neoliberal policy solutions and the institutionalization of gendered and racialized environmental violence, while transforming the decolonial contours and futurist imaginings of global environmental governance. The FEM GND Coalition looks forward to championing feminist foreign policy, feminist solutions for a just and equitable COVID recovery, and the continued integration of gender into climate policy.

Notes

1 Black, Indigenous, and People of Color (BIPOC).

2 After witnessing immigrant women and girls die horrifically in the Triangle Shirtwaist Factory Fire in NY, Frances Perkins dedicated her life to combatting labor exploitation and social inequality.

3 The Federal Council on Negro Affairs (i.e., the Black Cabinet) was coined and led by Dr. Mary McLeod Bethune, the leader of the Negro Affairs Division of the National Youth Administration (NYA) and a close friend of First Lady Eleanor Roosevelt. As head of the Negro Affairs Division of the NYA, Dr. Bethune was able to increase the representation of Black girls, women, and families in New Deal programs.

4 Healing justice is a Black, southern, queer, radical political strategy devised by BIPOC and Global South feminists, health practitioners and advocates for immigration reform, prison abolition, Indigenous sovereignty, disability justice, and LGBTQI+ rights in the early 2000s. Healing justice, according to Cara Page and the Kindred Southern Healing Justice Collective, critiques state-based violence and the medical industrial complex, politicizes the role of healers, and promotes practices of mutual aid, survival economies and collective care.

5 A more detailed description of our principles can be found on our website at feministgreennewdeal.com. They are also outlined in *Daniel & Dolan* (2020).

6 Other feminist and intersectional frameworks we support include Women Defend Commons, the Ecofeminist Impact Assessment Framework, A Vision for Equitable Climate Action, An Equitable and Just Climate Platform, the Blue-Green Alliance, the Sitting Bull Plan, and the Red, Black, and Green New Deal.

7 The ICLEI-Local Governments for Sustainability, the Global Covenant of Mayors for Climate & Energy, and the C40 Cities Climate Leadership Group are global diplomatic networks of hundreds of cities and local governments dedicated to urban sustainability, reducing greenhouse gas emissions, and climate resilience.

8 United Nations Framework Convention on Climate Change Conference of Parties

9 The 2021 Generation Equality Forum, co-hosted by Mexico and France and convened by UN Women, works to generate conversation on transformative and ambitious solutions for gender equality and celebrates the 25th anniversary of the 1995 Fourth World Conference in Beijing. These global conversations aim to ratchet progress on gender equality and women's rights and will be led by civil society and supported by governments, academia, corporations, social influencers, and artists.

10 The NDWA supports policy reforms that legislate universal child care, universal long-term support, paid leave, and family caregiver support (Palladino and Gunn-Wright 2021).

11 Eunice Foote was an American (amateur) scientist, inventor and women's rights advocate. In addition to signing the 1848 Seneca Falls Convention Declaration that advocated for women's rights, she was the first scientist to hypothesize the greenhouse effect, although the credit historically is attributed to (antifeminist) John Tyndall.

12 The C40 Women4Climate initiative aims to increase awareness of the leadership of women in negotiating international climate agreements, empower women in sustainability and city climate action, and inspire future environmental leaders through mentorship and community building.

References

Bäckstrand, K., Kuyper, J.W., Linnér, B-O. and Lövbrand, E. 2017. Non-State Actors in Global Climate Governance: From Copenhagen to Paris and Beyond. *Environmental Politics*. 26(4), 561–579. Available from: https://doi.org/10.1080/09644016.2017.1327485.

Baker, S.H. 2021. *Revolutionary Power: An Activist's Guide to the Energy Transition*. Washington, D.C.: Island Press.

Barbier, E.B. and UNEP. 2020. Building a Greener Recovery: Lessons from the Great Recession. Geneva. Available from: https://www.greengrowthknowledge.org/sites/default/files/learning-resources/action/Building a Greener Recovery_ Lessons from the great recession_UNEP.pdf.

Bauhardt, C. 2014. Solutions to the Crisis? The Green New Deal, Degrowth, and the Solidarity Economy: Alternatives to the Capitalist Growth Economy from an Ecofeminist Economics Perspective. *Ecological Economics*. 102, 60–68. Available from: https://doi.org/10.1016/j.ecolecon.2014.03.015.

Bell, S.E., Daggett, C. and Labuski, C. 2020. Toward Feminist Energy Systems: Why Adding Women and Solar Panels Is Not Enough. *Energy Research & Social Science*. 68, 1–13. Available from: https://doi.org/10.1016/j.erss.2020.101557.

Bloomfield, J., and Steward, F. 2020. The Politics of the Green New Deal. *The Political Quarterly*. 1–10. Available from: https://doi.org/10.1111/1467-923X.12917.

Burns, B. and Reyes, E. 2020. Feminist Solidarity for a Collective Response to COVID-19. 2020. Available from: https://worldat1c.org/feminist-solidarity-for-a-collective-response-to-covid-19-1ce3df2f38ca.

Clemmons, Z.E. 2020. Cut Her Some Slack: Examining 21st Century Ecofeminist Digital Opinion Lesder #AOC and the #Greennewdeal. Colorado State University.

Cohen, N.L. 2020. Toward a Feminist Future: A Political Strategy for Fighting Backlash and Advancing Gender Equity. *Signs*. 45(2), 328–336. Available from: https://doi.org/10.1086/704987.

Cohen, M. and MacGregor, S. 2020. Towards a Feminist Green New Deal for the UK: A Paper for the WBG Commission on a Gender-Equal Economy. London. Available from: https://www.wen.org.uk/wp-content/uploads/FEM-GND-POLICY-PAPER-2.pdf.

Daniel, T. and Dolan, M. 2020. Intersectionality and Collective Action: Visioning a Feminist Green New Deal in the US. *Gender and Development*. 28(3), 515–533. Available from: https://doi.org/10.1080/13552074.2020.1843829.

Dengler, C. and Seebacher, L.M. 2019. What About the Global South? Towards a Feminist Decolonial Degrowth Approach. *Ecological Economics*. 157, 246–252. Available from: https://doi.org/10.1016/j.ecolecon.2018.11.019.

Dolan, M. 2020. Planning for a Feminist Economic Recovery. *MsMagazine.Com*. May. Available from: https://msmagazine.com/2020/05/27/planning-for-a-feminist-economic-recovery/.

Fdr4freedoms. 2014. Women and the New Deal: Gaining Ground in Politics and Public Life. Four Freedoms Park Conservancy. Available from: https://fdr4freedoms.org/wp-content/themes/fdf4fdr/DownloadablePDFs/II_HopeRecoveryReform/15_WomenandtheNewDeal.pdf.

FEM GND. 2019. Feminist Green New Deal Principles. Available from: http://feministgreennewdeal.com/principles/.

FEM GND. 2021. Building Feminist Policies for Climate Justice. Available from: http://feministgreennewdeal.com/2021/03/11/building-feminist-policies-for-climate-justice/.

Foster, E.A. 2017. Gender, Environmental Governmentality, and the Discourses of Sustainable Development. In: S. MacGregor, ed. *Routledge Handbook of Gender and Environment*. New York: Earthscan. pp. 216–228.

FRIDA and YFA-AWID. 2016. Brave Creative Resilient: The Global State of Young Feminist Organizing. Available from: https://youngfeministfund.org/wp-content/uploads/2017/05/frida-awid_research_summary.pdf.

Gaard, G. 2018. Feminism and Environmental Justice. In: R. Holifield, J. Chakraborty and G. Walker, eds. *The Routledge Handbook of Environmental Justice*. Milton Park: Routledge. pp. 74–88.

Galvin, R. and Healy, N. 2020. The Green New Deal in the United States: What It Is and How to Pay for It. *Energy Research and Social Science*. 67, 1–9. Available from: https://doi.org/10.1016/j.erss.2020.101529.

Glickman, L. 2020. How White Backlash Controls American Progress. *The Atlantic*. May. Available from: https://www.theatlantic.com/ideas/archive/2020/05/white-backlash-nothing-new/611914/.

Guzda, H. 1980. Frances Perkins' Interest in a New Deal for Blacks. *Monthly Labor Review.* 103(4), 31–35.

Hansley, C. and Rye Butler, R. 2015. Why Environmental Activists Are Turning Out for Voting Rights. Greenpeace.Org. Available from: https://www.greenpeace.org/usa/environmental-activists-turning-voting-rights/.

Harcourt, W. and Nelson, I.L., eds. 2015. *Practising Feminist Political Ecologies: Moving Beyond the Green Economy.* London: Zed Books.

Hasler, O., Walters, R. and White, R. 2020. In and Against the State: The Dynamics of Environmental Activism. *Critical Criminology.* 28, 517–531. Available from: https://doi.org/10.1007/s10612-019-09432-0.

Hathaway, J.R. 2019. Climate Change, the Intersectional Imperative, and the Opportunity of the Green New Deal. *Environmental Communication.* 0(0), 1–10. Available from: https://doi.org/10.1080/17524032.2019.1629977.

HiveFund. 2020. Funding Healing Justice and Holistic Security. Available from: https://www.hivefund.org/learning-lab/funding-healing-justice.

HSCSW. 2020. Building Bridges, Not Walking on Backs: A Feminist Economic Recovery Plan for COVID-19. Available from: https://humanservices.hawaii.gov/wp-content/uploads/2020/04/4.13.20-Final-Cover-D2-Feminist-Economic-Recovery-D1.pdf.

Johnson, D. 2020. Viewing Social Security through the Civil Rights Lens. NAACP.Org. Available from: https://www.naacp.org/latest/viewing-social-security-civil-rights-lens/.

Lavelle, M. 2015. A 50th Anniversary Few Remember: LBJ's Warning on Carbon Dioxide. *Daily Climate.* Available from: https://www.jacksonfreepress.com/news/2015/feb/02/50th-anniversary-few-remember-lbjs-warning-carbon-/.

Levi-Uyeda, R. 2019. The Red Deal Is an Indigenous Climate Plan That Builds on the Green New Deal. *Teenvogue.Com.* Available from: https://www.teenvogue.com/story/red-deal-indigenous-climate-plan-green-new-deal-red-nation.

Littig, B. 2017. Good Green Jobs for Whom? A Feminist Critique of the Green Economy. In: S. MacGregor, ed. *Routledge Handbook of Gender and Environment.* London: Routledge. pp. 318–330.

Liu, M. and Lo, K. 2021. Pathways to International Cooperation on Climate Governance in China: A Comparative Analysis. *Journal of Chinese Governance.* 6(3), 417–434. Available from: https://doi.org/10.1080/23812346.2020.1721230.

MacGregor, S. 2010. A Stranger Silence Still: The Need for Feminist Social Research on Climate Change. *The Sociological Review.* 57(2), 124–140. Available from: https://doi.org/10.1111/j.1467-954X.2010.01889.x.

MacGregor, S. ed. 2017. *Routledge Handbook of Gender and Environment.* London: Routledge.

Mellor, M. 2017. Ecofeminist Political Economy: A Green and Feminist Agenda. In: S. MacGregor, ed. *Routledge Handbook of Gender and Environment.* London: Routledge. pp. 86–100.

Muchhala, B. 2020. Towards a Decolonial and Feminist Global Green New Deal. Rosa-Luxemburg-Stiftung. Available from: https://www.rosalux.de/en/news/id/43146/towards-a-decolonial-and-feminist-global-green-new-deal.

Nelson, J.A. and Morgan, J. 2020. Ecological and Feminist Economics: An Interview with Julie A. Nelson. *Real-World Economics Review.* 91, 146–153. Available from: http://www.paecon.net/PAEReview/issue91/NelsonMorgan91.pdf.

Palladino, L. and Gunn-Wright, R. 2021. Care & Climate: Understanding the Policy Intersections. Available from: http://feministgreennewdeal.com/wp-content/uploads/2021/04/FemGND-IssueBrief-Draft7-Apr15.pdf.

Pusey, A. 2017. The Woman behind America's Social Safety Net. *ABA Journal.* 103(8), 72.

Rao, S. and Teixeira, S. 2020. The Green New Deal: Social Work's Role in Environmental Justice Policy. *Social Work.* 65(2), 197–200. Available from: https://doi.org/10.1093/sw/swaa004.

Roberts-Gregory, F. 2020. My Petrochemical Love. *Anthropology News.* April. Available from: https://doi.org/10.1111/AN.1387.

Salleh, A. 2020. A Materialist Ecofeminist Reading of the Green Economy: Or, Yes Karl, the Ecological Footprint Is Sex-Gendered. In: H. Hosseini, J. Goodman, S. Motta and B. Gills, eds. *The Routledge Handbook of Transformative Global Studies.* New York: Routledge.

Sandler, J. and Goetz, A.M. 2020. Can the United Nations Deliver a Feminist Future? *Gender & Development.* 28(2), 239–263. Available from: https://doi.org/10.1080/13552074.2020.1753432.

Schwartz, J. 2020. Overlooked No More: Eunice Foote, Climate Scientist Lost to History. *New York Times*. 21 April. Available from: https://www.nytimes.com/2020/04/21/obituaries/eunice-foote-overlooked.html.

Sellers, S. 2020. Gender and Climate Change in the United States: A Reading of Existing Research. Available from: https://wedo.org/wp-content/uploads/2020/03/WEDO-RP-022920.pdf.

Stephens, J.C. 2020. *Diversifying Power: Why We Need Antiracist, Feminist Leadership on Climate and Energy*. Washington, DC: Island Press.

Thompson, L. 2020. Mexican Diplomacy Has Gone Feminist. *Foreignpolicy.com*. 14 January. Available from: https://foreignpolicy.com/2020/01/14/mexican-diplomacy-feminist-foreign-policy/.

Thompson, L., Patel, G., Kripke, G. and O'Donnell, M. 2020. *Toward a Feminist Foreign Policy in the United States*. Washington, DC: International Center for Research on Women.

Walker, R. 2019. Was the New Deal Racist? The Living New Deal. Available from: https://livingnewdeal.org/was-the-new-deal-racist-2/.

WEDO. 2019. Women's Rights and Climate Activists Launch a Feminist Agenda for a Green New Deal. WEDO.org. Available from: https://wedo.org/feminist-green-new-deal-press-release/.

WEDO. 2020. Global Feminist Frameworks for Climate Jusice Town Hall: Frameworks Reader. WEDO.org. Available from: https://wedo.org/wp-content/uploads/2021/02/Global-Feminist-Framework-Town-Hall-READER-FINAL.pdf.

Wichterich, C. 2015. Contesting Green Growth, Connecting Care, Commons and Enough. In: I.L. Nelson and W. Harcourt, eds. *Practising Feminist Political Ecologies: Moving Beyond the "Green Economy"*. London: Zed Books. pp. 67–100.

Wilkie, C. 2021. Democrats' $3.5 Trillion Budget Package Funds Family Programs, Clean Energy and Medicare Expansion. *CNBC*. 14 July. Available from: https://www.cnbc.com/2021/07/14/democrats-3point5-trillion-budget-package-funds-family-programs-clean-energy-medicare-expansion.html.

12
DEMOCRATIZING THE GREEN NEW DEAL[1]

Julie L. MacArthur, Christina E. Hoicka and Runa R. Das

Introduction

Green New Deals have the potential to harness the power of coordinated state policy to address the significant and interrelated challenges of environmental degradation, climate change, poverty and energy insecurity (Mazzucato and McPherson 2018; Aronoff et al. 2019; Pettifor 2019). In a post-COVID era many are also counting on a large sustainability transition stimulus to be a central part of economic re-build strategies, so that the stimulus helps us to "build back better." But what exactly does this "better" look like, and how might we achieve it? From green colonialism and ecological modernization on the one hand, to ecosocialism on the other, there are many variations in both the means and the ends of any one green stimulus design (Aşıcı and Bünül 2012; Tienhaara 2014; Aronoff et al. 2019; Heenan and Sturman 2020). In this chapter we examine the concept of energy democracy (ED) and what lessons this concept holds for our understanding of Green New Deals.

A decade ago, a Global Green New Deal (GGND) was proposed following the global financial crisis of 2007–2008. Early proponents argued that a state-led fiscal stimulus through coordinated policy interventions can simultaneously provide jobs in clean(er) industries, reduce emissions, spur technological innovation and ensure habitable living spaces for citizens (UNEP 2009). As Ann Pettifor, one of the "godmothers" of the United Kingdom's Green New Deal, argues:

> finance, economy, and the environment are integrated – [...] you need a joined-up policy that deals with all three. When I studied the history of Roosevelt's New Deal, I saw how he did the same thing; he met the challenges of unemployment and economic collapse, fixed the Dust Bowl, and had to subordinate the financial system to the interests of the democratic state.
>
> *(O'Brien 2019)*

This subordination and the degree to which it takes place are clearly political. However, even on instrumental grounds, recent research shows that COVID recovery plans focused on GND policies (energy efficiency, subsidies for renewables, investment in power grids,

DOI: 10.4324/9781003110880-15

electric vehicle schemes and tree planting) economically and environmentally outperform business as usual stimulus packages (Pollitt 2020).

The promise of an effective GND extends far beyond just physical infrastructural transformations though, to social and political transformation (Aronoff et al. 2019). There is potential as well to contribute to the 2030 Sustainable Development Goals (SDGs), including SDG 5 on gender equality, SDG 7 on clean affordable energy, SDG 8 for decent work and economic growth, SDG 9 on sustainable and resilient infrastructure, and SDG 10, which strives to address the needs of marginalized communities. We argue in this chapter that it is in these commitments to transforming not just the technologies we use, but also the social and political systems that design and utilize them, where GND proposals can be radical and transformative.

There are a number of overlaps between GND proposals and the literature on energy democracy, but also some important differences. One of the core focus areas for Green New Deal proposals is energy sector reform: increased renewables, policies for electrification of transport and heat, and often transition strategies for incumbent actors. Renewable energy systems can be seen as the solution to greater security with respect to energy supply and access, but even "low-carbon" transitions can distribute costs and benefits unequally (Eames and Hunt 2013; Jenkins, Sovacool, and McCauley 2018). Those currently denied a place at the policymaking table or in well-paid energy sector jobs are, therefore, not necessarily more likely to economically benefit from green technology than they did with fossil fuels. Furthermore, new renewable energy industries in some jurisdictions like the United States have much lower rates of unionization than centralized and fossil fuel incumbents, meaning that new "green jobs" won't necessarily be decent, secure or reflective of diverse worker's voices (Stevis and Felli 2015; Stevis 2019; Isser 2020). Democratizing energy decision-making and ownership so that those most affected by transitions have control over them is one way that green stimulus can become just and transformative as well (MacArthur 2016a; Jenkins, Sovacool, and McCauley 2018). In this chapter we ask: what can energy democracy teach us about a Green New Deal? We begin answering this question with a critical review of recent literature on energy democracy. We then turn to the "how" of energy democratization, as represented in decentralization, ownership and political participation, as well as the "who" in terms of gender, race and class based inclusivity. We draw examples from energy democracy initiatives internationally, but with a particular focus on Canada.

Energy democracy

Energy governance is dominated by elites across the globe: largely a matter for technical investors, large companies and policy insiders. Top-down planning with centralized, increasingly private ownership is the norm. The concept of energy democracy challenges this orientation by highlighting the normative value and strategic importance of including citizens and civil society organizations in the design, ownership and operation of energy infrastructure (van Veelen and van der Horst 2018; Stephens 2019). At its core, energy democracy represents the idea that "the people" should play a larger role than they currently do in deciding on and benefiting from energy-related activities. Under the slogan "power to the people," energy democracy emerged out of climate social movements on the basis that institutional (mis)incentives and captured regulatory bodies were (and are) to blame for slow progress on energy decarbonization (Sweeny 2013).

Calls for energy democracy are rationalized on both normative and pragmatic grounds. Democratization can be an end unto itself, or a tool to achieving other ends, such as decarbonization or political support. From a normative standpoint, broadening the actors and mechanisms for participation are congruent with a commitment to democratic politics more broadly. From a pragmatic standpoint, increasing the democratic participation in and control of energy systems is theorized to have a range of benefits for energy transitions. It can help to increase the social acceptability of new infrastructure (Shaw et al. 2015), distribute financial benefits to proximate affected populations (Yildiz et al. 2015), encourage energy literacy (Duguid 2007), include previously marginalized actors with new and innovative ideas, and aid in effective policy implementation (Berka and Creamer 2018). Effective transitions need to include actors outside the industry–policy nexus (Breetz, Mildenberger and Stokes 2018), with citizen involvement throughout policy processes, and must consider the role of asset ownership as a form of participation (Burke and Stephens 2018; Lennon, Dunphy and Sanvicente 2019).

Energy democracy is less an endpoint than a claim that increased empowerment of citizens can help to transition to a low-carbon and just energy future. It involves resisting the expansion of fossil fuel sectors, reclaiming ownership of energy industries for public purpose, and restructuring energy technologies for decentralized 100% renewable energy futures (Sweeny 2013; Stephens 2019). From its social movement origins, the concept of energy democracy has since spread to policymakers and academics, contributing to a rapidly expanding discussion of its aims, participants, mechanisms and outcomes (van Veelen and van der Horst 2018; Brisbois 2019; Szulecki and Overland 2020). Scholars researching the movement for energy democracy, and the theoretical roots upon which the movement is based, have identified two key mechanisms through which citizens can play a greater role in shaping energy system outputs and outcomes: (1) Participation in energy sector planning and decision-making (through citizens fora, policy co-design initiatives and public consultation on new energy strategies and initiatives); and (2) Increased direct energy asset ownership by citizens or their representative governments, particularly at the local level (through local and community energy ownership, remunicipalization of utilities) (MacArthur 2016a; Szulecki 2018; Wyse and Hoicka 2019; MacArthur et al. 2020).

Just as the academic interest in energy democracy has grown, so too have the criticisms of both the concept and the practice. The most frequent criticism, even by those who take an interest in and are broadly supportive of energy transitions that are "just," is the conceptual fuzziness of the term (Szulecki 2018). Democracy alone is a highly contested concept with significant variation between its deliberative, participatory, representative and cosmopolitan variants. It isn't immediately clear how the broader umbrella of energy democracy links to one (or more) of these, which already are theorized to lead to significantly different outcomes for political participation, social outcomes and other important elements of a transition (Kuzemko, Lockwood, Mitchell et al. 2016). Similarly, the "energy" element of energy democracy is also broad (van Veelen and van der Horst 2018). Is the target renewable electricity generation, heat and power consumption, transport fuel transitions, or all of the above? One of the benefits of the conceptual fuzziness and flexibility of energy democracy is that it can be tailored to specific circumstances or needs. This is a significant strength for broad mobilization, particularly in countries where "democracy" and "democratization" are viewed broadly as desirable and uncontroversial.

As with the literature on the Green New Deal, there are also large geographic variations in the mechanisms and goals proposed by specific energy democracy advocates, as broad ideals are mediated by the specific socio-technical regimes of a given country or region (Kuzemko et al. 2016; Creamer et al. 2018; Judson et al. 2020). This is where the conceptual variation can be problematic, since an approach to energy democracy in one jurisdiction emphasizing nationalization of fuel and power industries from extraction to retailing will differ in impact from an approach centered on enabling the participation of citizens in policy design or targeted transition areas (Thombs 2019). It matters who this democracy is meant to include, the mechanisms for it, and ultimate targets.

While GND proposals focus attention on state stimulus and industrial policy, the literature on energy democracy emphasizes more the role of non-state actors and decentralization, and in some cases does not have a clear articulation of the role of the state in this. The literature emphasizes the role of grassroots "bottom-up" actors, particularly those associated with the social and solidarity economy sectors: co-operatives, non-profits and community associations (Berka, MacArthur, and Gonnelli 2020; Brisbois 2020; Tarhan 2020). However, the role of the state and other corporate actors in this democratization is less consistent or clear. Because of these ambiguities, Szulecki and Overland (2020) argue that "proponents should not assume that more energy democracy will inherently mean faster decarbonization, improved energy access or social well being." Mechanisms and actors matter, but which, and how?

Decentralization, ownership and participation: mechanisms for energy democracy

Below we discuss how diverse mechanisms of energy democratization, from physical and political decentralization to ownership changes and decision-making reforms, can contribute to decarbonization.

Energy decentralization and democracy

Renewable energy transitions, which form a central element in most GND policies, consist of major spatial and economic reorganization (Bridge et al. 2013). Incumbent nuclear power or fossil fuels are more compatible with monopolistic ownership. Renewable energy is considered to be more compatible with distributed generation (Kuzemko et al. 2016, 2017). The potential of renewable energy sources is specific to a local context (Ramirez Camargo and Stoeglehner 2018; Risso, Beluco and De Cássia Marques Alves 2018; Lam et al. 2020), and they are more geographically decentralized (Pasqualetti 2012; Bridge et al. 2013). Renewable energy sources are therefore considered more compatible with decentralized ownership, and are viewed as a natural fit for local energy democracy (Berka and Creamer 2018; Burke and Stephens 2018). Renewable energy is more resilient during natural disasters than fossil fuels and nuclear power (Grant 2018).

Due to the low spatial energy density, intermittency and low dispatchability of renewable energy sources, a shift to renewable energy requires a different architecture and logic than centralized systems (Hoicka and MacArthur 2019; Lowitzsch, Hoicka and van Tulder 2020). This is because renewable energy is geography- and landscape-specific (Pasqualetti 2012) with a spatial density of production (in watts per square meter or W/m^2) that is orders of magnitude lower than that of traditional centralized generation (Smil 2015). A shift to increased shares of renewable energy leads to spatial pressures across landscapes and communities (Pasqualetti 2012; Smil 2015; Ramirez Camargo and Stoeglehner 2018; Hoicka and MacArthur 2019).

One important issue to decentralization, decarbonization and democratization of energy is that urban areas are densely populated with high energy density of demand (W/m^2), particularly as electric vehicle growth is expected in cities (quintupling the average peak household electricity load) (Hertzke et al. 2019; Hoicka and MacArthur 2019). Deep energy retrofits to buildings can significantly reduce energy demand (Hoicka and Das 2020). However, it remains unclear how urban areas can transition to renewable energy, which has spatial energy densities that are orders of magnitude lower than conventional power, requiring more area for similar energy output (Smil 2015).

Some argue that disruptive technological innovation can lead to decentralization. Disruptive innovations create major societal change, including introducing new social values and political beliefs; in this case, the emergence of new actors in renewable energy production and supply, and regulatory interventions (Dixon, Lannon and Eames 2018; Wilson 2018; Johnstone et al. 2020). Depending on how a renewable energy transition occurs, it can address or exacerbate inequalities in local contexts. In the case of renewable energy and its supporting infrastructure, the rapid or successful diffusion of singular innovations, such as solar panels or electric vehicles, can lead to negative disruption and consequential risk, such as major system instabilities (Islam 2017; Hahn and Viet Nam Energy Environment Climate 2019; Hertzke et al. 2019). For example, a feed-in tariff policy in Vietnam was so successful that solar power experienced exponential growth over the course of months (4,000 Mega-Watts (MW) installed, 23,000 MW awaiting approval in December 2019) (Hahn and Viet Nam Energy Environment Climate 2019). By comparison, the Ontario electricity system in Canada is 26,000 MW. This rapid growth overloaded and destabilized the grid, leading to the curtailment of solar and the need to revise the policy (Hahn and Viet Nam Energy Environment Climate 2019). While this was a very successful and well-intentioned rapid scale-up of solar power, these types of risks can be offset with careful policy design, including knowledge transfer from the innovation system to the local context in advance of and during implementation. Renewable energy integration requires flexible technologies and innovations – conservation, demand response, aggregators, storage, virtual power plants, peer-to-peer trading and microgrids (Martinot 2016). These elements are present in renewable energy clusters and multi-carrier energy systems (Mancarella 2014; Lowitzsch, Hoicka and van Tulder 2020).

Physical decentralization does not necessarily or automatically increase citizen agency in the energy system and enhance environmental performance (Judson et al. 2020). Judson et al. (2020) argue that decentralization pathways can block rapid decarbonization and entrench incumbent actors' interests, and that the institutional context is a key determinant to whether decentralization is accompanied by democratization and decarbonization. Buth et al. (2019) evaluate blockchain technology's impact on the energy sector, but conclude that the impact of blockchain does not seem to be as disruptive and decentralizing as may be expected. Renewable energy policy implementation has often ignored the benefits of complementarity, the asynchronicity of combining multiple variable renewable energy sources, when awarding contracts, thereby limiting renewable energy project contracts (Hoicka and Rowlands 2011).

Energy project ownership and democracy

Another mechanism by which energy can be democratized is through a shift in ownership from corporate actors to a broader range of civil society and community groups. Ownership changes in the sector can take place either through the transfer of existing assets (which is relatively rare) or the development of new infrastructure by community actors (MacArthur 2016b; Creamer et al. 2018; Brisbois 2020). The literature on the characteristics, role and growth of "community energy" (CE) has traced how non-traditional energy actors have played important roles in the energy transitions in both Denmark and Germany (Viardot 2013; MacArthur 2016b). One reason for the appeal of CE is that local investment and decision-making in energy activities can increase support for project approval. Another is that it creates the potential for these projects to redistribute and recirculate profits for economic development, creating co-benefits in housing, health and local businesses. Today, community renewable energy is a growing movement internationally (REN21 2017). Diverse actors from Indigenous tribes and nations, non-profit associations, cooperatives, local authorities, community trusts and others have been actively involved in energy activities from renewable power generation to energy efficiency, transport electrification and power distribution and storage (Seyfang, Jin and Smith 2013; Martiskainen 2017; Hicks and Ison 2018; Wierling et al. 2018; Berka, MacArthur and Gonnelli 2020).

In recent years, a number of researchers have attempted to capture the nature and extent of energy democracy in various jurisdictions, particularly with reference to asset ownership by local communities and municipalities (Capellán-Pérez, Campos-Celador and Terés-Zubiaga 2018; Hicks and Ison 2018; Hoicka and MacArthur 2018; Van Veelen 2018). Canada provides one example. Data collection for this kind of research in Canada is challenging, as ownership data for energy assets across the sector is not collected by a single government agency or in a consistent way. For specific non-traditional actor types, like cooperatives, researchers rely on self-reported surveys, first under the remit of Agriculture and Agri-Food Canada, and now Industry Canada (since 2015; MacArthur et al. 2020). Despite the challenges, one of the most comprehensive efforts to capture the nature and scope of local energy ownership in Canada illustrates that more than 785 distinct energy projects owned by municipalities, cooperatives, non-profits, Indigenous communities and charitable organizations operate in Canada (Hoicka and MacArthur 2018). These projects are engaged in a wide range of activities that have significant implications for the shape and effectiveness of future energy transitions, from renewable power generation to distribution and energy demand management (Lipp, Tarhan and Dixon 2016; Hoicka and MacArthur 2018).

As with other forms of democratization, the results can be mixed in terms of how radical and extensive these shifts can be, and institutional structures, policy implementation and capacity play an important role (Hoffman and High-Pippert 2009; Devine-Wright 2019). Due to the deployment of the *Green Energy and Green Economy Act*, in the province of Ontario, Canada, a study found that the majority of renewable energy cooperatives were controlled by corporations and were not community-based (Tarhan 2020). Membership in cooperatives appeared to come from the environmental sector, made up of mostly white and wealthy individuals. This was because corporate cooperatives had more resources to contribute through their parent companies for project development, whereas grassroots cooperatives did not. Some grassroots cooperatives were sold to larger renewable energy cooperatives in order to gain better access to capacity and experience for project development and to address complex and time-consuming regulatory requirements, even though they had access to financial capital. Tarhan (2020) argues that in order to address inequities and inclusion, there needs to be more access to time, money and experience in order to promote community energy. A further crucial element is that of the development and existence of trust in local communities for the success of energy democracy initiatives (Wiersma and Devine-Wright 2014). On the one hand, projects can play a role in building new networks and coalitions; for example, between landowners, social movement and anchor institutions, and local authorities. On the other, local ownership is particularly important for First Nations and Indigenous Peoples for whom trust in governments and large external actors has long been in short supply due to colonization (MacArthur and Matthewman 2018).

Policy participation and grassroots activism as democracy

A third mechanism for increased energy democracy can be found in the opening up of policymaking processes to citizen participation and stakeholder involvement (see also MacArthur 2016a; 2016b) as well as grassroots activism and protest. While distinct, both focus on the activities of citizens to shape or reshape policymaking. Brisbois argues that energy action, both sanctioned and subversive, is rescaling toward local levels (Brisbois 2020). From the Fridays for Future school strikes to the Extinction Rebellion movement,, protest actors have long been involved in expressing frustration and placing pressure on elected bodies to adopt more radical energy policy reforms (Patterson et al. 2018; Sovacool et al. 2020).

Policy scholarship for more than three decades now has noted a "deliberative turn," with an enhanced focus for both instrumental and normative rationales to increase stakeholder participation (Gorter 2011; Johnson 2011; Wittmayer et al. 2019). Of course, the nature and content of this participation can vary significantly, from citizens' assemblies with broad and open-to-revision goals to much narrower, prescribed and "consultative" activities driven by state or corporate authorities. Both mark a shift away from closed elite decision-making and discussions, but the former does so in a much more robust way. The question of course is not just whether there is participation by citizens, but what forms does this take and with what effect (Fung and Wright 2003; Fung 2006; MacArthur 2015; Lennon et al. 2019). There is also a crucial scalar dimension to these processes: at municipal and regional levels there are increased opportunities for participation in decision-making, whereas at national and international levels this is more circumscribed (Cowell, Ellis Sherry-Brennan et al. 2017).

The language of stakeholder involvement together with practices of citizen consultation is certainly on the rise. For example, the US Department of Energy and the European Commission each provide guidelines that outline the importance of stakeholder involvement in the articulation of actions in local energy plans (Wyse and Hoicka 2019). In Canada, efforts to hold deliberative consultations on energy policy have taken place in some specific provincial settings, such as Nova Scotia (Johnson 2011), but even with this the historical legacy of public inclusion is one of tokenistic consultation rather than significant policy empowerment or co-production. The interpretation of who is a "stakeholder" is revealing, as these are more likely to be those with economic or geographic interests (such as industry executives), and in the latter a more diverse (but not necessarily inclusive or representative) range of citizens. Other findings from Canada reveal that citizens rarely participate in local energy plans prior to the articulation of actions, and plans subsequently do not strategically address community energy goals (Wyse and Hoicka 2019). Clearly just as with economic ownership, there are deeper socio-economic mechanisms at play that prevent an opportunity for power and input in theory from translating into power in practice (Wolsink 2012; Avelino et al. 2020).

Diversifying democratization

Just as the mechanisms of energy democracy differ, so to do the actors. A neutral characterization of power for "the people" ignores in many respects the stratification of distinct groups of people and the challenges that some groups disproportionately face (Bouzarovski and Tirado Herrero 2017; Lieu et al. 2020). Here we discuss three important elements of the demographics of democratization focusing on race, gender and class-based issues of equity and inclusion. While we fully acknowledge that an intersectional lens is essential, we present the specific issues found in three separate categories based on the best available information, which is just emerging for each. This section draws predominantly from Canadian source material, but many of the challenges are echoed across the globe so are not limited to one country.

Indigenous Peoples and energy democracy

Indigenous Peoples' experiences with energy have not been inherently positive, particularly in settler colonial contexts. In Aotearoa New Zealand, Canada, the United States and around the world, the energy sector has been involved in the seizure, use and devastation of traditional territories. For example, in Canada, Indigenous communities were not consulted when rivers and land were flooded by hydroelectric dams, destroying traditional hunting and fishing areas, camps, trails and travel routes, and burial and sacred sites (Coates 2016). For McGregor:

> global economic systems and their 'false solutions' aggressively undermine Indigenous peoples, in particular Indigenous women, in systemic, ongoing, and violent ways. It is therefore simply not rational for Indigenous peoples to rely on these global, national, and regional economic and political frameworks for climate justice and a sustainable future.
>
> *(2020, 37)*

In exploring the alignment of community energy with self-determination, Smith and Scott (2019) argue that "Settler colonialism continues to structure the broader set of relations in which RE [renewable energy] projects, even equity projects, are situated." The United Nations Declaration on the Rights of Indigenous Peoples (UNDRIP) outlines self-determination, control of traditional lands, and the importance of free, prior and informed consent (FPIC) in relation to any project on traditional land or land Indigenous People have rights to. These are outlined in Articles 26, 28, 29:

- Article 26: Indigenous peoples exercise the right to the territory to which they belong and all of the resources and have the right to use, develop and control these territories and resources.
- Article 28: Indigenous peoples exercise the right to redress with just, fair and equitable compensation for the lands, territories and resources that were confiscated, taken, occupied, used and damaged without our free, prior and informed consent.
- Article 29: Indigenous peoples exercise the right to the conservation and protection of the environment and the productive capacity of our lands, territories and resources. (United Nations 2008)

Indigenous communities are now seeking equity and control in renewable energy projects on their land (see LaDuke, this volume). Some Indigenous communities and organizations view equity ownership and control of renewable energy as reconciliation (Cameron 2020; Hickling 2020) and argue that projects are unlikely to go forward without involvement of Indigenous communities in pre-planning and planning stages, and partnerships (Bull 2020). Increased equity ownership is important for the increased delivery of social goods and local regional development; reduced ecological impacts; accelerated permit approvals; reduced risk/lower cost of capital (Hickling 2020); and long-term stable revenue (Cameron 2020). According to Chief Ken Cameron of Saulteau First Nations, Moberly Lake: "Ownership is the only type of reconciliation we understand; ownership and partnership" (Cameron 2020). For these reasons, there is a trend away from impact and benefit agreements, which are considered weak and short-lived, and toward Indigenous equity partnerships in renewable energy projects (Hickling 2020). However, despite some policy support, the majority of projects associated with Indigenous communities in Canada that are on traditional land have no Indigenous ownership or control. Of 194 projects found, only 41 were controlled by Indigenous communities (Hoicka et al., under review).

Kimberly Scott (2020), co-chair of Indigenous Clean Energy Social Enterprise in Canada, views community energy as a way to address SDGs, reconciliation and Canada's equity goals as increasing local and democratic decision-making power over profits, jobs and investments contributes to reconciliation. She argues that organizations that have a "moral authority" should be leading community energy. Whether they are structured under settler institutions or grassroots community initiatives, "moral authorities include any traditional governance or leadership entities such as clan mothers, Elders' councils, and Indigenous governance structures. Contemporary examples of Indigenous moral authority include women's and health organizations as well as some, but not all, Indigenous governance structures created under colonial rule (i.e., the *Indian Act*) that function with collective interest at heart" (Scott 2020).

Decolonization in the context of climate change is to assert Indigenous knowledge and legal systems that include the rights of nature (Bargh, Douglas and Te One 2014; MacArthur and Matthewman 2018; Mcgregor, Whitaker and Sritharan 2020). For example, in the case of the Batchewana First Nation's project, the Chinodin Chigumi Nodin Kitagan (Bow Lake Wind Farm), while the Nation is governed by a settler, colonial-imposed legal structure, the community was able to assert principles deriving from its own legal order into the approval process. For example, more stringent environmental regulations than settler legislation are required. They were also able to arrange a less hierarchical legal structure by developing a community trust; the structure and spending were based on participatory community consultations. The institutional support of the Aboriginal Price Adder set up by the Province of Ontario specifically encouraged equity ownership.

Gender and energy democracy

Women's leadership is considered critical in a democratic renewable energy transformation (Allen, Lyons and Stephens 2019; Roberts-Gregory, Chapter 9, this volume). Gender diversity is about securing a wider, deeper talent pool to address our climate crisis (IRENA 2019), and gender diversity enhances innovation and creativity (Duguid 2007; Pearl-Martinez and Stephens 2016; Perkins 2017). The gender employment gap in energy industries is significant, and studies exploring women's experiences in the clean energy sector are sparse (Baruah 2017), and even less prevalent for gender-diverse or LGBTQ2S persons. Similar data gaps exist on the employment of people of color, but what has been published on the solar industry in the United States, for example, shows that Black Americans (8%) and women (26%) are underrepresented in solar industry employment compared to their overall share of the working population (women by a much larger amount), while Asian Americans were represented at a higher rate (The Solar Foundation 2019, 58). Global data on renewable energy employment addresses the issue of gender equity but does not mention racial diversity or the issue of unionization in energy industries anywhere (IRENA 2020b).

The latest research in this area shows that 19% of jobs in the energy industry overall go to women globally, but they work disproportionately in office support or administrative jobs;

the economic implications of gendered income gaps during working years spill from current earnings into broader challenges such as retirement pension savings and elder poverty (World Economic Forum 2016; Pacheco, Chao and Cochrane 2017). The renewable energy sector is projected to increase significantly, with the total number of jobs growing from 7 million in 2012 to 10.3 million in 2017 and an anticipated 29 million in 2050 (IRENA 2020a). According to a recent report by the Brookings Institution, clean energy jobs are generally better paid than other jobs in the US economy (by 8 to19%) but lack demographic diversity, skewing older, male and white (Muro et al. 2019).

Women make up only 32% of the global renewable energy workforce (IRENA 2019). There are also significant gendered employment patterns between subsectors. Recent research by MacArthur and Dyer in the New Zealand context found that the gender gap in employment as of 2019 was strongest in electricity distribution and oil and gas exploration employment, and smallest in fuel retailing (gas stations) and electricity retailing (2021). It also found that in some subsectors the share of women being hired in new jobs, even in growth areas, hasn't changed in more than two decades. They found a similar pattern in terms of a largely white (or pākeha) workforce as well as significantly above-average wages compared to the economy more broadly.

A 2017 survey attributed these gender gaps internationally to: a lack of understanding about the range of occupations and opportunities, a limited number of visible female role models, a male-dominated industry culture, (un)conscious biases of women's roles, and a lack of family-friendly policies and culture (Electricity Human Resources Canada 2017).

The International Renewable Energy Agency (IRENA) (2019) has recently identified ways to equitably engage women. First, "mainstreaming" gender across all clean energy frameworks is critical, which includes policies, programs, practices and a gendered analysis of data collection. Second, tailored training and skills development is needed rather than a one-size-fits-all approach. Third, attracting and retaining talented women can be achieved through responsive policies such as parental leaves and flexible working hours and conditions. Finally, and perhaps most importantly, is to structurally create a culture, and demonstrate through role modeling, a set of social norms that illustrates how gender diversity is valued in the workplace.

There are a number of mechanisms that can be leveraged to promote an equitable and more democratic energy transition. These include, the Equal by 30 Campaign: Equal Pay, Equal Leadership, Equal Opportunities, a joint Clean Energy Ministerial and IEA initiative prioritizing both SDGs 5 and 7 through existing frameworks, policies and programs (Electricity Human Resources Canada 2017; Williams et al. 2018). Two international networks of women in energy employment as well as women and non-binary people working in energy research are: Women in Renewable Energy (WiRE) and Women and Inclusivity in Sustainable Energy Research (WISER) Network (WiRE 2020; WISER 2020). Many more are developing globally as research begins to reveal just how large and persistent the employment gaps are for women.

Poverty and energy democracy

The importance of energy consumption to well-being is known (Day, Walker and Simcock 2016). However, beginning mostly in the 1980s, concerns over the "under-consumption" of energy started receiving more attention from researchers, policymakers and the general public (Day et al. 2016). Recent research finds millions of people, including those living in industrialized nations, to be energy-poor (Bouzarovski, Petrova and Sarlamanov 2012).

Consensus is lacking on strict definitions of energy poverty (Moore 2012). However, there is general agreement that energy poverty refers to an inability to attain necessary levels of domestic services for social and material needs (Bouzarovski and Petrova 2015).

In lower-income countries, energy poverty is associated with lacking access to electricity (Nussbaumer, Bazilian and Modi 2012), whereas in higher-income countries energy poverty is usually connected to high energy costs, low household income or inefficient housing (Boardman 2012). In fact, derived from seminal research, the dominant benchmark for energy poverty appears to be connected to a situation wherein households need to spend more than 10% of their income on maintaining comfortable indoor temperatures (Boardman 1991). According to Canada's independent federal energy regulator, the Canada Energy Regulator (CER) (formerly known as the National Energy Board), "a household may be described as experiencing [energy] poverty when it spends more than 10% of its income on utilities" (National Energy Board 2017). Consequently, the CER estimates 8% of households in Canada to be experiencing energy poverty.

Energy poverty, however, is importantly being recognized not solely as a technical or economic problem, but one that is also social (Baker, Mould and Restrick 2018). Certain demographic groups may be predisposed to higher levels of vulnerability by virtue of their social, family or housing arrangements (Dubois and Meier 2016; Bouzarovski and Tirado Herrero 2017; Robinson, Bouzarovski and Lindley 2018). For example, retirees who spend more time at home or families with young children can have higher end-use energy demands (Roberts 2008; Yohanis 2012; Das and Martiskaïnen 2018). Similarly, energy use can be viewed as a social practice such that the need for energy services is dynamic, variable and dependent on being able to engage in everyday practices stemming from culture, customs and shared conventions, such as showering versus bathing, or cooking a traditional meal (Shove 2003; Gram-Hanssen 2011).

The consequences of energy poverty have been linked to mental health impacts, social stress, reduced emotional resiliency and learning impediments in children (Liddell and Morris 2010; Dear and McMichael 2011; O'Sullivan et al. 2017). Physical health impacts associated with inadequate indoor temperatures have also been reported and linked to excess deaths, cases of asthma, respiratory problems, arthritis and rheumatism (Wright 2004; Rudge and Gilchrist 2005; Hernández and Bird 2010; Heyman, Harrington and Heyman 2011; Ormandy and Ezratty 2012).

Energy poverty research is currently at a pivotal point given the manner in which energy transitioning and its associated strategies, such as energy and climate change policies, can impact the everyday lives of people. In particular, policies attempting to disincentivize energy use and reduce greenhouse gas emissions can "disproportionally" impact marginalized groups (Teelucksingh et al. 2016). For example, a carbon tax on fuel has the potential to negatively impact new immigrants who live in low-income suburbs by constraining them to drive older, less fuel-efficient cars to several part-time jobs (Teelucksingh et al. 2016). In contrast, wealthier downtown residents in urban centers are more likely able to go without owning a car by virtue of their financial circumstances and thus their ability to live in walkable cities with adequate public transportation (Teelucksingh et al. 2016). Further, climate change policies that increase household energy bills can be regressive if they do not protect low-income customers. On the other hand, policies that simply reimburse customers may lead to more carbon emissions (Fitzpatrick 2011).

The movement for energy democracy has emphasized the need for voices previously not heard, including the energy-poor, not only to be heard, but to be invited into the conversations regarding inequities associated with energy use and just transitions.

Conclusion

Green New Deal plans often make bold promises for energy transitions, including the phasing out of fossil fuels, creation of decent (and sometimes inclusive) employment, and economies fit for the twenty-first century. Hundreds of billions of dollars in new infrastructure investment will be directed at the creation of local microgrids as well as supergrids to move large amounts of new renewable power (Mazzucato and McPherson 2018; Rifkin 2019). Jobs in the energy sector overall are projected to grow to 100 million by 2050, with an estimated 42 million of these in renewables (IRENA 2020b: 100). These developments provide huge opportunities, but no guarantees.

As pressure increases to develop new renewable energy infrastructure, tensions are likely to arise over the location and ownership of these assets (Walker, Stephenson and Baxter 2018; Brisbois 2020). Decentralized infrastructures will mean that many more local areas are going to be confronted by the physical, social and financial impacts of an energy transition (Bridge et al. 2013). Energy democracy is theorized to help facilitate energy transitions and energy justice through enhancing the social support for new infrastructures, distributing the costs (and benefits) more equitably, and improving informational exchange and bottom-up learning by industry and policy actors. Potential for positive change through both the overarching research agenda of energy democracy as well as through the social movement exists (Szulecki 2018; Feldpausch-Parker, Endres and Peterson 2019).

Energy democracy may advance transitions and approaches to sustainability from simple reform (or recovery) to a more revolutionary reconfiguration in which deep structural societal shifts occur (Geels et al. 2015). In part, this is because new actor networks are required to spur and push for particular transition pathways (Betsill and Stevis 2016; Patterson et al. 2018; Hurlbert et al. 2019). In Canada to date, the majority of renewable energy projects with Indigenous involvement are in British Columbia, Ontario and Quebec, but not often accompanied by significant project control (Savic and Hoicka 2021). Research on energy cooperatives and community ownership more broadly in Canada has also shown that there are more developments than many might first suspect, but they are plagued with a range of challenges, pressure to corporatize and prohibitive start-up costs (MacArthur 2016b; Tarhan 2015). Similarly, Canadian local energy plans have struggled to engage with participatory and inclusive processes (Wyse and Hoicka 2019).

Structural shifts to address these gaps are essential. Decades of centralized and elite-dominated energy institutions are deeply rooted in industry networks, policy processes, and ideas about the economic, social and environmental roles that energy has in modern society (Oreskes and Conway 2010; Breetz, Mildenberger and Stokes 2018; Carter 2020). Transitions scholars have identified targeted policy designs as essential to reorganizing socio-technical systems, and these are likely to be resisted by powerful incumbent actors, so both bottom-up and top-down mobilization is essential (Jenkins, Sovacool and McCauley 2018; Köhler et al. 2019). State sponsorship of new fossil fuel infrastructure, like the Keystone XL or Transmountain pipelines, has illustrated just how contested the energy transition terrain is, with powerful actors and a diverse array of voices opposing such projects.

Just as local buy-in is crucial for social acceptance and legitimacy of technological shifts, significant policy efforts will be required to address issues of democracy, redistribution and justice. As McGregor (2020, 35) argues, "Not only do current global, national and local systems of governance and law fail Indigenous Peoples, they fail all life," Bringing together the discourses of Green New Deal and Green Recovery with a conceptualization of energy democracy attendant to inclusive actors and processes is thus important. GND proposals that lack a significant component of democratization are unlikely to be deeply transformative and more likely to reproduce (or even intensify) existing socio-economic cleavages (Aronoff et al. 2019). This politicization of Green New Deal approaches will bring significant conflict, but it is difficult to see how the level and pace of decarbonization required today are possible without it.

Note

1 This chapter draws from MacArthur, J.L., C.E. Hoicka, H. Castleden, R.Das, J. Lieu 2020. "Canada's Green New Deal: Forging the Socio-Political Foundations of Climate Resilient Infrastructure?" Energy Research & Social Science 65 (July). Available from: https://doi.org/10.1016/J.ERSS.2020.101442

References

Allen, E., Lyons, H. and Stephens, J.C. 2019. "Women's Leadership in Renewable Transformation, Energy Justice and Energy Democracy: Redistributing Power." *Energy Research & Social Science* 57. Available from: https://doi.org/10.1016/j.erss.2019.101233.

Aronoff, K. et al. 2019. *A Planet to Win: Why We Need a Green New Deal*. New York: Verso.

Aşıcı, A.A. and Bünül, Z. 2012. "Green New Deal: A Green Way out of the Crisis?" *Environmental Policy and Governance* 22(5): 295–306. Available from: https://doi.org/10.1002/eet.1594.

Avelino, F. et al. 2020. "Translocal Empowerment in Transformative Social Innovation Networks." *European Planning Studies* 28(5): 955–977. Available from: https://doi.org/10.1080/09654313.2019.1578339.

Baker, K.J., Mould, R. and Restrick, S. 2018. "Rethink Fuel Poverty as a Complex Problem." *Nature Energy* 3(8): 610–612. Available from: https://doi.org/10.1038/s41560-018-0204-2.

Bargh, M., Douglas, S-L. and Te One, A. 2014. "Fostering Sustainable Tribal Economies in a Time of Climate Change." *New Zealand Geographer* 70(2): 103–115. Available from: https://doi.org/10.1111/nzg.12042.

Baruah, B. 2017. "Renewable Inequity? Women's Employment in Clean Energy in Industrialized, Emerging and Developing Economies." *Natural Resources Forum* 41: 18–29. Available from: https://doi.org/10.1111/1477-8947.12105.

Berka, A.L. and Creamer, E. 2018. "Taking Stock of the Local Impacts of Community Owned Renewable Energy: A Review and Research Agenda." *Renewable and Sustainable Energy Reviews* 82(February): 3400–3419. Available from: https://doi.org/10.1016/J.RSER.2017.10.050.

Berka, A.L., MacArthur, J.L. and Gonnelli, C. 2020. "Explaining Inclusivity in Energy Transitions: Local and Community Energy in Aotearoa New Zealand." *Environmental Innovation and Societal Transitions* 34: 165–182.

Betsill, M. and Stevis, D. 2016. "The Politics and Dynamics of Energy Transitions: Lessons from Colorado's (USA) 'New Energy Economy.'" *Environment and Planning C: Government and Policy* 34: 381–396. Available from: https://doi.org/10.1177/0263774X15614668.

Boardman, B. 1991. *Fuel Poverty: From Cold Homes to Affordable Warmth*. London: Bellhaven.

Boardman, B. 2012. "Fuel Poverty Synthesis: Lessons Learnt, Actions Needed." *Energy Policy* 49(October): 143–148. Available from: https://doi.org/10.1016/j.enpol.2012.02.035.

Bouzarovski, S and Petrova, S. 2015. "A Global Perspective on Domestic Energy Deprivation: Overcoming the Energy Poverty-Fuel Poverty Binary." *Energy Research & Social Science* 10: 31–40. Available from: https://doi.org/10.1016/j.erss.2015.06.007.

Bouzarovski, S., Petrova, S. and Sarlamanov, R. 2012. "Energy Poverty Policies in the EU: A Critical Perspective." *Energy Policy* 49: 76–82. Available from: https://doi.org/10.1016/j.enpol.2012.01.033.

Bouzarovski, S. and Tirado Herrero, S. 2017. "Geographies of Injustice: The Socio-Spatial Determinants of Energy Poverty in Poland, the Czech Republic and Hungary." *Post-Communist Economies* 29(1): 27–50. Available from: https://doi.org/10.1080/14631377.2016.1242257.

Breetz, H., Mildenberger, M. and Stokes, L. 2018. "The Political Logics of Clean Energy Transitions." *Business and Politics* 20(4): 492–522. Available from: https://doi.org/10.1017/bap.2018.14.

Bridge, G. et al. 2013. "Geographies of Energy Transition: Space, Place and the Low-Carbon Economy." *Energy Policy* 53: 331–340. Available from: https://doi.org/10.1016/j.enpol.2012.10.066.

Brisbois, M.C. 2019. "Powershifts: A Framework for Assessing the Growing Impact of Decentralized Ownership of Energy Transitions on Political Decision-Making." *Energy Research & Social Science* 50(April): 151–161. Available from: https://doi.org/10.1016/j.erss.2018.12.003.

Brisbois, M.C. 2020. "Rescaling, Reorganization and Battles for Influence: Shifting Political Power in an Era of Electricity Decentralization." *Environmental Innovation and Societal Transitions* 36(September): 49–69. Available from: https://doi.org/10.1016/j.eist.2020.04.007.

Bull, T. 2020. "Indigenous Green Energy: Policy and Finance for a Sustainable Future." In *Post-Pandemic Opportunities for a Sustainable Society*. Vancouver, BC: Canadian Climate Law Initiative. https://allard.ubc.ca/about-us/events-calendar/post-pandemic-opportunities-sustainable-society-e-conference.

Burke, M.J. and Stephens, J.C. 2018. "Political Power and Renewable Energy Futures: A Critical Review." *Energy Research & Social Science* 35(January): 78–93. Available from: https://doi.org/10.1016/J.ERSS.2017.10.018.

Buth, M.C., Wieczorek, A.J. and Verbong, G.P.J. 2019. "The Promise of Peer-to-Peer Trading? The Potential Impact of Blockchain on the Actor Configuration in the Dutch Electricity System." *Energy Research & Social Science* 53(July): 194–205. Available from: https://doi.org/10.1016/j.erss.2019.02.021.

Cameron, K. 2020. "Indigenous Green Energy: Policy and Finance for a Sustainable Future." In *Post-Pandemic Opportunities for a Sustainable Society*. Vancouver, BC: Canadian Climate Law Initiative. https://allard.ubc.ca/about-us/events-calendar/post-pandemic-opportunities-sustainable-society-e-conference.

Capellán-Pérez, I., Campos-Celador, A. and Terés-Zubiaga, J. 2018. "Renewable Energy Cooperatives as an Instrument towards the Energy Transition in Spain." *Energy Policy*. Available from: https://doi.org/10.1016/j.enpol.2018.08.064.

Carter, A. 2020. *Fossilized: Environmental Policy in Canada's Petro Provinces*. Vancouver: UBC Press.

Coates, K. 2016. "First Nations Engagement in the Energy Sector in Western Canada." Tsuu T'ina Nation, Alberta. Available from: http://www.irccanada.ca/sites/default/files/First Nations Engagement in the Energy Sector in Western Canada.pdf.

Cowell, R. et al. 2017. "Sub-National Government and Pathways to Sustainable Energy." *Environment and Planning C: Politics and Space* 35(7): 1139–1155. Available from: https://doi.org/10.1177/2399654417730359.

Creamer, E. et al. 2018. "Community Energy: Entanglements of Community, State, and Private Sector." *Geography Compass* June. Available from: https://doi.org/10.1111/gec3.12378.

Das, R. and Martiskaïnen, M. 2018. "Energy Deprivation in Everyday Living: Estimating, Profiling, and Escaping Energy Poverty in Canada." SPRU-Science Policy Research Unit Current Projects. 2018. Available from: http://www.sussex.ac.uk/spru/research/projects/energy-poverty-canada.

Day, R., Walker, G. and Simcock, N. 2016. "Conceptualising Energy Use and Energy Poverty Using a Capabilities Framework." *Energy Policy* 93(June): 255–264. Available from: https://doi.org/10.1016/j.enpol.2016.03.019.

Dear, K.B.G. and McMichael, A.J. 2011. "The Health Impacts of Cold Homes and Fuel Poverty." *BMJ* 342. British Medical Journal Publishing Group. Available from: https://doi.org/10.1136/bmj.d2807.

Devine-Wright, P. 2019. "Community versus Local Energy in a Context of Climate Emergency." *Nature Energy*. Available from: https://doi.org/10.1038/s41560-019-0459-2.

Dixon, T., Lannon, S. and Eames, M. 2018. "Reflections on Disruptive Energy Innovation in Urban Retrofitting: Methodology, Practice and Policy." *Energy Research & Social Science* 37(March): 255–259. Available from: https://doi.org/10.1016/j.erss.2017.10.009.

Dubois, U. and Meier, H. 2016. "Energy Affordability and Energy Inequality in Europe: Implications for Policymaking." *Energy Research & Social Science* 18: 21–35. Available from: https://doi.org/10.1016/j.erss.2016.04.015.

Duguid, F. 2007. "Part of the Solution: Developing Sustainable Energy through Co-Operatives and Learning." *OISE*. PhD Dissertation, University of Toronto, Toronto.

Eames, M. and Hunt, M. 2013. "Energy Justice in Sustainability Transitions Research." In Bickerstaff, K, G. Walker, H. Bulkeley (eds) *Energy Justice in a Changing Climate*. London: Zed Books. 46–50.

Electricity Human Resources Canada. 2017. "Profile of Women Working in the Clean Energy Sector in Canada. Final Report." Available from: https://www.nrcan.gc.ca/sites/www.nrcan.gc.ca/files/energy/energy-resources/Profile_of_Women_Working_in_the_Clean_Energy_Sector_in_Canada_compressed.pdf.

Feldpausch-Parker, A.M., Endres, D. and Peterson, T.R. 2019. "Editorial: A Research Agenda for Energy Democracy." *Frontiers in Communication* 4(October): 53. Available from: https://doi.org/10.3389/fcomm.2019.00053.

Fitzpatrick, T. 2011. *Understanding the Environment and Social Policy*. Bristol, UK: Policy Press.

Fung, A. 2006. "Varieties of Participation in Complex Governance." *Public Administration Review* December 2: 66–75.

Fung, A. and Wright, E.O. 2003. *Deepening Democracy: Institutional Innovations in Empowered Participatory Governance. Real Utopias Project*. London: Verso.

Geels, F.W. et al. 2015. "A Critical Appraisal of Sustainable Consumption and Production Research: The Reformist, Revolutionary and Reconfiguration Positions." *Global Environmental Change* 34(September): 1–12. Available from: https://doi.org/10.1016/j.gloenvcha.2015.04.013.

Gorter, R. 2011. "Towards Deliberative Environmental Governance: Rethinking Participation." University of Auckland.

Gram-Hanssen, K. 2011. "Understanding Change and Continuity in Residential Energy Consumption." *Journal of Consumer Culture* 11(1): 61–78. Available from: https://doi.org/10.1177/1469540510391725.

Grant, J. 2018. "Renewables: Bridging the US Energy Security Gap." *American Foreign Policy Council, Defense Dossier*, no. 23. Available from: https://www.afpc.org/publications/e-journals/resource-security-and-changing-global-environmental-conditions.

Hahn, D. and Viet Nam Energy Environment Climate. 2019. "Solar Power Development in Viet Nam." In *Achieving the NDCs through Energy Transition Acceleration, COP 25*. Madrid: UNFCCC. Retrieved from Twitter: https://twitter.com/cehoicka/status/1202658280679624706/photo/3.

Heenan, N. and Sturman, A. 2020. "Five Orientations to the Green New Deal." Progress in Political Economy, March 30 2020. Available at: https://www.ppesydney.net/5-orientations-to-the-green-new-deal/

Hernández, D. and Bird, S. 2010. "Energy Burden and the Need for Integrated Low-Income Housing and Energy Policy." *Poverty & Public Policy* 2(4): 668–688. Available from: https://doi.org/10.2202/1944-2858.1095.

Hertzke, P. et al. 2019. "Expanding Electric-Vehicle Adoption despite Early Growing Pains." *McKinsey & Company*. August.

Heyman, B., Harrington, B. and Heyman, A. 2011. "A Randomised Controlled Trial of an Energy Efficiency Intervention for Families Living in Fuel Poverty." *Housing Studies* 26(1): 117–132. Available from: https://doi.org/10.1080/02673037.2010.512787.

Hickling, J. 2020. "Indigenous Green Energy: Policy and Finance for a Sustainable Future." In *Post-Pandemic Opportunities for a Sustainable Society*. Vancouver: Canadian Climate Law Initiative.

Hicks, J. and Ison, N. 2018. "An Exploration of the Boundaries of 'Community' in Community Renewable Energy Projects: Navigating between Motivations and Context." *Energy Policy* 113(February): 523–534. Available from: https://doi.org/10.1016/j.enpol.2017.10.031.

Hoffman, S.M. and High-Pippert, A. 2009. "Community Energy: A Social Architecture for an Alternative Energy Future." *Bulletin of Science, Technology & Society* 25(5): 387–401. Available from: https://doi.org/https://doi.org/10.1177/0270467605278880.

Hoicka, C.E. and Das, R. 2020. "Ambitious Deep Energy Retrofits of Buildings to Accelerate the 1.5°C Energy Transition in Canada." *The Canadian Geographer/Le Géographe Canadien*. June. cag.12637. Available from: https://doi.org/10.1111/cag.12637.

Hoicka, C.E. and MacArthur, J.L. 2018. "From Tip to Toes: Mapping Community Energy Models in Canada and New Zealand." *Energy Policy* 121: 162–174. Available from: https://doi.org/https://doi.org/10.1016/j.enpol.2018.06.002.

Hoicka, C.E. and MacArthur, J.L. 2019. "The Infrastructure for Electricity: A Technical Overview." In K. Hancock and J. Allison, eds. *Oxford Handbook of Energy Politics*. [online] New York: Oxford University Press. Available from: https://doi.org/10.1093/oxfordhb/9780190861360.013.33.

Hoicka, C.E. and Rowlands, I.H. 2011. "Solar and Wind Resource Complementarity: Advancing Options for Renewable Electricity Integration in Ontario, Canada." *Renewable Energy* 36(1): 97–107. Available from: https://doi.org/10.1016/j.renene.2010.06.004.

Hurlbert, M. et al. 2019. "Transitioning from Coal: Toward a Renewables-Based Socio-Technical Regime in Saskatchewan." *Environmental Innovation and Societal Transitions*. Available from: https://doi.org/https://doi.org/10.1016/j.eist.2019.11.005.

IRENA. 2019. "Renewable Energy: A Gender Perspective." Abu Dhabi. Available from: https://irena.org/-/media/Files/IRENA/Agency/Publication/2019/Jan/IRENA_Gender_perspective_2019.pdf

IRENA. 2020a. "Global Renewables Outlook: Energy Transformation 2050." Abu Dhabi. Available from: https://www.irena.org/-/media/Files/IRENA/Agency/Publication/2020/Apr/IRENA_Global_Renewables_Outlook_2020.pdf

IRENA. 2020b. "Renewable Energy and Jobs – Annual Review 2020." Abu Dhabi. Available from: https://www.irena.org/-/media/Files/IRENA/Agency/Publication/2020/Sep/IRENA_RE_Jobs_2020.pdf

Islam, S. 2017. "Challenges and Opportunities in Grid Connected Commercial Scale PV and Wind Farms." *Proceedings of 9th International Conference on Electrical and Computer Engineering, ICECE 2016*, 1–7. Available from: https://doi.org/10.1109/ICECE.2016.7853843.

Isser, M. 2020. "Why Every Job in the Renewable Energy Industry Must Be a Union Job." *In These Times*. 3 September. Available from: https://inthesetimes.com/article/renewable-energy-industry-union-jobs-climate-labor-green-new-deal-environmentalism.

Jenkins, K., Sovacool, B.K. and McCauley, D. 2018. "Humanizing Sociotechnical Transitions through Energy Justice: An Ethical Framework for Global Transformative Change." *Energy Policy* 117(March): 66–74. Available from: https://doi.org/10.1016/j.enpol.2018.02.036.

Johnson, G.F. 2011. "The Limits of Deliberative Democracy and Empowerment: Elite Motivation in Three Canadian Cases." *Canadian Journal of Political Science* 44(1): 137–159.

Johnstone, P. et al. 2020. "Waves of Disruption in Clean Energy Transitions: Sociotechnical Dimensions of System Disruption in Germany and the United Kingdom." *Energy Research & Social Science* 59(January): 101287. Available from: https://doi.org/10.1016/j.erss.2019.101287.

Judson, E. et al. 2020. "De-Centralisation, The Centre Cannot (Always) Hold: Examining Pathways towards Energy System." *Renewable and Sustainable Energy Reviews* 118(February): 109499. Available from: https://doi.org/10.1016/j.rser.2019.109499.

Köhler, J. et al. 2019. "An Agenda for Sustainability Transitions Research: State of the Art and Future Directions." *Environmental Innovation and Societal Transitions* 31(June): 1–32. Available from: https://doi.org/10.1016/J.EIST.2019.01.004.

Kuzemko, C. et al. 2016. "Governing for Sustainable Energy System Change: Politics, Contexts and Contingency." *Energy Research & Social Science* 12(February): 96–105. Available from: https://doi.org/10.1016/J.ERSS.2015.12.022.

Kuzemko, C. et al. 2017. "Policies, Politics and Demand Side Innovations: The Untold Story of Germany's Energy Transition." *Energy Research & Social Science* 28(February): 58–67. Available from: https://doi.org/10.1016/J.ERSS.2017.03.013.

Lam, D.P.M. et al. 2020. "Scaling the Impact of Sustainability Initiatives: A Typology of Amplification Processes." *Urban Transformations* 2(1): 3. Available from: https://doi.org/10.1186/s42854-020-00007-9.

Lennon, B. et al. 2019. "Citizen or Consumer? Reconsidering Energy Citizenship." *Journal of Environmental Policy & Planning* 22(2): 1–14. Available from: https://doi.org/10.1080/1523908X.2019.1680277.

Lennon, B., Dunphy, N.P. and Sanvicente, E. 2019. "Community Acceptability and the Energy Transition: A Citizens' Perspective." *Energy, Sustainability and Society* 9(1): 35. Available from: https://doi.org/10.1186/s13705-019-0218-z.

Liddell, C. and Morris, C. 2010. "Fuel Poverty and Human Health: A Review of Recent Evidence." *Energy Policy* 38(6): 2987–2997. Available from: https://doi.org/10.1016/j.enpol.2010.01.037.

Lieu, J. et al. 2020. "Three Sides to Every Story: Gender Perspectives in Energy Transition Pathways in Canada, Kenya and Spain." *Energy Research & Social Science* 68(October): 101550. Available from: https://doi.org/10.1016/J.ERSS.2020.101550.

Lipp, J., Tarhan, M.D. and Dixon, A. 2016. "Accelerating Renewable Energy Co-Operatives in Canada: A Review of Experiences and Lessons." Available from: http://canada.coop/sites/canada.coop/files/files/documents/en/2016_coop-arecc_report_final_screen.pdf.

Lowitzsch, J., Hoicka, C.E. and van Tulder, F.J. 2020. "Renewable Energy Communities under the 2019 European Clean Energy Package – Governance Model for the Energy Clusters of the Future?" *Renewable and Sustainable Energy Reviews* 122(April). Available from: https://doi.org/10.1016/j.rser.2019.109489.

McGregor, D., Whitaker, S. and Sritharan, M. 2020. "Indigenous environmental justice and sustainability." *Current Opinion in Environmental Sustainability* 43(April): 35–40. Available from: doi: 10.1016/j.cosust.2020.01.007.

MacArthur, J.L. 2016a. "Challenging Public Engagement: Participation, Deliberation and Power in Renewable Energy Policy." *Journal of Environmental Studies and Sciences* 6(September): 631–640. Available from: https://doi.org/10.1007/s13412-015-0328-7.

MacArthur, J.L. 2016b. *Empowering Electricity: Co-Operatives, Sustainability, and Power Sector Reform in Canada*. Vancouver: UBC Press.
MacArthur, J. L, and C. Dyer. 2021. "Transition Inequity: Gendered Employment Trends in New Zealand's Energy Industries." *Policy Quarterly* 17 (3): 31–38. Available at: https://ojs.victoria.ac.nz › issue › download
MacArthur, J.L. and Matthewman, S. 2018. "Populist Resistance and Alternative Transitions: Indigenous Ownership of Energy Infrastructure in Aotearoa New Zealand." *Energy Research & Social Science* 43(January): 16–24. Available from: https://doi.org/10.1016/j.erss.2018.05.009.
MacArthur, J.L. et al. 2020. "Canada's Green New Deal: Forging the Socio-Political Foundations of Climate Resilient Infrastructure?" *Energy Research & Social Science* 65(July). Available from: https://doi.org/10.1016/J.ERSS.2020.101442.
Mancarella, P. 2014. "MES (Multi-Energy Systems): An Overview of Concepts and Evaluation Models." *Energy* 65(February): 1–17. Available from: https://doi.org/10.1016/j.energy.2013.10.041.
Martinot, E. 2016. "Grid Integration of Renewable Energy: Flexibility, Innovation, and Experience." *Annual Review of Environment and Resources* 41(1): 223–251. Available from: https://doi.org/10.1146/annurev-environ-110615-085725.
Martiskainen, M. 2017. "The Role of Community Leadership in the Development of Grassroots Innovations." *Environmental Innovation and Societal Transitions* 22(March): 78–89. Available from: https://doi.org/10.1016/J.EIST.2016.05.002.
Mazzucato, M. and McPherson, M. 2018. "The Green New Deal: A Bold Mission-Oriented Approach." London.
Mcgregor, D., Whitaker, S. and Sritharan, M. 2020. "Indigenous Environmental Justice and Sustainability." *Current Opinion in Environmental Sustainability* 43: 35–40. Available from: https://doi.org/10.1016/j.cosust.2020.01.007.
Moore, R. 2012. "Definitions of Fuel Poverty: Implications for Policy." *Energy Policy* 49(October): 19–26. Available from: https://doi.org/10.1016/j.enpol.2012.01.057.
Muro, M. et al. 2019. "Advancing Inclusion through Clean Energy Jobs." New York. Available from: https://www.brookings.edu/wp-content/uploads/2019/04/2019.04_metro_Clean-Energy-Jobs_Report_Muro-Tomer-Shivaran-Kane_updated.pdf.
National Energy Board. 2017. "Market Snapshot: Fuel Poverty across Canada – Lower Energy Efficiency in Lower Income Households." Available from: https://www.cer-rec.gc.ca/nrg/ntgrtd/mrkt/snpsht/2017/08-05flpvrt-eng.html?=undefined&wbdisable=true.
Nussbaumer, P., Bazilian, M. and Modi, V. 2012. "Measuring Energy Poverty: Focusing on What Matters." *Renewable and Sustainable Energy Reviews* 16(1): 231–243. Available from: https://doi.org/10.1016/j.rser.2011.07.150.
O'Brien, H. 2019. "How the Green New Deal Was Born." *New Statesman*. 24 September. Available from: https://www.newstatesman.com/politics/environment/2019/09/how-green-new-deal-was-born.
Oreskes, N. and Conway, E. 2010. *Merchants of Doubt*. New York: Bloomsbury Academic.
Ormandy, D. and Ezratty, V. 2012. "Health and Thermal Comfort: From WHO Guidance to Housing Strategies." *Energy Policy* 49(October): 116–121. Available from: https://doi.org/10.1016/j.enpol.2011.09.003.
O'Sullivan, K.C. et al. 2017. "Cool? Young People Investigate Living in Cold Housing and Fuel Poverty. A Mixed Methods Action Research Study." *SSM – Population Health* 3(December): 66–74. Available from: https://doi.org/10.1016/j.ssmph.2016.12.006.
Pacheco, G., Chao, L. and Cochrane, B. 2017. "Empirical Evidence of the Gender Pay Gap in New Zealand." Wellington, New Zealand.
Pasqualetti, M.J. 2012. "Reading the Changing Energy Landscape." In S. Stremke and A. van den Dobbelsteen, eds. *Sustainable Energy Landscapes. Designing, Planning and Development*. New York: CRC Press, Taylor & Francis Group. pp. 11–44. Available from: http://ebookcentral.proquest.com/lib/york/reader.action?docID=1019592&ppg=31.
Patterson, J.J. et al. 2018. "Political Feasibility of 1.5°C Societal Transformations: The Role of Social Justice." *Current Opinion in Environmental Sustainability* 31(April): 1–9. Available from: https://doi.org/10.1016/J.COSUST.2017.11.002.
Pearl-Martinez, R. and Stephens, J.C. 2016. "Toward a Gender Diverse Workforce in the Renewable Energy Transition." *Sustainability: Science, Practice, and Policy* 12(1): 8–15.
Perkins, P E. 2017. "Canadian Indigenous Female Leadership and Political Agency on Climate Change." In M. Cohen (ed.) *Climate Change and Gender in Rich Countries: Work, Public Policy and Action*. London: Routledge, 282–296.

Pettifor, A. 2019. *The Case for the Green New Deal.* London: Verso Press.

Pollitt, H. 2020. "Green Recovery Plans More Effective than Return-to-Normal Stimulus – Cambridge Econometrics." Cambridge, UK. Available from: https://www.camecon.com/news/green-recovery-plans-more-effective-than-return-to-normal-stimulus/.

Ramirez Camargo, L. and Stoeglehner, G. 2018. "Spatiotemporal Modelling for Integrated Spatial and Energy Planning." *Energy, Sustainability and Society* 8(1): 1–29. Available from: https://doi.org/10.1186/s13705-018-0174-z.

REN21. 2017. *Renewables Global Futures Report: Great Debates towards 100% Renewable Energy.* Paris: Renewable Energy Policy Network.

Rifkin, J. 2019. *The Green New Deal.* New York: St. Martin's Press.

Risso, A., Beluco, A. and De Cássia Marques Alves, R. 2018. "Complementarity Roses Evaluating Spatial Complementarity in Time between Energy Resources." *Energies* 11(7): 1–14. Available from: https://doi.org/10.3390/en11071918.

Roberts, S. 2008. "Energy, Equity and the Future of the Fuel Poor." *Energy Policy* 36(12): 4471–4474. Available from: https://doi.org/10.1016/j.enpol.2008.09.025.

Robinson, C., Bouzarovski, S. and Lindley, S. 2018. "'Getting the Measure of Fuel Poverty': The Geography of Fuel Poverty Indicators in England." *Energy Research & Social Science* 36(February): 79–93. https://doi.org/10.1016/j.erss.2017.09.035.

Rudge, J. and Gilchrist, R. 2005. "Excess Winter Morbidity among Older People at Risk of Cold Homes: A Population-Based Study in a London Borough." *Journal of Public Health* 27(4): 353–358. Available from: https://doi.org/10.1093/pubmed/fdi051.

Savic, K. and Hoicka, C.E. 2021. "Reconciliation and Self-determination through Renewable Energy? The Perspective of Economic Development Corporations of Grid-Connected First Nations Communities." Working Paper 01/21. Smart Prosperity Institute. Ottawa, Ontario.

Scott, K. 2020. "Reconciliation and Energy Democracy." *Canadian Journal of Program Evaluation* 34(3): 480–491. Available from: https://doi.org/10.3138/cjpe.6844.

Seyfang, G., Jin, J. and Smith, A. 2013. "A Thousand Flowers Blooming? An Examination of Community Energy in the UK." *Energy Policy* 61: 977–989. Available from: https://doi.org/10.1016/j.enpol.2013.06.030.

Shaw, K. et al. 2015. "Conflicted or Constructive? Exploring Community Responses to New Energy Developments in Canada." *Energy Research & Social Science* 8(8): 41–51. Available from: https://doi.org/10.1016/j.erss.2015.04.003.

Shove, E. 2003. "Converging Conventions of Comfort, Cleanliness and Convenience." *Journal of Consumer Policy* 26: 395–418. Available from: https://link.springer.com/content/pdf/10.1023/A:1026362829781.pdf.

Smil, V. 2015. "Chapter 7 Making Sense of Power Densities." In V. Smil (ed.) *Power Density: A Key to Understanding Energy Sources and Uses.* Cambridge, MA: MIT Press, 190–220.

Smith, A.A. and Scott, D.N. 2019. "Renewing Indigenous Power: A Case Study of Chinodin Chigumi Nodin Kitagan." In G. Atapattu and S. Seck, eds. *Environmental Justice, Sustainable Development and the Social Pillar/The Cambridge Handbook on Environmental Justice and Sustainable Development.* Cambridge, UK: Cambridge University Press.

Sovacool, B. et al. 2020. "Imagining Sustainable Energy and Mobility Transitions: Valence, Temporality, and Radicalism in 38 Visions of a Low-Carbon Future." *Social Studies of Science* 50(4): 642–679. Available from: https://doi.org/10.1177/0306312720915283.

Stephens, J.C. 2019. "Energy Democracy: Redistributing Power to the People Through Renewable Transformation." *Environment: Science and Policy for Sustainable Development* 61(2): 4–13. Available from: https://doi.org/10.1080/00139157.2019.1564212.

Stevis, D. 2019. "Labour Unions and Green Transitions in the United States." WP 108. Toronto.

Stevis, D. and Felli, R. 2015. "Global Labour Unions and Just Transition to a Green Economy." *International Environmental Agreements: Politics, Law and Economics* 15(1): 29–43. Available from: https://doi.org/10.1007/s10784-014-9266-1.

Sweeny, S. 2013. "Resist, Reclaim, Restructure: Unions and the Struggle for Energy Democracy." New York. Available from: http://unionsforenergydemocracy.org/wp-content/uploads/2014/05/resistreclaimrestructure_2013_english.pdf.

Szulecki, K. 2018. "Conceptualizing Energy Democracy." *Environmental Politics* 27(1): 21–41. Available from: https://doi.org/10.1080/09644016.2017.1387294.

Szulecki, K. and Overland, I. 2020. "Energy Democracy as a Process, an Outcome and a Goal: A Conceptual Review." *Energy Research & Social Science* 69(November). Available from: https://doi.org/10.1016/j.erss.2020.101768.

Tarhan, M.D. 2020. "Renewable Energy Co-Operatives and the Struggle for Energy Democracy: The Case of Ontario." University of Toronto.

Tarhan, M.D. "Renewable Energy Co-operatives: A Review of Demonstrated Impacts and Limitations." *Journal of Entrepreneurship and Organizational Diversity* 4(1): 104–120. Available from: https://ssrn.com/abstract=2605796.

Teelucksingh, C. et al. 2016. "Environmental Justice in the Environmental Non-Governmental Organization Landscape of Toronto (Canada)." *Canadian Geographer* 60(3): 381–393. Available from: https://doi.org/10.1111/cag.12278.

The Solar Foundation. 2019. "US Solar Industry Diversity Study." Available from: https://www.thesolarfoundation.org/wp-content/uploads/2019/05/Solar-Industry-Diversity-Study-2019-2.pdf.

Thombs, R.P. 2019. "When Democracy Meets Energy Transitions: A Typology of Social Power and Energy System Scale." *Energy Research & Social Science* 52(June): 159–168. Available from: https://doi.org/10.1016/J.ERSS.2019.02.020.

UNEP. 2009. "Global Green New Deal Policy Brief." Geneva. Available from: https://wedocs.unep.org/bitstream/handle/20.500.11822/7903/A_Global_Green_New_Deal_Policy_Brief.pdf?sequence=3&amp%3BisAllowed=.

United Nations. 2008. "United Nations Declaration on the Rights of Indigenous Peoples." Available from: https://www.un.org/esa/socdev/unpfii/documents/DRIPS_en.pdf.

Van Veelen, B. 2018. "Negotiating Energy Democracy in Practice: Governance Processes in Community Energy Projects." *Environmental Politics* 27(4): 1–22. Available from: https://doi.org/10.1080/09644016.2018.1427824.

Van Veelen, B. and Van der Horst, D. 2018. "What Is Energy Democracy? Connecting Social Science Energy Research and Political Theory." *Energy Research & Social Science* 46(February): 19–28. Available from: https://doi.org/https://doi.org/10.1016/j.erss.2018.06.010.

Viardot, E. 2013. "The Role of Cooperatives in Overcoming the Barriers to Adoption of Renewable Energy." *Energy Policy* 63: 756–764. Available from: https://doi.org/10.1016/j.enpol.2013.08.034.

Walker, C., Stephenson, L. and Baxter, J. 2018. "His Main Platform Is 'Stop the Turbines': Political Discourse, Partisanship and Local Responses to Wind Energy in Canada." *Energy Policy* 123(August): 670–681. Available from: https://doi.org/10.1016/j.enpol.2018.08.046.

Wierling, A. et al. 2018. "Statistical Evidence on the Role of Energy Cooperatives for the Energy Transition in European Countries." *Sustainability* 10(9): 3339. Available from: https://doi.org/10.3390/su10093339.

Wiersma, B. and Devine-Wright, P. 2014. "Decentralising Energy: Comparing the Drivers and Influencers of Projects Led by Public, Private, Community and Third Sector Actors." *Contemporary Social Science* 9(4): 456–470. Available from: https://doi.org/10.1080/21582041.2014.981757.

Williams, L. et al. 2018. *Women and Climate Change Impacts and Action in Canada: Feminist, Indigenous and Intersectional Perspectives*. Toronto, ON: Canada.

Wilson, C. 2018. "Disruptive Low-Carbon Innovations." *Energy Research & Social Science* 37(March): 216–223. Available from: https://doi.org/10.1016/j.erss.2017.10.053.

WiRE. 2020. Women in Renewable Energy. Available from: https://www.womeninrenewableenergy.ca/

WISER. 2020. Women and Inclusivity in Sustainable Energy Research. Available from: https://wseresearch.com/

Wittmayer, J.M. et al. 2019. "Narratives of Change: How Social Innovation Initiatives Construct Societal Transformation." *Futures* 112(September). Available from: https://doi.org/10.1016/J.FUTURES.2019.06.005.

Wolsink, M. 2012. "The Research Agenda on Social Acceptance of Distributed Generation in Smart Grids: Renewable as Common Pool Resources." *Renewable and Sustainable Energy Reviews* 16(2): 822–835. Available from: https://doi.org/10.1016/j.rser.2011.09.006

World Economic Forum. 2016. *The Industry Gender Gap Women and Work in the Fourth Industrial Revolution*. Geneva: World Economic Forum. Available at: https://www.weforum.org/whitepapers/the-industry-gender-gap-women-and-work-in-the-fourth-industrial-revolution.

Wright, F. 2004. "Old and Cold: Older People and Policies Failing to Address Fuel Poverty." *Social Policy and Administration* 38(5): 488–503. Available from: https://doi.org/10.1111/j.1467-9515.2004.00403.x.

Wyse, S.M. and Hoicka, C.E. 2019. "'By and For Local People': Assessing the Connection between Local Energy Plans and Community Energy." *Local Environment* 24(9): 1–18. Available from: https://doi.org/10.1080/13549839.2019.1652802.

Yildiz, Ö. et al. 2015. "Renewable Energy Cooperatives as Gatekeepers or Facilitators? Recent Developments in Germany and a Multidisciplinary Research Agenda." *Energy Research & Social Science* 6: 59–73. Available from: https://doi.org/10.1016/j.erss.2014.12.001.

Yohanis, Y.G. 2012. "Domestic Energy Use and Householders' Energy Behaviour." *Energy Policy* 41(February): 654–665. Available from: https://doi.org/10.1016/j.enpol.2011.11.028.

13

A GREEN NEW DEAL BEYOND THE "NORTH"

Both promise and peril[1]

Vijay Kolinjivadi and Ashish Kothari

Introduction

Since 2019, the world has seen the emergence of significant ecological and social crises. From wildfires raging in the Brazilian Amazon, unheard-of summer temperatures in Antarctica, 38-degree Celsius heat waves in Siberia, disastrous floods in the American Midwest and across parts of southern Africa, and the loss of billions of animals in Australia's catastrophic bushfires, the world is burning and drowning in front of our eyes. On top of this came the most dramatic societal shutdown since World Wars I and II in response to the global COVID-19 pandemic.

The spread of monoculture agri-business, the movement of people toward cities, and the destructive simplifications of landscapes shaped by a modern narrative of "development" have made increasingly populated urban centers a greater risk of zoonotic spillover (the spread of deadly pathogens from animal species to people. The lightning speed spread of pathogens is propagated along tightly interconnected supply chains and frenetic movement of people around the world. Recent research has shown that rapid changes in land use influence the risk and emergence of zoonotic diseases in humans (Gibb et al. 2020). The "just-in the-time" demands of this nature–labor orchestration extinguish the life-giving potential of the land, water, and human cultures. It is a system that also serves as an ideal conduit for a viral pathogen to penetrate new bodies faster than underfunded public health systems and existing knowledge can handle it.

The chapter is structured as follows: first, we sketch how ecological breakdown and social inequality are intertwined, and indeed co-constitutive of capitalist, statist, and patriarchal modernity. Next, we describe the response strategy to address these twinned crises by exploring prominent calls for a Green (New) Deal in the United States and Europe. We highlight the central focus on techno-solutions to ecological and social crises that have come to define these Northern-led Green New Deals (GNDs), namely, the global implications of Northern-led techno-optimism in bringing about progressive "eco-friendly" policies. These implications piggyback on historical relations of uneven development centered around resource imperialism and the continued dependency on racialized, gendered, and classed workers. We then highlight why a focus on techno-solutions cannot be separated from the growth imperative of capitalism and must also be contextualized within the current political

DOI: 10.4324/9781003110880-16

juncture, which offers a breeding ground for racial and patriarchal capitalism, authoritarian and far-right governments, and even ecofascist elements to thrive. We conclude by going beyond a techno-focus on growing "greener" and instead describe alternative just transitions and radical transformations that prioritize reparation and restorative justice, decolonization, autonomy for workers, and deliberative democracy in transforming what a global green new deal might look like. We highlight the transformative power of building global solidarity across autonomous social movements that remain politically and ethically committed to social and environmental justice outside the state and hence are not wooed by new streams of capital growth and profit.

Intertwined social and ecological crises

In the last two years there has been a spate of conflict flashpoints, violent coups, and increasingly visible evidence of shameful inequalities in wealth, which have resulted in unprecedented demands for social change around the world. Among the most dramatic of these have been movements in Chile, Ecuador, Bolivia, and elsewhere in Latin America. Social uprisings have also emerged in India, France, Lebanon, Haiti, Algeria, Sudan, and South Africa. Across Europe and North America before the pandemic, youth movements have been amassing on the streets every Friday demanding climate justice and a future worth living in.

India witnessed a general worker strike of 250 million on 26 November 2020, making it the biggest strike in world history, followed by months of sustained mobilizations against the three farm bills proposed by the increasingly authoritarian and neoliberal Bharatiya Janata Party (BJP) government in India. Hundreds of thousands of farmers mobilized in and around Delhi against the laws that sought to remove their guaranteed procurement prices and further marginalize them in favor of the agro-industrial lobby and digital agriculture technologies, and will erode their autonomy over their own production systems (Narasimhaiah and Kulriya 2021). Over the few months the farmers have been camping on the borders of Delhi, while other worker groups and unions, academics and students, environmental organizations, youth and feminist groups, human rights advocates, and many others have shown solidarity with the protest, contradicting many observers who dismissed it as a movement with a "narrow sectarian" base (Asher 2021; Kaur 2021; Siwach 2021).

The United States, a country built upon the backs of anti-Black racism and settler colonialism, has suffered the greatest number of COVID-19 cases and deaths, disproportionately impacting the most marginalized in society. In 2020, the combination of ongoing police violence, the pandemic's deeply uneven impacts, and the historical legacy of systemic racism resulted in the largest and most widespread social uprisings in the country in decades. Anti-racism protests rapidly surfaced globally, with demands to defund the police, the physical dismantling of colonial symbols and statues, and widespread reassessment of institutional and corporate strategies to "end white supremacy." Indigenous Peoples' movements for self-determination, such as the rail blockades held in solidarity with the Wet'suwet'en First Nation in Canada who are protesting the construction of a gas pipeline across their unceded land, and the reclaiming of territories taken over in colonial times, have joined this series of "beautiful trouble" (e.g., Boyd and Mitchell 2013), as have worker movements in South Africa and other countries.

While the causes of today's social and ecological crises are varied and have emerged from context-specific geographies, there is a striking commonality to the demands that social movements are making. They generally revolve around calls for autonomy from oppressive states; a growing resistance to profit- and power-hungry global elites constantly pushing people and nature to beyond the point of tolerance (e.g., Chile, Hong Kong, Algeria, Haiti, Sudan, Ecuador); and resisting and ending anti-Black racism, casteism, settler colonialism, Islamophobia, extractivism, and ecologically devastating policies (e.g., in the United States, Canada, India, Latin America). But the corresponding state response has been quite different, from crackdowns on and vilification of social movements by right-wing parties and governments, to appreciative nods and a semblance of positive policy moves by a few liberal or welfarist regimes. Only a few mainstream politicians have dared to say anything fundamentally different. Among these responses are: the "Green New Deal" manifesto of once-US-presidential hopeful Bernie Sanders; parallel statements and manifestos by former UK prime ministerial candidate Jeremy Corbyn (see Bailey and Hofferberth, this volume); the Green New Deal for Europe (not to be confused with the European Green Deal) (see Adler and Wargan, this volume); and the Pacto Ecosocial del Sur, a manifesto spearheaded by Latin American and Caribbean countries calling for the cancellation of external debt, tax reform, universal basic income, post-extractive economies, and food and cultural sovereignty from Northern economies, among other demands.[2] The Green New Deal (GND), in its different variants, proposes a corrective to the social and ecological destruction of the mainstream development model and to some of its key architects such as the fossil fuel and military industries.

A GND to sustainably modernize economies in overly developed regions of the world has implications for the lives, livelihoods and ecosystems of the rest of the world, which will invariably be transformed in the name of "greening." Before delving into the role that a GND might play, we first contextualize global calls for a GND with three priority concerns that illustrate how ecological degradation and pernicious social inequality are not only intertwined, but have become more pronounced due to the global COVID-19 pandemic. These concerns include worker precarity, climate change response strategies, and "saving nature."

Worker precarity

The unprecedented lockdowns imposed as a response to the pandemic initially caused local and global economies to come screeching to a halt, exposing the vulnerability of hundreds of millions of workers. In India, up to half a million migrants were forced to start walking to their ancestral villages after a 21-day lockdown was imposed without warning by the Modi government in April 2020 and carried out with shamefully inadequate consideration or groundwork to respond to the needs of the poorest and most vulnerable. Many days later, when the impacts became very visible and pressure from civil society and state governments ramped up, the Indian government announced some (rather inadequate) relief packages. As Jessica Faleiro of ActionAid International describes, internal displacements of workers in India associated with the pandemic are the tip of an iceberg of broader migrations and dislocations of the masses due to climate-induced natural disasters, resulting in the emergence of "ghost villages" in some hilly regions (Faleiro 2021): and building on a history of development-induced displacement of about 60 million people in the last few decades (Mathur 2008). A study by the Azim Premji University (2021) reports that about 230 million people were pushed into poverty in the first year of the pandemic.

Billions of workers around the world have had to continue providing "essential" services during the pandemic, often at low wages and putting their health on the line in the process. Others have been obliged to accept reductions in daily earnings or have lost their jobs entirely. The level of disposability of informal livelihoods was hardwired in the production and circulation of goods and services prior to the pandemic but has now reached astronomical proportions. Many workers have been touted as "guardian angels" (Lynes and Trepanier 2020), upholding a society in which certain privileged members can order all their needs from the comfort of home while the "angels" endure health risks and extreme economic precarity. They are often racialized migrant laborers brought to North America and Europe under specific conditions that restrict the possibility of attaining legal status in the country of arrival and the social services that can support their well-being and that of their families (Ferguson and McNally 2015). In countries like India, they are made up predominantly of Dalit (the so-called "outcastes") and other lower castes, religious minorities and Indigenous People.

As C.P. Chandrasekhar and Jayati Ghosh (2020) write, informal workers make up more than 60% of the global workforce (in countries like India, above 90%). Their role in a globalized economy of "just-in-time" capital accumulation is precisely to have a high turnover rate. There are always substitutes to replace those who are burned out, or made redundant, or forced to return to their country of origin (or domestically, to their village). John Bellamy Foster and Intan Suwandi (2020) note that another factor of migrant labor is their *cheapness*. For instance, unit labor costs of Indian nationals working in the United States are only 37% of that of their US citizen counterparts. This wage differential has nothing to do with differences in productivity but has much more to do with the continuation of a highly interconnected global network of racially driven exploitation. The racialized premise of global development is a point we will return to later in this chapter and which we argue challenges any attempt at building a "Green New Deal."

Climate response and adaptation

The rapid shutdown of various parts of the economy associated with the lockdowns did indeed lead to reduced greenhouse gas emissions, with between a 4% and 7% drop for the year 2020 (Le Quéré et al. 2020). However, this effect becomes negligible on a broader time horizon when understood as emerging from circumstance rather than directed planning (Forster et al. 2020). Moreover, the reduction in emissions is still a far cry from the minimum 7.6% drop per annum that would be required to remain below 1.5 degrees Celsius of warming (UNEP 2019). Focusing on the outcomes rather than on the intention is dangerously misleading, as increased Amazon deforestation due to the loosening of environmental regulations in Brazil has illustrated (Londoño et al. 2020). In India, the lockdown period was used by the government to roll out several ecologically devastating projects (e.g., industrial agriculture, mining, expressways) and dilute environmental laws and social protections for farmers at a time when mass mobilization was restricted due to the pandemic (Kothari 2020). The consequences of such decisions will be felt as we emerge from the pandemic.

The promise of powerful governments and multinational corporations to "return to normal" as soon as possible threatens to plunge people and nature into a spiral of unprecedented economic structural adjustments. It is not surprising that peoples' movements and civil society groups are resisting this with all their might. But it is not enough; a dangerous "return to normal" has already happened and this time it comes with a "green" face.

Scholars Bigger and Webber (2021) warn of the risks of "green structural adjustment" as a strategy by the World Bank to encourage cities across the Global South[3] to take on more debt through promises of marketizing urban renewal and climate change adaptation and resilience. The underlying driver of such strategies is to channel the liquidity of Northern investors (or as the authors claim, "spatially fix" their otherwise speculative capital) toward bankable urban projects that will not only generate trillions of dollars in climate transactions but also continue the colonial process of funneling those returns from the Global South back toward the Global North. In this sense, climate change adaptation and resilience, while viewed as a legitimate concern, also becomes itself a new frontier for capital accumulation (Chandrasekaran 2021). Bigger and Webber (2021) illustrate how "green structural adjustment" works in practice through the examples of Jakarta, Indonesia and Can ThoCity, Vietnam. In these, the World Bank undertakes a diagnostic assessment of these cities' climate vulnerabilities and recommends how to make them more investable for large-scale flood protection, transport, and sewage management infrastructure that will assure climate change "resiliency." Like previous forms of structural adjustment, generating a "resilient city" through urban renewal involves taking on World Bank loans and by turns repaying the debts that follow. The training programs associated with the World Bank's approach offer recommendations to municipal, local, and national governments on the obstacles that prevent private investment in climate resilience and how to remove those obstacles. These include improving credit ratings, fine-tuning methods for land value capture or the swapping of public land for infrastructure development rights, and encouraging blended finance through public–private partnerships.

Ultimately, this form of "greening" is geared toward making investment suitable for capital accumulation by Global North investors in the name of responding to climate change. At the same time, it entirely obfuscates the fact that climate impacts are the result of Global North development strategies in the 500-year quest for capital accumulation, falling disproportionately on the regions of the world least responsible for this modus of development even as these post-colonial nations are obliged (and tempted with the complicit acquiescence of their elites) to participate in its acceleration through market integration. The ethos of capital markets is a return on investment; it matters little whether the side objectives are couched as being eco-friendly, climate-resilient, LGBTQ-friendly or not. Potential returns on investment take precedence over any and all intentionality, however urgent or well-meaning. It is for this reason that development banks like the World Bank, national governments like the United States, or supranational governing blocs like the EU can spend billions in renewable energy infrastructure and in supporting Green Deals while simultaneously investing in the arms industry, coal-fired plants and natural gas pipelines. A form of "green" gaslighting becomes all too clear when unfair and unintended outcomes become viewed as profitable opportunities for the perpetrators of this logic, using narratives like pandemic recovery and climate resiliency to cover up their tracks.

"Saving nature"

The links between deforestation, expansion of extractivism and industrial agriculture, biodiversity loss, and the role that these play in encouraging the conditions for zoonotic disease spillover events from animals to humans leading to global pandemics, has led to renewed calls for protecting nature (Gibb et al. 2020; IPBES 2020). The clarion call has been resounding: the prevention of future pandemics can only happen by protecting nature. In the last year, urgent calls to protect nature have emerged from influential groups like National Geographic, the International Union for the Protection of Nature (IUCN), The Nature Conservancy, and the World Wide Fund for Nature (WWF). The so-called "suicidal" war on nature, as recently proclaimed by UN chief António Guterres, stands as a testament to the need for nature protection and will come to define the United Nations' biodiversity conservation strategy to be revealed later in 2022. Protecting nature was also recently emphasized in the UN Environment Programme's "Making Peace with Nature" report released in February 2021 (UNEP 2021).

Yet, it is never entirely clear how "nature" is defined, how it is to be protected, or by whom. Do the lifeworlds of the Penan of Sarawak, Malaysia, the Shuar of Ecuador, or the Anishinaabe of Turtle Island count in what "nature" refers to? How about the intricate rice terraces co-constructed by the Ifugao people in the Philippines or the Satoyama landscapes of Japan in which people not only actively construct "nature" but whose cultures are themselves profoundly shaped by these assembled landscapes? "Nature" is instead treated as a black box of pristine, depopulated landscapes requiring "protection" from human recklessness. The precise relationships between humans and the non-human world that characterize what "nature" refers to and how it is treated are assumed to default to a dualistic understanding of separation between humans and the non-human world (Moore 2015). At the same time, while human recklessness is purported as the instigator, rarely, if ever, are capital accumulation and settler colonialism singled out as the actual culprits for the modus of development that treats the non-human world as an expendable resource for extraction, consumption and waste. The continued treatment of "nature" and "people" as separate and unnuanced categories paves the way for overly simplistic and culturally skewed technical solutions that risk exacerbating twinned social and ecological crises.

One such proposed solution by biologist E.O. Wilson is the "half-earth" proposal to devote one-half of the earth's lands and waters to conservation; another comes from institutions urging for 30% of the earth to be protected by 2030. These proposals, well-meaning as they may be, continue a neo-colonial approach to conservation, as they: (1) are focused largely on separating the pursuits of modern development from a passive nature that requires protection, (2) are proposed and debated largely by academics and NGOs of the Global North, (3) do not involve communities living in the ecosystems and landscapes sought to be "protected," (4) ignore the immense knowledge and conservation practice of such communities, and (5) hardly challenge the planet-destroying production and consumption patterns of the Global North (Kothari 2021a and 2021b).

The influence held by figures like E.O. Wilson lies in the cultural matching they do (Richardson 2018). This refers to the ways in which problems and their solutions are determined according to established cultural habits, aesthetics, and deeply ingrained universalities in how relationships between humans and non-humans are demarcated and socio-culturally cemented. Half-earth conservation, or other models suggesting that the world's population should go entirely vegan (e.g., Springmann et al. 2018), for example, reflect a deeply white-washed cultural construction of "nature" and of human relations to their non-human kin. In the process, the failure to delink these solutions to hegemonic forms of cultural matching allows the white supremacist project of Western development and conservation to go unquestioned. This has a bearing on how one views GND-like proposals.

To conclude this section, the increasing precarity of workers, the urgent need to respond to multiple ecological crises (including those of biodiversity, pollution, and climate), and the imperative to recognize alternative relationships between people and our non-human kin, together illustrate the impossibility of separating social inequality from ecological degradation. A GND has the potential to recognize these intersections and intervene in ways that do not replicate a "return to normal" by simply "greening" growth. Green growth has potential adverse impacts in terms of how costs of development get shifted elsewhere. This often takes place through an ongoing legacy of racialized[4] and patriarchal patterns of resource extraction and the continued pattern of violent and humiliating land dispossession and cultural genocide in expanding the frontier of capital markets. Great care is required to reclaim a GND that does not get co-opted by "business as usual." This requires an unequivocal rejection of tendencies like "green structural adjustment" that fail to unmake the imperialist construction and continued dependence on a Global South as a source of extraction of cheap labor and natural resources for continued wealth accumulation in the North (Podur 2021). A GND must have clear positions against resource imperialism, racial capitalism, the securitization of the status quo by the nexus of state and capital, and the patriarchal project of shifting regenerative work to unpaid or unrecognized labor. It requires a specific call for a reparations ecology that takes decolonization and combating patriarchy as the guiding principles for conceptualizing what it means to be "green." In the next section, we briefly discuss how the GND, as championed in the United States by 2020 presidential hopeful Bernie Sanders, came to prominence. In doing so, and in also referring to the EU's Green Deal, we analyze how the GND gets framed as providing technological and managerial solutions, at times with a justice focus, to the intertwined social and ecological crises we have described and the implications of this focus particularly for the Global South.

"Green New Deal" or more efficient old deal?

Talk of a Green New Deal began after the global financial crisis of 2008 with the United Kingdom's New Economics Foundation issuing a report on "A Green New Deal" for a shift toward renewable energy production (Elliott et al. 2008). More recently in the United States, a youth-led grassroots climate mobilization known as the Sunrise Movement staged a sit-in on 13 November 2018 to occupy Speaker of the House of Representatives Nancy Pelosi's office (Roberts 2019). Their demands were that all Democrat leadership in the House refuse to accept donations from the fossil fuel industry and to establish a House Select Committee on a Green New Deal. Many Democratic representatives, including representatives Alexandria Ocasio-Cortez and Rashida Tlaib, voiced support for the movement and further publicized the message. Within a month, major environmental organizations including Greenpeace and Friends of the Earth, over 300 local elected officials, and numerous Democratic members of Congress were supporting the Committee for a GND that prioritized green jobs and green energy transitions. In early 2019, Senator Ed Markey and Representative Ocasio-Cortez released a Green New Deal Resolution at the 116th US Congress calling for public investments in public transportation, zero-emission energy sources twinned with social safeguards geared toward the most vulnerable communities, including universal health care, increased minimum wage, and affordable housing (H. Res. 109).

When Bernie Sanders announced he was running for the 2020 presidential race in the United States, he supported Ocasio-Cortez's resolution and promised his own version of a GND, noting that climate change is an "existential threat" to the nation and the planet at large (Rosane 2019). Bernie's version of the GND[5] had a clear focus on both ecological and social justice issues. It centered heavily around the need to tackle the climate crisis, moving completely away from fossil fuels and toward renewable energy, while explicitly supporting various grassroots movements (e.g., climate justice, divestment) that have demanded such measures. Importantly, unlike mainstream climate change proposals, it emphasized the need to address social justice issues in the transition period, especially for those most vulnerable (including low-income people, people of color, children, seniors, and people with disabilities). It stressed the need to create dignified, ecologically oriented jobs for workers likely to be affected by the transition away from a fossil fuel–based economy, and to place transport infrastructure and energy systems in public hands (including through worker cooperatives). Measures for conserving public lands for "ecologically regenerative and sustainable agriculture" and ecological restoration were also included, and touted as having the potential to create millions of jobs. The renegotiation of international trade deals to "ensure strong and binding climate standards, labor rights, and human rights" was another significant commitment. Bernie's GND also explicitly opposed continued exploration of oil and gas in rolling back mega-infrastructure projects such as the Keystone XL and Dakota Access Pipelines.

Bernie's campaign had gained momentum on the power of social movements demanding workers' rights and climate/environmental justice. It is important to note that relatively recent examples from Bolivia, Venezuela, Ecuador, and Greece have shown that leftist parties which have obtained power in government with the help of significant grassroots mobilization have, to varying extents, failed to maintain consistent and ongoing connections to these grassroots struggles or commitment to democratically driven political organization and socio-cultural transformation (Federici and Linebaugh 2018). Leftists, youth, workers, progressive liberals, and others rooting for transformation need to understand that a GND will only be successful to the extent that people's movements rise up on an unprecedented scale to build sufficient autonomy, and to hold the state (whomever it is composed of) accountable to political and economic democracy. This autonomous power is also known as "dual power," reflecting the establishment of "counter-institutions" that both meet the needs of marginalized populations and are also run by those very people (Broumas 2018). The most critical component of this is direct, radical power exercised by collectives on the ground (Zografos 2019).

Unfortunately, the GND, in its various incarnations, does not have an explicit focus on radical grassroots democracy in which centralized power withers away. There remains a great dependence on the nation-state, with its inevitable tendency to concentrate power, even if in the name of the people. Other such crucial flaws could severely hamper the potential for real change that the GND promises. There remains a significant dependence on technological solutions to problems that are not necessarily technological in nature – a fundamental flaw that has been seen in mainstream "solutions" for decades (Collard et al. 2016; Kallis 2017). Existing outlines of a US GND say nothing about reducing overall energy demand (apart from "weatherization" to reduce domestic consumption) or the consumption of materials. As such, they fail to acknowledge the unsustainable exploitation of nature and natural resources required to create electric cars, solar panels, and wind turbines (Hickel 2018; Riofrancos 2021). The US GND proposal commits to holding corporations accountable to domestic climate goals and labor standards, but is not explicit in whether they will also be held accountable globally. The failure to consider global corporate accountability is particularly worrying given the utter failure of previous institutionalized efforts. One such example is the UN's Global Compact, which lacks any monitoring or enforcement provisions and has been accused of perpetuating "bluewash," the practice of corporations purporting to voluntarily participate in philanthropic efforts in order to improve their bargaining power in the multilateral governance arena (Bruno and Karliner 2000).

While Bernie Sanders' campaign focused on putting an end to unprecedented inequality in the United States, his version of the GND was not clear on how such inequality can be addressed at its root, beyond taxing billion-dollar fossil fuel companies and providing "green jobs" to lift low-income sectors. Without clarity on the issue of systemic inequality inherent within capitalism, a GND cannot challenge its foundational structures of racism, gendered divisions of labor, and the precarity of working-class people.

Why does this detail on local, national and global inequality matter so much? As we describe below, many of the same people who wouldn't dare question a system responsible for the severance of life-support systems and centuries-long systemic dehumanization, are now throwing billions of dollars of investment into "green" development. The EU's Green Deal (described further in chapter by Adler and Walgan, this volume), while sounding impressive on paper in offering €100 billion/year over ten years for "green investment" in Europe, is one of several proposals (and historical culprits) pushing for a more inclusive capitalism (see further chapter by Selwyn, this volume). The concern with this "too little too late" approach is not about the amount of the financial support, but rather about how it shifts risk away from private enterprise (and wealthy individuals) and onto the public sphere and future generations.

The global implications of sidestepping systemic inequality within a GND paves the way for "green" colonialism, perpetuating the 500-year quest for cheap raw materials and the labor of Black and Brown bodies to achieve more efficient (call it "green" if you will) growth (Taylor and Kaur 2019). The impacts that this "greener" mode of development has on the Global South is anything but new (Podur 2021). Yet dominant actors of the global economy stand to benefit immensely from a GND that elevates "green" and remains unhinged from the global politics of class, race and gender. Often the depiction of "green" advocated by influential actors in global conservation, multilateral, and development lending arenas takes form through technological solutions.[6]

Green New Deal or green tech for profit?

It is worth reiterating a point from earlier that, despite stated commitments to social responsibilities and engagement with the communities in which industry operates, private finance always functions to ensure returns on investment as profit. Furthermore, there is no evidence to show that increasing profitable growth (measured as enhanced production throughput) can be accomplished without exploiting the biophysical environment and shifting costs of production to labor. In other words, any absolute decoupling of social and ecological impacts from economic growth remains a myth (Hickel and Kallis 2020; Parrique et al. 2019; Vadén et al. 2020).[7] The early stages of the global pandemic – which had shown improved ecological outcomes due to decreased economic growth – has never made the fallacy of decoupling so evident. When it comes down to the bottom line (financially and metaphorically), the interest of the private sector in the GND is to secure future profits and minimize their own risk. Issues such as workers' rights, demands for dignified jobs, wages, food security, housing, health care, and ecological sustainability are bound to be downplayed or ignored altogether in versions of a GND that do not challenge private sector investments.[8]

The existential fear of losing privileges as a result of the unexpected social and ecological "externalities" of "business as usual" has (likely unwillingly) forced global elites from the far-right to the center-left to reckon with climate change as an "investment risk" (Christianson and Pinchot 2020). From BlackRock CEO Larry Fink to Jeff Bezos, the world's richest man and CEO of Amazon, to former US President Donald Trump, those who throw billions of dollars into "solutions" like planting a trillion trees (Friedman 2020) do so not only as a good public relations exercise but also to achieve a good return on investment to stabilize such risk. Throwing a few hundred million more into funding environmental groups (the ones unlikely to challenge the fundamental structures of capitalism), is great for a "green" image while not making any dent in their wealth. In other words, big business does not deny the risks of climate change, but the response to these risks is only to maintain or enhance profit-making potential rather than address the uneven social impacts that ecological breakdown generates. Up until late 2020, Amazon even threatened to fire employees that spoke out about climate change (Milman 2020). Indeed, maintaining "business as usual" could not have been made any clearer than Microsoft's recent commitment to become "carbon negative" by 2030, with CEO Satya Nadella stating that a "corporation's purpose is to find *profitable solutions* to the *problems* of people and planet" (Clifford 2020). This view resonates with that of the United Nations, which has long espoused a triple bottom line putting people and planet on the same plane as profits. In the face of ecological breakdown, securitizing a future for capital accumulation will require increasingly centralized policy-making and authoritarian control (Mitchell and Chaudhary 2020). A GND that stems from the Global North and sets the terms for engaging with the Global South rather than be open to an equal and historically reparative relationship presents a perfect opportunity to justify such securitization.

The logic that profits can go on forever while protecting people and the planet is seductively dangerous at a time of unprecedented global inequality and ecological collapse resulting from that very same logic. Ecological economists have repeatedly argued that efficiency improvements in a profit-oriented enterprise will eventually run up against the Jevon's Paradox – that increasing energy and material efficiencies reduce prices and therefore enhance demand, effectively offsetting efficiency gains in a perpetually growing economy (Alcott et al. 2012; see also Schor and Tienhaara, this volume). The concern is not only that demand will rise for products made more efficient (energy-wise or materially), but that positive spinoffs in other areas of the economy will arise, making it difficult to measure the overall impact of material or energy efficiencies in terms of final throughput (Giampietro and Mayumi 2018; see also McCollum, this volume). For instance, while the shift to a digital economy might have resulted in reductions in material and energy expenditure per transaction (though see Greenford et al. 2020 for contradictions to this assumption), the broader shift to digital lifestyles and the use of smartphones have increased the need for rare earth mineral extraction. Cloud computing and artificial intelligence increase the demand for electricity, which is more often than not met by coal-fired power plants (Wonder Alorse 2019). While in 2002, you might have possessed a laptop computer and a cellphone, you now have a more energy-efficient smartphone or tablet that performs the same functions but is now also connected to a Wi-Fi–enabled stove, online banking, Amazon Prime, social media networks (powered by coal through giant computer farms), and to your electricity-powered car. Such all-pervasive digitization has serious consequences for the places where raw materials and energy are extracted (Caffentzis 2019). Similarly, digital agriculture platforms permit powerful agribusinesses to render yields more predictable and precise through digitized drones and sensors; consolidated contracts between farmers, fertilizer and pesticide suppliers, seed companies, and shipping companies; and more streamlined than ever production cycles to consumers through e-commerce arrangements (GRAIN 2021). In addition to reinforcing hegemonic control by agribusiness, the result is greater material and energy throughput even if digitization improves marginal efficiencies in energy expenditure. Technological improvements that stimulate energy efficiencies and cost savings *do not sit idle* in a capitalist system; they get reinvested back into growth, and, in turn, into further ecological and social degradation (Kallis 2017).

Returning to Microsoft CEO Satya Nadella, he claims that we must "trust in technology" and put a billion dollars in an "innovation fund." Elsewhere, billionaire and Tesla CEO Elon Musk has offered a prize of US$100 million to capture and store carbon dioxide from the atmosphere (Clifford 2021). Yet, it is the endless proliferation of hi-tech developments, from 4G and 5G to AI, to drones, deep learning and geographic information systems, which have only made capitalist development and expansion in the realms of mineral extraction, food, energy, urban development, communication and finance that much quicker and cheaper (Arboleda 2020). This is not to deny that some of these technologies have their own benefits and can empower people, but the overall political and economic relations in which these technologies are brought into being requires recognition. Meanwhile, the social alienation, worker displacement, inequality and ecological consequences of these technology-induced efficiencies are increasingly visible, and the uncertainties for future generations palpable. Quick technical fixes will usually produce social disparities and are by themselves entirely insufficient to generate the relational shifts needed among humans, and between humans and the rest of nature.

Technological innovation does not emerge out of a vacuum; it is embedded in structural power relations where there is a significant tendency for efficiencies to favor already privileged, socially mobile, wealthy groups and their government sponsors. The Pfizer-BioNTech and Moderna vaccines to combat COVID-19 offer a case in point. They were developed by giant pharmaceutical companies, sold for profit to the first bidders who had the wealth and infrastructure to store their vaccines in the appropriate conditions and vaccinate their populations. In the early months of 2021, a kind of "vaccine apartheid" has spread around the globe, with the bulk of available vaccines being cornered by the usual suspects of historically privileged countries (Thier 2021). Understanding and reversing the root causes of social inequality and ecological degradation – as they are based in systemic racism, classism, and patriarchy – was never meant to be part of the techno-fix strategy.

Situating "Green" in patterns of exploitation

A Green New Deal would do well to address how collective organization can play a part in directing the ways in which technology is developed and used. This would require engaging people through deliberative direct democracy to define the ethical and political parameters on the purpose and limits (both ecological and social) of technological development (Mumford 1964). Democratically defining the limits and potential of technological advancements might offer the space to oppose "green" tech that reinvests efficiency surpluses back into capital accumulation and hence sustains a status quo of entitlement and greed for a privileged few. The ramifications of such a shift are profound within Western modernity. Capital relations treat humans as separate from and dominant over a nature "out there," viewed as something to protect, manipulate or extract from, and ultimately to commodify and exchange in order to sustain profits. As Jason Moore argues, "nature can neither be saved nor destroyed, only transformed" (2015: 45). In this way, a sensitively crafted GND can serve to "restore nature" (including human labor land, air, sky, water, and non-human kin) by replenishing a multitude of socially mediated relations that build on an ethics of regeneration, and explicitly reject the instrumentalization or commodification of such relationships.

Moore explains how the availability of biophysical nature and unpaid or underpaid work is crucial for capital accumulation to proceed at an adequate rate of growth. He calls this the planet's "ecological surplus," or the ratio of system-wide capital assets to system-wide appropriation of unpaid work/energy (Moore 2015: 95). He also claims that this surplus is dwindling due to a contradiction between the rate of transforming nature and labor inputs for economic production, on the one hand, and the social reproduction of labor and the regeneration of biophysical structure to replenish natural resources, on the other. The rapid depletion of fertile soils and crucial pollinators, the emergence of superweeds from industrial pesticide resistance (and indeed zoonotic diseases and global pandemics), groundwater contamination, and a rapidly aging workforce all pose significant threats for maintaining an ecological surplus for capital accumulation to continue without disruption. It is partly for these reasons that interest in urban sustainability and green-friendly investments have been increasingly prioritized by multilateral lending agencies and urban planners as described earlier with the concept of "green structural adjustment." Cities are seen as hotbeds of "sustainability" innovation and as exemplars of what sustainable living has come to mean (Angelo and Wachsmuth 2020). The urban link to the rural gets increasingly severed as a steady stream of smallholder farmers and small producers flock to urban areas, dispossessed from their land and resource base by a combination of decreasing yields due to climate change and ecological collapse, threats from agribusiness and urban-industrial expansion, and shifts in demography influenced by unequal access to health, education, and civic amenities (Paprocki 2018). Domestic migrants (and in some cases refugees) serve as a burgeoning "cheap" labor source domestically in rapidly urbanizing centers in places like Nigeria and India, and are easy targets within networks of (often illegal) recruiting agencies peddling in migrant labor export to places like Canada and Australia (Ferguson and McNally 2015). The securitization of "cheap" labor along with investment in nature-based solutions and ecosystem services as instrumentalized "natures" are together imperative to overcome the problem of a dwindling ecological surplus to keep the machinery running. Some analysts have observed that the three new farm laws promulgated by the Government of India in late 2020, which spurred the farmer agitation referred to above, were an attempt to convert tens of millions of farmers into what is potentially the world's largest remaining pool of cheap labor, with a handful of corporate giants doubling-down their control of India's agriculture (Engdahl 2021; Todhunter 2021).

The word "green" obfuscates what is required to adequately respond to ecological breakdown by putting a certain kind of environmental crisis at the forefront, and in so doing, reinforcing dualistic binaries between humans and "nature." As Aldeia and Alves (2019) argue, the word "environment" is itself deeply problematic. To utter the word "environment" is to instantly speak about the world around "us," not including "us." Ecological relationships, on the other hand, very much include the social behavior and history of humans. They therefore offer a deeper understanding of the geographically and historically specific moments of shaping and transforming the material and energy of people and the rest of nature, in ways that have come to define global capitalism (Moore 2015). Going beyond capital relations, however, ecology also requires breaking through what Ferdinand (2019) calls the "double fracture" of environmentalism and coloniality that fail to inform each other. Understood in this manner, long struggles against oppression and exploitation of being considered sub-human to varying degrees (e.g., "lower" castes, Indigenous People, Black people, women, and people with disabilities), are neither secondary effects of ecological breakdown nor should they be considered as unrelated to ecological impacts. Yet, the fatally erroneous separation of social crises from a vision of untouched wilderness or pristine "environmental" crises continues to define many "eco" movements around the world and is especially encapsulated by the use of the word "green."

Wainwright and Mann (2018) take this concern further by describing how a GND similarly assumes that the state is somehow unrelated to capital accumulation. The authors question the assumption that the state can simply reassert itself to take control of the deleterious effects of capital while continuing to glorify liberalism as a means to respond to ecological breakdown. The (neo)liberal state should be understood as a consolidation of power through historically colonial and liberal advances that work toward neutralizing decolonial, feminist, LGBTQ, and class struggles into governable modalities; the state operates to unify heterogenous elements into a singular national jurisdiction. Such a "unified" jurisdiction is then obliged to compete for resources and power with other national jurisdictions in a global arena premised on the political and economic relations of capital. In the current state of affairs, this means prioritizing the flow of capital (migrant labor, goods, and services), militarizing national borders, and policing migrant (especially Black and Brown) people to ensure that those attempting to enter specific jurisdictions are vetted first and foremost in terms of their labor potential rather than their status as dignity-deserving human beings (Ferguson and McNally 2015).

In contrast to state-driven strategies, the Out of the Woods Collective in its 2020 book *Hope Against Hope: Writings on Ecological Crises* argue that collective identity can rather be considered "solidarity" when it unifies *against* (not in favor of) the consolidation of power associated with fixed notions of state and nationalistic forms of identity, and crucially without quashing difference. Such "no borders" solidarity can and should be global because the impacts of capitalist ecology intentionally weave through human and non-human bodies beyond national boundaries (Arboleda 2020). The false separation of state and capital ignores the ways that the two are co-dependent on each other. As the Collective argues, a GND risks being rife with contradictions that on the one hand involve the state implementing policy to end the use of fossil fuels and on the other hand pay for social welfare improvements, such as social housing, by taxing profits from fossil fuels. Recalling the impact of the original 1930s New Deal, the Collective claims that such reforms "not only helped stabilize capitalism (and its endless drive for profits), but the compromise helped undermine the disruptive power which had forced the concessions in the first place" (2020: 204). This is also reminiscent of the failures of orthodox leftist parties taking power in several countries in Latin America, or Greece, which funded their enhanced welfare programs through "neo-extractivism" (Hargreaves 2019).

So then does a Green New Deal need an entirely new name? Or perhaps more fundamentally, a more radical approach? A statist initiative that seeks to prioritize an abstracted notion of a pristine "green" environment excluding racial and patriarchal capitalism, settler colonialism, and the dependence on underpaid labor is perhaps just the ticket that half-earthers and eco-modernists are seeking. But liberal and statist approaches that co-opt diversity for national unity do not just engage with the anti-capitalist left; they also engage with far-right fascists. This ambivalence is utterly frightening, as we describe below.

Racial capitalism, (eco)fascism, and the Green New Deal

Tightening border imperialism, justified along ethno-nationalist and xenophobic lines, ensures that the divisions of labor remain confined to very specific working conditions that increase the precarity of migrants' lives. The imperial mode of living (e.g., Brand and Wissen 2012) to "get something" and not pay for any of the costs has increasingly taken on a far-right, fascist turn. The passing of the National Registry of Citizens and the Citizenship Amendment Act in India in late 2019, rooted in shoring up a Hindu supremacist vision of development while castigating any dissent against this vision as "anti-national," is a case in point (Crowley 2019). That India, under Narendra Modi, is also muscling up to the resource imperialist requirements of global capital allows it the space not only to extract resources and labor from people and planet, but also to victimize anyone suffering from its consequences. This is no different (albeit with visible local variations) from the United States under Trump, Brazil under Bolsonaro, Turkey under Erdogan, the Philippines under Duterte, China under Xi, or Russia under Putin.

Many environmentalist arguments that frame ecological crises as a "threat" have disturbingly Malthusian implications that must be reckoned with. In the 1968 book *The Population Bomb*, author and environmentalist Paul Ehrlich described a New Delhi slum from his taxi window as a "hellish mob," describing his fear of being unable to eventually return to his hotel and his recognition of "emotionally" experiencing what he called "over-population" (Purdy 2015). This perception is rooted in the fear that more bodies seeking a "good life" would not be sustainable for those who already hold such privileges. The imagery around "threat" erases colonial and imperial histories of Euro-American (or Hindu Brahminical for an Indian analog) domination. The richest 10% of the population are responsible for 50% of global emissions, for example (Lawson et al. 2020). In India, the richest person consumes 17 times the poorest (Shrivastava and Kothari 2012). A blanket statement that climate change is a "threat," without an obligatory attachment to global inequality in consumption (e.g., Wiedmann et al. 2020), or indeed in the control over production and consumption, could therefore be readily construed as ecofascist. The GNDs we have seen emerge are disappointingly silent on this. This is not to assert that human numbers on the planet do not have material consequences. Yet, such a position is a red herring when viewed in isolation from the political economy of resource flows and dependencies on cheap labor that underpin development. A decontextualized focus on demographics as having damaging environmental implications is frequently either a naive absence or willful dismissal of the underlying structures and historical relations of coloniality, Euro-American cultural hegemony, and resource imperialism in explaining uneven global production and consumption patterns. One outcome of this decontextualization is to point fingers at the "over-populated" and uneducated masses of the Global South as the culprit for environmental crises. This lack of historical context could also lead to justifications for depopulating large portions of the earth in the name of equitable and eco-centric conservation (e.g., Kopnina et al. 2018). It can also lead to frightening approaches like Hardin's "lifeboat ethics," which implicitly or explicitly consider people of the Global South to be expendable (Clark 2019).

In a world embedded in global capitalism and statism (building on patriarchy, racism, and casteism), "finance-rich, resource-poor" countries are increasingly looking to "resource-rich" countries and regions in the Global South to secure both their food and energy needs (Borras and Franco 2012). While traditional players (e.g., North America and Europe) that have been on the "frontier" of imperialist pursuits are still in the game, new players like India and China also want a piece of the pie. Indeed, the very notion of "national development" is becoming increasingly irrelevant in an era where transnational corporations have been active in dispossessing people of their lands, food and cultural sovereignty domestically, regionally and globally. India, for example, is active internally in "land-grabbing" strategies for biofuel, industrial development, "nature" conservation business parks and transport infrastructure, and abroad in fueling the investment boom in mineral deposits and agro-industrial projects (Ministerio de Minería Chile 2019). Examples of the latter include an Indian joint venture (backed by the Indian Ministry of Mines) known as Khanij Videsh India Limited (KABIL) involved in prospecting lithium extraction in Chile's Atacama desert and Bolivia's Uyuni salt flats for "green energy" production, under the aegis of so-called "sustainable development" in the mining sector. Elsewhere, Indian companies such as Karuturi Global have been involved in forcefully removing peasants from their ancestral lands in their intent to invest in industrial-scale sugarcane, palm oil, and rice plantations in Ethiopia, ostensibly to help the local economy (Chandran and Gardner 2017). Without paying attention to the broader political economy of globalized economic production that transcends national borders, a GND in Europe, the United States, Canada, South Korea, and its variants in China (e.g., "Ecological Civilization") will be mere window dressing to conceal an underlying imperialist quest for cheap nature and cheap labor to satisfy the (increasingly "eco-friendly") demands of the wealthiest people (Schwartzman 2019).

As Fuchs et al. (2020) have recently shown, the EU Green Deal does nothing to halt the offshoring or cost-shifting of ecologically destructive agricultural practices in the food that it imports, particularly meat and grains imported from places like Brazil and Indonesia that are experiencing some of the worst biodiversity losses. While outsourcing the harm, those spearheading GNDs take the "green" credit. Zografos and Robbins (2020) further elaborate on this point by illustrating how both the EU Green Deal and the Markey/Ocasio-Cortez–proposed GND resolution in the United States remain glaringly silent on their implied dependence on "green sacrifice zones." These refer to the resource extraction, transportation, and waste dump sites located largely in the Global South required for the transition to a low-carbon economy. The authors, echoing similar views of EU interventions toward the "underdeveloped" (e.g., Rutazibwa 2010), go on to argue that by invoking tropes of salvation from "existential crises," the EU GND reinforces the moral and ethical aspects of a European savior complex, in which it is the Global North that unquestionably holds the power to secure a (white) future worth living in. Yet, to be truly just, a GND must overhaul the "cost-shifting" culture that the historical and ongoing colonial relations that growth-oriented development invariably depends upon. This is *very* different than merely transitioning to a more efficient "green" energy economy.

In India, where solar energy generation has become the cheapest in the world (Wood 2019), the transition to renewable energy could not be more of a blessing. But while decentralizing energy production to ensure clean energy sovereignty at the panchayat (village council) or urban municipal level is one ray of hope, transitioning entire coal-based megacities to maintain and enhance inherently unsustainable commerce and production requires industrial-scale renewable energy generation, which is an entirely different matter. Mega-solar and wind parks are an increasing source of ecological damage and social dislocation across the world.

Nor is "energy-efficiency" by itself a solution if absolute demand itself is not called into question. Increasing demand for supposedly efficient digital technologies in the world's largest companies, including Google, Apple and Microsoft, has resulted in some of the world's most deplorable working conditions at the source of raw material extraction behind seemingly benign digital communication platforms (Caffentzis 2019). In some cases, pregnant women are often powerless to prevent themselves and their children from working in the mines to extract the rare earth minerals to fuel the (now pandemic-induced)virtual workforce (Langlois 2019). Competition over rare earth minerals for "green" tech has also directly perpetuated one of Africa's longest running armed conflicts (Totolo 2009). Harm reduction in industrialized and rapidly industrializing countries, including China and India, in their move away from polluting coal and unbreathable air toward a hi-tech society fueled by renewable energy, means harm creation in the Democratic Republic of the Congo (DRC), where lives deemed less valuable are made to shoulder the cost. It also means harm creation domestically. For instance, in the grasslands of Kachchh and Andhra Pradesh, the coasts of southern India, the fields of Assam, and the desert of Rajasthan, wildlife, farmers, and pastoralists face ever-increasing takeover of the territories they depend on for supposedly "clean" solar and wind energy production.

To the extent that a GND does not fundamentally reverse these patterns, it is highly unlikely that the kinds of transformational social changes that it seeks will be attained, even if it does offer a welcome dent in carbon emissions by the fossil fuel industry (Arnoff et al. 2019). The advancement of strong social welfare reforms in some Western European countries was the culmination of long-fought struggles of labor unions against their capitalist bosses. Similar wins are imperative to avoid racialized labor exploitation in global food production in the North and South alike, for example. The ultimate success of the 2020–2021 farmer mobilization in India, resulting in the eventual repeal of the proposed farm bills offers a case in point. Social and environmental workplace safeguards that have created high standards of living in Europe are necessary beyond its borders, and not as a zero-sum game in which Europe continues to benefit at the expense of others. Building social supports cannot therefore take place by cost-shifting the heavy burdens of material and surplus labor requirements for such transitions to places like the DRC. Likewise, the siting of intensive extractive agriculture and mineral extraction should not be justified in so-called "undervalued" areas or "wastelands" falsely characterized as devoid of history, people or nature, such as the Olusosun e-waste dumpsite in Nigeria. Entrenched hierarchies of racial and patriarchal capitalism, stemming from slavery (of people of color and women) and the amassing of wealth by colonial oppressors, have shaped both historical and contemporary global development and consumption patterns. They have allowed for countries like India and China to shoulder the manufacturing requirements for consumption in the EU, the United States, Canada, and Australia, while simultaneously preying upon African countries and their own marginalized ecosystems and peoples for raw material assets.

Toward a pluriverse of alternatives

As Indigenous Anishinaabe scholar Vanessa Watts (2013) writes, remedying historical mistakes that have led to ecological breakdown does not mean comparing or measuring Indigenous cosmologies with the mistakes made by Euro-Western development, including through post-structuralist critique. Instead, moving forward toward the re-flourishing of ecologies requires restoring socio-cultural relationships with the land as territory, as a living place that affords agency to both people and non-people alike. Eurocentric narratives of state and capital were historically (and continue to be) premised on the idea of a Global South, that presumably had/has nothing to contribute practically or intellectually to human flourishing (Dabashi 2015; Richardson 2018 and Amin 1989). Cultural genocide and assimilation of non-European ways of life has therefore been seen as acceptable, as a "sacrifice zone" or as the inevitable cost of "progress." The political economic relations of a "green" economy that cost-shifts production and waste dumps to the Global South and finds solutions in ideas like industrial-scale global veganism or half-earth conservation resonates deeply with what Mitchell and Chaudhury claim as plans that "involve the re-enactment and innovation of key techniques used by European colonizers to annex land, displace communities and undermine the sovereignty of BIPOC[9] peoples across the planet" (2020: 10). As we describe further below, a focus on replenishing social relations among and between humans and non-humans requires adopting an explicitly historical approach in the spirit of *reparations* from five centuries of colonial impositions. Moving beyond what Arturo Escobar (2018) defines as a "one world world," also means rejecting the interpretation of both "problems" and their "solutions" as technical-fixes to keep the overall structure intact and which replicate what Shiva (1993) calls "monocultures of the mind."

We need a reparations ecology

As Raj Patel and Jason Moore (2017) and later Táíwò (2022) argue, a "just" Deal ("Green," "New" or otherwise) should set in a motion a "reparations ecology" – directly opposed to the ecological relations of capitalism in which people, land, water, and non-human nature are treated as commodified resources. A "reparations ecology" relates the visceral historical memory and ongoing trauma of Western modernity's binaries of "nature" from "humans," and humans according to race, gender, class, and caste, to specific violent acts of cultural genocide, dispossession and ecocide. It involves reappropriating the flow of materials and energy to permit a plurality of ecological relationships, rendering the binary separations mentioned above irrational. The Western obsession of needing to rationalize (i.e., classify, quantify, predict and control) solutions would therefore be turned on its head by reparations ecology, which should provide unconditional payments for anti-capitalist and grassroots approaches to re-commoning social and ecological development pathways.

Reparations go much further than any kind of redistributive attempt (the least of which are restricted merely to monetary terms), and instead prioritize alternative knowledges and ontologies as legitimate without any requirement to be translated into Western Euro-descendent logics, settler colonial languages, or any other form of hegemonic ideology. Reparations undo centuries of privatization and reverse the logic of private property that perceives emerging values only as potential market opportunities for profit. In solidarity with recent arguments by Bagayoko (2021) and Nacpil (2021), ecological reparations mean, first and foremost, recognizing that "indebted" countries that have endured centuries of colonial crimes against humanity and stolen natural and cultural wealth deserve much more than debt cancellation. To this end, ecological reparations are not performative acts but involve material transfers such as giving land back to Indigenous populations. Neither reparations nor decolonization can be used in the abstract or metaphorically. Rather, they serve as both self-reflexive invitations and missile words to intentionally disrupt "comfortable" Euro-liberal humanist proposals that tend to window dress generations of cultural and ecological trauma in an effort to fashion more inclusive and "progressive" forms of domination. Reparations means holding space for emotionally sensitive and situated, experienced knowledge to be treated legitimately and at least on par with abstract or theoretical models, allowing for actions to take place according to the terms and conditions of those who have experienced and continue to experience ecological and cultural trauma (Murdock 2018). This is what being attentive to ecology means; this is what being "green" ignores.

We need holistic transformation

While reparation is crucial to deal with historical and ongoing Global North-South relations, also needed are transformations in other forms of inequity and exploitation, including gender, caste, and race. We need transformations across political, social, economic, cultural and other domains of life, consistent with ecological wisdom and sustainability. Across the world, there are hundreds of thousands of initiatives that are meeting human needs and aspirations without trashing the earth, and without worsening inequities and injustices. Rather, they take form by respecting the diversity and resilience of nature and of human cultures, by reducing socio-economic inequities, and by challenging and attempting to replace structures of oppression, injustice and unsustainability. Many have arisen from within movements resisting extractivist "development," others are currently relevant assertions of traditional practices and worldviews, and others still emerge from within industrialized societies and challenge their essentially exploitative narrative. A recent compilation of over 100 essays brings many of these together: global networks that compile thousands of practical examples of agroecology, commoning community conservation, alternative currencies and transition movements; worldviews and approaches building on Indigenous, spiritual, and other traditions such as swaraj, hurai, tao, and kyosei (from Asia), buen vivir, sumac kawsay, sentipensar (and many other parallels across Latin America), ubuntu (and its parallels across

Africa), caring for country (from Australian aboriginal peoples), minobimaatisiiwin (and other native North American cosmologies) (Kothari et al. 2019).[10] These essays also include radical reinterpretations of mainstream religions, and ideological and other approaches from within industrialized or modern societies (such as degrowth, ecosocialism, ecofeminism, alter-globalization, free software, and decolonial design).

Two of the most inspiring radical alternatives that have challenged multiple structures of domination and unsustainability, and have done it at scale, are found in the Zapatista autonomous region in Mexico and the Kurdish autonomous region at the intersection of Turkey, Iran, Iraq, and Syria (Aslan and Akbulut 2019; Leyva-Solano 2019).[11] In both cases, there is an attempt to create a radical, fully participatory form of political and economic governance, with strong adherence to ecological and feminist principles. In both, there is a strong challenge to the centrality of the state; both are also periodically attacked in various ways by the nation-states they are located within. Beyond these examples, there are the movements to reclaim spaces from privatization, such as of land, natural ecosystems and knowledge, and return them to the commons through democratic governance for the benefit of all. These include the conversion of car parking lots into collective urban gardening in some European cities, the re-assertion of "community economies," worker-led production systems, and the movements for open-source, "copyleft" technologies (De Angelis 2019; Halpin 2019; Karyotis 2019). There are also thousands of examples across the world of "territories of life," which are natural ecosystems governed by Indigenous Peoples and other local communities in ways that conserve biodiversity while securing dignified livelihoods.[12]

During the COVID-19 pandemic, even as states and corporations have ramped up authoritarian, profit-making tendencies, people's movements of the kinds mentioned above have demonstrated the remarkable resilience of communities that have always already been mobilized for self-determination and self-reliance.[13] The ones who had their food, water, and energy systems intact, having sustained them from the past or asserted them anew, have fared much better than those funneled into globalized markets governed by the state-corporate nexus.

Common threads linking a plurality of solutions

While enormously different from each other, such radical approaches do show some common values and principles: commons and collectives over selfish individualism (but not denying individual identities and aspirations), autonomy and freedom with responsibility, respect for the rights of humans and non-human nature, self-reliance and localization, simplicity or notions of "enoughness" and sufficiency, direct democracy enabling equitable participation by all, and so on. And they attempt transformation in at least five spheres of life (Kalpavriksh 2017):

a *Ecological wisdom, integrity, and resilience*, maintaining the eco-regenerative processes that conserve ecosystems, species, functions, and cycles; respect for ecological limits at various levels, local to global; and the infusion of ecological wisdom and ethics in all human endeavor, including the recognition of the rights of nature in law and policy;

b *Social well-being and justice*, including lives that are fulfilling and satisfactory physically, socially, culturally, and spiritually; where there is equity between communities and individuals in socio-economic and political entitlements, benefits, rights and responsibilities; where there is communal and ethnic harmony; where hierarchies and divisions based on faith, gender, caste, class, ethnicity, ability, and other attributes are replaced by non-exploitative, non-oppressive, non-hierarchical, and nondiscriminatory relations; and where collective and individual human rights are ensured;

c *Direct and delegated democracy*, where decision-making starts at the smallest unit of human settlement, in which every human has the right, capacity, and opportunity to take part, and builds up from this unit to larger levels of governance by delegates that are downwardly accountable to the units of direct democracy; and where decision-making is not simply on a "one-person, one-vote" basis but rather consensual, while being attentive to emerging power asymmetries, respectful and supportive of the needs and rights of those currently marginalized;

d *Economic democracy*, in which local communities and individuals (including producers and consumers, wherever possible combined into one as "prosumers") have control over the means of production, distribution, exchange, and markets; where localization is a key principle, and larger trade and exchange is built on it on the principle of equal exchange; where private property gives way to the commons, removing the distinction between owner and worker.

e *Cultural diversity and knowledge democracy*, in which pluralism of ways of living, ideas and ideologies is respected, where creativity and innovation are encouraged, where the generation, transmission and use of knowledge (traditional/modern, including science and technology) are accessible to all, and where spiritual and/or ethical learning and deepening are central to social life.

Achieving transformation in the above five spheres must be above all a decolonizing effort. Such an effort must also be in conversation with a global and transversal interweaving of radical alternatives, as for instance, what the Global Tapestry of Alternatives[14] and related platforms are attempting. At the same time, we recognize that these initiatives have their own internal complexities and uneven relations of power that define them in both space and time. Our aim is not to romanticize them, but rather to view them as openings continuously in the process of "becoming" and which show potential for remaking the world in more just ways. To summarize, a Green New Deal will further reinforce violence and will be a vast waste of effort and time if it is restricted to bringing in historically marginalized people to play the rules of "one-world world" development, "green" or otherwise. Without needing to engage with Northern-led GNDs like the EU Green Deal, innumerable alternatives from the many Global Souths of marginalized working-class people around the world can and should be facilitated to flourish on their own.

Postscript: a recent reflection on the implications of a "Global Green New Deal", spearheaded by War on Want, The Leap and others, is attempting to transcend the limitations of GND-like approaches by explicitly building upon Global North-South inequality, uneven patterns of consumption and resource imperialism, and the politically neutralizing efforts of liberal democracy.[15] Further, and as this chapter was being finalized, a new book entitled *A People's Green New Deal* by Max Ajl was published by Pluto Press in May, 2021. Ajl's work interrogates the presumption of "northern" accumulation and consumption patterns to realistically initiate ecological transformation of the kind needed to pull the breaks on the social and ecological crises we face. His works draws attention to the red flags of romanticized Keynesian social welfare programs and eco-modernism that risk further reinforcing the socially alienating class and racial divisions that fuel ecological breakdown. He centers his analysis on the transformative potential that anti-imperialist agroecological farming practice can play in opening up possibilities that are nowhere to be seen in any GND being proposed by the Global North. Ajl's "People's Green New Deal," instead, demands an internationalist convergence committed to decolonial climate reparations, and abolitionist and Indigenous self-determination in the twin struggle for social and climate justice.

Notes

1 This chapter is an updated and extended version of the two-part article, "Harm Here is Still Harm There: The Green New Deal and the Global South" published in *Jamhoor* in May 2020.

2 In this chapter, we focus primarily on the impacts of Northern-led GNDs, as these are becoming inscribed into policy and materially affecting development priorities within and beyond their boundaries.

3 We extend our understanding of "Global South" to go beyond colonized or economically weaker nations historically located in Latin America, Africa, and Asia, to include marginalized sections of society across the world, including within the so-called "developed" countries; and its counterpart, the "Global North" to go beyond economically powerful nations historically located primarily in Europe, North America, Australia, Singapore, and Japan, to include rich and powerful sections within the geographical South.

4 We use this word in the broadest sense, to both specify the underpinnings of global capitalism as rooted in anti-Blackness, but also the ways this extends to similar forms of discriminative "othering" and exploitation, such as casteism. In doing so, we do not intend to equate forms of racism, but rather to highlight how racialization serves as a crucial process in the making of contemporary capitalism.

5 Available from: https://berniesanders.com/issues/green-new-deal/

6 See critiques of several techno-managerial-market solutions in the section "Universalizing the Earth: Reformist Solutions," of Kothari et al. 2019.

7 See also the Jevon's Paradox, below.

8 We make here a distinction between "private" sector and community or collective processes, both being distinct from "state-led" sectors; as we show later, community-based initiatives can be a radical alternative to both the state and the private corporate sector.

9 Black, Indigenous, and People of Color (BIPOC)

10 Available for free PDF download at: https://radicalecologicaldemocracy.org/pluriverse

11 See also: Jineolojî (https://www.jineoloji/en/) and the Reworlding series on uprising democracy (https://www.youtube.com/watch?v=t3rWIHuKpIg)

12 For examples, see documents and case studies at www.iccaconsortium.org; on the conservation efficacy of such initiatives, see https://www.sciencedirect.com/science/article/abs/pii/S1462901119301042?via%3Dihub

13 For several examples from around the world, see https://www.interfacejournal.net; for examples from India, see several volumes of the series "Extraordinary Work of "Ordinary" People: Beyond Pandemics and Lockdowns", https://vikalpsangam.org/article/extraordinary-work-of-ordinary-people-in-multi-language-translation/

14 https://globaltapestryofalternatives.org

15 https://waronwant.org/our-work/global-green-new-deal

References

Ajl, M. 2021. *A People's Green New Deal*. Pluto Press, London.

Alcott, B., Giampietro, M., Mayumi, K., and Polimeni, J. 2012. *The Jevons Paradox and the Myth of Resource Efficiency Improvements*. Routledge, New York.

Aldeia, J., and Alves, F. 2019. Against the Environment. Problems in Society/Nature Relations. *Frontiers in Sociology* 4(29): 1–12.

Amin, S. 1989. *Eurocentricism*. NYU Press, New York.

Angelo, H., and Wachsmuth, D. 2020. Why Does Everyone Think Cities Can Save the Planet? *Urban Studies*. Available from: doi.org/10.1177/0042098020919081.

Arboleda, M. 2020. *Planetary Mine*. Verso, London.

Asher, M. 2021. Clash of the Toolkits: Where Farmers' Concerns and Environmental Activism Converge. *The Bastion*. 18 March. Available from: https://thebastion.co.in/politics-and/environment/climate-change/clash-of-the-toolkits-where-farmers-concerns-and-environmental-activism-converge/

Aslan, A. and Akbulut, B. 2019. Democracy Economy in Kurdistan. In: Kothari, A. et al. eds. *Pluriverse – A Post-Development Dictionary*. Tulika Books and Authors UpFront, New Delhi.

Azim Premji University. 2021. *State of Working India 2021: One Year of COVID-19*. Centre for Sustainable Employment, Azim Premji University, Bengaluru. Available from: https://cse.azimpremjiuniversity.edu.in/state-of-working-india/.

Bagayoko, B. 2021. Colonial Debt and Reparations. In: Kaur Paul, H. and Gebrial, D. eds. *Perspectives on a Global Green New Deal*. Rosa-Luxemburg Stiftung, London.

Bigger, P. and Webber, S. 2021. Green Structural Adjustment in the World Bank's Resilient City. *Annals of the American Association of Geographers*: 111(1): 36–51. Available from: doi.org/10.1080/24694452.2020.1749023.

Borras, S.M. Jr., and Franco, J.C. 2012. Global Land Grabbing and Trajectories of Agrarian Change: A Preliminary Analysis. *Journal of Agrarian Change* 12(1): 34–59.

Boyd, A., and Mitchell, D.O. eds. 2013. *Beautiful Trouble: A Toolbox for Revolution*. Or Books, New York, NY.

Brand, U., and Wissen, M. 2012. Global Environmental Politics and the Imperial Mode of Living: Articulations of State-Capital Relations in the Multiple Crisis. *Globalizations* 9(4): 547–560.

Broumas, A. 2018. Commons' Movements and 'progressive' Governments as Dual Power: The Potential for Social Transformation in Europe. *Capital and Class* 42(2): 229–251.

Bruno, K., and Karliner, J. 2000. Tangled Up in Blue: Corporate Partnerships in the United Nations. Available from: http://www.corpwatch.org/article.php?id=996.

Caffentzis, G.C. 2019. Digital Tools. In: Kothari, A. et al. eds. *Pluriverse – A Post-Development Dictionary*. Tulika Books and Authors UpFront, New Delhi.

Chandran, R. and Gardner, T. 2017. Calls to End Africa's 'horrific' Land Deals after Indian Firm's Fallout. *Reuters*. 28 November. Available from: https://www.reuters.com/article/us-ethiopia-landrights-india/calls-to-end-africas-horrific-land-deals-after-indian-firms-fallout-idUSKBN1DS1FK

Chandrasekaran, K. 2021. Can Land as a Carbon Sink Save us All? In: Kaur Paul, H. and Gebrial, D. eds. *Perspectives on a Global Green New Deal*. Rosa-Luxemburg Stiftung, London.

Chandrasekhar, C.P. and Ghosh, J. 2020. Informal Workers in the Time of Coronavirus. *International Development Economics Associates*. 24 March. Available from: http://www.networkideas.org/featured-articles/2020/03/informal-workers-in-the-time-of-coronavirus/

Christianson, G. and Pinchot, A. 2020. BlackRock Is Getting Serious about Climate Change. Is This a Turning Point for Investors? *World Resources Institute*. 27 January. Available from: https://www.wri.org/blog/2020/01/blackrock-getting-serious-about-climate-change-turning-point-investors

Clark, J.P. 2019. Lifeboat Ethics. In: Kothari, A. et al. eds. *Pluriverse – A Post-Development Dictionary*. Tulika Books and Authors UpFront, New Delhi.

Clifford, T. 2020. CNBC. Capitalism 'will fundamentally be in jeopardy' If Business Does Not Act on Climate Change, Microsoft CEO Satya Nadella Says. *CNBC*. 16 January. Available from: https://www.cnbc.com/2020/01/16/microsoft-ceo-capitalism-is-in-jeopardy-if-we-do-not-act-on-climate-change.html

Clifford, C. 2021. The Who, What and Where of Elon Musk's $100 Million Prize Money for Carbon Capture Innovation. *CNBC*. 8 February. Available from: https://www.cnbc.com/2021/02/08/who-what-where-of-elon-musks-100-million-prize-for-carbon-capture.html

Collard, R.C., Dempsey, J. and Sundberg, J. 2016. The Moderns' Amnesia in Two Registers. *Environmental Humanities* 7(1): 227–232.

Crowley, T. 2019. Modi Might Have Finally Gone Too Far. *Jacobin*. 22 December. Available from: https://jacobinmag.com/2019/12/narendra-modi-india-citizenship-amendment-act-muslims-bjp

Dabashi, H. 2015. *Can Non-Europeans Think?* Zed Books Ltd., London.

De Angelis, M. 2019. Commons. In: Kothari, A. et al. eds. *Pluriverse – A Post-Development Dictionary*. Tulika Books and Authors UpFront, New Delhi.

Elliott, L. et al. 2008. A Green New Deal. Green New Deal Group. Available from: https://greennewdealgroup.org/wp-content/uploads/2019/06/a-green-new-deal.pdf.

Engdahl, F.W. 2021. The WEF Agenda Behind Modi Farm Reform. Counter Currents. 17 February. Available from: https://countercurrents.org/2021/02/the-wef-agenda-behind-modi-farm-reform/

Escobar, A. 2018. *Designs for the Pluriverse: Radical Interdependence, Autonomy, and the Making of Worlds.* Duke University Press, Chapel Hill.

Faleiro, J. 2021. Intersecting Crises: A Case Study of Climate Migration in India in the Wake of Covid-19. In: Kaur Paul, H. and Gebrial, D. eds. *Perspectives on a Global Green New Deal.* Rosa-Luxemburg Stiftung, London.

Federici, S. and Linebaugh, P. 2018. *Re-enchanting the World: Feminism and the Politics of the Commons.* PM Press, Oakland.

Ferdinand, M. 2019. *Une Écologie Décoloniale.* Éditions du Seuil, Paris.

Ferguson, S., and McNally, D. 2015. Precarious Migrants: Gender, Race, and the Social Reproduction of a Global Working Class. *Socialist Register* 51: 1–23.

Forster, P.M. et al. Current and Future Global Climate Impacts Resulting from COVID-19. *Nature Climate Change* 10: 913–919. Available from: doi.org/10.1038/s41558-020-0883-0.

Foster, J.B. and Suwandi, I. 2020. COVID-19 and Catastrophe Capitalism. *Monthly Review.* 1 June. Available from: https://monthlyreview.org/2020/06/01/covid-19-and-catastrophe-capitalism/

Friedman, L. 2020. A Trillion Trees: How One Idea Triumphed over Trump's Climate Denialism. *New York Times.* 12 February. Available from: https://www.nytimes.com/2020/02/12/climate/trump-trees-climate-change.html

Fuchs, R., Brown, C. and Rounsevell, M. 2020. Europe's Green Deal Offshores Environmental Damage to Other Nations. *Nature* 586: 671–673.

Giampietro, M. and Mayumi, K. 2018. Unraveling the Complexity of the Jevons Paradox: The Link Between Innovation, Efficiency, and Sustainability. *Frontiers in Energy Research* 6: 6–26.

Gibb, R. et al. 2020. Zoonotic Host Diversity Increases in Human-Dominated Ecosystems. *Nature* 584: 398–402. Available from: doi.org/10.1038/s41586-020-2562-8

GRAIN. 2021. Digital Control: How Big Tech Moves into Food and Farming (and What it Means). Grain.org. 21 January. Available from: https://grain.org/en/article/6595-digital-control-how-big-tech-moves-into-food-and-farming-and-what-it-means

Greenford, D.H. et al. 2020. Shifting Economic Activity to Services has Limited Potential to Reduce Global Environmental Impacts Due to the Household Consumption of Labour. *Environmental Research Letters* 15(6), 064019.

Halpin, H. 2019. Free Software. In: Kothari, A. et al. eds., *Pluriverse – A Post-Development Dictionary.* Tulika Books and Authors UpFront, New Delhi.

Hargreaves, S. 2019. Neo-extractivism. In: Kothari, A. et al. eds., *Pluriverse – A Post-Development Dictionary.* Tulika Books and Authors UpFront, New Delhi.

Hickel, J. 2018. Why Growth can't be Green. *Australian Options* 89: 12.

Hickel, J. and Kallis, G. 2020. Is Green Growth Possible? *New Political Economy* 25(4): 469–486.

IPBES. 2020. Workshop Report on Biodiversity and Pandemics of the Intergovernmental Platform on Biodiversity and Ecosystem Services. Daszak, P., Amuasi, J., das Neves, C. G., Hayman, D., Kuiken, T., Roche, B., Zambrana-Torrelio, C., Buss, P., Dundarova, H., Feferholtz, Y., Földvári, G., Igbinosa, E., Junglen, S., Liu, Q., Suzan, G., Uhart, M., Wannous, C., Woolaston, K., Mosig Reidl, P., O'Brien, K., Pascual, U., Stoett, P., Li, H., Ngo, H. T. Bonn: IPBES Secretariat. Available from: doi.org/10.5281/zenodo.4147317.

Kallis, G. 2017. *In defense of Degrowth: Opinions and Minifestos.* Uneven Earth Press, Hansbeke, Belgium.

Kalpavriksh. 2017. The Search for Radical Alternatives: Key Elements and Principles. Kalpavriksh. Available from: https://vikalpsangam.org/wp-content/uploads/migrate/Resources/alternetives-frameworkbookletrevisedfinal1512.pdf

Karyotis, T. 2019. Worker-led Production. In: Kothari, A. et al. eds., *Pluriverse – A Post-Development Dictionary.* Tulika Books and Authors UpFront, New Delhi.

Kaur, R. 2021. The Protest has Opened New Space for Workers, Farmers to Forge Solidarity in their Struggle. *The Indian Express.* 7 March. Available from: https://indianexpress.com/article/opinion/columns/solidarity-that-keeps-farm-protests-going-7217479/

Kaur Paul, H. and Gebrial, D. eds. 2021. *Perspectives on a Global Green New Deal.* Rosa-Luxemburg Stiftung, London.

Kopnina, H., Washington, H., Gray, J., and Taylor, B. 2018. The 'future of conservation' Debate: Defending Ecocentricism and the Nature Needs Half Movement. *Biological Conservation* 217: 140–148.

Kothari, A. 2020. Stop Messing with the Environment and People's Rights! *Vikalp Sangam*. 10 September. Available from: http://vikalpsangam.org/article/stop-messing-with-the-environment-and-peoples-rights/

Kothari, A. 2021a. Colonial Conservation in New Avatars. *Wall Street International Magazine*. 13 January. Available from: https://wsimag.com/economy-and-politics/64574-colonial-conservation-in-new-avatars

Kothari, A. 2021b. Half-earth or Whole-earth: Green or Transformative Recovery? Where Are the Voices from the Global South? *Oryx* 55(2): 161–162. Available from: doi:10.1017/S0030605321000120.

Kothari, A. et al. eds. 2019. *Pluriverse – A Post-Development Dictionary*. Tulika Books and Authors Up-Front, New Delhi.

Langlois, S. 2019. Du sang dans nos cellulaires. *Radio Canada*. 12 May. Available from: https://ici.radio-canada.ca/info/2019/05/coltan-republique-democratique-congo-mines-enfants/

Lawson, M. et al. 2020. Time to Care. *Oxfam*. 20 January. Available from: https://www.oxfam.org/en/research/time-care

Le Quéré, C. et al. 2020. Temporary Reduction in Daily Global CO_2 Emissions During the COVID-19 Forced Confinement. *Nature Climate Change* 10: 647–653.

Leyva-Solano, X. 2019. Zapatista Autonomy. In: Kothari, A. et al. eds., *Pluriverse – A Post-Development Dictionary*. Tulika Books and Authors UpFront, New Delhi.

Londoño, E. et al. 2020. Amazon Deforestation Soars as Pandemic Hobbles Enforcement. *New York Times*. 6 June. Available from: https://www.nytimes.com/2020/06/06/world/americas/amazon-deforestation-brazil.html

Lynes, K. and Trépanier, A-M. 2020. Who Guards the 'guardian angels' Upholding our Pandemic Response? *Ricochet Media*. 16 July. Available from: https://ricochet.media/en/3222/who-guards-the-guardian-angels-whose-work-upholds-our-pandemic-response

Mathur, H.M. ed. 2008. *India: Social Development Report 2008*. Council for Social Development, New Delhi. Available from: http://www.csdindia.org/social-development-report/india-social-development-report-2008

Milman, O. 2020. Amazon Threatened to Fire Employees for Speaking Out on Climate, Workers Say. *The Guardian*. 2 January. Available from: https://www.theguardian.com/technology/2020/jan/02/amazon-threatened-fire-employees-speaking-out-climate-change-workers-say

Ministerio de Minería Chile. 2019. Chile and India Advance in Lithium Investment Agreement BN Americas. 15 October. Available from: https://www.bnamericas.com/en/news/chile-and-india-advance-in-lithium-investment-agreement

Mitchell, A., and Chaudhury, A. 2020. Worlding Beyond 'the' 'end' of 'the world': White Apocalyptic Visions and BIPOC Futurisms. *International Relations* 34(3): 309–332. Available from: https://doi.org/10.1177/0047117820948936

Moore, J.W. 2015. *Capitalism in the Web of Life: Ecology and the Accumulation of Capital*. Verso Books, London.

Mumford, L. 1964. Authoritarian and Democratic Technics. *Technology and Culture* 5(1): 1–8.

Murdock, E.G. 2018. Unsettling Reconciliation: Decolonial Methods for Transforming Social-Ecological Systems. *Environmental Values* 27: 513–533.

Nacpil, L. 2021. Debt Cancellation and Reparations – Southern Movement Perspectives. In: Kaur Paul, H. and Gebrial, D. eds. *Perspectives on a Global Green New Deal*. Rosa-Luxemburg Stiftung, London.

Narasimhaiah, S., and Kulriya, M. 2021. India's Farmers' Protests: "This is History in the Making." *ROAR Magazine*. 5 February.

Out of the Woods Collective. 2020. *Hope Against Hope: Writings on Ecological Crisis*. Common Notions, Brooklyn.

Paprocki, K. 2018. Threatening Dystopias: Development and Adaptation Regimes in Bangladesh. *Annals of the American Association of Geographers* 108(4): 955–973.

Parrique, T. et al. 2019. *Decoupling Debunked: Evidence and Arguments against Green Growth as a Sole Strategy for Sustainability*. Brussels: European Environmental Bureau.

Patel, R., and Moore, J.W. 2017. *A History of the World in Seven Cheap Things: A Guide to Capitalism, Nature, and the Future of the Planet*. University of California Press, Berkeley.

Podur, J. 2021. Leaving behind the Racist and Imperialist Baggage of the Original New Deal. In: Kaur Paul, H. and Gebrial, D. eds. *Perspectives on a Global Green New Deal*. Rosa-Luxemburg Stiftung, London.

Purdy, J. 2015. Environmentalism's Racist History. *The New Yorker.* 13 August. Available from: https://www.newyorker.com/news/news-desk/environmentalisms-racist-history

Recognizing the Duty of the Federal Government to Create a Green New Deal. H. Res. 109, 116th Congress. 2019. Available from: https://ocasio-cortez.house.gov/sites/ocasio-cortez.house.gov/files/Resolution%20on%20a%20Green%20New%20Deal.pdf.

Richardson, W.J. 2018. Understanding Eurocentricism as a Structural Problem of Undone Science. In: Bhambra, G.K., Gebrial, D. and Nişancioğlu, K. eds. *Decolonising the University.* Pluto Press, London.

Riofrancos, T. 2021. The Rush to 'go electric' Comes with a Hidden Cost: Destructive Lithium Mining *The Guardian.* 14 June. Available from: https://www.theguardian.com/commentisfree/2021/jun/14/electric-cost-lithium-mining-decarbonasation-salt-flats-chile

Roberts, D. 2019. The Green New Deal, Explained. *Vox.* 30 March. Available from: https://www.vox.com/energy-and-environment/2018/12/21/18144138/green-new-deal-alexandria-ocasio-cortez.

Rosane, O. 2019. Bernie Sanders Enters 2020 Race, Promises Own Version of Green New Deal. *EcoWatch.* 19 February. Available from: https://www.ecowatch.com/bernie-sanders-2020-2629410846.html.

Rutazibwa, O.U. 2010. The Problematics of the EU's Ethical (Self) Image in Africa: The EU as an 'Ethical Intervener' and the 2007 Joint Africa-EU Strategy. *Journal of Contemporary European Studies* 18(2): 209–228.

Schwartzman, D. 2019. China and the Prospects for a Global Ecological Civilization. *Climate and Capitalism.* 17 September. Available from: https://climateandcapitalism.com/2019/09/17/china-and-the-prospects-for-a-global-ecological-civilization/

Shiva, V. 1993. *Monocultures of the Mind.* Zed Books, London.

Shrivastava, A., and Kothari, A. 2012. *Churning the Earth: The Making of Global India.* Penguin Books, New Delhi.

Siwach, S. 2021. What Is Leading to Massive Gatherings at Mahapanchayats; What Is its Relevance?. *The Indian Express.* 13 February. Available from: https://indianexpress.com/article/explained/explained-kisan-mahapanchats-farmer-agitation-relevance-7185221/

Springmann, M. et al. 2018. Options for Keeping the Food System within Environmental Limits. *Nature* 562: 519–525.

Táíwò, O.O. 2022. *Reconsidering Reparations.* Oxford University Press, Oxford.

Taylor, A. and Kaur, P. 2019. A Green New Deal Needs to be Global, Not Local. *Chain Reaction* 136: 14–15.

Thier, H. 2021. Vaccine Apartheid. Africa Is a Country. March. Available from: https://www.africasacountry.com/2021/03/vaccine-apartheid

Todhunter, C. 2021. Farmers' Protest in India: Price of Failure Will be Immense. *CounterPunch.* 9 February. Available from: https://www.counterpunch.org/2021/02/09/farmers-protest-in-india-price-of-failure-will-be-immense/

Totolo, E. 2009. ISN Security Watch. Coltan and Conflict in the DRC. Available from: https://reliefweb.int/report/democratic-republic-congo/coltan-and-conflict-drc

United Nations Environment Programme. 2019. *Emissions Gap Report 2019.* UNEP, Nairobi, Kenya.

United Nations Environment Programme. 2021. *Making Peace with Nature: A Scientific Blueprint to Tackle the Climate, Biodiversity and Pollution Emergencies.* UNEP, Nairobi, Kenya.

Vadén, T. et al. 2020. Raising the Bar: On the Type, Size and Timeline of a 'successful' Decoupling. *Environmental Politics.* Available from: doi.org/10.1080/09644016.2020.1783951

Wainwright, J., and Mann, G. 2018. *Climate Leviathan: A Political Theory of Our Planetary Future.* Verso, London.

Watts, V. 2013. Indigenous Place-Thought and Agency Amongst Humans and Non-Humans (First Woman and Sky Woman go on a European World Tour). *Decolonization: Indigeneity, Education and Society* 2(1): 20–34.

Wiedmann, T., Lenzen, M., Keyβer, L.T., and Steinberger, J.K. 2020. Scientists' Warning on Affluence. *Nature Communications* 11(3107): 1–10.

Wonder Alorse, R. 2019. The Digital Economy's Environmental Footprint Is Threatening the Planet. *The Conversation.* 8 December. Available from: https://theconversation.com/the-digital-economys-environmental-footprint-is-threatening-the-planet-126636

Wood, J. 2019. INDIA IS NOW PRODUCING the World's Cheapest Solar Power. *World Economic Forum*. 28 June. Available from: https://www.weforum.org/agenda/2019/06/india-is-now-producing-the-world-s-cheapest-solar-power/

Zografos, C. 2019. Direct Democracy. In: Kothari, A. et al. eds. *Pluriverse – A Post-Development Dictionary*. Tulika Books and Authors UpFront, New Delhi.

Zografos, C., and Robbins, P. 2020. Green Sacrifice Zones, or Why a Green New Deal Cannot Ignore the Cost Shifts of Just Transitions. *One Earth Cell Press* 3(5): 543–546.

PART III

The Green New Deal in practice

14

CHINESE GREEN JOB GUARANTEE

A roadmap for sustainable prosperity

Vincent (Yijiang) Huang

Introduction

The primary purpose of this article is to propose a tailored Green Job Guarantee program (thereafter Green JG) for the Chinese economy to coordinate economic growth, employment, structural adjustments, and environmental sustainability. I first demonstrate that a Job Guarantee program is far more effective in creating jobs than the conventional macroeconomic policies that indirectly create jobs by stimulating economic growth. I then explain why China would especially benefit from a Green JG and why China's time to implement it is ripe. I then show that the benefits of a Chinese Green JG outweigh its costs. Increasing China's fiscal deficit by 1.58% of 2019 GDP would have financed a complete Chinese Green JG to eliminate China's 24.27 million urban unemployment total and elevate China's GDP growth rate to the 2019 range of 9.23%–10.65%. Moreover, since a Green JG entails increased deficit spending, I examine the sustainability and functionality of Chinese government deficits by constructing and examining China's sector balances. Finally, I explore the design of a Chinese Green JG, such as how it should be administered, what jobs it could create, and why China should adopt a gradualist approach in order to implement it.

What is a job guarantee?

A Job Guarantee (JG) or Employer of Last Resort (ELR) is a publicly funded and locally administered employment program to (1) eliminate unemployment in a market economy by offering a job to anyone willing, able, and ready to work and (2) achieve public purposes by creating these jobs in appropriate fields (such as infrastructure, environmental service, and cultural heritage programs). It is a different public policy approach advocated by many to address unemployment (Minsky 1986; Forstater 2003; Wray 2004; Fullwiler 2005; Kaboub 2007a). Conventional macroeconomic policies – fiscal and monetary – aim to indirectly create jobs by stimulating economic growth. The problem, however, is that labor-displacing technical change (i.e. the machine process, robotics, and automation) is a structural trend that continues to undermine the causality from economic growth to job growth.[1] The result is that economic stimulus policies generate jobless growth (Ricardo 1911; Forstater 2000).

DOI: 10.4324/9781003110880-18

In comparison, a JG offers an unorthodox but logical solution to unemployment: eliminate joblessness by directly creating jobs. Then, these new jobs not only achieve public purposes (such as reforestation to address desertification) but also contribute to the growth of the market economy as the JG workers' wages translate into consumer spending, business sales, revenue, profits, and investments. Hence, while conventional economic stimulus policies indirectly create jobs by promoting economic growth, a JG program creates jobs first, which then organically generates economic growth.

The above logical difference between conventional macroeconomic policies and the Job Guarantee program has important implications regarding the quantitative relationship between China's GDP growth rate and unemployment rate. Chinese Premier Li Keqiang was clear when he discussed the purpose of China's economic growth: "the reason we care about GDP is because we care about employment stability" (Li 2013). However, his calculations expressed concerns about the effectiveness of stimulating GDP growth to create jobs, as he said in 2013,

> In the past, each one percent of China's GDP growth can create employment opportunities for 1 million Chinese. With the economy's structural adjustments, especially with the accelerating growth of the service sector, now [in 2013] each one percentage of China's GDP growth can create 1.3 or even 1.5 million jobs.
>
> *(Li 2013)*

This means that even if we assume that 1% GDP growth generates 1.5 million more jobs, China's GDP would have needed to grow for an additional 16% to eliminate its 24.27 million urban unemployment figure in 2019. This unrealistic requirement precisely demonstrates the difficulty of translating GDP growth to job growth using conventional economic stimulus policies in a world that is increasingly automated and capital-intensive.

If, however, we aim to create jobs directly and let economic growth become a residual, my calculation later in this chapter shows that a complete Chinese Green JG (assuming an average JG wage of 3700 RMB per month) will eliminate China's 24.27 million urban unemployment while generating an additional 3.13%–4.55% GDP growth in 2019. This means that to employ the same 24.27 million urban people unemployed in China in 2019, a JG approach now "requires"[2] the GDP to grow only 3.13%–4.55% more, as opposed to the 16% more as calculated before. The discrepancy reflects the fundamental advantage a JG program has over conventional macroeconomic stimulus policies – conventional economic stimulus policies only indirectly create jobs by promoting economic growth whereas a JG program creates jobs first, which then organically generates economic growth. Hence, echoing the importance of stabilizing employment, a JG approach is undoubtedly the more viable choice for China. In a nutshell, the "job growth creates GDP growth" approach is functional whereas the "GDP growth creates job growth" approach is inefficient and often contradictory to environmental and structural adjustments goals.

It is not only conventional macroeconomic policies that are ineffective at promoting employment; so are the conventional tools of education and training/retraining. Keynes' principle of effective demand argues that unemployment is a structural defect in a capitalist market economy because the firms' profit-maximizing level of output generally does not coincide with the full employment level of output (Keynes 1936). While training and education are important, they cannot alone explain aggregate unemployment. An individual's hard work, education, and training may lead him/her to a job. But that only changes the composition of unemployment; it does not alter joblessness in the aggregate level.

Hence, the Job Guarantee is an innovative policy response to the failures of conventional macroeconomic policies and education and training programs in achieving and maintaining full employment in a market economy.

Another important advantage of a JG program, when compared to conventional macroeconomic policies, is that it reduces policy instability and uncertainty. This is because a JG program is an institutionalized countercyclical automatic stabilizer to manage the macroeconomy. When the market economy slows down, the market sector (including both privately owned businesses and state-owned enterprises) will release workers into the JG program to produce more publicly desirable goods (such as environmental service, cultural heritage preservation programs, and other quality-of-life-enhancing works). When the market economy expands, workers will be incentivized by the higher wages offered by the private sector to re-enter market employment and produce more market goods. A JG program thus complements the market, rather than replacing it. A JG program therefore not only *achieves* full employment at a point in time but also *maintains* full employment through time (Forstater 2000). Employment fluctuations during the business cycles are shown in Figure 14.1.[3]

Moreover, JG programs are generally affordable, especially for countries with monetary sovereignty. Research has demonstrated the financial affordability of a JG in a number of countries, including the United States, Australia, Tunisia, India, Saudi Arabia, and even Greece (Gordon 1997; Kitson, Michie and Sutherland 1997; Mitchell and Watts 1997; Fullwiler 2003; Kaboub 2007b; Forstater, Kaboub and Kelsey 2015). In this chapter, I demonstrate that even the most conservative estimates of the benefits of a Chinese Green JG far outweigh the costs of implementing it. I also show that the fiscal deficit needed to finance a Chinese Green JG is not only sustainable but also functional to stabilize Chinese private sector balance sheets.

Note that the benefits of a JG are enormous precisely due to the tremendous economic and social costs of unemployment for the macroeconomy, individuals, households, communities,

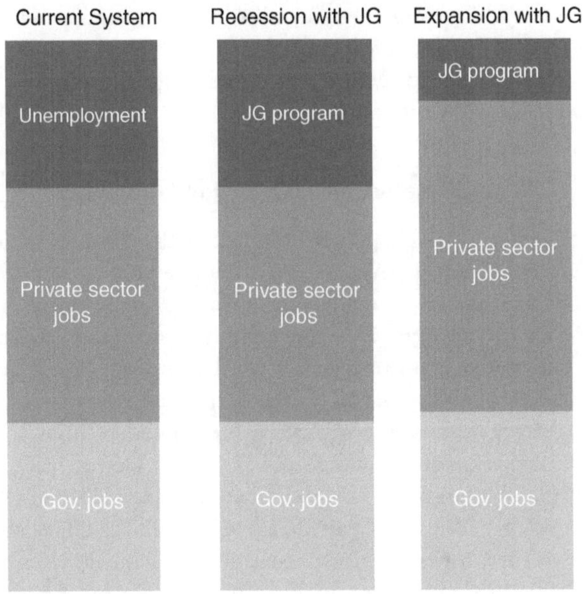

Figure 14.1 The job guarantee approach to full employment
Source: Forstater, Kaboub and Kelsay (2015).

and the nation-state. In macroeconomic terms, unemployment entails a loss of potential GDP should the unemployed remain unable to contribute to production. Individually, unemployment presents substantial economic and psychological hardship that threatens one's material provisioning and mental health. Socially, unemployment is discouraging and detrimental to cultivate social trust and harmony. For the nation-state, unemployment generates social and political instabilities that could result in right-wing populism.[4]

A final introductory note about the JG concerns its applications in the real world. While a variety of countries (such as the United States, Sweden, Australia, Argentina, and India) have experimented with JG in some forms, the design and implementation of their job creation programs have been partial and incomplete. Even when a program was clearly functioning well, it could still be discontinued, as evidenced by the American New Deal after WWII. The most important factors that have constrained the development of JG worldwide are not economical but rather political and ideological. This is because even though JG is complementary to a market economy, it is socialist in nature and entails changes in the structure of society that may undermine the power of the owners of capital. As such, it faces strong political and ideological opposition in capitalist countries, particularly those with a laissez-faire/neoliberal model of economic governance. Kalecki, for instance, was skeptical that a program granting full employment would be possible given the likely opposition from powerful actors in a capitalist society. He notes that a full employment capitalism entails essential social and institutional changes:

> 'Full employment capitalism' will, of course, have to develop new social and political institutions which will reflect the increased power of the working class. If capitalism can adjust itself to full employment, a fundamental reform will have been incorporated in it. If not, it will show itself an outmoded system which must be scrapped
>
> *(Kalecki 1943: 5)*

Hence, various forms of JG have only been adopted in these countries when unemployment issues became too acute to be ignored. China, on the other hand, is in a unique position to use JG as a means to an end due to the Chinese state's pragmatic and developmental role in shaping China's socialist market economy.

Why China needs a Green Job Guarantee

In addition to the benefits of a Job Guarantee described in the previous section, China would especially benefit from a Green JG because it has the potential to help the Chinese economy coordinate economic growth, employment, structural adjustments and environmental sustainability. I first identify four major changes and challenges that have pressured China's economic growth and employment in recent years. I then show how a Chinese Green JG enhances the Chinese state's ability to tackle each of these four changes and challenges.

The four major changes and challenges that have pressured the Chinese economy in recent years are domestic, international, structural and technical. Domestically, the Supply-Side Structural Reform (SSSR) announced by President Xi in late 2015 – while necessary to reduce excessive capacity, address pollution and upgrade China's industry – inevitably put downward pressure on the Chinese economy in the short and medium term. Internationally, Trump's initiation of the trade war against China in 2018 (which has been accompanied by a technology war, currency war, media war, etc.) has pressured China's economic growth through the exports channel. Structurally, China's population growth slowdown due to urbanization presents a serious long-term challenge for the Chinese economy to transition from export-led to domestic consumption-led. Finally, in the technical dimension, the Chinese state's macroeconomic policy over the last few years had (until 2019–2020[5]) preferred corporate tax cuts and monetary policies to direct government spending, which reduced the effectiveness of budget deficits.

The job creation part of the Green JG effectively addresses China's economic growth and employment concerns while enhancing the Chinese state's ability to tackle each of these changes and challenges. First, the JG program not only supports the SSSR by creating employment opportunities to counteract the unemployment pressure from reducing excess capacity. It also enriches the SSSR by increasing shortage capacity (such as the Chinese economy's ability to perform environmental service, preserve, and disseminate Chinese traditional culture, and other quality-of-life-enhancing works). This is because the types of jobs created through the JG depend on the need of the Chinese economy. A Chinese Green JG program thus enables China's Supply-Side Structural Reform by stabilizing employment and enriches it by increasing needed capacity within the Chinese economy.

Second, my proposed JG program supports the Chinese economy's structural transition from export-led to domestic consumption-led growth. As Trump's trade war against China in the context of global populism, nationalism, isolationism, and protectionism signals a "new normal," the Chinese economy must develop its resilience against external demand shocks by promoting its domestic demand (China State Council 2018). A JG program can facilitate this process through increasing the purchasing power of the previously unemployed Chinese workers (who have a greater marginal propensity to consume).[6] As the JG program creates employment, it increases workers' disposable income, thereby increasing workers' consumption and stabilizing firms' profits and balance sheets. Hence, the JG program begins with creating public sector employment to achieve public purposes and ends by stimulating the market economy to promote economic growth.

Third, a JG program alleviates macroeconomic pressure arising from China's slowdown in population growth rate. The decline in China's population growth rate entails two macroeconomic issues. First, China's labor supply growth will decelerate, which implies that cheap labor cannot be a long-term strategy to secure international competitiveness for Chinese manufacturing. Second, China's domestic demand will be harder to manage since unborn Chinese people would not buy goods and services. A JG program helps address both issues. By offering a job to any Chinese willing, able and ready to work, a JG allows the Chinese economy to operate at full utilization of labor at a point in time. By guaranteeing employment, a JG program also brings economic security to Chinese households that should positively impact China's population growth rate, thereby increasing China's labor supply over time. In terms of its impact on domestic demand, a JG program stabilizes domestic consumption by paying wages to the previously unemployed workers. These new wages translate into consumption more effectively, since JG workers tend to exhibit much higher marginal propensity to consume than high-income earners.

Fourth, I mentioned before that the Chinese state's macroeconomic policy in the last few years had preferred tax cuts and monetary policies to direct government spending, which reduced the effectiveness of budget deficits. A JG program can be much more economically simulative even with the same amount of impact on the fiscal budget. For instance, a 1 million RMB personal income tax cut for Ma Yun[7] produces limited macroeconomic simulative effects since Ma Yun's consumption habit will hardly be affected by the additional income. Similarly, a 1 million RMB corporate tax cut does little to stimulate the economy when the corporation uses the money not to invest but to buy back its stock in the financial market. However, a 1 million RMB wage in the hands of Chinese JG workers will likely translate most (if not all) of that amount into consumption (and most likely consumption of domestically produced goods and services), thereby stimulating economic growth via the multiplier effect. Both tax cuts and JG spending in my example have the same impact on the fiscal budget. Yet, they produce dramatically different simulative and distributional effects.

It is also important to note that the JG program does not compete with the private sector in the end market since they produce different goods and services. The JG program does, however, compete with the private sector in the input market for workers. This allows the JG to ensure the basic benefits of workers, since a worker can always earn a living wage in the JG program if they are mistreated by a private employer. The JG wage thus effectively becomes the minimum wage. However, the JG wage needs to be appropriate – high enough to be a living wage and low enough to not cause wage-led inflation or impair private employers' ability to hire. If the JG wage rate is set too high, exporting industries could see their international competitiveness undermined due to increased labor costs. Considering the Chinese state's vision to maintain China's industrial dominance, I use 3700 RMB[8] as an average JG worker's monthly income to estimate the cost of a Chinese Green JG further on.

Another reason that China would especially benefit from a Green JG results from the strategic role of Chinese State-Owned Enterprises (SOEs) in the Chinese economy. A JG program should be considered a more desirable solution to address unemployment and economic deceleration than having the SOEs expand hiring and investments when there are no market demands.[9] A Chinese JG program thus allows Chinese SOEs to focus on their industrial strategies, improve operational efficiency, and thereby expand international competitiveness. This, of course, does not mean that a JG program will or should take away the many other important responsibilities shouldered by the SOEs, such as investments in R&D.

Why China's time to implement a Green Job Guarantee is ripe

I have demonstrated in the previous section that China would especially benefit from a Green JG program. Whether it is to counteract the unemployment pressure from structural adjustments, to cope with the US-China trade war in an increasingly conflictual international political climate, to better transition the Chinese economy from export-led to domestic consumption-led in the context of declining population growth, or to promote economic growth without sacrificing the environment, a Green JG program is an effective policy tool. These are the *demand-side* reasons for why China's time to implement a Green JG is ripe. In this section, I explain the *supply-side* reasons why China is ready and capable to implement a Green JG.

First, from the political economy perspective, a Green JG can be an important component of the "Chinese Characteristics" of China's socialist market economy. As I concluded in my essay, *Transformation, not Transition: A Critical Survey of China's Political Economy*, in order to understand the future of the Chinese economy, the question to ask is not whether China should have the market or not, or whether the Chinese state is interfering too much, but rather what kind of a market economy best fulfills the developmental vision set by the Chinese state. Following Deng Xiaoping's "black cat, white cat" principle, a market economy is simply a tool, not an end for the Chinese state. Hence, compared with capitalist market economies, China faces no significant political and ideological barriers to adopt a socialist labor policy.[10]

By definition, a Job Guarantee program creates employment opportunities for those who are left behind by the market economy. Hence, it complements the market economy as opposed to replacing it. This is consistent with the Chinese state's two primary visions for its economy: a continuous determination to the market economy and a continuous search for and expansion of the Chinese characteristics of that market economy. A full-employment market economy is therefore a concrete reflection of China's socialist market economy. As it becomes increasingly clear that China's political economy ushers a different yet viable political and economic order that challenges Western liberal democracy and free market ideals, China is in a stronger political and institutional position to implement the Green JG.

Furthermore, while President Xi's "confidence doctrine"[11] enables the implementation of a socialist labor market policy like a Green JG, the "confidence doctrine" itself can be strengthened and enriched by the Green JG. This reason is simple: if the Chinese state successfully implements a Green JG to eliminate unemployment (which, as Keynes argues, is a persistent structural problem of the market economy), it would truly be enriching the meaning of China's "socialist market economy with Chinese characteristics." A full employment socialist market economy has every reason to be confident in its "path, theory, system, and culture" (Xi 2017).

Second, China's time to implement a *Green* JG is ripe because China's environmental policy climate today seeks synthesized environmental-economic policies to address the contradiction between economic growth and environmental sustainability. Like implementing synthesized environmental-industrial policies and laws to improve energy efficiency and conservation, the Chinese state since 2005 has also positioned the renewable energy sector at the core of its national industrial planning to ensure energy security for the future. Though it is not always possible to align monetary efficiency and environmental efficiency, there exists substantial synthesis between economic growth and environmental sustainability. For example, as Chen estimates, "spending within three segments of the renewable energy sectors – solar, wind and bioenergy – will produce in combination about twice as many jobs per dollar of expenditure than an equal amount of spending on fossil fuels [in China]" (Chen 2019).

Considering this positive development in China's environmental policy climate in recent years, the time for China to implement a *Green* JG is ripe. This is because a Green JG can contribute to environmental sustainability in two primary ways. As Forstater, Kaboub and Kelsay state:

> There are two main ways in which the JG program can promote ecological sustainability. First, JG workers can be directly employed in activities that enhance the environment. Examples include recycling, clean up, community gardens, and so on. Second, even if JG workers are not directly engaged in activities related to the environment, an economy brought to full employment through the JG will be more sustainable than one in which the job creation comes through stimulating private sector growth. JG activities need not use scarce natural resources or methods of production that pollute. There is a whole spectrum of near pure services that use virtually no natural resources at all.
>
> *(2015: 25)*

Third, China's time to implement a Green JG is ripe because empirical lessons are abundant from a variety of foreign, domestic, formal, and informal adoptions of JG programs. Internationally, from WWII to the 1970s, a variety of Western countries adopted informal job guarantees. For example, the American New Deal included job creation programs such as the Civilian Conservation Corp (CCC) and the Works Progress Administration (WPA) that were responsible for building much of the US infrastructure that remains in use to this day. Sweden developed broad-based employment programs that substantially increased the availability of public goods and virtually guaranteed employment to anyone willing, able and ready to work. A number of countries including Australia maintained

> a close approximation of full employment through a combination of high aggregate demand plus loosely coordinated direct job creation. Often there would be an informal 'employer of last resort,' such as the national railroads, that would hire just about anyone.
>
> *(Wray 2012: 233)*

After its 2001 economic crisis that saw the collapse of its currency sovereignty, Argentina created a formal employment Plan *Jefes y Jefas* that guaranteed a job for poor heads of households (Kostzer 2008; Tcherneva 2012). The program "created 2 million new jobs that not only provided employment and income for poor families, but also provided needed services and free goods to poor neighborhoods" (Wray 2012: 235). Another example of a formal but partial job guarantee is India's 2005 National Rural Employment Guarantee Act.

Domestically, China has also adopted informal and partial JG programs. For example, China's traditional infrastructure stimulus programs are in effect partial experiments of the JG program. The difference is that infrastructure investments stimulus stabilizes employment temporarily while the JG program permanently eliminates unemployment. Moreover, infrastructure investment stimulus only targets China's infrastructure while the JG program aims to address deficiencies in the Chinese economy, including but not limited to infrastructure needs. As another example, China has also experimented with partial JG programs in conjunction with its ecological immigration. In her essay, *Ningxia's Ecological Immigration Program: An Embryonic Employer of Last Resort Program*, Li found that, "NEIP [Ningxia Ecological Immigration Program] bears some embryonic characteristics of JG green jobs programs" and concluded that:

> It is likely that the personnel responsible for NEIP were never directly exposed to the JG literature. However, through their own trial and error from real-world experimentation of NEIP over 30 years, the local government in Ningxia has figured out a unique program that has made quite some achievements and possesses a few features of the JG program.
>
> *(Li 2013: 64)*

Finally, the Chinese state is capable of implementing a Green JG because the Chinese central government, as the monopoly issuer of RMB, possesses the monetary sovereignty necessary to sustainably finance a Chinese Green JG, which I discuss in the final section of this chapter.

The economic benefits and costs of a Chinese Green JG

In this section, I calculate the true cost of implementing a full-fledged Chinese Green JG program by computing the economic benefit of JG and the economic cost of financing it. Since JG eliminates unemployment, the economic benefit of JG lies in eliminating the output loss arising from unemployment. Therefore, to calculate the economic benefits of JG, I use two methods to estimate China's lost output arising from its unemployment – the "average product" method (which estimates the lost output by multiplying the average GDP per Chinese worker/peasant[12] by the number of Chinese unemployed workers) and the "Okun's Law" method (which is a generally accepted empirical rule that describes a quantitative relationship between changes in unemployment and changes in GDP). The logic is that as China achieves full employment, its GDP growth will expand. My work is simply to estimate the size of that GDP expansion due to the elimination of unemployment.

I first use the "average product" method, which requires knowing the number of unemployed workers in China and the average GDP per worker in China. According to the National Bureau of Statistics of China, as of December 2019, China had an urban labor force survey unemployment rate of 5.2% and a total urban employment of 442.47 million (NBSC 2020). This means that in 2019, China had a total urban labor force of 466.74 million. Combined with the 5.2% urban unemployment rate, China had 24.27 million unemployed workers in 2019. Note that this figure assumes that the rural Chinese who worked as peasants in 2019 had no intention to migrate to cities to become peasant-workers.[13] Hence, the 24.27 million urban unemployment figure is a conservative estimate of China's overall unemployment. Considering that Chinese peasants are guaranteed access to at least some land in rural China, this is probably a reasonable assumption as well.

In 2019, China's GDP reached 99.0865 trillion RMB by employing a total of 774.71 million workers, which included 442.47 million in urban employment and 332.24 million in rural employment (NBSC 2020). This means that the average GDP per Chinese worker/peasant is 127,901 RMB in 2019. Multiplying China's 24.27 million urban unemployment by the average GDP per Chinese worker/peasant (127,901 RMB) yields a lost output arising from China's unemployment in 2019 of 3.104 trillion RMB, which was 3.13% of China's 2019 GDP. In other words, the "average product" method shows that the 24.27 million urban people unemployed cost the Chinese economy approximately 3.13% of GDP in 2019.

Note that the "average product" method assumes that the unemployed Chinese workers are, on average, contributing the same amount of value-added to China's GDP as an average employed worker/peasant in China. It is possible that the average unemployed urban Chinese worker, once employed, contributes less value-added to GDP than the average currently employed urban Chinese worker. However, an argument can also be made that the average unemployed urban Chinese worker is more productive, in terms of their total value-added contribution to GDP, than the average currently employed rural peasant (which account for 43% of China's total labor force in 2019) (NBSC 2020). Hence, by accounting for both urban and rural labor's value-added contribution to GDP, the average GDP per worker/peasant figure that I used in my calculation should serve as a reasonable measurement for estimating the potential value-added contribution of GDP from an average urban unemployed worker in China.

To ensure that my assumption above was reasonable and even conservative, I use the "Okun's Law" method to cross-examine China's lost GDP arising from unemployment. As mentioned before, Okun's Law is a generally accepted and tested empirical rule that describes a quantitative correlation between changes in unemployment and changes in GDP. Okun, in his 1962 paper, *Potential GDP: Its Measurement and Significance*, found that a 1% reduction in the unemployment rate corresponded with a 3% increase in real GDP, which implied an "Okun coefficient" of 3. Since Okun, there have been some revisions to Okun's method and extensions to other time periods and other countries (Altig, Fitzgerald and Rupert 1997; Lee 2000; Dritsaki, Chaido and Nikolaos Dritsakis 2009). Consequently, the empirically tested Okun coefficients have varied by time and by country and have mostly fallen between 1.5 and 3. In order to be conservative in estimating the benefits of JG, I use an Okun coefficient of 1.5 to estimate China's lost GDP arising from unemployment.

A conservative Okun coefficient of 1.5, combined with China's 5.2% urban labor force survey unemployment rate in 2019, suggests that China's lost GDP amounts to 7.8% in 2019. This means that a full-fledged JG program would have contributed an additional 7.8% to

China's existing 6.1% GDP growth rate in 2019, reaching a whopping 13.9% GDP growth rate. However, this calculation exaggerates the economic benefit of JG because it would be a mistake to use the 5.2% urban labor force survey unemployment rate as a measurement for China's overall unemployment rate (NBSC 2020). This is because the unemployment rate for the rural Chinese is supposedly zero as Chinese peasants are guaranteed access to at least some land in rural China. It is for this reason that the National Bureau of Statistics of China only reports the urban unemployment rate. Therefore, I compute China's overall unemployment rate by dividing China's total number of urban unemployed workers by its total labor force, which includes both urban and rural labor forces.

My calculation before already showed that China's total urban unemployment in 2019 was 24.27 million. In 2019, China's total labor force equals the sum of total rural labor force (332.24 million) and total urban labor force (466.74 million), which is 798.98 million. The 24.27 million urban unemployment, combined with China's total labor force of 798.98 million in 2019, suggests that China's overall unemployment rate in 2019 should be 3.03% (NBSC 2020). Then, using an Okun coefficient of 1.5, I determine that China's lost output arising from unemployment in 2019 amounted to approximately 4.55% of 2019 GDP.

Recall that the "average product" method suggests that China's lost output arising from unemployment in 2019 equals to 3.13% of GDP. The "Okun's Law" method computes a greater output loss even with my conservative choice of the Okun coefficient. This discrepancy, however, is expected. This is because the "average product" method assumes the number of unemployed workers to be fixed, while the "Okun's Law" method considers actual historical patterns that each additional percentage point reduction in unemployment rate requires even more jobs to be created, as Forstater, Kaboub, and Kelsay explained:

> Okun's coefficients take into account actual historical patterns. One of the theorized reasons why the coefficients are consistently above 1 is that as more jobs become available, more people will enter the labor force to look for jobs. Thus, an economy will actually have to be employing a higher number of people in order for the unemployment rate to fall each additional percentage point.
>
> *(2015: 16)*

Above I have estimated the GDP cost of unemployment in China using the "average product" method and the "Okun's Law" method. The conclusion is that urban unemployment in China costs between 3.13% and 4.55% of GDP per year. Note that in both methods, I used the more conservative estimates whenever possible to calculate the GDP cost of unemployment. Since my proposed Green JG eliminates unemployment by offering a publicly funded job to anyone willing, able and ready to work, the economic benefit of JG is precisely in eliminating the lost GDP arising from Chinese unemployment. This means that a full employment Chinese economy would have grown an additional 3.13%–4.55% of GDP in 2019, reaching a total GDP growth rate in the 9.23%–10.65% range.

To complete the cost-benefit analysis of a Chinese JG, I now calculate the cost of financing it. For consistency, I continue to use 24.27 million as the total number of unemployed workers in China. I assume the JG wage to be 3,700 RMB per month. On top of that, I assume an additional 35% of the total wage bill to cover the "Five Insurances"[14] benefit costs and another 10% of the total wage bill to pay for all the logistical and material costs associated with executing the JG program. The financial costs of implementing a JG in China are shown in Table 14.1.

Table 14.1 Job Guarantee Cost Estimates

Average JG Wage (RMB)	*Number of JG Workers Employed*	*Total Wage Bill (RMB)*	*Total Annual Benefits (RMB)*	*Logistical and Material Costs (RMB)*	*Total Financing Cost of JG (RMB)*	*Cost of JG as Percentage of 2019 GDP*
3700	24.27 million	1.077588 trillion	0.3771558 trillion	0.1077588 trillion	1.5625026 trillion	1.58%

Hence, from a strictly economic point of view, the economic benefit of having a JG program is between 3.13% and 4.55% of China's 2019 GDP. The cost of having a JG program is 1.58%. The net economic benefit for a Chinese JG program is therefore overwhelmingly positive. Increasing China's fiscal deficit by 1.58% of 2019 GDP would be enough to finance a complete Chinese Green JG to eliminate China's 24.27 million urban unemployment and elevate China's GDP growth rate from 6.1% to the 9.23% and 10.65% range in 2019.

It is important to note that, in my analysis, I have purposefully underestimated the benefits of JG and overestimated the costs of implementing it in order to make a more compelling case. I underestimated the benefits of JG because I only conservatively quantified the economic growth benefit as a result of full employment. Other benefits of a Green JG, such as social stability, environmental sustainability, and economic security for the Chinese people, are arguably more valuable despite not being assigned a monetary value. On the other hand, I purposefully overestimated the cost of implementing it. For instance, a full employment Chinese economy will spend less on unemployment insurance and crime prevention. Spending by JG workers will also contribute to tax revenue. Hence, financing the JG program reduces government spending in other areas and increases tax revenue through the macroeconomic simulative effects from increased consumption from JG workers.

Sustainability and functionality of China's deficit spending

Even though a Chinese Job Guarantee makes economic sense for the Chinese economy, some may be concerned about the sustainability of China's deficit spending and national debt. In this section, I debunk the myth of sound finance by examining China's sector balances. My analysis is based on the vast literature from functional finance, Modern Money Theory, credit theory of money, and state theory of money (Lerner 1943; Knapp 1973; Minsky 1993; Goodhart 1998; Wray 1998; Bell 2000; Forstater 2000; see also Nersisyan, in this volume). My conclusion is that for a country like China that has sovereign control of its monetary system, government deficits are not only sustainable but also functional to stabilize private sector balance sheets.

Before presenting China's sector balances, it is necessary to explain what a sector balance is. At the level of a country's macroeconomy, aggregate spending is, by accounting identity, equal to aggregate income (i.e. every RMB spent is received as income). Wynne Godley in 1996 suggested that it would be useful to divide a country's macroeconomy into three sectors: domestic government (central and local), domestic private (firms and households), and foreign sector (the rest of the world). This means that

> if one sector spends more than its income (deficit), at least one other must spend less than its income (surplus) to maintain the aggregate identity that total spending equals total income. The balances (income minus expenditure) of the three sectors have to add up

to zero since we are adding up all the income in the economy and subtracting all the spending, which are equal by identity.

(*Wray 2019*)

Hence, as a macroeconomic accounting identity, "Domestic Private Sector Balance + Domestic Government Sector Balance + Foreign Sector Balance = 0" holds true for any country. Based on this accounting identity, I produced China's three-sector balances as a percentage of GDP from 1978 to 2018. The result is as follows (Figure 14.2):

Important insights can be gathered by examining China's three-sector balances as a percentage of GDP from 1978 to 2018. First, the Chinese private sector balances (blue bars) have mostly been in the surplus territory, which were made possible by the foreign sector deficits (green bars) and the Chinese government sector deficits (red bars). Indeed, it is healthy that the Chinese private sector (firms and households) has been net accumulating financial wealth at around 5% of GDP per year since 1997. In 2015, the Chinese private sector achieved its highest surplus as a percentage of GDP at around 8%. Since 2015, however, the Chinese private sector surplus as a percentage of GDP has declined noticeably, mostly due to the decline of foreign sector deficits (green bars), which meant that China's trade surpluses as a percentage of GDP had declined.

Second, the Chinese government's balance, which includes central and local governments' balances, has consistently been in the negative territory (represented by the red bars). This is desirable since Chinese government deficits, together with China's foreign trade surpluses, have been necessary to enable the Chinese private sector to run surpluses historically. Moreover, the Chinese government deficits from 2015 to 2018 had expanded as a percentage of GDP, which offset some of the pressure arising from China's reduced foreign trade surpluses as a percentage of GDP during the same period. However, since 2015, the increases in China's government deficit as a percentage of GDP have not been large enough to offset the decreases in China's trade surplus as a percentage of GDP. As a result, China's private sector surplus as a percentage of GDP has declined from around 8% in 2015 to 6% of GDP in 2018.

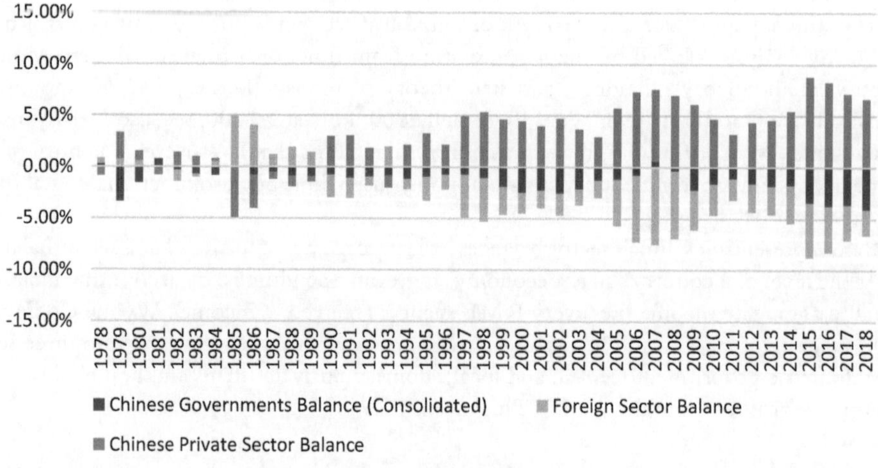

Figure 14.2 China's Sectoral Balances as % of GDP (1978–2018)

Source: National Bureau of Statistics of China.

Third, China's three-sector balances suggest that China's financial system has been in a sound position for most of the years since 1978. This is because China's three sectors have been in their sustainable territories most of the time. First, it is sustainable for the foreign sector (green bars) to remain in the deficit territory since that simply means that China runs an international trade surplus against the rest of the world.[15] Second, it is sustainable for the Chinese government sector (red bars) to remain in the deficit territory since the Chinese government (the Chinese central government, to be precise), as the sole issuer of RMB, faces no default risk on RMB-denominated debt. The default risk for the Chinese central government bonds is zero not because the international credit market deems RMB bonds trustworthy but because the Chinese central government pays interests on its bonds (which are denominated in RMB) by crediting RMB into existence.[16] Third, it is sustainable and even necessary for the Chinese private sector to remain in the surplus territory. This is because private sector surpluses represent accumulation of private savings that strengthen the financial positions of firms and households who, as currency users of RMB, face real default risk. An implication is that if China's foreign trade surpluses as a percentage of GDP decline, the Chinese government deficits must expand to facilitate surpluses for the Chinese private sector.

It is important to note that functional finance by no means suggests unlimited government spending, nor does it ignore the fact that government deficits may create inflationary pressures. Indeed, if the economy is already at full employment, any additional deficit spending will be purely inflationary without creating jobs or increasing economic growth. If the economy is below full employment, however, deficit spending increases aggregate demand and aggregate supply at the same time, which may or may not cause substantial inflation. The other issue is that due to automation, conventional government deficit spending may promote economic growth but not job growth. It is therefore particularly desirable that deficits be used to finance a Chinese Green JG since such a program directly creates jobs and consequently promotes economic growth.

Designing a Chinese Green Job Guarantee

A Chinese Job Guarantee program should be designed and implemented in a way that embraces China's particular needs and priority concerns. Therefore, in my previous analysis, in addition to introducing what a JG is, I have theorized why China would especially benefit from a Green JG, why China's time to implement a Green JG is ripe, how much a Chinese JG would contribute to China's GDP growth and cost China's fiscal budget, and why the financing cost of a JG is not only sustainable but also functional for China. I apply the same logic now to inquire how a Chinese Green JG should be administered, what types of jobs a Chinese Green JG should create, and why China's implementation of a Green JG should follow a gradualist approach.

Administration of a Chinese Green Job Guarantee

Considering that the Chinese central government as an RMB issuer is not revenue-constrained and that the Chinese provincial and local governments as RMB users face real default risks, the Chinese central government should fund the bulk, if not all, of the JG program. Contributions from other entities, such as provincial and local governments and social philanthropists, are not necessary for financing purposes, but may still be encouraged to achieve other desirable outcomes. For example, requiring provincial and local governments to finance a part of the JG program might encourage more attentive implementation of JG at the provincial and local level. On the other hand, encouraging social philanthropists to contribute to the JG program could be worthwhile to create a public-private partnership platform for interested social philanthropists.

While the central government provides the financing, provincial and local governments should administer the JG. Specifically, provincial and local governments should identify local needs, submit corresponding JG proposals that would address these needs to the central government, administer the local JG programs by training and organizing the JG workers, and evaluate the program. Hence, once identifying an appropriate need, the JG administrator (provincial and local governments) should: (1) consult with experts to assess what specific works need to be done to address that need and (2) propose the corresponding jobs to the central government for approval and funding. The central government should play the financier and the supervisory role by monitoring the performance of the JG program.

For example, jobs that enhance China's environmental service capabilities are important and urgent given the substantial costs of environmental pollution on public health. However, the private sector normally has little incentive to produce environmental service goods since it is not profitable. Green jobs that aim to enhance China's environmental service capabilities therefore seem a natural candidate to be included in a JG for the environmentally degraded regions in China. So, administrators of the JG program in these regions should consult with environmental engineers to figure out what specific works need to be done and then propose to create the corresponding jobs. If the identified need is to tackle desertification and it has been determined that (re)forestation is an effective way to address desertification, then provincial and local governments should make a tree-planting JG proposal to the central government to be approved and funded.

Should the Chinese state adopt a gradualist approach to implement the Green JG (I argue that it should), there is the added question about who the JG should prioritize in hiring in the early stages. Again, this should depend on China's particular needs and priority concerns. I suggest that military veterans be prioritized; a JG program can help them gain skills and work experience in the civilian economy and aid them in the transition to employment in the market economy in the future.

Types of jobs in a Chinese Green Job Guarantee

After discussing the administration of the Green JG in China, I explore the types of jobs that could be created in a Chinese Green JG. In principle, the types of jobs created through a Chinese JG program will change over time because they are intended to address deficiencies in the Chinese market economy at any given point. However, all jobs created by a JG program should be in areas that are important and urgent but have been neglected by the market due to the lack of opportunities for profit. It should be noted that the development of a JG program would greatly benefit from consultation with local communities and governments at all levels to identify neglected areas of particular significance. The recommendations below reflect my assessment of the important areas that could be improved in the Chinese market economy as of the time of writing (October 2020). I propose three broad categories of jobs that I believe would be feasible and beneficial to the Chinese economy and society.

The first category consists of those jobs that aim to directly employ JG workers in activities that enhance the environment. The goal is to promote employment *and* environmental sustainability. As Forstater suggests, "it may be desirable to create an Environmental Service Corps, or Green Corps… [that] help society satisfy the biophysical conditions for a sustainable economy" (2003). I believe that the Chinese economy would especially benefit from establishing a Green Corps as a major component of its JG program to increase its environmental service capabilities and to better tackle environmental issues. Examples of Green Corps jobs include reforestation, recycling, environmental cleanup, wildlife preservation, and community gardening. Many of these tasks are labor-intensive and require little job training, making them particularly suitable for a JG program. As Forstater further explains, a Green Corps program has potential educational implications in addition to their direct environmental service efforts:

> PSE [Public Service Employment] workers can visit classrooms and workplaces and do presentations. They can set up tables in the community to demonstrate the effectiveness and simplicity of many sustainable practices... Doubtless there are many other areas where PSE workers can perform environmental services. The development of a Green Corps will provide a reservoir of labor that can contribute to sustainability in many ways.
>
> *(Forstater 2003: 404)*

The second category covers jobs aimed at the preservation of cultural heritage. Globalization and modernization of the Chinese economy has turned China into a net importer of culture. While this brings some benefits, it also creates many challenges. One notable challenge is that Western values and culture (e.g. Hollywood films) are often presented as superior to the traditional values and culture of China and other countries in East Asia. This has the potential to create a clash of civilizations or an ideological war within China among different generations and social classes. A cultural heritage preservation program would not reject Western culture, but would help Chinese society to be more familiar with traditional Chinese values and culture and its contemporary relevance. Many cultural heritage preservation jobs require specialized knowledge, which is perfect for the millions of Chinese university graduates majoring in humanities and arts who are not able to find suitable employment in the market economy.[17] As Kaboub describes:

> [cultural heritage preservation workers are] devoted to information dissipation, conservation of local/regional history, culture, and traditions. Such projects would involve higher education graduates with degrees/specializations in history, anthropology, sociology, computer science, geology, psychology, ethnography, social work, folklore studies, literature, religious studies, art, art history, photography, journalism, communications, statistics, music, dance, graphic design, and architecture.
>
> *(Kaboub 2007b: 10)*

Cultural heritage preservation is currently largely conducted by the Chinese state. Instead of the government preaching traditional values to Chinese citizens, the JG workers (such as university graduates majoring in Chinese literature, history, and arts) are likely to do a more effective job communicating to the public, especially through social media. For example, my mother initiated an early childhood philosophy education program that, in my view, presented the contemporary relevance and charm of Chinese traditional values, such as the roles of altruism and collectivism in a modern competitive society. While she continues to make all educational materials (in the forms of cartoon videos and audio stories) free to the public, her program can certainly benefit from the help of cultural heritage preservation workers to create new content and reach a greater audience.

As another example, the word "economics" in traditional Chinese culture came from the writings of Jin Dynasty scholar Ge Hong (known under the pen name Baopuzi) (283–343 AD). The term derived from "manage worldly affairs" (经世) and "help the people (济民)," which emphasized the managing role of the political state in economic affairs as opposed to promoting a free market. This certainly is consistent with China's economic system today. In other instances, JG workers in the cultural heritage preservation program can help document, interpret, recreate, and celebrate China's traditional culture, philosophy, and multiethnic heritage. It is through these efforts that cultural heritage preservation jobs help promote confidence in the Chinese path, system, theory and culture within the Chinese society to achieve a balance with the Western cultural hegemony brought by globalization.

The third category covers jobs that broadly serve the public interest. This includes jobs associated with the construction of public infrastructure such as high-speed rail. It also includes quality-of-life-enhancing activities that are underproduced by the market. Forstater, Kaboub, and Kelsay listed the following examples: (1) data gathering, as JG workers can be hired to gather data to inform better policy-making; (2) supporting the operations of the JG program itself, as "some Job Guarantee workers can be hired to provide transportation, childcare, elderly care, community meals, or any other services needed within the Job Guarantee program"; and (3) upgrading China's existing charitable infrastructure by

> transforming from one that primarily relies on volunteers with minimal experience to… organizations that employ professionally trained full-time staff to support the specific mission of the organizations [that are] assisting pilgrims, the elderly, people with disabilities, low-income families, orphans, emigrants, and victims of domestic violence.
>
> *(Forstater, Kaboub and Kelsay 2015: 51)*

A gradualist approach to implementing the Chinese Green JG

Inspired by Fagg Foster's theory of Institutional Adjustment, I propose a two-phase gradualist approach for the Chinese state to implement the Chinese Green JG. Foster's theory of Institutional Adjustment has three components: instrumental primacy, recognized interconnectedness and minimal dislocation (Foster 1981). The significance of Foster's theory lies in the fact that while organizations can change overnight, institutions as habits of thought and routines of behaviors cannot (Kaboub 2007a). Therefore, to successfully implement a public policy, policy-makers must be aware of their own ignorance of the proposed policy and social reality (instrumental primacy); policymakers must recognize all interconnected institutions that need to be adjusted when implementing the policy (recognized interconnectedness); and policymakers should implement the policy in a way that causes minimal dislocation to the existing institutional structure (minimal dislocation). Hence, Foster's theory of Institutional Adjustment is a gradualist and pragmatist approach to public policy, which has astounding similarities to the Chinese state's reform gradualism and reform pragmatism after 1978.

Therefore, even though a Green JG makes sense economically, politically, socially, and environmentally, and the Chinese central government faces no financial constraint to finance it, it is a new public policy that tests the organizational capabilities of the local governments as well as the coordination capabilities among different levels of governments and ministries in China. Given that different localities in China face different economic, labor, and environmental realities, and that the local governments in these localities exhibit different levels of competency in organizing and administering a program like the Green JG, it is sensible to select representative regions to experiment the Green JG before rolling it out as a national economic policy. Initial evaluations of the JG programs can also be done during this phase.

The successful administrators of the JG program during phase one, including local and provincial officials, can then serve as mentors to help guide other localities and provinces. For example, as the Ningxia local government's ecological migration program possesses a few features of the JG program (Li 2013), it would be reasonable to include Ningxia in the first phase of Green JG. Then, lessons and experiences can be learned and shared for other regions like Ningxia to implement in their JG programs.

Again, it is important to emphasize that the above "experiment, evaluate, and expand" two-phase approach is consistent with Foster's theory of Institutional Adjustment and the Chinese state's reform gradualism and pragmatism in shaping China's socialist market economy since 1978. Since China is a large country with roughly 20% of the world population, any benefits or mistakes in the national policy level have far-reaching consequences. Hence, a reasonable amount of caution is warranted. More importantly, a gradualist approach allows the Chinese state to figure out the best practices concerning the implementation of a Chinese Green JG. Promoting best practices is certainly a much more pragmatic approach than having all local governments try adopting the Green JG at the same time. Finally, a gradualist approach to implementing the Chinese Green JG gives Chinese governments at all levels the time necessary to develop, organize, coordinate and evaluate their capabilities and experiences for the successful implementation of the Chinese Green JG.

Conclusion

Compared to conventional macroeconomic policies, a Green Job Guarantee is much more effective at coordinating a country's economic growth, employment, structural adjustments, and environmental sustainability. A Green JG especially benefits China in terms of counteracting the unemployment pressure from its domestic structural adjustments, coping with the US-China trade war in an increasingly conflictual international political climate, transitioning the Chinese economy from export-led to domestic consumption-led in the context of declining population growth, and promoting economic development without sacrificing the environment. Institutionally, the Chinese state possesses the capability to implement a Green JG due to its political pragmatism, vision for environmental sustainability, and monetary sovereignty.

It has been estimated that increasing China's fiscal deficit by 1.58% of 2019 GDP would have financed a complete Chinese Green JG to eliminate China's 24.27 million urban unemployment and elevate China's GDP growth rate to the 9.23% and 10.65% range in 2019. Furthermore, it has also been shown that for a monetarily sovereign country like China, the government deficits required to finance the Green JG are not only sustainable but also functional to stabilize private sector balance sheets. Considering the other benefits of a Green JG, such as social stability, environmental sustainability, and economic security for the Chinese people, a Chinese Green JG is well worth it. A green and full employment Chinese economy may be the best testament of a socialist market economy with Chinese characteristics.

Notes

1 Some argue that historically we have seen manufacturing jobs replacing agricultural jobs and service jobs replacing manufacturing jobs. The problem, however, is that service jobs are now themselves being lost to the machine process, which begs the question, "where do we go from here?"

2 "Require" may not be the precise word, since GDP growth is a consequence of job creation in a JG, not a cause as in conventional economic tools.

3 Figure taken from "The Cost of Unemployment and the Job Guarantee Alternative in Saudi Arabia," by Mathew Forstater, Fadhel Kaboub, and Michael Kelsay in 2015.
4 As seen in the United States, Taiwan, Hong Kong, etc., in recent years.
5 There was a reversal in 2019 and 2020, as infrastructure investment was reinvigorated under Li Keqiang's leadership.
6 Keynes in *The General Theory* argues that lower-income workers spend a larger proportion of additional income on consumption and therefore have a greater marginal propensity of consumption.
7 Founder of Alibaba, the largest e-commerce company in China by revenue.
8 3700 RMB per month is selected because it is the average wage for Chinese peasant-workers in 2018. The 2019 figure is not yet available.
9 During the 2008 Global Financial Crisis, for example, many Chinese SOEs were directed to scale up production despite making a loss at the time in order to stabilize employment.
10 Bernie Sanders included a new "New Deal" as his core economic policy when he ran for the US presidency in 2016. Many criticized this policy for being too socialist.
11 The four confidences include: confidence in path, confidence in system, confidence in theories and confidence in culture.
12 China's Household Registration System specifies a Chinese citizen's origin as either rural or urban. "Peasant" is the official term in China to describe a Chinese citizen with a rural origin that lives and works in rural China.
13 "Peasant-worker(s)" is the official term used in China to describe a peasant (with a specified "rural" status in the Household Registration Book) who works and lives in urban China, often in precarious conditions.
14 "Five Insurances" are considered a generous benefits package for Chinese employees. Together, they account for about 35% of an employee's wage bill.
15 However, the size of the green bars (i.e. China's trade surplus as a percentage of GDP) may decrease as China transitions to a consumption-led economy. Also, it is not sustainable for every country to accumulate trade surpluses – for there to be a trade surplus, there must generate a trade deficit.
16 This is the same reason why the United States Federal Government can never be forced to default on USD-denominated liabilities.
17 Doing so also alleviates pressure for the Chinese STEM (Science, Technology, Engineering, and Mathematics) majors to find employment in the market economy sector.

References

Altig, D., Fitzgerald, T. and Rupert, P. 1997. Okun's Law Revisited: Should We Worry about Low Unemployment. Federal Reserve Bank of Cleveland. 5 May. Available from: https://www.clevelandfed.org/research/Commentary/1997/0515.htm.

Bell, S. 2000. Do Taxes and Bonds Finance Government Spending? *Journal of Economic Issues*. 34(September), 603–620.

Chen, Y. 2019. Renewable Energy Investment and Employment in China. *International Review of Applied Economics*. 33(3), 314–334.

China State Council. 2018. Positioning Domestic Demand as the Main Engine of Economic Growth. Available from: http://www.gov.cn/guowuyuan/2018-09/16/content_5322363.htm

Dritsaki, C. and Dritsakis, N. 2009. Okun's Coefficient for Four Mediterranean Member Countries of the EU: An Empirical Study. *International Journal of Business and Management*. 4(5), 18–26.

Forstater, M. 2000. Full Employment and Economic Flexibility. *Economic and Labour Relations Review*. 11(June), 69–88.

Forstater, M. 2003. Public Employment and Environmental Sustainability. *Journal of Post Keynesian Economics*. 25(3), 385–406.

Forstater, M., Kaboub, F. and Kelsay, M. 2015. The Cost of Unemployment and the Job Guarantee Alternative in Saudi Arabia. Policy Report No. 101. *Global Institute for Sustainable Prosperity*. Available from: http://www.global-isp.org/policy-report-101/

Forstater, M. and Wray, R. 2004. Full Employment and Social Justice. In: D.P. Champlin and J.T. Knoedler, eds. *The Institutionalist Tradition in Labor Economics*. Armonk, NY: M.E. Sharpe. pp. 253–272.

Foster, J.F. 1981. Syllabus for Problems of Modern Society: The Theory of Institutional Adjustment. *Journal of Economic Issues.* 15, 929–935.

Fullwiler, Scott T. 2003. Further Simulation of an Employer of Last Resort Policy. Center for Full Employment and Price Stability. Working Paper # 27. August. Available from: http://www.cfeps.org/pubs/

Fullwiler, Scott T. 2005. Macroeconomic Stabilization through an Employer of Last Resort. Center for Full Employment and Price Stability. Working Paper # 44. August. Available from: http://www.cfeps.org/pubs/

Godley, W. 1996. Money, Finance and National Income Determination: An Integrated Approach. Working Paper No. 167. *Levy Economics Institute of Bard College.* June. Available from: http://www.levyinstitute.org/publications/money-finance-and-national-income-determination

Goodhart, C.A.E. 1998. The Two Concepts of Money: Implications for the Analysis of Optimal Currency Areas. *European Journal of Political Economy.* 14(3), 407–432.

Gordon, W. 1997. Job Assurance: The Job Guarantee Revisited. *Journal of Economic Issues.* 32(September), 826–834.

Kaboub, F. 2007a. Institutional Adjustment for Full Employment. *Journal of Economic Issues.* 41(June), 495–502.

Kaboub, F. 2007b. ELR-led Economic Development: A Plan for Tunisia. Working Paper No. 499. The Levy Economics Institute.

Kalecki, M. 1943. Political Aspects of Full Employment. *Political Quarterly.* 14(4), 322–330.

Keynes, J.M. 1936. *The General Theory of Employment, Interest and Money.* London: Macmillan.

Kitson, M., Michie, J. and Sutherland, H. 1997. A Price Well Worth Paying? The Benefits of a Full-Employment Strategy. In: J. Michie and J.G. Smith, eds. *Employment and Economic Performance: Jobs, Inflation, and Growth.* Oxford: Oxford University Press.

Knapp, G.F. 1973 [1924]. *The State Theory of Money.* Clifton, NY: Augustus M. Kelley.

Kostzer, D. 2008. Argentina – A Case Study on the Plan Jefes y Jefas de Hogar Desocupados, or the Employment Road to Economic Recovery. Working Paper No. 534. Levy Economics Institute. May. Available from: http://www.levyinstitute.org/publications/argentina-a-case-study-on-the-plan-jefes-y-jefas-de-hogar-desocupados-or-the-employment-road-to-economic-recovery

Lee, J. 2000. The Robustness of Okun's Law: Evidence from OECD Countries. *Journal of Macroeconomics.* 22(2), 331–356.

Lerner, A.P. 1943. Functional Finance and the Federal Debt. *Social Research.* 10(February).

Li, J. 2013. Ningxia's Ecological Immigration Program: An Embryonic Employer of Last Resort Program. Drafted Book Chapter. [Unpublished item].

Li, K. 2019. Premier Li Calls for Fulfilling Major Economic Targets. Available from: http://www.xinhuanet.com/english/2019-10/15/c_138471612.htm

Liu, X. and Wray, R. 2014. Options for China in a Dollar Standard World: A Sovereign Currency Approach. Working Paper No. 783. Levy Economics Institute at Bard College. Available from: http://www.levyinstitute.org/publications/options-for-china-in-a-dollar-standard-world-a-sovereign-currency-approach

Minsky, H.P. 1986. *Stabilizing an Unstable Economy.* New Haven, CT: Yale University Press.

Minsky, H.P. 1993. *Modern Money: A Blueprint for Successful Capitalism.* Draft book. [Unpublished item].

Mitchell, W.F. and Watts, M.J. 1977. The Path to Full Employment. *Australian Economic Review.* 30(4), 433–435.

National Bureau of Statistics of China. 2020. 2019 Chinese Economy Report. Available from: http://www.stats.gov.cn/tjsj/zxfb/202001/t20200117_1723383.html

Okun, A.M. 1962. Potential GDP: Its Measurement and Significance. Proceedings of the Business and Economic Statistics Section of the American Statistical Association.

Ricardo, D. 1911. *The Principles of Political Economy & Taxation.* London, New York: J.M. Dent; E.P. Dutton.

Tcherneva, P. 2012. Beyond Full Employment: The Employer of Last Resort as an Institution for Change. Working Paper No. 732. The Levy Economics Institute at Bard College. Available from: http://www.levyinstitute.org/publications/beyond-full-employment

Wray, L.R. 1998. *Understanding Modern Money: The Key to Full Employment and Price Stability.* Northampton, MA: Edward Elgar Publishing.

Wray, L.R. 2007. The Employer of Last Resort Programme: Could It Work for Developing Countries? Economic and Labour Market Papers, Geneva, Switzerland: International Labor Organization. August.

Wray, L.R. 2012. *Modern Money Theory: A Primer on Macroeconomics for Sovereign Monetary Systems*. New York: Palgrave Macmillan.

Xi, J. 2017. Report in the 19th Congressional Meeting of the Communist Party of China. Available from: http://www.xinhuanet.com/2019-04/26/c_1124419194.htm.

15

SOUTH KOREA'S GREEN NEW DEAL 2.0

Old wine in new bottles?

Kyla Tienhaara,[1] Sun-Jin Yun[2] and Ryan Gunderson

Introduction

It is rarely acknowledged in discussions about the Green New Deal that South Korea was the first country to formally adopt a policy under this banner. In 2009, the government released a stimulus package – the Korean Green New Deal (KGND) – in response to the Global Financial Crisis (GFC). The KGND was dubbed by several commentators outside the country as the "greenest" stimulus package in the world (see, e.g., Bernard et al. 2009). However, within Korea it was highly controversial.

Just over a decade later, a new crisis – the COVID-19 pandemic and subsequent economic downturn – sparked the development of a new Green New Deal, embedded within a broader Korean New Deal (we will abbreviate to KND to distinguish the two). The Korean government was inspired by both the Ocasio-Cortez/Markey proposal for a GND in the US (H. Res. 109) as well as the European Green Deal (see further chapter by Alder and Wargan, this volume), but many have questioned whether the KND represents a substantial shift in Korean policy (S. Lee 2020). This chapter aims to compare the form and content of the KGND and KND and assess how the developments within South Korea line up with the broader evolution of GND discourse that was outlined in the Introduction (Tienhaara and Robinson, this volume).

With that objective in mind, it is important to note at the outset that South Korea has been more closely associated with the "green growth" policy paradigm than any other country in the world. The chief architect of the first KGND – former President Lee Myung-bak – was dubbed "the father of green growth" by the OECD secretary-general in 2011 (Shin 2011). Some have hypothesized that Lee embraced green growth to gain international recognition for Korea and himself as a green leader (Shim 2010; Yun, Cho and von Hippe 2011). Therefore, it is hardly surprising that in addition to developing a five-year development plan around green growth (for overviews, see Jones and Yoo 2010; UNEP 2010; Yun et al. 2011; Kang et al. 2012), he also actively pushed this onto the G20 agenda when the country became the first non-G8 member to host a summit in 2010 (Cho et al. 2014). During Lee's presidency, Korea also launched the Global Green Growth Institute (GGGI) to share knowledge and promote the development of domestic green growth platforms around the world (predominantly in developing countries; GGGI n.d.). Initially, GGGI was a nonprofit

DOI: 10.4324/9781003110880-19

foundation, but at the Rio+20 Earth summit in 2012, it was converted into an international organization. Korea committed USD 5 million to a new "green new deal fund" within GGGI in May 2021 (Shin 2021).

Despite the rhetoric around green growth, South Korea is an environmental laggard. The country was the seventh-biggest emitter of carbon dioxide in 2018 (IEA 2020a). The Korean economy remains focused on energy-intensive manufacturing industries including electronics, cars, shipbuilding and steel. Coal and oil dominate the country's energy supply, with a growing share for methane gas, the vast majority of which is imported (IEA 2020b). While the country does not export fossil fuels, it has been a major financer of coal plants abroad, although President Moon has recently committed to ending new finance for coal (H. Lee 2021). Renewables like solar and wind have not been developed at scale. Nuclear power is currently the only significant low-carbon energy source, and it is highly controversial with the Korean public.

At the same time, the country is increasingly experiencing the impacts of climate change. Average temperatures in the country have already risen by 1.4°C, which is higher than the global average, and summers have become longer (Gabbatiss 2020). Typhoons, heavy rains, landslides, and droughts have already cost the country billions of dollars (Moon et al. 2021). A 2019 study by the Pew Research Centre found that more Koreans (86%) view climate change as a major threat to the country than North Korea's nuclear program (67%) (Poushter and Huang 2019). Local air pollution is also a major health issue, with the average South Korean anticipated to lose 1.4 years of life expectancy because of fine particulate pollution (AQLI 2019). Although some of the pollution is blown in from neighboring countries, domestic coal power generation and automotive emissions also contribute to the problem.

South Korea ratified the Paris Agreement in November 2016, having submitted a nationally determined contribution (NDC) of a reduction of its emissions to 37% below business as usual (BAU) by 2030, which would amount to levels 78% higher than in 1990 or 10% lower than in 2010 (excluding land use, land use change and forestry) (Climate Action Tracker 2020). The form of the NDC (but not the ambition of the emissions reductions) was modified in December 2020 to a 24.4% reduction of the total national GHG emissions in 2017 (709.1 $MTCO_2eq$[3]) by 2030 (Republic of Korea 2020).

One of the main cross-sectoral policy instruments implemented to achieve emissions reductions is the Korea Emission Trading Scheme (ETS) launched in 2015; the first nationwide mandatory ETS in East Asia and the second-largest carbon market after the EU ETS (Lee and Woo 2020). However, because the vast majority of trading certificates are still provided for free, the ETS has not yet had a substantial impact on emissions (IEA 2020b). Additionally, the Renewable Portfolio Standard, which replaced a previous feed-in tariff scheme in 2012, requires major electric utilities with capacity over 500 MW to increase their new and renewable energy[4] share in the electricity mix to 10% by 2023 (Lee and Woo 2020). The target will be raised to 25% as of October 2021 (Hong 2021).

Both the NDC and the policies in place to achieve it have been classified by Climate Action Tracker (2020) as "highly insufficient." The government plans to submit a more ambitious NDC in October 2021 in the lead-up to the 26th Conference of the Parties (COP) of the United Nations Framework Convention on Climate Change.

The remainder of this chapter outlines the key elements of the KGND and the major controversies surrounding it and provides a first look at the KND, highlighting some potential areas of concern. We argue that the KND appears to be an improvement on its predecessor. However, it is still early days, and there are some areas, like just transition planning, where not a lot of detail had been provided by the Korean government at the time of writing. We also suggest that the substantial investments in hydrogen technologies in the KND are risky in both economic and environmental terms. Finally, both Korean green new deals ultimately rest on the flawed assumption that environmental impacts and CO_2 emissions can be decoupled from economic growth at the scale and pace necessary to meeting emissions targets. Admittedly, the same is true for the EU Green Deal and other proposals for GNDs being considered around the world. We conclude with some suggestions of policies that Korea could consider adding to the KND to bring about a more significant transformation of the economy.

The Korean Green New Deal (2009)[5]

As an export-oriented country heavily focused on medium- and high-technology products, Korea's economy was severely affected by the GFC. In November 2008, a KRW[6] 14-trillion (USD 10.9 billion) package was introduced, focused largely on tax cuts, infrastructure, and support for the construction industry (Nanto 2009). This was followed by a KRW 50-trillion (USD 38.1 billion) "Green New Deal" in January 2009.

In a widely cited report by a research team at HSBC, Korea's green stimulus up to May 2009 was calculated to be USD 30.7 billion (Robins et al. 2009). The report does not mention the first Korean stimulus, although it does mention the stimulus plans of other countries developed in 2008. Consequently, Korea's proportion of green stimulus was reported as 80.5%, leading to claims that the country had the "greenest" stimulus package in the world. Had the earlier stimulus been included (bringing the total stimulus to USD 49 billion), the green percentage would have fallen to 63%, placing Korea on par with the European Union. The controversial centerpiece of the KGND – the Four Major Rivers Project – was allocated almost a third of the total budget (see Table 15.1).

Table 15.1 KGND Budget in Trillions of KRW

Project		*Total Budget*
Core Projects	Four Major Rivers Project	14.48
	Green transportation	9.65
	Integrated territory management	0.37
	Water resource catchment	0.94
	Green cars and clean energy	2.05
	Water resource reuse	0.93
	Forest protection	2.42
	Green Home Green School	8.05
	Eco-River	0.48
Related Projects	Disaster risk area management	2.50
	Clean Korea	0.21
	Green waterside area	0.80
	Bio-mass energy	1.12
	Disaster prevention, forest restoration	0.73
	Public facility LED replacement	1.34
	Green IT technology	0.11
	Other	3.96
Total		**50.15**

Source: Adapted from Tienhaara 2018.

The KGND was eventually incorporated into the National Strategy for Green Growth, which had an additional budget of KRW 3.796 trillion in 2009 (see Table 15.2). KRW 1.3 trillion (34.5% of the total budget) was allocated to green technology development. Nuclear and nuclear fusion technologies received the largest portion of funds (35.8%). Renewable energy technology development only received an 18.5% share of the green technology budget, down from 19.2% in 2008 (Yun 2009).

Expansion of nuclear power became a core feature of green growth in Korea under the Lee administration. By 2010, there were plans for 13 new nuclear power units to be constructed by 2024, which would increase the total number of units to in the country to 34 and increase the share of electricity produced by nuclear power to 49% (IEA 2012). President Lee argued that nuclear power would both improve the country's energy independence and help to mitigate climate change (O'Donnell 2013). However, many in the country have long-held concerns about the issue of storing spent nuclear fuel. Some environmental groups, such as Green Korea United, have also called into question the climate credentials of nuclear power, arguing that emissions from the mining and refining of the uranium fuel source must be considered (O'Donnell 2013).

Renewable energy was largely sidelined in the KGND and the National Strategy for Green Growth. In 2018, Korea had the lowest share of energy from renewable sources in energy supply among all International Energy Agency (IEA) countries (IEA 2020b).

Table 15.2 Low-Carbon Green Growth-Related Budgets in 2008 and 2009 in Billions of KRW

Category	*2008*	*2009*	*Details*	*2008*[a]	*2009*[a]	*Change*[b]
Green technology development	10,812	13,069	New and renewables	2,079 (19.3%)	2,424 (18.5%)	+16.6%
				3,775 (34.9%)	4,683 (35.8%)	+24.1%
	+23.7%		Nuclear and fusion	1,324 (12.2%)	1,375 (10.5%)	+3.9%
			Eco-friendly industry	372 (3.4%)	662 (5.1%)	+78.0%
				3,262 (30.2%)	3,927 (30.0%)	+20.4%
			Green car and LED			
			Climate change-related			
Diffusion of renewables and energy-saving facilities	11,058	13,820	New and renewables	3,103 28.1(%)	4,482 (32.4%)	+44.4%
				4,837 (43.7%)	5,337 (38.6%)	+10.3%
			Loan for energy-saving facilities	1,054 (9.5%)	2,085 (15.1%)	+97.8%
	+24.1%		New mass transit including CNG			
Promotion of eco-friendly business	879	1,408	Energy recovery from waste	32 (3.6%)	344 (24.4%)	+975.0%
	+3.9%					
Capacity building for climate change response	7,895	9,619	GHG reduction in agriculture	2,200 (27.9%)	2,683 (27.9%)	+22.0%
				42 (0.5%)	420 (4.4%)	+900.0%
	+20.4%		International cooperation			
Total	30,644	37,916				
	+23.7%					

Source: National Assembly Budget Office 2008 and 2009.

a Figures in () means the share of budget in each category.

b Change means growth rate of budget from 2008 to 2009.

In addition to the substance of these strategies, there have also been critiques focused on the way in which they were developed. There was no process to consult or engage with civil society about funding decisions (Gunderson and Yun 2017). It was a top-down approach (Bluemling and Yun 2016) or what Han (2015) calls "environmental authoritarianism." For example, civil society members were not well represented in the Presidential Commission on Green Growth, the top governance entity that initiated the Five-Year Plan for Green Growth (Lee and Yun 2011). The project that most exemplifies this environmental authoritarianism is the disastrous Four Major Rivers Project.

The Four Major Rivers Project

During his presidential election campaign, Lee Myung-bak – who in addition to being the former mayor of Seoul was also the former CEO of a construction company – proposed a Pan-Korean Grand Waterway involving a series of canals, including one stretching 335.5 miles (540 km) connecting Seoul and Busan (Korea's two largest cities) (Kim 2012). Lee won the election, but this proposal proved very controversial. Polls suggested that more than 80% of the country's citizens opposed the project (Kim 2012). In February 2008, college professors across Korea formed the Professors' Organization for Movement against the Grand Korean Canal (POMAC), the membership of which would eventually swell to over 2,500 academics (Yun 2014). In the summer of 2008, to regain the public's favor following his incredibly unpopular decision to allow the importation of US beef during the mad cow disease crisis, Lee promised to drop the canal project. Stocks of construction companies across the nation immediately fell (Card 2009).

When the KGND was released in January 2009, Korean critics immediately pointed out that the Four Major Rivers Project was simply the Pan-Korean Grand Waterway under a different name. The government refuted this claim, but a 2013 report from the Board of Audit and Inspection (an arm's-length government body) suggests that the critics were correct. According to the report, when President Lee publicly abandoned the Pan-Korean Grand Waterway, the Ministry of Land, Transport and Maritime Affairs was secretly ordered to develop an alternative plan to revive the project (Chosunilbo 2013).

The Four Major Rivers Project was initially allocated almost KRW 14.5 trillion (USD 11.3 billion). By the time it was completed in late 2011, costs had ballooned to KRW 22 trillion (USD 20 billion).[7] The project involved dredging 570 billion m^3 of sediment and creating 16 dams across the country's four largest rivers. Three dams were built on the Han River, eight on the Nakdong River, three on the Geum River, and two on the Yeosang River. It was the first time that Korea had built dams on the main bodies of four major rivers that were sources of drinking water.

The government framed the project primarily in terms of climate change adaptation (protection against flooding) with other specific benefits including increased water storage capacity and improved water quality (Republic of Korea n.d.; Cha et al. 2011; MLTM 2012). The government argued that "repeated flooding and droughts have caused human casualties, ecosystem loss and habitat degradation, property damage and forced displacement of riverine residents" (Cha et al. 2011, 1). However, critics of the project countered that the major rivers in Korea had already been well prepared against floods, and that it is along the tributaries of those rivers where most serious flooding now occurs (Chang et al. 2012; Yun 2014). Critics also questioned the need for increased water storage, as water scarcity is not an issue in South Korea, "a country which has sufficient annual rainfall, a number of mountains, and is well equipped with water supply facilities" (Chang et al. 2012, 157). Experts argued instead that the problem facing the country was "excessive per capita water consumption" (10.5 gallons [40.02 liters] per person daily, which is two to six times the consumption rate of other developed countries) (Chang et al. 2012, 157). The government's own water resource planning document from 2006 suggests that even in a worst-case scenario of dramatic droughts and increased demand, water shortfalls would not have been large enough to justify the scale of the Four Major Rivers Project and could have been addressed through much smaller and simpler management systems (J-S. Kim 2013).

The issue of water quality is perhaps the most controversial aspect of the Four Major Rivers Project. The government claimed that by 2012, "the water quality of the mainstream will be improved to an average of level two (Biochemical Oxygen Demand less than 3 ppm)" (Cha et al. 2011, 4). The government seems to have hoped that in addition to reducing the introduction of contaminants through new water treatment facilities, it could also rely on the dictum that "the solution to pollution is dilution." The Lee administration claimed that enlarging the "water bowl" through dredging and installing dams would improve water quality by diluting pollutants (Nam 2011). However, the National Institute of Environmental Research found that increased water levels during the dry season and decreased rates of water flow would encourage algae growth in the stagnant water and lead to a reduction in water quality (Nam 2011).

In addition to these issues, the NGO Birds Korea (2010) predicted that 50 bird species would be negatively affected by the project and the conservation value of at least one Ramsar-listed wetland would be reduced. In 2012, the World Water Network awarded Korea a "Grey Globe Award" (the award highlights wetlands that are being actively degraded or neglected). The award announcement (World Water Network 2012) noted:

> The wetlands are home to many endangered species such as hooded cranes (Globally Vulnerable) whose numbers have declined from 3,000 to 1,000 since the Four Major Rivers Project started in 2009. Established resting sites for white-naped cranes have also been lost, as well as most of the habitats of freshwater clams. The Nakdong Estuary has seen a drop of 75% in its wintering bird populations, despite being nationally designated.

In October 2013, a representative of the main opposition party (the Democratic Party) used an Environment Ministry report to argue that 28 protected species had disappeared from the river ecosystem during the implementation of the project (P. Kim 2013).

In addition to environmental issues, there were several injuries and deaths among laborers on the project, as well as structural flaws in the completed bridges and weirs (Chang et al. 2012). The Board of Audit and Inspection reported in 2013 that the concrete riverbeds built to protect the weirs had subsided or been swept away for 11 out of 16 weirs (Stedman 2013; Lah et al. 2015). Korean economists were concerned that the cost of maintaining the system would burden the country's recovering economy (Tienhaara 2018). The Board of Audit and Inspection also determined that large-scale corruption and collusion had occurred in the bidding process for construction work on the project (Chosunilbo 2013). Eight contractors involved in the scheme were fined by the South Korean Fair Trade Commission for bid rigging, and in September 2013, the Supreme Prosecutor's Office in Seoul charged 22 individuals at 11 construction companies with bid rigging (Sleight 2013).

Pundits dispute the number of genuine jobs created by the Four Major Rivers Project as opposed to those that already existed and were simply reclassified as part of the project (Chang et al. 2012; Kim et al. 2012). The government aimed to create as many as 340,000 jobs through the project, but Lah et al. (2015) estimated that only 4,162 jobs were actually created (including temporary jobs). Concern has also been expressed about the quality of the jobs created (Yun et al. 2011; Chang et al. 2012; Kim et al. 2012). It has been suggested that the government's much smaller investment in renewable energy created higher-quality jobs than the Four Major Rivers Project did (Chang et al. 2012).

It was the construction industry, not the environment or the Korean people, that stood to benefit most from the Four Major Rivers Project, and President Lee had strong ties to that industry as the former CEO of a major construction firm. Han (2015, 823) argues that:

> The president and a small group of technocrats dominated the policy-making process and concentrated bureaucratic authority under a development-oriented ministry, which in turn reinforced its symbiotic relationship with the construction industry through project implementation. The Lee administration failed to incorporate policy input from local governments, NGOs, the media, and the public, despite their intense attention and opposition to the project for environmental, economic, and procedural reasons.

Speculation over why Lee pursued this project so relentlessly range from the extremely cynical suggestion that he "owed" the construction industry for their help with his election campaign, to the more forgiving argument that he was simply misguided and truly believed that the project would benefit the country (Tienhaara 2018). Once Lee had left office, the Board of Audit and Inspection conducted three further investigations into the project (an unprecedented number). President Moon made a campaign promise that the weirs would be opened fully and that some would be dismantled, and the government is now doing so at a cost of nearly 90 billion won (USD 75 million) (Kang et al. 2019; MacDonald 2020).

The failure of "green growth"

As noted above, the KGND and subsequent investments and policies of the Lee administration were heavily focused on the idea of "green growth." There are two key underlying assumptions of the green growth policy paradigm. The first is that economic growth and environmental pressure can be decoupled (UNEP 2010). In other words, through investments in energy efficiency measures and non-fossil-fuel-based energy, it will be possible for GDP to increase while environmental pressures, such as GHG emissions, decline. A second assumption is that the development of green technologies can act as a new engine for economic growth: i.e., that the economy can grow *through* environmental protection (Jacobs 2013).

A growing literature questions these assumptions, particularly with respect to decoupling. While there is evidence of *relative decoupling* (i.e., when the growth rate of emissions is lower than the rate of economic growth) in some developed countries (Jorgenson and Clark 2012), there is debate about the existence, extent, and prevalence of absolute decoupling (i.e., absolute reductions in emissions despite economic growth), especially when emissions related to trade are considered (Knight and Schor 2014; Cohen et al. 2017; Haberl et al. 2020; Hubacek et al. 2021). Even Nordic countries that have made large strides in mitigation (e.g., Denmark) "cannot be said to have demonstrated genuine green growth in this century" if one accounts for trade-related emissions and a stringent climate target is used as the reference point for "sufficient" decoupling (Tilsted et al. 2021, 7). There has "never been a global pattern of absolute decoupling of CO_2 from economic growth" (Parrique et al. 2019, 24) and, assuming continued economic growth, it is very unlikely that absolute decoupling could occur at the scale and pace necessary to avoid catastrophic climate change (Anderson and Bows 2012; Hickel and Kallis 2019). Compared to mitigation pathways that assume continued economic growth and unprecedented technological development, Keyßer and Lenzen (2021) show that "degrowth" scenarios, where GDP would decline due to strong mitigation policies, are better suited to keep warming within 1.5°C above preindustrial levels.

As predicted in early critical evaluations (Shim 2010; Yun 2009 and 2010), Korea has provided evidence in practice of the problems with the green growth paradigm (Dale 2015; Bluemling and Yun 2016; Gunderson and Yun 2017). While the growth objective was achieved (GDP rose 16.2% from KRW 1,188,118 billion in 2009 to KRW 1,380,833 billion in 2013, based on 2010 prices) (KEEI 2018) and energy efficiency also improved, absolute decoupling did not occur (Gunderson and Yun 2017). Instead, common measures of environmental pressure *increased* during the rollout of the KGND and National Strategy for Green Growth. Not only did GHG emissions increase 16.6% during the period 2009–2013 (598.0 $MTCO_2eq$ to 697.4 $MTCO_2eq$), but they also *exceeded* BAU emissions (Republic of Korea 2014). Total primary energy supply also increased 14.5% (from 243.5 MTOE[8] to 278.9 MTOE) during this period (Korea Energy Economics Institute 2015).

The Korean New Deal (2020)

In the run-up to Korea's parliamentary election on 15 April 2020, the ruling centrist Democratic Party of Korea (DPK), the center-right Party for People's Livelihoods (PPL), the center-left Justice Party (JP) and the left Green Party Korea (GPK) all made pledges around a "Green New Deal" (S. Lee 2020). DPK's climate manifesto included a pledge to pass a "Green New Deal Special Act" to steer the country's transformation to a low-carbon economy with the aim of achieving net-zero carbon emissions by 2050 (Ha 2020). The manifesto explicitly referenced the US GND and EU Green Deal as inspiration. The DPK achieved a landslide victory in 2020 general election, returning President Moon Jae-in to the Blue House and securing the party and its allies 180 seats in the 300-seat National Assembly.

The government released the Korean New Deal (KND) on 14 July 2020. The KND has two main pillars – the Digital New Deal and the Green New Deal – along with several policies to create a "Stronger Safety Net" (e.g., increases to employment insurance and worker compensation). The overall funding package for the KND is KRW 160 trillion (USD 140 billion) with approximately KRW 73.4 trillion (USD 60.9 billion) for "green" investments in the period 2020–2025 (KRW 42.7 trillion of which would come from the treasury and the rest from local governments and the private sector). Table 15.3 outlines how these funds are expected to be allocated. The government anticipates that the KND will create 1.9 million jobs by 2025 of which 659,000 will be "green jobs" (Ministry of Economy and Finance 2020).

The government additionally committed KRW 1.1 trillion to a job training program that would include training 20,000 Koreans in "green-integrated fields."

As with the KGND, the government has received a great deal of international praise for the KND. The UN Secretary General (2020) called it "exemplary," and the International Energy Agency (IEA 2020b, 11) described it as "a significant step towards accelerating Korea's energy transition." Some voices within the country, particularly those associated with the Green Party, have suggested that the KND is not radically different from the KGND (Bae 2020; Ko 2020; S. Lee 2020) and is largely a "repackaging" of existing plans and policies (Smith and Cha 2020). Lee Yujin (2020) has gone so far as to argue that it is "unworthy" of the green new deal name and "is merely a rather disappointing green stimulus package."

As we write, much of the KND remains in development and it is too soon to provide a comprehensive assessment of it. Nevertheless, it is promising that there is a clear shift away from funding for coal and nuclear power and a much-needed emphasis on renewable energy

Table 15.3 KND Budget (Green New Deal pillar) in Trillion KRW

Focus Area	*Projects*	*Total Budget*
Green transition of infrastructures	Turning public facilities into zero-energy buildings	6.2
	Restoring the terrestrial, marine and urban ecosystems	2.5
	Building a management system for clean and safe water	3.4
Low-carbon and decentralized energy	Building a smart grid for more efficient energy management	2.0
	Promoting renewable energy use and supporting a fair transition	9.2
	Expanding the supply of electric and hydrogen vehicles	13.1
Innovation in green industry	Promoting prospective businesses to lead green industry and establishing low-carbon and green industrial complexes	3.6
	Laying the foundation for green innovation via the R&D and financial sectors	2.7
Total		**42.7**

Source: Ministry of Economy and Finance 2020.

development. The Moon government has committed to phase out 30 coal power plants after 30 years of operation by 2034 (Ministry of Industry, Trade and Energy 2020). This is approximately half of the country's coal fleet. Much of the impetus for the coal phase-out has come from regional governments. The province of South Chungcheong – where around half the country's coal plants are located – joined the international Powering Past Coal Alliance (PPCA) in 2018. Six more subnational governments from Korea had joined by May 2021 (PPCA 2021). It is also worth noting that several analyses have indicated that coal power could (and should) be completely phased out much faster than the Moon government's plan (Parra et al. 2020; Ehrenheim et al. 2021). In June 2021, the UK's COP26 Envoy and Canada's Ambassador for Climate Change called on Korea to completely phase out coal by 2030 (Murton and Fuller 2021).

The Moon government has additionally committed to a gradual phase-out of nuclear power generation (IEA 2020b). As of 2021, the country had 24 nuclear power plants operating across the country's relatively small land area, giving it the highest density of nuclear power plants in the world. Nuclear power has become very controversial in the country, especially since the 2011 Fukushima disaster in Japan. The unexpected 5.8 magnitude earthquake in Gyeongju in September 2016, one of the strongest earthquakes in Korean modern history, and an earthquake in Pohang in November 2017 have also magnified public concerns about the safety of nuclear power. Two planned nuclear plants have been cancelled by the Moon government, while two that were already under construction when he was elected have been allowed to proceed after a public engagement process in 2017.

In terms of increasing the supply of renewable energy, the KND is expected to add 12.8 gigawatts to the government's initial midterm goal of increasing solar and wind to 29.9 gigawatts by 2025 (B. Kim 2020). In the allocation of funding for renewables, there is an effort to incorporate some consideration of "justice" in the KND, which has been the hallmark of the US GND discourse but is also increasingly discussed by domestic environmental groups and unions within Korea (Yun and Jung 2017). There is specific mention of community benefit sharing for renewable energy projects and greater support for renewable energy for residents of rural areas and industrial complexes. The KND also highlights that a "fair transition will be ensured for those regions that foresee difficulties coming from a reduced use of coal power and other traditional sources of energy" (Ministry of Economy and Finance 2020, 28), although a detailed plan was not provided (Lee and Woo 2020). Nevertheless, research suggests that support in the form of wage subsidies and unemployment insurance for displaced workers can play an important role in a just transition from coal to renewables (Garg et al. 2017), and these are policies that the Korean government is adopting or expanding under the "Stronger Safety Net" component of the KND.

In addition to the shift in focus to renewable energy and increased acknowledgement of the distributive effects of the energy transition, the Moon administration has taken a welcome approach to public participation in the development of the KND. In contrast with the "environmental authoritarianism" of the Lee administration, the Moon government has been inclusive and engaged with civil society. The presidential commission on policy and planning has held "hearing and consensus discussion" by region to collect public opinions about KND and explore regional KND projects.

Although these elements suggest that the KND is an improvement over its predecessor in both environmental and social terms, there are some valid concerns about the plan that are worth exploring. One is that hydrogen technologies receive substantial funding under the KND. Another is that the overall strategy remains premised on decoupling environmental impact from growth through technological innovation, i.e., green growth.

Betting big on hydrogen

The largest allocation of green funding in the KND is for transportation. Transportation is the second-largest energy consuming sector and the second-largest source of emissions in Korea (IEA 2020b). The automobile industry also makes up 12% of total employment in the country. Therefore, the government's focus on this sector is hardly surprising. However, in addition to subsidizing battery electric vehicles (BEVs) and investing in charging infrastructure, like many governments around the world, South Korea is making substantial investments in hydrogen fuel cell electric vehicles (FCEVs) and hydrogen refueling infrastructure. The KND sets a target to have 200,000 FCEVs on the road by 2025 and to increase the number of hydrogen refueling stations from 37 to 450. The specific type of FCEVs (e.g., passenger vehicles versus trucks and buses) is not specified in the KND. However, the government's 2019 Hydrogen Economy Roadmap anticipates that passenger vehicles will make up 95% of FCEV production by 2040 (Clifford Chance 2020).

Investing in hydrogen is a risky move in both economic and environmental terms. The idea of hydrogen as a clean energy solution has had several false starts (Van der Graaf et al. 2020). This time may be different, and many argue that hydrogen will play an essential role in decarbonizing economies. However, there are substantial uncertainties and debates about whether this will be a niche role in hard-to-electrify sectors like shipping, aviation and steel, or will instead result in a more encompassing "hydrogen economy" (Evans and Gabbatiss 2020). With respect to passenger vehicles, many experts argue that FCEVs have already lost the race against BEVs (Morris 2020). FCEVs are more expensive than BEVs, although they do currently have some advantages in terms of range. There are commercial vehicles like long-haul heavy payload trucks where a battery electric model is more challenging, and hydrogen may play a more important role (BloombergNEF 2020). Still, companies like Korea's Hyundai continue to focus on passenger vehicles alongside commercial ones because mass production is required to reduce costs, and "truck volumes can't come close to volumes of passenger cars" (Park 2020).

Importantly, given the export-focused nature of Korea's automotive industry, strong support for the technology within Korea will not be enough. The Hydrogen Economy Roadmap envisions Korea becoming a global leader in the market for hydrogen-based technology in transportation. Of the 6.2 million cars planned for in the Roadmap, only 2.9 million are intended for sale in the domestic market, whereas 3.3 million would be exported. As Stangarone (2021, 510) notes, "much of the plan will rest on South Korea's ability to expand the acceptance of fuel cell electric vehicles (FCEVs) first in South Korea's domestic market and in time in markets around the world." For such a plan to work, governments in key export markets will have to invest in refueling infrastructure. However, public concerns about the safety of hydrogen fueling stations and their siting may limit attempts to expand infrastructure for FCEVs both within Korea and abroad (IEA 2020b, 15).

On the environmental side, it is important to understand that "hydrogen is not an energy source but an energy *carrier*" (Van de Graaf et al. 2020, 2). While hydrogen itself burns cleanly, producing only water vapor, it is currently mainly produced using fossil fuels – either methane gas ("grey" hydrogen) or coal ("black" hydrogen). While there is a lot of hype about the use of carbon capture and storage (CCS) technologies to create "blue" hydrogen, such technology has been deployed at an underwhelming pace. Furthermore, blue hydrogen would only be carbon neutral if methane at the point of extraction was also successfully captured. One study found that even if the release of fugitive methane is kept very low, greenhouse gas emissions from blue hydrogen are still greater than from simply burning natural gas and that, therefore, "the use of blue hydrogen appears difficult to justify on climate grounds" (Howarth and Jacobson 2021, 1).

"Green" hydrogen created through electrolysis powered by renewables is currently negligible but could rapidly become dominant with the right policies and investments. At present, South Korea's hydrogen needs are supplied from byproducts in the petrochemical process. It is anticipated that increased demand will be met by domestic production using liquefied natural gas (LNG; Stangarone 2021) and hydrogen imports (Anderson 2021). The Hydrogen Economy Roadmap assumes that CCS will be viable to convert domestic grey hydrogen to blue hydrogen and that green hydrogen is not likely to be cost-competitive before 2030 (IEEFA 2020). It is not clear how Korea will achieve the transition from grey to blue to green. As law firm Clifford Chance (2020, 4) has pointed out, the government's hydrogen strategy

> appears to be driven more by the perceived opportunities for economic growth and industrial competitiveness than by climate change objectives. It remains to be seen what concrete steps or plans will be devised for the shift from grey to green hydrogen on the production/supply side.

Still green growth?

Green growth became an unpopular term in Korea following the Four Major Rivers Project, and President Park's administration, which followed Lee's, was very reluctant to use the term even though they are from the same political party (Gunderson and Yun 2017). Nevertheless, a second Five-Year Plan for Green Growth was adopted in 2014 in accordance with the Framework Act on Low Carbon Green Growth, which maintained a focus on improving energy efficiency and "greening" industry and technology (Global Green Growth Institute [GGGI] 2015). A third Five-Year Plan for Green Growth (2019–2023) was adopted after President Moon Jae-in (Democratic Party of Korea) took office in 2017. However, the DPK has been trying to legislate a Framework Act on Carbon Neutrality Implementation to replace the Framework Act on Low Carbon Green Growth. Furthermore, President Moon's main policy platform did not mention green growth, instead outlining a vision of "A Nation of the People, a Just Republic of Korea." When speaking at the 2018 Partnering for Green Growth and Global Goals 2030 (P4G) summit in Denmark, Moon (2018) noted that "Korea has had various successes in reducing greenhouse gas emissions through green growth policies over the past 10 years, all the while maintaining growth," but otherwise the speech focused much more heavily on "inclusiveness." At the second P4G held in Seoul in May 2021, Moon did not address green growth in his remarks and instead mainly focused on carbon neutrality and the Green New Deal, with an emphasis again on inclusiveness, as well as public-private partnerships and international cooperation (Kim 2021).

Moon's rhetorical approach may indicate that the term "green growth" continues to be associated in Korea with Lee's highly controversial term in office, and the Four Major Rivers Project in particular. However, a larger question is whether the KND still relies on decoupling to achieve carbon emissions reductions as the KGND and other green growth policies have, despite the failure of this approach over the last decade. The answer to this question appears to be yes. The text of the KND suggests that growth remains a predominant concern for the government even if the term "green growth" is not used: "The economic risks from the pandemic have shed light on the need for a growth strategy that also ensures sustainability including environmental and ecological protection" (Ministry of Economy and Finance 2020, 25). Moreover, while the enhancements to the social safety net in the KND are an important first step, more transformative initiatives, such as a job guarantee or Universal Basic Income/Services, would likely be required to ensure that increased employment and improved quality of life for Koreans could be achieved in the absence of GDP growth.

Conclusions

Carbon emissions and other environmental pressures increased following the adoption of the KGND, which took a green growth approach and was plagued by controversies surrounding the Four Major Rivers Project and the expansion of nuclear energy. By prioritizing renewable energy development instead of nuclear energy development, increasing inclusiveness and taking some first steps toward a just transition away from coal power, the KND is socially and environmentally superior to the KGND. Despite these improvements, the Moon government may repeat some of the failings of the Lee administration, including strong support for projects with questionable "green" outcomes and the continued focus on green growth as an overriding strategy. While the latter is hardly surprising – economic growth is one of the imperatives of liberal states (Dryzek et al. 2002) and none have fully embraced a shift away from this as a basis for policy – it does place a limit on our expectations for what the KND can achieve. Of course, other green new deals, such as the EU's Green Deal, are marked by similar ambiguities; they are peppered with potentially transformative tendencies while simultaneously maintaining a commitment to the power structures and economic processes that drive environmental harm (Ossewaarde and Ossewaarde-Lowtoo 2020; Adler and Wargan, this volume).

Unlike some scholars and activists in Korea, we do not believe that the shortcomings of the KND amount to a complete failure. We adopt the more pragmatic approach taken by several commentators who, while recognizing the limits of GND initiatives that have been developed (see Stoner 2020 on the US), view them as a springboard that can potentially lead to more effective and transformational measures over time (e.g., Foster 2019; Klein 2019; Smith 2020). This is in line with Schwartzman's (2011) call to avoid resolutely rejecting GND proposals as just another manifestation of green capitalism, and, instead, to view them as a potential starting point to begin transitioning out of the ecologically unsustainable dynamics of the current political-economic order (cf. White 2020).

To make the KND truly transformative, the Moon government should consider further policies that can reduce GHG emissions and increase human well-being. For example, the government could expand energy democracy programs like the energy cooperatives already found in Seoul (Gunderson and Yun 2021). As a more overarching policy, we recommend that Korea abandon Gross Domestic Product (GDP) as the key indicator of the health of the economy. GDP is not a valid measure of human well-being or progress, and the goals of increasing economic growth and reducing GHG emissions at the rate and pace necessary are likely incompatible. There are numerous alternative metrics available and examples, such as New Zealand's "well-being budget," that Korea can learn from. Finally, given that South Koreans have historically worked more hours per week on average than all but one other OECD country (there is even a Korean word – "gwarosa" – for "death by overwork"), adopting a shorter working week (see Schor and Tienhaara, this volume) is also a potentially important approach to improving both climate outcomes and the well-being of Koreans. The government has already made a critical first step in this direction by reducing the maximum working hours from a 68 per week to 40. President Moon noted when the legislation was passed that it was an "important opportunity to move away from a society of overwork and move toward a society of spending time with families" (Kwon and Field 2018). However, it is possible to go further in reducing working hours; some countries, such as Spain, are now considering adopting a 4-day (32-hour) work week (Kassam 2021).

We do not suggest that any of these policy proposals will be easy to achieve in Korea, particularly in the current political climate (local elections in 2021 indicated a swing to the conservative opposition). Nevertheless, over the long term they can help Korean society transition out of its currently unsustainable form into a qualitatively different order organized around meeting human needs and protecting the environment.

Notes

1 The first author was supported by funding from the Canada Research Chairs Program.
2 The second and third authors' contributions were supported by the Ministry of Education of the Republic of Korea and the National Research Foundation of Korea (NRF-2017S1A3A2067220).
3 $MTCO_2eq$ = Metric tons of carbon dioxide equivalent.
4 In Korea, the term "renewable energy" is not used but instead "new and renewable energy," which refers to energies that are not traditional fossil fuels (coal, oil, gas) or nuclear energy. New energies include hydrogen, fuel cell, coal liquefied/gasified energy and heavy oil residue, and renewable energies include solar, photovoltaic, biomass, wind, small hydro power, geothermal, ocean energy and waste energy.
5 This section and the following one are adapted from content in *Green Keynesianism and the Global Financial Crisis* by Kyla Tienhaara, Copyright 2018. Reproduced by permission of Taylor and Francis Group, LLC, a division of Informa PLC.
6 KRW = South Korean won.
7 Using an average KRW–USD exchange rate for 2011 of 0.0009.
8 MTOE = Millions of tons of oil equivalent.

References

Air Quality Life Index (AQLI). 2019. South Korea Fact Sheet. University of Chicago. Available from: https://aqli.epic.uchicago.edu/wp-content/uploads/2019/05/EPIC_SouthKorea_FactSheet_31319.pdf

Anderson, J. 2021. Experts Debate US Capacity Market Reform, Need for New Ancillary Service Product. *S&P Global*. Available from: https://www.spglobal.com/platts/en/market-insights/latest-news/electric-power/052821-experts-debate-us-capacity-market-reform-need-for-new-ancillary-service-product

Anderson, K. and Bows, A. 2012. A New Paradigm for Climate Change. *Nature Climate Change.* 2(9), 639–640.

Aşıcı, A.A. and Bünül, Z. 2012. Green New Deal: A Green Way Out of the Crisis? *Environmental Policy and Governance.* 22(5), 295–306.

Bae, H. 2020. How Green and New Is Moon's Deal? *Korea Herald.* 9 August.

Bernard, S., S. Asokan, H. Warrell, and J. Lemer. 2009. "The Greenest Bail-Out?" *The Financial Times*, August 17.

Birds Korea. 2010. *The Anticipated Impacts of the Four Rivers Project (Republic of Korea) on Waterbirds.* Birds Korea Preliminary Report, Busan: Birds Korea. Available from: http://birdskorea.org/Habitats/4-Rivers/Downloads/Birds-Korea-4-River-Report-March-12-2010.pdf

BloombergNEF. 2020. *Hydrogen Economy Outlook.* Available from: https://data.bloomberglp.com/professional/sites/24/BNEF-Hydrogen-Economy-Outlook-Key-Messages-30-Mar-2020.pdf

Bluemling, B., Yun, S.J. 2016. Giving Green Teeth to the Tiger? A Critique of 'green growth' in South Korea. In G. Dale, M.V. Mathai and J.A. Puppim de Oliveira, eds. *Green Growth: Ideology, Political Economy and the Alternatives.* London: Zed Books. pp. 114–130.

Card, J. 2009. Korea's Four Rivers Project: Economic Boost or Boondoggle? *Yale Environment 360* [blog]. 21 September. Available from: http://e360.yale.edu/features/koreas_four_rivers_project_economic_boost_or_boondoggle

Cha, Y.J., Shim, M.P. and Kim, S.K. 2011. The Four Major Rivers Restoration Project. Paper Presented at the *UN Water International Conference, 3–5 October, Zaragoza, Spain.* Available from: http://www.un.org/waterforlifedecade/green_economy_2011/pdf/session_8_water_planning_cases_korea.pdf

Chang, Y.-B., Han, J.-K. and Kim, H.-W. 2012. Green Growth and Green New Deal Policies in the Republic of Korea. *International Journal of Labour Research.* 4(2), 151–171.

Cho, H., Leitner, J., Lee, J. and S. Heo. 2014. Korean Green Growth: A Paradigm Shift in Sustainability Policy, and its International Implications. *Journal of Korean Law.* 13, 301–333.

Chosunilbo. 2013. Probe Finds Massive Underhand Dealings in 4 Rivers Project. *Chosunilbo.* 11 July. Available from: http://english.chosun.com/site/data/html_dir/2013/07/11/2013071101465.html.

Clifford Chance. 2020. Focus on Hydrogen: Korea's New Energy Roadmap. Available from: https://www.cliffordchance.com/content/dam/cliffordchance/briefings/2020/10/focus-on-hydrogen-korea-new-energy-roadmap.pdf

Climate Action Tracker. 2020. South Korea: Pledges and Targets (30 July Update). Available from: https://climateactiontracker.org/countries/south-korea/pledges-and-targets/

Cohen, G., Jalles, J.T., Loungani, M.P., and Marto, R. 2017. *Emissions and Growth: Trends and Cycles in a Globalized World.* Washington, D.C.: International Monetary Fund.

Dale, G. 2015. Origins and Delusions of Green Growth. *International Socialist Review.* 97. Available from: http://isreview.org/issue/97/origins-and-delusions-green-growth

Dietz, T., Rosa, E.A. and York, R. 2012. Environmentally Efficient Well-being: Is There a Kuznets Curve? *Applied Geography.* 32(1), 21–28.

Dryzek, J. et al. 2002. Environmental Transformation of the State: the USA. Norway, Germany and the UK. *Political Studies.* 50, 659–682.

Easterlin, R.A. 1974. Does Economic Growth Improve the Human Lot? Some Empirical Evidence. In P.A. Dagvid and M.W. Reder, eds. *Nations and Households in Economic Growth.* New York: Academic Press. pp. 89–125.

Ehrenheim, V., Kim, S., Song, Y. and Kim, J. 2021. End In Sight: How South Korea Can Force Coal Offline by 2028. Carbon Tracker, Chungnam National University and Solutions for Our Climate. Available from: https://carbontracker.org/reports/end-in-sight/

Evans, S. and Gabbatiss, J. 2020. In-depth Q&A: Does the World Need Hydrogen to Solve Climate Change? *Carbon Brief.* Available from: https://www.carbonbrief.org/in-depth-qa-does-the-world-need-hydrogen-to-solve-climate-change

Feindt, P.H. and Cowell, R. 2010. The Recession, Environmental Policy and Ecological Modernization–What's New About the Green New Deal? *International Planning Studies.* 15(3), 191–211.

Fitzgerald, J.B., Jorgenson, A.K. and Clark, B. 2015. Energy Consumption and Working Hours: A Longitudinal Study of Developed and Developing Nations, 1990–2008. *Environmental Sociology.* 3(1), 213–223.

Foster, J.B. 2019. A Green New Deal Is the First Step toward an Eco-revolution. *Truthout.* Available from: https://truthout.org/articles/a-green-new-deal-is-the-first-step-toward-an-eco-revolution/

Gabbatiss, J. 2020. The Carbon Brief Profile: South Korea. 6 April. Available from: https://www.carbonbrief.org/the-carbon-brief-profile-south-korea

Galvin, R. and Healy, N. 2020. The Green New Deal in the United States: What it Is and How to Pay for it. *Energy Research & Social Science*. 67, 101529.

Garg, A., Steckel, J. et al. 2017. Bridging the Gap: Phasing Out Coal. In *Emissions Gap Report 2017*. Nairobi: UN Environment. Available from: https://wedocs.unep.org/bitstream/handle/20.500.11822/22106/EGR_2017_ch_5.pdf?isAllowed=y&sequence=1

Georgescu-Roegen, N. 1971. *The Entropy Law and the Economic Process*. Cambridge, MA: Harvard University Press.

GGGI 2015. Global Green Growth Institute. 2015. *Korea's Green Growth Experience: Process, Outcomes and Lessons Learned*. Seoul: Global Green Growth Institute.

Gowan, P. 2018. A Plan to Nationalize Fossil-Fuel Companies. *Jacobin*. Available from: https://www.jacobinmag.com/2018/03/nationalize-fossil-fuel-companies-climate-change

Green Europe Foundation. 2009. A Green New Deal for Europe. Brussels. Available from: https://epub.wupperinst.org/files/3336/3336_Green_New_Deal.pdf

Gunderson, R. 2019. Work Time Reduction and Economic Democracy as Climate Change Mitigation Strategies: Or Why the Climate Needs a Renewed Labor Movement. *Journal of Environmental Studies and Sciences*. 9(1), 35–44.

Gunderson, R. and Yun, S-J. 2017. South Korean Green Growth and the Jevons Paradox: An Assessment with Democratic and Degrowth Policy Recommendations. *Journal of Cleaner Production*. 144, 239–247.

Gunderson, R. and Yun, S-J. 2021. Building Energy Democracy to Mend Ecological and Epistemic Rifts: An Environmental Sociological Examination of Seoul's One Less Nuclear Power Plant Initiative. *Energy Research & Social Science*. 72 (2), 101884.

Ha, T. 2020. In East Asian first, South Korea Announced Ambitions to Reach Net Zero by 2050. *Eco-Business*. Available from: https://www.eco-business.com/news/in-east-asian-first-south-korea-announces-ambitions-to-reach-net-zero-by-2050/

Halberl, H., Wiedenhofer, D., Virag, D., Kalt, G., Plank, B., Brockway, P., Fishman, T., Hausknost, D., Krausmann, F., Leon-Gruchalski, B. and Mayer, A. 2020. A Systematic Review of the Evidence on Decoupling of GDP, Resource Use and GHG Emissions, Part II: Synthesizing the Insights. *Environmental Research Letters*. 15 (6), 065003.

Han, H. 2015. Authoritarian Environmentalism Under Democracy: Korea's River Restoration Project. *Environmental Politics*. 24(5), 810–829.

Han, P. 2010. Sustainable and Green Tourism Korea's Green New Deal and 4 Rivers Restoration Project. *Presentation to the OECD Workshop on Sustainable Development Strategies and Tourism*, June 18. Available from: https://www.oecd.org/cfe/tourism/45558102.pdf

Herman, C. 2015. Green New Deal and the Question of Environmental and Social Justice (No. 31). Global Labour University Working Paper.

Hickel, J. and Kallis, G. 2019. Is Green Growth Possible? *New Political Economy*. 25(4), 469–486.

Hong, S. 2021. South Korea Raises Renewable Energy Target to 25pc. *Argus Media*. 19 April. Available from: https://www.argusmedia.com/en/news/2206528-south-korea-raises-renewable-energy-target-to-25pc

Howarth, R. and Jacobson, M. 2021. How Green Is Blue Hydrogen? *Energy Science and Engineering* (early view), 1–12. Available from: https://doi.org/10.1002/ese3.956

Hubacek, K., Chen, X., Feng, K., Wiedmann, T., and Shan, Y. 2021. Evidence of Decoupling Consumption-Based CO_2 Emissions from Economic Growth. *Advances in Applied Energy*. 4, 100074.

International Energy Agency (IEA). 2012. Energy Policies of IEA Countries: Republic of Korea (2012 Review). Available from: https://iea.blob.core.windows.net/assets/f95918d7-ed55-44ef-81a7-3609261894db/Korea2012_free.pdf

International Energy Agency (IEA). 2020a. IEA Atlas of Energy. Available from: http://energyatlas.iea.org/#!/tellmap/1378539487

International Energy Agency (IEA). 2020b. Korea Energy Policy Review. Available from: https://www.iea.org/reports/korea-2020

IPCC (Intergovernmental Panel on Climate Change). 2018. Summary for policymakers. In: *Global Warming of 1.5°C*. Geneva: World Meteorological Organization.

Jackson, T. 2009. *Prosperity Without Growth*. London: Earthscan.

Jacobs, M. 2013. Green Growth. In R. Falkner, ed. *Handbook of Global Climate and Environmental Policy*. Malden, MA: Wiley-Blackwell. pp. 197–214.

Johanisova, N. and Wolf, S. 2012. Economic Democracy: A Path for the Future? *Futures*. 44(6), 562–570.

Jones, R.S. and Yoo, B. 2010. Korea's Green Growth Strategy: Mitigating Climate Change and Developing New Growth Engines. OECD Economics Department Working Papers, No. 798. OECD Publishing.

Jung, M.-K. 2020. "Korean New Deal" Aims to Revive Economy through Digitalization. *Korea Herald*. 7 May. Available from: http://www.koreaherald.com/view.php?ud=20200507000889

Kallis, G., Kerschner, C. and Martinez-Alier, J. 2012. The Economics of Degrowth. *Ecological Economics*. 84, 172–180. Available from: https://www.sciencedirect.com/science/article/abs/pii/S0921800912003333

Kang, C. et al. 2019. Weirs Now Open Remain Mired in Controversy. *Korea JoongAng Daily*. 20 March. Available from: https://koreajoongangdaily.joins.com/news/article/article.aspx?aid=3060839

Kang, S.I., Oh, J.G. and Kim, H. 2012. Korea's Low-Carbon Green Growth Strategy. OECD Development Center, Working Paper No. 310.

Kassam, A. 2021.Spain to LAUNCH trial of Four-Day Working Week. *The Guardian*. 15 March. Available from: https://www.theguardian.com/world/2021/mar/15/spain-to-launch-trial-of-four-day-working-week

Keyßer, L.T. and Lenzen, M. 2021. 1.5°C Degrowth Scenarios Suggest the Need for New Mitigation Pathways. *Nature Communications*. 12(1), 1–16.

KEEI (Korea Energy Economics Institute). 2018. *2018 Energy Info. Korea*. Available from: http://www.keei.re.kr/web_keei/en_publish.nsf/by_allv/CF91294F488178C5492583C800006A0D/$-file/EnergyInfo2018.pdf

Kim, B. 2020. Korea Sets 42% Renewable Energy Target by 2034. *The Korea Herald*. 16 December. Available from: https://ieefa.org/korea-sets-42-renewable-energy-target-by-2034/

Kim, J.-S. 2013. The Environmental Fallout of the Four Major Rivers Project. *The Hankyoreh*. 3 August. Available from: http://www.hani.co.kr/arti/english_edition/e_national/598190.html

Kim, J-W. 2012. Four Major River Project and Environmental Ordeal under the Lee Myung-bak Government in South Korea. In A. Mori, ed. *Democratization, Decentralization, and Environmental Governance in Asia*. Kyoto: Kyoto University Press. pp. 72–85.

Kim, P. 2013. 28 Endangered Species Gone Due to 4-River Project. *The Korea Observer*. 21 October. Available from: http://www.koreaobserver.com/dozens-endangered-species-perish-following-river-project-8163/

Kim, S. 2021. P4G Summit Opens with Pledge for "inclusive green recovery" from Moon. *Korea JoongAng Daily*. 30 May. Available from: https://koreajoongangdaily.joins.com/2021/05/30/national/socialAffairs/P4G-Summit-green-recovery-climate-change/20210530193200533.html

Klein, N. 2019. *On Fire: The (Burning) Case for a Green New Deal*. New York: Simon and Schuster.

Knight, K.W., Rosa, E.A. and Schor, J.B. 2013. Could Working Less Reduce Pressures on the Environment? A Cross-National Panel Analysis of OECD Countries, 1970–2007. *Global Environmental Change*. 23(4), 691–700.

Knight, K.W. and Schor, J.B. 2014. Economic Growth and Climate Change: a Cross-National Analysis of Territorial and Consumption-Based Carbon Emissions in High-Income Countries. *Sustainability*. 6(6), 3722–3731.

Ko, J. 2020. Environment Minister Defends Green New Deal, Promises Carbon Neutrality. *The Korea Herald*. 22 July.

Korea Energy Economics Institute. 2015. *2015 Energy Info Korea*. Ulsan.

Kunze, C. and Becker, S. 2015. Collective Ownership in Renewable Energy and Opportunities for Sustainable Degrowth. *Sustainability Science*. 10(3), 425–437.

Kwon, J. and Field, A. 2018. South Koreans Are Working Themselves to Death. Can they Get their Lives Back? *CNN*. 5 November. Available from: https://www.cnn.com/2018/11/04/asia/korea-working-hours-intl/index.html

Lah, T.J., Park, Y. and Cho, Y.J. 2015. The Four Major Rivers Restoration Project of South Korea: An Assessment of Its Process, Program, and Political Dimensions. *Journal of Environment & Development*. 24(4), 375–394. Available from: http://dx.doi.org/10.1177/1070496515598611

LaJeunesse, R. 2009. *Work Time Regulation as Sustainable Full Employment Strategy: The Social Effort Bargain*. New York: Routledge.

Lawn, P.A. 2003. A Theoretical Foundation to Support the Index of Sustainable Economic Welfare (ISEW), Genuine Progress Indicator (GPI), and Other Related indexes. *Ecological Economics*. 44(1), 105–118.

Lee, H. 2021. South Korea Shuns Coal-Power Financing Amid Rising U.S. Pressure. *Bloomberg*. 22 April. Available from: https://www.bloomberg.com/news/articles/2021-04-22/south-korea-shuns-coal-power-financing-amid-rising-u-s-pressure

Lee, H-J. 2020. Moon's Korean New Deal detailed. *Korea JoongAng Daily*. Available from: https://koreajoongangdaily.joins.com/2020/06/01/economy/newdeal-digitalnewdeal-greennewdeal/20200601193300201.html.

Lee, J-H. and Woo, J. 2020. Green New Deal Policy of South Korea: Policy Innovation for a Sustainability Transition. *Sustainability*. 12(23), 10191. Available from: http://dx.doi.org/10.3390/su122310191

Lee, J-H. and Yun, S-J., 2011. A comparative study of governance in state management: Focusing on the Roh Moo-hyun government and the Lee Myung-bak government. *Development and Society*. 40(2): 289–318.

Lee, S. 2020. The Substance of a Korean Green New DEAL IS STILL BEING DEFINED. *China Dialogue*. 1 July. Available from: https://chinadialogue.net/en/climate/the-substance-of-a-korean-green-new-deal-is-still-being-defined/

Lee, Y. 2020. South Korea's Reforms Should Not be Called a Green New Deal. *Heinrich Boll Stiftung Blog*. Available from: https://hk.boell.org/en/2020/09/14/south-koreas-reforms-should-not-be-called-green-new-deal

Luke, T.W. 2009. A Green New Deal: Why Green, How New, and What Is the Deal? *Critical Policy Studies*. 3(1), 14–28.

MacDonald, S. 2020. How Green Is South Korea's Green New Deal? *The Diplomat*. 12 August. Available from: https://thediplomat.com/2020/08/how-green-is-south-koreas-green-new-deal/

Martinez, C. 2017. From Commodification to the Commons: Charting the Pathway for Energy Democracy. In D. Fairchild and A. Weinrub, eds. *Energy Democracy: Advancing Equity in Clean Energy Solutions*. Washington, DC: Island Press. pp. 21–36.

Mathews, J.A. 2012. Green Growth Strategies – Korean Initiatives. *Futures*. 44, 761–769.

Mazur, A. and Rosa, E. 1974. Energy and Lifestyle: Cross-National Comparison of Energy Consumption and Quality of Life Indicators. *Science*. 186(4164), 607–610.

Ministry of Economy and Finance. 2020. *Korean New Deal (English version)*. Available from: https://english.moef.go.kr/pc/selectTbPressCenterDtl.do?boardCd=N0001&seq=4948

Ministry of Industry, Trade and Energy. 2020. *2018 Year Energy Statistics*. [in Korean]

Ministry of Land, Transport and Maritime Affairs (MLTM). 2012. *Four Rivers Restoration Project*. Seoul.

Moon, J. 2018. Address by President Moon Jae-in at Partnering for Green Growth and the Global Goals 2030 (P4G) Summit. Available from:
https://english1.president.go.kr/briefingspeeches/speeches/85

Moon, T.H., Chae, Y., Lee, D.S. et al. 2021. Analyzing climate change impacts on health, energy, water resources, and biodiversity sectors for effective climate change policy in South Korea. Scientific Reports. 11, 18512. https://doi.org/10.1038/s41598-021-97108-7

Morris, J. 2020. Why Hydrogen Will Never be the Future of Electric Cars. *Forbes*. 4 July. Available from: https://www.forbes.com/sites/jamesmorris/2020/07/04/why-hydrogen-will-never-be-the-future-of-electric-cars/?sh=4411f78c12fa

Murton, J. and Fuller, P. 2021. UK and Canada Climate Envoys Call on South Korea to Set a 2030 Coal Phase-Out Date. Powering Past Coal Alliance. 16 June. Available from: https://www.poweringpastcoal.org/news/PPCA-news/uk-and-canada-climate-envoys-call-on-south-korea-to-set-a-2030-coal-phase-out-date

Nam, J.-Y. 2011. Experts of Government-Affiliated Institute Say the Impacts of Deteriorated Water Quality Have Removed the Economic Basis Used to Justify the Project. *The Hankyoreh*. 22 March. Available from: http://english.hani.co.kr/arti/english_edition/e_national/469236.html.

Nanto, D.K. 2009. The Global Financial Crisis: Analysis and Policy Implications. CRS Report for Congress. DIANE Publishing.

National Assembly Budget Office. 2008. *National Finance of Korea 2008*. Seoul: National Assembly Budget Office. [in Korean]

National Assembly Budget Office. 2009. *National Finance of Korea 2008*. Seoul: National Assembly Budget Office. [in Korean]

O'Donnell, J. 2013. Nuclear Power in South Korea's Green Growth Strategy. *Green Growth Quarterly Update III-2013.* Council on Foreign Relations.

O'Neill, D.W. 2012. Measuring Progress in the Degrowth Transition to a Steady State Economy. *Ecological Economics.* 84, 221–231.

Ossewaarde, M. and Ossewaarde-Lowtoo, R. 2020. The EU's Green Deal: A Third Alternative to Green Growth and Degrowth? *Sustainability.* 12(23), 9825.

Park, K. 2020. Hyundai Hydrogen Chief on Why the Company Bet on Fuel Cells. *Bloomberg.* 9 June. Available from: https://www.bloomberg.com/news/articles/2020-06-09/hyundai-s-hydrogen-chief-on-why-the-auto-giant-bet-on-fuel-cells

Parra, P. et al. 2020. Transitioning Towards a Coal-Free Society: Science-Based Coal Phase-Out Pathway for South Korea under the Paris Agreement. *Climate Analytics.* Available from: https://climateanalytics.org/publications/2020/transitioning-towards-a-coal-free-society-science-based-coal-phase-out-pathway-for-south-korea-under-the-paris-agreement/

Parrique T. et al. 2019. *Decoupling Debunked: Evidence and Arguments Against Green Growth as a Sole Strategy for Sustainability.* Brussels: European Environmental Bureau.

Pollin, R., Garrett-Peltier, H., Heintz, J. and Scharber, H. 2008. *Green Recovery: A Program to Create Good Jobs & Start Building a Low-Carbon Economy.* Political Economy Research Institute, University of Massachusetts at Amherst.

Poushter, J. and Huang, C. 2019. Climate Change Still Seen as the Top Global Threat, but Cyberattacks a Rising Concern. Pew Research Center. Available from: https://www.pewresearch.org/global/wp-content/uploads/sites/2/2019/02/Pew-Research-Center_Global-Threats-2018-Report_2019-02-10.pdf

Powering Past Coal Alliance (PPCA). 2021. South Korea's Cities and Provinces Pave the Way for Faster Coal Phase-Out. 18 May. Available from: https://www.poweringpastcoal.org/news/member-news/south-koreas-cities-and-provinces-pave-the-way-for-faster-coal-phase-out

Recognizing the duty of the Federal Government to create a Green New Deal. H. Res. 109, 116th Congress. 2019. Available from: https://www.congress.gov/bill/116th-congress/house-resolution/109/text.

Redefining Progress. 1995. *Gross Production vs Genuine Progress.* Excerpt from the Genuine Progress Indicator: Summary of Data and Methodology. Redefining Progress, San Francisco.

Republic of Korea. n.d. *The River Revitalization of Korea.* Seoul (on file with authors).

Republic of Korea. 2014. *First Biennial Update Report of the Republic of Korea under the United Nations Convention on Climate Change.* Seoul: Greenhouse Gas Inventory & Research Center of Korea #501.

Republic of Korea. 2020. *Submission under the Paris Agreement: The Republic of Korea's Update of its First Nationally Determined Contribution.* Available from: https://www4.unfccc.int/sites/ndcstaging/PublishedDocuments/Republic%20of%20Korea%20First/201230_ROK%27s%20Update%20of%20its%20First%20NDC_editorial%20change.pdf

Robins, N., Clover, R. and Singh, C. 2009. *Building a Green Recovery* London: HSBC Global Research. Available from: https://www.unglobalcompact.org/docs/issues_doc/Environment/Building_a_Green_Recovery.pdf

Rosnick, D. and Weisbrot, M. 2006. *Are Shorter Working Hours Good for the Environment? A Comparison of U.S. and European Energy Consumption.* Washington, DC: Center for Economic and Policy Research.

Salleh, A. 2010. Green New Deal-or Globalisation Lite? *Arena Magazine.* 105, 15–19.

Santarius, T. 2012. *Green Growth Unravelled. How Rebound Effects Baffle Sustainability Targets When the Economy Keeps Growing.* Berlin: Wuppertal Institute.

Schor, J.B. and Jorgenson, A.K. 2019. Is it too Late for Growth? *Review of Radical Political Economics.* 51(2), 320–329.

Schwartzman, D. 2011. Green New Deal: An Ecosocialist Perspective. *Capitalism Nature Socialism.* 22(3), 49–56.

Sen, A. 1992. *Commodities and Capabilities.* Oxford: Oxford University Press.

Shim, D. 2010. Green Growth: South Korea's Panacea? In F. Rudiger, J. Hoare, P. Kollner, and S. Pares, eds. *Korea, 2010—Politics, Economy and Society.* Leiden: Brill. pp. 165–188.

Shin, H. 2011. Global Forum Touts Green Growth Paradigm. *The Korea Herald.* 20 June. Available from: http://www.koreaherald.com/view.php?ud=20110620000810.

Shin, H. 2021. S.Korea Pledges Bigger Cuts to Emissions, $5 mln for New Green Deal Fund. *Reuters.* 30 May. Available from: https://www.reuters.com/business/environment/skorea-pledges-bigger-cuts-emissions-5-mln-new-green-deal-fund-2021-05-30/

Sleight, C. 2013. Price-Fixing Charges on US$20.5 Billion Four Rivers Project. *International Construction*, https://www.khl.com/news/Price-fixing-charges-on-US-20.5-billion-Four-Rivers-project/1088539.article

Smith, J. and Cha, S. 2020. Jobs Come First in South Korea's Ambitious "Green New Deal" Climate Plan. *Reuters*. 8 June.

Smith, R. 2011. Green Capitalism: The God that Failed. *Real-World Economics Review*. 56, 112–144.

Smith, R. 2020. An Ecosocialist Path to Limiting Global Temperature Rise to 1.5°C. *Real-World Economics Review*. 87, 149–180.

Stangarone, T. 2021. South Korean efforts to Transition to a Hydrogen Economy. *Clean Technologies and Environmental Policy*. 23, 509–516. Available from: https://doi.org/10.1007/s10098-020-01936-6

Stedman, L. 2013. Audit Claims Extensive Four Rivers Project Problems. *Water 21*. London: IWA Publishing. 22 January. Available from: https://www.iwapublishing.com/?name=news1448.

Stoner, A.M. 2020. Critical Reflections on America's Green New Deal: Capital, Labor, and the Dynamics of Contemporary Social Change. *Capitalism Nature Socialism*. Available from: DOI: 10.1080/10455752.2020.1775860.

Stuart, D., Gunderson, R. and Petersen, B. 2020. *Climate Change Solutions: Beyond the Capital-climate Contradiction*. Ann Arbor: University of Michigan Press.

Svampa, M. and Viale, E. 2020. A View of the Green New Deal from Argentina. *Jacobin*. Available from: https://jacobinmag.com/2020/06/green-new-deal-argentina-gran-pacto

Szulecki, K. 2018. Conceptualizing Energy Democracy. *Environmental Politics*. 27(1), 21–41.

Taylor, M. and Nelsen, A. 2019. Yanis Varoufakis: Green New Deal Can Unite Europe's Progressives. *Guardian*. 22 May. Available from: https://www.theguardian.com/world/2019/may/22/yanis-varoufakis-green-new-deal-can-unite-europes-progressives.

Tienhaara, K. 2018. *Green Keynesianism and the Global Financial Crisis*. London: Routledge.

Tilsted, J.P., Bjørn, A., Majeau-Bettez, G. and Lund, J.F. 2021. Accounting Matters: Revisiting Claims of Decoupling and Genuine Green Growth in Nordic Countries. *Ecological Economics*. 187, 107101.

United Nations Development Programme. 2020. *Human Development Index*. Available from: http://hdr.undp.org/en/content/human-development-index-hdi.

UNEP. 2009. *Global Green New Deal Policy Brief.* United Nations Environmental Programme. Available from: https://unep.ch/etb/publications/Green%20Economy/UNEP%20Policy%20Brief%20Eng.pdf.

United Nations Environment Programme. 2010. *Overview of the Republic of Korea's National Strategy for Green Growth*. Available from: http://www.unep.org/PDF/PressReleases/201004_unep_national_strategy.pdf

United Nations Secretary General. 2020. *Statement Attributable to the Spokesperson for the Secretary-General – on ROK President Moon Jae-in's Net-Zero Announcement*. Available from: https://www.un.org/sg/en/content/sg/statement/2020-10-27/statement-attributable-the-spokesperson-for-the-secretary-general-rok-president-moon-jae-'s-net-zero-announcement

Van de Graaf, T., Overland, I., Scholten, D. and Westphal, K. 2020. The New Oil? The Geopolitics and International Governance of Hydrogen. *Energy, Research & Social Science*. 70, 101667.

Watts, J. 2020. Could a Green New Deal Turn South Korea from Climate Villain to Model? *Guardian*. 23 May. Available from: https://www.theguardian.com/world/2020/may/23/could-a-green-new-deal-turn-south-korea-from-climate-villain-to-model.

White, D. 2020. Just Transitions/Design for Transitions: Preliminary Notes on a Design Politics for a Green New Deal. *Capitalism Nature Socialism*. 31(2), 20–39.

World Water Network. 2012. *Wetland Globes, Category: Grey Globe Award Asia*. Available from: http://www.worldwetnet.org/docs/files/awards_2012/4_Rivers_poster.pdf.

Xu, A. and Lee, J. 2020. President Moon to Quickly Push for "Korean New Deal". *KOREA.net*. Available from: http://www.korea.net/NewsFocus/policies/view?articleId=185745

Yonhap. 2020. S. Korea to Include Green Projects in "New Deal" Plan. *Korea Herald*. 20 May. Available from: http://www.koreaherald.com/view.php?ud=20200520000815.

Yun, S., Cho, M. and von Hippel, D. 2011. The Current Status of Green Growth in Korea: Energy and Urban Security. *The Asia-Pacific Journal*. 9(44), 4.

Yun, S.-J. 2009. The Ideological Basis and the Reality of Low Carbon, Green Growth. *ECO*. 13(1), 219–266. [in Korean]

Yun, S.-J. 2010. Not So Green: A Critique of South Korea's Growth Strategy. *Global Asia*. 5(2), 70–74.

Yun, S.-J. 2014. Experts' Social Responsibility in the Process of Large-Scale Nature-Transforming National Projects: Focusing on the Case of the Four Major Rivers Restoration Project in Korea. *Development and Society*. 43(1), 109–141.

Yun, S.-J. and Jung, Y.-M. 2017. *Energy Policy at a Crossroads in the Republic of Korea*. Friedrich-Ebert-Stiftung. Available from: https://library.fes.de/pdf-files/bueros/seoul/14488.pdf

16

DECARBONIZATION WITHOUT DEMOCRACY

Tennis-ball politics and the EU Green Deal

David Adler and Pawel Wargan

Introduction

In December 2019, in an opening speech to the plenary of the European Parliament, President of the European Commission Ursula von der Leyen announced the arrival of the European Green Deal.

> Seventy years ago, Europeans invested in coal and steel. And it turned out to be a historic reconciliation, and an economic miracle. Today we are investing in renewables and algorithms… The European Green Deal is about reconciling our economy with our planet, reconciling the way we produce, the way we consume with our planet and respecting the environment we live in. That is the core of the European Green Deal.
>
> *(Von der Leyen 2019b)*

By von der Leyen's account, then, the Green Deal would mark a new era for Europe and for the world. On the former, it promised to shift the entire axis of economic development that undergirded European integration in the course of the twentieth century. On the latter, it promised to make Europe into the world's first carbon-neutral continent, setting an example for other nations and for future generations striking in city streets, plazas, and courtyards across the continent. "Our European Green Deal is for them," von der Leyen assured her audience.

The announcement of the Green Deal was hailed as a momentous step forward in the global movement for a Green New Deal. "EU Beats US, Adopts Its Own Green New Deal," one headline ran (Keating 2019). Another article read: "Unlike the US Democrats' Green New Deal, the European Union's version is technically feasible. Because of that, it could do much more to pave the way for future environmental gains" (Valatsas 2019). EU officials were happy to claim the mantle of the Green New Deal movement from their US counterparts and displace them as global leaders in the push toward a decarbonized future. "I bring back a message from Madrid," EU Commission Vice-President Frans Timmermans told the Parliament following a visit to the UN Climate Change Conference in 2019. "The message is this: we need European leadership. The message is also this: some of us are insecure what we should do, but if Europe leads we might go in the same direction." Europe – not the

DOI: 10.4324/9781003110880-20

United States – was to give birth to the Green New Deal before spreading it around the world. "It is our man-on-the-moon moment," von der Leyen concluded in her speech to Parliament.

This chapter makes the case for a radical reassessment of the European Green Deal and its place in the history of the Green New Deal movement. We advance three core claims – about the Green Deal (GD), the Green New Deal (GND), and the politics of decarbonization, respectively.

We argue first that the Green Deal is less a pathbreaking vision for an ecological future than an historic effort to greenwash Europe's political and economic status quo. We show that the differences between the GD in Europe and the GND popularized by political representatives like Alexandria Ocasio-Cortez are not merely semantic. Rather, the policy package introduced in December 2019 by the institutional managers of the EU bears almost no relation to the Green New Deal paradigm. The latter is rooted in a Keynesian model of the economy and a Rooseveltian theory of political change. Specifically, it begins from the premise of high private savings, low public investment, and a political concern for the extensive suffering of workers and their families in a prolonged period of stagnation. Linking the crisis of underinvestment to the crisis of environmental breakdown, the GND presses idle savings into public investments and delivers millions of new jobs in service of the ecological transition (Pettifor 2019; Aronoff et al. 2019). The EU Green Deal, by contrast, leverages public money toward private investments, socializing costs and privatizing the gains from the green transition. Against the Rooseveltian tradition, the GD is a program of upward, rather than downward, economic distribution, seeking explicitly to deepen the logic of private competition over the promise of public cooperation. We move systematically through the components of the Green Deal to reveal that the green transformation promised by EU officials is better described as a strategy of green preservation. In other words, Ursula von der Leyen was right in her assessment that the GD is Europe's "man-on-the-moon moment," insofar as its primary impact on the lives of Europe's citizens is indirect: through "spillover effects" of decarbonization technologies, and through the continental pride that comes with Europe leading the world toward decarbonization targets.

We argue second that the hollow promise of the GD in Europe holds critical implications for the politics of the GND everywhere. Many advocates of the GND have advanced the policy under the banner of "climate populism," suggesting that its sweeping scope has the power to unite a broad coalition of workers, communities, and concerned citizens (Bosworth 2020). The experience of the GD suggests the need for more careful attention to the coalitional politics that underpin the GND. Specifically, the GD was framed primarily as a response to the youth movement that marched on the streets of Europe in the months that preceded its announcement. "Let me say here today," Timmermans told the European Parliament in December 2019, "I want to congratulate Greta Thunberg for having been nominated Person of the Year by *Time Magazine*." Largely absent from Europe's climate movement, however, were the trade unions and community organizations that were central to the original New Deal in the 1930s (Goldfield 1989). On the contrary, workers were time and again portrayed as opponents of the Green Deal, a political barrier that the EU would have to dodge, transcend, or bulldoze if it were to achieve its sustainability targets. We argue that the construction of an activism-to-policy pipeline that moved around – rather than through – the labour movement enabled EU policymakers to craft a green agenda that lacked the spirit and substance of the Green New Deal. We refer to this phenomenon as *tennis-ball politics*: green on the outside, and hollow on the inside. On the outside, EU officials performed a listening exercise for the youths of Europe. On the inside, the EU ensured that fossil fuel lobbyists kept their seats at the table in the construction of the Green Deal agenda, while trade unions and front-line communities were kept at its margins. The adoption of the Green Deal, therefore, does not reflect the democratic responsiveness of the European Union, but rather the capacity for its central decision-makers to co-opt democratic demands and repurpose their rhetoric in order to inject fresh legitimacy into an existing, unpopular paradigm.

We argue third that the divergence between the Green Deal and the Green New Deal reveals an ugly truth about the politics of decarbonization. The contemporary climate movement has emerged in large part from the left side of the political spectrum, with the result that its most ambitious proposals – like the GND – reflect principles of equity and democracy that are held close by climate activists themselves. In many cases, this has led advocates of the GND to suggest that decarbonization is in and of itself a progressive or redistributive project. Our analysis of the Green Deal suggests, instead, that decarbonization can equally serve to preserve the unequal distribution of power between rich and poor, North and South, creditor nations and debtor ones. The danger of tennis-ball politics is not only its deception, promising a transformation it does not intend to deliver; it is also the prospect of its success, decarbonizing the continental economy from inside the democratic deficit.

The rest of the chapter is divided into three sections. The first provides an overview of the European Green Deal and its contents. The second dives into the differences between the Green Deal and its pseudo-namesake, the Green New Deal, providing a careful and detailed analysis of its pitfalls and empty promises. And third derives some implications for our theoretical understanding of climate politics and the project of decarbonization around the world.

Overview of the EU Green Deal

The roots of the European Union are stained with fossil fuel. Back in 1950, French Foreign Minister Robert Schuman advanced a declaration for "Franco-German production of coal and steel as a whole be placed under a common High Authority, within the framework of an organization open to the participation of the other countries of Europe." The Schuman Declaration, as it came to be known, formed the basis of the European Coal and Steel Community (ECSC), which would bind countries across the bloc to a common market and a cartelized system of carbon emissions (Hassan and Duncan 1994; Gillinham 2004). The ECSC was a vision of fossil fuel production not as an engine of continental integration. "The coming together of the nations of Europe requires the elimination of the age-old opposition of France and Germany," the declaration stated. A united Europe would be built on the basis of carbon diplomacy, taking the same resources that had once fuelled war between nations and putting them to service in the project of collective reconstruction. In the years that followed, from the formation of the European Economic Community to the European Union that succeeded it, the production, distribution, and consumption of carbon remained central to the advance of the European project.

The climate crisis, then, is not merely a policy question to which EU officials would have to apply their technical skills. Instead, it cuts across the core of Europe's political settlement. Consider the Common Agricultural Policy. Introduced in 1962, the concept of a unified approach to agriculture was considered central to the prospects for Europe's internal cohesion and external defence against the Communist threat. Walter Hallstein, a German politician who became the first President of the European Commission on the passage of the Treaty of Rome, gave special emphasis to the "rural class" as a key component of the European project:

> The European rural class will count among the most trustworthy pillars of our unified European market. Because its fate is also at stake, and is one of the first threatened. In this room there is no one whose family tree doesn't reach back, sooner or later, to farming roots. We know what the rural class means to Europe, not only through its economic values, but also by its moral and social values.
>
> *(Hallstein 1958)*

Since the post-war years, agricultural policy in the EU has grown to €60 billion in annual investment in that "rural class," from olive oil in Europe's south to meat production in its north. Protections for Europe's farmers, however, have come at the cost of the climate; Europe's meat farming today produces more greenhouse emissions than all of its cars and vans combined (Greenpeace 2020), while its pesticides have contributed heavily to severe biodiversity loss (Petrequin 2020). Decarbonizing the Common Agricultural Policy – as in other areas of EU competence – would mean completely rewiring the political economy of Europe.

As the hallmark of Ursula von der Leyen's mandate at the Commission, the Green Deal was presented as precisely this holistic overhaul. Both in breadth and ambition, the Green Deal offered to transform key pillars of the European economy. These included plans for a Farm to Fork Strategy that would "cherish and preserve our rural areas and invest in their future," aiming to reduce agricultural emissions and align farming practices with the EU's new climate goals (von der Leyen 2019a: 7). They included a New Circular Economy Action Plan that would support Europe's construction and textile industries to pollute less and curb the production of plastics. And they included a Sustainable Europe Investment Plan – soon to be renamed InvestEU – that would leverage €1 trillion in sustainable investments over the following decade, including a Just Transition Fund to ensure that "we leave nobody behind" (Ibid).

Taken together, the components of von der Leyen's Green Deal suggest a paradigm shift in European political economy – and were hailed as such. "Europe's Green Deal could be the most important in a generation," wrote economist Mariana Mazzuato in the pages of the *Financial Times*. The perils of the EU's democratic deficit were here turned on their heads: it was the experts at Brussels – not the voters in Europe's member-states – that had succeeded to develop this vision of a sustainable Europe. All they needed was a little inspiration from Europe's youth. "I have been inspired by the passion, conviction and energy of the millions of our young people making their voice heard on our streets and in our hearts," von der Leyen wrote in her political guidelines for the Commission. "It is our generational duty to deliver for them."

The EU Green Deal vs. the Green New Deal for Europe

The warm reception of the GD at the outset of von der Leyen's mandate presents a puzzle. The European Union is historically riven with deep cleavages that cut across the dimensions of its economic organization: North and South, creditor and debtor, core and periphery (Schmidt 2019). These cleavages are widely recognized to have both widened and deepened in the course of its recent crisis period, with conflicts over sovereign debt and the policy of austerity erupting into existential prospects of member-state exit and EU disintegration (Mudde 2007; De Vries and Edwards 2009). How, then, did Ursula von der Leyen succeed to unite the bloc in such a radical vision of the green transition, as signalled by the name of the GD?

The answer to this question requires a close analysis of the content of the Green Deal, rather than simply tracing its contours. Specifically, we must interrogate the core claim, put forward by its authors at the Commission, that the Green Deal will deliver a "just transition for all." Who stands to benefit from the GD? Who stands to lose? What does the Green Deal change about the ordo-liberal architecture of the European Union? What does it preserve? Finally – and most relevant to this volume – how does the Green Deal of the twenty-first century live up to the legacy of the New Deal in the twentieth?

Other chapters in this volume have examined the New Deal of the 1930s and the role that it has played in the inspiration of the Green New Deal movement today. Summarized briefly, the New Deal was designed as a response to the collapse of the US economy as it spiralled into its Great Depression. Recognizing the historic rise in household poverty, President Roosevelt sought to provide immediate relief for struggling Americans, introducing policies like the Federal Emergency Relief Act (FERA) and agencies like the Civil Works Administration (CWA) that provided immediate cash payments and employment opportunities in the public sector. In response to the collapse of US industry, Roosevelt sought to drive economic recovery with policies like the National Industrial Recovery Act (NIRA) and agencies like the Tennessee Valley Authority (TVA) that mobilized massive public investments in infrastructure and created jobs for thousands of unemployed Americans along the way. Finally, in recognition of the role that reckless finance played in the 1929 stock market crash, Roosevelt initiated deep reforms of the banking sector, including the Emergency Banking Act and the Glass-Steagall Act, imposing regulations on risks and leverage.

We argue here that the Green Deal bears no resemblance to the original New Deal. While borrowing its rhetoric, the authors of the Green Deal stripped the program of its original intention to confront the failures of speculative capitalism and drive an economic transformation to replace it. If Roosevelt "welcomed the hatred" of high finance and the capitalist class at large, Ursula von der Leyen has sought to accommodate their interests, if not to serve them outright. If Roosevelt's New Deal aimed to instantiate a new set of rights for workers and their families, Ursula von der Leyen's Green Deal contains no social dimension, and virtually no provisions for the social dislocation associated with its decarbonization project. In short, we argue not only that the Green Deal does not qualify as a Green New Deal, as Roosevelt would have understood it. Instead, we argue that these two policy visions – in their politics, as in their policy – are in direct and irresolvable conflict. And to make this case, we point to the "Six Ss" that separate the Green Deal from the Rooseveltian project from which it steals so much legitimacy: Speed, Size, Scope, Scale, Structure, and Strategy.

Speed

With the ecological clock ticking rapidly away, the most basic measure of any climate program is its speed. Can it respond – in sufficient time to ensure our continued survival – to the irreversible environmental tipping points that are already in motion? When von der Leyen announced the Green Deal at the end of 2019, she pledged to raise the EU's emissions reduction target from 40% to 50%–55% below 1990 levels by 2030, reaching "net-zero" emissions by 2050 (von der Leyen 2019a). Since then, that ambition has found growing support within the EU. Before Germany assumed the Presidency of the European Council in 2020, Chancellor Angela Merkel reaffirmed her commitment to the targets, calling for a "comprehensive package of measures to this end" (Merkel 2020). In October 2020, the European Council also voiced support for the new targets, but fell short of a firm commitment to supporting them (European Council 2020).

But the proposed pace of decarbonization fails to align with Europe's legal responsibilities, let alone live up to the claim of world leadership. First, the commitment is incommensurate with Europe's current and historical contributions to pollution across the world. The EU is today the world's third-largest emitter of greenhouse gases. It is responsible for nearly 8% of all emissions globally (Ge and Friedrich 2020) and it has played an outsized role in driving historical emissions. According to *Climate Analytics*, Germany on its own will account for roughly 3.9% of the global temperature increase by 2,100 – taking into account its historical legacy (Rocha et al. 2015). And the EU's economy continues to depend on globalized trade flows, which export emissions and pollution to other parts of the world. This is particularly acute in agriculture. While European forests expanded significantly between 1994 and 2014, for example, Europe's appetite for agricultural imports has led to rampant deforestation abroad (Fuchs 2020). There is no sign of a change in approach under the GD.

Second, the commitment to "net-zero" emissions is itself misleading, masking the environmental destruction required to achieve it. The "net" is predicated on the assumption that continued CO_2 emissions will be offset by largely unproven and environmentally destructive carbon sequestration technologies. More crucial than a fixed date for achieving decarbonization, then, is the pace at which the transition happens and the size of the "net." A transition based on unabated emissions and the exploitation of vast tracts of land – as much as 40% of all arable land, according to recent estimates (Phys 2018) – to generate the biomass needed for carbon offsets cannot live up to the principles of global justice.

Third, Europe's greater historical contribution to climate change and its greater technological and financial capacities carry a heightened responsibility to address the crisis. The 1992 Earth Summit in Rio de Janeiro formalized the Common But Differentiated Responsibility (CBDR), a principle that is reflected in the 2016 Paris Agreement. The principle holds that wealthier countries should be expected to shoulder a greater share of the burden of climate action. The EU Green Deal shirks this responsibility outright. "We consider it somewhat unfortunate to see that some countries are reverting to rigid and somewhat outdated rhetoric that divides the world into developed and developing countries," the EU's lead climate negotiator, Elina Bardram, said (Yeo 2015).

That division is coming into clearer focus as the climate and environmental crises grind on. The most severe impacts of hurricanes, droughts, floods, fires, landslides, and other disasters occur in countries across the Global South. Unequal distribution of both impacts and capacities to respond amount to "a massive transfer of value from the hot parts of the world to the cooler parts of the world" (Burke, Hsiang and Miguel 2015). Such inequality becomes clearer when we look beyond climate alone. Around the world, soil depletion caused by intensive farming techniques is threatening food supplies for billions of people (Yang 2015). Within underground aquifers – the primary source of potable water for nearly 2 billion people and 40% of the water used for irrigation globally – the rate of freshwater extraction now dramatically exceeds the rate at which that water is replenished (Thomas and Famiglietti 2019). In addition, the planet is on the brink of a mass extinction on a scale not witnessed for millions of years, with one-fifth of invertebrate species facing extinction. These are pollinators, the caretakers of soil, safeguards against pests, and feed for the animals that sustain a careful balance within the natural world – the very foundation, in other words, of all terrestrial ecosystems.

Through initiatives like "farm-to-fork" and biodiversity strategies, the Green Deal has committed to take on these challenges. The biodiversity strategy, for example, promises to protect 30% of the land and the sea in Europe (European Commission 2020). But Europe's actions have not lived up to its promises. Consider the EU's Common Agricultural Policy, a system of agricultural subsidies that represents nearly 40% of the EU's budget. Eighty percent of these subsidies are funnelled to the largest landowners and most industrialized farms on the continent, representing only 20% of the EU's farms. The corollary to this is that 80% of Europe's farms – many of them practising sustainable, agroecological models of food production – receive only 20% of available funding. In October 2020, the European Parliament voted against reducing these subsidies, a decision that climate lobbyists described as a "death sentence on nature" (Dalton 2020).

The proposals put forward under the Green Deal, then, fail to address the complex and interlinked crises of climate, environment and ecology at the pace that these crises demand.

Size

The transition to a zero-carbon economy, even at the timescale proposed by the European Commission, is expensive. Have they pledged the resources to deliver it, with attention to the principles of justice and fairness that it claims to underpin the Green Deal?

To answer this question, we turn first to the Sustainable Europe Investment Plan, a flagship policy under the Green Deal. Von der Leyen promised to turn the European Investment Bank into a climate bank, mobilizing €1 trillion over the next decade toward the green transition. Though large in absolute terms, that figure falls far short of all estimated costs of transition. The European Commission itself put the cost at approximately €260 billion per year in additional funding to secure Europe's climate and energy targets by 2030 (European Commission 2019). And this figure is also likely to underestimate the true cost of a just transition. It is based on emissions reduction targets that pre-date the announcement of the Green Deal. What's more, it does not include the cost of other environmental and social measures that comprise the policy package.

In March 2020, the COVID-19 pandemic took centre stage in EU budget negotiations. Lockdowns imposed across the continent took a significant toll on national economies, with GDP figures plummeting across the board (Statista 2020). In July, the European Council agreed on a €1.8 trillion COVID-19 recovery package, comprising €1,074.3 billion from EU budgets for 2021–2027 (the Multiannual Financial Framework) and €750 billion from an investment plan known as Next Generation EU – representing the first time the European Union committed to using sovereign debt to fund grants. When announcing the package, von der Leyen and European Council President Charles Michel pledged to make climate a "top priority" of the COVID-19 recovery plan. Thirty percent of spending under the package was set to go toward Europe's new climate targets – an additional €547 billion in new funding between 2021 and 2027. "Sooner or later our scientists and researchers will develop a vaccine against coronavirus. For climate change, however, there is no vaccine," von der Leyen said. "This is why Europe must now invest in a clean future" (Von der Leyen 2020).

Concerns about the overall size of the climate commitment, however, are compounded by the risk that a large part of the available funds will be misallocated in the course of the Green Deal's execution. Within the EU's accounting framework, not every investment labelled as green meets the standards of sustainability. According to a 2020 report by the European Court of Auditors, the EU's methodology for deciding what investments qualify as "green" is susceptible to overestimation – and does not conform to the World Bank's widely accepted "conservativeness principle," which gives preference to the underreporting of climate data (European Court of Auditors 2020). In other cases, the data is plainly misleading. Under the Renewable Energy Directive, for example, bioenergy is classified as sustainable. But its primary source, forest biomass – in other words, wood – is driving deforestation in countries like Latvia and Estonia (Flach et al. 2018). The use of forest biomass for energy production increased 140% between 1990 and 2016, and bioenergy now contributes to 65% of all "renewable" energy inputs in the EU (*Peter Sabo and Others v. the European Commission and European Council* 2019, 7). If the accounting models for sustainability remain biased toward the continued exploitation of natural resources – including through mass deforestation in the EU's "peripheral" countries and more so in parts of the world that fall outside the Commission's purview – the European Green Deal may aggravate the crisis it promises to repair.

The criticism of the Green Deal's size only applies to the Sustainable Europe Investment Plan. As we will argue later in this section, proposals for a "Just Transition Fund" reveal a similar tendency of the Commission to overstate their fiscal commitments with co-opted rhetoric. We focus here on the €1 trillion centrepiece of the Green Deal to highlight the ways in which the decarbonization agenda of the European Union is only partial on its own terms. Even if we exclude the social dimension that sits at the heart of the Green New Deal movement, the Green Deal presents major risks of greenwashing by its private sector partners. We turn now to examine the distributional consequences of this decarbonization agenda.

Scope

The just transition, as we have argued, presents a real opportunity for the European Union to respond to the intersecting economic, environmental, and political crises sweeping across the continent. But when she introduced the Green Deal, von der Leyen reasserted her commitment to the constraints set out in the Stability and Growth Pact (SGP). The SGP – sometimes referred to as Europe's "fiscal straightjacket" – effectively sets a limit on public expenditure in the eurozone. This policy has been responsible for the plummeting levels of public investment in the region. Since 2015, net public investment across the euro area has been close to zero (Klein 2019) – a shadow of the politics of austerity that governed Europe's response to the 2008 financial crisis and the sovereign debt crises that followed.

In introducing, for the first time, a mutualized debt instrument into the EU's economic toolkit, the Next Generation EU program (also known as the EU Recovery Fund) promised to break through these fiscal constraints. The logic is simple: by consolidating risk among eurozone states into a single financial product, mutualized debt reduces the cost of borrowing for those eurozone countries that continue to suffer from poor sovereign credit ratings. But the financing program does not challenge the underlying logic of austerity. Rather than abandon the SGP in favour of long-term strategies that can deepen public investment across the continent, it merely defers questions of fiscal responsibility to the next round of budget talks. Since the Next Generation EU funds are distributed unequally, with poorer nations receiving a greater share, the imperative to balance the books will primarily fall on them – a concern that is already deeply felt in debtor capitals like Rome (Giuffrida 2021). The narrow scope of Next Generation EU, and the Green Deal more broadly, therefore risks intensifying the programs of austerity that have already brought the EU to the brink of disintegration.

These constraints become clearer when we consider the institutional arrangements that scaffold the Green Deal. While the European Green Deal portfolio was delegated to centre-left Dutch politician Frans Timmermans – himself once a contender for von der Leyen's seat – many of the substantive elements of the Green Deal were stripped from that portfolio. Green finance, for example, does not fall within Timmermans' remit. Instead, it falls within the so-called "Economy that Works for People" portfolio. This portfolio is led by Valdis Dombrovskis, the former prime minister of Latvia and chief designer of its austerity program. The stripping away of the core mechanisms through which the Green Deal can be implemented from the European Green Deal portfolio is itself a strong signal that, beneath the lid, the Green Deal is less a path toward a sustainable future than a strategy to manoeuver within the institutional constraints of the past (Adler and Wargan 2019).

Scale

The climate crisis is planetary, although its origins are uneven. Seventy-one percent of all emissions between 1988 and 2017 can be traced to 100 multinational corporations (CDP 2017). According to Oxfam, the wealthiest 1% of the world's population accounts for more than double the combined emissions of the bottom 50% (Oxfam 2020). As the IPCC has long warned, the unequal distributional impacts of climate change will lead to the mass displacement of populations (IPCC 1992), with hundreds of millions seeking relief from flooding, droughts, famines, or wars.

To ensure a just and sufficient transition, the scale of the policy response must meet the scale of the challenge. This brings us to the next deficiency in the design of the Green Deal: the program does very little to advance the politics of the just transition beyond Europe's borders, even as Europe itself bears significant historic responsibility for accelerating climate and environmental breakdown in countries around the world, as we have shown above. Beyond a commitment to introducing a carbon border adjustment mechanism if "differences in levels of ambition worldwide persist" (Commission 2019) – effectively a policy of taxing imports that do not comply with EU regulations – there is very little about so-called "third countries" in the Green Deal: there are no provisions for technology transfers or infrastructural support, let alone reparations that fall in line with standard definitions of a global just transition.

If such expectations of global stewardship are too high, the EU's claim to justice at least requires it to refrain from exporting further environmental destruction beyond its borders. A recent study by Greenpeace and Public Eye revealed, for example, that in 2018, EU member states approved the export of 81,615 tonnes of pesticides containing 41 substances that are banned in Europe because of their impacts on both the environment and on health (Gaberell and Viret 2020). The pesticides, produced in Europe's wealthier countries, have predominantly been exported to low- and middle-income countries in the Global South (Nicolás 2020).

Agriculture is one of the clearest examples of the dangers of a climate policy that advances sustainability at home even as it creates environmental and social damage abroad. As we have set out above, a significant portion of the EU's annual budget goes toward subsidizing large agricultural concerns as part of the Common Agricultural Policy. Much of that investment supports agricultural exports to support the growing food dependency of Global South countries whose own agricultural industries have been dismantled in the course of structural adjustment, which has mandated measures like the cutting of state subsidies for agriculture, and the transition from food production for local markets to the development of cash crops for export (Fritz 2011, 38). Today, developing countries account for more than half of global cereal imports, measured by price (FAO 2020, 22–23). This undermines their resilience to external food shocks and to increases in prices on global markets. Between 2002 and 2008, for example, food import costs more than doubled for the 48 "Least Developed Countries," rising from $9 billion to $24 billion (UNCTAD 2010). That figure continues to rise, leaving many countries unable to provide for the needs of their citizens. As a major exporter of cereals to the developing world, the EU has been a clear beneficiary of these trends (Fritz 2011, 42–44). The risk of the proposed carbon border adjustment mechanism is that it will merely introduce punitive measures against states producing food for European consumers using European fertilizers, further widening the inequalities between the Global North and Global South that the climate crisis is aggravating. Unless the geographical scale of the Green Deal expands beyond the borders of the EU, the program cannot hope to make meaningful gains toward a true, planetary just transition.

Structure

As we have argued, the Green Deal was framed as a response to grassroots demands for change. And in its name, it held the promise of a break with the economic heterodoxy that has both caused climate and environmental breakdown and prevented its repair. But in its structure, the Green Deal sustains the logic that has underpinned over a decade of financial and democratic crisis in Europe. As we have seen, the European Union suffers from a prolonged crisis in public investment. Today, rather than investing directly in the green transition, the Green Deal proposes to mobilize public funding to incentivize private sector investment. "We must move away from fossil fuels and towards renewable energies and greater energy efficiency," Angela Merkel said in April 2020, "we believe and I believe that market economy incentives are most important."

In this regard, the Green Deal resembles its immediate predecessor – the Investment Plan for Europe, also known as the "Juncker Plan." Like the Green Deal, the Juncker Plan sought to mobilize roughly €100 billion per year by using public funds to guarantee private loans – socializing the risk of investment while privatizing the gains. This model allows the EU to mobilize significant amounts of funding without incurring the full balance sheet costs of investment. Its logic is "to nudge private finance toward the public good," as EIB President Werner Hoyer said in 2019. But this approach of public-private co-financing not only elevates short-term budgetary considerations over long-term sustainability – the products of these investments do not remain in public hands – it has also been shown to generate disproportionate gains for private investors. In a 2018 report, the European Court of Auditors said that the risk allocation between private and public partners in such arrangements "was often inappropriate, incoherent and ineffective" with "remuneration rates (up to 14%) on the private partner's risk capital" that did not reflect the risk borne (Herics et al. 2018). In other words, the model has served to siphon public wealth into private hands.

For that reason, the Green Deal fails on the basic premise of the just transition – that we all gain – and runs contrary to commitments made by von der Leyen herself. "This transition will either be working for all and be just," she said in remarks to the press, "or it will not work at all" (von der Leyen 2019c). The proposals she put forward cannot deliver on that commitment. Europe already suffers from rising levels of poverty, including among workers. In 2016, 118 million Europeans, nearly one out of four, were at risk of poverty or social exclusion (Di Meglio et al. 2018). Rates of homelessness have been rising steadily in every country across the continent except for Finland, which eliminated homelessness through policy interventions (FEANTSA 2017). According to the World Health Organization, over 100,000 people die in Europe each year because of inadequate housing (World Health Organization 2011). Even in Germany, poverty and inequality have been on the rise for decades (Grevenbrock et al. 2017). A program that relies predominantly on private investment – and private ownership of the products of that investment – does not have the redistributive capacities to reverse these trends. In its structure, then, the Green Deal is firmly wedded to the structural imbalances that continue to generate economic injustice in Europe.

Strategy

In its political strategy, the Green Deal risks aggravating Europe's deepening crisis of democratic legitimation. As we set out above, the Green New Deal was pitched in the United States as a project of climate populism: a vehicle that could unite workers, communities, activists, and citizens in a program that promised the restoration both of nature and the national economy. The European Green Deal, by contrast, makes no such promises. It was designed primarily in response to the historic youth movement that began to sweep across Europe in the year before its announcement. Workers were portrayed as opponents of the green agenda, and a political obstacle that EU officials would need to placate or silence to push through policies they framed as "unpopular." The resulting activism-to-policy pipeline entirely side-stepped the labour movement. This coalitional constraint – which also limits the climate movement's capacities to build material power – is now mirrored in the politics of the Green Deal. While EU officials met with young activists to signal that they were "listening," they surreptitiously met with over 11 business lobbyists each week to delve into the substance of the policies (Corporate Europe Observatory 2020).

The exclusion of workers from the coalitional politics underpinning the Green Deal may prove to be its self-defeat. French President Emmanuel Macron's proposed 2018 tax on diesel is a case in point. In France, the poor spend approximately 2.7 times more – as a proportion of total income – on diesel than the wealthy (Réseau Action Climat 2019). By taxing diesel at a flat rate, the measure disproportionately impacted the poor. In doing so, it opened Europe's first major battleground between workers and the climate agenda, and came to serve as a warning of the "perils" of climate action for states that are more heavily dependent on fossil fuels than France. It is clear that without robust social protections, support for reskilling, and other vital measures – designed in cooperation with workers and communities – it will be very difficult to advance an agenda that is green or just.

To address these concerns, von der Leyen put forward a proposal for a Just Transition Mechanism (JTM), a set of policies and a fund with the "ambition to mobilise EUR 100 billion precisely targeted to the most vulnerable regions and sectors" (Von der Leyen 2019c). The JTM relies on the same policy tools we have critiqued above: it uses public funds to guarantee and incentivize private investments. Von der Leyen also introduced proposals for a Just Transition Fund (JTF): a pool of money intended to support states with their own transitions. The JTF has been the subject of controversy, and saw significant opposition during the EU's 2020 budget negotiations. At the latest meeting of the European Council, the budget of the JTF was more than halved – from €40 billion to €17.5 billion. By comparison, the Coal Commission set up by the city of Berlin to finance the green transition of Germany's mining regions has a budget of €40 billion. The conflicts over the paltry sums promised for the JTF speak to the challenges of building political consensus without democratic accountability.

Indeed, the flawed coalitional politics of the Green Deal are already eroding its policy ambitions. In March 2020, lobby group BusinessEurope wrote to European Council President Charles Michel, demanding derogations to regulatory requirements and the delay of key elements of Green Deal legislation, including the Climate Law that would put legislative brakes on emissions in Europe (Gattaz and Beyrer 2020). Just a few months later, in October 2020, reports began to emerge that EU officials were considering delays to the legislation to better assess its economic impacts (Chrysoloras and Krukowska 2020). At the time of writing, no agreement is in sight for the core provisions of the Climate Law – its binding emissions reduction targets for 2050 (Abnett 2021). Policies necessarily reflect the coalitional forces that shape them. In excluding workers and communities, superficially consulting with activists, and including lobby groups in substantive deliberations about the shape of the Green Deal, the Commission has fatally constrained its political ambitions while foreclosing strategic possibilities for advancing a more robust plan for the just transition.

Discussion

European Commission President Ursula von der Leyen is fond of referring to the EU Green Deal as Europe's "man-on-the-moon moment" as a signal of its historical import and innovative edge. The primary argument of this chapter is that von der Leyen's description is accurate, but for entirely different reasons than she intended. Her Green Deal, we have shown, is similar to John F. Kennedy's moon landing in its origins (in the closed boardrooms of high politics), ambitions (to raise Europe's stature on the world stage), and impact in the lives of its citizens (indirect "spillover" effects). It bears no similarity, however, to the New Deal of Franklin D. Roosevelt three decades prior. On the contrary, the Green Deal aims to entrench the economic model that Roosevelt's New Deal sought to upend. Rather than mobilizing public investment to generate public wealth, the Green Deal uses public finances to pave the road for private investors to reap the rewards of the green transition. Rather than providing relief for the poor and unemployed, the Green Deal pays off the owners of capital that may lose out in the course of decarbonization, while leaving their workers without a safety net to catch them. The Green Deal succeeds to set ambitious and world-leading targets for decarbonizing Europe's economy in the years to come – a significant feat of diplomacy within the framework of an international Union. But in terms of size, scope, scale, speed, structure and strategy, it bears no relation to the policy paradigm that shepherded the United States out of its Great Depression, nor to the contemporary Green New Deal modelled on it.

Given these fundamental, irreconcilable differences, what can the passage of the EU Green Deal tell us about the trajectory of the Green New Deal elsewhere? We propose three main implications.

The first is that it is possible to decarbonize without democracy. The development of the EU Green Deal has seen the deployment of tennis-ball politics to address the climate crisis – green on the outside, hollow on the inside. Citizens were granted "consultations" with little influence on the Green Deal's overall design; lobbyists, by contrast, were given seats at the table to advance the corporate agenda throughout the policy development process. The process offers a stark contrast to New Deal programs like the Tennessee Valley Authority, which actively aimed to foster "the active daily participation of the people themselves." If the ambition of the New Deal was to mobilize citizens in a new public spirit of industry, prosperity, and recovery, the ambition of the Green Deal is to demobilize them – "to put an end to all the marching, to get the children back in school and the rebels off the streets." Advocates of the Green New Deal often depict democracy and decarbonization as twin ambitions. But the EU's model suggests that decarbonization is equifinal: many roads lead to a low-carbon economy. We have argued that the EU is unlikely to succeed in its grand vision for the Green Deal because of the many sacrifices it has made to the integrity of the decarbonization agenda. However, those shortcomings do not imply that democracy is a necessary component of the green transition. The project of democratization must be actively woven into the plan for decarbonization, if it is to advance at all.

The second implication, then, is that the boundaries of climate politics remain very fuzzy, open to political entrepreneurs who wish to draw or redraw them. The comparative histories of climate denialism on the right and climate activism of the left can give the appearance of eternal advantage: environmentalism is, was, and will be the province of social democratic forces. But the denialism of the right is fading into a new and hardened climate realism, which accepts the premise of a changing climate while advancing hard borders and welfare chauvinism as its answer. This new political conflict suggests that the climate agenda remains up for grabs, and largely undefined. In the case of Europe, we have shown that the EU has sought to circumscribe the climate issue to exclude the "social" dimension entirely. Roughly 140 million people in the EU are at risk of poverty (Dauderstädt 2019); according to the Commission's own estimates, one in three people inside the EU cannot "cope with unexpected financial expenses" (Eurostat 2020). These statistics are inseparable from the green transition, both in terms of energy production – 50 million people in the EU cannot afford to heat their homes (Thomson and Bouzarovski 2018) – and in terms of economic justice. But these concerns are completely missing from the Green Deal. The inclusion of a Just Transition Fund, initially proposing to mete out a paltry €7 billion over the next seven years, adds insult to injury for advocates of a Green New Deal. In other words, the conflict at the heart of the Green New Deal is not only over the "how" of the green transition, but also the "what" of the climate crisis itself.

Third and finally, our understanding of the politics and prospects for a Green New Deal must be grounded in a detailed analysis of the coalition that is driving it. The youth movements of Europe may have succeeded to put climate onto the agenda. But their appeal to conscience created room for EU officials to act as the patrons of their movement, representing them as responsible "adults in the room" while depriving them of meaningful say in the development of the Green Deal that was – in von der Leyen's words – "for them." The absence of labour rights and regulations from the Green Deal, meanwhile, is a reflection of the absence of workers from the climate movement. The absence of social protections and community investment is a reflection of the generational divide of the climate movement, and the ways in which the latter failed to incorporate these concerns into its core agenda. In a word, power resources will determine the fact of the Green New Deal more than symbolic social movements. A transformation of that depth and breadth can only come about with the organization and mobilization of the people it claims to represent.

Altogether, our analysis in this chapter suggests that the EU is a critical case for scholars of the Green New Deal – as a foil, rather than a representative case. Von der Leyen's program attests to the capacity of the European Union to co-opt its street-level movements, and to the power of prime movers to reap political rewards in spite of the defects in the policy agenda they actually put on the table. The EU may well succeed in putting its man on the moon. But the more important questions – at what cost, to whose benefit, and with what meaning in the lives of ordinary citizens in whose name it was all done – are likely to remain unasked and unanswered in the halls of Berlaymont. Roosevelt shrugs, and from Brussels, the New Deal moves further into the distance.

References

Abnett, K. 2021. "EU climate law talks dodge the 'elephant in the room.'" *Associated Press*. 2 February. Available from: https://www.reuters.com/article/us-climate-change-eu-law/eu-climate-law-talks-dodge-the-elephant-in-the-room-idUSKBN2A22KM

Adler, D. and Wargan, P. 2019. "Ursula von der Leyen's Green Deal is doomed." *Politico*. 16 October. Available from: https://www.politico.eu/article/ursula-von-der-leyens-green-deal-is-doomed-climate-change-european-commission/

Aronoff, K., Battistoni, A., Cohen, D.A. and Riofrancos, T. 2019. *A Planet to Win: Why We Need a Green New Deal*. London: Verso.

Bosworth, K. 2020. "The people's climate March: Environmental populism as political genre." *Political Geography* 83, 102281.

Burke, M., Hsiang, S.M. and Miguel, E. 2015. "Global non-linear effect of temperature on economic production." *Nature* 527, 235–239. Available from: http://web.stanford.edu/~mburke/climate/BurkeHsiangMiguel2015.pdf

Chrysoloras, N. and Krukowska, E. 2020. "European Green law risks delay as leaders seek to defer decision." *Bloomberg Green*. 5 October. Available from: https://www.bloomberg.com/news/articles/2020-10-05/european-green-law-risks-delay-as-leaders-seek-to-defer-decision

Corporate Europe Observatory. 2020. "Disclosed: Intense fossil industry lobby undermines EU Green Deal." *Corporate Europe Observatory*. 8 July. Available from: https://corporateeurope.org/en/2020/07/disclosed-intense-fossil-industry-lobby-undermines-eu-green-deal

Dalton, J. 2020. "'Death sentence on nature': European Parliament accused of killing Green Deal." *The Independent*. 22 October. Available from: https://www.independent.co.uk/climate-change/news/eu-agricultural-policy-cap-mep-vote-reform-farming-climate-change-extinction-b1226540.html

Dauderstädt, M. 2019. "Addressing poverty and inequality in Europe." *Social Europe*. 15 January. Available from: https://www.socialeurope.eu/poverty-and-inequality-in-europe

De Vries, C.E., and Edwards, E.E. Taking Europe to its extremes: Extremist parties and public Euroscepticism. *Party Politics* 15(1), 5–28.

Di Meglio, E., Kaczmarek-Firth, A., Litwinska, A. and Rusu, C. 2018. *Living Conditions in Europe*. Eurostat. March. Available from: https://ec.europa.eu/eurostat/documents/3217494/9079352/KS-DZ-18-001-EN-N.pdf/884f6fec-2450-430a-b68d-f12c3012f4d0

European Commission. 2020. "EU biodiversity strategy for 2030." European Commission. Available from: https://ec.europa.eu/info/strategy/priorities-2019-2024/european-green-deal/actions-being-taken-eu/eu-biodiversity-strategy-2030_en

European Council. 2020. "European Council conclusions on COVID-19 and climate change." *European Council*. 16 October. Available from: https://www.consilium.europa.eu/en/press/press-releases/2020/10/16/european-council-conclusions-on-covid-19-and-climate-change-15-october-2020/

European Court of Auditors. 2020. "Tracking climate spending in the EU budget." *European Court of Auditors*. 17 June. Available from: https://www.eca.europa.eu/Lists/ECADocuments/RW20_01/RW_Tracking_climate_spending_EN.pdf

Eurostat. 2020. "Quality of life indicators-economic security and physical safety." *Eurostat, Statistics Explained*. July. Available from: https://ec.europa.eu/eurostat/statistics-explained/pdfscache/30565.pdf

FAO. 2020. *Food Outlook – Biannual Report on Global Food Markets – November 2020*. Rome. Available from: https://doi.org/10.4060/cb1993en

FEANTSA. 2017. *Homeless in Europe*. FEANTSA. Available from: https://www.feantsa.org/download/increases-in-homelessness4974810376875636190.pdf

Flach, B., Lieberz, S., Lappin J. and Bolla, S. 2018. *EU Biofuels Annual 2018*. USDA Foreign Agricultural Service. 7 March. Available from: https://apps.fas.usda.gov/newgainapi/api/report/downloadreportbyfilename?filename=Biofuels%20Annual_The%20Hague_EU-28_7-3-2018.pdf

Fritz, T. 2011. Globalising Hunger – Food Security and the EU's Common Agricultural Policy. Berlin: Transnational Institute. Available from: https://thomas-fritz.org/english/globalising-hunger-food-security-and-the-eu-s-common-agricultural-policy-174

Fuchs, R. 2020. "Europe's Green Deal offshores environmental damage to other nations." *Nature*. 26 October. Available from: https://www.nature.com/articles/d41586-020-02991-1

Gaberell, L. and Viret, G. 2020. "Banned in Europe: How the EU exports pesticides too dangerous for use in Europe." *Public Eye*. 10 September. Available from: https://www.publiceye.ch/en/topics/pesticides/banned-in-europe

Gattaz, P. and Beirer, M.J. 2020. "Message to the video conference of the Members of the European Council on 26 March 2020: Overcoming the COVID-19 crisis and focussing on the essential." *Business Europe*. 24 March. Available from: https://www.businesseurope.eu/sites/buseur/files/media/public_letters/dirgen/2020-03-24_message_to_the_spriing_european_council_26_march_2020.pdf

Ge, M. and Friedrich, J. 2020. "4 Charts explain greenhouse gas emissions by countries and sectors." *World Resources Institute*. 6 February. Available from: https://www.wri.org/blog/2020/02/greenhouse-gas-emissions-by-country-sector

Gillingham, J. 2004. *Coal, Steel, and the Rebirth of Europe, 1945–1955: The Germans and French from Ruhr Conflict to Economic Community*. Cambridge: Cambridge University Press.

Giuffrida, A. 2021. "Italian PM battles for coalition's survival over Covid recovery plan." *The Guardian*. 18 January. Available from: https://www.theguardian.com/world/2021/jan/18/conte-battles-for-his-coalitions-survival-over-covid-recovery-plan

Goldfield, M. 1989. "Worker insurgency, radical organization, and New Deal labor legislation." *The American Political Science Review* 83(4), 1257–1282.

Greenpeace. 2020. *Farming for Failure*. Greenpeace. September. Available from: https://storage.googleapis.com/planet4-eu-unit-stateless/2020/09/20200922-Greenpeace-report-Farming-for-Failure.pdf

Grevenbrock, N. et al. 2017. *Germany: Selected Issues*. Country Report No. 17. 193. *International Monetary Fund*. 13 June. Available from: https://www.imf.org/~/media/Files/Publications/CR/2017/cr17193.ashx

Hallstein, W. 1958. Cited in Fennell, R. 1997. *The Common Agricultural Policy: Continuity and Change*. Oxford: Oxford University Press, p. 12.

Hassan, J.A. and Duncan, A. 1994. Integrating energy: The problems of developing an energy policy in the European Communities, 1945–1980. *Journal of European Economic History* 23(1), 159.

Herics, O. et al. 2018. *Public Private Partnerships in the EU: Widespread Shortcomings and Limited Benefits*. Luxembourg: European Court of Auditors. Available from: https://www.eca.europa.eu/Lists/ECADocuments/SR18_09/SR_PPP_EN.pdf

Hoyer, W. 2019. "The EU climate bank: Channeling private capital into sustainable finance." European Investment Bank. 22 March. Available from: https://www.eib.org/en/press/news/the-eu-climate-bank-channeling-private-capital-into-sustainable-finance

IPCC. 1992. *Climate Change: The IPCC 1990 and 1992 Assessments*. Intergovernmental Panel on Climate Change. June. Available from: https://www.ipcc.ch/report/climate-change-the-ipcc-1990-and-1992-assessments/

Keating, D. 2019. EU Beats U.S., Adopts Its Own Green New Deal. *Forbes*. 11 December. https://www.forbes.com/sites/davekeating/2019/12/11/eu-beats-us-adopts-its-own-green-new-deal/?sh=4fb2d00b15de

Klein, M.C. 2019. "Italy embraces China, and Europe's elites have only themselves to blame." *Barron's*. 5 April. Available from: https://www.barrons.com/articles/europes-elites-have-only-themselves-to-blame-for-italys-embrace-of-china-51554481025 [accessed 15 May 2019]

Merkel, A. 2020. "Speech by Federal Chancellor Dr Angela Merkel at the XIth Petersberg climate dialogue on 28 April 2020." Press and Information Office of the Federal Government. 28 April. Available from: https://www.bundesregierung.de/breg-en/news/speech-by-federal-chancellor-dr-angela-merkel-at-the-xith-petersberg-climate-dialogue-on-28-april-2020-video-conference--1749602

Mudde, C. 2007. *Populist Radical Right Parties in Europe*. Cambridge: Cambridge University Press.

Nikolás, E.S. 2020. "EU urged to stop export of toxic pesticides to third countries." *Euobserver*. 6 November. Available from: https://euobserver.com/green-deal/149966

Oxfam. 2020. "Confronting carbon inequality." *Oxfam Briefing Paper*. 20 September. Available from: https://www.oxfamamerica.org/explore/research-publications/confronting-carbon-inequality/

Peter Sabo and Others v. the European Commission and European Council. 2019. Court of Justice of the European Union. 4 March. Available from: http://eubiomasscase.org/wp-content/uploads/2019/08/EU-Biomass-Case-Main-Arguments.pdf

Petrequin, S. 2020. "EU urged to act against pesticides to fight insect decline." *AP News*. 9 June. Available from: https://apnews.com/article/46c52a31c79b0628d07d5d5fa44b5806

Pettifor, A. 2019. *The Case for the Green New Deal*. London: Verso.

Phys.org. 2018. "Crisis management: Seven ways to engineer climate." Phys.org. 8 October. Available from: https://phys.org/news/2018-10-crisis-ways-climate.html

Réseau Action Climat. 2019. *Pas de Transition Écologique sans Justice Sociale*. Available from: https://reseauactionclimat.org/wp-content/uploads/2019/04/presentation.pdf

Rocha, M. et al. 2015. *Historical Responsibility for Climate Change — From Countries Emissions to Contribution to Temperature Increase*. Climate Analytics. November. Available from: https://climateanalytics.org/media/historical_responsibility_report_nov_2015.pdf

Schmidt, V. 2019. "Politicization in the EU: between national politics and EU political dynamics." *Journal of European Public Policy* 26(7), 1018–1036.

Statista. 2020. "GDP growth rate forecasts in Europe 2020–2021." *Statista*. November. Available from: https://www.statista.com/statistics/1102546/coronavirus-european-gdp-growth/

Thomas, B.F. and Famiglietti, J.S. 2019. "Identifying climate-induced groundwater depletion in GRACE observations." *Nature*. 11 March. Available from: https://www.nature.com/articles/s41598-019-40155-y

Thomson, H. and Bouzarovski, S. 2018. "Addressing energy poverty in the European Union: State of play and action." *EU Energy Poverty Observatory*. August. Available from: https://www.energypoverty.eu/sites/default/files/downloads/publications/18-08/paneureport2018_final_v3.pdf

UNCTAD. 2010. The Least Developed Countries Report 2010. New York: United Nations. Available from: https://unctad.org/system/files/official-document/ldc2010_en.pdf

Valatsas, D. 2019. Green Deal, Greener World. *Foreign* Policy. 17 December. Available from: https://foreignpolicy.com/2019/12/17/united-states-democrats-green-new-deal-eu-europe-technically-feasible-environment-progress/

Von der Leyen, U. 2019a. *A Union that Strives for More- My Agenda for Europe,* European Commission. Available from: https://op.europa.eu/en/publication-detail/-/publication/43a17056-ebf1-11e9-9c4e-01aa75ed71a1

Von der Leyen, U. 2019b. "Speech by President von der Leyen in the Plenary of the European Parliament at the debate on the European Green Deal." *EU Commission Press*. Available from: https://www.pubaffairsbruxelles.eu/speech-by-president-von-der-leyen-in-the-plenary-of-the-european-parliament-at-the-debate-on-the-european-green-deal-eu-commission-press/

Von der Leyen, U. 2019c. "Press remarks by President von der Leyen on the occasion of the adoption of the European Green Deal Communication." *European Commission*. 11 December. Available from: https://ec.europa.eu/commission/presscorner/detail/en/speech_19_6749

Von der Leyen, U. 2020. "Speech by President von der Leyen at the European Parliament Plenary on the new MFF, own resources and the Recovery Plan." *European Commission*. 14 May. Available from: https://ec.europa.eu/cyprus/news/20200514_2_en

World Health Organization. 2011. "New evidence from WHO: Inadequate housing causes more than 100 000 annual deaths in Europe." *World Health Organization*. 23 June. Available from: https://www.euro.who.int/en/media-centre/sections/press-releases/2011/06/new-evidence-from-who-inadequate-housing-causes-more-than-100-000-annual-deaths-in-europe

Yang, S. 2015. "Human security at risk as depletion of soil accelerates, scientists warn." *UC Berkeley*. 7 May. Available from: https://news.berkeley.edu/2015/05/07/soil-depletion-human-security/

Yeo, S. 2015. "Old battlelines resurface as countries meet for last time ahead of Paris climate summit." *Carbon Brief*. 26 October. Available from: https://www.carbonbrief.org/old-battlelines-resurface-as-countries-meet-for-last-time-ahead-of-paris-climate-summit

17

THE EVOLUTION OF THE UK'S GREEN NEW DEAL

"Green Industrial Revolution," "Building Back Better," and beyond

Daniel Bailey and Elena Hofferberth

> Momentum is growing for a comprehensive Green New Deal that will transform our economy, society, and almost every aspect of life in Britain.
>
> *(GND Group 2019)*

Introduction

As one of the epicentres of the industrial revolution, the UK has a profound historical accountability for the ecological degradation that is unfolding on a global scale. The ecologically intensive systems of production and consumption established under British stewardship since the industrial revolution render the country a significant contributor to environmental harm. The UK's depiction as a "climate-progressive" country today is belied both by consumption-based measurements of carbon emissions and by resource use, which reveal that the UK continues to be culpable for planetary overshoot (Sayers and Trebeck 2015; Good Life Leeds 2020). Including estimations of historical carbon debt only further underscore the need for the UK to take responsibility and assume a leadership role on environmental protection (Hickel 2020). According to Anderson, Broderick and Stoddard (2020: 8), the "UK emissions pathway implies a carbon budget at least a factor of two greater than the UK's Paris-compliant budget estimated here." In short, the UK is highly responsible for the change in the climate system, which is increasingly affecting much more severely the countries of the Global South than the countries of the Global North.

In addition to ecological overshoot, the UK economy is also characterized by a series of other failings which require political attention. The libertarian approach to economic governance has allowed financialization, rentierism, labour market precarity and vast inequalities between classes, ethnicities, genders, regions and generations – all pronounced characteristics of British capitalism (cf. McCann 2018; Christophers 2019; ONS 2019, 2020a, b, c; Equality Trust 2020). The country also experiences relatively high levels (approximately 8%) of poverty (including child and "in-work" poverty) (ONS 2018). The dysfunctions of the status quo indicate that the UK's political economy is simply not working for many of its citizens as well as the natural world. The calls for a Green New Deal in the UK can be seen

DOI: 10.4324/9781003110880-21

as a reaction against the persistent economic and social dysfunctions of the UK economy, as well as the desire to mitigate the ecological crisis.

The Green New Deal has been a sporadic feature of British politics since it was first proposed in 2008. In 2018, the international momentum behind the Green New Deal led to its appearance on the UK political agenda in the lead-up to a general election. The British iteration shared the fundamental vision of change of Green New Deals elsewhere – to simultaneously address multiple different crises and pave the way for a just, low-carbon economy via state interventionism and investment – albeit with some important national idiosyncrasies.

This chapter discusses political and economic dimensions of the Green New Deal in the UK. The following section charts the evolution of the British Green New Deal since its inception in the midst of the financial crash through to the COVID-19 pandemic. Thereafter, in the context of the inequalities exposed and exacerbated by the pandemic, we examine the need for a "new social contract" with significant implications for the evolution of the Green New Deal for the UK. Finally, we provide an overview of the key considerations for developing and advancing a Green New Deal policy program in the 2020s that can "transform our economy, society, and almost every aspect of life in Britain" (GND Group 2019).

The politics of the Green New Deal in the UK

The Green New Deal agenda began in London in 2008. A combination of politicians, economists, trade unionists, activists and public intellectuals – including Caroline Lucas, Richard Murphy, Ann Pettifor, Larry Elliot, Colin Hines, Clive Lewis, Jeremy Leggett, Charles Secrett, Geoff Tily and Andrew Simms – combined to form the Green New Deal Group and launch a report which outlined the principles and policies of green interventionism (Green New Deal Group 2008).

Roosevelt's New Deal was, of course, to some degree an economic policy response to an environmental catastrophe. The "dustbowl" in the midwestern US coincided with the Great Depression and compounded the socio-economic trauma of the 1930s. Accordingly, the original New Deal contained a variety of environmental protection measures including the establishment of the Civilian Conservation Corps that planted 3 billion trees, built shelter belts across the Great Plains to reduce the risk of dust storms and created 700 state parks.

The Green New Deal in 2008, however, was tailored to an era of climate change, high oil prices in the purported era of "peak oil," and a paralyzing credit crunch. The initial report of the Green New Deal Group (2008: 2) recommended "a sustained program to invest in and deploy energy conservation and renewable energies, coupled with effective demand management," and also called for the re-regulation of the financial sector which had fuelled "irresponsible" and "often fraudulent" patterns of lending, created asset bubbles and empowered environmentally unsustainable consumption. The boldness of its vision and the scale of the structural transformation it proposed were immediately striking.

The proposals received support from numerous figures and organizations in the aftermath of the 2008 financial crash, including the United Nations (UNEP 2009). Of the UK's fiscal stimulus expenditure, 16.3% was initially earmarked for investments in low-carbon economic sectors (Barbier 2010), although it has been argued that most countries ultimately spent less than was earmarked (Tienhaara 2018). The "public debt crisis" narration of contemporaneous political events, which rationalized the turn to austerity, rendered any Keynesian stimulus politically unviable. As public investment contracted during the period of austerity, the economy entered a second recession and the growth model that had produced both the crash and ecological degradation was left largely unmodified.

Inspired by the success of Alexandria Ocasio-Cortez and the Sunrise Movement in the US in 2018, a collection of grassroots campaigners, trade unionists and politicians sought to revive a British version of the idea after a decade of dormancy. Green New Deal proposals were embraced and developed by think tanks, NGOs and activists before they were embraced by political parties. The New Economics Foundation and the Common Wealth think tank (and the Institute for Public Policy Research to a lesser extent) both mobilized around the Green New Deal, fusing a focus on decarbonization with a case for transforming production systems, ownership structures and distributional patterns in the language of global social justice. Those organizations worked alongside other NGOs and activists to found the "Green New Deal UK" in 2019 to build a decentralized mass movement and orchestrate political campaigns in support of their "ambitious ten-year national action plan to tackle climate breakdown in a way that improves peoples' lives and builds a fairer, more democratic society and economy" (GND UK 2020a). The agenda gathered momentum in 2019 as it found support in environmental activist movements, trade unions and the UK Green Party and Labour Party (Miliband et al. 2019; Satow 2019).

Ahead of the 2019 general election, the Labour Party's leadership eschewed the term "green new deal" in favour of "green industrial revolution," on the basis that the former is not part of Britain's "national political memory" (McDonnell 2019). Nonetheless the activities of Green New Deal campaigners are regularly acclaimed (McDonnell 2019; NEF 2019), and a Green New Deal bill was put forward in the House of Commons by the Labour Party's Clive Lewis MP in collaboration with Caroline Lucas of the UK Green Party. Building on prior calls for a "green jobs revolution" (BBC 2018), the "green industrial revolution" became a key pillar of Labour's electoral campaigning.

The 2019 Labour Party Manifesto pledged investment in a Green Transformation Fund worth £250 billion as well as a National Investment Bank tasked with allocating a further £250 billion of credit over ten years for the purpose of funding the types of production, infrastructure, enterprise and innovation compatible with decarbonization goals (Labour Party 2019). It was projected that 1 million green jobs would be created through this investment. These commitments were substantial – albeit dwarfed by the ambitions of the UK Green Party, which pledging to reach net zero by 2030 through enacting a Green New Deal that would have entailed borrowing £1 trillion over ten years (Green Party UK 2019). The Labour Party's public investment pledge was complemented by an intention to strengthen the powers of financial regulators in order to "mobilize green investment" and "manage the risk to financial stability posed by short-sighted investment in polluting assets" (Labour Party 2019). Through mobilizing both public investment and attempting to "crowd in" private investment, Labour sought to transform a range of industries, transport systems, energy sources and buildings in ways that achieve "the majority" of the UK's emission reduction by 2030 (Labour Party 2019).

The Labour Party's industrial policy proposals were designed to usher in a structural economic transformation by vertically supporting the growth of low-carbon economic sectors through subsidies and tax incentives, financing the expansion of renewable energy production, improving energy efficiency through retrofitting residential and commercial buildings, enforcing stronger environmental regulations and tax disincentives on fossil fuel companies and the finance sector, and rolling out low-carbon public infrastructure. As with other Green New Deals around the world, the agenda sought to make these industrial policies part of a "new social contract," but in the UK the emphasis was primarily on ameliorating regional and class inequalities through public investment, rather than racial or gender inequalities. It also emphasized the importance of reversing austerity measures and expanding public ownership and democratic control of industry.

For the Labour Party this agenda represented not only a commensurate and electorally expedient response to the climate emergency; it also reflected an opportunity to transform the unstable and unbalanced UK economic growth model and a rationale for investment after a prolonged period of fiscal austerity. Addressing regional inequalities through the creation of green jobs has long been a theme of Labour rhetoric but it has become increasingly prevalent. Rebecca Long-Bailey has hailed the Green Industrial Revolution as an opportunity to rebuild Britain and address inequality on behalf of those communities that have been "left behind" (NEF 2019). She stated that a future Labour government should "transform the UK through a green jobs revolution, tackling the environmental crisis in a way that brings hope and prosperity back to parts of the UK that have been held back for too long" (Long-Bailey 2019). This represents not only an inclination toward decarbonization but also an economic transformation that could potentially appeal to working-class voters feeling alienated due to decades of deindustrialization, public service cuts and Brexit.

This electoral strategy was ultimately unsuccessful. The Labour Party's defeat in the December 2019 general election, and the subsequent changes to the Labour leadership, substantially damaged the level of support for a political offering akin to the Green New Deal in Westminster. Although the principles and ideas underpinning the policy package were not entirely vanquished, the notion of large-scale green interventionism had suffered a devastating electoral blow.

The approach of the victorious Conservative government to the environment, in contrast, was based on market-based solutions and heralding environmental achievements made so far (typically based on misleading statistics rooted in methodological nationalism and production-based carbon accountancy). Under the leadership of Boris Johnson, the Conservative Party manifesto re-stated the belief that "free markets, innovation and prosperity can protect the planet" (Conservative Party 2019). The manifesto did recognize the need to reach net-zero emissions by 2050 and promised to invest in the energy efficiency of public sector buildings, homes and certain systems of energy production. It also pledged to provide budgets to deal with specific environmental issues such as flood defences (Conservative Party 2019). In this sense, the manifesto did represent a degree of evolution in Conservative Party policy. Yet the ideological commitment to market-based solutions rather than interventionist political action means that the manifesto refrains from offering an industrial strategy that remedies the root economic drivers of the crisis.

COVID-19 and calls to "Build Back Better"

After the decisive general election victory of December 2019, it appeared that the prospects of a Green New Deal had inauspiciously diminished. The pandemic of 2020, however, dramatically reshaped the Overton window. The emergence of COVID-19 – itself a manifestation of the "Capitalocene" insofar as the inimical relationship between market forces and the natural world set the conditions for its emergence (Moore 2017; Carrington 2020a) – brought about a public health crisis and a partial shutdown of the UK economy.

The Conservative government marshalled a remarkable fiscal policy response, which was strongly supported by the Bank of England's Quantitative Easing program and backstopped by the "Ways and Means" facility (Bank of England 2020a; 2020b; 2020c). The scale of the British state's economic response to the pandemic-induced downturn made it clear that, however temporarily, the Conservative Government's antipathy toward economic interventionism and concern over government debt had been shelved (Bailey 2020). In this context, the question was not one of the capacity to mobilize resources but rather the extent and character of the government intervention.

Under the guise of "Building Back Better," the new maxim for progressives, the Green New Deal ideas gained a new lease on life. The widespread desire for public investment to be utilized for green economic recovery revived support for green Keynesian fiscal measures despite their electoral rejection only a few months prior. The Build Back Better campaign was heavily informed by the ideas contained within the Green New Deal proposals, which had been devised by a variety of academics, politicians and movements in the interim. This included the All-Party Parliamentary Group (APPG) on the Green New Deal, a platform designed to develop a Green New Deal policy program that cut across party lines. Many of the original Green New Deal proposals are now reflected in the agendas for Building Back Better (NEF 2020a; Green New Deal UK 2020b), a Green and Just recovery (NEF 2020b; Labour for a Green New Deal 2020), or a Green New Deal Recovery (Common Wealth 2020).

The Build Back Better campaign claimed a strange assortment of fans, including business owners, trade unions, activists and the members of the Royal family. In April 2020, in the midst of the first wave of the coronavirus pandemic, an Ipsos MORI poll even discovered that 66% of the British public believed climate change to be just as serious a crisis as COVID-19, and the majority favoured prioritizing environmental sustainability during the economic recovery (Ipsos MORI 2020). The APPG on the Green New Deal meanwhile orchestrated the Reset enquiry, which gathered evidence from experts and a representative sample of the population (55,000 people), and found "widespread public support for the government to take steps to completely reshape everyday life in Britain" including a green economic recovery, shorter and more flexible working arrangements, and more meaningful opportunities to "act for the common good" (Reset 2020). The desire for a policy response that responded to the climate crisis, the economy's other deep-seated issues, and discontent with the "old normal" was palpable. Concurrently, a study from the University of Oxford – co-authored by Joseph Stiglitz and Nicholas Stern among others – found that government spending on green growth projects would yield higher returns on government spending than a conventional fiscal stimulus (Hepburn et al. 2020). Based on an examination of 700 stimulus policies since 2008 and a survey of 230 senior officials from central banks and finance ministries in 53 countries, the timely report concluded that the time was ripe for the types of public investment long advocated by the green new deal movement (Hepburn et al. 2020).

Ahead of COP26, to be held in Glasgow, the Conservative government found itself under pressure to launch an economic recovery package that would help the UK meet its decarbonization targets. In June 2020, Boris Johnson went as far as to proclaim a new "Rooseveltian approach" to the COVID-19 crisis, stating that "the country has gone through a profound shock, but in those moments you have the opportunity to change and to do things better. We really want to build back better" (Walker 2020). Standing in front of a light green sign with "Build Build Build" emblazoned on it, Prime Minister Johnson promised to "build back better, greener and stronger," and referencing Roosevelt's New Deal he declared that

> it's time now not just for a new deal, but for a fair deal for the British people.... If it sounds like a prodigious amount of government intervention, if it sounds like a New Deal, all I can say is if that is so, then that is how it is meant to sound.
>
> *(BBC 2020)*

In this context, many questioned whether the pandemic has shifted the Overton window significantly enough to act as a historical inflection point in economic governance. However, shaping the "new normal" would still be subject to political contestation and struggle.

COVID-19 and the revealing and exacerbation of inequalities: a growing need for a new social contract

The pandemic and consequential economic impacts exposed and intensified many of the dysfunctions of the current British economy. The pre-existing UK growth model had been criticized for, among other pathologies, its tendency to generate rising inequalities and instability, as well as unsustainable levels of greenhouse gas emissions. The dysfunctions of the economic status quo – which was already failing many in the UK – were aggravated and laid bare during lockdown.

During the pandemic, a combination of market forces and policy decisions exacerbated inequalities across numerous axes. These inequalities had distinctive class, race, gender, regional and generational characteristics.

The lowest-paid workers had their hours cut or were made unemployed – particularly in sectors such as hospitality and retail that were subject to lockdown restrictions – or were "key workers" in sectors that exposed them to viral contagion (ONS 2020b). This dual inequality was compounded by the disproportionate need for the lowest-paid to live in housing that was crowded, lacked access to a garden or other immediate green spaces, and suffered poor air quality. In contrast, more affluent people were able to work from home remotely, in more comfortable and spacious environments, and were relatively insulated from fears of unemployment. Moreover, the Quantitative Easing programs of Central Banks enhanced demand for assets despite the economic downturn and thereby protected asset prices and portfolios (Berry et al 2020; Dempsey, Elder and Lockett 2020). For those still too young to participate in the labour market, the differing ability to pay expensive private tuition and obtain equipment during the closure of schools could plausibly widen the gap in educational attainment between those of different socio-economic backgrounds, creating a long-term legacy of lockdown. The pandemic has thus dramatically amplified disparities of income and wealth in the UK.

Income inequalities intersect with racial and gender equalities. Black and minority ethnic (BAME) households were the worst hit financially by COVID-19 – with 20% of BAME workers made unemployed and a further 31% experiencing a drop in working hours (Doward 2020) – as well as being at greater risk of contracting the coronavirus due to socio-economic conditions (Carrington 2020b; Siddique 2020). The injustices of systemic racism highlighted by Black Lives Matter movement have only been compounded by these entwined socio-economic and health inequalities.

Women, meanwhile, disproportionately occupy precarious roles in the labour market, and were more likely to be furloughed or experience a reduction in working hours as a result (NEF 2020c). Simultaneously, young mothers have been disproportionately subject to the additional caring duties and other forms of unpaid work in the household created by the closure of schools and nurseries (IFS 2020). This only adds to the imperative for a policy response that recognizes and reduces the gender pay gap and the inequalities of social reproduction.

The pandemic has also raised questions of intergenerational equality, with those under 25 years of age being far more likely to suffer from early career unemployment and the long-term scarring effects with which it is associated (IFS 2020), while being far less likely to be the beneficiaries of political efforts to protect asset prices (Berry et al 2020).

Inequality is already a profoundly important environmental issue, given the clear relationship between wealth and attributable greenhouse gas emissions (Oxfam 2020), but it has become even more imperative to attune any public investment comprising the Green New Deal to the existent inequalities exacerbated by the pandemic. The "new social contract" must be attuned to the Conservative government's purported desire to "level up" the UK, and it must be sensitive to the accelerating inequalities between class, gender, race and generations.

There are fears though that "levelling up" the UK via a Green New Deal may not be as simple as it first appears. Although public investment could alleviate unequal socio-economic conditions if deployed effectively, the parallel measures designed to curtail the profitability of unsustainable economic activities are projected to have unfortunately uneven social effects. The UK2070 Commission Report suggested that it is the poorest regions of the UK that are the most reliant on the jobs provided by carbon-intensive industries (UK2070 Commission 2020), suggesting great struggles to reconcile social justice and ecological justice in the formulation of transitional policies. In addition, a green industrial strategy would have deep environmental impacts in the Global South (Rehman 2019; see also Kolinjivadi and Kothari, this volume), which will compound the responsibility of the Global North for the generation of a climate emergency (Oxfam 2020). A Green New Deal will thus require a multifaceted program of policies that ensures a "just transition."

Systemic change via a Green New Deal

Ongoing socio-economic crises and political uncertainty present the opportunity for path-shaping policy interventions that address the various pathologies of British capitalism, including the systemic risks, inequalities, inequities and forms of ecological exploitation that characterize the existing economic model. As many GND proposals in the UK have stated, what is needed is no less than the transformation of the economic system (Common Wealth 2019; GND Group 2019; GND UK 2020a). Only a policy package that promises systemic change can be considered commensurate to the scale of the systemic crises we face. Acknowledging the UK's historical carbon debt as well as the divergence between the UK's current and Paris-compliant emissions pathway, much tougher targets should be set, and tighter carbon budgets and emission pathways should be adopted. Anderson, Broderick and Stoddard (2020: 12) call for "an immediate increase in their proposed mitigation rates by a factor of two to over 10% per annum, with full decarbonisation achieved across all sectors by 2035–40." Raising climate ambitions clearly raises the bar for the efforts required to meet these targets and renders more radical forms of political action apposite. This, in essence, demands "a deep and purposeful reorganisation of our economy" (Common Wealth 2019: 3) based on a critique of the current economic system and a strong vision of the future.

This entails – most obviously – the advancement of a green industrial strategy, coordinated with trade unions, that channels public investment toward the infrastructure and sectors conducive to decarbonization and the abatement of other forms of ecological degradation. The revamping of energy systems, transport and housing are vital components of a green economy transformation. If the UK is to meet its strict environmental targets, however, stricter regulations of carbon-intensive and resource-intensive industries, and the explicit phasing out of some, will be simultaneously required. Policies will particularly need to steer the energy industry, the automotive industry and aviation industries toward alternative trajectories, in order to address planetary overshoot (Newell 2013; Barth et al. 2020).

As the winding down of industries poses a threat to the workforce in these sectors, clear strategies to prevent unemployment and other adverse impacts of the phase-out are required. Green economic transformation runs the risk of having socially uneven impacts on the livelihoods of citizens. Those already living in less affluent areas of the country appear to be the most reliant on carbon-intensive industries for their employment (UK2070 Commission 2020). Given these circumstances, there are fears that ecological justice could be achieved in socially unjust ways. The socially uneven effects of a green economic transformation – both within the UK and internationally (lest we forget that investment in low-carbon technologies can be seen as a form of "green colonialism," cf. Gebrial 2019; Táíwò 2019; Kolinjivadi and Kothari, this volume) – only further underscores the need for a broader transition strategy that mitigates the risks of inequalities being further exacerbated.

Ensuring that a Green New Deal is part of "just transition," benefiting from a broad base of political support drawn from a diverse alliance of societal interests, demands a multifaceted economic policy agenda that can forge a new economic trajectory and a new social contract. The approach will require attuning public investment in low-carbon sectors to existing inequalities, coordinating parallel investment in childcare and other measures to mitigate gender inequalities, and ensuring that the green jobs created are not simply "jobs for the boys" (Cohen and MacGregor 2020; see also Roberts-Gregory, this volume). It must also include structural alterations to patterns of distribution and the concentration of power, a political challenge to processes of financialization, and fundamental changes in ownership and the control of resources and assets.

Existing structures of ownership and control in Britain contribute to the exacerbation of multiple forms of inequality – producing tendencies toward ever-greater financialization and rentierism – and prevent the effective public management of essential resources and assets in a socially desirable, democratically grounded and ecologically sound manner. The democratization of the economy should be a key pillar of the Green New Deal, and new proposals of reform have been made by UK activists, think tanks and the Labour Party (Labour Party 2017; Common Wealth 2019b; NEF 2019).

At the firm level, the strengthening of trade unions and encouraging increased worker participation and ownership may be powerful ways of altering existing distributional patterns in the transition to a low-carbon economy. Ensuring workers have stronger collective bargaining power, a voice in the boardroom and a participatory role in decision-making processes, a greater provision of stakes in companies, and the encouragement of worker-owned cooperative organization are trends that would be conducive to shifting the distribution of power over the key resources and structures of the economy. By the same token, it would empower front-line communities to shape their future world of work; as part of a broader adjustment of work in the context of labour automation and digitization. In the just transition to a low-carbon economy, this will include decisions over retraining schemes and apprenticeships designed to re-equip workers with the skills corresponding to a more sustainable economy. The Trade Union Congress lays out a clear vision for how to organize a transition in ways that meets working people's needs (TUC 2020).

Integrating principles of "community wealth building" into Green New Deal proposals may also advance economic democratization. Decentralized community-owned energy production projects, worker or community ownership, new codes of procurement as pioneered in Preston, and new principles of managing land and property are all instances of this emerging approach to local economic development, which aims to tackle the concentration of wealth and economic power (Centre for Local Economic Strategies and Preston City Council 2019; Guinan and O'Neill 2019). This amounts to a restructuring of production, distribution and consumption that empowers local communities to distribute resources more equitably while shaping the trajectory of their low-carbon transition.

Meanwhile, a state inclined to democratize the economy while governing a transition to sustainability could capitalize on corporate crises by taking an equity stake in return for financial support. This approach would not only allow the state to gain greater steering capacity in the economy, potentially allowing for the prioritization of socio-ecological goals in corporate boardrooms, but would also allow for the creation of a Sovereign Wealth Fund which bolsters state capacity (Bailey 2020). This would clearly disrupt the ongoing tendency to socialize losses and privatize costs across the business cycle. A truly "green state" could also democratize the economy by undertaking land reform, bringing certain industries into public or common ownership, decommodifying labour via welfare renewal and decommodifying numerous services via public and potentially more democratic and participatory delivery (Gough 2019; Guinan and O'Neill 2019). Reorganizing the provisioning of essential goods and services (such as health care, food, education or transport) in a holistic way may be required to achieve social well-being without breaching ecological boundaries (O'Neill et al. 2018).

Ensuring that the transition to sustainability is swift and just will also necessitate political interventions into the UK's finance sector. The continuing attraction of investment capital to unsustainable sectors of the economy in hubs of financial activity such as Canary Wharf renders the financial sector a formidable barrier to economic transformation. These investment patterns, reinforced by the "market neutral" Quantitative Easing programs of Central Banks, have sustained business operations that are incompatible with decarbonization targets, including in the fossil fuel energy and automotive industries (NEF 2020e). Indeed, Britain's role in today's global monetary and financial system renders it imperative that a progressive Green New Deal align investments in financial hubs with environmental targets (Steinberger and Hofferberth 2019). Credit guidance (e.g., via differential reserve), capital or liquidity requirements for clearly defined green and brown investment, or prudential regulation should be considered as policy options, for instance (Campiglio et al. 2018). Monetary reform, which strengthens the hand of public authorities to create and distribute money, while tightening regulations on the financing of sectors not aligned with decarbonization would enable a truly "green state" to allocate resources in ways conducive to a swift and equitable sustainability transition (Bailey 2018). Stronger coordination of fiscal and monetary policy alongside the establishment of a democratic Public Investment Bank imbued with a socio-ecological agenda would powerfully render global financial patterns more sustainable.

Any steering of financial investment in the UK's jurisdiction – by monetary authorities and financial regulators – will have global reach. Support for a fundamental transformation of the architecture of global economic and financial governance, as part of an equitable low-carbon transition, has been voiced by a wide assortment of academics, international institutions, thinks tanks and campaign groups (Aronoff et al. 2019; Gallagher and Kozul-Wright 2019; Pettifor 2019; C40 2020; Chomsky and Pollin 2020; Ghosh 2020). The financial sector occupies a systemically significant role in the UK economy – and we cannot underestimate the scale of its power – but greater regulations on allocative decisions and perhaps even a deeper rethinking of its purpose may increasingly be seen as a predicate of any effective transformation (Campiglio et al. 2018).

The multifaceted policy response needed to bring about systemic change will not emerge from conventional approaches to economic governance. Any seismic shift in the directionality of economic development is predicated upon philosophical debates and democratic deliberation of the economy's purpose and understandings of value, which offer alternative rationales and frameworks for the formulation of policy. The current paradigm of economic governance serves as a formidable barrier to the implementation of policies comprising a just transition.

In particular, the political and economic tendency to prioritize short-term economic growth – regardless of the social and ecological cost – must be contested if the Green New Deal is to be transformational. The strong correlation between economic growth and ecological degradation since the industrial revolution (Hickel and Kallis 2019; Haberl et al. 2020) indicates the challenges of reconciling *ad infinitum* economic growth with genuine environmental sustainability. Scrutinizing the evidence that exists for a decoupling of final energy consumption from economic growth in the UK reveals the strong impact of offshoring of energy-intensive production. These insights do not only put in question the success of decoupling but make it necessary to "adopt a holistic approach, taking into account [...] the relationship between the structural change in the UK and in the global supply chains delivering the goods and service for consumption and investment in the UK" (Hardt et al. 2018, 124).

Even a program of "Green Keynesianism" designed to nurture the growth of low-carbon sectors is likely to lead to increased consumer demand in sectors of the global economy that are distinctly and inauspiciously un-green. Incorporating a challenge to undifferentiated economic growth as the predominant objective of UK economic governance is thus vital for the orchestration of a green economic transformation (Barry 2012). Any successful program of decarbonization will require policies designed to stymie the growth of certain sectors while encouraging the growth of others. Strengthening the critique of undifferentiated growth will become more important as we move closer to decisive deadlines for emission reductions. As noted at the outset, it is incumbent on the UK, given its past and present contribution to climate change, to adopt even more ambitious climate targets and transformative political action than currently envisioned (cf. Anderson, Broderick and Stoddard 2020; Hickel 2020).

Ensuring that a Green New Deal is sufficiently transformative to meet decarbonization targets will thus likely mean explicating a critique of undifferentiated economic growth. Calls to eschew the obsession with economic growth have intensified in recent years anyway, given its power to disguise unequal income distributions and unpaid work in the household as well as rationalize policies that exacerbate environmental degradation and societal well-being (Bakker 2007; Stern 2009; Wilkinson and Pickett 2011; Barry 2012; Skidelsky and Skidelsky 2012; Costanza et al. 2014). Proponents of doing so instead call for the prioritization of interconnected social and environmental indicators (Sen et al. 2008; Fitoussi and Stiglitz 2012; Juniper 2013; Sachs et al. 2018). These calls have been rendered all the more salient because COVID-19 and the climate emergency both seem to result from an inimical relationship between economic systems and the natural world (Carrington 2020a). Contemplating what we truly value, and thus what we want the economy to provide for society, is not only acute in the context of the public health crisis but also germane to the design of an economic recovery (Mazzucato 2018; Steinberger 2020).

The prospect of weaning the UK economy and UK political authorities off the levels of economic growth it has historically been accustomed to only further underscores the importance of developing "just transition" strategies that prevent seismic negative impacts on the livelihoods of UK citizens. It implores us to develop further our understanding of the complementarities between moving beyond growth and the GND policy agenda (cf. Hofferberth 2019; Mastini et al. 2021). Equally, it underscores the importance of enacting institutional changes that reduce the UK economy's various dependencies on economic growth, such as welfare reform and monetary reform (Bailey 2016, 2018), which will safeguard well-being and prosperity beyond growth.

Kate Raworth's pioneering work on Doughnut Economics can serve as a starting point for the governance of systemic change (Raworth 2017). Her accessible framework incorporates a diverse range of alternative measurements of progress – including measurements of well-being and environmental sustainability – drawn from the insights of the natural sciences, feminist economics, the foundational economy and ecological economics *inter alia*. The logic of her approach is nothing less than a repurposing of the economy in aid of promoting a just transition to sustainability. Institutionalizing a more holistic dashboard of progress indicators to formulate and evaluate the success of policy-making would not only be conducive to the design of a Green New Deal with genuinely transformative potential, but it would also help ensure that a Green New Deal addresses existing inequalities. It would, for example, help rationalize investment in the restoration of peatland and rewilding, or alert policy-makers to the inequities of creating green jobs that disproportionately privilege a particular gender or region. In other words, it would help disrupt current patterns of economic governance and inculcate an approach that takes systemic change seriously. Stratford and O'Neill (2020) offer a practical application of Raworth's framework to the pandemic context in the UK and offer a number of policy proposals that would help achieve a "Doughnut-shaped recovery." Setting up a dedicated "Well-being Budget," of the type pioneered and institutionalized in New Zealand under the leadership of Prime Minister Jacinda Ardern, would allow government to explicitly align investment decisions with both the social-ecological transformation agenda and the need for a recovery package in the aftermath of COVID-19. An institutionalized recognition of social and environmental goals could reorient policy-making around alternative priorities (Barth et al. 2020).

Equally, systemic change requires a re-evaluation of what we currently understand to be valuable. Current frameworks of economic governance are underpinned by a sensitivity to commodity and asset prices as primary representations of economic value, while non-monetized ecosystems, natural resources and social reproduction remain unvalued and underappreciated (Mazzucato 2018). Recognizing and institutionalizing a recognition of the indispensable and un-exchangeable value of the natural world would challenge perceptions on commodification in sites of power (O'Neill 2017). Re-thinking economic governance for the twenty-first century in this way dovetails with the need to govern systemic change and implement a truly transformative Green New Deal.

Accomplishing the systemic change of British capitalism via a Green New Deal thus requires the development of a Green New Deal policy package in the wake of the pandemic. It must complement industrial policies with a broader transformation of the economic policy agenda. As revealed by the GND APPG, however, the desire for genuine change is strong among the British population at the present moment (Reset 2020). Calls to "build back better" have gained momentum, and an opportunity for radical change has, however fleetingly, presented itself. Nurturing this appetite and strengthening public support is the task that lies ahead.

Conclusion

The UK Green New Deal has evolved significantly since its first iteration in 2008, and it must continue to evolve if it is to represent a commensurate response to an increasingly urgent climate crisis and the palpable need and appetite for a new social contract. The need to achieve drastic and rapid cuts to levels of greenhouse gas emissions and alleviate rising inequalities means that the proponents of a Green New Deal in the UK must countenance increasingly radical forms of systemic change. This, in all likelihood, means not only developing a conception of a green industrial strategy for modern-day Britain but also embedding it within a broader multifaceted policy agenda guided by a more holistic understanding of the economy's purpose in an age of climate crisis.

However, this is far from the current direction of travel in British politics. The Conservative government's response to the pandemic-induced economic downturn has been to mobilize public investment in the service of preserving – rather than transforming – the economic status quo. Corporate bailouts and other emergency interventions have been orchestrated with no "green strings" attached (as was the case in other countries, including France), while the Bank of England's Quantitative Easing programs have helped rescue businesses with business models not compatible with a transition to sustainability. Only a handful of small budgets conducive to decarbonization have been announced at the time of writing (e.g., £3 billion set aside to ensure energy efficiency in public buildings and homes), but these are peripheral elements of the UK Government's crisis management response. The British state has thereby mobilized public resources in aid of restoring and "locking in" pre-existing economic patterns of ecological degradation. The prospects of accomplishing an economic transformation that meets decarbonization targets are thus greatly diminished as a result of current crisis management policies.

On an issue where winning slowly is the same as losing, as Bill McKibben (2017) put it, it is difficult to envisage how the political barriers to a sustainability transition can be overcome in the timeframes necessary. The current political and economic developments in the UK certainly evoke pessimism. Processes of geo-political fragmentation – of which Brexit is one iteration – will only make it more difficult to stage a coordinated international response to ecological degradation. Yet, the diverse but growing calls internationally for a "new normal," a green recovery, or "Building Back Better" represent an important and heartening counter-tendency. The intellectual and political advancement of Green New Deal proposals means they remain among the most viable strategies for instigating systemic change at this critical historical juncture. In order to achieve this in the UK, the "overwhelming public appetite for a fairer, greener, kinder Britain after COVID" (Reset 2020) will need to be harnessed by the development of GND proposals – in collaboration with trade unions and social movements – in order to create and mobilize a shared vision of the future.

References

All Party Parliamentary Group on the Green New Deal, 2020. Time to reset. *The Public Desire for a Fairer, Greener Britain after Covid.* Available from: https://reset-uk.org/static/TimeToReset-3a6ee92ce4fff64d024c62404f53fe5c.pdf

Anderson, K., Broderick, J.F. and Stoddard, I. 2020. A factor of two: How the mitigation plans of 'climate progressive' nations fall far short of Paris-compliant pathways. *Climate Policy* 20(10), 1290–1304.

Aronoff, K., Battistoni, A., Aldana cohen, D. and Riofrancos, T. 2019. *A Planet to Win. Why We Need A Green New Deal.* London & New York: Verso.

Bailey, D. 2016. The environmental paradox of the welfare state: The dynamics of sustainability. *New Political Economy* 20(6), 793–811.

Bailey, D. 2018. Re-thinking the fiscal and monetary political economy of the green state. *New Political Economy* 25(1), 5–17.

Bailey, D. 2020. Shaping the new normal. *Renewal* 28(2). Available from: https://renewal.org.uk/articles/shaping-the-new-normal

Bakker, I. 2007. Social reproduction and the constitution of a gendered political economy. *New Political Economy* 12(4), 541–556.

Bank of England. 2020a. Asset Purchase Facility (APF): Asset Purchases and TFSME – Market Notice. 19 March. Available from: https://www.bankofengland.co.uk/markets/market-notices/2020/apf-asset-purchases-and-tfsme-march-2020

Bank of England. 2020b. HM treasury and Bank of England announce temporary extension to Ways and Means facility. 9 April. Available from: https://www.bankofengland.co.uk/news/2020/april/hmt-and-boe-announce-temporary-extension-to-ways-and-means-facility

Bank of England. 2020c. Asset Purchase Facility: Gilt purchases – Market Notice. 18 June. Available from: https://www.bankofengland.co.uk/markets/market-notices/2020/asset-purchase-facility-gilt-purchases-june-2020

Barbier, E.B. 2010. Green stimulus is not sufficient for a global green recovery. *VoxEU*. 3 June. Available from: https://voxeu.org/article/urgently-needed-global-green-new-deal

Barry, J. 2012. *The Politics of Actually Existing Unsustainability: Human Flourishing in a Climate-Changed, Carbon Constrained World*. Oxford: Oxford University Press.

Barth, J. and Coscieme, L. et al. 2020. *Analysing Options for Systemic Change to Transform the World's Economic* and *Financial Systems*. Bonn: ZOE-Institute for future-fit economies.

BBC. 2018. Reality check: Labour's green energy plans. 26 September. Available from: https://www.bbc.co.uk/news/uk-politics-45655310

BBC. 2020. NY restricts travellers from nearly half of US. 30 June. Available from: https://www.bbc.co.uk/news/live/world-53230389

Berry, C., Macfarlane, L. and Nanda, S. 2020. Who wins and who pays? Rentier power and the Covid crisis. *IPPR*. 13 May. Available from: https://www.ippr.org/research/publications/who-wins-and-who-pays

C40 Cities. 2020. Principles of the global green new deal. Available from: https://www.c40.org/other/the-global-green-new-deal

Campiglio, E. et al. 2018. Climate change challenges for central banks and financial regulators. *Nature Climate Change* 8, 462–468.

Carrington, D. 2020a. Halt destruction of nature or suffer even worse pandemics, say world's top scientists. *The Guardian*. 27 April. Available from: https://www.theguardian.com/world/2020/apr/27/halt-destruction-nature-worse-pandemics-top-scientists

Carrington, D. 2020b. Omission of air pollution from report on Covid-19 and race 'astonishing'. *The Guardian*. 7 June. Available from: https://www.theguardian.com/environment/2020/jun/07/omission-of-air-pollution-from-report-on-covid-19-and-race-astonishing

Centre for Local Economic Strategies and Preston City Council. 2019. How we built community wealth in preston. *Achievements and Lessons*. Available from: https://www.preston.gov.uk/media/1792/How-we-built-community-wealth-in-Preston/pdf/CLES_Preston_Document_WEB_AW.pdf?m=636994067328930000

Chomsky, N. and Pollin, R. 2020. *Climate Crisis and the Global Green New Deal. The Political Economy of Saving the Planet*. London & New York: Verso.

Christophers, B. 2019. The rentierization of the United Kingdom economy. *EPA: Economy and Space*, 1–33. https://journals.sagepub.com/doi/10.1177/0308518X19873007

Cohen, M. and MacGregor, S. 2020. Towards a feminist green new deal for the UK. *Women's Budget Group*. Available from: https://wbg.org.uk/wp-content/uploads/2020/05/Feminist-Green-New-Deal.pdf

Common Wealth. 2019a. Roadmap to a green new deal. *From Extraction to Stewardship*. Available from: https://www.common-wealth.co.uk/reports/road-map-to-a-green-new-deal-from-extraction-to-stewardship

Common Wealth. 2019b. *Owning the Future: Toward the Democratic Economy*. Available from: https://www.common-wealth.co.uk/reports/owning-the-future-toward-the-democratic-economy

Common Wealth. 2020. Covid-19. Available from: https://www.common-wealth.co.uk/project-streams/covid-19

Conservative Party. 2019. Our plan: Conservative party manifesto 2019. Available from: https://vote.conservatives.com/our-plan

Constanza, R. et al. 2014. Development: Time to leave GDP behind. *Nature* 505(7483), 283–285.

Dempsey, H., Elder, B. and Lockett, H. 2020. US stocks erase all losses for the year. *Financial Times*. 8 June. Available from: https://www.ft.com/content/1dfaeb58-6d65-4f17-b710-b1ebc6622649

Doward, J. 2020. BAME and single-parent families worst hit financially by Covid-19. *The Guardian*. 7 June. Available from: https://www.theguardian.com/world/2020/jun/07/bame-and-single-parent-families-worst-hit-financially-by-covid-19

Equality Trust. 2020. *The Scale of Economic Inequality in the UK*. Available from: https://www.equalitytrust.org.uk/scale-economic-inequality-uk

Fitoussi, J.P. and Stiglitz, J.E. 2012. "On the measurement of social progress and wellbeing: Some further thoughts." In: Stiglitz, J.E., Gordon, R., and Fitoussi, J., eds. *The Global Macro Economy and Finance*. London: Palgrave Macmillan. pp. 13–24.

Gallagher, K.P. and Kozul-Wright, R. 2019. Breaking out of the double squeeze: The need for fiscal and policy space during the COVID-19 crises. *Global Policy Journal*. 26 June. Available from: https://www.globalpolicyjournal.com/blog/26/06/2020/breaking-out-double-squeeze-need-fiscal-and-policy-space-during-covid-19-crises

Gebrial, D. 2019. As the left wakes up to climate injustice, we must not fall into 'green colonialism.' *The Guardian*. 8 May. Available from: https://www.theguardian.com/commentisfree/2019/may/08/left-climate-injustice-green-new-deal?%20CMP=share_btn_tw

Ghosh, J. 2020. How to build the global green new deal. *Progressive International*. Available from: https://progressive.international/blueprint/80b03a68-68ca-4322-a3ad-c91775f167b9-jayati-ghosh-how-to-build-the-global-green-new-deal/en

Good Life Leeds. 2020. A good life for all within planetary boundaries. *Country Comparisons*. United Kingdom. Available from: https://goodlife.leeds.ac.uk/countries/#UnitedKingdom

Gough, I. 2019. Universal basic services: A theoretical and moral framework. *The Political Quarterly* 90(3), 534–542.

Green New Deal Group. 2008. A green new deal. Joined-up policies to solve the triple crunch of the credit crisis, climate change and high oil prices. *The First Report of the Green New Deal Group*. July. Available from: www.neweconomics.org/publications/green-new-deal

Green New Deal Group. 2019. *The Green New Deal. A Bill to Make it Happen*. London: The Green New Deal Group.

Green New Deal UK. 2020a. Green new deal UK. *Our Principles*. Available from: https://www.greennewdealuk.org/about-us/our-principles/

Green New Deal UK. 2020b. Green new deal UK is fighting to build back better. Available from: https://www.greennewdealuk.org/stories/green-new-deal-uk-is-fighting-to-build-back-better/

Green Party. 2019. If not now, When? green party manifesto. Available from: https://www.greenparty.org.uk/assets/files/Elections/Green%20Party%20Manifesto%202019.pdf

Guinan, J. and O'Neill, M. 2019. From community wealth-building to system change. *IPPR Progressive Review* 25(4), 382–392.

Haberl, H. et al. 2020. A systematic review of the evidence on decoupling of GDP, resource use and GHG emissions, part II: Synthesizing the insights. *Environmental Research Letters* 15, 1–42.

Hartd, L. et al. 2018. Untangling the drivers of energy reduction in the UK productive sectors: Efficiency or offshoring? *Applied Energy* 223, 124–133.

Hepburn, C. et al. 2020. Will Covid-19 fiscal recovery packages accelerate or retard progress on climate change?. *Oxford Review of Economic Policy* 36(S1). Available from: https://www.smithschool.ox.ac.uk/publications/wpapers/workingpaper20-02.pdf

Hofferberth, E. 2019. A green new deal beyond growth (II). *Some Steps Forward*. Available from: https://www.degrowth.info/en/2019/05/a-green-new-deal-beyond-growth-ii-some-steps-forward/

Hickel, J. 2020. Quantifying national responsibility for climate breakdown: An equality-based attribution approach for carbon dioxide emissions in excess of the planetary boundary. *Lancet Planet Health* 4, e399–404.

Hickel, J. and Kallis, G. 2019. Is green growth possible? *New Political Economy*. Available from: https://www.tandfonline.com/doi/abs/10.1080/13563467.2019.1598964

IFS. 2020. Covid-19: The impacts of the pandemic on inequality. 11 June. Available from: https://www.ifs.org.uk/publications/14879

Ipsos MORI. 2020. Two thirds of britons believe climate change as serious as coronavirus and majority want climate prioritised in economic recovery. Available from: https://www.ipsos.com/ipsos-mori/en-uk/two-thirds-britons-believe-climate-change-serious-coronavirus-and-majority-want-climate-prioritised

Juniper, A. 2013. *What Has Nature Ever Done For Us? How Money Really Does Grow On Trees*. London: Profile Books.

Labour Party. 2017. Alternative models of ownership. *Report to the Shadow Chancellor of the Exchequer and Shadow Secretary of State for Business, Energy and Industrial Strategy*. Available from: https://labour.org.uk/wp-content/uploads/2017/10/Alternative-Models-of-Ownership.pdf

Labour Party. 2019. Time for real change: The labour party manifesto 2019. Available from: https://labour.org.uk/wp-content/uploads/2019/11/Real-Change-Labour-Manifesto-2019.pdf

Labour for a Green New Deal. 2020. Available from: https://www.labourgnd.uk/green-recovery/#gr-intro

Long-Bailey, R. 2019. Labour to set out plans to decarbonise UK and fulfil green jobs pledge. *The Guardian*.12 February. Available from: https://www.theguardian.com/environment/2019/feb/12/labour-plan-decarbonise-uk-green-jobs-climate-crisis

Mastini, R., Kallis, G. and Hickel, J. 2021. A green new deal without growth?. *Ecological Economics* 179, 106832.

Mazzucato, M. 2018. *The Value of Everything: Making and Taking in the Global Economy*. New York: PublicAffairs.

McCann, P. 2018. *Perceptions of Regional Inequality and the Geography of Discontent: Insights from the UK*. UK2070 Commission.

McDonnell, J. 2019. A green new deal for the UK. *Jacobin*. 30 May. Available from: https://jacobinmag.com/2019/05/john-mcdonnell-labour-green-industrial-revolution?fbclid=-IwAR1S7s75Uea75fY9O8RC4wF4kgHIQ-LOQWiWw2J8t0Ulr0AJq9pn2jIsW6g

McKibben, B. 2017. Winning slowly is the same as losing. *Rolling Stone*. Available from: https://www.rollingstone.com/politics/politics-news/bill-mckibben-winning-slowly-is-the-same-as-losing-198205/

Miliband, E., Lucas, C. and Sandys, L. 2019. Let's seize the moment and create a green new deal for the UK. *The Guardian*. 30 April. Available from: https://www.theguardian.com/commentisfree/2019/apr/30/green-new-deal-climate-change-social-transformation

Moore, J.W. 2017. The capitalocene, Part I: On the nature and origins of our ecological crisis. *The Journal of Peasant Studies* 44(3), 594–630.

NEF. 2019. *A Green New Deal in the UK*. London: New Economics Foundation.

NEF. 2020a. Coronavirus response. *New Economics Foundation*. Available from: https://neweconomics.org/campaigns/coronavirus-response/

NEF. 2020b. Building a green stimulus for Covid-19. A recovery plan for a greener, fairer future. *New Economics Foundation*. Available from: https://neweconomics.org/2020/07/building-a-green-stimulus-for-covid19

NEF. 2020c. Who's losing income during the pandemic?. *New Economics Foundation*. Available from: https://neweconomics.org/2020/06/whos-losing-income-during-the-pandemic

NEF. 2020d. *Change the Rules. New Rules for the Economy*. London: New Economics Foundation.

NEF. 2020e. Decarbonising the Bank of England's pandemic QE. *New Economics Foundation*. 4 August. Available from: https://neweconomics.org/2020/08/decarbonising-the-bank-of-englands-pandemic-qe

Newell, P. 2013. *Globalization and the Environment: Capitalism, Ecology and Power*. New York: John Wiley & Sons.

O'Neill, J. 2017. Life beyond capital. *Centre for Understanding Sustainable Prosperity*. Available from: https://www.cusp.ac.uk/wp-content/uploads/Life-beyond-capital-online.pdf

O'Neill, D.W., Fanning, A.L., Lamb, W.F. and Steinberger, J.K. 2018. A good life for all within planetary boundaries. *Nature Sustainability* 1, 88–95.

ONS. 2018. Persistent poverty in the UK and EU: 2017. *Office for National Statistics*. Available from: https://www.ons.gov.uk/peoplepopulationandcommunity/personalandhouseholdfinances/incomeandwealth/articles/persistentpovertyintheukandeu/2017

ONS. 2019. Total wealth in Great Britain: April 2016 to March 2018. *Office for National Statistics*. Available from: https://www.ons.gov.uk/peoplepopulationandcommunity/personalandhouseholdfinances/incomeandwealth/bulletins/totalwealthingreatbritain/april2016tomarch2018

ONS. 2020a. Household income inequality, UK: Financial year ending 2020 (provisional). *Office for National Statistics*. Available from: https://www.ons.gov.uk/peoplepopulationandcommunity/personalandhouseholdfinances/incomeandwealth/bulletins/householdincomeinequalityfinancial/financialyearending2020provisional

ONS. 2020b. Deaths involving COVID-19 by local area and socioeconomic deprivation: Deaths occurring between 1 March and 31 May 2020. *Office for National Statistics*. Available from: https://www.ons.gov.uk/peoplepopulationandcommunity/birthsdeathsandmarriages/deaths/bulletins/deathsinvolvingcovid19bylocalareasanddeprivation/deathsoccurringbetween1marchand31may2020

Oxfam. 2020. Carbon emissions of richest 1 percent more than double the emissions of the poorest half of humanity. 21 September. Available from: https://www.oxfam.org/en/press-releases/carbon-emissions-richest-1-percent-more-double-emissions-poorest-half-humanity

Pettifor, A. 2019. *The Case for a Green New Deal*. London: Verso.

Raworth, K. 2017. *Doughnut Economics. Seven Ways to Think Like a 21st-Century Economist*. New York: Random House.

Rehman, A. 2019. The 'green new deal' supported by Ocasio-Cortez and Corbyn is just a new form of colonialism. *The Independent*. 4 May. Available from: https://www.independent.co.uk/voices/green-new-deal-alexandria-ocasio-cortezcorbyn-colonialism-climate-change-a8899876.html

Reset. 2020. Available from: https://reset-uk.org/

Sachs, J.D., Layard, R. and Helliwell, J.F. 2018. *World Happiness Report 2018*. Working Paper 12761. Available from: https://ideas.repec.org/p/ess/wpaper/id12761.html

Satow, A. 2019. Our new movement aims to propel labour into a radical green new deal. *The Guardian*. 22 March. Available from: https://www.theguardian.com/commentisfree/2019/mar/22/movement-propel-labour-radical-green-new-deal

Sayers, M. and Trebeck, K. 2015. *The UK Doughnut. A Framework for Environmental Sustainability and Social Justice*. Oxfam Research Report.

Sen, A., Stiglitz, J. and Fitoussi, J.P. 2008. *Report by the Commission on the Measurement of Economic Performance and Social Progress*. Paris.

Siddique, H. 2020. BAME Britons still lack protection from Covid, says doctors' chief. *The Guardian*. 20 September. Available from: https://www.theguardian.com/world/2020/sep/20/bma-chair-act-now-stop-further-disproportionate-bame-covid-deaths

Skidelsky, R. and Skidelsky, E. 2012. *How Much is Enough? Money and the Good Life*. London: Penguin Books.

Steinberger, J. 2020. Pandenomics: A story of life versus growth. *Open Democracy*. 8 April. Available from: https://www.opendemocracy.net/en/oureconomy/pandenomics-story-life-versus-growth/

Steinberger, J. and Hofferberth, E. 2019. UK financial investment and action on climate change consistent with 1.5 degrees celsius. *SRI Briefing Note Series No. 24*. Available from: https://www.see.leeds.ac.uk/fileadmin/Documents/research/sri/briefingnotes/SRI_Briefing_Note_24.pdf

Stern, N.H. 2009. Rich nations will have to forget about growth to stop climate change. *The Guardian*. 11 September. Available from: http://www.guardian.co.uk/environment/2009/sep/11/stern-economic-growth-emissions

Stratford, B. and O'Neill, D.W. 2020. *The UK's Path to a Doughnut-Shaped Recovery*. Leeds: University of Leeds.

Táíwò, O.O. 2019. How a green new deal could exploit developing countries. Available from: https://psmag.com/social-justice/how-the-gnd-can-avoid-climate-colonialism

Tienhaara, K. 2018. *Green Keynesianism and the Global Financial Crisis*. London: Routledge.

Trade Union Congress. 2020. *Voice and Place: How to Plan Fair and Successful Paths to Net Zero Emissions*. Available from: https://www.tuc.org.uk/research-analysis/reports/voice-and-place-how-plan-fair-and-successful-paths-net-zero-emissions

UK2070 Commission. 2020. *Make No Little Plans: Acting at Scale for a Fairer and Stronger Future: Final Report of the UK2070 Commission*. February. Available from: http://uk2070.org.uk/wp-content/uploads/2020/02/UK2070-FINAL-REPORT.pdf

United Nations Environment Programme. 2009. *Global Green New Deal*. Policy Brief. Available from: https://www.unenvironment.org/resources/report/global-green-new-deal-policy-brief-march-2009

Walker, P. 2020. Boris Johnson says Covid-19 disaster for UK and pledges 'Rooseveltian' strategy. *The Guardian*. 29 June. Available from: https://www.theguardian.com/world/2020/jun/29/boris-johnson-calls-for-rooseveltian-approach-to-help-uk-economy-recover

Wilkinson, R. and Pickett, K. 2011. *The Spirit Level: Why Equality is Better for Everyone*. London: Allen Lane.

18
A MADE-IN-CANADA GREEN NEW DEAL

Seth Klein

> We need the federal government to step up and guarantee that every single worker, family and community impacted by this transition will be supported. The best way to do that is to borrow from the Green New Deal and implement a federal job guarantee that tells every single person in Canada that they don't have to choose between putting food on the table and ensuring our children inherit a liveable planet.
>
> —*Clayton Thomas-Müller, Cree activist and campaigner with 350.org Canada*

In the 1930s, Canada did not have a Keynesian economic plan comparable to Franklin Delano Roosevelt (FDR)'s New Deal in the United States (US). The Canadian prime minister for the early years of the Great Depression was Conservative R.B. Bennett, who was replaced as of 1935 by "Liberal" William Lyon Mackenzie King. Yet notwithstanding Mackenzie King's alleged liberal leanings, and despite calls from many in civil society and at least one premier for Canada to follow the US in adopting an ambitious New Deal, Mackenzie King stubbornly resisted, needlessly prolonging the Depression's cruel hardships.

But where the Depression failed to shake loose the constraints of what today we would call neoliberal thinking, the demands of war succeeded. In Canada, the Second World War was our New Deal. Canada declared war on Germany in September 1939 (two years earlier than the US), and it was only then, as the country marshalled a military (which would ultimately see nearly 1 in 11 Canadians enlist) and ramped up wartime production, that unemployment was banished and the long tail of the Great Depression extinguished. It was also during the Second World War that the architecture of the modern Canadian welfare state was developed. The war saw the introduction of Canada's first major income support programs (unemployment insurance and the family allowance), and a promise was made to returning soldiers that they would not come home to the same sort of unequal and harsh society as the one they had left behind. A similar promise must be at the root of climate emergency mobilization today.

The Canadian call for a Green New Deal

Notwithstanding the fact that the New Deal has no historic roots in Canada, the idea of a "made-in-Canada" *Green* New Deal (GND) has found great excitement and receptivity.

DOI: 10.4324/9781003110880-22

Like elsewhere, youth-led initiatives have been vital to climate mobilization in Canada, most notably the student climate strikes and 350.org Canada's Our Time youth initiative,[1] and these movements have coalesced around the call for a GND. There is a new generation of millennials who are now in leadership roles within the Canadian non-governmental organizations that are pushing for a made-in-Canada GND.

For many young people, the Second World War is an old story from high school history textbooks; it struggles to find resonance. Yet a growing number of them intimately understand the climate emergency and young climate activists have started to employ a wartime frame, linked to the idea of a GND. In early 2019, as 350.org Canada was ramping up its plans ahead of a federal election scheduled for the fall, their national call-out for volunteers stated:

> A Green New Deal for Canada means mobilizing a WWII scale response to climate change that addresses not just the environmental crisis, but enshrines Indigenous rights into law. It means climate policies that transition us off fossil fuels in line with what the science demands by making massive investments in renewable energy and public transportation and guaranteeing green jobs for workers all across Canada.[2]

Similarly, as one of the Vancouver climate strike leaders, Rebecca Hamilton, told CBC radio,

> During World War II, everybody knew there was a war on. It was the lens through which every individual and government decision was made, and I want the climate crisis to be seen with the same level of urgency and addressed with the same level of scale.[3]

Among the first to call for a Canadian version of the GND was Cree climate activist Clayton Thomas-Müller of 350.org's Canadian team. Inspired by what he saw unfolding south of the border, Thomas-Müller wrote in late 2018,

> That's the same thing we need here in Canada – a climate plan that stops fossil fuel expansion, gets us to 100% renewables and guarantees a good job for impacted workers. And, it has to do it all in full partnership with Indigenous peoples.
>
> *(Thomas-Müller 2018)*

In Canada, the linkages between the GND and the defence of Indigenous rights and title is of particular significance. Over and over again, as our mainstream politics have dithered and dodged on meaningful and coherent climate action, implementing contradictory and inadequate policies, it is the assertion of Indigenous title and rights that has come to our collective aid – blocking new fossil fuel projects and buying us time, until such time as our politics comes into alignment with the reality of the climate emergency. This has been particularly true in British Columbia, where most of the land is "unceded," meaning land was never relinquished by treaty or conquest. Relatedly, some of Canada's most inspiring renewable energy projects are also happening under First Nations' leadership.[4] Given this, it has become increasingly understood by climate mobilization activists that it is imperative to honour and support such efforts, first by embedding the UN Declaration on the Rights of Indigenous Peoples into law at all levels of government, and second by ensuring that Indigenous communities and nations are full partners in the development of our climate emergency plans.

Ahead of Canada's 2019 federal election, young activists called for ambitious climate action, but also seamlessly integrated demands for social and Indigenous justice into their agenda. Climate Strike Canada, a national network of groups organizing student climate strikes, set seven conditions for any candidates who hoped to earn the youth vote,[5] including:

- Legislated emission reduction targets of 65% by 2030 and 100% by 2040;
- "Separation of oil and state" by rejecting new fossil projects and ending fossil subsidies;
- A just transition for fossil fuel workers;
- Commitment to an environmental bill of rights;
- Full implementation of the UN Declaration on the Rights of Indigenous Peoples;
- Conservation of biodiversity; and
- Protection of vulnerable groups – including recognition of climate displacement as a basis for refugee status.

In a push to mobilize millennials during the election, 350.org Canada launched the Our Time initiative. The aim was to encourage younger voters to get behind those candidates who were serious about the climate emergency and committed to implementing a made-in-Canada Green New Deal. Atiya Jaffar, a campaigner for 350.org and one of the founders of the initiative, explained in an interview that a great appeal of the GND is how it challenges the "jobs-versus-environment" narrative, turning this trope on its head and seizing the initiative with a bold plan to create a million-plus jobs building the future economy we want and need. In the face of a federal government that ceaselessly insists that pipeline expansion is necessary to the Canadian economy, Jaffar and her colleagues realized that "winning this broader, populist narrative meant moving beyond fighting for climate action one pipeline at a time or one fossil fuel project at a time."[6]

Just as Jaffar and her 350.org team were re-evaluating their strategy, they started to witness the rise of the youth-led Sunrise Movement and Alexandria Ocasio-Cortez in the US, who were taking on the Democratic Party establishment and demanding real climate action, and whose campaign was focussed around the call for a Green New Deal, a federal jobs guarantee, and a 100% renewable energy economy. They could see the appeal taking off, not only in the US, but in other countries as well.

> We were really inspired by that, and of course we were planning for what our campaigning would look like in an election year... And so we turned our attention to this more populist narrative around the Green New Deal and toward what it would take to have a massive shift in the structure of Canadian society.

"The Green New Deal packages everything really nicely," notes Jaffar.

> It invokes historical examples of massive state spending for a massive transition, social safety nets for people that are impacted, and it is really what we need in order to address the scale of the climate crises. If we were to win something like the Green New Deal, things like the Trans Mountain Pipeline would not even be on the table.

The coalition of Canadian organizations calling for a GND grew to over 60 environmental organizations and civil society groups, including Leadnow (a Canadian NGO similar to MoveOn.org in the US), Greenpeace, The Leap, the Canadian Union of Postal Workers, the Union of BC Indian Chiefs, Indigenous Climate Action, Confédération des syndicats nationaux (CSN – a major Quebec labour federation), the Council of Canadians, and the Ontario division of the Canadian Union of Public Employees.

Avi Lewis, co-founder of The Leap, in a cross-Canada tour promoting a Green New Deal ahead of the 2019 federal election, called it "the greatest anti-austerity program of our time." Like Jaffar, Lewis emphasizes that a great benefit of the GND (like the earlier Leap Manifesto) is that it turns the "jobs-versus-environment" barrier to action on its head, and instead seizes the mantle of job creation. "The Green New Deal will be a massive job creator, swell the ranks of unions, and increase workers' rights for all, especially the most vulnerable," declares Lewis.

On 28 October 2019, one week after the federal election, 27 young people were arrested during a sit-down protest in the foyer of the federal House of Commons. They were all from 350.org's Our Time initiative, and they were calling on all of the newly elected members of Parliament to work across party lines and govern for a Green New Deal.[7]

Five months later, the global COVID-19 pandemic struck, and climate emergency and GND organizing were pushed off the front burner. But the central ideas of a GND were not lost. Rather, they became embedded in the call to "Build Back Better," with many of the same civil society groups mentioned above joining forces again in a call for a "Just Recovery"[8] they saw as a path to a GND.[9]

The logic of linking climate mobilization with tackling inequality

At the heart of the call for a GND is the principle of linking the two great "inconvenient truths" of our time – inequality and the climate crisis. The logic of doing so is compelling. To succeed in a mass mobilization in the face of an existential threat, a vital ingredient is social solidarity – a shared belief that *everyone* is in the fight. People need to feel confident that all are contributing according to their means, and making sacrifices in equal measure – the rich as well as the poor. And equally important, people need to know that the society that will emerge after their efforts will be a more just and fairer one. In contrast, the social divisions fuelled by economic inequality, racism and sexism are toxic to such efforts.

During the First World War, inequality and rampant profiteering in Canada undermined social solidary and mobilization efforts. Consequently, at the outset of the Second World War, the Canadian government took remarkable and bold steps to lessen inequality, substantially raising taxes on the wealthy and corporations and introducing an excess profits tax (Granatstein 2005, 8). Such measures are needed again today.

There is a common argument made against linking the need for climate action with inequality and social justice issues which goes: "Why make this any more complicated? Getting society off fossil fuels is challenging enough. So why make the task even *more* difficult by requiring our transition plans to rectify the other injustices of the world?" The Green New Deal and other climate justice campaigns frequently encounter this position, often made by climate policy wonks and even some mainstream environmental organizations.

The rebuttal is two-fold. First, it is only by linking these issues that we win over and mobilize broad popular support. And second, these issues are actually deeply intertwined.

Inequality itself, along with economic and job insecurity, is a key obstacle to bold climate action. Its corrosive effect operates at both the concrete and psycho-social level. With respect to the latter, inequality undermines trust that "we are all in this together." Many doubt that the task at hand will be undertaken in a manner that is fair. It is hard to rally the public if many believe the rich are merely buying their way out of making change – fortifying their homes, walling their communities or purchasing carbon offsets in the hopes that others will lower their actual emissions. Equally troubling is a cultural narrative that sees climate action as part of an elite project, with the poor, or those currently working in the fossil fuel sector, viewed as expendable.

But while inequality makes tackling the climate crisis harder, the reverse is also true – less inequality helps to galvanize climate action. Those countries with less inequality, such as Denmark, Norway, Finland and Sweden, are also where we tend to see the strongest climate policies. British epidemiologists Richard Wilkinson and Kate Pickett, in their groundbreaking book on inequality, *The Spirit Level*, highlight that societies with less income inequality are also more open to embracing environmental actions (Wilkinson and Pickett 2009).

At a concrete and material level, inequality is interwoven with the climate crisis because the growing income gap exacerbates climate change, while climate change's impacts and many of the policies seeking to tackle it are unequally felt. The Canadian Centre for Policy Alternatives' Climate Justice Project is a research alliance that has spent many years exploring these connections. The work of the project has been guided by an overarching question: what does it look like to dramatically reduce our greenhouse gas (GHG) emissions, but to do so in a manner that reduces inequality and ensures that societal and industrial transitions are just and equitable?

A few years ago, the project's director, economist Marc Lee, along with evaluation consultant Amanda Card, calculated GHG emissions in Canada by household income. Not surprisingly, as the accompanying chart shows (see Figure 18.1), Canadian household emissions are highly unequal; the wealthiest 20% are responsible for almost double the GHG emissions of the poorest 20% (Lee and Card 2011). The richer a person is, the greater their carbon footprint – more disposable income means more consumption, bigger homes, more flights, etc. This mirrors results in more recent global studies (Weidmann et al. 2020).

Consider the implications of this distribution. Even if those in the richest quintile successfully reduce their household emissions by 30% by 2030 – Canada's official goal at the time of writing – they will *still* be emitting more than the poorest 20% of households do today.

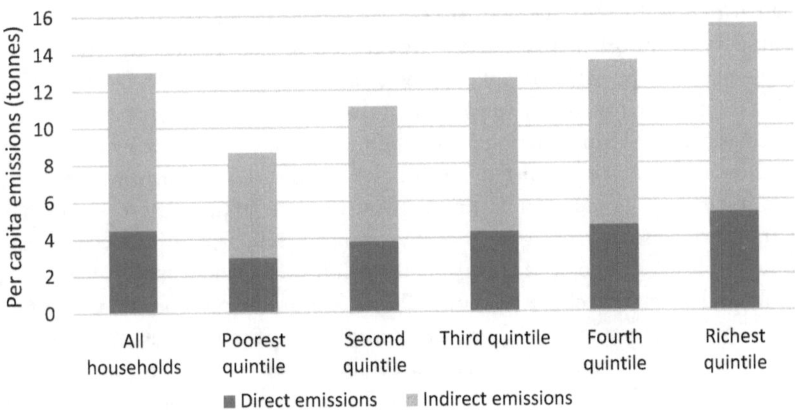

Figure 18.1 Canada's GHG emissions per person (2009)

Notes: Direct Emissions include motor fuel and in-home fuel; indirect emissions are those from the production, transportation and use of goods and services that households consume.

Source: Calculated by Marc Lee, based on data from Statistics Canada, Survey of Household Spending, Energy Statistics Hand, and Canada Year Book; Environment Canada, National Inventory Report 1990–2009: Greenhouse Gas Sources and Sinks in Canada.

This surely exposes a fundamental equity challenge and suggests as a matter of justice that higher-income households should bear a greater burden of reducing emissions.

On the flip side, issues of fairness and justice must also be effectively addressed in the design of GHG reduction policies. That's because most conventional climate action policies (such as carbon pricing), in isolation (meaning, in the absence of lower-income carbon tax credits or dividends), have regressive impacts; they hit lower-income families harder as a share of their income. Almost all climate actions have household costs or will increase energy prices in the short and medium term, and those costs are harder for low- and modest-income households (not to mention poorer countries) to contend with. This means that redistribution measures – both within and between states – must be at the core of climate action agendas.

A Green New Deal invites us to do precisely that. A vision with maximum public appeal emerges when our post-carbon society also includes a comprehensive plan to tackle poverty, a bold national affordable housing strategy that ends homelessness, a commitment to living wages and the introduction of the next generation of social programs: universal public elder care and child care, public pharmacare and dental care, tuition-free post-secondary education and free public transit – programs that effectively socialize these costs and remove them from the affordability anxieties of families.

Contrary to the view espoused by some climate policy purists, when tackling inequality and the climate emergency are linked, support for bold government action actually increases. In the summer of 2019, as part of research for my book on the climate emergency, I commissioned an extensive national public opinion poll from Abacus Data (one of Canada's leading polling firms). The results were fascinating. The full results of the online poll of 2,000 representative Canadians can be found on the Abacus website.[10] Overall, the results were very hopeful, revealing a Canadian public that is ahead of our politics. A large share of Canadians is already deeply worried about the climate crisis and increasingly ready for bold and ambitious climate actions.

Among the most interesting findings, and highly relevant to discussions of a Green New Deal, are these:

- **The more a bold climate plan is seen as linked to an ambitious plan to tackle inequality, economic insecurity, poverty and job creation, the more likely people are to support it.** People are concerned about climate change, but they are also very worried about inequality and affordability. So, when these social equity issues are tackled as part of a climate action plan, support for bold action to reduce GHG emissions rises dramatically. The poll listed five policy actions that could help with the transition, including extending income and employment supports to those more vulnerable during the transition, and increasing taxes on the wealthy and corporations to help pay for the transition. It asked people if such policies would make them more or less supportive of bold and ambitious climate actions. Those five policy options and the responses are shown in the accompanying chart (see Figure 18.2). If government provided financial support to low- and modest-income households to help them pay for the transition away from fossil fuels, 79% of people became more supportive of bold climate action. Similarly, if the government increased taxes on the wealthy and corporations to help pay for the transition, 78% of respondents became more supportive of a bold climate plan. And if the government were to commit to a "good jobs guarantee" for current fossil fuel workers – a signal that the government was ready to actively help with a just transition plan for workers – 73% became more supportive of ambitious climate action.

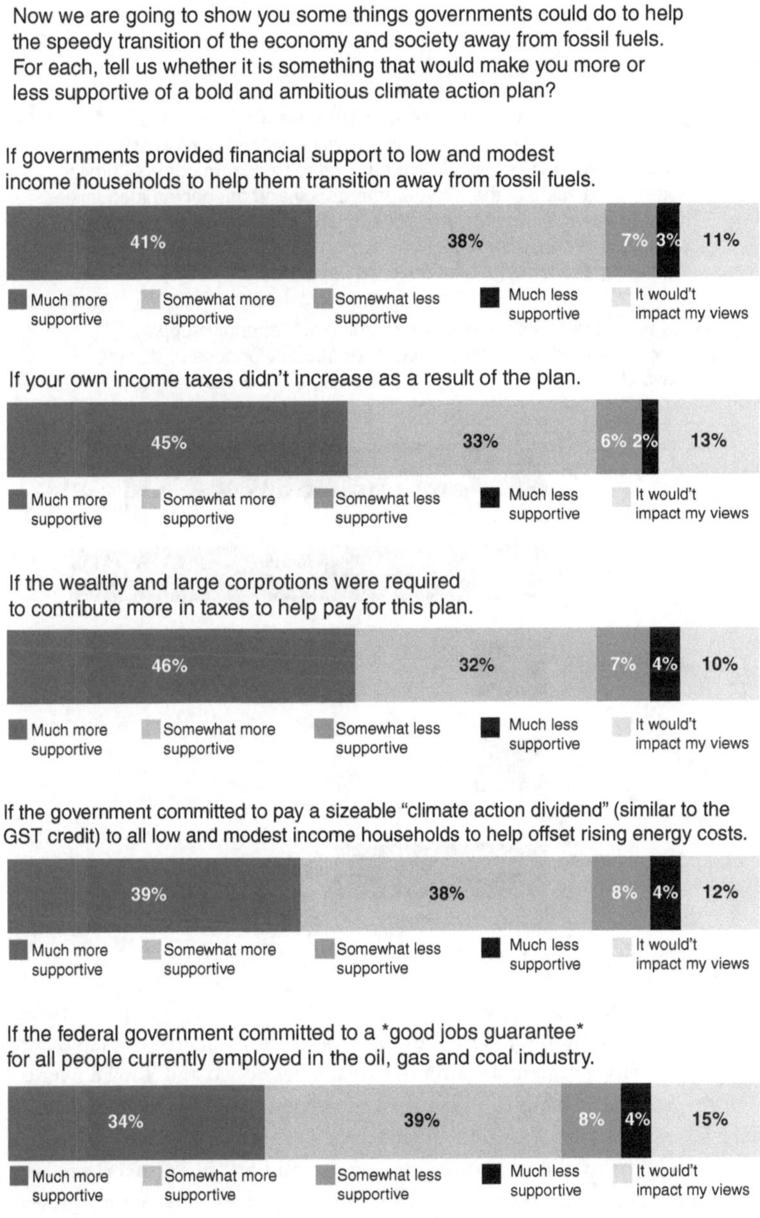

Figure 18.2 Government policies in support of bold climate action

- **Few Canadians had, at the time of the poll, heard of the Green New Deal. But once they learnt about it, they liked it**. Unsurprisingly, only 14% of respondents were certain that they had heard of the Green New Deal (GND), and another 19% thought they might have. However, after being given a short description of the GND (see Figure 18.3), 72% responded that they support the key principles of a Green New Deal.

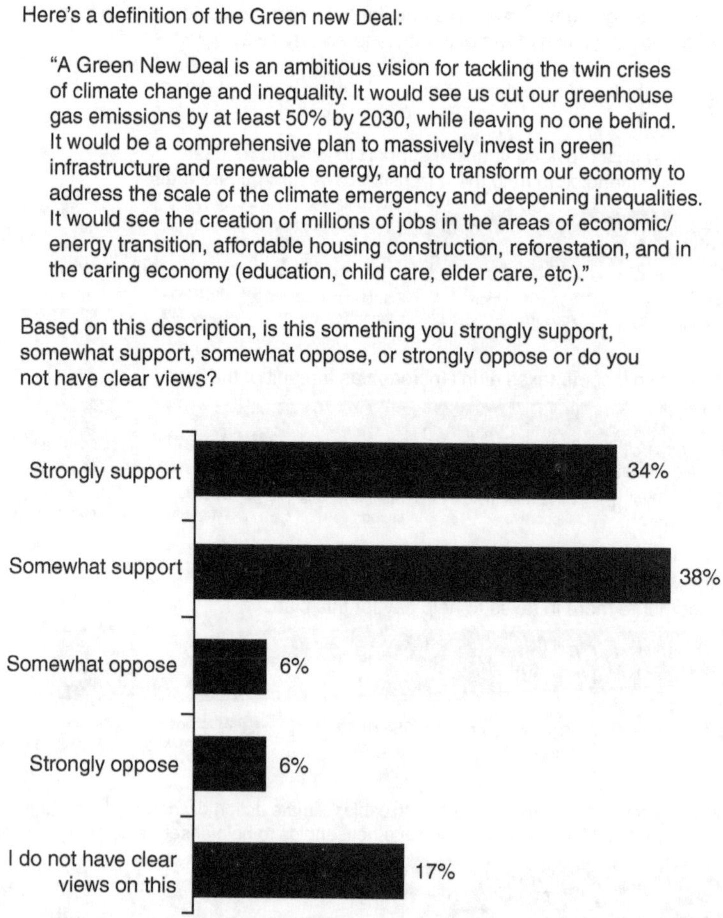

Figure 18.3 Support for a Green New Deal

Some see hopeful climate poll findings like this and worry such positive results will not hold, particularly as income and job insecurity becomes more acute (as it has during the pandemic). Support for environmental action in Canada has ebbed and flowed over the decades, generally in reverse relationship to the state of the economy.

Yet therein lies the solution, and the strength of a GND. The answer is not to treat these concerns separately, or to allow them to forever rise and fall in an inverse relationship, but to link them and tackle them together. A vital dimension to recent opinion research is that, in addition to people's growing concern about climate change, they are also increasingly distressed about affordability, employment security and inequality. The Abacus results show that concern about climate change is very high, second only to concerns about the rising cost of living. A bold climate program then that is tied to fairness, equality and affordability finds maximum resonance and durability, which helps to explain the appeal of the Green New Deal. We can best motivate and rally people with a big and bold transformative program that tackles the twin crises of climate and inequality. That is how we make common cause across class, race and gender.

For years, Canadian public opinion polls have highlighted a paradox: respondents indicate high levels of concern regarding climate change and strong support for policies that would reduce GHG emissions, yet low levels of willingness to personally pay for climate action. But there is no great mystery to this mixed response. It only stands to reason; affordability is a more immediate concern to most people. Hence the powerful need to link these issues. When we do so, the appeal is dramatic, far surpassing the levels of support for any one political party.

Elements of a Canadian Green New Deal

As we prepare to leap into a carbon-free society and economy, it is entirely understandable that many, particularly those whose livelihoods are currently derived from the fossil fuel industry, feel anxious and economically insecure. But the good news is that, as we experienced in the Second World War, the climate mobilization means there are many jobs to be had and a lot of work to be done. The transition requires care and planning, as the jobs of the future will not be all the same jobs in the same places. Nor will most of the new jobs pay as highly as what some in the oil patch have come to expect. But overall, there is every reason to believe that there will be more jobs, and that those jobs will be meaningful, decent, well-paid, and considerably more secure than the jobs in or related to the fossil fuel industry today.

We also need to ensure that those new jobs are complemented by enhanced public services and social supports that result in a better standard of living for all. When we decide as a society to collectively pay for key needs like child care, elder care, post-secondary education, pharmaceutical drugs, dental and eye care, decent pensions, public transit and affordable housing, we are all liberated from a great deal of anxiety about how much our employment pays. In such a rebalancing of what we pay for by ourselves and what we pay for together, many will find more work-life balance, and the fulfilment that comes from more time with family, community, nature, the arts and more.

In my view, an overall plan for economic transformation aligned with the climate emergency needs to include seven core elements.

First, as occurred in the war, we need to conduct a "national needs inventory" of all the items required to electrify everything with renewable power. How many heat pumps will be needed? How many electric buses, cars and trucks? How many electric charging stations and where should they be located? How many solar panels should we install on homes, public buildings and commercial buildings? How many additional solar fields will be needed, and how much power do we need them to generate? How much wind power is needed, and how many turbines will we need to deploy to produce that? Where should tidal and wave power be produced? What is needed to electrify our ferry fleets and our government vehicles? Which communities will be best served by geothermal power, and which neighbourhoods can be serviced by community renewable energy utilities? And so on.

The good news is that many of these core estimates have already been done. Stanford University's Mark Z. Jacobson and his team have not only calculated how every US state can meet its energy needs through renewables (and without relying on new mega hydro dams, new nuclear power, biofuels or carbon capture), but they have also very kindly done so for Canada and 138 other countries. Jacobson's work is both hopeful and practical. For each jurisdiction his team takes on, they meticulously calculate how much energy is needed; how much can be produced by each of wind, water and solar power; how many wind turbines, solar arrays and, to a lesser extent, tidal/wave turbines will be needed; how much it would cost to produce this new power; what materials and land will be needed; and approximately how many jobs will be created producing this new capacity. It's a remarkable body of work, showing that we already have the technological capacity for the world to get to nearly 100%

renewable energy. (There remain some technological challenges to meet the final 5–10% of our energy needs, mainly with respect to air travel, shipping and a few industrial processes, but new technology is quickly coming online to meet these needs too.)[11]

For Canada, Jacobson and his team calculate that 100% renewable energy can be attained by 2050 through a combination of:

- 27.5% onshore wind power;
- 22.9% offshore wind power;
- 14.5% hydro power;
- 9.8% concentrating solar plants;
- 9.1% commercial and government rooftop solar power;
- 6.9% solar plants;
- 5.3% residential solar rooftop power;
- 2.2% from wave devices;
- 1.7% geothermal power; and
- 0.2% tidal turbines.

Were Canada to adopt this plan, Jacobson and his team calculate we would generate 315,138 construction jobs, and 367,889 operating jobs (with each of these jobs representing 40 years of continuous employment). They estimate all this new power generation will require only 0.25% of Canada's land mass. They also contend that overall demand for energy would be 38% less than under status quo conditions, as fossil fuel extraction and combustion is much less efficient than renewable electric technology. And they estimate this energy shift will result in $110 billion in health cost savings (due mainly to reduced air pollution).[12]

Second, informed by the inventory requirements outlined above, and again as occurred in the war, we must coordinate the mass production and deployment of the equipment needed to realize our new GHG reduction targets. We will need factories to produce solar panels, wind turbines, electric heat pumps and electric buses at a mass scale. It is worth appreciating, however, that the technical challenge of such production is far less than building complex planes and warships. And the technology needed already exists. As much as possible, we should seek to manufacture these items domestically. (For a discussion of the challenges of mandating local manufacturing under current trade and investment agreements, see Tucker and Meyer, in this volume.)

Third, we must develop a clear wind-down pathway for all fossil fuel extraction in Canada, guided by a robust just transition plan for existing fossil fuel workers and communities that currently rely on these industries.

An essential starting point is to declare that there will be no *new* fossil fuel infrastructure. While we have two to three decades to wind down the fossil fuel industry, it makes no economic or ecological sense to spend billions of dollars on new projects, particularly when that infrastructure has a working lifespan and expected financial returns that well exceed 30 years. Decisions we make today about infrastructure such as pipelines and new processing plants matter greatly because they tend to lock in place a certain development path. If we know we need to set out on a path toward fossil fuel wind-down, then the time is past to be investing in new infrastructure that supports ramp-up.

Fourth, in place of fossil fuel infrastructure, we need to develop a massive green public infrastructure plan involving all levels of government. We need to invest billions of dollars in renewable energy, building retrofits, high-speed rail, mass public transit, electric vehicle charging stations and methane capture from farms and landfills. And we need it at a scale well beyond what any political party has campaigned on to date. This would represent the foundation of a wartime-level employment plan.

And because even under the best-case scenario a certain amount of global warming is already locked in, we also now need to undertake major investments in climate adaptation and resilience infrastructure, with a focus on ensuring that vulnerable communities are better protected from climate disasters and related events (extreme weather events, forest fires, extreme heat events, flooding, etc.). For example, we need to construct and reinforce dykes that threaten vulnerable communities. And we need to significantly invest in forest management that will lessen wildfire risks to rural and Indigenous communities, while providing thousands of sustainable jobs in resource-based communities.

Fifth, we need a large-scale program to repair and enhance Canada's natural climate sequestration systems – helping nature suck carbon from the atmosphere. That includes an extensive reforestation program, and of course the preservation of existing old-growth forests (the world's intact forests, of which Canada is home to a large share, represent a vital element of slowing climate change (Wieting 2019)). We also need to encourage value-added wood production and building (which locks away carbon), and develop new sources of fibre such as hemp and bamboo (see further discussion of the potential for hemp production in LaDuke, in this volume). There is scope for extensive job creation in this area. We should adopt an ambitious goal, such as planting 5 or10 billion trees (currently, the Trudeau government has committed to plant 2 billion trees over the next ten years).

Sixth, as advocates of a Green New Deal have made clear, we need more than just direct climate infrastructure investments – we also need large-scale investments in social infrastructure and the caring economy if we are to realize the equality goals outlined earlier and keep everyone on the bus. That means investments from all levels of government in zero-carbon public and non-profit housing – a bold commitment to build hundreds of thousands of new units of non-market housing. And it means federal and provincial funding for universal, public, accessible, quality child care and home care for seniors and people with disabilities. These are public services that are already virtually carbon-free and would represent a major enhancement to household affordability.

Seventh and finally, we need to set in law and regulation clear dates by which certain things *must* happen. For example:

- Cutting Canada's GHG emissions by at least 60% by 2030
- Ensuring Canada achieves net-zero GHG emissions by 2050. (These first two targets require interim benchmarks that must be hit along the way, and we should establish rolling and declining three-year carbon budgets for the country, each province and major industrial sectors to ensure we stay on a pathway to meet our targets.)
- Banning the sale of all new fossil fuel-combustion vehicles by 2025.
- Phasing out the business licenses of conventional gas stations, with all of them expired by 2040 (unless they have converted to electric-vehicle charging stations).
- Prohibiting the use of natural gas or any other fossil fuel in all new buildings by 2022.
- Regulating that, by 2025, if a furnace or boiler needs to be replaced in any type of building of any age, it cannot be legally replaced with a fossil-fuel-fired unit.
- Cutting off *all* natural gas (and any other fossil fuels) to homes and buildings by 2040. Meaning, by this date, all pre-2022 buildings will need to have been retrofitted so they are no longer using a fossil fuel heating or energy source. This is important, because more than half the existing stock of buildings today will still be standing in 2050, when

the IPCC says we must be off fossil fuels entirely. Given this, energy retrofits cannot be voluntary by this point – they need to be mandated.
- Ending the use of all fossil fuels for electricity generation by 2030. Canada is already on track to do this for coal-generated power, but this must also be extended to natural gas-fired electricity generation. And we need a plan to get all remote and Indigenous communities off diesel-powered electricity.
- Phasing out the use of hydrofluorocarbons, HFCs (a highly potent greenhouse gas), as Europe is doing.
- Ending the extraction and export of all fossil fuels by 2050, if not 2040.

Clear targets such as these – embedded in law and well publicized – will send a much stronger signal to the market than any form of carbon pricing. They communicate to businesses and consumers that they must reorient their plans accordingly. If effectively enforced, these targets will push manufactures, builders, installers and extraction companies to make investment plans that align with these dates. What are now small industries (such as electric heat pump or geothermal installers) will quickly scale up to meet the demands that will result from such regulations. Many low- and middle-income families will need financial help to get their homes off fossil fuels, and that must be part of a just transition plan.

The challenges of Canadian federalism

In Canada, climate mobilization is additionally complicated by the realities of Canadian confederation, but once again, a robust Green New Deal could help bridge the divides. Progress on any number of files needs support and cooperation from the provinces and territories. Natural resource policy falls, for the most part, under provincial jurisdiction in Canada's constitution (Indigenous rights and title aside). And at any given time, provincial leaders may seek to make political hay by picking a fight with the federal government. Were Canada a unitary state, acting in the face of an emergency might be easier. For better or worse, we are not. Indeed, Canada is arguably one of the most decentralized federations in the world.

The oil and gas industry's importance to the overall Canadian economy is often overstated. The industry represents 8–9% of Canada's GDP, and only about 1.5% of national employment[13] (the gap between these two statistics gives some indication of how capital-intensive the industry is, and how much of our oil and gas is exported in low-value, unprocessed form). From a trade perspective, oil and gas account for about 5% of the total value of Canada's exports.[14] But as many economists have noted over the years (Vallée and Bimenyamana 2011), oil and gas exports are a double-edged sword – they inflate the value of the Canadian dollar, thereby hurting the competitiveness of other non-energy exports. These numbers should provide reasonable confidence that we can plan for a two- to three-decade wind down of the industry.

But while the overall Canadian economy is not highly dependent on the extraction and export of fossil fuels, the same is not true of certain regions, notably the provinces of Alberta and Saskatchewan, but also northeastern British Columbia and parts of Atlantic Canada.

In Alberta, for example, fossil fuels are the single-largest sector of the provincial economy, accounting for 31–34% of provincial GDP in recent years and employing over 160,000 people (or about 7% of total provincial employment). In Saskatchewan, fossil fuels represent 21–23% of provincial GDP and just under 3% of employment. In Newfoundland and Labrador, now home to a massive offshore industry, oil and gas is responsible for about 25% of the province's GDP and about 3% of their employment. And while oil and gas represent only between 1 and 2% of British Columbia's employment, in northeastern B.C., the sector is of much greater significance, representing about 9% of regional employment.[15]

Almost 40% of Canada's GHG emissions are from Alberta[16] (a staggering reality), and thus, climate action needs Alberta. Given this, I have proposed that as part of a Canadian Green New Deal, we should institute a new federal transfer program to the provinces – a Climate Emergency Just Transition Transfer. Such a transfer could be specifically linked to funding green infrastructure projects that would create thousands of jobs, along with training and/or apprenticeships. It could be a mechanism to renew confederation while rising to the climate crisis.

The transfer's distribution could be based on a formula linked to recent GHG emissions in each province (but fixed from that point onward, so that it does not perversely incentivize continued high GHGs). Doing so would recognize that jurisdictions such as Alberta, Saskatchewan and Newfoundland and Labrador face a more challenging task and will have to do more of the heavy lifting to transition their local economies. As Alberta currently produces about 40% of Canada's GHG emissions, it would receive about 40% of the transfer money. Alternatively, the formula could be linked to how many people are currently employed in the oil and gas sector; again, the bulk of the support would go to the regions where it is most needed.

Rather than this transfer money being handed over to provincial governments, however, I recommend the establishment of new just-transition agencies – one in each province – jointly governed by the federal government, provincial and local governments, and, vitally, Indigenous nations from each province, with civil society representatives too from labour, business and academia/NGOs. This would ensure the transfer money isn't simply absorbed into provincial budgets or used to displace other infrastructure or training funds. It would ensure the money is used for its intended purpose. There are already models for a joint structure like this in Canada, such as the Port Authorities.

There is a long list of worthwhile projects such a transfer could fund. The key is that this transfer would represent *real* dollars for *actual* transition and new jobs (not vague assurances and the historic false promises of just transition). It could include a good job guarantee for energy workers. There should be other conditions tied to the transfer: ending fossil fuel subsidies; minimum apprenticeship placements for women and Indigenous People; minimum royalty rates charged to fossil fuel companies; and no new fossil fuel infrastructure. It could also, over time, be tied to demonstrated reductions in GHGs. An innovation such as this could be a linchpin within an overall transition plan that is fair and just.

New crown corporations: Let's get this done!

In Canada, given our continued membership in the British Commonwealth, federal and provincial public enterprises are known as *crown corporations*. There is a long legacy of these enterprises in the story of Canada's economic development, although in more recent decades, like elsewhere, the dominant story has been of privatization.

Sadly, contemporary Canadian social democratic governments have been disinclined to consider forming new crown corporations in order to respond to modern-day emergencies. The same is not true for social democratic parties elsewhere, which in some cases (such as the UK Labour Party) are not only re-embracing the need for state enterprise but are reimagining what modern public ownership can look like and how it could be more democratically and locally governed (McDonnell and Wainwright 2018).

A central dilemma facing transition is that oil and gas companies continue to put billions of dollars on the table for new fossil fuel infrastructure (pipelines, oil sands projects, liquified natural gas plants), while investment in new economy infrastructure on the scale required has not been forthcoming (notwithstanding the fact that the jobs produced per dollar invested in renewables, public transit and building retrofits exceed those in oil and gas). How then might public enterprise (at all levels of government), or Indigenous development corporations, or worker or community cooperatives, or social enterprises help to break this logjam?

Amazingly, during the Second World War, in order to expedite wartime production, the Canadian government established 28 crown corporations. This history leads one to ask: what might a new generation of crown corporations be today, as we seek to expedite rapid decarbonization?

First, recall some of the reasons *why* Canada's leaders during the Second World War and other times past felt the need for public corporations:[17]

- To secure supply chains for needed production, while also gaining the cost benefits that come from bulk purchasing some inputs or from the economies of scale that come from mass production.
- To ensure a public competitor operates within core sectors, to keep the private players honest and prices/costs down, and to avoid profiteering in the face of an emergency.
- To develop a technology that the private sector either won't or cannot develop, perhaps because the endeavour is too risky or costly or sensitive or short-term.
- To provide a good or service that the private sector won't because there is not enough profit to be made, or to ensure that the good or service will be universally provided at an affordable price.
- To ensure that needed technology is made widely available, rather than tightly held as a private proprietary asset for the purposes of maximum profit.
- To ensure that the public gains maximum return from the development or commercialization of a public resource.
- And lastly, as was certainly the case in the Second World War, to make something happen quickly at a mass scale when the private sector proves unwilling or unable to do so.

Given such considerations, what follows is a list of possible candidates for *new* crown corporations for meeting the climate emergency:

- A federal high-speed rail corporation. The original railroads were foundational to the creation of Canada. Why not keep those of the next-generation public (particularly given the private-sectors apparent disinterest in this prospect given Canada's population densities)? Nationalize a GM auto plant (or others) to expedite the production of electric vehicles, with a focus on electric vans, trucks and buses to replace public and commercial fleets.
- Renewable energy corporations, likely in every province, that focus both on building large-scale renewable projects (solar fields, wind farms, wave/tidal power generation and neighbourhood geothermal/heat exchange systems) and on the widespread installation of solar and geothermal systems at the individual building level. Much like the development of large hydro dams in Canada's past, there is a logic to doing this work

publicly. These projects will frequently require public land. And, starkly different from oil and gas, once a project is built, the energy itself is free. Nature, in its bountiful generosity, provides the sun's rays and the wind and the warmth of the earth, day after day, at no monthly charge to the user, making these activities less attractive to massive for-profit corporations. Oil has produced the most profitable corporations on the planet. That's never going to happen with solar.

- New municipal and/or provincial public corporations focussed on the mass installation of electric heat-pumps. This would simplify what is currently a very complicated exercise for many homeowners, keep the price down by bulk purchasing/importing heat pumps and eliminate profit margins from the installation work.
- If the mass importation of heat pumps proves too challenging or costly, then consider a new crown corporation to manufacture heat pumps for the millions of homes and buildings across Canada. Most electricity utilities in Canada are already public, so this could be undertaken by new subsidiary of the country's existing crown utilities.
- Similarly, if we no longer wish to import most solar panels and wind turbines, then we should consider new crown corporations that would mass produce them in Canada.
- A crown corporation to expedite the development, manufacture and deployment of new non-fossil fuel agricultural equipment (freeing farmers from the costs of oil). Given how well the management of food production worked during the war for both consumers and farmers, Canada should restore and expand the use of public supply management boards (jointly governed with farmers and communities).
- Federal and/or provincial crown corporations to oversee the decommissioning of abandoned oil and gas wells and mines, funded by the oil and gas industry – an activity that could employ thousands in Alberta and Saskatchewan, as the group Reclaim Alberta has documented.[18]
- New public housing development corporations focussed on building low-income carbon-zero homes.
- New building retrofit corporations, staffed with an army of expert tradespeople who can advise both residential and commercial owners on the best way to maximize their building's energy efficiency, without fear of getting fleeced, and then ensure the work gets done.
- A new crown corporation to coordinate waste re-use. Given the crisis and market failures in the global recycling market, and understanding that so much of what we call "waste" is in fact a resource that has already been semi-processed, a crown agency could oversee the deconstruction (as opposed to the demolition) of buildings and the collection of other reusable items, and then direct these resources to various remanufactures. Where no local remanufactures exist, the corporation could seek to establish them (Lee, Maxwell, Legg and Rees 2013).
- New provincial and/or federal crown corporations to undertake mass reforestation and forest revitalization.
- A "Right to Repair" crown corporation that would allow consumers (including farmers) to open and repair consumer goods, combined with a national network of neighbourhood repair centres staffed with skilled technicians who can fix electronics and other household items. Such centres could even spearhead the use of 3D printing for replacement parts.
- A new crown corporation to develop and produce an alternative to asphalt, using recycled plastic, as some companies have already done in other countries.[19]

- The 350.org Our Time initiative proposed a "No-Crown Corporation," an Indigenous-run project to end all boil-water advisories in a single year, while upgrading every Indigenous community across the land to 100% renewable energy by year two.
- A new public steel manufacturer, using innovative electric arc furnaces. Right now, Canada exports most of the metals we recycle, as well as the metallurgic coal we mine that is used for steel production overseas. A crown corporation in this field could innovatively combine the metals we recycle with some modest amount of mined metallurgic coal to produce steel in Canada, and could, as occurred in the war, ensure that steel resources are deployed to manufacture the goods we need for the transition – electric buses, new rail lines, bikes, wind turbines, etc.
- A crown corporation to coordinate the mass production of non-methane plant-based protein foods (Bartels 2001).
- A labour market matchmaking corporation to assist with just transition – a public agency that would link current fossil fuel employees and other workers with the green jobs in the above corporations and building new climate and social infrastructure.

There are, no doubt, more possibilities worthy of consideration. The point is simply this: if something that needs to happen isn't happening through the market at the scale and speed that the emergency requires, then – through our governments – we can and should do it ourselves.

In some cases, it will make more sense for "public" or "collective" ownership of a new enterprise to be at the municipal level, the Indigenous nation level, or in some other non-profit or social enterprise form. For example, Aki Energy is an Indigenous social enterprise that installs geothermal heating in northern Manitoba communities (working in partnership with the larger Manitoba Hydro crown corporation; Fernandez 2016).

Governments could also use either existing or new crown corporations to support fossil-fuel-dependent communities going through transition. If a community reliant on fossil fuels, like a coal town, is facing collapse, the government has the power to move a crown corporation or agency there, as an anchor employer, so people can stay and their home values are sustained.

Sadly, thus far, the Trudeau government has seen fit to establish only two new crown corporations during its time in office – the Canada Infrastructure Bank, a vehicle for effectively privatizing the building and operating of public infrastructure, and the Trans Mountain Corporation, the agency established in 2018 so that the government, on our collective behalf, could purchase the aging oil pipeline from Texas-based Kinder Morgan and then build the expansion project that will triple the volume of bitumen carried from the oil sands to Metro Vancouver (Tienhaara and Walker forthcoming).

GND job creation and just transition

The job creation potential of a GND is immense, if and when we marshal green and social infrastructure investments at the scale envisioned. The number of jobs created per dollar invested in these sectors far outstrips the fossil fuel industry (Garrett-Peltier 2017). That's mainly because the latter is so capital-intensive, whereas the alternatives are more labour-intensive. This is especially true for public services and the caring economy – to state the obvious, services are delivered by people. As economist Marjorie Griffin Cohen notes, these service and caring jobs – more often done by women – are just as much a part of the "real" economy as goods-producing ones are, and "the huge growth in the services sectors of advanced industrial nations indicates that real prosperity may not be tied, ultimately, to manufacturing and resource extraction" (Cohen 2017, 306). Similarly, zero-waste management, agriculture, value-added forestry, energy efficiency work such as building retrofits, and construction work building new low-income housing are all more labour-intensive than fossil fuel extraction and processing. The comparative job-creation can be seen in the accompanying chart (see Figure 18.4).

"So, when people tell you that the GND will hurt workers, set them straight," insisted Avi Lewis at a GND townhall in the summer of 2019. "Tell them that the Green New Deal is a job program of epic proportions."

That said, as noted earlier, while true climate mobilization surely means a net increase in jobs, the jobs of the future will not be all the same jobs in the same places. And thus, care and planning are needed to ensure a just transition.

The notion of just transition, however, should be understood as bigger than the issue of support for individual workers in industries we seek to wind down. Shannon Daub, British Columbia director of the Canadian Centre for Policy Alternatives and co-director of the Corporate Mapping Project (an academic alliance tracking the power and influence of the fossil fuel industry in Canada), proposes three levels of just transition.[20] First, at an individual worker level, it captures issues such as income support, early retirement, training and education, relocation costs, counselling and, ideally, help finding new "green jobs" in the renewable economy or other industries. Second, at a community level, it can address issues such as economic diversification for communities that have been heavily reliant on one industry such as fossil fuels, the recruitment of new industries and employers, and green infrastructure and renewable energy projects. Third, at the macro level, just transition captures broader issues of climate justice and the transition to a post-fossil fuel economy, decolonization and Indigenous rights, particularly for Indigenous communities that have been harmed by fossil fuel extraction, tackling inequalities in the labour market, particularly between traditionally male-oriented versus female-oriented jobs, and energy democracy, meaning who owns and controls energy resources and infrastructure. A truly just transition plan would see us address all these dimensions.

Drawing upon on the work of the Canadian Centre for Policy Alternatives, and based on past Canadian experiences with industrial transitions, here are what I believe should constitute core government commitments at the heart of a robust just transition plan:

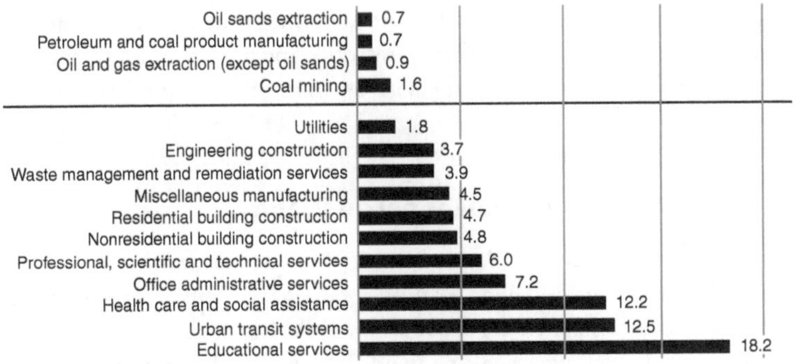

Figure 18.4 Direct jobs per $1 million of output (Canada, 2016)

Source: Statistics Canada: Tables 36-10-0594-01 and 36-10-0013-01.

- Massive public investment in new green and social infrastructure, as outlined above.
- A "Good Jobs Guarantee," not only for workers and communities that currently rely on the fossil fuel sector and for those whose communities have been most harmed by the fossil fuel industry, but for *anyone* who wants employment building the green and social infrastructure we will need. The guarantee should be for well-paid and unionized jobs. This may sound too radical or ambitious. But why? We did it during the war and we can do it again. Moreover, as in the war, our most likely challenge in the coming decades is not going to be finding enough jobs for workers, but rather the reverse – finding enough workers for all the jobs that need doing (for further discussion on the role of a job guarantee, see Robinson, in this volume).
- Given that some will need to retrain and/or relocate for some of those new jobs, the Good Jobs Guarantee should include training commitments (with income support during that time) and relocation allowances. The training should include a renewed focus on apprenticeship programs, with minimum quotas for women, Indigenous People and other underrepresented groups in the building trades that will be most in demand.
- Early retirement bridge financing for older workers whose jobs in the fossil fuel sector are lost.
- Community transition support will also be needed and, arguably, is often more necessary that individual transition supports. Most current fossil fuel workers will retire over the next 20–30 years, in line with the wind-down period, and those still too young to retire have transferable skills. Given this, just transition requires specific supports and new opportunities for small and rural communities that are currently highly reliant on the fossil fuel sector. This could mean the government buying out homes that lose their value, but preferably it would mean locating major anchor employers in these communities (either crown corporations or enticing other employers). Our governments should seek to foster renewable energy projects, value-added forestry ventures and sustainable agriculture growth in smaller and rural communities so that people see local options beyond the fossil fuel sector.
- Generous income transfers – a "Climate Action Dividend" – for *all* low- and middle-income households to offset transition costs and rising energy prices. These should come in the form of a refundable tax credit, so that cheques go to all who qualify regardless of how much tax they pay. And the Climate Action Dividend should have a long phase-out tail, so that most in the middle class receive at least some benefit.
- In addition to the Climate Action Dividend (which will likely need to be provided for at least a couple decades), low- and middle-income homeowners should be provided with one-time rebates for home energy retrofits and fuel-switching their homes and appliances (such as furnaces and stoves). A separate program will be needed to offset these costs in rental properties.

Canada is not an island

Canada's population is relatively small, yet we have punched above our weight before – we certainly did in the Second World War – and we can again. This lesson applies at multiple levels as we confront the climate emergency. First, while Canada's domestic GHG emissions may be small at a global level, we are also a major international exporter of fossil fuels. Second, in addition to taking climate action at home, Canada must embrace our responsibilities to the rest of the world. Our per capita GHG emissions are among the highest in the world,[21] and we are one of the world's wealthiest countries. Given this, it is incumbent on Canada to substantially boost our financial transfers to poorer countries, particularly in those regions hardest hit by the climate crisis and extreme weather. This is not a matter of charity, but of necessity and justice. Third, we must make right one of the most shameful chapters of Canada's Second World War legacy – the response to refugees. Before, during and after the war, Canada refused to open its doors to people fleeing persecution, particularly Jews seeking to escape Nazi-occupied Europe. In the coming decades, the crises of people displaced by climate impacts will surely be a defining issue. This time, we need to act with honour.

Paying for a GND

In a society as wealthy as Canada's we can absolutely afford to dramatically boost our public spending. We have the capacity to spend billions more each year on both operating programs and capital/infrastructure investments to meet the climate emergency head-on and make real the vision of a made-in-Canada Green New Deal. The 2008–2009 financial crisis laid bare just how much money the national governments of Canada, the US, the UK and others were quickly able to muster when hundreds of billions were needed to bail out the banks and auto companies, and to pump liquidity into the economy. The response to the COVID-19 pandemic even more so. But the wealth of our country is currently very unevenly shared. According to the CCPA's David Macdonald (2018), the richest 87 families in Canada have the same combined wealth as everyone living in Newfoundland and Labrador, New Brunswick and PEI combined.

How much per year should Canada be spending on tackling the climate emergency? The path-breaking 2006 *Stern Review of the Economics of Climate Change* (commissioned by the then UK government and headed by former World Bank chief economist Nicholas Stern), recommended that governments spend 1% of their respective GDP on climate mitigation investments, although two years later Stern boosted that recommended target to 2% given evidence of accelerating climate change (Jowit and Wintour 2008).

In either scenario, this is certainly a much lower share of GDP than Canada or other Allied nations spent on the war effort. For Canada, with an annual GDP currently of about $2.4 trillion, a target of 2% of GDP would mean our governments joining forces to spend approximately $48 billion a year on green infrastructure and climate action. In fact, we should spend more, given Canada's comparative wealth and disproportionate role in historic GHG emissions, with an additional sum directed toward financial assistance for climate mitigation and adaptation in poorer countries.

Achieving such investment and spending levels is well within our means, given the political will. Yet so far, no political party in Canada has proposed spending anything close to this, even in the context of a post-COVID just recovery.

If we add into the mix investments to tackle the urgent needs of Indigenous communities, the housing crisis, instituting public child care, transforming public health care, ending post-secondary tuition and other spending related to a Green New Deal, the target should be well higher than the Stern recommendation, something closer to $100 billion a year – an amount that would jolt a transformative leap into a new and more caring post-carbon economy. That sounds like a lot, and it is. It represents an increase in overall federal spending of about 25%. But to put that into perspective, in an economy such as Canada's, with an annual GDP of $2.4 *trillion*, a bold spending and investment plan of $100 billion represents a little more than 4% of GDP. That's significant, but still pales in comparison to what we did in the war years. And as we did then, Canada should raise the needed revenues to confront the climate emergency with a combination of borrowing and new taxes and other revenues.

Conclusion

The approach Canada has been taking with respect to the climate crisis for the last 30 years is, quite simply, not working. Canada's GHG emissions have only flatlined since the year 2000 – they are not going down. Our emissions in the year 2018 (the last year for which we have statistics at the time of writing) were almost exactly where they were in the year 2000.[22] We are not on a path to stave off a horrific future for our children and future generations. We have run out the clock with distracting debates about incremental changes. But where it matters most – actual GHG emissions – we have accomplished precious little. And so, a new approach is needed.

A Canadian Green New Deal – undertaken at "wartime scale" – is how we can truly make "common cause" as we rally in the face of the climate emergency. Its framework for linking climate action with tackling inequality and economic insecurity is vital if those who currently feel tied to the fossil fuel economy are to be prepared to leap into the next one.

As I write, the world has been struck by a pandemic crisis that has pushed the climate emergency, for now at least, off the front pages. But the emergency response to the pandemic has also reminded us all of how quickly society, our politics and the economy can pivot, when we truly see emergencies for what they are.

There is a key difference, however, between the wartime and climate crises, on the one hand, and the coronavirus pandemic on the other. The war effort and climate mobilization demand that we get out and build what was/is required for the transition, while the pandemic has obliged us to stay home. Consequently, whereas the war and climate action were and can be a boost to the economy and job creation, the COVID-19 crisis represents a massive hit to both. The fact that bold climate action is a positive on these fronts, however, is welcome news; just as the Second World War ended the Great Depression, as we rebuild from this pandemic, an ambitious climate plan with massive green infrastructure spending – the Green New Deal – can be just what the doctor ordered.

Here in Canada, the COVID-19 pandemic has reaffirmed the role and value of ambitious government action. It has reminded us of our mutual reliance. Social solidarity and support for public services is likely at a generational high. There is a new spirit of national cooperation in the land upon which we must now capitalize. The public emerges from the COVID-19 crisis with new respect for scientists and scientific evidence. We collectively now understand that the more our economy is localized, the more resilient we are to disruptions. The economy now urgently requires public investment to rebuild from the pandemic. Combine all these new realities, and the time has never been more opportune for true climate emergency mobilization.

Notes

1 For more on 350.org Canada's Our Time initiative, see: https://our-time.ca/

2 350.org Canada email to supporters, February 20, 2019.

3 "Cutting Classes to Stop Climate Change: Young Canadian Strike for the Planet," *CBC Radio's Day 6*, February 1, 2019, https://www.cbc.ca/amp/1.5001974.

4 According to Catherine Abreu of Climate Action Network Canada, about 20% of renewable energy projects in Canada are Indigenous. For example, an Indigenous social enterprise in Manitoba, Aki Energy, has been engaged in geothermal installations in northern First Nations communities since 2012. The T'Sou-ke First Nation on southern Vancouver Island was among the first Indigenous nations to undertake a large solar project, developing a three-pronged initiative in 2009 that includes a 75 kilowatt solar system (feeding excess power into the BC Hydro grid when it's not needed locally), 40 solar hot-water systems in member residences, and an energy

conservation program (see http://www.tsoukenation.com/first-nation-takes-lead-on-solar-power/). In October 2019, the Tsilhqot'in Nation cut the ribbon on the largest solar farm in B.C., a 1.25 megawatt solar farm that is wholly developed, built, owned and operated by the Tsilhqot'in Nation (see http://www.tsilhqotin.ca/Portals/0/PDFs/Press). Cree climate activist Melina Laboucan-Massimo hosts a 13-part documentary series called *Power to the People*, on the Aboriginal Peoples Television Network (APTN), which profiles more such initiatives.

5 See https://actionnetwork.org/petitions/call-for-emergency-climate-justice-plan

6 Interview with the author, Vancouver, March 19, 2019.

7 For more on this action, see: https://our-time.ca/lead/

8 For more on the Just Recovery principles and coalition, see: https://justrecoveryforall.ca/#principles

9 See: https://www.toronto350.org/just_recovery_principles_launched

10 Abacus conducted this national survey of 2,000 people between July 16 and 19, 2019. A random sample of panelists were invited to complete the survey online from a set of partner panels based on the Lucid exchange platform. The margin of error for a comparable probability-based random sample of the same size is +/– 2.19%, 19 times out of 20. The data were weighted according to census data to ensure that the sample matched Canada's population according to age, gender, educational attainment and region. The full public results from the poll can be found on the Abacus website at https://abacusdata.ca/wp-content/uploads/2019/08/Climate-Emergency-Polling-July-2019-RELEASE.pdf.

11 For more on Jacobson's work, see The Solutions Project (co-founded by Jacobson) website: https://thesolutionsproject.org/

12 The Solutions Project roadmap for Canada to reach 100% renewable energy by 2050 can be found at: https://thesolutionsproject.org/why-clean-energy/#/map/countries/location/CAN

13 Author's calculations, based on Statistics Canada, Table 36-10-0402-01 and 2016 Census, Catalogue Number 98-400-X2016290

14 Author's calculations, based on Statistics Canada, Table 12-10-0092-01.

15 All of the provincial GDP and employment data are author's calculations, based on Statistics Canada, Table 36-10-0402-01 and 2016 Census, Catalogue Number 98-400-X2016290.

16 Environment and Climate Change Canada, Tables IPCC Sector Canada.

17 I offer a history of Canada's WWII crown corporations in my book *A Good War: Mobilizing Canada for the Climate Emergency* (Toronto: ECW Press, 2020). Further, for an excellent history of crown corporations in Canada, see Linda McQuaig's *The Sport and Prey of Capitalists: How the Rich Are Stealing Canada's Public Wealth* (Toronto: Dundurn Publishers, 2019).

18 For more on the work of Reclaim Alberta, see: http://www.reclaimalberta.ca/

19 For more on this alternative, see: https://science.howstuffworks.com/recycled-plastic-waste-creates-roads.htm

20 From a presentation by Shannon Daub at a Just Transition workshop hosted by the Parkland Institute, Edmonton Alberta, June 2019.

21 For the latest GHG data and global rankings, see the World Resources Institute site at https://www.wri.org/blog/2014/11/6-graphs-explain-world-s-top-10-emitters

22 Environment and Climate Change Canada, Tables IPCC Sector Canada.

References

Bartels, D. 2001. Wartime Mobilization to Counter Severe Global Climate Change. *Human Ecology*. 10(January).

Cohen, M.G. 2017. Using Information About Gender and Climate Change to Inform Green Economic Policies. In: M.G. Cohen, ed. *Climate Change and Gender in Rich Countries: Work, Public Policy and Action*. New York: Routledge.

Fernandez, L. 2016. *How Government Support for Social Enterprise Can Reduce Poverty and Greenhouse Gases*. Winnipeg: Canadian Centre for Policy Alternatives.

Garrett-Peltier, H. 2017. Green Versus Brown: Comparing the Employment Impacts of Energy Efficiency, Renewable Energy, and Fossil Fuels Using an Input-Output Model. *Economic Modelling*. 61(February), 439–447.

Granatstein, J.L. 2005. *Arming the Nation: Canada's Industrial War Effort, 1939–1945*. Ottawa: Canadian Council of Chief Executives.

Jowit, J. and Wintour, P. 2008. Cost of Tackling Global Climate Change has Doubled, Warns Stern. *The Guardian*. 26 June.
Klein, S. 2020. *A Good War: Mobilizing Canada for the Climate Emergency*. Toronto: ECW Press.
Lee, M. and Card, A. 2011. *Who Occupies the Sky? The Distribution of GHGs in Canada*. Ottawa: Canadian Centre for Policy Alternatives.
Lee, M., Maxwell, S., Legg, R. and Rees, W. 2013. *Closing the Loop: Reducing Greenhouse Gas Emissions Through Zero Waste in BC*. Vancouver: Canadian Centre for Policy Alternatives.
MacDonald, D. 2018. *Born to Win: Wealth Concentration in Canada Since 1999*. Ottawa: Canadian Centre for Policy Alternatives.
McDonnell, J. and Wainwright, H. 2018. The New Economics of Labour. *Open Democracy*. 25 February.
McQuaig, L. 2019. *The Sport and Prey of Capitalists: How the Rich Are Stealing Canada's Public Wealth*. Toronto: Dundurn Publishers.
Stern, N. 2006. *Stern Review of the Economics of Climate Change*. Cambridge: Cambridge University Press.
Thomas-Müller, C. 2018. Canada Needs Its Own Green New Deal. Here's What It Could Look Like. *National Observer*. 29 November.
Tienhaara, K. and Walker, J. 2021. Fossil Capital, 'Unquantifiable Risk' and Neoliberal Nationalizations: The Case of the Trans Mountain Pipeline in Canada. *Geoforum*. 124, 120–131.
Vallée, L. and Bimenyimana, C. 2011.Curing the Dutch Disease in Canada. *Policy Options*. 1 November.
Wiedmann, T. et al. 2020. Scientists' Warning on Affluence. *Nature Communications*. 19 June.
Wieting, J. 2019. *Clearcut Carbon*. Victoria: Sierra Club of BC.
Wilkinson, R. and Pickett, K. 2009. *The Spirit Level: Why More Equal Societies Almost Always Do Better*. London; New York: Allen Lane.

19

CITIES AND THE GREEN NEW DEAL

Addressing the financialization of urban production

Christopher W. Gibson

Introduction

Mobilizing resources to combat and adapt to the effects of climate change will require coordination of all levels of government. In general, national governments receive the bulk of attention by commentators, press outlets, and analysts as lawmakers debate and discuss proposals and legislation. Adding to the noise in the discourse, environmental reform faces fierce opposition, including from certain elected officials, representatives of industries, and a network of activist organizations. While the upper levels of governments – like the US Congress – are most often pointed out as being responsible for climate policy, local levels of government, particularly cities and special districts, have major roles to play in bringing about and enacting major institutional reforms. These include the types of reforms proposed in the Green New Deal (GND) put forth in the US House of Representatives, and similar GND packages proposed in other countries. In short, the national governments may establish broadly applicable plans through legislation, but cities and special districts are responsible for the day-to-day efforts that carry out such plans. This includes the administration of complex and diverse financial arrangements and relationships that underpin the raising of capital and the allocation of state funds. Therefore, I argue in this chapter for a focus on municipal governance that accounts for how the financialization of urban production intersects with environmental governance. The concept of *financialization* describes the increasing influence of financial markets and financial logics throughout society, especially in previously non-financial areas of activity (Epstein 2005; Krippner 2005). *Urban production* refers to the financial systems and circuits underpinning the "design, construction, exploitation, and ownership of the urban built environment" (Halbert and Attuyer 2016). *Urban governance*, a closely related term, refers to the maintenance and decision-making that distributes and allocates resources pertaining to urban production and infrastructures (O'Brien, O'Neill and Pike 2019).

Such a focus on the financialization of urban production and governance can help scholars and policymakers to be mindful of the ways in which financial markets lean on public officials. The weight of this influence is felt by the directors on boards of special governance districts and cities as well as others in decision-making positions in departments of local government. Representatives of financial markets, seeking to maximize the value for investors who hold

DOI: 10.4324/9781003110880-23

municipal bonds, influence even the most well-intended plans toward the interests of financial gains while sacrificing public and social goods. The most prominent of such financial market representatives are the credit rating agencies – Moody's, Standard & Poor's, and Fitch – which effectively function as financial gatekeepers (Sinclair 1994, 2008; Hackworth 2002). By rating the perceived creditworthiness of debt issuers with categorical scales, they determine the cost of and access to financial capital markets (Poon 2012; Carruthers 2013).

My original research to date has focused on the case of water governance in the western US as an illustrative case to understand the effects of financialization on environmental governance. Examples noted in this chapter therefore draw from research on water governance, and I contend that water management shares a great deal with other sectors of public services and utilities, making it an effective case from which many lessons can be drawn regarding urban governance organizations and environmental policy.

Why cities?

Cities and urban spaces are particularly important to any discussion of climate policy (Bulkeley 2010), with local governments having a key role to play in addressing global problems (Bulkeley and Betsill 2003, 2005). To illustrate the point broadly, the majority of the world's population live in cities, rather than rural spaces (United Nations 2019), and this trend is expected to continue with significant consequences for climate change adaptation pathways (Jiang and O'Neill 2017). Furthermore, urban areas create the majority of carbon emissions (Seto et al. 2014; Creutzig et al. 2015), with one study pointing out that the 100 areas with the highest urban emissions generate 18% of global CO_2 emissions (Moran et al. 2018). Thus, cities represent the lived experiences of most of humanity and are a primary contributor to global carbon emissions.

Besides these broad characteristics, there is a multitude of geophysical, social, and economic linkages that center urban spaces in the climate change discussion. For instance, urbanization can increase warming effects and intensify rainfall (IPCC 2020 Summary for Policymakers, A.4.6). Thus, the policies of city officials as well as patterns of development and consumption behaviors, make a unique contribution to climate concerns. Moreover, the expansion of urban spaces can compromise croplands and lead to declining food production within globally integrated food supply chains, while the implementation of urban green infrastructure and expansion management can alleviate climate risks for city residents (IPCC 2020 Summary for Policymakers, A.6.5). Evidence from efforts to model pathways to limit warming to 1.5 degrees Celsius demonstrate unequivocally the need for extensive transitions in "urban systems and infrastructure" (IPCC 2020 Summary for Policymakers, B.7.4).

Cities and their elected leaders have key roles to play in bringing about policy changes, like a GND, at higher levels of government through advocacy and information exchange networks. For instance, the C40 is an organization that brings cities from around the world together to coordinate efforts to achieve the goals of the Paris Agreement. The C40 provides a mechanism to amplify the voices of mayors and bring their city-level perspectives to bear on the global climate agenda. In one instance that highlights how ambitions of local officials can be discordant with actions of the federal government, Mayor Eric Garcetti in Los Angeles, California, announced "Los Angeles' Green New Deal," which seeks to meet the goals of the Paris Agreement and embraces the principles contained in the GND resolution proposed in the US House of Representatives (Office of Los Angeles Mayor Eric Garcetti 2019). In doing so, Garcetti sought to fashion himself as a global leader on climate change action (Roth 2019). Although activist groups criticized the plan for not setting ambitious enough targets, Garcetti's action directly challenged the pro-industry, anti-reform policies and messages contemporaneously coming from the federal government run by the administration of Donald Trump, whose rhetoric on climate change frequently shifts, but has referred to it at times as a "hoax" and "mythical" (Cheung 2020).

Since cities are central to understanding the causes, consequences and solutions to climate change, it is important to interrogate the structures of how cities govern public and social goods and what this means for environmental resources and ecological sustainability. Furthermore, social science research on economic trends in recent decades demonstrates the growing influence of financial markets in previously non-financial areas of social life and public policy (Epstein 2005; Krippner 2005; van der Zwan 2014). The term *financialization* is applied to describe this shift as it manifests in, and creates consequences for, a wide variety of settings including higher education (Eaton et al. 2016), household behaviors (Fligstein and Goldstein 2015), municipal development policies (Pacewicz 2013, 2016), and land ownership and forestry (Gunnoe and Gellert 2011; Gunnoe 2014, 2016) to name a few relevant to governance and the environment.

Accordingly, this chapter seeks to draw lessons from previous research on financialization of urban productions and governance that can inform our expectations, strategies, and research pertaining to GND proposals and environmental reform in general. In this chapter, I first describe the general contours of urban governance organizations and networks and how financing unfolds in this arena. Next, I examine the key concepts of financialization and urban production in greater depth, emphasizing the relevance for sustainability and broad-based environmental reform policies. Thereafter, I discuss case studies of municipalities that illustrate how financial processes can impede action on sustainability and environmental reform, seeking to tell a cautionary tale that calls for attentiveness to the influence of financial market actors and representatives. Finally, I conclude the chapter with a brief discussion emphasizing the role of financialization in shaping socio-environmental relations through the influences historically wielded by financial interests over governance policies and priorities.

Urban governance and finance

Urban governance and public policy implementation occur through a variety of institutional and organizational forms that can overlap in competition and cooperation. Despite the potential for climate change to have drastic worldwide effects on society, throughout domestic and international contexts there is no integrated governance regime to mitigate the effects of climate change or to minimize greenhouse gas emissions. Rather, governance over climate change is best understood as a regime complex (Keohane and Victor 2011). While city governments, water agencies, energy utilities, and other public service providers are not tasked with specifically addressing climate change, I argue that they are important players in the regime complex because their actions and policies have direct implications for the societal response to climate change. Although there is a wide range of geographical variability of institutions and organizations within the regime complex, there are some generalities to urban governance in cities that can help explain how city and regional governance unfolds.

The increasingly fragmented structure of governance organizations is an important consideration. This fragmentation refers to the how public services and goods – i.e., water, sanitation, public transportation, energy, among others – rely on a network of special districts, joint power authorities, regional governments, and various forms of partially public and partially privatized utility systems (Mullin 2009). Each one functions as a fiscally independent organization with costs, revenues, investments and debts.

To illustrate what this can look like in practice, let us consider the delivery of water in a Southern California town that delivers a mix of imported water and locally available water, as is the case with most urban areas in the region. First, the organization closest to the end user, to whom the user pays their water bill, is the local water agency, many of which have the legal structure of a "special district" that is governed by an elected board of directors and is independent of the city government. However, in some cases, the local water agency may be a department of the city government taking direction from elected officials of the city. Next, the local water agency acquires imported water that it distributes from the wholesale agency, Metropolitan Water District of Southern California (MWD). MWD is run by a board of directors comprised of representatives of agencies to whom they sell water. In addition to MWD, most local agencies also work with an agency that manages groundwater withdrawals – another fiscally and politically independent organization. Furthermore, these agencies also coordinate with independent sanitation districts where their duties intersect (with grey water recycling efforts, for instance).

Water delivery is also energy intensive, so these providers share overlapping interests with energy utilities. Some water districts – like MWD, which manages hydroelectric dams – are also energy producers. Additionally, there are independent organizations responsible for multibenefit projects, habitat conservation, public outreach, and other initiatives. For instance, the Santa Ana Watershed Project Authority is a joint power authority, another fiscally independent agency comprised of various stakeholders that addresses water-related issues along the watershed. One could also consider how the consumption of water in Southern California has effects on habitats upstream, like the out-of-balance and declining ecosystems of the San Francisco Bay Delta or the Salton Sea. Work and oversight on these habitat areas is performed and managed by other organizations that are fiscally independent and have unique interests. Ultimately, the end user likely knows little about this extensive web of organizations that exists behind their local municipal water supplier. However, these organizations, and how they are run and financed, are consequential for a range of social and environmental concerns.

The independence and multitudes of governance agencies results in a fragmented organizational landscape containing inefficiencies and problems that are unique to issues commonly associated with public utility pricing like, "the conservation conundrum" (Beecher 2010) or "institutional inertia" that characterizes many public agencies (Brown and Farrelly 2009). Considering that these areas are well-trodden territory, this discussion will focus on the implications of organizational fragmentation and how this interacts with an increasingly financialized economy. Mullin (2009) analyzed fragmented special district governance networks that provide water in California, pointing out, among other issues, that "fragmentation of authority introduces new actors into the policy process who represent multiple political constituencies" (178). This points to the fact that governance organizations have amorphous jurisdictional boundaries that are both incongruent with environmental landscapes and pit multiple constituencies against each other in competition for access to limited financial resources.[1] Abers and Keck demonstrate that one potential solution is the creation of new democratic institutions and arrangements, purposely constructed to address issues of resource management (2013). While new institutions may offer promising pathways to reform, I contend that, within old or new institutions, developing sustainable environmental governance requires an examination of how the current institutions and organizations are funded to understand the role of financial markets in shaping socio-environmental relations through governance organizations.

Public municipal organizations generally manage capital-intensive infrastructure projects and, as a result, they have relatively sophisticated financial operations, especially among the mid-sized to larger special districts and city governments, which easily count annual revenues and expenses in hundreds of millions of US dollars. To understand how financialization intersects with fragmented governance, it is important to consider *how* the costs of governance are paid. There are essentially three ways to pay for things. First, pay-as-you-go (PAYGO) financing refers to paying with cash held by the district and requires no issuance of debt. This is uncommon for many special districts and cities. However, in my research on water districts, I found that some agencies have board members with strong preferences toward conservative financial positions based in ideological distaste for debt accumulation, which ultimately encourages an embrace of PAYGO financing at some smaller-scale organizations.

Second, regional special districts and cities can participate in projects that are funded by higher levels of government, like the state or federal government. However, as Hackworth (2007) points out, the neoliberal turn in urban governance left municipalities with more responsibilities, privatized public assets, and reduced the redistributive elements of the federal government. The early and mid-twentieth century saw the federal government funding many large-scale infrastructure and other projects seeking to deliver broadly relevant public goods, like the Hoover Dam (1931), the GI Bill (1944), the Interstate Highway System (1954), and Title 1 funding of the Elementary and Secondary Education Act (1965). In the current era, projects like these are uncommon, leaving regional governing bodies responsible to contribute greater amounts of funding through their ability to issue municipal debt. Additionally, this trend also encourages greater privatization of governance duties and infrastructure development as the involvement of private firms is necessitated by the lack of investment of public funds.

The third mode of funding is debt. To avoid the challenges associated with saving huge sums of cash to fund projects through PAYGO financing, municipal organizations finance construction, maintenance, and operations by issuing debt in the form of municipal bonds. In the US, public municipal debt has a long history, as bond debt in simple forms has been fundamental for infrastructure projects like roads, bridges, railroads, and ports. Emphasizing the point, *The Wall Street Journal* reports that the first recorded general obligation bond was issued by New York City to build a canal in 1812 (Malanga 2010). However, the deep reliance on revenue-backed debt as opposed to tax-backed debt is relatively new and presents challenges for the administration of public goods and public services. General obligation (GO) bonds refer to debt that is backed by the taxing power of a jurisdiction and must be approved by voters. Revenue bonds, on the other hand, refer to debt that is backed by the future revenues of a municipality (Sbragia 1996).[2] Bonds enable municipalities to avoid paying up front for the costs of capital-intensive infrastructure and incurring immediate expenses that are often untenable for political constituencies. Additionally, GO bonds can also be issued by the state government, and once the line of debt is secured, the state can distribute GO bond proceeds to regional agencies as grants or as low-interest debt. Since revenue bonds are backed by a specific revenue stream – like electricity sales, water revenues, or usage tolls – rather than by the potential to tax, revenue bonds are not subject to voter approval. Revenue bonds typically imply more risk for the investors, rendering the credit ratings of the issuing agency an important piece of information that influences access to capital. Therefore when agencies issue revenue bonds, credit rating agencies look very closely at revenue streams and anything that might compromise steady and predictable revenues, like reduced sales due to climatological realities.

Most significantly, the desire of agencies to obtain the lowest interest rates on borrowed capital creates internal contradictions for the municipal agency. This is formalized through the credit rating agencies whose primary function is to identify the traits that are favored by investors and apply these standards through a system of categorical ranks accompanied by a negative or stable outlook prediction. In short, this financial system leans on agencies to serve the interests of investors through favorable credit ratings, at the expense of serving by following moral principles or technical calculations. For governance organizations, rating agencies issue favorable credit ratings where agencies maximize revenues, minimize costs, have predictable leadership and limited political oversight. This means that ratings suffer when governance organizations reduce consumption of natural resources *(this reduces revenue)*, spend to provide equitable services and invest in decarbonization *(this increases costs)*, are open and responsive to constituencies' democratically expressed concerns *(this can destabilize leadership)*, and are supportive of state and federal regulations to alleviate environmental harms *(this results in greater oversight)*.

For investors, municipal bond ratings simply provide information, but for critics, ratings can upset and undermine democratic politics. Bond ratings give a small group of firms – the three main rating agencies: Moody's, Standard and Poor's, and Fitch – the power to effectively determine the cost of funding public services outside the reach of electoral politics (Goodman 1968; Sinclair 1994, 2008; Appadurai 1996). Even if they strictly adhere to their intended purpose – to signal creditworthiness to the market – this signal may have powerful repercussions for the debt issuers. Moreover, the judgments of rating agencies have been written into regulatory laws of nations, cementing their position as the gatekeepers to capital (Kerwer 2002; King and Sinclair 2003; Thomas 2004; Sinclair 2008; Altman et al. 2011; Carruthers 2013). However, under the current conditions where governance must meet the challenges of adapting to climate change, conserving non-renewable resources, and mitigating our impact on the environment, it is important to analyze how credit ratings not only impact the pocketbooks of citizens and undermine democratic institutions, but also influence our collective impact on the environment.

Credit ratings embody the general commensuration processes that are essential to a variety of social actions (Espeland and Stevens 1998, 2008), distilling qualitative and quantitative information about an organization's creditworthiness into discrete categories that investors use to judge the desirability of an investment. Although it is the dominant tool for investors to manage and interpret financial uncertainties, the credit rating agencies have a questionable track record of predicting risk, especially at important moments like the 2008 financial crisis (Rona-Tas and Hiss 2010; Altman et al. 2011; Carruthers 2013).

Financialization and urban production

Financialization is a concept that broadly describes the increasing influence of financial markets and financially oriented activities in social, economic and political matters occurring in the later decades of the twentieth century (Epstein 2005; Krippner 2005; Foster 2007). Moreover, it is particularly salient for understanding the growing influence of finance in previously non-financial areas of activity (for reviews of the concept see: van der Zwan 2014; Davis and Kim 2015). As the financial sector of the economy grew in size and influence, it came to have significant impacts on urban municipal governance. A primary consideration is that financial actors view public goods and infrastructure as potential streams of revenue to be made into a class of assets – municipal bonds – and rendered tradable on global capital markets (Leyshon and Thrift 2007; Torrance 2008; Halbert and Attuyer 2016; O'Neill 2017). The outcome is that a public service – e.g., providing water, transportation, land management, etc. – is a site of accumulation by holders of private capital, despite maintaining a publicly run structure with the trappings of democratic representation of constituencies. In essence, the financialization of urban governance masks the commodification and privatization of public goods by opening a backdoor for financial interests to secure an undue portion of revenues and use financial gatekeepers to influence the policymaking process.

The neoliberal era beginning in the 1970s created an opening for financial markets to fill a gap created by the retrenchment of economic support from the federal government, as local governments turned to capital markets in need of funding (Sbragia 1996; Hackworth 2007). Neoliberal policies continued hollowing out funding for public services, making a pronounced impact on water supply privatization in the 1990s (Bakker 2010) and increasing the need for public water agencies to turn to private capital. As reliance on financial markets grew, so did the need to please financial gatekeepers – a necessity to keep the access to financial capital open and maintain investor demand. Furthermore, the state institutionalized and deepened the role of credit ratings since non-market actors like oversight boards in state governments also use credit ratings as a measure to judge the perceived success and organizational merit of special districts and cities. Similarly, research shows that financialization of urban governance is not simply a case of outside, autonomous markets being imposed on local officials; rather, local actors in governments are better understood as objects *and* agents of financialization as they engage in creating institutional conditions to attract financial market activities (Weber 2010; O'Brien et al. 2019). The blurring of lines between public and private actors and interests highlights that, in the financialized economy, the operative logics that drive decision-making in local governance center on financial objectives and normalize the primacy of utilizing financial capital as a necessity for governing.

Before concluding, the remainder of this chapter will examine four case studies focusing on various governance–finance assemblages and their respective social consequences. Taken together, these case studies illustrate how the financialization of urban production and governance influences policy and has the potential to shape socio-environmental relations.

Case studies

New York: A Social Agenda Faces the Financial Squeeze

Martha Poon offers an insightful book chapter (2012) in which she points to 1960s New York City as a key moment that illustrates the ascent of credit rating agencies to a position of political power and domination over municipal policies. New York City's lead finance official, Roy M. Goodman, spoke before Congress in 1968, proclaiming in opening remarks that a "double-barreled financial threat confronts the municipalities of our great nation" (Goodman 1968, 59). At the center of his argument was his increasing concern regarding "the inadequacies of the private bond-rating system and the incursions of industrial revenue financing" that he observed during his appointment as the city's Commissioner of Finance (Goodman 1968, 59).

In Goodman's account, Moody's and Standard & Poor's downgraded New York City's tax-backed debt in 1965 and 1966, resulting in the city receiving interest costs of about ten basis points more than previously. The downgrade was triggered by the issuance of $250 million in additional bonds – an amount that is, at the most, only moderately consequential in the broader context of the budget belonging to the nation's largest city. Referring to claims made by municipal finance experts who took issue with the downgrade, he describes the debt issuance at the heart of the matters as merely a "transitory policy of one Administration" (61), asserting that the negative evaluation was unjustified when accounting for the broader, long-term standing of the city. Goodman makes this case to Congress, pointing to a variety of financial evidence that includes New York's enormous portfolio of property assets, revenue-producing facilities, and history of meeting debt requirements, among others. His central complaint was that the rating agencies – privately run and responsible to clients and subscribers – wield a nearly automatic ability to determine the interest rate that the city must pay on its bonds. Such interest hikes, as Goodman observed in the case of New York City, are problematic because regular citizens incur the costs of interest payments on government bonds, and cities lose resources that could otherwise provide public goods and services. In making his case to Congress, he walks through estimates of these effects and what they mean for citizens of New York City. He points out that a lower-rated Baa bond receives a 5.2% net interest cost compared to 4.7% for an A-rated bond. Based on the typical amount of new debt that the city issues each year, he estimates an extra cost of about $20 million per year and argues that this is "enough to provide hospital space for 500 patients or build seven elementary schools or put 2,000 policemen on the beat" (62).

Poon (2012) underscores a key tension by pointing to the fact that credit ratings were written into federal laws and regulations in order to protect *investors*; but, since ratings are tied to interest payments, they end up costing, rather than protecting, *citizens*. This tension creates competing perspectives where on one hand, credit ratings "enforce financial prudence for the benefit of a greater good," and on the other hand, they are "seen as infringing upon the smooth functioning of democratic politics" (Poon 2012, 11). Goodman described this infringement as shortchanging the city out of "hundreds of millions of dollars" that were "vitally needed for basic services" (Goodman 1968, 60).

The argument in Goodman's testimony in the 1960s makes a compelling case that financial gatekeepers – i.e., the credit rating agencies – impose a set of financial logics on municipal officials as they seek to provision the city's resources for public goods and social services. This episode in the 1960s was a precursor for the city's deeper financial troubles in the 1970s. Hackworth (2002) points out that in this period, New York City had no choice but to leave behind policies of significant redistribution and regulation, "in favor of a business-friendly pro-growth form of governance," citing several noteworthy monographs focused explicitly on this well-studied case (Tabb 1982; Lichten 1986; Fainstein 1992; Schefter 1992). In 1975, New York City saw an even deeper downgrade than the one with which Goodman took issue. This time the Caa rating issued by Moody's placed the city into the "speculative-grade" category, which practically removes its ability to issue debt in open capital markets. Eventually the State of New York helped the city to restructure its finances and, in the process, the city came under new leadership who imposed deeper austerity measures – cutting social services, affordable housing and hospital funding – while they also allocated public money to assist finance, insurance and real estate industries.

The example of New York City illustrates a case in which a city government openly conflicted with rating agencies. The conflict can be characterized as one between two opposing forces. In one corner was a City Hall generally embracing Keynesian redistributive policies, labor unions, and a large public sector workforce.

This policy agenda created friction with the rating agencies in the other corner. The rating agencies championed financialized governance logics and a neoliberal vision for the city. In this case, we can observe that the persistent and durable influence of financial gatekeepers inevitably wins out as city officials have scant alternatives to funding social services and deep economic incentives to capitulate to the austerity favored by financial investors.

Detroit: Business-Friendly Leaders with Dwindling Industries and a Shrinking Population

In the next case study, there are similar dynamics at play as in New York; however, in Detroit, city leadership tended toward a greater embrace of fiscally conservative policies and still faced troubling downgrades (Hackworth 2002; Peck and Whiteside 2016; see also Rector, in this volume). This demonstrates that under the conditions of a financialized economy, the sway of financial gatekeepers is unavoidable and unremitting. Throughout the ladder decades of the twentieth century, Detroit received relatively poor credit ratings.[3] In Hackworth's description of this era, he points to a "severe version of deindustrialization and suburban capital flight during the 1970s and 1980s" (2002, 721) as the reasons behind the city's financial troubles, budget deficits, and the subsequent unfavorable evaluations by the rating agencies. However, city officials, led by a very business-friendly, financially oriented mayor, managed to eventually achieve an investment-grade rating issued by Moody's in 1986 that brought the city out of speculative – also known as "junk" – bond status (Eisinger 1998).

Despite a decade of aggressive efforts to pursue economic development and shape the city's finances according to the financial logics sought by the rating agencies, the investment-grade rating did not last (Hackworth 2002). Only six years later, Moody's downgraded the city's credit again, back to a rating in the speculative category. A New York Times report at the time, citing a financial adviser for the city, argued that the downgrade reflected Moody's evaluation of Detroit's revenue prospects in the future, rather than its current credit standing (Presley Noble 1992). The downgrade illustrates the broader trend of financial divestment from cities with lasting social problems that have the potential to impede economic development and tax revenues. Following the downgrade, Detroit's next mayor pledged to go even further in attracting businesses, cutting expenditures, and encouraging gentrification. After the continued cutbacks from the city, Moody's rewarded the city with bond rating upgrades in 1996, which further demonstrates the pattern wherein financial gatekeepers coerce city governments to implement financially favorable policies by dangling the reward of access to necessary investment capital.

In the early 2000s, city officials focused on economic development and revenue-seeking initiatives like constructing casinos and sports stadiums. Regardless of these efforts, some, but not all, of the city's lines of credit fell out of the "investment-grade" range again. By 2009, all of the city's credit was rated below "investment-grade," further restricting access to financial capital for social services and public goods, and ramping up pressure to orient the city's activities toward revenues and cost cutting. Detroit's population shrank to a 100-year low in 2010. With property taxes comprising a large share of city budgets, the declining population created significant budget shortfalls on the horizon. As the city tumbled down a path of insolvency, public employees lost pay, pension obligations were compromised, and people lost vital healthcare benefits. Eventually, the city experienced even deeper credit rating downgrades and filed for the largest municipal bankruptcy in US history in 2013. A 2018 article in the Detroit Free Press profiles the lingering human cost of the financial struggles of the city by profiling a number of impacted citizens, like a retiree of the Detroit Public Library who lost health coverage and monthly income due to the city's bankruptcy restructuring (Tompor 2018). The experiences of residents in Detroit point to how a city under financial distress is disciplined by financial gatekeepers to maximize bondholder value and is thus coerced into prioritizing debt repayments and fiscal conservation over social services, redistribution, and public goods (Peck and Whiteside 2016).

The circumstances of New York and Detroit discussed here highlight the fact that city governments are unable to adequately provide for the public when under such financial pressures. Moreover, in the context of a financialized economy that leaves governments with no viable funding alternatives to debt markets, financial gatekeepers impose a strict set of logics on city officials. In these examples, we see how financial logics encourage and coerce officials to seek policies that benefit the financial well-being of Wall Street investors over the livelihoods of their Main Street constituents. Research over the years has explicated how financialization pairs with neoliberal austerity reforms to shape systems of urban production and limit social provisioning and redistribution; however, we would benefit from further examination of how these financial concerns intersect with the role of regional and city governments in crafting and implementing environmental governance and policy. The following two examples illustrate some of these possible connections, linking financialization to environmental policies in water governance as it unfolds in urban areas. The first focuses on how privatization leads to the financialization of urban infrastructure, and the second presents a case of a public governance system entrenched in financial interests that shape socio-environmental relations.

Privatization and Financialization in the UK: The Case of Thames Water

According to the official company website, Thames Water supplies water and provides wastewater treatment to 15 million people in London, England and other areas in the UK, making it the largest water company in the UK. Thames Water formed following the privatization of the public water authority in 1989. The company was acquired by an international consortium associated with an Australian bank, which subsequently spread shares of the water company to investors around the world. The largest shareholders include a major Canadian pension fund (Reuters 2017) and a pension fund of a British telecom company (Kavanagh 2012). Behind the pension funds, the next major investors include the sovereign wealth funds of Abu Dhabi (Reuters 2011), China (Sakoui 2012), and Kuwait (Plimmer 2017). Under this globalized ownership structure, the consumption of water by urban residents in London becomes a key site for the extraction of wealth by global financial elites. Moreover, with profit as the primary objective, the company has been repeatedly found responsible for environmental damages, including in 2013 when the government imposed the largest regulatory fine in UK history on Thames Water for river pollution associated with raw sewage spilling from improperly maintained equipment. Meanwhile, according to the Financial Times, the company was simultaneously paying billions in dividends to their global base of shareholders while dodging corporate taxes, paying enormous compensation to executives, and significantly growing its debt holdings.[4] The Financial Times also posits that the complex regulatory system in which Thames Water operates creates incentives for the company to spend on capital investments – regardless of what is in the interest of customers – and not on operational tasks that prevent environmental damages and enhance efficiency. Allen and Pryke summarize the dealings of Thames Water in their analysis of how household water has been financialized in the UK as a "shift that has taken place in treating infrastructure as a stable, long-term asset class by pension funds and the like" (2013, 421). They also suggest that "it points to the introduction of a less-familiar funding model in the sector, one based upon debt refinancing largely through the securitization of revenue streams" (2013, 421).

One example of Thames Water's financialized infrastructure development is the Thames Water Desalination Plant (TWDP). Loftus and March argue that the TWPD exemplifies an "infrastructure-heavy solution to the demands of financialization" (2016, 46). The essential question they seek to ask is if London needed a 270-million euro desalination plant at all. They find that, under the conditions of financialized urban governance, big infrastructure projects, like the TWDP, offer significant rewards for financial investors and few risks, as the risks are largely shouldered by the city government. The financial motivations of the project exist in an opaque and obfuscated background context of which many rate payers are unaware. On the surface, the company argued that the TWDP was a necessary addition to London's water supply portfolio due to reduced rainfall and climate change. However, critics, including Loftus and March (2016) point to more mundane, less costly, and proven strategies like demand management and leakage reduction. They argue that these options are summarily dismissed as they fail to fit with the company's prioritization of large infrastructure projects. This is because, in crafting such large projects, opportunities arise to establish lasting financial arrangements that provide a channel for global financial investors to extract wealth from households, in the current moment and indefinitely into the future. The transformation of public infrastructure into lasting financial channels for the private accumulation of wealth is the product of a system that normalizes the financialization of urban production and public goods.

Another example of what critics consider to be a questionable infrastructural investment by Thames Water with potential for immense financial gain is the Thames Tideway Tunnel (TTT). Loftus and March (2019) argue that the TTT is less a response to the needs of the people of London or for environmental protection and more guided by the extraction of wealth from Londoners through murky and complex financial arrangements. More specifically, as urban production becomes more financialized, investors take on a greater role in shaping infrastructure and policy. As Loftus and March point out, "the more important consideration for investors is how best to expand the terrain over which rents can be captured," as opposed to debating the efficiency gains, public goods, or environmental benefits that one form of infrastructure may produce over others (2019, 2282). The logical conclusion of prioritizing the interests of investors is demand for "more and larger infrastructure rather than for necessarily smarter infrastructure (2019, 2282). Loftus and March make this case by pointing to a number of alternatives that were swiftly dismissed despite support from key figures in the UK's water sector and regulatory agencies. Additionally, Chris Binney, the chairman of the group that initially recommended the tunnel, stated that the data on which the recommendation was made turned out to be incorrect and argues that the 4-billion euro project is an unnecessary waste that will cost customers. An article in the Guardian discusses how Binney arrived at this conclusion and asserts that the financing of the project leaves the government with all the risk, while private investors, supplying 2.8 billion euros in capital, begin receiving income from the very start of construction (Gayle and Taylor 2016). Loftus and March summarize their examination of the TTT asserting:

> Financial and political interests come to be integrated into an elite fix that will generate returns for the pension funds, insurance companies and sovereign wealth funds now integral to the hydrosocial cycle of the city. Rather than an ambitious project to avoid a polluted Thames, generate clean energy, and build creatively on the challenges of the water-energy nexus, the Thames Tideway Tunnel is a concrete tunnel for extracting rents, a pure financial asset.
>
> (2019, 2293)

The TWDP and the TTT projects illustrate how financial markets and financial actors shape the development of urban infrastructure. In these cases, we see that a large-scale infrastructure project takes precedence over other options, even when alternatives have potential for greater social and environmental benefits. Moreover, under the conditions of financialization, global financial elites drive the development of infrastructure projects designed as tools for financial advantages. Instead of creating public goods with broad social and environmental benefits, elements of urban production are created for their financial structures that enable the extraction of wealth from the city government and its residents, at the expense of public resources and costing residents in their monthly bills. Ultimately, the financialization of urban governance highlights a significant channel of capital accumulation in the highly privatized field of water supply management in the UK (Bakker 2003).

Public Governance and Financialization: The Case of Water in Southern California

Urban development and population growth in Southern California are predicated upon importing water from hundreds of miles away, requiring massive infrastructure systems of water conveyance and storage. Since water governance is critical to urban production, it makes a prime case study to understand what financialization means for the nexus of urban production and environmental policy under publicly run systems of governance. Furthermore, the organizational infrastructure in the US is dominated by publicly run organizations. This makes it a strategic case that enhances our understanding of financialization by offering a juxtaposition to governance systems reliant upon dominant private corporations, like the case of Thames Water in London.

The provisioning, management and delivery of water supplies throughout the US occurs through a vast network of mostly public organizations. With a few exceptions, the large majority of water supply organizations are publicly run, with democratically elected boards of directors and subject to the transparency requirements of local governments. Issues associated with water resources and infrastructure are particularly pronounced in Southern California, where the water demands from the sprawling urban and suburban spaces in the greater Los Angeles and San Diego regions far exceed the locally available water supplies (Erie and Brackman 2006).

The public agencies overseeing water delivery do not have shareholders, nor do they pay dividends like private companies do. Instead, they are reliant upon investment capital in the form of municipal bonds, like the budgets of city governments. Public water managers face a variety of financial pressures to treat water as a commodity, rather than a public good, as a result of prioritizing financial objectives for bondholder value. These pressures, which essentially squeeze elements of water delivery to create value for bondholders, are distilled, quantified and evaluated by the bond rating agencies (Gibson 2021; 2022). Original research (publications forthcoming) conducted between 2017 and 2019 with elected and career water officials in the region reveal a dominant financially oriented posture as policymakers seek to receive and maintain favorable credit ratings. For example, one general manager of a water district explained to me that they get very high credit ratings because "the nice thing they [the rating agencies] like about us is that we have the ability to raise our rates, and have historically done that in the past to support building projects" (interview with GM, 2/8/2019). Nearly all other officials observed and interviewed echoed similar sentiments about water districts seeking to demonstrate to credit rating agencies that they operate in ways that privilege financial objectives that create bondholder value (Peck and Whiteside 2016; Apkarian 2018) over social and environmental objectives that might compromise financial objectives.

Archival research on water districts from the same period and region reveal the primary concerns and practices in which the credit rating agencies are interested when making their evaluations. Qualitative coding of bond rating reports show that water districts are incentivized to increase water sales, regardless of climatological realities. This is illustrated in the fact that water districts face the threat of downgrades due to declining revenues during times of widespread drought. For instance, in May 2011, the Metropolitan Water District of Southern California, which is the wholesale district selling imported water to the region's retail districts and the largest provider of treated drinking water in the US, received a downgrade by Fitch. As the district slipped from the highest rank to the second-highest rank, Fitch reported that the evaluation was due to volatility in the demand for water. Coming on the heels of three years of drought from 2007 to 2009, the assessment illustrates that the financial gatekeepers fail to take into considerations the climatological realities facing public water districts as they seek to steward natural resources. During times of drought, the state (and common sense) encourages water users to reduce consumption, which directly contributes to volatility in water demands. Reduced resource consumption during times of scarcity is a reasonable element to foster in sustainable socio-environmental relations. However, we see that the financialization of the economy encourages public water managers to commodify water and shirk actions that reduce our collective environmental footprint.

Other conditions that are incentivized by the rating agencies include maintaining a monopoly over access to water supply, minimal democratic turnover of leadership, a demonstrated willingness to raise rates despite public interests and economic circumstances, limited spending on environmental conservation initiatives, and a regulatory environment with limited pressures to conserve resources. Taken together, these data point to how the reliance on financial capital empowers financial gatekeepers to shape the activities and priorities of public governance agencies in ways that are potentially antithetical to the public interest and sound environmental stewardship. Ultimately, the lesson to learn here is that privatization is not necessarily the main impediment to sustainable environmental governance in urban settings, because even the publicly run agencies effectively treat environmental resources as commodities to leverage for financial advantages. Rather, there is a need to attend to the role of financial markets in creating institutional and structural processes that cripple the ability of public agencies to implement ambitious and environmentally oriented policies.

Conclusion

Under the current conditions, where urban governance officials must meet the challenges of adapting to a changing climate by conserving non-renewable resources and mitigating our impact on the environment, we must consider how reliance on private financial capital not only impacts the pocketbooks of citizens and undermines democratic institutions, but also influences our collective impact on the environment. This chapter explores four case studies to demonstrate how financial markets intersect with urban production. The first two cases examine city governments. New York City offers a case of a city in conflict with financial gatekeepers over an agenda of more liberal redistributive policies. As a contrast, Detroit presents a case of a city embracing business-friendly policies, but still facing a tightening grip of financial market interests due to a shrinking tax base. The final two cases show that financialization also influences resource governance and other arms of regional governments. The case of Thames Water in London shows that privatization intersects with financialization in ways that allow private capital to leverage infrastructure projects as investment tools and shape urban production to be conducive to the long-term extraction of wealth and public resources. And, the case of public water management in Southern California shows that even under environmental circumstances of scarcity and relatively transparent public governance, financial interests have a strong influence over organizations and policies due to an entrenched reliance on municipal bond markets for capital funding.

The financialization of urban infrastructure is unique from other characterizations or concepts that explain aspects of urban political economy like neoliberalism, privatization or commodification. These concepts usually reinforce each other, as the underlying condition is the siphoning of public resources into avenues of private accumulation. The financialization of urban production emphasizes that even well-intended, seemingly "fiscally responsible" policies exist in a macrostructural context that, for public officials in city governments and special districts, renders public goods and sound environmental stewardship tertiary concerns behind financial objectives of maximizing revenues.

There is a cautionary tale within these case studies that relates to climate change policy and local governance. Climate change can be seen as a type, or variation, of the social problems and challenges to city revenues that have historically resulted in disfavor by financial gatekeepers, downgraded credit ratings, and a diminished capacity to invest in city governance initiatives. While there may be ways in which climate change presents opportunity for revenues – for instance, the development of new green energy sectors – there will surely be major economic costs incurred in implementing climate change adaptation and defense measures. If we continue to allow the governance capacities of cities to be determined by the calculations of financial gatekeepers and actors who represent investors, we are likely to see financial divestment in cities hardest hit by climate change. Just as Detroit was hit with a downgrade over a poor outlook for the future and water districts face penalties for conservation during drought, cities and special governance districts will similarly take financial hits over a future that promises seasonal destruction (e.g., wildfires, hurricanes, storm surges), compromised long-term viability (e.g., sea-level rise, drought, extreme heat), and expensive capital investments (e.g., water infrastructure, sea walls, retreat and rebuilding efforts).

The GND presents an opportunity to reshape the relationship between urban production and financial markets in a way that brings environmental sustainability to the forefront of decision-making. A reorientation of how we fund urban governance is necessary to ensure that environmental considerations are not precluded by the financial logics forced upon city officials by financial gatekeepers and the need to create bondholder value. As such, the following suggestions should be considered in the development of GND initiatives:

1 Distribute state and federal grants and low-interest loans according to principles that do not consider credit ratings or use credit ratings as a metric of performance for regional governance organizations.
2 Provide state and federal funding directly to communities with minimal involvement of financial intermediaries and minimal processes that force municipalities to compete for access to scarce discretionary funds. Such competitive governance conditions tend to marginalize low-income areas with limited tax bases and resources.
3 Encourage intermunicipal cooperation across geographies and sectors, and centralization where applicable, to reduce organizational competition and unnecessary redundancies.
4 Engage the public in participatory forums and leverage existing scientific agencies and regulatory boards in identifying highest-need locations for GND investments and interventions. Ideally, scientific analysis in concert with public engagement will drive the classification of high-need areas, so funds will be distributed according to need and not according to historical financial performance, perceived financial futures, nor the evaluations of credit rating agencies.

Keohane and Victor (2011) remind us of the fragmentation of multilevel governing efforts as they pertain to climate change, arguing that a *regime complex for climate change* is the best way to understand climate change governance. Within this framework, local and regional governance agencies occupy a place in the regime complex where a great deal of policy implementation occurs in highly consequential urban spaces (Betsill and Bulkeley 2003). Urban governance agencies settle important decisions and implement policies on things like development patterns, water supply management, and distribution of public goods, among others. As the cases discussed in this chapter illustrate, the tentacles of financialization are deep within public and privatized urban governance organizations. In the absence of an integrated, environmentally minded regulatory regime, financial gatekeepers, and capital investors retain the capacity to shape and constrain the priorities and policies of governance organizations, twisting their objectives toward private accumulation and bondholder value and away from public good and social justice. The Green New Deal and other ambitious efforts at climate change governance will benefit from considering how lasting environmental reform will require financial reforms in order to empower governance agencies to act in the public interest.

Notes

1 Feldman (2012) provides essential background and adroit summation of the structures of public utilities, private enterprises, and "mixed" arrangements common in the US. Chapter 4, "Who's in Control" (pp. 92–123) is particularly helpful in this regard.

2 See Sbragia (1996: 112–119) for a detailed overview of "The Evolution of Debt Instruments" and a compelling argument that revenue bonds emerged as a tool to circumvent legal regulations on public debt.

3 Following the high-profile municipal bankruptcy in 2013, Reuters reporting staff authored a timeline of events pertaining to the financial history of Detroit. https://www.reuters.com/article/usa-detroit-timeline/timeline-a-brief-history-of-detroits-fiscal-problems-idUSL1N0FP00F20130719

4 The FT offers several useful descriptive accounts of the financial dealings of Thames Water. This piece offers a critical take on Thames Water's business structures and dealings over the years of private ownership: https://www.ft.com/content/5413ebf8-24f1-11e7-8691-d5f7e0cd0a16

References

Abers, R. and Keck, M.E. 2013. *Practical Authority: Agency and Institutional Change in Brazilian Water Politics*. Oxford: Oxford University Press.

Allen, J. and Pryke, M. 2013. Financialising Household Water: Thames Water, MEIF, and 'Ring-Fenced' Politics. *Cambridge Journal of Regions, Economy and Society*. 6(3), 419–439. Available from: https://doi.org/10.1093/cjres/rst010.

Altman, E. et al. 2011. Regulation of Rating Agencies. In Acharya, V.V. et al. (eds.), *Regulating Wall Street*. Hoboken, NJ: John Wiley & Sons, Inc. Available from: https://doi.org/10.1002/9781118258231.ch15.

Apkarian, J. 2018. Opposition to Shareholder Value: Bond Rating Agencies and Conflicting Logics in Corporate Finance. *Socio-Economic Review*. 16(1), 85–112. Available from: https://doi.org/10.1093/ser/mwx041.

Appadurai, A. 1996. *Modernity at Large: Cultural Dimensions of Globalization*. Public Worlds, V. 1. Minneapolis, MN: University of Minnesota Press.

Bakker, K.J. 2003. *An Uncooperative Commodity: Privatizing Water in England and Wales*. Oxford Geographical and Environmental Studies. Oxford; New York: Oxford University Press.

Bakker, K.J. 2010. *Privatizing Water: Governance Failure and the World's Urban Water Crisis*. Ithaca, NY: Cornell University Press.

Beecher, J.A. 2010. The Conservation Conundrum: How Declining Demand Affects Water Utilities. *American Water Works Association Journal*. 102(2), 78–80.

Brown, R.R. and Farrelly, M.A. 2009. Challenges Ahead: Social and Institutional Factors Influencing Sustainable Urban Stormwater Management in Australia. *Water Science & Technology*. 59(4), 653. Available from: https://doi.org/10.2166/wst.2009.022.

Bulkeley, H. 2010. Cities and the Governing of Climate Change. *Annual Review of Environment and Resources*. 35(1), 229–253. Available from: https://doi.org/10.1146/annurev-environ-072809-101747.

Bulkeley, H. and Betsill, M. 2003. *Cities and Climate Change: Urban Sustainability and Global Environmental Governance*. Routledge Studies in Physical Geography and Environment 4. London; New York: Routledge.

Bulkeley, H. and Betsill, M. 2005. Rethinking Sustainable Cities: Multilevel Governance and the 'Urban' Politics of Climate Change. *Environmental Politics*. 14(1), 42–63. Available from: https://doi.org/10.1080/0964401042000310178.

Carruthers, B.G. 2013. From Uncertainty Toward Risk: The Case of Credit Ratings. *Socio-Economic Review*. 11(3), 525–551. Available from: https://doi.org/10.1093/ser/mws027.

Cheung, H. 2020. What Does Trump Actually Believe on Climate Change? *BBC News*. 23 January. Available from: https://www.bbc.com/news/world-us-canada-51213003.

Creutzig, F. et al. 2015. Global Typology of Urban Energy Use and Potentials for an Urbanization Mitigation Wedge. *Proceedings of the National Academy of Sciences*. 112(20), 6283–6288. Available from: https://doi.org/10.1073/pnas.1315545112.

Davis, G.F. and Kim, S. 2015. Financialization of the Economy. *Annual Review of Sociology*. 41(1), 203–221. Available from: https://doi.org/10.1146/annurev-soc-073014-112402.

Eaton, C. et al. 2016. The Financialization of US Higher Education. *Socio-Economic Review*. 8 February. Available from: https://doi.org/10.1093/ser/mwv030.

Eisinger, P. 1998. City Politics in an Era of Federal Devolution. *Urban Affairs Review*. 33(3), 308–325. Available from: https://doi.org/10.1177/107808749803300302.

Epstein, G.A. ed. 2005. *Financialization and the World Economy*. Cheltenham: Elgar.

Erie, S.P. and Brackman, H.D. 2006. *Beyond Chinatown: The Metropolitan Water District, Growth, and the Environment in Southern California*. Stanford: Stanford University Press.

Espeland, W.N. and Stevens, M.L. 1998. Commensuration as a Social Process. *Annual Review of Sociology*. 24(1), 313–343. Available from: https://doi.org/10.1146/annurev.soc.24.1.313.

Espeland, W.N. and Stevens, M.L. 2008. A Sociology of Quantification. *European Journal of Sociology*. 49(3), 401. Available from: https://doi.org/10.1017/S0003975609000150.

Feldman, D.L. 2012. *Water Resources*. Cambridge; Malden, MA: Polity.

Fligstein, N. and Goldstein, A. 2015. The Emergence of a Finance Culture in American Households, 1989–2007. *Socio-Economic Review*. 13(3), 575–601. Available from: https://doi.org/10.1093/ser/mwu035.

Foster, J.B. 2007. The Financialization of Capitalism. *Monthly Review*. 58(11), 1.

Gayle, D. and Taylor, M. 2016. London Super-sewer Is Waste of £4bn, Says Assessor. *The Guardian*. 14 November. Available from: https://www.theguardian.com/uk-news/2016/nov/14/london-super-sewer-is-waste-of-4bn-says-assessor#:~:text=The%20original%20assessor%20who%20backed,begin%20work%20on%20the%20project.

Goodman, R.M. 1968. Municipal Bond Rating Testimony. *Financial Analysts Journal*. 24(3), 59–65. Available from: https://doi.org/10.2469/faj.v24.n3.59.

Gibson, C.W. 2021. Financialized Savings in Public Water Governance: An Illustrative Case Study in the Arid American West. Finance and Society. 7(2), 94-112. Available from: https://doi.org/10.2218/finsoc.v7i2.6627

Gibson, C.W. 2022. 'How Will This Affect Our Credit Rating?': Municipal Debt and Governing the Environment. Environmental Sociology. Available from: https://doi.org/10.1080/23251042.2022.2054131

Gunnoe, A. 2014. The Political Economy of Institutional Landownership: Neorentier Society and the Financialization of Land. *Rural Sociology*. 79(4), 478–504. Available from: https://doi.org/10.1111/ruso.12045.

Gunnoe, A. 2016. The Financialization of the US Forest Products Industry: Socio-Economic Relations, Shareholder Value, and the Restructuring of an Industry. *Social Forces*. 94(3), 1075–1101. Available from: https://doi.org/10.1093/sf/sov108.

Gunnoe, A. and Gellert, P.K. 2011. Financialization, Shareholder Value, and the Transformation of Timberland Ownership in the US. *Critical Sociology*. 37(3), 265–284. Available from: https://doi.org/10.1177/0896920510378764.

Hackworth, J. 2002. "Local Autonomy, Bond-Rating Agencies and Neoliberal Urbanism in the United States." International Journal of Urban and Regional Research 26 (4): 707–725.

Hackworth, J. R. 2007. The Neoliberal City: Governance, Ideology, and Development in American Urbanism. Ithaca: Cornell University Press.

Halbert, L. and Attuyer, K. 2016. Introduction: The Financialisation of Urban Production: Conditions, Mediations and Transformations. *Urban Studies*. 53(7), 1347–1361. Available from: https://doi.org/10.1177/0042098016635420.

IPCC. 2020. Climate Change and Land: Summary for Policymakers. *Intergovernmental Panel on Climate Change, 2020*. Available from: https://www.ipcc.ch/srccl/chapter/summary-for-policymakers/.

Jiang, L. and O'Neill, B.C. 2017. Global Urbanization Projections for the Shared Socioeconomic Pathways. *Global Environmental Change*. 42, 193–199. Available from: https://doi.org/10.1016/j.gloenvcha.2015.03.008.

Kavanagh, M. 2012. BT Pension Scheme Buys Thames Water Stake. *Financial Times*. 30 May. Available from: https://www.ft.com/content/4ebe15ec-aa7c-11e1-9331-00144feabdc0.

Keohane, R.O. and Victor, D.G. 2011. The Regime Complex for Climate Change. *Perspectives on Politics*. 9(1), 7–23. Available from: https://doi.org/10.1017/S1537592710004068.

Kerwer, D. 2002. Rating Agencies Setting a Standard for Global Financial Markets. *Economic Sociology_the European Electronic Newsletter*. 3(3), 40–46.

King, M.R. and Sinclair, T.J. 2003. Private Actors and Public Policy: A Requiem for the New Basel Capital Accord. *International Political Science Review*. 24(3), 345–362. Available from: https://doi.org/10.1177/0192512103024003004.

Krippner, G.R. 2005. The Financialization of the American Economy. *Socio-Economic Review*. 3(2), 173–208. Available from: https://doi.org/10.1093/SER/mwi008.

Leyshon, A. and Thrift, N. 2007. The Capitalization of Almost Everything: The Future of Finance and Capitalism. *Theory, Culture & Society*. 24(7–8), 97–115. Available from: https://doi.org/10.1177/0263276407084699.

Loftus, A. and March, H. 2019. Integrating What and for Whom? Financialisation and the Thames Tideway Tunnel. *Urban Studies*. 56(11), 2280–2296. Available from: https://doi.org/10.1177/0042098017736713.

Malanga, S. 2010. The Muni-bond Debt Bomb. *Wall Street Journal*. 31 July. Available from: https://www.wsj.com/articles/SB10001424052748703999304575399591906297262.

Moran, D. et al. 2018. Carbon Footprints of 13 000 Cities. *Environmental Research Letters*. 13(6), 064041. Available from: https://doi.org/10.1088/1748-9326/aac72a.

Mullin, M. 2009. *Governing the Tap: Special District Governance and the New Local Politics of Water*. American and Comparative Environmental Policy. Cambridge, MA: MIT Press.

O'Brien, P., O'Neill, P. and Pike, A. 2019. Funding, Financing and Governing Urban Infrastructures. *Urban Studies*. 56(7), 1291–1303. Available from: https://doi.org/10.1177/0042098018824014.

O'Neill, P. 2017. Managing the Private Financing of Urban Infrastructure. *Urban Policy and Research*. 35(1), 32–43. Available from: https://doi.org/10.1080/08111146.2016.1235034.

Office of Los Angeles Mayor Eric Garcetti. 2019. Mayor Garcetti Launches L.A.'s Green New Deal. *LAmayor.Org*. 29 April. Available from: https://www.lamayor.org/mayor-garcetti-launches-las-green-new-deal.

Pacewicz, J. 2013. Tax Increment Financing, Economic Development Professionals and the Financialization of Urban Politics. *Socio-Economic Review*. 11(3), 413–440. Available from: https://doi.org/10.1093/ser/mws019.

Pacewicz, J. 2016. The City as a Fiscal Derivative: Financialization, Urban Development, and the Politics of Earmarking. *City & Community*. 15(3), 264–288. Available from: https://doi.org/10.1111/cico.12190.

Peck, J. and Whiteside, H. 2016. Financializing Detroit. *Economic Geography*. 92(3), 235–268. Available from: https://doi.org/10.1080/00130095.2015.1116369.

Plimmer, G. 2017. Macquarie Sells Final Stake in Thames Water for £1.35bn. *Financial Times*. 14 March. Available from: https://www.ft.com/content/63ae6f88-08a5-11e7-97d1-5e720a26771b.

Plimmer, G. and Espinoza, J. 2017. Thames Water: The Murky Structure of a Utility Company. *Financial Times*. 4 May. Available from: https://www.ft.com/content/5413ebf8-24f1-11e7-8691-d5f7e0cd0a16.

Poon, M. 2012. Rating Agencies. In Cetina, K.K. and Preda, A. (eds.), *The Oxford Handbook of the Sociology of Finance*. Oxford: Oxford University Press. Available from: https://doi.org/10.1093/oxfordhb/9780199590162.013.0015.

Presley Noble, B. 1992. A Downgraded Detroit Cries Foul. *New York Times*. 3 November. Available from: https://www.nytimes.com/1992/11/03/business/a-downgraded-detroit-cries-foul.html.

Reuters. 2011. Abu Dhabi Sovereign Fund Buys Thames Water Stake. *Reuters*. 13 December. Available from: https://www.reuters.com/article/adia-thames/abu-dhabi-sovereign-fund-buys-thames-water-stake-idUSL6E7ND50J20111213.

Reuters. 2017. Borealis Buys Additional 5.5 Percent in Thames Water from AMP Capital. *Reuters*. 26 July. Available from: https://www.reuters.com/article/uk-thameswater-borealis/borealis-buys-additional-5-5-percent-in-thames-water-from-amp-capital-idUKKBN1AB0SC?edition-redirect=uk.

Rona-Tas, A. and Hiss, S. 2010. The Role of Ratings in the Subprime Mortgage Crisis: The Art of Corporate and the Science of Consumer Credit Rating. In: *Markets on Trial: The Economic Sociology of the U.S. Financial Crisis: Part A*. Bingley: Emerald Publishing, 115–55. Available from: https://doi.org/10.1108/S0733-558X(2010)000030A008.

Roth, S. 2019. L.A. Mayor Garcetti's 'green new deal' Would Phase Out Gas-Fueled Cars. *Los Angeles Times*. 29 April. Available from: https://www.latimes.com/business/la-fi-garcetti-green-new-deal-los-angeles-20190429-story.html.

Sakoui, A. 2012. China buys Stake in Thames Water. *Financial Times*. 20 January. Available from: https://www.ft.com/content/7b19ca2e-42c0-11e1-b756-00144feab49a.

Sbragia, A.M. 1996. *Debt Wish: Entrepreneurial Cities, U.S. Federalism, and Economic Development*. Pitt Series in Policy and Institutional Studies. Pittsburgh, PA: University of Pittsburgh Press.

Seto, K.C. et al. 2014. Chapter 12 – Human Settlements, Infrastructure and Spatial Planning. In: *Climate Change 2014: Mitigation of Climate Change. IPCC Working Group III Contribution to AR5*. Cambridge: Cambridge University Press. Available from: http://www.ipcc.ch/pdf/assessment-report/ar5/wg3/ipcc_wg3_ar5_chapter12.pdf.

Sinclair, T.J. 1994. Passing Judgement: Credit Rating Processes as Regulatory Mechanisms of Governance in the Emerging World Order. *Review of International Political Economy*. 1(1), 133–159. Available from: https://doi.org/10.1080/09692299408434271.

Sinclair, T. 2008. *The New Masters of Capital: American Bond Rating Agencies and the Politics of Creditworthiness*. Cornell Studies in Political Economy. Ithaca, NY: Cornell Paperbacks.

Thomas, G.S. 2004. Rating Agencies: An American Policy Arm? *Economic and Political Weekly*. 39(42), 4613–4615.

Tompor, S. 2018. Even 5 Years Later, Retirees Feel the Effects of Detroit's Bankruptcy. *Detroit Free Press*. 18 July. Available from: https://www.freep.com/story/money/personal-finance/susan-tompor/2018/07/18/detroit-bankruptcy-retirees-pension/759446002/.

Torrance, M.I. 2008. Forging Glocal Governance? Urban Infrastructures as Networked Financial Products. *International Journal of Urban and Regional Research*. 32(1), 1–21. Available from: https://doi.org/10.1111/j.1468-2427.2007.00756.x.

United Nations, Department of Economic and Social Affairs, and Population Division. 2019. *World Urbanization Prospects: The 2018 Revision*. New York: United Nations.

van der Zwan, N. 2014. "Making Sense of Financialization." *Socio-Economic Review* 12 (1): 99–129.

Weber, R. 2010. Selling City Futures: The Financialization of Urban Redevelopment Policy. *Economic Geography*. 86(3), 251–274. Available from: https://doi.org/10.1111/j.1944-8287.2010.01077.x.

APPENDIX

Examples of Green New Deals and legislative proposals

1. The European Green Deal (Communication from the Commission to the European Parliament, The European Council, The Council, The European Economic and Social Committee and the Committee of the Regions, Brussels, 11.12.2019 COM(2019) 640 final).

EUROPEAN
COMMISSION

Brussels, 11.12.2019
COM(2019) 640 final

COMMUNICATION FROM THE COMMISSION TO THE EUROPEAN PARLIAMENT, THE EUROPEAN COUNCIL, THE COUNCIL, THE EUROPEAN ECONOMIC AND SOCIAL COMMITTEE AND THE COMMITTEE OF THE REGIONS

The European Green Deal

1. INTRODUCTION - TURNING AN URGENT CHALLENGE INTO A UNIQUE OPPORTUNITY

This Communication sets out a European Green Deal for the European Union (EU) and its citizens. It resets the Commission's commitment to tackling climate and environmental-related challenges that is this generation's defining task. The atmosphere is warming and the climate is changing with each passing year. One million of the eight million species on the planet are at risk of being lost. Forests and oceans are being polluted and destroyed[1].

The European Green Deal is a response to these challenges. It is a new growth strategy that aims to **transform the EU into a fair and prosperous society, with a modern, resource-efficient and competitive economy** where there are **no net emissions of greenhouse gases in 2050 and where economic growth is decoupled from resource use.**

It also aims to **protect, conserve and enhance the EU's natural capital, and protect the health and well-being of citizens from environment-related risks** and impacts. At the same time, this transition must be **just and inclusive**. It must put people first, and pay attention to the regions, industries and workers who will face the greatest challenges. Since it will bring substantial change, active public participation and confidence in the transition is paramount if policies are to work and be accepted. A new pact is needed to bring together citizens in all their diversity, with national, regional, local authorities, civil society and industry working closely with the EU's institutions and consultative bodies.

The EU has the collective ability to transform its economy and society to put it on a more sustainable path. It can build on its strengths as a global leader on climate and environmental measures, consumer protection, and workers' rights. Delivering additional reductions in emissions is a challenge. It will require massive public investment and increased efforts to direct private capital towards climate and environmental action, while avoiding lock-in into unsustainable practices. The EU must be at the forefront of coordinating international efforts towards building a coherent financial system that supports sustainable solutions. This upfront investment is also **an opportunity to put Europe firmly on a new path of sustainable and inclusive growth**. The European Green Deal will accelerate and underpin the transition needed in all sectors.

The environmental ambition of the Green Deal will not be achieved by Europe acting alone. The drivers of climate change and biodiversity loss are global and are not limited by national borders. The EU can use its influence, expertise and financial resources to mobilise its neighbours and partners to join it on a sustainable path. The EU will continue to lead international efforts and wants to build alliances with the like-minded. It also recognises the need to maintain its security of supply and competitiveness even when others are unwilling to act.

This Communication presents an **initial roadmap of the key policies and measures needed to achieve the European Green Deal.** It will be updated as needs evolve and the

---

1 Sources: (i) Intergovernmental Panel on Climate Change (IPCC): Special Report on the impacts of global warming of 1.5°C; (ii) Intergovernmental Science-Policy Platform on Biodiversity and Ecosystem Services: 2019 Global assessment report on biodiversity and ecosystem services; (iii) The International Resource Panel: Global Resources Outlook 2019: Natural Resources for the Future We Want; (iv) European Environment Agency: the European environment — state and outlook 2020: knowledge for transition to a sustainable Europe

policy responses are formulated. All EU actions and policies will have to contribute to the European Green Deal objectives. The challenges are complex and interlinked. The policy response must be bold and comprehensive and seek to maximise benefits for health, quality of life, resilience and competitiveness. It will require intense coordination to exploit the available synergies across all policy areas[2].

The Green Deal is an integral part of this Commission's strategy to implement the United Nation's 2030 Agenda and the sustainable development goals[3], and the other priorities announced in President von der Leyen's political guidelines[4]. As part of the Green Deal, the Commission will refocus the European Semester process of macroeconomic coordination to integrate the United Nations' sustainable development goals, to put sustainability and the well-being of citizens at the centre of economic policy, and the sustainable development goals at the heart of the EU's policymaking and action.

The figure below illustrates the various elements of the Green Deal.

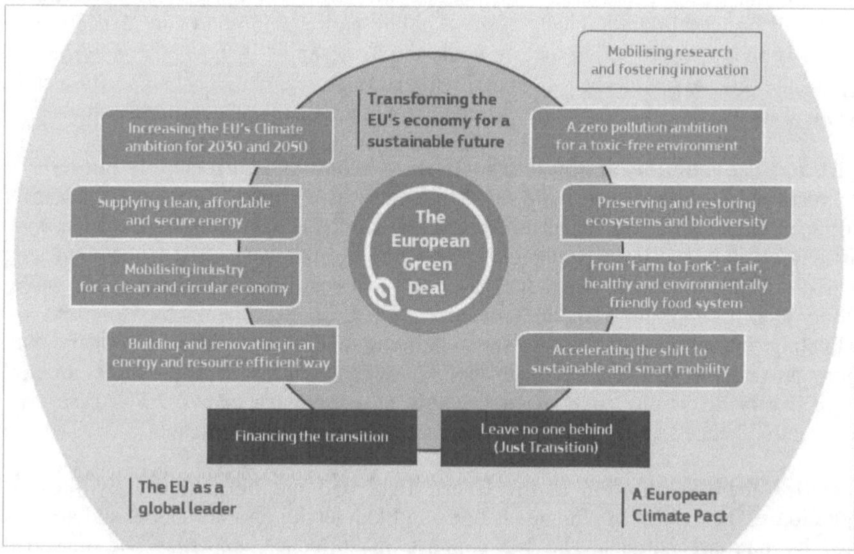

Figure 1: The European Green Deal

---

2 In line with the findings of the 2020 European environment — state and outlook 2020: knowledge for transition to a sustainable Europe (European Environment Agency)

3 https://sustainabledevelopment.un.org/post2015/transformingourworld

4 See Political Guidelines of President elect Ursula von der Leyen: *Political guidelines for the next Commission (2019-2024) – 'A Union that strives for more: My agenda for Europe'*:

2. Transforming the EU's economy for a sustainable future

2.1. Designing a set of deeply transformative policies

To deliver the European Green Deal, there is a need to rethink policies for clean energy supply across the economy, industry, production and consumption, large-scale infrastructure, transport, food and agriculture, construction, taxation and social benefits. To achieve these aims, it is essential to increase the value given to protecting and restoring natural ecosystems, to the sustainable use of resources and to improving human health. This is where transformational change is most needed and potentially most beneficial for the EU economy, society and natural environment. The EU should also promote and invest in the necessary digital transformation and tools as these are essential enablers of the changes.

While all of these areas for action are strongly interlinked and mutually reinforcing, careful attention will have to be paid when there are potential trade-offs between economic, environmental and social objectives. The Green Deal will make consistent use of all policy levers: regulation and standardisation, investment and innovation, national reforms, dialogue with social partners and international cooperation. The European Pillar of Social Rights will guide action in ensuring that no one is left behind.

New measures on their own will not be enough to achieve the European Green Deal's objectives. In addition to launching new initiatives, the Commission will work with the Member States to step up the EU's efforts to ensure that current legislation and policies relevant to the Green Deal are enforced and effectively implemented.

2.1.1. Increasing the EU's climate ambition for 2030 and 2050

The Commission has already set out a clear vision of how to achieve climate neutrality by 2050[5]. This vision should form the basis for the long-term strategy that the EU will submit to the United Nations Framework Convention on Climate Change in early 2020. To set out clearly the conditions for an effective and fair transition, to provide predictability for investors, and to ensure that the transition is irreversible, the **Commission will propose the first European 'Climate Law' by March 2020.** This will enshrine the 2050 climate neutrality objective in legislation. The Climate Law will also ensure that all EU policies contribute to the climate neutrality objective and that all sectors play their part.

The EU has already started to modernise and **transform the economy with the aim of climate neutrality.** Between 1990 and 2018, it reduced greenhouse gas emissions by 23%, while the economy grew by 61%. However, current policies will only reduce greenhouse gas emissions by 60% by 2050. Much remains to be done, starting with more ambitious climate action in the coming decade.

By summer 2020, the Commission will present an impact assessed plan **to increase the EU's greenhouse gas emission reductions target for 2030 to at least 50% and towards 55% compared with 1990 levels in a responsible way.** To deliver these additional greenhouse gas emissions reductions, the Commission will, by June 2021, review and propose to revise where necessary, all relevant climate-related policy

---

5 A Clean Planet for all - A European strategic long-term vision for a prosperous, modern, competitive and climate neutral economy COM (2018) 773

instruments. This will comprise the Emissions Trading System[6], including a possible extension of European emissions trading to new sectors, Member State targets to reduce emissions in sectors outside the Emissions Trading System[7], and the regulation on land use, land use change and forestry[8]. The Commission will propose to amend the Climate Law to update it accordingly.

These policy reforms will help to ensure effective carbon pricing throughout the economy. This will encourage changes in consumer and business behaviour, and facilitate an increase in sustainable public and private investment. The different pricing instruments must complement each other and jointly provide a coherent policy framework. Ensuring that taxation is aligned with climate objectives is also essential. The Commission will propose to revise the Energy Taxation Directive[9], focusing on environmental issues, and proposing to use the provisions in the Treaties that allow the European Parliament and the Council to adopt proposals in this area through the ordinary legislative procedure by qualified majority voting rather than by unanimity.

As long as many international partners do not share the same ambition as the EU, there is a risk of carbon leakage, either because production is transferred from the EU to other countries with lower ambition for emission reduction, or because EU products are replaced by more carbon-intensive imports. If this risk materialises, there will be no reduction in global emissions, and this will frustrate the efforts of the EU and its industries to meet the global climate objectives of the Paris Agreement.

Should differences in levels of ambition worldwide persist, as the EU increases its climate ambition, **the Commission will propose a carbon border adjustment mechanism, for selected sectors, to reduce the risk of carbon leakage.** This would ensure that the price of imports reflect more accurately their carbon content. This measure will be designed to comply with World Trade Organization rules and other international obligations of the EU. It would be an alternative to the measures[10] that address the risk of carbon leakage in the EU's Emissions Trading System.

The Commission will adopt a new, more ambitious EU strategy on adaptation to climate change. This is essential, as climate change will continue to create significant stress in Europe in spite of the mitigation efforts. Strengthening the efforts on climate-proofing, resilience building, prevention and preparedness is crucial. Work on climate adaptation should continue to influence public and private investments, including on nature-based solutions. It will be important to ensure that across the EU, investors, insurers, businesses, cities and citizens are able to access data and to develop instruments to integrate climate change into their risk management practices.

---

6 Consolidated version of Directive 2003/87/EC of the European Parliament and of the Council establishing a scheme for greenhouse gas emission allowance trading within the Community and amending Council Directive 96/61/EC

7 Regulation (EU) 2018/842 on binding annual greenhouse gas emission reductions by Member States from 2021 to 2030 contributing to climate action to meet commitments under the Paris Agreement and amending Regulation (EU) No 525/2013

8 Regulation (EU) 2018/841 on the inclusion of greenhouse gas emissions and removals from land use, land use change and forestry in the 2030 climate and energy framework, and amending Regulation (EU) No 525/2013 and Decision No 529/2013/EU

9 Council Directive 2003/96/EC restructuring the Community framework for the taxation of energy products and electricity

10 Such as the free allocation of emission allowances or compensation for the increase in electricity costs

2.1.2. *Supplying clean, affordable and secure energy*

Further decarbonising the energy system is critical to reach climate objectives in 2030 and 2050. The production and use of energy across economic sectors account for more than 75% of the EU's greenhouse gas emissions. Energy efficiency must be prioritised. A power sector must be developed that is based largely on renewable sources, complemented by the rapid phasing out of coal and decarbonising gas. At the same time, the EU's energy supply needs to be secure and affordable for consumers and businesses. For this to happen, it is essential to ensure that the European energy market is fully integrated, interconnected and digitalised, while respecting technological neutrality.

Member States will present their revised energy and climate plans by the end of 2019. In line with the Regulation on the Governance of the Energy Union and Climate Action[11], these plans should set out ambitious national contributions to EU-wide targets. The Commission will assess the ambition of the plans, and the need for additional measures if the level of ambition is not sufficient. This will feed into the process of increasing climate ambition for 2030, for which the Commission will review and propose to revise, where necessary, the relevant energy legislation by June 2021. When Member States begin updating their national energy and climate plans in 2023, they should reflect the new climate ambition. The Commission will continue to ensure that all relevant legislation is rigorously enforced.

The clean energy transition should involve and benefit consumers. Renewable energy sources will have an essential role. Increasing offshore wind production will be essential, building on regional cooperation between Member States. The smart integration of renewables, energy efficiency and other sustainable solutions across sectors will help to achieve decarbonisation at the lowest possible cost. The rapid decrease in the cost of renewables, combined with improved design of support policies, has already reduced the impact on households' energy bills of renewables deployment. The Commission will present by mid-2020 measures to help achieve smart integration. In parallel, the decarbonisation of the gas sector will be facilitated, including via enhancing support for the development of decarbonised gases, via a forward-looking design for a competitive decarbonised gas market, and by addressing the issue of energy-related methane emissions.

The risk of energy poverty must be addressed for households that cannot afford key energy services to ensure a basic standard of living. Effective programmes, such as financing schemes for households to renovate their houses, can reduce energy bills and help the environment. In 2020, the Commission will produce guidance to assist Member States in addressing the issue of energy poverty.

The transition to climate neutrality also requires smart infrastructure. Increased cross-border and regional cooperation will help achieve the benefits of the clean energy transition at affordable prices. The regulatory framework for energy infrastructure, including the TEN-E Regulation[12], will need to be reviewed to ensure consistency with the climate neutrality objective. This framework should foster the deployment of innovative technologies and infrastructure, such as smart grids, hydrogen networks or carbon capture, storage and utilisation, energy storage, also enabling sector integration. Some existing infrastructure and assets will require upgrading to remain fit for purpose and climate resilient.

---

11 Regulation (EU) 2018/1999 on the Governance of the Energy Union and Climate Action

12 Trans-European Networks - Energy (TEN-E) Regulation

2.1.3. Mobilising industry for a clean and circular economy

Achieving a climate neutral and circular economy requires the full mobilisation of industry. It takes 25 years – a generation – to transform an industrial sector and all the value chains. To be ready in 2050, decisions and actions need to be taken in the next five years.

From 1970 to 2017, the annual global extraction of materials tripled and it continues to grow[13], posing a major global risk. About half of total greenhouse gas emissions and more than 90% of biodiversity loss and water stress come from resource extraction and processing of materials, fuels and food. The EU's industry has started the shift but still accounts for 20% of the EU's greenhouse gas emissions. It remains too 'linear', and dependent on a throughput of new materials extracted, traded and processed into goods, and finally disposed of as waste or emissions. Only 12% of the materials it uses come from recycling[14].

The transition is an opportunity to expand sustainable and job-intensive economic activity. There is significant potential in global markets for low-emission technologies, sustainable products and services. Likewise, the circular economy offers great potential for new activities and jobs. However, the transformation is taking place at a too slow pace with progress neither widespread nor uniform. The European Green Deal will support and accelerate the EU's industry transition to a sustainable model of inclusive growth.

In March 2020, the Commission will adopt an EU industrial strategy to address the twin challenge of the green and the digital transformation. Europe must leverage the potential of the digital transformation, which is a key enabler for reaching the Green Deal objectives. Together with the industrial strategy, **a new circular economy action plan** will help modernise the EU's economy and draw benefit from the opportunities of the circular economy domestically and globally. A key aim of the new policy framework will be to stimulate the development of lead markets for climate neutral and circular products, in the EU and beyond.

Energy-intensive industries, such as steel, chemicals and cement, are indispensable to Europe's economy, as they supply several key value chains. The decarbonisation and modernisation of this sector is essential. The recommendations published by the High Level Group of energy-intensive industries show the industry's commitment to these objectives[15].

The circular economy action plan will include a 'sustainable products' policy to support the circular design of all products based on a common methodology and principles. It will prioritise reducing and reusing materials before recycling them. It will foster new business models and set minimum requirements to prevent environmentally harmful products from being placed on the EU market. Extended producer responsibility will also be strengthened.

While the circular economy action plan will guide the transition of all sectors, **action will focus in particular on resource-intensive sectors such as textiles, construction, electronics and plastics**. The Commission will follow up on the 2018 plastics strategy focusing, among other things, on measures to tackle intentionally added micro plastics

---

13 Global Resources Outlook 2019: Natural Resources for the Future We Want: The International Resource Panel.

14 https://ec.europa.eu/eurostat/tgm/table.do?tab=table&init=1&language=en&pcode=cei_srm030&plugin=1

15 https://ec.europa.eu/commission/presscorner/detail/en/IP_19_6353

and unintentional releases of plastics, for example from textiles and tyre abrasion. The Commission will develop requirements to ensure that all packaging in the EU market is reusable or recyclable in an economically viable manner by 2030, will develop a regulatory framework for biodegradable and bio-based plastics, and will implement measures on single use plastics.

The circular economy action plan will also include **measures to encourage businesses to offer, and to allow consumers to choose, reusable, durable and repairable products.** It will analyse the need for a 'right to repair', and curb the built-in obsolescence of devices, in particular for electronics. Consumer policy will help to empower consumers to make informed choices and play an active role in the ecological transition. New business models based on renting and sharing goods and services will play a role as long as they are truly sustainable and affordable.

Reliable, comparable and verifiable information also plays an important part in enabling buyers to make more sustainable decisions and reduces the risk of 'green washing'. Companies making 'green claims' should substantiate these against a standard methodology to assess their impact on the environment. The Commission will step up its regulatory and non-regulatory efforts to tackle false green claims. Digitalisation can also help improve the availability of information on the characteristics of products sold in the EU. For instance, an electronic product passport could provide information on a product's origin, composition, repair and dismantling possibilities, and end of life handling. Public authorities, including the EU institutions, should lead by example and ensure that their procurement is green. The Commission will propose further legislation and guidance on green public purchasing.

A sustainable product policy also has the potential to reduce waste significantly. Where waste cannot be avoided, its economic value must be recovered and its impact on the environment and on climate change avoided or minimised. This requires new legislation, including targets and measures for tackling over-packaging and waste generation. In parallel, EU companies should benefit from a robust and integrated single market for secondary raw materials and by-products. This requires deeper cooperation across value chains, as in the case of the Circular Plastics Alliance. The Commission will consider legal requirements to boost the market of secondary raw materials with mandatory recycled content (for instance for packaging, vehicles, construction materials and batteries). To simplify waste management for citizens and ensure cleaner secondary materials for businesses, the Commission will also propose an EU model for separate waste collection. The Commission is of the view that the EU should stop exporting its waste outside of the EU and will therefore revisit the rules on waste shipments and illegal exports.

Access to resources is also a strategic security question for Europe's ambition to deliver the Green Deal. Ensuring the supply of sustainable raw materials, in particular of critical raw materials necessary for clean technologies, digital, space and defence applications, by diversifying supply from both primary and secondary sources, is therefore one of the pre-requisites to make this transition happen.

EU industry needs 'climate and resource frontrunners' to develop the first commercial applications of breakthrough technologies in key industrial sectors by 2030. Priority areas include clean hydrogen, fuel cells and other alternative fuels, energy storage, and carbon capture, storage and utilisation. As an example, the Commission will support clean steel breakthrough technologies leading to a zero-carbon steel making process by 2030 and will explore whether part of the funding being liquidated under the European

Coal and Steel Community can be used. More broadly, the EU Emissions Trading System Innovation Fund will help to deploy such large-scale innovative projects.

Promoting new forms of collaboration with industry and investments in strategic value chains are essential. The Commission will continue to implement the Strategic Action Plan on Batteries and support the European Battery Alliance. It will propose legislation in 2020 to ensure a safe, circular and sustainable battery value chain for all batteries, including to supply the growing market of electric vehicles. The Commission will also support other initiatives leading to alliances and to a large-scale pooling of resources, for example in the form of Important Projects of Common European Interest, where targeted time-bound State aid can help build new innovative value chains.

Digital technologies are a critical enabler for attaining the sustainability goals of the Green deal in many different sectors. The Commission will explore measures to ensure that digital technologies such as artificial intelligence, 5G, cloud and edge computing and the internet of things can accelerate and maximise the impact of policies to deal with climate change and protect the environment. Digitalisation also presents new opportunities for distance monitoring of air and water pollution, or for monitoring and optimising how energy and natural resources are used. At the same time, Europe needs a digital sector that puts sustainability at its heart. The Commission will also consider measures to improve the energy efficiency and circular economy performance of the sector itself, from broadband networks to data centres and ICT devices. The Commission will assess the need for more transparency on the environmental impact of electronic communication services, more stringent measures when deploying new networks and the benefits of supporting 'take-back' schemes to incentivise people to return their unwanted devices such as mobile phones, tablets and chargers.

2.1.4. *Building and renovating in an energy and resource efficient way*

The construction, use and renovation of buildings require significant amounts of energy and mineral resources (e.g. sand, gravel, cement). Buildings also account for 40% of energy consumed. Today the annual renovation rate of the building stock varies from 0.4 to 1.2% in the Member States. This rate will need at least to double to reach the EU's energy efficiency and climate objectives. In parallel, 50 million consumers struggle to keep their homes adequately warm.

To address the twin challenge of energy efficiency and affordability, the EU and the Member States should **engage in a 'renovation wave' of public and private buildings.** While increasing renovation rates is a challenge, renovation lowers energy bills, and can reduce energy poverty. It can also boost the construction sector and is an opportunity to support SMEs and local jobs.

The Commission will rigorously **enforce the legislation related to the energy performance of buildings**. This will start with an assessment in 2020 of Member States' national long-term renovation strategies[16]. The Commission will also launch work on the possibility of including emissions from buildings in European emissions trading, as part of broader efforts to ensure that the relative prices of different energy sources provide the right signals for energy efficiency. In addition, the Commission will review the Construction Products Regulation[17]. It should ensure that the design of new and

16 As part of the requirements under the Energy Performance of Buildings Directive

17 Regulation (EU) No 305/2011 laying down harmonised conditions for the marketing of construction products and repealing Council Directive 89/106/EEC

renovated buildings at all stages is in line with the needs of the circular economy, and lead to increased digitalisation and climate-proofing of the building stock.

In parallel, the Commission proposes to work with stakeholders on a new initiative on renovation in 2020. This will include an open platform bringing together the buildings and construction sector, architects and engineers and local authorities to address the barriers to renovation. This initiative will also include innovative financing schemes under InvestEU. These could target housing associations or energy service companies that could roll out renovation including through energy performance contracting. An essential aim would be to organise renovation efforts into larger blocks to benefit from better financing conditions and economies of scale. The Commission will also work to lift national regulatory barriers that inhibit energy efficiency investments in rented and multi-ownership buildings. Particular attention will be paid to the renovation of social housing, to help households who struggle to pay their energy bills. Focus should also be put on renovating schools and hospitals, as the money saved through building efficiency will be money available to support education and public health.

2.1.5. Accelerating the shift to sustainable and smart mobility

Transport accounts for a quarter of the EU's greenhouse gas emissions, and still growing. To achieve climate neutrality, a 90% reduction in transport emissions is needed by 2050. Road, rail, aviation, and waterborne transport will all have to contribute to the reduction. Achieving sustainable transport means putting users first and providing them with more affordable, accessible, healthier and cleaner alternatives to their current mobility habits. The Commission will adopt a strategy for sustainable and smart mobility in 2020 that will address this challenge and tackle all emission sources.

Multimodal transport needs a strong boost. This will increase the efficiency of the transport system. As a matter of priority, a substantial part of the 75% of inland freight carried today by road should shift onto rail and inland waterways. This will require measures to manage better, and to increase the capacity of railways and inland waterways, which the Commission will propose by 2021. The Commission will also consider withdrawing and presenting a new proposal to revise the Combined Transport Directive[18] to turn it into an effective tool to support multimodal freight operations involving rail and waterborne transport, including short-sea shipping. In aviation, work on adopting the Commission's proposal on a truly Single European Sky will need to restart, as this will help achieve significant reductions in aviation emissions.

Automated and connected multimodal mobility will play an increasing role, together with smart traffic management systems enabled by digitalisation. The EU transport system and infrastructure will be made fit to support new sustainable mobility services that can reduce congestion and pollution, especially in urban areas. The Commission will help develop smart systems for traffic management and 'Mobility as a Service' solutions, through its funding instruments, such as the Connected Europe Facility.

The price of transport must reflect the impact it has on the environment and on health. Fossil-fuel subsidies should end and, in the context of the revision of the Energy Taxation Directive, the Commission will look closely at the current tax exemptions including for aviation and maritime fuels and at how best to close any loopholes.

---

[18] Proposal for a directive amending Directive 92/106/EEC on the establishment of common rules for certain types of combined transport of goods between Member States COM(2017) 648

Similarly, the Commission will propose to extend European emissions trading to the maritime sector, and to reduce the EU Emissions Trading System allowances allocated for free to airlines. This will be coordinated with action at global level, notably at the International Civil Aviation Organization and International Maritime Organization. The Commission will also give fresh political consideration as to how to achieve effective road pricing in the EU. It calls on the European Parliament and the Council to maintain the high level of ambition in the Commission's original proposal for the 'Eurovignette' Directive[19], and is ready to withdraw it if necessary and to propose alternative measures.

The EU should in parallel **ramp-up the production and deployment of sustainable alternative transport fuels.** By 2025, about 1 million public recharging and refuelling stations will be needed for the 13 million zero- and low-emission vehicles expected on European roads. The Commission will support the deployment of public recharging and refuelling points where persistent gaps exist, notably for long-distance travel and in less densely populated areas, and will launch as quickly as possible a new funding call to support this. These steps will complement the measures taken at national level. The Commission will consider legislative options to boost the production and uptake of sustainable alternative fuels for the different transport modes. The Commission will also review the Alternative Fuels Infrastructure Directive[20] and the TEN-T Regulation to accelerate the deployment of zero- and low-emission vehicles and vessels.

Transport should become drastically less polluting, especially in cities. A combination of measures should address emissions, urban congestion, and improved public transport. The Commission will propose more stringent air pollutant emissions standards for combustion-engine vehicles. The Commission will also propose to revise by June 2021 the legislation on CO_2 emission performance standards for cars and vans, to ensure a clear pathway from 2025 onwards towards zero-emission mobility. In parallel, it will consider applying European emissions trading to road transport, as a complement to existing and future CO_2 emission performance standards for vehicles. It will take action in relation to maritime transport, including to regulate access of the most polluting ships to EU ports and to oblige docked ships to use shore-side electricity. Similarly, air quality should be improved near airports by tackling the emissions of pollutants by aeroplanes and airport operations.

2.1.6. From 'Farm to Fork': designing a fair, healthy and environmentally-friendly food system

European food is famous for being safe, nutritious and of high quality. It should now also become **the global standard for sustainability.** Although the transition to more sustainable systems has started, feeding a fast-growing world population remains a challenge with current production patterns. Food production still results in air, water and soil pollution, contributes to the loss of biodiversity and climate change, and consumes excessive amounts of natural resources, while an important part of food is wasted. At the same time, low quality diets contribute to obesity and diseases such as cancer.

There are new opportunities for all operators in the food value chain. New technologies and scientific discoveries, combined with increasing public awareness and demand for sustainable food, will benefit all stakeholders. The Commission will present

19 Proposal for a directive amending Directive 1999/62/EC on the charging of heavy goods vehicles for the use of certain infrastructure COM(2017) 275

20 Directive 2014/94/EU on the deployment of alternative fuels infrastructure

the 'Farm to Fork' Strategy in spring 2020 and launch a broad stakeholder debate covering all the stages of the food chain, and paving the way to formulating a more sustainable food policy.

European farmers and fishermen are key to managing the transition. The Farm to Fork Strategy will strengthen their efforts to tackle climate change, protect the environment and preserve biodiversity. The common agricultural and common fisheries policies will remain key tools to support these efforts while ensuring a decent living for farmers, fishermen and their families. The Commission's proposals for the common agricultural policy for 2021 to 2027 stipulate that at least 40% of the common agricultural policy's overall budget and at least 30% of the Maritime Fisheries Fund would contribute to climate action.

The Commission will work with the European Parliament and the Council **to achieve at least this level of ambition in the proposals.** Given that the start of the revised Common Agricultural Policy is likely to be delayed to the beginning of 2022, the Commission will work with the Member States and stakeholders to ensure that from the outset the national strategic plans for agriculture fully reflect the ambition of the Green Deal and the Farm to Fork Strategy. The Commission will ensure that these strategic plans are assessed against robust climate and environmental criteria. These plans should lead to the use of sustainable practices, such as precision agriculture, organic farming, agro-ecology, agro-forestry and stricter animal welfare standards. By shifting the focus from compliance to performance, measures such as eco-schemes should reward farmers for improved environmental and climate performance, including managing and storing carbon in the soil, and improved nutrient management to improve water quality and reduce emissions. The Commission will work with the Member States to develop the potential of sustainable seafood as a source of low-carbon food.

The strategic plans will need to reflect an increased level of ambition to reduce significantly the use and risk of chemical pesticides, as well as the use of fertilisers and antibiotics. The Commission will identify the measures, including legislative, needed to bring about these reductions based on a stakeholder dialogue. The area under organic farming will also need to increase in Europe. The EU needs to develop innovative ways to protect harvests from pests and diseases and to consider the potential role of new innovative techniques to improve the sustainability of the food system, while ensuring that they are safe.

The Farm to Fork Strategy will also contribute to achieving a circular economy. It will aim to reduce the environmental impact of the food processing and retail sectors by taking action on transport, storage, packaging and food waste. This will include actions to combat food fraud, including strengthening enforcement and investigative capacity at EU level, and to launch a process to identify new innovative food and feed products, such as seafood based on algae.

Lastly, the Farm to Fork Strategy will strive **to stimulate sustainable food consumption and promote affordable healthy food for all.** Imported food that does not comply with relevant EU environmental standards is not allowed on EU markets. The Commission will propose actions to help consumers choose healthy and sustainable diets and reduce food waste. The Commission will explore new ways to give consumers better information, including by digital means, on details such as where the food comes from, its nutritional value, and its environmental footprint. The Farm to Fork strategy will also contain proposals to improve the position of farmers in the value chain.

2.1.7. Preserving and restoring ecosystems and biodiversity

Ecosystems provide essential services such as food, fresh water and clean air, and shelter. They mitigate natural disasters, pests and diseases and help regulate the climate. However, the EU is not meeting some of its most important environmental objectives for 2020, such as the Aichi targets under the Convention on Biological Diversity. The EU and its global partners need to halt biodiversity loss. The Intergovernmental Science-Policy Platform on Biodiversity and Ecosystem Services' 2019 Global Assessment Report[21] showed worldwide erosion of biodiversity, caused primarily by changes in how land and sea are used, direct exploitation of natural resources, and with climate change as the third most important driver of biodiversity loss.

The Conference of the Parties to the Convention on Biological Diversity in Kunming, China, in October 2020 is an opportunity for the world to adopt a robust global framework to halt biodiversity loss. To ensure that the EU plays a key role, the Commission will present a **Biodiversity Strategy by March 2020**, to be followed up by specific action in 2021. The strategy will outline the EU's position for the Conference of the Parties, with global targets to protect biodiversity, as well as commitments to address the main causes of biodiversity loss in the EU, underpinned by measurable objectives that address the main causes of biodiversity loss.

The biodiversity strategy will identify specific measures to meet these objectives. These could include quantified objectives, such as increasing the coverage of protected biodiversity-rich land and sea areas building on the Natura 2000 network. Member States should also reinforce cross-border cooperation to protect and restore more effectively the areas covered by the Natura 2000 network. The Commission will identify which measures, including legislation, would help Member States improve and restore damaged ecosystems to good ecological status, including carbon-rich ecosystems. The biodiversity strategy will also include proposals to green European cities and increase biodiversity in urban spaces. The Commission will consider drafting a nature restoration plan and will look at how provide funding to help Member States to reach this aim.

All EU policies should contribute to preserving and restoring Europe's natural capital[22]. The Farm to Fork Strategy, outlined in section 2.1.6, will address the use of pesticides and fertilisers in agriculture. Work will continue under the common fisheries policy to reduce the adverse impacts that fishing can have on ecosystems, especially in sensitive areas. The Commission will also support more connected and well-managed marine protected areas.

Forest ecosystems are under increasing pressure, as a result of climate change. The EU's forested area needs to improve, both in quality and quantity, for the EU to reach climate neutrality and a healthy environment. Sustainable re- and afforestation and the restoration of degraded forests can increase absorption of CO_2 while improving the resilience of forests and promoting the circular bio-economy. Building on the 2030 biodiversity strategy, the Commission will prepare a new EU forest strategy covering the whole forest cycle and promoting the many services that forests provide.

The new EU forest strategy will have as its key objectives effective afforestation, and forest preservation and restoration in Europe, to help to increase the absorption of CO_2,, reduce the incidence and extent of forest fires, and promote the bio-economy, in

21 https://ipbes.net/news/ipbes-global-assessment-preview

22 EU guidelines SWD (2019)305 FINAL "EU guidance on integrating ecosystems and their services into decision-making"

full respect for ecological principles favourable to biodiversity. The national strategic plans under the common agricultural policy should incentivise forest managers to preserve, grow and manage forests sustainably. Building on the Communication on Stepping up EU Action to Protect and Restore the World's Forests[23], the Commission will take measures, both regulatory and otherwise, to promote imported products and value chains that do not involve deforestation and forest degradation.

A sustainable 'blue economy' will have to play a central role in alleviating the multiple demands on the EU's land resources and tackling climate change. The role of oceans in mitigating and adapting to climate change is increasingly recognised. The sector can contribute by improving the use of aquatic and marine resources and, for example, by promoting the production and use of new sources of protein that can relieve pressure on agricultural land. More generally, lasting solutions to climate change require greater attention to nature-based solutions including healthy and resilient seas and oceans. The Commission will analyse the findings of the International Panel on Climate Change special report on oceans[24] and propose measures in the maritime area. This will include ways to manage maritime space more sustainably, notably to help tap into the growing potential of offshore renewable energy. The Commission will also take a zero-tolerance approach to illegal, unreported and unregulated fishing. The 2020 United Nations Ocean Conference in Portugal will be an opportunity for the EU to highlight the importance of action on ocean issues.

2.1.8. A zero pollution ambition for a toxic-free environment

Creating a toxic-free environment requires more action to prevent pollution from being generated as well as measures to clean and remedy it. To protect Europe's citizens and ecosystems, the EU needs to better monitor, report, prevent and remedy pollution from air, water, soil, and consumer products. To achieve this, the EU and Member States will need to look more systematically at all policies and regulations. **To address these interlinked challenges, the Commission will adopt in 2021 a zero pollution action plan for air, water and soil.**

The natural functions of ground and surface water must be restored. This is essential to preserve and restore biodiversity in lakes, rivers, wetlands and estuaries, and to prevent and limit damage from floods. Implementing the 'Farm to Fork' strategy will reduce pollution from excess nutrients. In addition, the Commission will propose measures to address pollution from urban runoff and from new or particularly harmful sources of pollution such as micro plastics and chemicals, including pharmaceuticals. There is also a need to address the combined effects of different pollutants.

The Commission will draw on the lessons learnt from the evaluation of the current air quality legislation[25]. It will also propose to strengthen provisions on monitoring[26], modelling and air quality plans to help local authorities achieve cleaner air. The Commission will notably propose to revise air quality standards to align them more closely with the World Health Organization recommendations.

The Commission will review EU measures to address pollution from large industrial installations. It will look at the sectoral scope of the legislation and at how to make it

[23] COM/2019/352 final

[24] Special Report on the Ocean and Cryosphere in a Changing Climate

[25] Fitness check of the Ambient Air Quality Directives SWD(2019) 427

[26] Including by making use of new monitoring opportunities provided by digitalisation

fully consistent with climate, energy and circular economy policies. The Commission will also work with Member States to improve the prevention of industrial accidents.

To ensure a toxic-free environment, the Commission will present a chemicals strategy for sustainability. This will both help to protect citizens and the environment better against hazardous chemicals and encourage innovation for the development of safe and sustainable alternatives. All parties including industry should work together to combine better health and environmental protection and increased global competitiveness. This can be achieved by simplifying and strengthening the legal framework. The Commission will review how to use better the EU's agencies and scientific bodies to move towards a process of 'one substance – one assessment' and to provide greater transparency when prioritising action to deal with chemicals. In parallel, the regulatory framework will need to rapidly reflect scientific evidence on the risk posed by endocrine disruptors, hazardous chemicals in products including imports, combination effects of different chemicals and very persistent chemicals.

2.2. Mainstreaming sustainability in all EU policies

2.2.1. Pursuing green finance and investment and ensuring a just transition

To achieve the ambition set by the European Green Deal, there are significant investment needs. The Commission has estimated that achieving the current 2030 climate and energy targets will require €260 billion of additional annual investment[27], about 1.5% of 2018 GDP[28]. This flow of investment will need to be sustained over time. The magnitude of the investment challenge requires mobilising both the public and private sector.

The Commission will present a Sustainable Europe Investment Plan to help meet the additional funding needs. It will combine dedicated financing to support sustainable investments, and proposals for an improved enabling framework that is conducive to green investment. At the same time, it will be essential to prepare a pipeline of sustainable projects. Technical assistance and advisory services will help project promoters to identify and prepare projects and to access sources of finance.

The EU budget will play a key role. The Commission has proposed a 25% target for climate mainstreaming across all EU programmes. The EU budget will also contribute to achieving climate objectives on the revenue side. The Commission has proposed new revenue streams ("Own Resources"), one of which is based on the non-recycled plastic-packaging waste. A second revenue stream could involve allocating 20% of the revenue from the auctioning of EU Emissions Trading System to the EU budget.

At least 30% of the InvestEU Fund will contribute to fighting climate change. Moreover, projects will be subject to sustainability proofing to screen the contribution that they make to climate, environmental and social objectives. InvestEU also offers Member States the option to use the EU budgetary guarantee e.g. to deliver on climate-related cohesion policy objectives in their territories and regions. InvestEU also strengthens cooperation with national promotional banks and institutions, which can encourage an overall greening of their activities to deliver on EU policy objectives.

27 Communication "United in delivering the Energy Union and Climate Action - Setting the foundations for a successful clean energy transition" COM(2019) 285

28 These estimates are conservative, as they do not consider, for instance, the investment needs for climate adaptation or for other environmental challenges, such as biodiversity. They also exclude the public investment needed to address the social costs of the transition and the costs of inaction

Moreover, as part of the revision of the EU Emission Trading System, the Commission will review the role of the Innovation and Modernisation Funds, which are not financed by the EU's long-term budget. The ambition will be to strengthen their role and their effectiveness in deploying innovative and climate neutral solutions across the EU. In the revision of the EU Emissions Trading System, the allocation of additional revenues from allowances to the EU budget with a view to strengthening the financing of the just transition will also be considered.

The Commission will also work with the European Investment Bank (EIB) Group, national promotional banks and institutions, as well as with other international financial institutions. The EIB set itself the target of doubling its climate target from 25% to 50% by 2025, thus becoming Europe's climate bank.

As part of the Sustainable Europe Investment Plan, the Commission will propose a Just Transition Mechanism, including a Just Transition Fund, to leave no one behind. The transition can only succeed if it is conducted in a fair and inclusive way. The most vulnerable are the most exposed to the harmful effects of climate change and environmental degradation. At the same time, managing the transition will lead to significant structural changes in business models, skill requirements and relative prices. Citizens, depending on their social and geographic circumstances, will be affected in different ways. Not all Member States, regions and cities start the transition from the same point or have the same capacity to respond. These challenges require a strong policy response at all levels.

The Just Transition Mechanism will focus on the regions and sectors that are most affected by the transition because they depend on fossil fuels or carbon-intensive processes. It will draw on sources of funding from the EU budget as well as the EIB group to leverage the necessary private and public resources. Support will be linked to promoting a transition towards low-carbon and climate-resilient activities. It will also strive to protect the citizens and workers most vulnerable to the transition, providing access to re-skilling programmes, jobs in new economic sectors, or energy-efficient housing. The Commission will work with the Member States and regions to help them put in place territorial transition plans.

The mechanism will come in addition to the substantial contribution of the EU's budget through all programmes directly relevant to the transition, as well as other funds such as the European Regional Development Fund and the European Social Fund Plus.

In order to bring an answer to the long-term financing needs of the transition, the Commission will continue to explore with relevant partners, as part of the Sustainable Europe Investment Plan, additional sources that could be mobilised and innovative ways to do so.

The need for a socially just transition must also be reflected in policies at EU and national level. This includes investment to provide affordable solutions to those affected by carbon pricing policies, for example through public transport, as well as measures to address energy poverty and promote re-skilling. Coherence of climate and environment policies and a holistic approach are often a precondition for ensuring they are perceived as fair, as illustrated by the debate on taxation of various modes of transport. For companies and their workers, an active social dialogue helps to anticipate and successfully manage change. The European Semester process of macroeconomic coordination will support national policies on these issues.

The private sector will be key to financing the green transition. Long-term signals are needed to direct financial and capital flows to green investment and to avoid stranded assets. The Commission will present a renewed sustainable finance strategy in the third quarter of 2020 that will focus on a number of actions.

First, the strategy will strengthen the foundations for sustainable investment. This will require notably that the European Parliament and Council adopt the taxonomy for classifying environmentally sustainable activities. Sustainability should be further embedded into the corporate governance framework, as many companies still focus too much on short-term financial performance compared to their long-term development and sustainability aspects. At the same time, companies and financial institutions will need to increase their disclosure on climate and environmental data so that investors are fully informed about the sustainability of their investments. To this end, the Commission will review the Non-Financial Reporting Directive. To ensure appropriate management of environmental risks and mitigation opportunities, and reduce related transaction costs, the Commission will also support businesses and other stakeholders in developing standardised natural capital accounting practices within the EU and internationally.

Second, increased opportunities will be provided for investors and companies by making it easier for them to identify sustainable investments and ensuring that they are credible. This could be done via clear labels for retail investment products and by developing an EU green bond standard that facilitates sustainable investment in the most convenient way.

Third, climate and environmental risks will be managed and integrated into the financial system. This means better integrating such risks into the EU prudential framework and assessing the suitability of the existing capital requirements for green assets. We will also examine how our financial system can help to increase resilience to climate and environmental risks, in particular when it comes to the physical risks and damage arising from natural catastrophes.

2.2.2. Greening national budgets and sending the right price signals

National budgets play a key role in the transition. A greater use of green budgeting tools will help to redirect public investment, consumption and taxation to green priorities and away from harmful subsidies. The Commission will work with the Member States to screen and benchmark green budgeting practices. This will make it easier to assess to what extent annual budgets and medium-term fiscal plans take environmental considerations and risks into account, and learn from best practices. The review of the European economic governance framework will include a reference to green public investment in the context of the quality of public finance. This will inform a debate on how to improve EU fiscal governance. The outcome of the debate will form the basis for any possible future steps including how to treat green investments within EU fiscal rules, while preserving safeguards against risks to debt sustainability.

Well-designed tax reforms can boost economic growth and resilience to climate shocks and help contribute to a fairer society and to a just transition. They play a direct role by sending the right price signals and providing the right incentives for sustainable behaviour by producers, users and consumers. At national level, the European Green Deal will create the context for broad-based tax reforms, removing subsidies for fossil fuels, shifting the tax burden from labour to pollution, and taking into account social considerations. There is a need to ensure rapid adoption of the Commission's proposal on value added tax (VAT) rates currently on the table of the Council, so that Member States can make a more targeted use of VAT rates to reflect increased environmental ambitions, for example to support organic fruit and vegetables.

Evaluations are underway of the relevant State aid guidelines including the environmental and energy State aid guidelines. The guidelines will be revised by 2021 to reflect the policy objectives of the European Green Deal, supporting a cost-effective transition to climate neutrality by 2050, and will facilitate the phasing out of fossil fuels, in particular those that are most polluting, ensuring a level-playing field in the internal market. These revisions are also an opportunity to address market barriers to the deployment of clean products.

2.2.3. Mobilising research and fostering innovation

New technologies, sustainable solutions and disruptive innovation are critical to achieve the objectives of the European Green Deal. To keep its competitive advantage in clean technologies, the EU needs to increase significantly the large-scale deployment and demonstration of new technologies across sectors and across the single market, building new innovative value chains. This challenge is beyond the means of individual Member States. Horizon Europe, in synergy with other EU programmes, will play a pivotal role in leveraging national public and private investments. At least 35% of the budget of Horizon Europe will fund new solutions for climate, which are relevant for implementing the Green Deal.

The full range of instruments available under the Horizon Europe programme will support the research and innovation efforts needed. Four 'Green Deal Missions' will help deliver large-scale changes in areas such as adaptation to climate change, oceans, cities and soil. These missions will bring together a wide range of stakeholders including regions and citizens. Partnerships with industry and Member States will support research and innovation on transport, including batteries, clean hydrogen, low-carbon steel making, circular bio-based sectors and the built environment. The knowledge and innovation communities run by the European Institute of Innovation and Technology will continue to promote collaboration among higher education institutions, research organisations and companies on climate change, sustainable energy, food for the future, and smart, environmentally-friendly and integrated urban transport. The European Innovation Council will dedicate funding, equity investment and business acceleration services to high potential start-ups and SMEs for them to achieve breakthrough Green Deal innovation that can be scaled up rapidly on global markets.

Conventional approaches will not be sufficient. Emphasising experimentation, and working across sectors and disciplines, the EU's research and innovation agenda will take the systemic approach needed to achieve the aims of the Green Deal. The Horizon Europe programme will also involve local communities in working towards a more sustainable future, in initiatives that seek to combine societal pull and technology push.

Accessible and interoperable data are at the heart of data-driven innovation. This data, combined with digital infrastructure (e.g. supercomputers, cloud, ultra-fast networks) and artificial intelligence solutions, facilitate evidence-based decisions and expand the capacity to understand and tackle environmental challenges. The Commission will support work to unlock the full benefits of the digital transformation to support the ecological transition. An immediate priority will be to boost the EU's ability to predict and manage environmental disasters. To do this, the Commission will bring together European scientific and industrial excellence to develop a very high precision digital model of the Earth.

2.2.4. *Activating education and training*

Schools, training institutions and universities are well placed to engage with pupils, parents, and the wider community on the changes needed for a successful transition. The Commission will prepare a European competence framework to help develop and assess knowledge, skills and attitudes on climate change and sustainable development. It will also provide support materials and facilitate the exchange of good practices in EU networks of teacher-training programmes.

The Commission has been working to provide Member States with new financial resources to make school buildings and operations more sustainable. It has strengthened collaboration with the European Investment Bank and created stronger links between structural funds and the new financial instruments with the aim of leveraging €3 billion in investment in school infrastructure in 2020.

Pro-active re-skilling and upskilling are necessary to reap the benefits of the ecological transition. The proposed European Social Fund+ will play an important role in helping Europe's workforce to acquire the skills they need to transfer from declining sectors to growing sectors and to adapt to new processes. The Skills Agenda and the Youth Guarantee will be updated to enhance employability in the green economy.

2.2.5. *A green oath: 'do no harm'*

All EU actions and policies should pull together to help the EU achieve a successful and just transition towards a sustainable future. The Commission's better regulation tools provide a solid basis for this. Based on public consultations, on the identification of the environmental, social and economic impacts, and on analyses of how SMEs are affected and innovation fostered or hindered, impact assessments contribute to making efficient policy choices at minimum costs, in line with the objectives of the Green Deal. Evaluations also systematically assess coherence between current legislation and new priorities.

To support its work to identify and remedy inconsistencies in current legislation, **the Commission invites stakeholders to use the available platforms[29] to simplify legislation and identify problematic cases.** The Commission will consider these suggestions when preparing evaluations, impact assessments and legislative proposals for the European Green Deal.

In addition, building on the results of its recent stock taking of better regulation policy, the Commission will **improve the way its better regulation guidelines and supporting tools address sustainability and innovation issues.** The objective is to ensure that all Green Deal initiatives achieve their objectives in the most effective and least burdensome way and all other EU initiatives live up to a green oath to 'do no harm'. To this end, the explanatory memorandum accompanying all legislative proposals and delegated acts will include a specific section explaining how each initiative upholds this principle.

[29] *'Have Your Say – Lighten the Load'* website: https://ec.europa.eu/info/law/better-regulation/lighten-load

3. THE EU AS A GLOBAL LEADER

The global challenges of climate change and environmental degradation require a global response. The EU will continue to promote and implement ambitious environment, climate and energy policies across the world. It will develop a stronger 'green deal diplomacy' focused on convincing and supporting others to take on their share of promoting more sustainable development. By setting a credible example, and following-up with diplomacy, trade policy, development support and other external policies, the EU can be an effective advocate. The Commission and the High Representative will work closely with Member States to mobilise all diplomatic channels both bilateral and multilateral – including the United Nations, the G7, G20, the World Trade Organization and other relevant international fora.

The EU will continue to ensure that the Paris Agreement remains the indispensable multilateral framework for tackling climate change. As the EU's share of global emissions is falling, comparable action and increased efforts by other regions will be critical for addressing the global climate challenge in a meaningful way. The debate on climate ambition will intensify in the coming months in line with the Paris Agreement provisions for regular stocktaking and updates. The Conference of Parties in Glasgow in 2020 will be an important milestone before the global stocktake in 2023. It will assess progress towards achieving long-term goals. As it currently stands, it is clear that the level of global ambition is insufficient[30]. The EU will engage more intensely with all partners to increase the collective effort and help them to revise and implement their nationally determined contributions and devise ambitious long-term strategies. This will build on the EU's own increased ambition as outlined in section 2.

In parallel, the EU will step up bilateral engagement with partner countries and, where necessary, establish innovative forms of engagement. The EU will continue to engage with the economies of the G20 that are responsible for 80% of global greenhouse gas emissions. Stepping up the level of climate action taken by international partners requires tailor-made geographic strategies that reflect different contexts and local needs – for example for current and future big emitters, for the least developed countries, and for small island developing states. **The EU is also working with global partners to develop international carbon markets** as a key tool to create economic incentives for climate action.

The EU will put emphasis on supporting its immediate neighbours. The ecological transition for Europe can only be fully effective if the EU's immediate neighbourhood also takes effective action. Work is underway on a green agenda for the Western Balkans. The Commission and the High Representative are also envisaging a number of strong environment, energy and climate partnerships with the Southern Neighbourhood and within the Eastern Partnership.

The 2020 EU-China summits in Beijing and Leipzig will be an opportunity to reinforce the partnership between the EU and China on climate and environmental issues, notably ahead of the **Kunming Biodiversity Conference**, and the Conference of Parties in Glasgow.

Likewise, the forthcoming Comprehensive Strategy with Africa, and the 2020 summit between the African Union and the EU, should make climate and environmental

---

[30] United Nations Environment emissions gap report 2019

issues key strands in relations between the two continents. In particular, the Africa-Europe Alliance for sustainable investment and jobs will seek to unlock Africa's potential to make rapid progress towards a green and circular economy including sustainable energy and food systems and smart cities. The EU will strengthen its engagement with Africa for the wider deployment and trade of sustainable and clean energy. Renewable energy and energy efficiency, for example for clean cooking, are key to closing the energy access gap in Africa while delivering the required reduction in CO_2. The EU will launch a "NaturAfrica" initiative to tackle biodiversity loss by creating a network of protected areas to protect wildlife and offer opportunities in green sectors for local populations.

More generally, **the EU will use its diplomatic and financial tools to ensure that green alliances are part of its relations with Africa and other partner countries and regions,** particularly in Latin America, the Caribbean, Asia and the Pacific.

The EU should also reinforce current initiatives and engage with third countries on cross-cutting climate and environment issues. This may include ending global fossil fuel subsidies in line with G20 commitments, phasing-out financing by multilateral institutions of fossil fuel infrastructure, strengthening sustainable financing, phasing out all new coal plant construction, and action to reduce methane emissions.

The EU also recognises that the global climate and environmental challenges are a significant threat multiplier and a source of instability. The ecological transition will reshape geopolitics, including global economic, trade and security interests. This will create challenges for a number of states and societies. The EU will work with all partners to increase climate and environmental resilience to prevent these challenges from becoming sources of conflict, food insecurity, population displacement and forced migration, and support a just transition globally. Climate policy implications should become an integral part of the EU's thinking and action on external issues, including in the context of the Common Security and Defence Policy.

Trade policy can support the EU's ecological transition. It serves as a platform to engage with trading partners on climate and environmental action. Commitments to sustainability have been continuously strengthened in EU trade agreements, in particular with regard to enhancing climate change action. The Commission has also been stepping up efforts to implement and enforce the sustainable development commitments of EU trade agreements, and these efforts will be further enhanced with the appointment of a Chief Trade Enforcement Officer. On climate change more specifically, the EU's most recent agreements all include a binding commitment of the Parties to ratify and effectively implement the Paris Agreement. The Commission will propose to make the respect of the Paris agreement an essential element for all future comprehensive trade agreements. The EU's trade policy facilitates trade and investment in green goods and services and promotes climate-friendly public procurement. Trade policy also needs to ensure undistorted, fair trade and investment in raw materials that the EU economy needs for the green transition. It can help address harmful practices such as illegal logging, enhance regulatory cooperation promote EU standards and remove non-tariff barriers in the renewable energy sector. All chemicals, materials, food and other products that are placed on the European market must fully comply with relevant EU regulations and standards. The EU should use its expertise in "green" regulation to encourage partners to design similar rules that are as ambitious as the EU's rules, thus facilitating trade and enhancing environment protection and climate mitigation in these countries.

As the world's largest single market, the EU can set standards that apply across global value chains. The Commission will continue to work on new standards for sustainable growth and use its economic weight to shape international standards that are in line with EU environmental and climate ambitions. It will work to facilitate trade in environmental goods and services, in bilateral and multilateral forums, and in supporting open and attractive EU and global markets for sustainable products. It will work with global partners to ensure the EU's resource security and reliable access to strategic raw materials.

The EU's international cooperation and partnership policy should continue to help channel both public and private funds to achieve the transition. While the EU and its Member States remain the world's leading donors of development assistance and provide over 40% of the world's public climate finance. As public funds will not suffice, the EU and its Member States will coordinate their support to engage with partners to bridge the funding gap by mobilising private finance. The Commission proposal for a Neighbourhood, Development and International Cooperation Instrument proposes to allocate a target of 25% of its budget to climate-related objectives. The Commission will also support the commitment made by national public financial resources to improve the investment climate and achieve contributions from the private sector. This work will need to be accompanied by opportunities to de-risk investments in sustainable development through tools such as funding guarantees and blended financing.

To mobilise international investors, the EU will also remain at the forefront of efforts to set up a financial system that supports global sustainable growth. The EU will build on the International Platform on Sustainable Finance that was recently established to coordinate efforts on environmentally sustainable finance initiatives such as taxonomies, disclosures, standards and labels. The Commission will also encourage discussions at other international fora, in particular the G7 and G20.

4. TIME TO ACT - TOGETHER: A EUROPEAN CLIMATE PACT

The involvement and commitment of the public and of all stakeholders is crucial to the success of the European Green Deal. Recent political events show that game-changing policies only work if citizens are fully involved in designing them. People are concerned about jobs, heating their homes and making ends meet, and EU institutions should engage with them if the Green Deal is to succeed and deliver lasting change. Citizens are and should remain a driving force of the transition.

The Commission will launch a European Climate Pact by March 2020 to focus on three ways to engage with the public on climate action. First, it will encourage information sharing, inspiration, and foster public understanding of the threat and the challenge of climate change and environmental degradation and on how to counter it. It will use multiple channels and tools to do so, including events in Member States, on the model of the Commission's on-going citizens' dialogues. Second, there should be both real and virtual spaces for people to express their ideas and creativity and work together on ambitious action, both at individual and collective level. Participants would be encouraged to commit to specific climate action goals. Third, the Commission will work on building capacity to facilitate grassroots initiatives on climate change and environmental protection. Information, guidance and educational modules could help exchange good practice. The Commission will ensure that the green transition features prominently in the debate on the future of Europe.

The Climate Pact will build on the Commission's on-going series of citizens' dialogues and citizens' assemblies across the EU, and the role of social dialogue committees. It will continue to work to empower regional and local communities, including energy communities. The urban dimension of cohesion policy will be strengthened, and the proposed European Urban Initiative will provide assistance to cities to help them make best use of opportunities to develop sustainable urban development strategies. The EU Covenant of Mayors will continue to be a central force. The Commission will work with it to continue to provide assistance to cities and regions that want to commit to ambitious pledges on climate and energy policies. It will remain an essential platform to share good practices on how to implement change locally.

The Commission is also keen to reduce its environmental impact as an institution and as an employer. It will present a comprehensive action plan in 2020 to implement itself the objectives of the Green Deal and to become climate neutral by 2030. It calls on all the other institutions, bodies and agencies of the EU to work with it and come forward with similar ambitious measures.

In addition to the Climate Pact, the Commission and Member States should work to ensure that all available planning tools for the European Green Deal are used coherently. The most important of these are the national energy and climate plans and the proposed strategic national plans to implement the common agricultural policy. The Commission will ensure that they are fit for purpose and that Member States are implementing them effectively, and will use tools such as the European Semester as appropriate.

European funds, including for rural development, will help rural areas to harness opportunities in the circular and bio-economy. The Commission will reflect this in its long-term vision for rural areas. It will pay particular attention to the role of outermost regions in the European Green Deal, taking into account their vulnerability to climate change and natural disasters and their unique assets: biodiversity and renewable energy sources. The Commission will take forward the work on the Clean Energy for EU Islands Initiative to develop a long-term framework to accelerate the clean energy transition on all EU islands.

The Commission and the Member States must also ensure that policies and legislation are enforced and deliver effectively. The environmental implementation review will play a critical role in mapping the situation in each Member State. The Commission will also present a new environmental action programme to complement the European Green Deal that will include a new monitoring mechanism to ensure that Europe remains on track to meet its environmental objectives. The Commission will also launch a dashboard to monitor progress against all of the European Green Deal objectives.

The Commission will consider revising the Aarhus Regulation to improve **access to administrative and judicial review at EU level for citizens and NGOs who have concerns about the legality of decisions with effects on the environment**. The Commission will also take action to improve their access to justice before national courts in all Member States. The Commission will also promote action by the EU, its Member States and the international community to step up efforts against environmental crime.

The European Green Deal launches a new growth strategy for the EU. It supports the transition of the EU to a fair and prosperous society that responds to the challenges posed by climate change and environmental degradation, improving the quality of life of current and future generations. The Commission invites the European Parliament and the European Council to endorse the European Green Deal and to give their full weight to the measures it contains.

2. Korean New Deal – Green New Deal (English version). Government of Korea, 2020.

National Strategy for a Great Transformation

KOREAN NEW DEAL

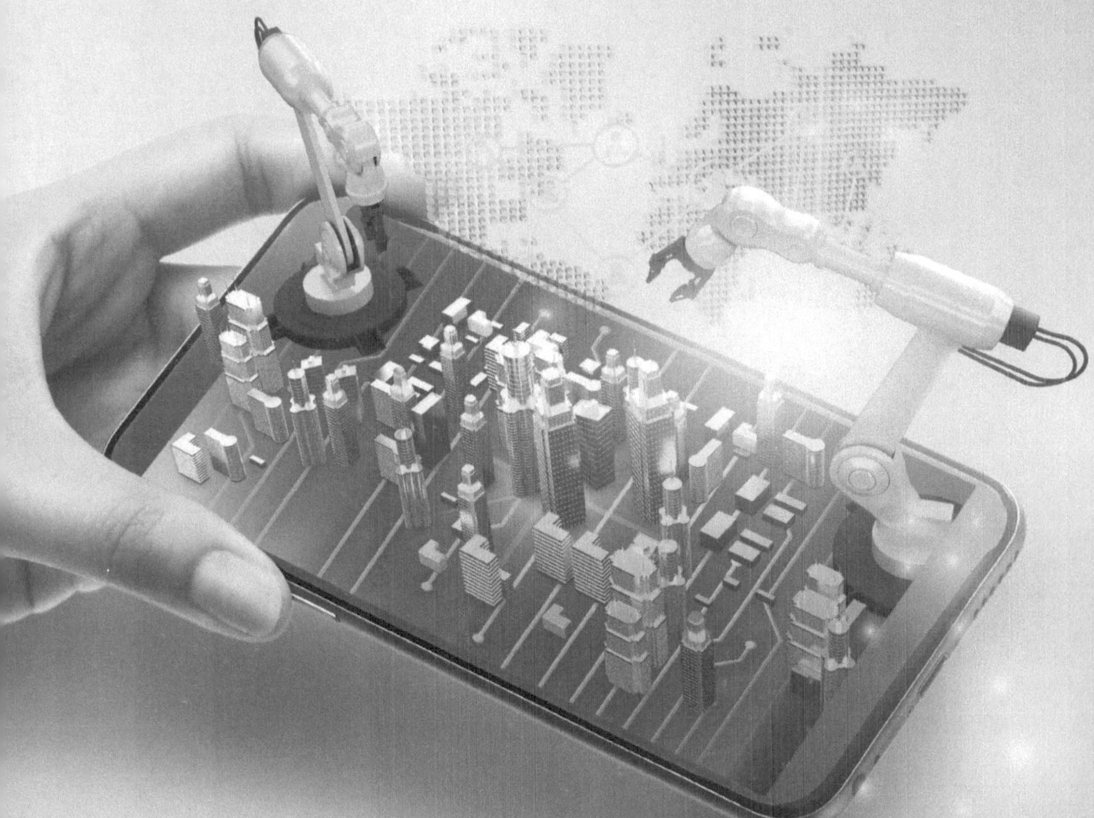

Government of the Republic of Korea

The Korean New Deal

National Strategy for a Great Transformation

July 2020

"The Korean New Deal will set the foundation for Korea's next 100 years."

President Moon Jae-in
at Presentation of Korean New Deal Initiative

CONTENTS

I. INTRODUCTION 1

1. Background 3
2. Structural Changes from COVID-19 5

II. KOREAN NEW DEAL 7

1. Overview 9
2. Digital New Deal 17
3. Green New Deal 25
4. Stronger Safety Net 33

III. WHAT WE ENVISION FOR 2025 37

IV. IMPLEMENTATION PLAN 41

ANNEX: 10 KEY PROJECTS 45

REFERENCES 61

I. INTRODUCTION

1. **Background**
2. **Structural Changes from COVID-19**

Background

The Republic of Korea has achieved remarkable economic growth over the past several decades, becoming the seventh country to join the 30-50 club[1] in 2017. As Korea's economy matured, however, the country began to see a decline in its growth rate, while its insufficient social security system further widened levels of polarization. The average annual growth rate reached 6.9% in the 1990s, and then declined to 4.4% and 2.9% in the 2000s and the 2010s, respectively, while the income quintile share ratio increased from 3.86 in the 1990s to 4.52 and 4.57 in the 2000s and the 2010s, respectively. Against the challenges of slower growth and polarization, Korea has been shifting its paradigm towards a people-centered economy to realize President Moon's vision for an innovative and inclusive country for all.

Economic Impact due to COVID-19 and Expected Recovery Pathways

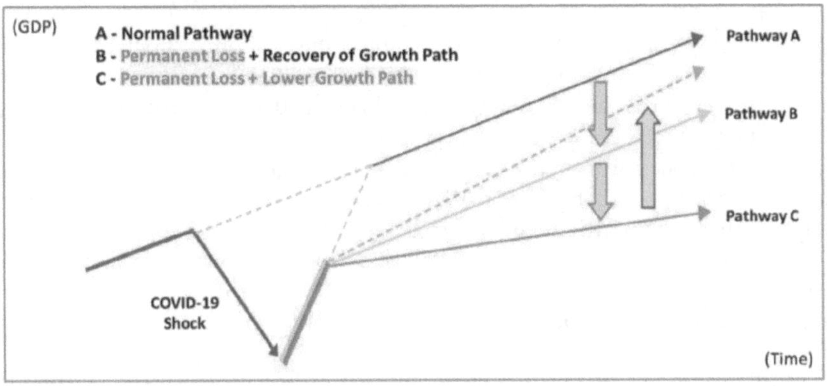

In the face of the COVID-19 pandemic, the Korean economy has encountered two major challenges: aiding recovery from a severe economic recession while addressing the structural transformation. The unforeseen shock of the pandemic has resulted in the worst economic downturn that the world has seen since the Great Depression. Border closures and travel restrictions have affected economies and job markets around the world, and the Organization for Economic Cooperation and Development (OECD) has predicted that the income loss by the end of 2021 will exceed that of any previous recession over the last 100 years outside wartime.[2] Without the government efforts protecting the job market and boosting domestic consumption, the pandemic could result in a vicious cycle of income loss, demand contraction and mass unemployment.

According to the OECD, economic activity will not be able to return to normal under the current circumstances,[3] which means that it is inevitable for the shock of the pandemic to permanently damage the economy. Furthermore, the International

---

[1] '30-50 club' denotes countries with per capital gross national income (GNI) surpassing USD 30,000 and a population of over 50 million.

[2] OECD. (2020). *OECD Economic Outlook.*

[3] Ibid.

Monetary Fund (IMF) expects the current crisis to unevenly affect certain groups that are socially or economically more vulnerable.[4] Failing to address the crisis early on may lead to hysteresis in the labor market, shrinking investments, and ultimately, may have a bigger and longer-lasting impact on the economy.

The unparalleled challenges of the pandemic have completely changed the world's overall economic and social structures. In addition to the increased use of 'untact[5]' services accelerating the transition towards a digital economy, there has also been a growing demand for a green economy, making it a common consensus in the international community. Delayed action against such structural changes, therefore, may hurt productivity and result in a lower growth path.

Against such backdrop, the Korean New Deal was introduced as a national development strategy to support the country's recovery from the pandemic crisis and lead the global action against structural changes. Its three main objectives are as follows:

First, the Korean New Deal aims to minimize the economic shock by creating jobs. It creates not only government-supported jobs for low-skilled workers, but also jobs that support the structural transition towards a digital and green economy. Second, this strategy supports the Korean economy's quick return to its normal growth path by building the necessary infrastructure for a digital and green economy that will restore investments and support job creation. Third, it sets the groundwork for Korea not only to adapt to the structural changes but also to lead the global community in the post COVID-19 era. This plan forms an institutional basis on which a digital and green economy can be supported. At the same time, it also establishes a universal employment insurance system and sets a path towards net-zero emissions.

---

[4] IMF. (2020). *World Economic Outlook Update.*

[5] 'Untact,' a term combining 'un' with 'contact,' is used in Korea to refer to a non-contact or non-face-to-face operations such as remote work.

Structural Changes from COVID-19

The pandemic is expected to change people's behaviors and perceptions, and ultimately, bring structural changes to economies and societies the world over. These structural changes include a rising demand for 'untact' services, a growing call for an environmentally friendly economy, and rapid labor market changes that widen polarization. As a result of such changes, government action is essential to accelerate the transition towards a digital economy, drive the shift towards a green economy, and alleviate the polarization.

First, the rising demand for 'untact' services can accelerate the transition towards a digital economy. The need for online services that allow consumers to enjoy normal everyday activities while conforming to quarantine rules has been growing rapidly. Korea's online consumption, which made up 22.9% of overall consumption in January 2020, rose to a monthly average of 26.9%[6] from February to May, indicating that e-commerce and delivery services are replacing offline purchases. In addition, the increase in Microsoft Teams users around the world, from 20 million in November 2019 to 75 million in April 2020,[7] also shows that areas such as remote working and virtual learning are rapidly being digitalized.

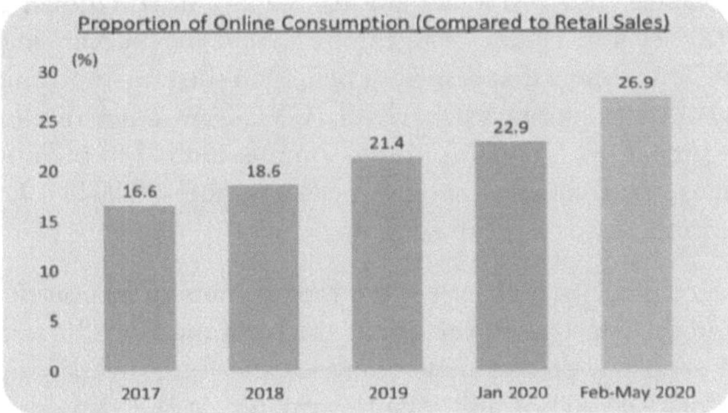

In line with such changes, the traditional service industry, and small and medium-sized manufacturing businesses with less digital capacity have been hit the hardest by the pandemic. On the contrary, sales of online and platform businesses have been growing, as evidenced by the 169% hike in the sales of Zoom, a video telephony platform, in the first quarter of 2020 compared to a year ago. This highlights how the speed of the transition towards a digital economy can affect the competitiveness of a country's industries and businesses, and emphasizes the need to invest in digital infrastructure.

Second, the growing demand for a low-carbon and environmentally friendly economy will drive the shift towards a green economy. Climate change has undermined the safety of people and the economy. According to the US management consulting firm McKinsey & Company, pandemics and climate change share similarities in that both are

[6] Statistics Korea. (2020, July 3). *Press Release: Online Shopping Trend of May 2020.*

[7] Rosalie Chan. (2020, April 30). Microsoft Teams now has 75 million daily active users, adding 31 million in just over a month. *Business Insider*.

difficult to prepare for despite the continued warnings of experts, and can only be remedied by addressing the underlying physical causes. The two are also similar in that past probabilities and distributions of occurrences are inadequate for future projections, and that their socioeconomic impact grows disproportionally and even catastrophically once certain thresholds are breached.[8] As the world currently experiences the effects of a pandemic, it is now recognizing greater the urgent need for climate actions.

The transition to a green economy does not simply enhance the quality of life for people, but also offers opportunities to create new industries and jobs through growing investment. The European Union (EU) plans to mobilize at least 1 trillion euros of sustainable investment over the next decade through the European Green Deal,[9] while the International Renewable Energy Agency (IRENA) predicted that 130 trillion dollars of investment would be needed until the year 2050 to reach zero emissions.[10] This green transition is supportive of long-term growth and can create new project opportunities, according to the OECD.[11] The IMF has also stated that green investments will be able to drive the recovery from the COVID-19 pandemic by creating many new employment opportunities.[12]

Furthermore, businesses have also accelerated the transition towards a green economy. Apple, Google, and BMW are among the 242 multinational firms that have joined the RE100 (Renewable Energy 100) campaign and are encouraging their suppliers to go carbon-free[13]. This means that being left behind in the transition could mean losing a competitive edge in the global value chain (GVC). As countries introduce green recovery policies similar to the European Commission's 750-billion-euro stimulus package[14] that focuses on climate-friendly measures, the COVID-19 pandemic may expedite the transition towards a green economy.

The third type of structural change is the radical transformation of economic and social structures, and the consequent reform of the labor market. The transition towards a digital and green economy creates new industries and jobs, diversifying the forms of work and enabling platform labor and remote working. At the same time, it could also lead to a mismatch between jobs and skills, as well as a lower demand for low-skilled labor. The growing burden of unemployment and intensifying polarization, therefore, calls for a tighter and stronger employment safety net that provides advanced job training while protecting new types of employment.

---

8 Pinner, D., Rogers, M., and Samandari, H. (2020, April 7). Addressing climate change in a post pandemic world, *McKinsey Quarterly*.

9 European Commission. (2020, January 14). *Press Release: Financing the Green Transition: The European Green Deal Investment Plan and Just Transition Mechanism*.

10 IRENA. (2020). *Global Renewables Outlook*.

11 OECD. (2019). Innovation and Business/ Market Opportunities associated with Energy Transitions and a Cleaner Global Environment. *Issue Paper*.

12 IMF. (2020, April 20). Greening the Recovery. *IMF Special Series on COVID-19*.

13 Renewable Energy 100. *Website: www.there100.org. Accessed on 22, July 2020.*

14 European Parliament. (2020, May 27). *Press Release: Europe's moment: Repair and prepare for the next generation*.

II. KOREAN NEW DEAL

1. Overview
2. Digital New Deal
3. Green New Deal
4. Stronger Safety Net

Overview of the Korean New Deal

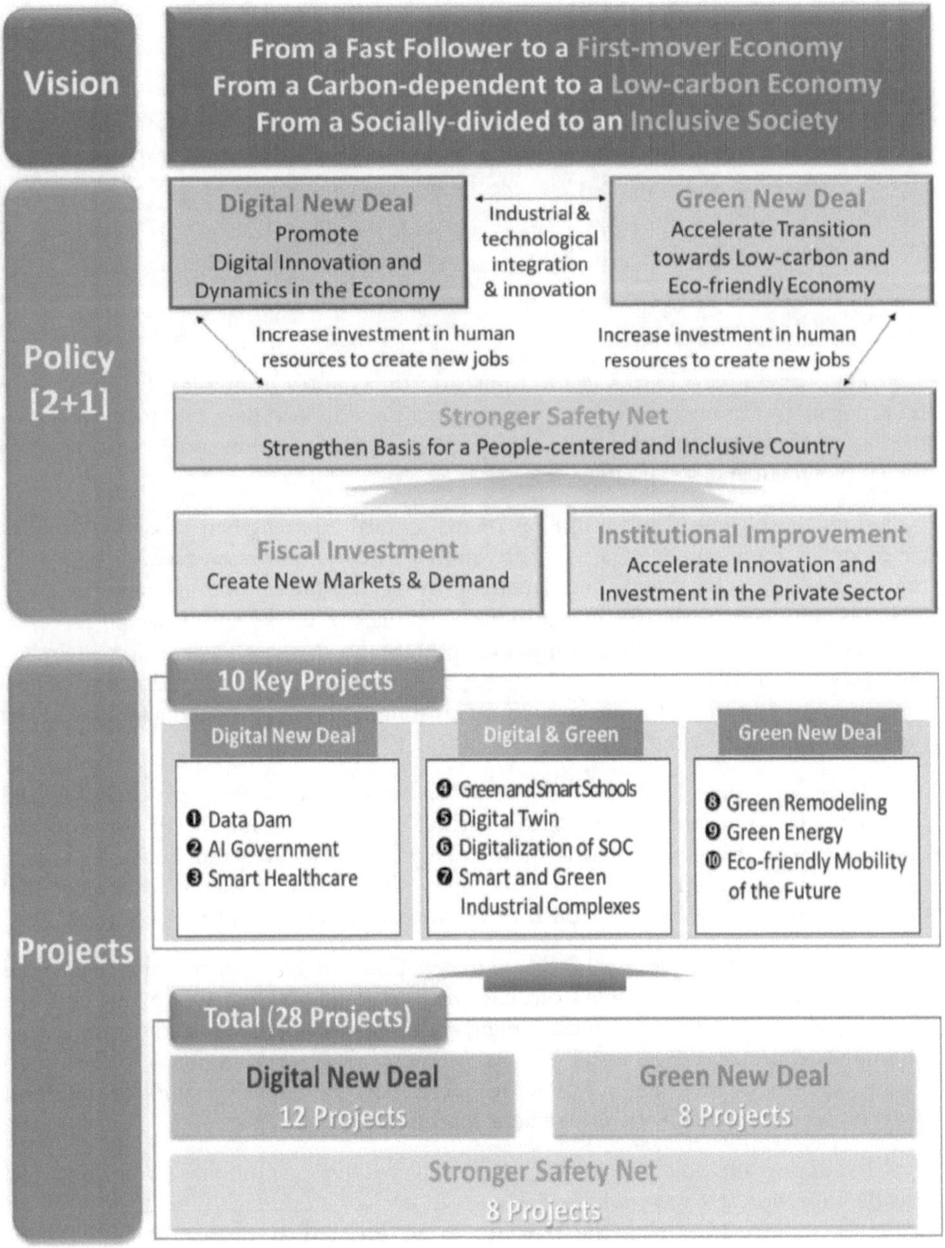

The Korean New Deal seeks to transform Korea into:

- **a smart country** that is at the center of a digital transition based on data, network and artificial intelligence (DNA) infrastructure[1];
- **a green country** that achieves a balance among people, nature and growth through a green transition towards net-zero emissions as a responsible member of the global community; and
- **a safe country** that invests in human resources for a strong employment and social safety net.

The Korean New Deal seeks to transform the country from a fast follower into a first mover. To this end, the Korean government plans to introduce two main policies – the Digital New Deal and the Green New Deal – and an overarching policy to strengthen the employment and social safety net.

With the Digital New Deal, Korea aims to further strengthen its digital capacity based on its competitive edge in information and communication technology (ICT), thereby promoting innovation and dynamics throughout the economy. The government plans to build large-scale ICT infrastructure including a 'Data Dam,[15]' which serves as the foundation for a digital economy. This promotes a data-driven economy including the collection, standardization, processing and combining of data, and ultimately secures a competitive advantage for the country by creating new industries and accelerating the digital transition of key industries.

At the same time, Korea's Green New Deal aims to achieve net-zero emissions and accelerates the transition towards a low-carbon and green economy. To this end, the government plans to build eco-friendly energy infrastructures that promote energy saving and an increased use of renewable energy. The mobility, energy, technology and other types of climate-friendly industries will be strengthened in all possible ways.

The Korean New Deal will increase the resilience of economic agents against the uncertainty of times that result from changing economic structures. To this end, the Korean government will work to close blind spots in the employment and social security system based on social consensus. The government will establish a 'future-oriented job training system' by investing in human resources, thereby allowing a smooth transition between occupations and nurturing talent for innovation.

To support the objectives of the Korean New Deal, institutional frameworks will also be improved upon to mobilize large scale private investment. With an investment of 114.1 trillion won from the treasury to be injected in phases until 2025, the

---

[15] large collection of data to support big data development

government plans to create new markets and stimulate private demand. The institutional base for the transition towards a digital and green economy will be prepared along with regulatory improvements, in order to accelerate innovation and additional investment from the private sector.

Among the Korean New Deal projects, 10 key projects that contribute significantly to the creation of jobs and new industries, and to a well-balanced form of regional development have been selected as the building blocks of the forthcoming transformation. These projects will be explained in detail in the Annex.

List of Projects*

(trillion won, thousand jobs)

	Focus Areas	Projects	2020 SB -2022	2020 SB -2025	# of Jobs
Aggregated Total			**49.0**	**114.1**	**1,901**
Digital New Deal	**Total**		**18.6**	**44.8**	**903**
	1. Stronger Integration of DNA[16] throughout the Economy	**Sub-total**	**12.5**	**31.9**	**567**
		1) Collecting, disclosing and utilizing data in areas closely related to people's lives	3.1	6.4	295
		2) Expanding the integration of 5G and AI into industries	6.5	14.8	172
		3) Making a smart government that utilizes 5G and AI	2.5	9.7	91
		4) Advancing cyber security	0.4	1.0	9
	2. Digitalization of Education Infrastructure	**Sub-total**	**0.6**	**0.8**	**9**
		5) Creating technology-based education infrastructure for grades 1-12	0.3	0.3	4
		6) Strengthening the online education system of universities and job training institutions	0.3	0.5	5
	3. Fostering the 'Untact' Industry	**Sub-total**	**1.1**	**2.1**	**134**
		7) Building smart medical and care infrastructures	0.2	0.4	5
		8) Promoting remote working in SMEs	0.6	0.7	9
		9) Supporting online activities of microbusinesses	0.3	1.0	120
	4. Digitalization of Social Overhead Capital (SOC)	**Sub-total**	**4.4**	**10.0**	**193**
		10) Building a smart management system in four sectors	3.7	8.5	124
		11) Adding digital innovation to urban spaces and industrial complexes	0.6	1.2	14
		12) Building a smart logistics and distribution system	0.1	0.3	55

[16] DNA refers to data, network and artificial intelligence (AI), the three innovative industries selected by the Presidential Committee on the Fourth Industrial Revolution.

<table>
<tr><td rowspan="14">Green New Deal</td><td colspan="2">Total</td><td>19.6</td><td>42.7</td><td>659</td></tr>
<tr><td rowspan="4">5. Green Transition of Infrastructures</td><td>Sub-total</td><td>6.1</td><td>12.1</td><td>387</td></tr>
<tr><td>13) Turning public facilities into zero-energy buildings</td><td>2.6</td><td>6.2</td><td>243</td></tr>
<tr><td>14) Restoring the terrestrial, marine and urban ecosystems</td><td>1.2</td><td>2.5</td><td>105</td></tr>
<tr><td>15) Building a management system for clean and safe water</td><td>2.3</td><td>3.4</td><td>39</td></tr>
<tr><td rowspan="4">6. Low-carbon and Decentralized Energy</td><td>Sub-total</td><td>10.3</td><td>24.3</td><td>209</td></tr>
<tr><td>16) Building a smart grid for more efficient energy management</td><td>1.1</td><td>2.0</td><td>20</td></tr>
<tr><td>17) Promoting renewable energy use and supporting a fair transition</td><td>3.6</td><td>9.2</td><td>38</td></tr>
<tr><td>18) Expanding the supply of electric and hydrogen vehicles</td><td>5.6</td><td>13.1</td><td>151</td></tr>
<tr><td rowspan="3">7. Innovation in the Green Industry</td><td>Sub-total</td><td>3.2</td><td>6.3</td><td>63</td></tr>
<tr><td>19) Promoting prospective businesses to lead the green industry and establishing low-carbon and green industrial complexes</td><td>2.0</td><td>3.6</td><td>47</td></tr>
<tr><td>20) Laying the foundation for green innovation via the R&D and financial sectors</td><td>1.2</td><td>2.7</td><td>16</td></tr>
</table>

<table>
<tr><td rowspan="12">Stronger Safety Net</td><td colspan="2">Total</td><td>10.8</td><td>26.6</td><td>339</td></tr>
<tr><td rowspan="6">1. Employment and Social Safety Net</td><td>Sub-total</td><td>9.3</td><td>22.6</td><td>159</td></tr>
<tr><td>21) Building a universal employment safety net</td><td>0.8</td><td>3.2</td><td>-</td></tr>
<tr><td>22) Strengthening the social safety net for an inclusive society for all</td><td>4.3</td><td>10.4</td><td>-</td></tr>
<tr><td>23) Ensuring livelihoods and employment stability for those not covered by employment insurance</td><td>3.0</td><td>7.2</td><td>39</td></tr>
<tr><td>24) Helping new employees in the labor market and those looking for new positions</td><td>0.9</td><td>1.2</td><td>118</td></tr>
<tr><td>25) Innovating the working environment and industrial safety standards</td><td>0.3</td><td>0.6</td><td>2</td></tr>
<tr><td rowspan="4">2. Investment in Human Resources</td><td>Sub-total</td><td>1.5</td><td>4.0</td><td>180</td></tr>
<tr><td>26) Training digital and green talents</td><td>0.5</td><td>1.1</td><td>25</td></tr>
<tr><td>27) Restructuring the job-training system to be future-oriented</td><td>0.6</td><td>2.3</td><td>126</td></tr>
<tr><td>28) Enhancing the accessibility to digital infrastructure for rural residents and vulnerable people</td><td>0.4</td><td>0.6</td><td>29</td></tr>
</table>

*This table shows the list of projects with the amount of investment from the treasury from the Third Supplementary Budget 2020 (2020SB) to years 2022 and 2025, and the total number of jobs to be created.

Investment Timeline

Projects that can be carried out immediately this year will be implemented while investment will be concentrated in the 'innovative projects on national transformation' by 2025.

2020, Starting the Transformation – Investment will be made in projects that help overcome the crisis or that can be implemented immediately. *(6.3 trillion won including 4.8 trillion won from the treasury will be invested through the 3rd Supplementary Budget 2020.)*

2021-2022, Scaling up the Investments – Investment will be increased to achieve the new growth path. *(67.7 trillion won including 49 trillion won from the treasury will be invested and 887,000 jobs will be created.)*

2023-2025, Settling the Transformation – Final touches will be added to solidify the new growth path. (*160 trillion won including 114.1 trillion won from the treasury will be invested, and 1,901,000 jobs will be created.)*

Focus Areas of the Korean New Deal:

Breakdown of Investments

1. Digital New Deal: 58.2 trillion won (44.8 trillion won from the treasury) will be invested; and 903,000 jobs will be created. With the aim to accelerate the transition towards a digital economy, investment will focus on the integration of data, network and AI (DNA) throughout the economy (31.9 trillion won from the treasury), promoting the 'untact' industry (2.1 trillion won from the treasury), and digitalizing the social overhead capital (10 trillion won from the treasury).

2. Green New Deal: 73.4 trillion won (42.7 trillion won from the treasury) will be invested; and 659,000 jobs will be created. With the aim to strengthen climate action and realize a green economy, investment will focus on green infrastructures (12.1 trillion won from the treasury), renewable energy (24.3 trillion won from the treasury), and fostering green industry (6.3 trillion won from the treasury).

3. Stronger Safety Net: 28.4 trillion won (26.6 trillion won from the treasury) will be invested; and 339,000 jobs will be created. In response to the uncertainties resulting from structural transformation, employment and the social safety net will be strengthened (22.6 trillion won from the treasury), and investment in people, such as capacity building in digital and green sectors, will be increased (4 trillion won from the treasury).

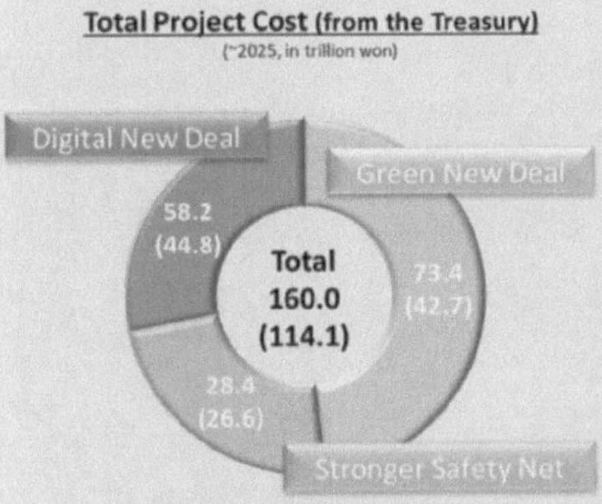

Investment Plan

[Project Cost (from treasury), trillion won]

	2020 SB-2022	2020 SB-2025
Total	67.7 (49.0)	160.0 (114.1)
Digital New Deal	23.4 (18.6)	58.2 (44.8)
Green New Deal	32.5 (19.6)	73.4 (42.7)
Stronger Safety Net	11.8 (10.8)	28.4 (26.6)

Number of Jobs Created

[In thousand]

	2020 SB-2022	2020 SB-2025
Total	887	1,901
Digital New Deal	390	903
Green New Deal	319	659
Stronger Safety Net	178	339

*The tables above show the amount that will be invested and the number of jobs that will be created through the Korean New Deal from the Third Supplementary Budget 2020 (2020 SB) to years 2022 and 2025.

PART 1. Digital New Deal

Focus Areas:

- Stronger Integration of DNA throughout the Economy
- Digitalization of Education Infrastructure
- Fostering the 'Untact' Industry
- Digitalization of Social Overhead Capital (SOC)

Overview of the Digital New Deal

Against the accelerated transition towards a digital economy since the beginning of the COVID-19 pandemic, digitalization has become a key factor both driving innovation and determining the competitiveness of a country and its industries. The overall transformation of economic and social structures, including the greater use of web-based services, has once again emphasized the importance of digital capabilities. Businesses providing 'untact' services such as e-commerce and remote working tools are becoming a promising industry, while small and medium-sized enterprises (SMEs) and micro-businesses that lack a digital capacity lag behind.

The Digital New Deal aims to build a digital economy and promote growth in promising 'untact' industries. It heightens the competitiveness of Korea and its industries by establishing digital infrastructures in areas such as data, network and artificial intelligence (DNA). At the same time, major infrastructures including those for transportation, water resources, urban planning, and logistics will be digitalized.

In addition, the Digital New Deal fosters 'untact' industries, which are critical for the post COVID-19 era, while also strengthening support for SMEs and micro-businesses against the changing business environment. Through these efforts, Korea seeks to generate greater added-value and create more jobs in the future while bridging digital gaps.

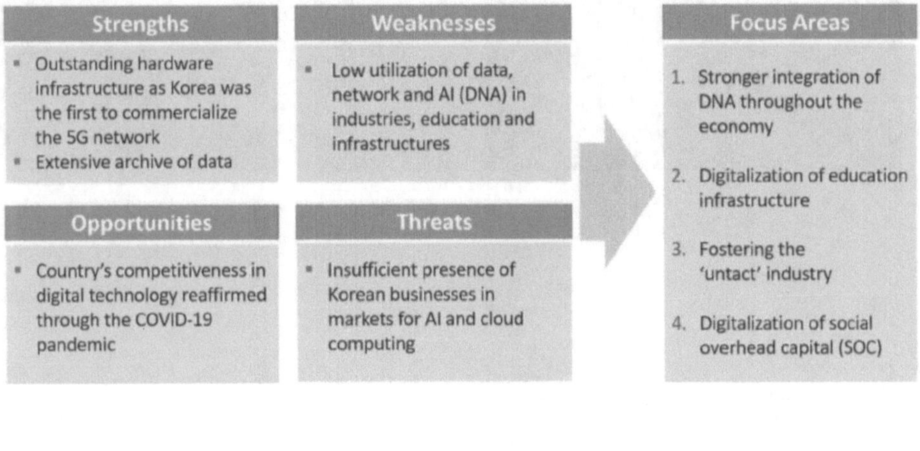

Focus Areas of the Digital New Deal

1. Stronger Integration of DNA throughout the Economy – promoting the use and integration of data, the 5G network and AI (DNA) throughout all sectors to create new digital products and services, while also enhancing the productivity of the Korean economy. (*38.5 trillion won including 31.9 trillion won from the treasury will be invested by 2025 to create 567,000 jobs.)*

<u>Collecting, disclosing and utilizing data in areas closely related to people's lives:</u> The 'data ecosystem,' which involves the collection, utilization, disclosure, integration and distribution of data will be reinforced. A data control tower will be established for the integrated management of public and private data.

- Disclosure of 142,000 public data; and the expanded collection and utilization of data in fields such as manufacturing and medical industries
- Establishment of big data platforms for different sectors, and the introduction of vouchers for data purchasing and processing to 8,400 companies
- Collection of additional data for AI-learning (1,300 types of data), and the introduction of vouchers on processing the data for AI-learning for 6,700 SMEs

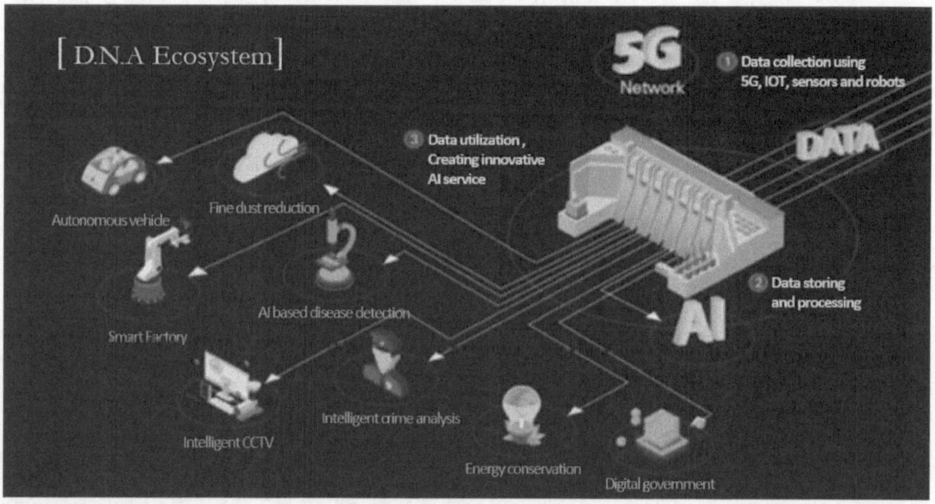

Expanding the integration of 5G and AI into industries: Projects that integrate 5G and AI technology into primary, secondary, and tertiary sectors of the economy will be introduced for the digitalization of all industries and the creation of new markets.

- Production of 195 immersive contents in areas such as culture, sports and transportation; the construction of 160 smart museums and galleries based on ICT; and the development of technology to commercialize self-driving vehicles and self-navigating vessels
- Construction of 12,000 smart factories; the provision of AI-based home services (e.g. indoor purification of fine dust); and the implementation of leading projects that integrate AI with other technologies in areas close to people's lives (e.g. medical image readers, etc.)
- Support for 1,000 startup businesses providing 'untact' services; the creation of a new 'Smart Korea Fund' worth 6 trillion won; and the provision of vouchers for AI solutions to 3,400 SMEs, and smart service solutions to 1,350 SMEs

Making a smart government that utilizes 5G and AI: The government will adopt a smart working environment by utilizing 5G and cloud networks, while also being innovative to quickly provide customized public services.

- Implementation of pilot projects based on blockchain technology (e.g. to prevent duplicate claims on welfare benefits) and the provision of customized information on government subsidy and pension plans
- Phased establishment of 5G at all government complexes; and the transition to cloud computing of public information system

Advancing cyber security: Cyber security will be strengthened nationwide to effectively respond to the accelerated digitalization and the consequent increase in cyber threats. Support will be provided to promising businesses and technologies in relevant areas.

- Provision of customized consulting on security, and installation support on security programs to 6,650 SMEs; and the diagnosis and reinforcement of the software security
- Development of 100 promising businesses for AI security; and the distribution of security models to 500 industrial sites for integrated technologies (e.g. self-driving vehicles)

2. Digitalization of Education Infrastructure – expanding digital infrastructure and educational materials to incorporate a blend of online and offline methods into learning environments of all elementary, middle and high schools, universities and job training institutions across the country. (*1.3 trillion won including 0.8 trillion won from the treasury will be invested by 2025 to create 9,000 jobs.)*

Creating technology-based education infrastructure for grades 1-12:

Full coverage of high-speed classroom Wi-Fi will be provided to all elementary, middle and high schools across country *(Timeline: from 80,000 classrooms in June 2020 to 240,000 classrooms based on the Supplementary Budget of 2020, and to all 380,000 classrooms by 2022).*

A total of 200,000 old computers and laptops of faculty members will be replaced with new ones, and 240,000 tablet PCs will be provided to 1,200 schools that will test out the 'online textbook' program in order to develop new teaching and learning models.

An integrated platform for online learning that utilizes various educational materials and big data to provide customized learning materials will be launched. This new platform provides both public and private learning materials, and supports all stages of learning.

Strengthening the online education system of universities and job training institutions:

Old servers and network facilities will be replaced with new ones at 39 national universities; to set the basis for online learning, 10 remote education support centers for shared use by universities will be installed; and to build the digital capacity of faculty members, 28 training centers will be installed.

A total of 2,045 lectures that address the demands of the Fourth Industrial Revolution, such as AI and robotics, will be developed and made available to the general public via the Korean Massive Open Online Course (K-MOOC) by 2025. In collaboration with other MOOC providers worldwide, 50 lectures that are globally recognized will also be introduced each year.

The Smart Training Education Platform, a comprehensive job training system that combines online and offline courses, will be further enhanced with the development of 3,040 e-learning and virtual training (AR and VR) programs by 2025.

Consulting services will be provided to occupational training institutions on adopting online programs, and 585 businesses will be eligible for subsidies on online learning management systems (LMS) for up to 18 million won a year.

3. Fostering the 'Untact' Industry – laying the groundwork to promote the 'untact' industry by setting up relevant infrastructures that are closely related to people's daily lives (e.g. medical, work-related and businesses-related infrastructures). *(2.5 trillion won including 2.1 trillion won from the treasury will be invested by 2025 to create 134,000 jobs.)*

Building smart medical and care infrastructures:

By utilizing digital technology such as 5G and IoT, 18 smart hospitals will be built to allow real-time monitoring of inpatients and interdisciplinary diagnosis and treatment. To provide safer medical treatment, 1,000 specialized clinics for patients with respiratory symptoms and fever will be established.

Digital health care services, such as IoT sensors that measure the heart rate, blood-sugar levels and activities, and AI speakers that engage in conversations to enhance cognitive functions, will be provided to 120,000 elderlies and others vulnerable to health implications. Wearable devices will be provided to 200,000 people with chronic conditions, such as high blood pressure or diabetes, to help them manage their conditions.

Promoting remote working in SMEs:

Vouchers will be provided to support remote working solutions and consulting services will be provided to 160,000 businesses. In areas where SMEs and venture companies are concentrated, 1,562 videoconferencing rooms will be established.

The development of ways to utilize new digital technologies in remote working (e.g. technology to enhance the quality and security of videoconferencing programs, and software on task management, etc.) will be supported.

Supporting online activities of microbusinesses:

A space on online exhibitions, shopping malls or live commerce markets will be offered to 320,000 microbusinesses. Each year, 5,000 pilot projects on subscription services will be supported to help microbusinesses secure a stable demand.

Smart technology based on 5G or AI will be integrated into microbusiness workplaces to set up 100,000 smart stores, which use kiosks and other 'untact' ordering systems, and 10,000 smart workshops, which are manufacturing businesses that consist of less than 10 employees and utilize smart technology.

4. Digitalization of Social Overhead Capital (SOC) – applying ICT technologies to key SOC infrastructure for safer and more convenient lifestyles and adding 'smart' components to urban spaces, industrial complexes and logistics systems to strengthen the competitiveness of relevant industries. *(15.8 trillion won including 10 trillion won from the treasury will be invested by 2025 to create 193,000 jobs.)*

<u>Building a smart management system in four sectors:</u>

In terms of transportation, Cooperative-Intelligent Transportation System (C-ITS) will be adopted on major roads; IoT sensors will be installed on all railroads; and digital management systems that utilize CCTV and IoT will be established at 3 national fishing harbors.

Regarding the geographic information system, a precise road map and a comprehensive 3D map will be prepared on 15 types of underground structures; measuring instruments will be installed on 120 km of underground utility-pipe conduit; and a digital platform will be set up at 29 harbors.

For safer water management, real-time monitoring and remote controlling systems will be set up for national rivers (73 rivers; 3,600 km), 27 reservoirs, and 37 nationally managed dams.

In terms of disaster management, 510 early-warning systems will be installed for slope land and other areas with high risk for disasters. Additional flood warning systems will be set up in 180 parking lots located near high water levels.

<u>Adding digital innovation to urban spaces and industrial complexes:</u>

Regarding smart cities, 108 platforms utilizing closed-circuit televisions (CCTVs) will be set up not only for traffic management but also for crime prevention in urban areas. The use of smart city solutions such as smart crosswalks, demand responsive transportation and drone delivery will be promoted, and two smart city pilots will be implemented as signature projects.

In terms of smart industries, comprehensive control centers will be established for the real-time management of safety, traffic and crimes in 10 industrial complexes. A remote monitoring system on leaking toxic chemical substances will be established in 15 old industrial complexes.

<u>Building a smart logistics and distribution system:</u>

In terms of land logistics, 11 smart distribution centers to be shared by SMEs, and large e-commerce distribution complexes will be established. A certification system on smart distribution centers will also be introduced.

A smart distribution center will be established in two port complexes, and an integrated blockchain platform for harbors, which provides real-time information on harbor activity for efficient transshipment, will be expanded.

An integrated platform on the trading and management of agricultural products and other food supplies for public meal services, and a platform for the online auctioning of livestock will be established.

Research and development of logistics technology such as high-tech delivery systems utilizing robotics, IoT and big data will be supported.

PART 2. Green New Deal

Focus Areas:

- Green Transition of Infrastructures
- Low-carbon and Decentralized Energy
- Innovation in the Green Industry

Overview of the Green New Deal

The economic risks from the pandemic have shed light on the need for a growth strategy that also ensures sustainability including environmental and ecological protection. Many countries are shifting towards a low-carbon economy to combat climate change, secure a stable source of energy and foster green industries. In Korea, meanwhile, greenhouse gas (GHG) emissions have seen a steady increase of 2% a year from 2000 to 2017, and the country's industrial structure remains to be carbon-dependent.

Against such backdrop, the Korean government plans to move towards a net-zero society by supporting ongoing policies such as the 2030 target for GHG emissions reduction, and the plan to have renewables account for 20% of the country's generation capacity by 2030. This includes a green transitioning of infrastructure to strengthen the safety net against climate and environmental risks. In addition, the use of low-carbon and decentralized energy will be promoted, while those regions and groups that lag behind the transition will be protected. Moreover, the foundations for innovation and growth will be consolidated for the green industry.

With an investment of 73.4 trillion won including 42.7 trillion won from the treasury by 2025, the Green New Deal will create 659,000 jobs.

Strengths	Weaknesses
▪ Strong social awareness in environmental issues ▪ High-end digital & IT technology that can be integrated into the green industry	▪ Carbon-intensive industrial ecosystem ▪ Low generation of clean energy due to geographical constraints
Opportunities	**Threats**
▪ Growing interest in climate change and sustainable development due to COVID-19 ▪ Worldwide growth of the market for environmental industry	▪ Deviation of domestic manufacturing industry due to strict environmental regulations and standards ▪ Global trends on stronger environmental regulations on trades

Focus Areas

1. Green transition of infrastructures
2. Low-carbon and decentralized economy
3. Innovation in the green industry

Focus Areas of the Green New Deal

1. Green Transition of Infrastructures – creating a green-friendly environment towards a future where humans and nature coexist. (*Investment of 30.1 trillion won including 12.1 trillion won from the treasury will be made by 2025 to create 387,000 jobs.)*

Turning public facilities into zero-energy buildings:

Renewable energy equipment and high-performance insulation will be used to make public buildings green and energy-efficient *(Targets: 225,000 public rental housings, 440 public daycare centers and 1,148 cultural facilities.).*

Energy efficiency of old school buildings, including at least 2,890 elementary, middle and high school buildings, will be enhanced through the installation of solar panels and eco-friendly insulation. This project will be funded both by government finances and through Public-Private Partnership (PPP) via the Build-Transfer-Lease (BTL) method. The private-sector component of the project is planned to be expanded with a new SOC fund open to the public. In addition to this green component, the plan to provide Wi-Fi coverage in 380,000 classrooms by 2024 will be completed by 2022 to integrate digital components into learning environments.

Restoring the terrestrial, marine and urban ecosystems:

By conducting a comprehensive diagnosis on the climate and environmental challenges of a city, customized solutions based on environmental technology and ICT will be introduced in 25 regions by 2022.

Urban green spaces will be created with 630 ha of forest acting as a barrier against fine dust; 216 forest sites in close proximity to local communities; and 370 green sites near school zones to separate sidewalks from streets.

The health of the ecosystems will be restored in 16 national parks, 25 damaged urban spaces, and 4.5 km^2 of tidelands.

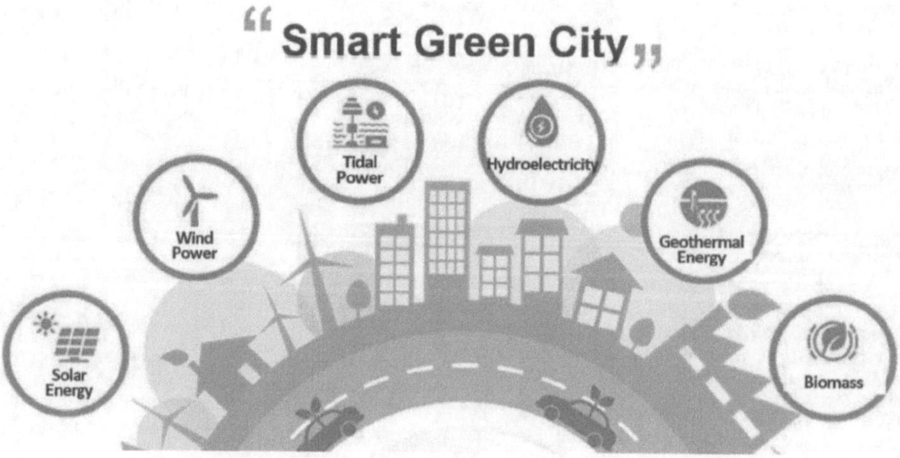

Building a management system for clean and safe water:

The entire water supply system will be made smart through the use of ICT and AI *(Targets: 48 inter-regional and 161 local water supply systems.).*

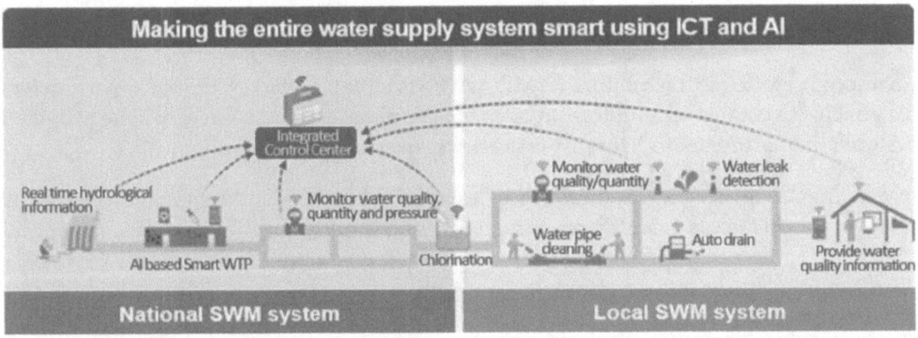

Smart components will be added to 15 sewage treatment plants by 2022, and a smart sewage management project controlling urban flooding and wastewater odor will be piloted at 10 locations until 2024.

To improve water quality and prevent leakages, 12 water purification plants for inter-regional supply and old water supply pipes will be remodeled *(3,332 km by 2024.).*

2. Low-carbon and Decentralized Energy Supply – preparing for a paradigm shift towards future energy by actively investing in R&D facilities that promote the use of sustainable and renewable energy throughout the country. *(Investment of 35.8 trillion won including 24.3 trillion won from the treasury will be made by 2025 to create 209,000 jobs.)*

Building a smart grid for more efficient energy management:

Advanced metering infrastructure (AMI), which is an integrated system of smart meters that enables two-way communication between suppliers and consumers, will be provided to 5 million apartments to help disperse energy needs and save energy.

An eco-friendly generation system will be established in 42 island regions to reduce the emission of pollutants from diesel-powered generators *(Renewable energy facilities installed in 34 island regions; new facilities to improve air quality built in three regions; and high-performance hybrid generator installed in five regions).*

Overhead cables providing electrical power or telecommunication will be replaced with underground cables in school zones and other areas in need *(Investment of 2 trillion won by 2025).*

Promoting Renewable Energy Use and Supporting a Fair Transition:

Support will be provided to measure the wind conditions and conduct feasibility studies on up to 13 regions to find sites for large-scale offshore wind farms of either the floating or fixed-bottom types. Demonstration complexes will be established in phases.

Community benefit sharing for renewable energy projects will be introduced. Higher support on loans for renewable energy will be provided to participating residents of farming areas and industrial complexes. Support will also be provided to 200,000 households for renewable energy facilities installed in residential or commercial buildings for private use.

A fair transition will be ensured for those regions that foresee difficulties coming from a reduced use of coal power and other traditional sources of energy by supporting their adjustment to the renewable energy sector (e.g. green mobility, digital management of renewable energy, platform for offshore wind farm, etc.).

<u>Expanding the Supply of Electric and Hydrogen Vehicles:</u>

The provision of 1.13 million EVs including passenger cars, buses, and freight vehicles, will be supported along with the installation of 15,000 rapid chargers and 30,000 slow chargers.

The provision of 200,000 hydrogen vehicles including passenger cars, buses and freight vehicles will be supported along with the installation of 450 charging facilities. Fuel cell plants and other infrastructure for the distribution of hydrogen will also be established.

The scrappage of old diesel cars and the transition to liquefied petroleum gas (LPG) or electric vehicles will be supported *(Scrappage of 1,160,000 diesel cars and construction equipment, and 32,000 farming machinery; and the transition of 135,000 freight and 88,000 school buses to LPG vehicles).*

3. Innovation in the Green Industry – finding areas of the green industry that strategically address climate change and environmental risks, and building infrastructure in support of this to create an innovative environment. (*7.6 trillion won including 6.3 trillion won from the treasury will be invested by 2025 to create 63,000 jobs.)*

<u>Promoting prospective businesses to lead the green industry, and establishing low-carbon and green industrial complexes:</u>

For 123 SMEs in environmental and energy sectors, the entire process of developing a business item (from R&D, testing and commercialization) will be supported. A 'green startup town,' a concentrated complex of startups that help improve environmental, transportation and residential infrastructures, will be set up by 2021.

A 'green-integrated cluster' will be set up as a regional hub that supports the technological development, testing, manufacturing and marketing in the five leading areas, which are clean air, biomaterial, hydrothermal energy, future waste resources and recycling of resources.

To enable the real-time monitoring and control of energy generation and consumption, 10 smart energy platforms based on a micro power grid will be established. These platforms allow for the collection of data based on ICT, the visualization of energy flow, and the operation of an integrated control center for electricity.

Support for facilities that prevent fine dust will be provided to 9,000 small businesses; and 100 smart ecological plants and 1,750 clean factories that reduce pollution will be established.

Laying the foundation for green innovation via the R&D and financial sectors:

The foundation will be set to test and support the commercialization of large-scale carbon capture utilization and storage (CCUS) by 2023, and the technology to produce chemical stock and other useful materials from CO_2 will be developed.

Measures against fine dust will be reinforced through the development of technology for the comprehensive management of fine dust in Northeast Asia based on regional cooperation and techniques against blind spots in fine dust management (e.g. military vehicles, agricultural machinery, construction equipment, etc.).

To promote resource recycling, support will be provided to develop remanufacturing technology (e.g. the disassembling and reassembling of old electric materials and machineries, engines and exhausts of special vehicles, etc.) and technology on collecting and utilizing rare materials.

A loan of 1.9 trillion won will be introduced for the green sector including investment to prevent the environmental pollution of businesses; and a joint fund made up by the public and the private sectors will be set up for 215 billion won to foster green businesses.

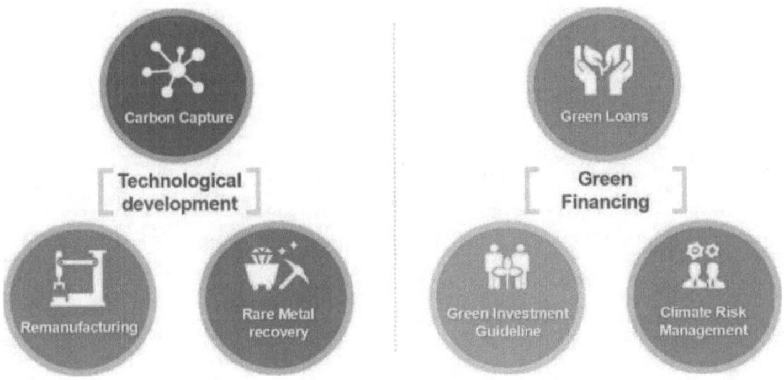

PART 3. Stronger Safety Net

Focus Areas:

- Employment and Social Safety Net
- Investment in Human Resources

Overview of the Stronger Safety Net

Countries around the world have taken strong measures to overcome the sudden shock on employment arising from the pandemic. Unemployment benefits are being provided for up to 39 weeks in the US, while France has introduced policies to limit layoffs during the pandemic. The large-scale shift towards a digital and green economy has intensified the challenge for governments to reinforce employment safety to address the mismatch between jobs and skills, and the growing polarization. Against this backdrop, countries are increasing the amount of investment being made in people with measures to support job training and re-employment in order to overcome the employment shock and prepare for structural changes such as digitalization in the labor market.

This part of the Korean New Deal adds protection through stronger employment and social safety systems, while also increasing the levels of investment in human resources. As a result, vulnerable groups will be better protected against employment shocks during times of crisis. In addition, investment in human resources aims to close the digital gap and build human capacity for the future, allowing Korea to respond preemptively to the changing labor market and to drive innovation.

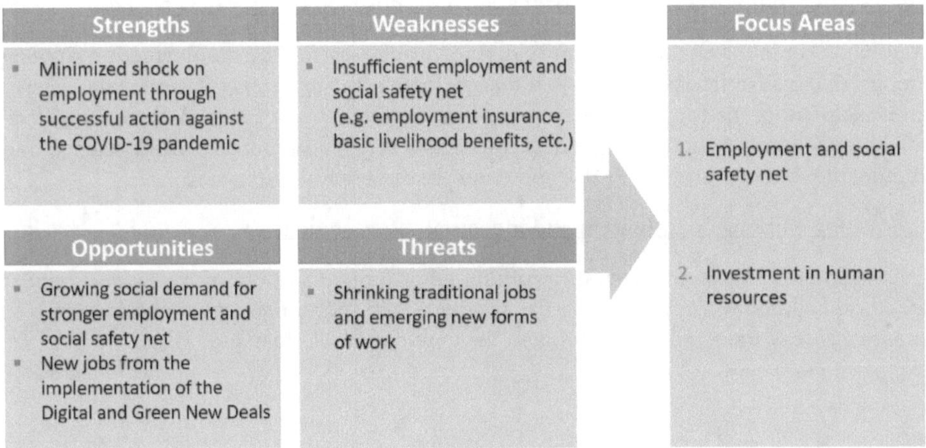

Focus Areas

1. Employment and Social Safety Net – protecting those who are particularly vulnerable in times of crisis, and building a stronger and tighter employment and social safety net. *(24 trillion won including 22.6 trillion won from the treasury will be invested by 2025 to create 159,000 jobs.)*

Building a universal employment safety net:

The employment insurance system will be expanded in phases to cover workers in non-standard forms of employment such as artists and freelancers.

Workers' compensation insurance will be expanded to cover approximately 88,000 additional workers in non-standard forms of employment.

Strengthening the social safety net for an inclusive society for all:

To provide an increased level of benefits to wider populations, the eligibility criteria for the basic livelihood security benefits will be relaxed in phases by 2022.

To introduce a Korean version of invalidity benefits, a study and a pilot project for low-income groups will be carried out.

Ensuring livelihoods and employment stability for those not covered by employment insurance:

Job Search Promotion Scheme, which includes Employment Success Package Program, Job Search Promotion Subsidy, job-training programs and internship opportunities for the vulnerable including low-income workers, will be expanded. Up to 500,000 won will be provided for six months through the Job Search Promotion Subsidy, and up to 1,500,000 won will be provided through the Employment Success Package Program depending on the period of continued employment after starting at the job.

Helping new employees in the labor market and those looking for new positions:

A subsidy on labor costs will be provided to businesses for the employment of young employees in IT-related fields *(up to 1,800,000 won for up to six months)* and a short-term internship program for young employees *(up to 800,000 won for up to six months)*. Job-matching support will also be provided to connect young graduates from science and engineering backgrounds to SMEs and enterprises of middle standing.

Innovating working environment and industrial safety standards:

Improvements will be made to the working environment through ways such as regular technical training to prevent industrial accidents; the recruitment of dedicated staff to ensure a safe working environment; and the elimination of dust and noise.

2. Investment in Human Resources – Against the changing economic structure, investment will be made in human resources to build talent and provide employment support for new types of jobs, and to reduce the digital gap. *(4.4 trillion won including 4 trillion won from the treasury will be invested by 2025 to create 180,000 jobs.)*

Training digital and green talents:

With the aim to train 100,000 individuals on AI and software, two additional research organizations will be selected under the Korea Initiative for fostering University of Research and Innovation (KIURI), and support will be provided to 40 universities to focus on software knowledge.

To support the training of 20,000 individuals in green-integrated fields, specialized graduate schools in the fields of climate change and green engineering, and job-training in the environmental industry will be provided.

Restructuring the job-training system to be future-oriented:

With the aim to nurture 180,000 individuals for future-oriented industries, training will be provided through businesses, universities and institutions for innovation.

Training on digital integration will be supported for 40,000 trainees in 2021 and 50,000 trainees a year from 2022, and a curriculum that integrates new technologies for 10,000 university students will be established in 40 campuses.

Digitally based training platforms will be provided to SMEs and training institutions by granting them access to local co-training centers, which had previously been available for affiliated businesses.

Enhancing the accessibility to digital infrastructure for rural residents and vulnerable people:

An ultrahigh-speed internet network will be built in 1,200 rural villages including island and other remote areas.

In addition to the replacement of 18,000 old Wi-Fi equipment, 41,000 high-performance Wi-Fi equipment will be installed in public places such as community centers.

Through the operation of 6,000 digital capacity-building centers, digital education including mobile finance and digital ethics will be provided to all residents.

The production and provision of alternative materials for the disabled, such as braille and audio books, will be expanded to enhance their access to information.

III. WHAT WE ENVISION FOR 2025

The Korean New Deal is expected to transform Korea into:

1. **a smart country** that leads the way for future industries and innovative public services.

- A newly established 'data dam' that allows the processing, trading and secure utilization of data will digitalize key industries of the country and create new markets.
- Based on digital technology such as blockchain and 5G, customized government services for different needs will be made available anywhere at any time.
- The digitalization of geographic data will create various types of new industries, and enable safe and convenient lifestyles through ICT and home services.
- The establishment of 'untact' infrastructure will protect the country from external shocks including infectious diseases by ensuring a stable provision of medical services and a safe working environment for medical staff.

2. **a green country** that engages deeply in global discussions on climate action, and strives to achieve a balance among growth, people and nature.

- Public facilities will be transformed into zero-energy buildings to enhance energy efficiency and create pleasant living spaces.
- Terrestrial and marine ecosystems will be restored, and nature will be integrated into urban spaces.
- The generation of more renewable energy will enable a faster transition towards a low-carbon economy and secure sustainable energy sources.
- An eco-friendly transportation system will be established to address concerns of greenhouse gas and fine dust.
- The Internet of Things (IoT), 5G and other digital technologies will support the transition of industrial complexes into innovative spaces with high energy efficiency and productivity.

3. **a safe country** that protects against unemployment and disparities.

- A secure employment safety net will provide protection against unemployment, and build capacity for reemployment opportunities.
- A social welfare system with no blind spots will ensure the minimum cost of living for all, and provide necessary support for the sick.
- The benefits of a digitally-advanced country will be made available to all, regardless of their social/income status of where they live, to realize an inclusive country.

IV. IMPLEMENTATION PLAN

Strategy Meeting on the Korean New Deal Chaired by the President:

Going forward, a strategy meeting will be established for the implementation of the Korean New Deal. Key decisions will be made at this meeting, which will be chaired by the president with participation from the entire government, a committee on the Korean New Deal within the Democratic Party, local governments and private businesses. This strategy meeting will be organized once or twice a month, taking various forms such as comprehensive reporting to the public and progress updates on key projects.

Joint Committee between the Government and the Democratic Party:

Within the government, the existing meetings of economy-related ministers will be utilized as ministerial meetings on the Korean New Deal. The K-New Deal Committee, which is the committee on the Korean New Deal within the Democratic Party, will also be continuing the discussions independently. To establish a channel for cooperation and discussion between the political community and the government, a joint headquarters for the implementation of the Korean New Deal will also be established. Co-chaired by the deputy prime minister of economy and the chief of the K-New Deal Committee, the headquarters will invite the heads of the subcommittee on the three components of the Korean New Deal and relevant ministers including those for the Ministry of Science and ICT (MSIT), the Ministry of Environment (MOE), the Ministry of Trade, Industry and Energy (MOTIE), and the Ministry of Employment and Labor (MOEL).

Working-level Task Force Led by the Vice Minister of Economy and Finance:

A working-level task force will be established within the Ministry of Economy and Finance with staff from other relevant ministries.

ANNEX: 10 KEY PROJECTS

1. Data Dam
2. AI Government
3. Smart Healthcare
4. Green and Smart Schools
5. Digital Twin
6. Digitalization of SOC
7. Smart and Green Industrial Complexes
8. Green Remodeling
9. Green Energy
10. Eco-friendly Mobility of the Future

Selection Criteria for 10 Key Projects

Among the Korean New Deal projects, 10 key projects have been selected in cooperation among the legislature, the government, and the public based on the following criteria:

- a project with a great impact including boosting the economy;
- a project that effectively stimulates regional economies and supports a balanced regional development;
- a project that creates not only short-term jobs but also a large quantity of sustainable jobs;
- a project that can lead to tangible changes which can be experienced by the people; and
- a project that can mobilize private investments, promoting business activities in new industries

1. Data Dam

The transition towards a digital economy will be accelerated, and 5G and AI will be integrated throughout all sectors by strengthening the foundation for data collection, processing, trading and utilization.

Policy Target Timeline:

	2020	2022	2025
Data market size	16.8 trillion won (in 2019)	30 trillion won	43 trillion won
5G provision	14.3% (as of June 2020)	45%	70%
Number of AI corporations	56	100	150

Key Investments and System Reforms:

- Invest 8.5 trillion won (including 7.1 trillion won from the treasury) by 2022 and create 207,000 new jobs
- Invest 18.1 trillion won (including 15.5 trillion won from the treasury) by 2025 and create 389,000 new jobs

Additional big data platforms will be established across industries including financial and environmental platforms *(20 additional platforms to make 30 total)*; a total of 142,000 public data will be made available to the public; and 1,300 types of data will be collected for AI learning.

The installation of 5G across the country will be supported by providing tax incentives and exemption of fees.

The 5G network will be integrated to produce 195 immersive contents in areas such as education, tourism and culture, and to develop technology for commercialization of self-driving vehicles and self-navigating vessels.

Support will be provided for the construction of 12,000 smart factories; the provision of AI-based home services (e.g. indoor purification of fine dust); and the implementation of leading projects that integrate AI with other technology in areas close to people's lives (e.g. medical image readers, etc.).

An integrated digital platform will be established to archive library databases, educational materials, and immersive contents of museums and galleries that are scattered nationwide. This will allow for the convenient searching and utilization of data.

A joint control tower between the public and the private sectors will be prepared to design national policies on data, to promote the integrated management, convergence and utilization of public and private data, and to support data-related industries.

2. Smart Government

A 'smart' government will utilize the 5G network, blockchain technology and other new digital technologies to quickly process and provide customized public services.

Policy Target Timeline:

	2020	2022	2025
Digital transition of public services	Mostly F2F services	Digital transition in 50% of major public services	Digital transition in 80% of major public services
Nationwide 5G Network	Government work based on wired networks	Installation of 5G wireless network	5G wireless network in all government complexes
Cloud Transition of Public Services	17% (of 224,000 digitization H/W)	50%	100%

Key Investments and System Reforms:

- Invest 2.5 trillion won from the treasury by 2022 and create 23,000 new jobs
- Invest 9.7 trillion won from the treasury by 2025 and create 91,000 new jobs

Provision of 'untact' public services will be expanded. This includes issuance of government documents based on a mobile identification system and provision of customized information on government subsidy and pension plans.

Blockchain technology will be adopted in 120 pilot projects in areas closely related to people's lives, such as the receipt of welfare benefits, real estate transactions and online voting.

To adopt a smart working environment in the government, the 5G network will be established in phases at all government complexes, and public information system will be transferred to cloud networks.

To build a knowledge platform, 1.25 million academic journals and books owned by the National Assembly and the National Library of Korea will be digitalized every year, and subscription to international academic journals will be expanded to five key academic journals and 76 general journals by 2025.

3. Smart Healthcare

The establishment of a smart medical infrastructure based on digital technology will protect patients and healthcare professionals from infectious diseases, while enhancing the convenience of treatment for patients.

Policy Target Timeline:

	2020	2022	2025
Medical models	Insufficient infrastructure for smart hospitals	9 smart hospital models	18 smart hospital models
Anti-infectious disease infrastructure	Lack of specialized system for respiratory diseases	1,000 specialized respiratory clinics	1,000 specialized respiratory clinics
AI-based precision medicine	Immature environment for AI medical diagnosis	Diagnosis of 8 diseases using AI	Diagnosis of 20 diseases using AI

Key Investments and System Reforms:

- Invest 100 billion won from the treasury by 2022 and create 1,000 new jobs
- Invest 200 billion won (including 100 billion won from the treasury) by 2025 and create 2,000 new jobs

Utilizing digital technology such as 5G and IoT, 18 smart hospitals will be built to allow for the real-time monitoring of inpatients and interdisciplinary diagnosis and treatment.

To provide safer medical treatment, 1,000 specialized clinics for patients with respiratory symptoms and fever will be established to diagnose them before they visit medical institutions.

AI-based software on the precise diagnosis of 12 diseases including lung cancer, diabetes and liver diseases will be developed and piloted.

To respond to infectious diseases and provide the convenience to the public, the Ministry of Health and Welfare will work to institutionalize 'untact' medical treatments based on full discussions with stakeholders including the medical sector. Measures will be prepared to address concerns over patient safety, accountability for medical mishaps and the overconcentration of patients at tertiary hospitals.

The government will continue to expand pilot projects extending health insurance coverage on remote medical treatment by utilizing ICT.

4. Green and Smart Schools

The installation of energy-saving facilities supports environmentally friendly classrooms, while the use of technology-based educational materials provides a learning environment that incorporates a blend of both online and offline methods.

Policy Target Timeline:

	2020	2022	2025
Remodeling of school buildings	-	1,299 schools	over 2,890 schools
Provision of classroom Wi-Fi	14.8%	100%	100%
EduTech industry size	3.8 trillion won (in 2018)	7 trillion won	10 trillion won

Key Investments and System Reforms:

- Invest 5.3 trillion won (including 1.1 trillion won from the treasury) by 2022 and create 42,000 new jobs
- Invest 15.3 trillion won (including 3.4 trillion won from the treasury) by 2025 and create 124,000 new jobs

Energy efficiency of old school buildings, including at least 2,890 elementary, middle and high school buildings, will be enhanced through the installation of solar panels and eco-friendly insulation. This project will be funded both by government finances and through Public-Private Partnership (PPP) via the Build-Transfer-Lease (BTL) method. The private-sector component of the project is planned to be expanded with a new SOC fund open to public.

The plan to provide full Wi-Fi coverage in 380,000 classrooms by 2024 will be completed by 2022. *(Timeline: 80,000 classrooms by June 2020; 240,000 classrooms based on the Supplementary Budget of 2020; and all 380,000 classrooms by 2022)*

A total of 200,000 old computers and laptops of school faculty members will be replaced with new ones, and 240,000 tablet PCs will be provided to 1,200 schools that will test out the 'online textbook' program in order to develop new teaching and learning models.

An integrated platform for online learning that utilizes various educational contents and big data to provide customized learning materials, will be launched. This new platform provides both public and private learning materials, and supports all stages of learning.

The enactment of the Basic Act on Distance Learning (tentative) will reinforce and promote virtual learning methods by defining and basic plan on distance learning and support measures for schools.

5. Digital Twin

Digital twin (a digital replica of an object that can be used for the analysis and prediction of the future through simulation) will be made for roads, underground spaces, harbors and dams to lay the foundation for new industries such as drones and self-driving vehicles, and to allow for the safe management of land and facilities.

Policy Target Timeline:

	2020	2022	2025
High-definition road mapping	For all national expressways	For all national roads	For local roads with more than 4 lanes
Management system on old underground utility-pipe conduit	on 10 km	on 30 km	on 130 km

Key Investments and System Reforms:

- Invest 0.5 trillion won from the treasury by 2022 and create 5,000 new jobs
- Invest 1.8 trillion won (including 1.5 trillion won from the treasury) by 2025 and create 16,000 new jobs

A high-resolution image map and Digital Elevation Models (DEMs), which provide 3D representation of a terrain, will be prepared to show the altitude of key regions including urban areas.

Precise digital road maps will be prepared on local roads with more than four lanes and national roads.

An intelligent management system including measuring instruments will be installed on 120 km of old underground utility-pipe conduit; and systems for the real-time monitoring of safety will be set up at 37 nationally managed dams.

Testbeds for harbor automation based on digital twin technology (4 berths), and a digital platform for the real-time monitoring of harbor facilities (29 locations) will be set up.

Two smart city pilots will be implemented as signature projects that enhance the quality of life and provide urban solutions based on AI, digital twin and other types of new technologies.

With the amendment of Security Management Regulations of the National Spatial Data, the online provision of point cloud data will be authorized to produce high-definition road maps to be used in developing private sector services including the commercialization of self-driving vehicles.

6. Digitalization of SOC

Key infrastructure that ensure safe and convenient lifestyles will be digitalized, and systems will be prepared to efficiently prevent and respond to disasters.

Policy Target Timeline:

	2020	2022	2025
Installation of C-ITS* in national expressways	85 km (2%)	2,085 km (51.2%)	4,075 km (100%)
Smart water supply system	Draft basic plans on inter-regional & local water supply system	39 interregional & 161 local systems	48 interregional & 161 local systems
Installation of early-warning system for disasters	-	510 locations	510 locations

*Cooperative-Intelligent Transport Systems

Key Investments and System Reforms:

- Invest 8.2 trillion won (including 5.5 trillion won from the treasury) by 2022 and create 73,000 new jobs
- Invest 14.8 trillion won (including 10 trillion won from the treasury) by 2025 and create 143,000 new jobs

Cooperative-Intelligent Transportation System (C-ITS) will be adopted on major roads; IoT sensors will be installed on all railroads; and fourth generation networks for railways will be built.

'Untact' biometric systems will be introduced into 15 airports, and digital management systems that utilize CCTV and IoT will be established at 3 national fishing harbors.

For safer water management, real-time monitoring and remote controlling systems will be set up for national rivers (73 rivers; 3,600 km) and 27 reservoirs; and the entire water supply system will be made smart through the use of ICT and AI. *(Targets: 48 inter-regional and 161 local water supply systems)*

In terms of disaster management, 510 early-warning systems will be installed for slope land and other areas that are considered high risk for disasters. Additional flood warning systems will be set up in 180 parking lots located near high water levels.

For the stable operation and management of smart water networks, the enforcement decree and the enforcement regulation of the Water Supply and Waterworks Installation Act will be amended to authorize the managing operators of pipe networks, and improve the technology diagnosis process.

The Framework Act on the Management of Disasters and Safety and other relevant acts will be enacted and amended to allow for the utilization of necessary private resources in disaster management.

7. Smart and Green Industrial Complexes

Industrial complexes will be made smart and eco-friendly (high productivity, high energy efficiency and low pollution) based on digital technology.

Policy Target Timeline:

	2020	2022	2025
Smart industrial complexes	7	10	15
Clean factories	-	700	1,750
Industrial complexes to share industrial waste for reuse	-	27	81
Pollution-preventive facilities for small businesses	4,182	10,182	13,182

Key Investments and System Reforms:

- Invest 2.1 trillion won (including 1.6 trillion won from the treasury) by 2022 and create 17,000 new jobs
- Invest 4 trillion won (including 3.2 trillion won from the treasury) by 2025 and create 33,000 new jobs

To test the manufacturing processes of industrial complexes, 3 simulation centers will be established. A remote monitoring system on leaking toxic chemical substance will be established utilizing AI and drones in 15 industrial complexes.

To enable the real-time monitoring and control of energy generation and consumption, 10 smart energy platforms based on micro power grid will be established. These platforms allow for the collection of data based on ICT, the visualization of energy flow, and the operation of an integrated control center for electricity.

Smart ecological plants minimizing pollution (e.g. by using renewable energy and reusing waste heat and other wastes) and clean factories reducing pollution based on individualized solutions for businesses will be established. *(100 plants and 1,750 factories)*

Support will be provided to help businesses build networks to share waste materials for reuse in 81 industrial complexes.

Support for facilities that prevent fine dust will be provided to 9,000 small businesses.

To measure and monitor the business pollutants, measuring instruments using IoT will be made mandatory in phases with the amendment of the Enforcement Decree of the Clean Air Conservation Act.

8. Green Remodeling

To encourage the energy efficiency of private sector buildings, the government will take the initiative and enhance the energy efficiency of public buildings by installing solar panels, eco-friendly insulation systems, etc.

Policy Target Timeline:

	2020	2022	2025
Improvement of old rental housing	-	186,000	225,000
Energy-efficient daycare centers	-	194	440
Energy-saving cultural facilities	-	287	1,148

Key Investments and System Reforms:

- Invest 3.1 trillion won (including 1.8 trillion won from the treasury) by 2022 and create 78,000 new jobs
- Invest 5.4 trillion won (including 3.0 trillion won from the treasury) by 2025 and create 124,000 new jobs

Solar panels will be installed and insulation system will be replaced with high-performance ones in 225,000 public rental housings that are over 15 years old; and in 2,170 daycare centers, public health centers and medical institutions.

High-efficiency energy equipment and eco-friendly materials will be used to build 440 public daycare centers and 51 public sports facilities.

Energy-saving facilities such as solar power systems and LED lights will be installed in 1,148 cultural facilities including museums and libraries.

The insulation of 3 old government complexes will be reinforced, and energy management systems will be made more efficient in 6 government complexes.

With an investment of 2 trillion won by 2025, overhead cables providing electrical power or telecommunication will be replaced with underground cables in school zones and other areas in need.

A roadmap to mandate the zero-energy of public buildings will be accelerated with the amendment of the Enforcement Decree of the Green Buildings Construction Support Act.

9. Green Energy

R&D and pilot projects will be expanded, and additional facilities provided to promote industries for renewable energy such as solar and wind power.

Policy Target Timeline:

	2020	2022	2025
Generation capacity (solar and wind energy)	12.7GW (in 2019)	26.3GW	42.7GW
Core and original technologies for hydrogen	Basic-level research	-	Possession of core and original technologies (by 2026)
Standards on hydrothermal technologies	-	Testing standards prepared (by 2023)	-

Key Investments and System Reforms:

- Invest 4.5 trillion won (including 3.7 trillion won from the treasury) by 2022 and create 16,000 new jobs
- Invest 11.3 trillion won (including 9.2 trillion won from the treasury) by 2025 and create 38,000 new jobs

Support will be provided to measure wind conditions and conduct feasibility studies on up to 13 regions to find sites for large-scale offshore wind farms of either floating or fixed-bottom types. Demonstration complexes will be established in phases.

Community benefit sharing for renewable energy projects will be introduced. Higher support on loans for renewable energy will be provided to participating residents of farming areas and industrial complexes. Support will also be provided to 200,000 households for renewable energy facilities installed in residential or commercial buildings for private use.

Support will be provided to develop all the core and original technologies needed from the generation to consumption of hydrogen, and to establish hydrogen cities.

A fair transition will be ensured for those regions that foresee difficulties arising from the reduced use of coal power and other traditional sources of energy by supporting their adjustment to the renewable energy sector (e.g. green mobility, digital management of renewable energy, platform for offshore wind turbine, etc.).

10. Eco-friendly Mobility of the Future

The green transition away from old diesel cars and vessels will be accelerated and the provision of electric vehicles (EVs) and hydrogen vehicles will be supported to reduce the emission of greenhouse gases and to enhance competitiveness in the future car market.

Policy Target Timeline:

	2020	2022	2025
Number of electric vehicles	91,000 (in 2019)	430,000	1,130,000
Number of hydrogen vehicles	5,000	67,000	200,000
Scrappage of old diesel cars	1,060,000	1,720,000	2,220,000 (by 2024)
Transition of old diesel freight cars to LPG	15,000	60,000	150,000

Key Investments and System Reforms:

- Invest 8.6 trillion won (including 5.6 trillion won from the treasury) by 2022 and create 52,000 new jobs
- Invest 20.3 trillion won (including 13.1 trillion won from the treasury) by 2025 and create 151,000 new jobs

The provision of 1.13 million EVs including passenger cars, buses, and freight vehicles, will be supported along with the installation of 15,000 rapid chargers and 30,000 slow chargers.

The provision of 200,000 hydrogen vehicles including passenger cars, buses and freight vehicles will be supported along with the installation of 450 charging facilities. Fuel cell plants and other infrastructure for the distribution of hydrogen will also be established.

The scrappage of old diesel cars and the transition to liquefied petroleum gas (LPG) or electric vehicles will be supported. *(Scrappage of 1.2 million diesel cars and construction equipment, and 32,000 farming machinery; and the transition of 135,000 freight and 88,000 school buses to LPG vehicles)*

The green transition (e.g. to liquefied natural gas, hybrid, etc.) of public vessels and navy fleets, and private vessels will be supported; and 80 public vessels will be equipped with diesel particulate filters (DPF).

Support will be provided to develop parts for future electric cars, hydrogen fuel cell systems, and eco-friendly fuels for vessels.

A medium to long-term fiscal management strategy will be prepared, reflecting the expected decline in the manufacturing costs of electric and hydrogen vehicles due to technological development and economies of scale.

To expand the supply of hydrogen cars, a fuel subsidy on hydrogen vehicles for commercial use will be introduced in phases with the amendments of the Passenger Transport Service Act and the Trucking Transport Business Act.

References

European Commission. (2020, January 14). *Press Release: Financing the Green Transition: The European Green Deal Investment Plan and Just Transition Mechanism.* Retrieved from: https://ec.europa.eu/regional_policy/en/newsroom/news/2020/01/14-01-2020-financing-the-green-transition-the-european-green-deal-investment-plan-and-just-transition-mechanism

European Parliament. (2020, May 27). *Press Release: Europe's moment: Repair and prepare for the next generation.* Retrieved from: https://ec.europa.eu/commission/presscorner/detail/en/ip_20_940

IMF. (2020). *World Economic Outlook Update.*

IMF. (2020, April 20). Greening the Recovery. *IMF Special Series on COVID-19.* Retrieved from: https://www.imf.org/~/media/Files/Publications/covid19-special-notes/en-special-series-on-covid-19-greening-the-recovery.ashx?la=en

IRENA. (2020). *Global Renewables Outlook.*

OECD. (2020). *OECD Economic Outlook.*

OECD. (2019). Innovation and Business/Market Opportunities associated with Energy Transitions and a Cleaner Global Environment. *Issue Paper.*

Pinner, D., Rogers, M., and Samandari, H. (2020, April 7). Addressing climate change in a post pandemic world, *McKinsey Quarterly.* Retrieved from: https://www.mckinsey.com/business-functions/sustainability/our-insights/addressing-climate-change-in-a-post-pandemic-world

Renewable Energy 100. Website: www.there100.org. Accessed on July 22, 2020.

Rosalie Chan. (2020, April 30). Microsoft Teams now has 75 million daily active users, adding 31 million in just over a month. *Business Insider.* Retrieved from: https://www.businessinsider.com/microsoft-teams-hits-75-million-daily-active-users-2020-4

Statistics Korea. (2020, July 3). *Press Release: Online Shopping Trend of May 2020.* Retrieved from: http://kostat.go.kr/assist/synap/preview/skin/doc.html?fn=synapview383635_2&rs=/assist/synap/preview

Government of
the Republic of Korea

This booklet has been prepared by the Green Climate Policy Division of the Ministry of Economy and Finance based on the Korean original text.

Ministry of Economy and Finance
Development Finance Bureau
Green Climate Policy Division
Government Complex Sejong (30109)
Republic of Korea

Government of
the Republic of Korea

3. M-1 Green New Deal (Canada). Private Member's Motion (Peter Julian), 2019.

HOUSE OF COMMONS, CANADA
MEMBERS OF PARLIAMENT – PRIVATE MEMBER'S MOTIONS
M-1 GREEN NEW DEAL
(PETER JULIAN, MP NEW WESTMINSTER—BURNABY, BC)

43rd PARLIAMENT, 1st SESSION

MOTION TEXT

That, in the opinion of the House:

(a) it is the duty of the government to create a Green New Deal (i) to achieve net-zero greenhouse gas emissions through a fair and just transition for all communities and workers, (ii) to create millions of good, high-wage jobs and ensure prosperity and economic security for all Canadians, (iii) to invest in Canada's infrastructure and industry to sustainably meet the challenges of the 21st century, (iv) to secure for all people of Canada for generations to come clean air and water, climate and community resiliency, healthy food, access to nature, and a sustainable environment, (v) to promote justice and equity by stopping current, preventing future, and repairing historic oppression of Indigenous Peoples (First Nations, Métis, and Inuit), racialized persons, non-dominant cultural, ethnic, religious and linguistic communities, immigrants and newcomers, youth, LGBTQ2S+ persons, the poor, low-income workers, women, the elderly, the unhoused, people with disabilities, migrant communities, deindustrialized communities and depopulated rural communities (referred to in this motion as "frontline and vulnerable communities");

(b) the goals described in paragraph (a) above (referred to in this motion as the "Green New Deal goals") should be accomplished through a 10-year national mobilization (referred to in this resolution as the "Green New Deal mobilization") that will require (i) building resiliency against climate-change-related disasters, such as extreme weather, including by leveraging funding and providing investments for community-defined projects and strategies, (ii) repairing and upgrading Canada's infrastructure, including by eliminating pollution and greenhouse gas emissions as much as technologically feasible, by guaranteeing universal access to clean water by reducing the risks posed by flooding and other climate impacts, and by ensuring that any infrastructure spending considered by Parliament addresses climate change, (iii) meeting 100 percent of the power demand in Canada through clean, renewable, and zero-emission energy sources, including by dramatically expanding and upgrading existing renewable power sources and by deploying new capacity, (iv) building or upgrading to energy-efficient, distributed, and ''smart'' power grids, and working to ensure affordable access to electricity, (v) upgrading all existing buildings in Canada and building new buildings to achieve maximal energy efficiency, water efficiency, safety, affordability, comfort, and durability, including through electrification, (vi) spurring massive growth in clean manufacturing in Canada and removing pollution and greenhouse gas emissions from manufacturing and industry as much as is technologically feasible, including by expanding renewable energy manufacturing and investing in existing manufacturing and industry, (vii) working collaboratively with Canada's farmers to eliminate pollution and greenhouse gas emissions from the agricultural sector as much as is technologically feasible, including by supporting family farming, by investing in sustainable farming and land use practices that increase soil health, and by building a more sustainable food system that ensures universal access to healthy food, (viii) overhauling Canada's transportation systems to eliminate pollution and greenhouse gas emissions from the transportation sector as much as is technologically feasible, including through investment in zero-emission vehicle infrastructure and manufacturing, and clean, affordable, and accessible public transportation, and high-speed rail, (ix) mitigating and managing the long-term adverse health, economic, and other effects of pollution and climate change, including by providing funding for community-defined projects and strategies, (x) removing greenhouse gases from the atmosphere and reducing pollution, including by restoring natural ecosystems through proven low-tech solutions that increase soil carbon storage, such as preservation and afforestation, (xi) restoring and protecting threatened, endangered, and fragile ecosystems through locally appropriate and science-based projects that enhance biodiversity and support climate resiliency, (xii) cleaning up existing hazardous waste and abandoned sites to promote economic development and sustainability, (xiii) identifying other emission and pollution sources and creating solutions to eliminate them, (xiv) promoting the international exchange of technology, expertise, products, funding, and services, with the aim of making Canada the international leader on climate action, and to help other countries achieve a Green New Deal;

(c) a Green New Deal must be developed through transparent and inclusive consultation, collaboration, and partnership with Indigenous Peoples, frontline and vulnerable communities, labour unions, worker cooperatives, civil society groups, academia, and businesses; and

(d) to achieve the Green New Deal goals and mobilization, a Green New Deal will require (i) providing and leveraging, in a way that ensures that the public receives appropriate ownership stakes and returns on investment, adequate capital (including through community grants, public banks, and other public financing), technical expertise, supporting policies, and other forms of assistance to communities, organizations, federal, provincial, and municipal governments, and businesses working on the Green New Deal mobilization, (ii) ensuring that the government takes into account the complete environmental and social costs and impacts of emissions through existing laws, new policies and programs, and ensuring that frontline and vulnerable communities shall not be adversely affected, (iii) providing resources, training, and high-quality education, including higher education, to all Canadians, with a focus on frontline and vulnerable communities, so those communities may be full and equal participants in the Green New Deal mobilization, (iv) making public investments in the research and development of new clean and renewable energy technologies and industries, (v) directing investments to spur economic development, deepen and diversify industry in local and regional economies, and build wealth and community ownership, while prioritizing high-quality job creation and economic, social, and environmental benefits in frontline and vulnerable communities that may otherwise struggle with the transition away from greenhouse gas intensive industries, (vi) ensuring the use of democratic and participatory processes that are inclusive of and led by frontline and vulnerable communities and workers to plan, implement, and administer the Green New Deal mobilization at the local level, (vii) ensuring that the Green New Deal mobilization creates high-quality union jobs that pay prevailing wages, hires local workers, offers training and advancement opportunities, and guarantees wage and benefit parity for workers affected by the transition, (viii) guaranteeing a job with a family-sustaining wage, adequate family and medical leave, paid vacations, and retirement security to all Canadians, (ix) strengthening and protecting the right of all workers to organize, unionize, and collectively bargain free of coercion, intimidation, and harassment, (x) strengthening and enforcing labour, workplace health and safety, antidiscrimination, and wage and hour standards across all employers, industries, and sectors, (xi) enacting and enforcing trade rules, procurement standards, and border adjustments with strong labor and environmental protections to stop the transfer of jobs and pollution overseas, and to grow domestic manufacturing in Canada, (xii) ensuring that public lands, waters, and oceans are protected, and that eminent domain is not abused, (xiii) obtaining the free, prior, and informed consent of First Nations, Métis, and Inuit people for all decisions that affect First Nations, Métis, and Inuit people and their traditional territories, honouring all treaties and agreements with First Nations, Métis, and Inuit people, and protecting and enforcing the sovereignty and land rights of First Nations, Métis, and Inuit people, (xiv) ensuring a commercial environment where every businessperson is free from unfair competition and domination by domestic or international monopolies, (xv) providing all Canadians with high-quality health care, affordable, safe, and adequate housing, economic security, and access to clean water, clean air, healthy and affordable food, and nature.

4. Recognizing the duty of the Federal Government to create a Green New Deal. H. Res. 109, 116th Congress (United States) 2019.

[~116HR109]

....

(Original Signature of Member)

117TH CONGRESS
1ST SESSION

H. RES. ______

Recognizing the duty of the Federal Government to create a Green New Deal.

IN THE HOUSE OF REPRESENTATIVES

Ms. OCASIO-CORTEZ submitted the following resolution; which was referred to the Committee on ______________________________

RESOLUTION

Recognizing the duty of the Federal Government to create a Green New Deal.

Whereas the October 2018 report entitled "Special Report on Global Warming of 1.5 °C" by the Intergovernmental Panel on Climate Change and the November 2018 Fourth National Climate Assessment report found that—

(1) human activity is the dominant cause of observed climate change over the past century;

(2) a changing climate is causing sea levels to rise and an increase in wildfires, severe storms, droughts, and other extreme weather events that threaten human life, healthy communities, and critical infrastructure;

(3) global warming at or above 2 degrees Celsius beyond preindustrialized levels will cause—

(A) mass migration from the regions most affected by climate change;

(B) more than $500,000,000,000 in lost annual economic output in the United States by the year 2100;

(C) wildfires that, by 2050, will annually burn at least twice as much forest area in the western United States than was typically burned by wildfires in the years preceding 2019;

(D) a loss of more than 99 percent of all coral reefs on Earth;

(E) more than 350,000,000 more people to be exposed globally to deadly heat stress by 2050; and

(F) a risk of damage to $1,000,000,000,000 of public infrastructure and coastal real estate in the United States; and

(4) global temperatures must be kept below 1.5 degrees Celsius above preindustrialized levels to avoid the most severe impacts of a changing climate, which will require—

(A) global reductions in greenhouse gas emissions from human sources of 40 to 60 percent from 2010 levels by 2031; and

(B) net-zero global emissions by 2050;

Whereas, because the United States has historically been responsible for a disproportionate amount of greenhouse gas emissions, having emitted 20 percent of global greenhouse gas emissions through 2014, and has a high technological capacity, the United States must take a leading role in reducing emissions through economic transformation;

Whereas the United States is currently experiencing several related crises, with—

(1) life expectancy declining while basic needs, such as clean air, clean water, healthy food, and adequate health care, housing, transportation, and education, are inaccessible to a significant portion of the United States population;

(2) a 4-decade trend of wage stagnation, deindustrialization, and antilabor policies that has led to—

(A) hourly wages overall stagnating since the 1970s despite increased worker productivity;

(B) the third-worst level of socioeconomic mobility in the developed world before the Great Recession;

(C) the erosion of the earning and bargaining power of workers in the United States; and

(D) inadequate resources for public sector workers to confront the challenges of climate change at local, State, and Federal levels; and

(3) the greatest income inequality since the 1920s, with—

(A) the top 1 percent of earners accruing 91 percent of gains in the first few years of economic recovery after the Great Recession;

(B) a large racial wealth divide amounting to a difference of 20 times more wealth between the average white family and the average black family; and

(C) a gender earnings gap that results in women earning approximately 80 percent as much as men, at the median;

Whereas climate change, pollution, and environmental destruction have exacerbated systemic racial, regional, social, environmental, and economic injustices (referred to in this preamble as "systemic injustices") by disproportionately affecting indigenous peoples, communities of color, migrant communities, deindustrialized communities, depopulated rural communities, the poor, low-income workers, women, the elderly, the unhoused, people with disabilities, and youth (referred to in this preamble as "frontline and vulnerable communities");

Whereas, climate change constitutes a direct threat to the national security of the United States—

(1) by impacting the economic, environmental, and social stability of countries and communities around the world; and

(2) by acting as a threat multiplier;

Whereas the Federal Government-led mobilizations during World War II and the New Deal created the greatest middle class that the United States has ever seen, but many members of frontline and vulnerable communities were excluded from many of the economic and societal benefits of those mobilizations; and

Whereas the House of Representatives recognizes that a new national, social, industrial, and economic mobilization on a scale not seen since World War II and the New Deal era is a historic opportunity—

(1) to create millions of good, high-wage jobs in the United States;

(2) to provide unprecedented levels of prosperity and economic security for all people of the United States; and

(3) to counteract systemic injustices: Now, therefore, be it

Resolved, That it is the sense of the House of Representatives that—

(1) it is the duty of the Federal Government to create a Green New Deal—

(A) to achieve the greenhouse gas and toxic emissions reductions needed to stay under 1.5 degrees Celsius of warming, through a fair and just transition for all communities and workers;

(B) to create millions of good, high-wage unions jobs and encourage collective bargaining agreements to ensure prosperity and economic security for all people of the United States;

(C) to invest in the infrastructure and industry of the United States to sustainably meet the challenges of the 21st century;

(D) to secure for all people of the United States for generations to come—

(i) clean air and water;

(ii) climate and community resiliency;

(iii) healthy food;

(iv) access to nature; and

(v) a sustainable environment; and

(E) to promote justice and equity by stopping current, preventing future, and repairing historic oppression of indigenous peoples, communities of color, migrant communities, deindustrialized communities, depopulated rural communities, the poor, low-income workers, women, the elderly, the unhoused, people with disabilities, and youth (referred to in this resolution as "frontline and vulnerable communities");

(2) the goals described in subparagraphs (A) through (E) of paragraph (1) (referred to in this resolution as the "Green New Deal goals") should be accomplished through a 10-year national mobilization (referred to in this resolution as the "Green New Deal mobilization") that will require the following goals and projects—

(A) building resiliency against climate change-related disasters, such as extreme weather, including by leveraging funding and providing investments for community-defined projects and strategies;

(B) repairing and upgrading the infrastructure in the United States, including—

(i) by eliminating pollution and greenhouse gas emissions as much as technologically feasible;

(ii) by guaranteeing universal access to clean water;

(iii) by reducing the risks posed by climate impacts; and

(iv) by ensuring that any infrastructure bill considered by Congress addresses climate change;

(C) meeting 100 percent of the power demand in the United States through clean, renewable, and zero-emission energy sources, including—

(i) by dramatically expanding and upgrading renewable power sources; and

(ii) by deploying new capacity;

(D) building or upgrading to energy-efficient, distributed, and "smart" power grids, and ensuring affordable access to electricity;

(E) upgrading all existing buildings in the United States and building new buildings to achieve maximum energy efficiency, water efficiency, safety, affordability, comfort, and durability, including through electrification;

(F) spurring massive growth in clean manufacturing in the United States and removing pollution and greenhouse gas emissions from manufacturing and industry as much as is technologically feasible, including by expanding renewable energy manufacturing and investing in existing manufacturing and industry;

(G) working collaboratively with farmers and ranchers in the United States to remove pollution and greenhouse gas emissions from the agricultural sector as much as is technologically feasible, including—

(i) by supporting family farming;

(ii) by investing in sustainable farming and land use practices that increase soil health; and

(iii) by building a more sustainable food system that ensures universal access to healthy food;

(H) overhauling transportation systems in the United States to remove pollution and greenhouse gas emissions from the transportation sector as much as is technologically feasible, including through investment in—

(i) zero-emission vehicle and non-motorized alternative modes of transportation infrastructure and manufacturing;

(ii) clean, affordable, and accessible public transit; and

(iii) high-speed rail;

(I) mitigating and managing the long-term adverse health, economic, and other effects of pollution and climate change, including by providing funding for community-defined projects and strategies;

(J) removing greenhouse gases from the atmosphere and reducing pollution by restoring natural ecosystems through proven low-tech solutions that increase soil carbon storage, such as land preservation and afforestation;

(K) restoring and protecting threatened, endangered, and fragile ecosystems through locally appropriate and science-based projects that enhance biodiversity and support climate resiliency;

(L) cleaning up existing hazardous waste and abandoned sites, ensuring economic development and sustainability on those sites;

(M) identifying other emission and pollution sources and creating solutions to remove them; and

(N) promoting the international exchange of technology, expertise, products, funding, and services, with the aim of making the United States the international leader on climate action, and to help other countries achieve a Green New Deal;

(3) a Green New Deal must be developed through transparent and inclusive consultation, collaboration, and partnership with frontline and vulnerable communities, labor unions, worker cooperatives, civil society groups, academia, and businesses; and

(4) to achieve the Green New Deal goals and mobilization, a Green New Deal will require the following goals and projects—

(A) providing and leveraging, in a way that ensures that the public receives appropriate ownership stakes and returns on investment, adequate capital (including through community grants, public banks, and other public financing), technical expertise, supporting policies, and other forms of assistance to communities, organizations, Federal, State, and local government agencies, and businesses working on the Green New Deal mobilization;

(B) ensuring that the Federal Government takes into account the complete environmental and social costs and impacts of emissions through—

(i) existing laws;

(ii) new policies and programs; and

(iii) ensuring that frontline and vulnerable communities shall not be adversely affected;

(C) providing resources, training, and high-quality education, including higher education, to all people of the United States, with a focus on frontline and vulnerable communities, so that all people of the United States may be full and equal participants in the Green New Deal mobilization;

(D) making public investments in the research and development of new clean and renewable energy technologies and industries;

(E) directing investments to spur economic development, deepen and diversify industry and business in local and regional economies, and build wealth and community ownership, while prioritizing high-quality job creation and economic, social, and environmental benefits in frontline and vulnerable communities, and deindustrialized communities, that may otherwise struggle with the transition away from greenhouse gas intensive industries;

(F) ensuring the use of democratic and participatory processes that are inclusive of and led by frontline and vulnerable communities and workers to plan, implement, and administer the Green New Deal mobilization at the local level;

(G) ensuring that the Green New Deal mobilization creates high-quality union jobs that pay prevailing wages, hires local workers, offers training and advancement opportunities, and guarantees direct replacement of lost wages, health care, retirement, and other benefits for workers affected by the transition;

(H) guaranteeing a job with a family-sustaining wage, adequate family and medical leave, paid vacations, and retirement security to all people of the United States;

(I) strengthening and protecting the right of all workers to organize, unionize, and collectively bargain free of coercion, intimidation, and harassment;

(J) strengthening and enforcing labor, workplace health and safety, antidiscrimination, and wage and hour standards across all employers, industries, and sectors;

(K) enacting and enforcing trade rules, procurement standards, and border adjustments with strong labor and environmental protections—

(i) to stop the transfer of jobs and pollution overseas; and

(ii) to grow domestic manufacturing in the United States;

(L) ensuring that public lands, waters, and oceans are protected and that eminent domain is not abused;

(M) obtaining the free, prior, and informed consent of indigenous peoples for all decisions that affect indigenous peoples and their traditional territories, honoring all treaties and agreements with indigenous peoples, and protecting and enforcing the sovereignty and land rights of indigenous peoples;

(N) ensuring a commercial environment where every businessperson is free from unfair competition and domination by domestic or international monopolies; and

(O) providing all people of the United States with—

(i) high-quality health care;

(ii) affordable, safe, and adequate housing;

(iii) economic security; and

(iv) clean water, clean air, healthy and affordable food, and access to nature.

INDEX

Note: Bold page numbers refer to tables; *italic* page numbers refer to figures; and page numbers followed by "n" denote endnotes.

agriculture: agrarian reform 98; agroecology 99–100; and COVID-19 90–94; decommodifying food 98–99; rewilding 101; socialist transition 89–90; subsidies 96–97; technologies 100–101; unsustainability of capitalist agro-industry 90–94, 91; urban greening and agriculture 102; workers' rights 97
agroecology 99–100
Ajl, Max 12, 249, 250; *People's Green New Deal* 249
Alexandria Ocasio-Cortez (AOC) *see* Ocasio-Cortez, Alexandria
American Green New Deal movement 28–29
American Recovery and Reinvestment Act (2009) 166, 168
Ardern, Jacinda 108, 325
Aronoff, Kate 3, 4, 9, 109

Beyond Oil and Gas Alliance 8
Bezos, Jeff 239
Biden, Joe 8, 14, 24, 26, 28, 32, 33, 47, 83, 89, 120, 122, 126, 128, 129, 131, 145, 152, 205
Black Lives Matter 6, 89, 143, 320
Bolsonaro, Jair 98, 243
border carbon adjustment (BCA) 125–127
Bretton Woods system 26, 37
Buffalo Treaty 177–178, 189
Build Back Better Agenda in the United States 16, 122, 134, 145, 152, 199, 205, 211, 318–319, 325
"Buy American" conditions 122, 128–129

Canadian Green New Deal: challenges of Canadian Federalism 342–343; Federal Government 474–488; elements of Canadian Green New Deal 339–342; GND job creation and just transition 346–348; logic of linking climate mobilization with tackling inequality 334–339; New Crown Corporations 343–346; paying for GND 349
capitalism 9, 90, 102: credit creation 31; environmental problems of 79; green capitalism 13, 89; metabolic rift 77–78; "pitfalls of capitalism" 83–85; state capitalism and problem of entrenched political power 78–83; re-regulate capital flows 31; restore policy autonomy 31; treadmill of production 75–77; working within 12–13
carbon adjustment fee (CAF) 125, 126
"carbon army" of workers 31
Carbon Capture and Storage (CCS) 11, 289
"carbon leakage" problem 125, 127, 378
carbon tariff 125, 132
carbon tax 5, 121, 122, 125, 135n5, 142–143, 221, 336
care and repair, concepts of 144
central banks: annual consumer price *52*; bonds and yields 50; combined monetary-fiscal approach 59–67; as defenders of financial system 54–55; and democratic control 48–53; GDP per capita 61–62; government control 58–59; government fiscal deficit 61–62; inflation rate 62; population growth 61; reserve accounts 60–61; toward proactive approach: buying green bonds 55–57

Chinese Green Job Guarantee (JG): administration of 271–272; designing 271–275; economic benefits and costs of 266–269, **269**; types of jobs 272–274
cities: Boston Green New Deal Detroit 6, 361–362; New York 359–361; water in 364–366; urban governance and finance 355–358; and urban spaces 354–355
Civilian Conservation Corps (CCC) 2, 157, 195, 265, 316
Civil Works Administration (CWA) 303
class: capitalist 81–83, 303; middle-class professionals 80–81, 83, 145, 161, 348, 478; ruling 6; rural 302; social 79; working 4, 12, 76–78, 80–81, 83–85, 121, 158, 163–164, 166, 238, 249, 262, 318
climate change/climate crisis 12, 23; adaptation and resilience 234–235, 283, 354, 358, 367, 387–389, 391, 393; carbon pricing, nuclear, and geoengineering 203; catastrophic 80, 108, 285; central banks 54; concern about 338; decolonization 219; devastation of 141–142, 144; EU strategy 378, 386; existential emergency 4; financial crisis of 2007–2008 23; gender equality 202; and inequality 145, 146, 151, *338*; material contribution 129; mitigation project 47–48, 52–59, 63, 68–69, 144, 282; Operation Noah 26; policies 221; Quantum Leap 24; threat of 120, 128, 141, 237, 244
climate justice 6, 14, 142–144, 150–152, 194, 196–197, 200–201, 204–205, 207, 218, 232, 237, 250, 334–335, 347
colonialism 2, 12, 15, 186, 197, 211, 218, 232, 236, 239, 322
Convention on Biological Diversity 386
Copenhagen Summit (2009) 24, 26
Corporate Mapping Project 347
COVID-19 pandemic 16, 141–142; and "Build Back Better" 318–319; and revealing and exacerbation of inequalities 320–321

decarbonization: EU Green Deal 300, 301–302; with existing trade and investment rules 124–127; rewriting trade rules 128; in United States and Europe 120–122, 124; using domestic trade law 131–132
degrowth: "bottom-up" grassroots initiatives 6, 110; economics 77, 82, 83; embracing (explicitly or implicitly) 9, 11–12; explicitly or implicitly embracing 9; opponents of 110; proponents 14, 116; redistributive 102; "top-down" GND approach 6; Transition Town movement 186
democracy: diversifying democratization 217–221; and energy decentralization 214–215; direct and delegated democracy 249; economic democracy 249; energy democracy 212–214; and energy project ownership 215–216; gender and energy democracy 219–220; indigenous peoples and energy democracy 218–219; policy participation and grassroots activism 216; poverty and energy democracy 220–221
Democratic Party 284, 333, 449
Democratic Party of Korea (DPK) 286, 289
Dish With One Spoon Treaty 188–189

electric vehicles (EVs) 11, 215, 288, 289, 344, 382, 464
energy democracy 212–214; and gender 219–220; and indigenous peoples 218–219; and poverty 220–221
energy justice 180–181, 222
environmental health disasters 163–165
environmental justice 122, 143, 158, 166–168, 196, 198–202, 232, 238
equity: class-based issues 217; economic 5; gender 142, 219; global 112; investment 391; and justice 3–7, 29, 168, 471, 479; ownership 218–219; partnerships 219; racial 73; in renewable energy projects 218; social 48, 336
EU Green Deal 300, 373; challenges 375–376; development of 310; food system 384–385; EU as a global leader 393–395; European Climate Pact 395–397; just transition 388–390; *vs.* Green New Deal for Europe 302–303
EU Recovery Fund 306
European Coal and Steel Community (ECSC) 301
European Environment Agency (EEA) 116
Extinction Rebellion 89, 217

Fair Labor Standards Act of 1938 115, 161
Feminist Agenda for a Green New Deal: opportunities 204–205; origins and principles 198–200
financing GND: conventional approach 36–37; MMT approach (*see* Modern Money Theory (MMT) approach); real resource constraints 38–39
Fossil Fuel Non-Proliferation Treaty 8
fossil fuels/fossil fuel industry 8, 11, 14, 40, 95, 96, 237, 245, 339–340, 346–348

G20 agenda 279, 393–395
Gates, Bill 28
gender: and energy democracy 219–220; equality 202, 206, 212, 320; inequities 121, 142, 199, 201, 247, 317, 322; just transition 200, 201; and racial justice 89, 198
General Agreement on Tariffs and Trade (GATT) 129–131
General Agreement on Trade in Services (GATS) 129

global financial crisis (GFC) 3, 35, 49, 51, 53, 65, 211, 237, 279, 281
Global Green New Deal (GGND) 2, 10, 111, 132–134, **133**, 211, 232, 249
Global South: climate debt 202; climate debt payments or climate reparations 12; development and growth 78; emissions/GDP per capita 111; environmental impacts in 321; export industries 197; greener mode of development 239; growing food dependency 307; issues of funding GNDs 10; low-carbon economy 245; metabolic rift 14; socioeconomic inequality 197; *see also* developing countries
global trade and investment law: approaches to decarbonization (*see* decarbonization); global GND 132–133, 134; International and National Dimensions **123**; making trade safe for green economic development policies 128–130; possible global counterparts of domestic GND **133**
Great Depression 158–162, 168
Great Recession 39, 43, 168
Green Deal (GD) 300; *see also* Green New Deal (GND)
"green growth" policy paradigm 2, 11, 15, 94, 110–111, 116, 236, 279–280; failure of 285–286; Korean Five-Year Plan 283, 289; low-carbon 282, **282,** 289
greenhouse gas (GHG) emissions 24, 27, 29, 54, 88, 101, 108, 141, 145, 147, 181, 289–290, 355
greening the economy 36, 40, 42, 44
green jobs 2, 6, 7, 15, 63, 145, 147–148, 166–168, 212, 237–238, 286, 317–318, 322, 325, 332, 346–347; *see also* jobs
Green New Deal Group (GNDG) 2–3
Gunn-Wright, Rhiana. 7, 30, 166, 168, 194

Hickel, Jason 110, 114
Hines, Colin 24, 316
hydrogen vehicles 464

Indigenous communities/knowledge: decolonization 219; and energy democracy 218–219; harms to 12; importance of 12; Indigenous rights 347; needs of 349; pillars for Indigenous-led GND 150; on renewable energy projects 179; uranium extraction and waste disposal 11
industrial policy: environmental 265; federal 5; green 5; Labour Party's 317; state stimulus 214
Intergovernmental Panel on Climate Change (IPCC) 1, 112
International Energy Agency (IEA) 112, 282, 286
International Labour Organization (ILO) conventions 97, 134
International Maritime Organization 384
International Renewable Energy Agency (IRENA) 220, 412

Job Guarantee (JG) 14, 261; in Canada 343, 348; in China (*see* Chinese Green Job Guarantee (JG)); in Korea 290; part of MMT 42
jobs: in care work 143; creation of 147, 158, 167, 259–260, 262–263, 265, 266, 271, 334, 336, 341, 346–348, 350, 410, 412, 417, 472; in Detroit 166–167; discrimination 161–163, 168; *vs.* environment dilemma 145, 333–334; "good paying union jobs" 32; green collar jobs 2, 6, 7, 15, 63, 145, 147–148, 166–168, 212, 237–238, 286, 317–318, 322, 325, 332, 346–347; guarantee (*see* Job Guarantee (JG)); in health and education 143; high-wage jobs 29, 121, 471, 478; intensive economic activity 380; losses in oil and gas sector 146–147, 149; lower-wage jobs 147, 158; low- or zero-carbon sectors of the economy 14; markets 409; pink collar jobs 7, 11; positive messages 12; poverty-wage jobs 145; promotion opportunities 115; and protecting environment 144–146; in renewable energy 143, 146–147; through Urban Climate Corps 6; well-paying jobs 14, 143–144; worker precarity 233–234; workers' rights 97
Johnson, Boris 318, 319
Johnson, Lyndon B. 84, 197
justice: climate 6, 14, 142–144, 150–152, 194, 196–197, 200–201, 204–205, 207, 218, 232, 237, 250, 334–335, 347; decarbonization efforts 3–4; decolonization and indigenous justice 150; ecological 321–322; economic 144, 145, 150, 151, 158, 168, 182–183, 205, 311; energy 180–181, 222; environmental 122, 143, 158, 166–168, 196, 198–202, 232, 238; and equity 3–7, 29, 168; gender 198, 201, 204; healing 196, 205, 207n4; oriented GND 151; racial 89, 168; restorative 182, 184, 186–188, 232; social 24, 47, 67, 147, 152, 237, 317, 321, 334
Just Transition: decolonization and Indigenous justice 150; energy justice 180–181; five-point plan 146; fund 302, 306, 311; geographic regions, impacted by green economy 124; GND job creation 345–348; Indigenous just transition 174, 185–186; industrial agriculture 177; infrastructure justice 178–179; Just Transition Mechanism (JTM) 309; regional-focus 5; training and jobs in renewable energy and transportation 146–147

Keynes 30, 115, 260, 265, 276n6; *see also* Keynesianism
Keynesianism 13, 30, 31, 62, 63, 249, 291, 300, 324

Klein, Naomi 2, 4, 7, 8, 10, 16, 99, 109, 142, 146, 148
Korean Green New Deal (KGND) (2009) 279, 281; budget in trillions of KRW **281**; carbon emissions reductions 290; expansion of nuclear power 282; failure of "green growth" 285–286; Four Major Rivers Project 281, **281,** 283–285, 289–290; "greenest" stimulus package 281; renewable energy 282; *see also* South Korea's Green New Deal 2.0
Korean New Deal (2020) 286–288, 398; background 409–410; projects 418–419
Krugman, Paul 37, 44
Kyoto Protocol 24, 121

Leap Manifesto 3, 8, 174
Lee Myung-bak 279, 282–285, 288–290
local content requirements 122, 124, 128, 129

Macron, Emmanuel 121, 309
Markey, Ed 6, 29, 35, 47, 110, 194, 237, 245, 279
Marshall Plan 174, 186
Mazzuato, Mariana 29, 302
McKibben, Bill 28, 29, 326
Medicare for All (M4A) 36, 41, 42, 44n1
Merkel, Angela 303, 308
Modern Money Theory (also referred to as Modern Monetary Theory) (MMT) approach 9, 14, 37–38; guaranteed jobs 42; inflation and tax policy for Green New Deal 43; MMT approach to costing the GND 39–43; transitioning to green energy 40–41; universal single-payer healthcare (Medicare for All) 41
Modi, Narendra 233, 243
monetary-fiscal approach 59–67; effects of increasing "high-powered" money 63–66; Green new deals and government deficits 59, 61–62; inflationary pressures in the productive economy 62–63; price stability 66; real economic growth and asset price inflation 66–67, *67*
Montreal Protocol (1987) 24
Moon Jae-in 280, 285–291, 409
Musk, Elon 240

neoliberalism 53, 74, 163–165
New Deal 2, 15, 29, 31, 45n10, 47, 73, 79, 81, 82, 85, 94, 158–162, 168, 195, 204, 243, 300, 303, 310, 311, 316, 319, 331
Northern Tribes Buffalo Treaty 178
"not-in-my-backyard" or "NIMBY" campaigns 84

Obama, B. 26, 121, 130, 131, 166, 197
Ocasio-Cortez, Alexandria 2, 6, 8, 12, 15, 24, 29, 35, 47, 110, 116, 121, 132, 149, 157, 194, 237, 300, 317, 333
Occupy Movement 27
350.org campaign 28, 332, 333, 334, 346
over-population 244

Paris Agreement 24, 27, 57, 131, 145n8, 202, 206, 280, 304, 354, 378, 394
Paris Conference of the Parties (COP21) 3
pink collar jobs 7, 11; *see also* jobs
Putin, Vladimir 243

quantitative easing (QE) 68

race/racism 5, 6, 96, 149, 157, 161, 163–165, 203, 207, 212, 217, 232, 237, 238, 239, 241, 247, 288, 320–321, 334, 338
racial justice 89, 168
Raworth, Kate 324, 325
Red Deal 6, 9, 10, 13, 201
renewable energy 291n4; corporations 344;democratic 219–220; equity and control 218; fuel production and consumption 75; Indigenous communities 179; infrastructure 235; initiatives 197; investments in 152, 194; for job growth 10, 11, 143, 146–147; laws in Canada and India 124; policy makers 145; solar and wind power 10, 150; technology development 282–283; transitions 201, 212, 214–215, 245; use of fossil fuels 40, 237
restorative justice 182, 184, 186–188, 232
Rio+20 Earth Summit (2012) 197, 280, 304
Roosevelt, Franklin D. 2, 23, 30–32, 47, 73, 79, 81, 115, 134, 159, 161, 168, 173, 211, 303, 310, 311, 316, 319, 331

Sanders, Bernie 9, 11, 15, 24, 36, 47, 149, 233, 237, 238
Sitting Bull Plan 15, 150, 174; Dish with One Spoon Treaty and the Rights of Mother Earth 188–189; just transition (*see* Just Transition, Sitting Bull Plan); land back and restorative justice 186–188
social justice 24, 47, 67, 147, 152, 237, 317, 321, 334
South Korea *see Korean Green New Deal, Korean New Deal*
Stern, Nicholas 94, 95, 319, 349
Stiglitz, Joseph 94, 111, 319
Sunrise Movement 2, 24, 28, 151, 194, 201, 237, 317, 333
sustainable development 201, 204, 244, 394, 395
Sustainable Europe Investment Plan 302, 305–306, 388, 389

Tennessee Valley Authority (TVA) 303, 310
Thunberg, Greta 24, 141, 144, 300
Timmermans, Frans 299, 300, 306

trade: coverage of trade flows 126; determination of embedded emissions 127; emissions scope 127; geographic scope 126; sectoral scope 127
Transition Town movement 186
Trump, Donald 121, 129, 132, 142, 178, 187, 194, 239, 243, 262, 263, 355

UK GND: 2008 30–31; COVID-19 and "Build Back Better" 318–319; COVID-19 and revealing and exacerbation of inequalities 320–321; politics of 316–318; systemic change via GND 321–325
UK Green Party 317
UK Labour Party 78, 317, 318, 322; 2019 Labour Party Manifesto 317
United Nations Declaration on the Rights of Indigenous Peoples (UNDRIP) 150, 218, 332, 333
United Nations Environment Programme (UNEP) 2
United Nations Framework Convention on Climate Change(UNFCCC) Conferences of the Parties(COPs) 198, 299, 280, 377
United States Green New Deal for Public Housing Act 13, 149

Von der Leyen, Ursula 299, 300, 302, 303, 305, 306, 308–311, 376

Wall Street power 31–32
Waxman-Markey climate bill 121
working class 4, 12, 76–78, 80–81, 83–85, 121, 158, 163–164, 166, 238, 249, 262, 318
Works Progress Administration (WPA) 159–160
worktime reduction: debate about growth and GND 110–112; incorporating policies into GND 114–115; social and environmental benefits 112–114
World Health Organization (WHO) 308, 387
World Trade Organization (WTO) 14, 124, 129–131, 378, 393
World War II 2, 52, 78, 94, 111, 152, 158, 161, 174, 176, 185, 331–332, 334, 339, 344, 349–350, 478
Wu, Michelle 6

Xi Jinping 243, 262, 265